New Advances in Distributed Computing and Its Applications

New Advances in Distributed Computing and Its Applications

Guest Editors

Zhiwei Xu
Jianer Zhou
Xueshuo Xie
Zhao Huang

MDPI • Basel • Beijing • Wuhan • Barcelona • Belgrade • Novi Sad • Cluj • Manchester

Guest Editors

Zhiwei Xu
Research Center of Unmanned Systems
Haihe Laboratory of Information Technology Application Innovation
Tianjin
China

Jianer Zhou
School of System Design and Intelligent Manufacturing
Southern University of Science and Technology
Shenzhen
China

Xueshuo Xie
Research Center of Digital Health
Haihe Laboratory of Information Technology Application Innovation
Tianjin
China

Zhao Huang
School of Computer Science and Technology
Xi'an University of Posts and Telecommunications
Xi'an
China

Editorial Office
MDPI AG
Grosspeteranlage 5
4052 Basel, Switzerland

This is a reprint of the Special Issue, published open access by the journal *Electronics* (ISSN 2079-9292), freely accessible at: https://www.mdpi.com/journal/electronics/special_issues/Distributed_Computing.

For citation purposes, cite each article independently as indicated on the article page online and as indicated below:

Lastname, A.A.; Lastname, B.B. Article Title. *Journal Name* **Year**, *Volume Number*, Page Range.

ISBN 978-3-7258-4582-8 (Hbk)
ISBN 978-3-7258-4581-1 (PDF)
https://doi.org/10.3390/books978-3-7258-4581-1

Contents

About the Editors

Zhiwei Xu

Dr. Xu is a professor at the Haihe Laboratory of Information Technology Application Innovation, Tianjin, China, while working as an adjunct professor with the Institute of Computing, Chinese Academy of Sciences. His research interests include trusted interactions of embodied intelligence and dependable VLA models and multi-agent systems.

Jianer Zhou

Jianer Zhou is an associate professor with the School of System Design and Intelligent Manufacturing, Southern University of Science and Technology, Shenzhen, 518055, China. His research interests lie in network performance optimization, future Internet architecture, and Internet measurement.

Xueshuo Xie

Xueshuo Xie is an associate professor with the Research Center of Digital Health, Haihe Laboratory of Information Technology Application Innovation, Tianjin, 300450, China. His research interests include digital health and related security and privacy problems.

Zhao Huang

Zhao Huang received his Ph.D. degree from Xidian University, Xi'an, China, in 2020. He is currently a Lecturer at Xi'an University of Posts and Telecommunications. His research interests include hardware security, hardware Trojan detection, PUF, TRNG, secure system architecture, and blockchain consensus security.

Preface

The content in this reprint is drawn from New Advances in Distributed Computing and Its Applications, a Special Issue of MDPI's journal *Electronics*. This Special Issue includes 20 papers, covering topics such as CNN model offloading in mobile networks, blockchain-based data security, throughput optimization for distributed blockchain systems, and resource scheduling in FPGA systems for edge computing. We have selected the most relevant papers and organized them into four chapters based on their themes.

Part 1: Edge Computing, Chapters 1–5;
Part 2: AI Algorithm Optimization for Distributed Computing, Chapters 6–11;
Part 3: Hardware Optimization for Computing Platforms, Chapters 12–13;
Part 4: Security and Privacy in Distributed Computing, Chapters 14–20.

Zhiwei Xu, Jianer Zhou, Xueshuo Xie, and Zhao Huang
Guest Editors

electronics

MDPI

Article

Collaborative Online Learning-Based Distributed Handover Scheme in Hybrid VLC/RF 5G Systems

Saidiwaerdi Maimaiti [1,2,†], Shuman Huang [3,†], Kaisa Zhang [3,*], Xuewen Liu [4], Zhiwei Xu [5] and Jihang Mi [6]

1 School of Information Engineering, Xinjiang Institute of Engineering, Urumqi 830023, China; saidi216@xjie.edu.cn
2 College of Physics and Electrical Engineering, Kashi University, Kashi 844008, China
3 School of Information and Communication Engineering, Beijing University of Posts and Telecommunications, Beijing 100876, China; huangsm@bupt.edu.cn
4 Department of Electronics and Communication Engineering, Beijing Electronics Science and Technology Institute, Beijing 100070, China; xuewen_liu1990@bupt.cn
5 Haihe Laboratory of Information Technology Application Innovation (ITAI), Tianjin 300459, China
6 Digital Technology Company Limited of Aerospace Science and Industry Corp., Beijing 100048, China
* Correspondence: kaisa@bupt.edu.cn
† These authors are co-first authors of this article.

Abstract: This paper investigates handover in hybrid visible light communication (VLC)/radio frequency (RF) networks. In such a network, mobile users are prone to experience frequent handovers (FHOs). To this end, we propose a collaborative online learning-based handover scheme (COLH) in hybrid VLC/RF 5G systems. By selecting the next access point (AP) to which a user should handover, our goal is to make the user–AP connection as long as possible after the handover, defined as a reward that is learned online through a multi-armed bandit (MAB) framework. Unlike previous schemes based on independent and collective learning, first, our scheme dynamically clusters users with similar feedback on a given AP. Second, the users in the same cluster collaborate in estimating the expected reward for that AP, and the one with the maximum expected reward is selected as the next AP. This scheme can be implemented without extensive offline training and location information; thus, its practicality is greatly enhanced. The simulation results show that the proposal outperforms existing benchmarks on reducing handovers.

Keywords: collaborative learning; distributed handover; hybrid visible light communication (VLC)/radio frequency (RF) 5G network; multi-armed bandit (MAB)

1. Introduction

With the explosive growth of mobile traffic, the tolerance for transmission delay, operational costs, user experience, and spectrum compression of radio frequency (RF) will become an urgent crisis in the future. Visible light communication (VLC) has many advantages over RF, including access to an abundant, free, and unregulated light spectrum and the ability to provide hyper-speed data transmission. Moreover, there is no electromagnetic interference between VLC and RF. Therefore, VLC in the existing RF network can overcome RF limitations and improve system performance [1,2]. In addition, compared with independent VLC networks, VLC access to existing RF networks also improves system throughput [3].

The resulting hybrid VLC/RF 5G network, which combines the high-speed data transmission of VLC and the ubiquitous coverage of RF, has been proven to provide better network performance than a standalone VLC or RF network [3]. However, mobile users in this network readily experience frequent handovers (FHOs) due to three factors: (i) the small coverage of a VLC access point (AP); (ii) the vulnerability of VLC links to blockage; and (iii) the tricky handover decisions in the case of multiple candidate APs with overlapping coverage. The large number of handovers will cause heavy signaling overhead, higher outage probability, and increased power consumption. As such, designing an efficient handover scheme to address the FHO issue is highly important in hybrid VLC/RF 5G networks.

Conventional handover schemes rely on the current channel state while ignoring its future variations and, thus, are regarded as "short-sighted" [4]. Such schemes are not efficient in VLC-enabled networks due to the abrupt VLC channel variations. Research on reducing handovers in hybrid VLC/RF 5G networks has only just begun. Analyses based on historical data are often used to optimize handover [5,6]. The Analytic Hierarchy Process and Cooperative Game Method are used to determine whether to perform vertical switching [7]. Researchers have also proposed an improved genetic algorithm method [8], which uses time series classification to minimize the number of handovers in VLC systems. To avoid unnecessary handovers, the authors of [9] leveraged the rate of variation in received signal strength to indicate whether a user is moving towards a certain AP, and the authors of [10] proposed a power-based handover scheme to skip unnecessary handovers. On this basis, the authors of [11] further optimized the dynamic adjustment of the selection preference between VLC and RF via machine learning. Nevertheless, these methods only capture very near-future variations in the channel state within the time-to-trigger period (i.e., hundreds of milliseconds). Once the user alters its moving direction or encounters an unexpected obstacle soon after performing the decision, a new unnecessary handover will be triggered. An intuitive solution is to make a "long-sighted" decision by predicting the post-decision trajectory [12] or link blockage [13]. Interestingly, the author of [14] stated that the trajectories of different users have similarities. This trajectory similarity was then exploited to improve the prediction accuracy in [15]. More recently, the authors of [16] described a classification model used to predict the type of user's trajectory and assist a reinforcement learning model to make handover decisions that can dynamically adapt to new network conditions. Despite this, the prediction-based solutions require extensive offline training and users' location information, which are not always available in practice. In [17], the researchers developed a neural network-based handover scheme that classifies the handover moments between light fidelity (LiFi)and wireless fidelity (WiFi) based on channel quality, user movement, and device direction.

Multi-armed bandit (MAB) is a powerful online learning technique in which an agent learns from interactions with the network to maximize its expected reward, enabling it to reach the "long-sighted" decision in dynamic networks. Accordingly, this paper proposes a collaborative online learning-based handover scheme (COLH) in hybrid VLC/RF 5G networks, aiming to maximize the expected user–AP connection time after each handover. Aided by the clustering of bandits (CBA) approach [18], our scheme can be divided into two modules, i.e., MAB-based AP selection (BAPS) and feedback sharing (FBS). First, FBS dynamically clusters similar users according to the shared feedback, which indirectly exploits the trajectory similarity without requiring location information. Then, in BAPS, the users in the same cluster can select APs in a collaborative way. That is, each user selects the AP by learning from the historical handover experiences of both themselves and similar users.

Briefly, the main contributions are as follows: (1) unlike independent and collective learning [19], we are the first to propose the collaborative online learning framework for handovers in hybrid VLC/RF 5G networks; (2) instead of using users' location information, our scheme can exploit the trajectory similarity across users using only the shared feedback, making it practical and privacy-protective; (3) and the results verify the superiority of our scheme over the benchmarks in reducing handovers.

2. System Model

We consider a multi-user hybrid network with one WiFi AP and multiple VLC APs, as depicted in Figure 1. Let $\mathrm{N} = \{1,\ldots,n,\ldots,N\}$ and $\mathrm{M} = \{1,\ldots,m,\ldots,M\}$ denote the set of users and APs, respectively. The WiFi AP (denoted as AP 1), as a typical indoor RF technique, is deployed at the center. The VLC APs are deployed on the ceiling in a lattice topology. Specially, the number 1 indicates WiFi AP, and the number 2–10 indicates VLC AP. All the WiFi and VLC APs are linked via fiber to a central controller (CC), which takes charge of handover in this network. There is no interference between the WiFi and any VLC AP, while co-channel interference (CCI) exists where the coverage of the VLC APs overlap. We apply a frequency reuse factor of 4 to mitigate the CCI [9]. In addition, we use the time division multiple accessing to allow the APs to serve multiple users [11]. The widely used random waypoint mobility (RWP) [20] and geometric model [21] are employed to generate the user's mobility pattern and link blockage, respectively.

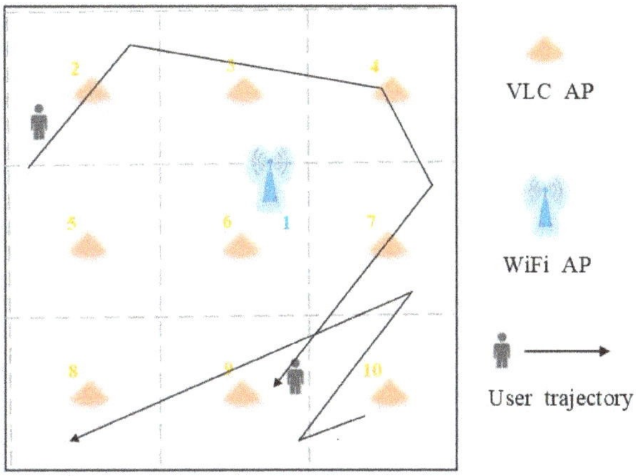

Figure 1. Hybrid VLC/RF network diagram.

If the LOS path is unblocked, the VLC channel gain is given by [2]

$$G_{m,n} = \begin{cases} \frac{(k+1)l^2 A}{2\pi d_{m,n}^2 \sin^2(\Psi)} g_f \cos^k(\phi)\cos(\varphi) & 0 \le \varphi \le \Psi \\ 0 & \varphi > \Psi \end{cases} \tag{1}$$

Otherwise, $G_{m,n} = 0$, where $m \in \{2,\ldots,M\}$. $d_{m,n}$ is the distance between AP m and user n; ϕ and φ are the angles of irradiance and incidence, respectively. For transmitter m, $k = \frac{-1}{\log_2(\cos(\Phi_{1/2}))}$ is the Lambertian order, and $\Phi_{1/2}$ is the half-intensity radiation angle. For receiver n, l is the refractive index, g_f is the optical filter gain, and A and Ψ are the physical area and field-of-view of photodiode, respectively. The signal-to-interference-plus-noise ratio (SINR) of the link between AP m and user n is

$$\gamma_{m,n} = \frac{(\eta P_V G_{m,n})^2}{B_V N_V + \sum_{i \in I/m} (\eta P_V G_{i,n})^2} \tag{2}$$

where η is the detector responsivity; P_V and B_V denote the optical power and bandwidth of the VLC AP, respectively; N_V is the noise power spectral density in VLC; and I denotes the set of VLC APs that use the same frequency spectrum as AP m. Here, the achievable data rate can be approximated as [22]

$$R_{m,n} = \tau_{m,n}\frac{B_V}{2}\log_2(1 + \frac{e}{2\pi}\gamma_{m,n}) \tag{3}$$

where $\tau_{m,n}$ is the fraction of resources assigned to user n by AP m, which is determined by a proportional fairness scheduler.

According to [23], the WiFi channel gain is written as

$$G_{1,n} = |H_{1,n}|^2 10^{(\frac{-L(d_{1,n})+Z_\sigma}{10})} \tag{4}$$

where $H_{1,n}$ is the channel transfer function that conforms to a Rayleigh distribution; Z_σ is the shadow fading; $L(.)$ is the free-space path loss, which is expressed as

$$L(d) = \begin{cases} 20\log_{10}(f_c d) - 147.5 & d < d_{ref} \\ 20\log_{10}(f_c \frac{d^{2.75}}{d_{ref}^{1.75}}) - 147.5 & d \geq d_{ref} \end{cases} \tag{5}$$

f_c is the carrier frequency, and d_{ref} is the reference distance. The SINR of the link between WiFi AP and user n is

$$\gamma_{1,n} = \frac{P_W G_{1,n}}{B_W N_W} \tag{6}$$

where P_W and B_W are the power and bandwidth of the WiFi AP, respectively; N_W is the noise power spectral density in WiFi. The data rate obtained is computed as

$$R_{1,n} = \tau_{1,n} B_W \log_2(1 + \gamma_{1,n}) \tag{7}$$

3. Collaborative Online Learning-Based Handover Scheme

In this Section, the framework of the proposed COLH is illustrated in Figure 2. On the user side, the handover is triggered by Event A2 (i.e., the achieved rate falls below the minimum required rate) and is initiated by sending measurement reports to the CC. On the CC side, the decision to select the next AP is made by learning from the historical handover experiences of the users themselves and similar users. The CC includes two modules, BAPS and FBS, which are elaborated on below.

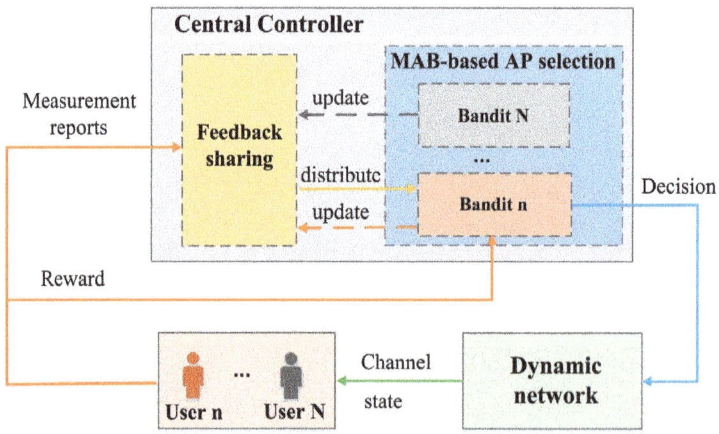

Figure 2. Framework of collaborative online learning-based handover scheme.

3.1. MAB-Based AP Selection Module

In the dynamic network, the handover process involves a sequence of AP selection decisions. This means that addressing the FHO issue boils down to finding the sequential APs that maximize the long-term reward. Here, the reward is defined as the user–AP connection time after the handover. In fact, the MAB is exactly the problem in which an agent decides which arm to pull in a number of rounds. In this regard, the AP selection problem for each user can be modeled as the MAB problem.

The BAPS module consists of N bandits, each of which serves a user by selecting the next AP when Event A2 occurs. Each bandit has M arms, each representing an AP. The BAPS module proceeds in discrete times. Upon the handover of user n is triggered by A2 at time t, and its context vectors with respect to all candidate APs are observed, denoted as $C_t = \{X_{t,m},\ m \in \mathrm{M}_t\} \subseteq \mathbb{R}^M$, where $\mathrm{M}_t = \{m \in \mathrm{M} :\ R_{m,n} \geq R_{\min}\}$ is the candidate AP set and $R_{\min}$ is the minimum required rate. In particular, the context vector $X_{t,m}$ is generated by applying one-hot encoding with one at the m-th position and zero everywhere else. The bandit serving user n then selects an AP m_t from the candidate APs based on their expected rewards and will observe the reward (feedback) associated with m_t at the next handover trigger time t', denoted as $r_{t,m_t} = t' - t$. The observation (C_t, m_t, r_{t,m_t}) is learned to improve the AP selection policy. The practical goal of the BAPS module is to find the optimal policy that maximizes the total reward over time. Equivalently, we interpret the goal as minimizing total regret $\sum q_t$, where the regret at time t is defined as the difference between the reward of the optimal AP in hindsight and the reward of the AP actually selected, i.e., $q_t = \max\limits_{m \in \mathrm{M}_t}\{r_{t,m_t}\} - r_{t,m_t}$.

One promising solution to the MAB problem is using the CBA approach [18]. In CBA, each bandit of user n at time t maintains a coefficient vector $w_{n,t} \in \mathbb{R}^M$, an additively updated vector $b_{n,t} \in \mathbb{R}^M$, and a correlation matrix $K_{n,t} \in \mathbb{R}^{M \times M}$. The expected reward for any AP m is estimated as a linear regression on the context vector, given by $w_{n,t}^T X_{t,m}$. In addition, the standard confidence bound function is derived as $CB_{n,t}(X_{t,m}) = \alpha\sqrt{X_{t,m}^T K_{n,t}^{-1} X_{t,m}}$, where α is the exploration parameter. Here, below, we present how the BAPS module selects Aps and updates the bandits:

(1) AP selection. The bandit of user n estimates the expected reward for each candidate AP m using the corresponding cluster-level parameters $w_{\widehat{\mathrm{N}}_m,t}$ and $CB_{\widehat{\mathrm{N}}_m,t}(X_{t,m})$, which are distributed by FBS (see Section 3.2 for details).

Based upon this, the bandit of n selects the AP with the highest upper confidence bound, given by

$$m_t = \underset{m \in \mathrm{M}_t}{\operatorname{argmax}}[w_{\widehat{\mathrm{N}}_m,t}^T X_{t,m} + CB_{\widehat{\mathrm{N}}_m,t}(X_{t,m})] \tag{8}$$

In this way, the users in the same cluster can select Aps in a collaborative way. In contrast, if any bandit of user n uses only its own parameters $w_{n,t}$ and $CB_{n,t}(X_{t,m})$, this means that the user selects the AP independently. This scheme is termed Non-COLH and serves as our benchmark.

(2) Bandit update. After handing over user n to the selected AP m_t, the observed reward is normalized to $\bar{r}_{t,m_t} = r_{t,m_t} / \max\limits_{m \in \mathrm{M}_t}\{r_{t,m_t}\}$, which is further utilized to update the bandit of user n with the following equations:

$$K_{n,t} = K_{n,t} + X_{t,m_t} X_{t,m_t}^T \tag{9}$$

$$b_{n,t} = b_{n,t} + \bar{r}_{t,m_t} X_{t,m_t} \tag{10}$$

$$w_{n,t} = K_{n,t}^{-1} X_{t,m_t} \tag{11}$$

The updated parameters are then shared by FBS.

3.2. Feedback Sharing Module

We define the users who have similar trajectories to user n in the vicinity of AP m as its neighborhoods with respect to AP m, denoted as N_m. Intuitively, user n's estimation of expected reward for AP m can benefit from learning its neighborhoods' historical experiences of handing over to AP m. Unfortunately, the user neighborhoods clustered according to trajectory similarity cannot be obtained directly without users' location information. In this subsection, we design the FBS module, which can estimate users' neighborhoods based on feedback similarity only.

The idea comes from the fact that the users within N_m typically have similar feedback when handing over to AP m since the feedback $r_{t,m}$ is determined by the user's post-handover trajectory. Consequently, the estimated neighborhood of user n with respect to AP m, denoted as $\widehat{\mathrm{N}}_m$, can be given by [18]

$$\widehat{\mathrm{N}}_m = \left\{ j \in \mathrm{N} : \left| w_{n,t}^T X_{t,m} - w_{j,t}^T X_{t,m} \right| \le CB_{n,t}(X_{t,m}) + CB_{j,t}(X_{t,m}) \right\} \tag{12}$$

This indicates that user j will be involved in the neighborhood of user n with respect to AP m if their feedback related to the context vector $X_{t,m}$ is sufficiently close. Afterward, the cluster-level parameters $w_{\widehat{\mathrm{N}}_m,t}$ and $CB_{\widehat{\mathrm{N}}_m,t}(X_{t,m})$ are, respectively, calculated by

$$w_{\widehat{\mathrm{N}}_m,t} = \frac{1}{\left|\widehat{\mathrm{N}}_m\right|} \sum_{j \in \widehat{\mathrm{N}}_m} w_{j,t} \tag{13}$$

and

$$CB_{\widehat{\mathrm{N}}_m,t}(X_{t,m}) = \frac{1}{\left|\widehat{\mathrm{N}}_m\right|} \sum_{j \in \widehat{\mathrm{N}}_m} CB_{j,t}(X_{t,m}) \tag{14}$$

Note that $\left|\widehat{\mathrm{N}}_m\right|$ denotes the cardinality of set $\widehat{\mathrm{N}}_m$.

The overall procedure of the proposed COLH is depicted in Algorithm 1.

Algorithm 1: The Proposed COLH

Input: exploration parameter a.
Init: $b_{n,0} = 0 \in \mathbb{R}^M$, and $K_{n,0} = I \in \mathbb{R}^{M \times M}, \forall \in_n \mathrm{N}$.
while The handover of any user n is triggered by A2 **do**
  Record current time t.
    Idenitify context vector set $C_t = \{X_{t,m},\ m \in \mathrm{M}_t\}$.
FBS module:
    for all $m \in \mathrm{M}_t$ **do**
        Compute neighborhood $\widehat{\mathrm{N}}_m$ for AP m according to (12).
        Set $w_{\widehat{\mathrm{N}}_m,t}$ and $CB_{\widehat{\mathrm{N}}_m,t}(X_{t,m})$ according to (13) and (14), resp.
  end for
  Distribute the cluster-level $w_{\widehat{\mathrm{N}}_m,t}$ and $CB_{\widehat{\mathrm{N}}_m,t}(X_{t,m})$ to the BAPS.
BAPS module:
Select AP m_t according to (8) and handover user n to this AP.
Observe reward $\bar{r}_{t,m_t}$ at the user n's next handover trigger time t'.
Update $K_{n,t}$, $b_{n,t}$, and $w_{n,t}$ according to (9), (10), (11), resp.
Share $K_{n,t}$ and $w_{n,t}$ with the FBS.

---

4. Performance Evaluation

For simulations, we consider an $16 \times 16 \times 3$ m^3 office-type indoor room with 1 WiFi AP and 16 VLC APs. The separation between the nearest VLC APs is set to 4 m, and the vertical distance between each user and the VLC AP is set to 2.5 m. Similar to [15], we generate a series of trajectories for each user over N_d consecutive days and introduce a random mobility parameter $\gamma \in [0,1]$ to control the inter-trajectory dependence. For example, $\gamma = 0.4$ means that the user follows random trajectories in 40% of the total days (i.e., $0.4 * N_d$) and follows a regular trajectory in the other days. Each day, the user moves at a speed of 1 m/s according to the RWP model [20] until reaching 1000 iterations (time units), and a trajectory is thus generated. Note that the trajectories for different users are generated independently. Following [21], we use a cylindrical object with a height of 1.75 m and a radius of 0.15 m to model the obstacle, which is assumed to be randomly distributed. If the line segment between the user and the obstacle intersects, the LOS path is considered to be blocked. The parameters related to WiFi and VLC channels refer to [2]. The hyper-parameter α is set to 0.16 empirically. Unless otherwise stated, the number of users and the number of obstacles (Note: An obstacle refers to any physical or environmental object that can interfere with or attenuate a signal's propagation path, strength, or quality), γ and $R_{\min}$, are set to $3, 20, 0.4$ and 120 Mbps, respectively. To reflect the average QoE of an arbitrary user, we introduce two metrics as in [5], namely the average number of handovers per user (ANH) and the average lasting time per each connection (ALT). The results are averaged over 500 times to mitigate the randomness of the trajectory and obstacle distribution.

First, Figure 3 shows the convergence of the proposed COLH in terms of the ANH under different values (i.e., $0, 0.4$, and 1). Here, $N_d = 20$. We can see that COLH gradually converges under all values as the number of iterations increases. Nevertheless, under a larger value of γ, COLH converges to a higher ANH at a slower convergence rate. This is because the larger mobility randomness during the learning process of COLH requires more samples.

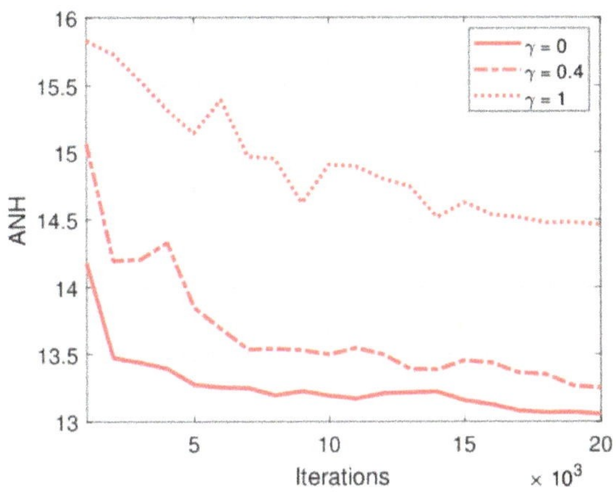

Figure 3. Convergence performance of COLH.

Next, we compare COLH with three benchmarks over the ANH and ALT: (1) rate-first handover (RFH); (2) non-COLH (NCOLH); and (3) SMART [19]. Specifically, RFH selects the AP that provides the highest rate in the present, while both NCOLH and SMART select the AP that provides the longest connection time in the future. In NCOLH, each user has its own bandit and performs independent learning. In SMART, all users share a common bandit and perform collective learning.

Figure 4 depicts the comparison of the ANH and ALT obtained under different schemes by varying the number of users from one to nine after 15,000 iterations. We see that the performance of all schemes degrades as the number of users increases due to the ensuing resource competition. More importantly, the "shortsighted" RFH exhibits the worst performance, while COLH exhibits the best one among its "long-sighted" counterparts. Moreover, the gap between COLH and its benchmarks grows. Although all users are of the same service type (because of the same rate requirements [19]), their trajectories are different but somewhat similar. As a result, the increase in the number of users exacerbates the disadvantage of collective learning in SMART and enlarges the advantage of collaborative learning in COLH. Concretely, when nine users are involved, the ALT obtained under COLH is larger than that under NCOLH, SMART, and RFH by 4.3%, 13.4%, and 38.5%, respectively. The performance gains obtained reflect not only the superiority of making "long-sighted" decisions through online learning but also the effectiveness of the collaborative effects incorporated by using feedback similarity.

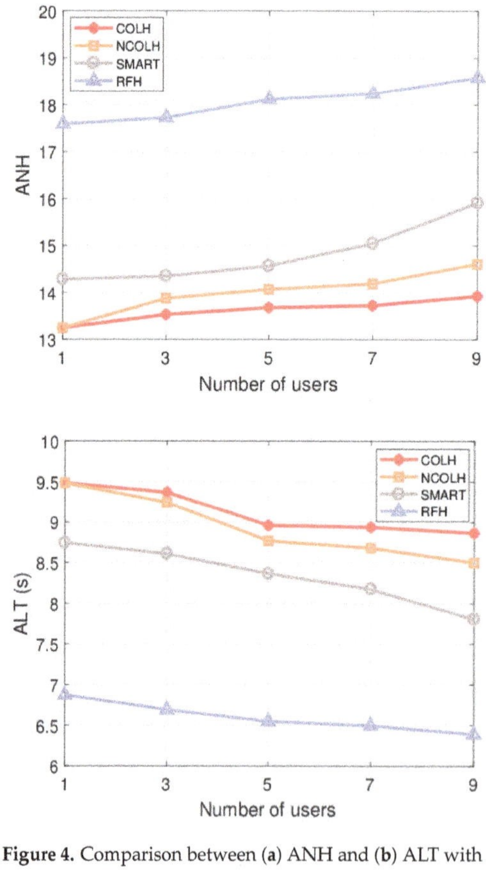

(a)

(b)

Figure 4. Comparison between (**a**) ANH and (**b**) ALT with different numbers of users.

Figure 5 depicts the comparison of the ANH and ALT obtained under different schemes by varying the numbers of obstacles from 10 to 30 after 15,000 iterations. With the number of obstacles increases, the ANH increases and the ALT decreases no matter the scheme. This trend is consistent with the intuition that more handovers occur in complex environments with many obstacles than in simple environments with few obstacles. Furthermore, COLH always outperforms the benchmarks, especially in complex environments.

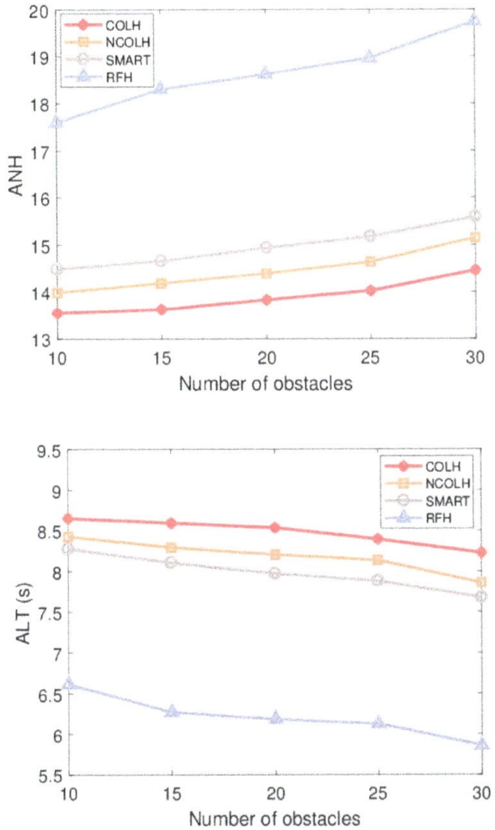

(**a**)

(**b**)

Figure 5. Comparison between (**a**) ANH and (**b**) ALT with different numbers of obstacles.

5. Conclusions

In this paper, a novel handover scheme in hybrid VLC/RF networks was proposed, through which the users in the same cluster collaborate to select APs. By sharing feedback, this scheme clusters similar users without involving any user trajectory, which improves its practicality and protects user privacy. On this basis, the feedback similarities across users are utilized for a smarter estimation of expected rewards and further reduction in handovers in the long run. By incorporating the collaborative effects of the user clusters, the proposal has been verified to outperform its benchmarks on reducing handovers.

Author Contributions: Conceptualization, data curation, investigation, methodology, resources, and simulation, S.M. and S.H.; formal analysis and supervision, K.Z.; visualization and writing—original draft, S.M. and X.L.; validation and writing—review and editing, S.M., S.H., Z.X. and J.M. All authors have read and agreed to the published version of the manuscript.

Funding: This work was supported by the Basic research funds for universities in the Xinjiang Uygur Autonomous Region in 2024 under Grant No. XJEDU2024P064. This work was also supported by the natural science foundation of Xinjiang Uygur Autonomous Region in 2024 under Grant No. 2024D01A12. This work was also supported by the doctoral research projects of Xinjiang Institute of Engineering under Grant No. 2025XGYBQJ31.

Data Availability Statement: Data are contained within the article.

Conflicts of Interest: Author Jihang Mi was employed by the company Digital Technology Company Limited of Aerospace Science and Industry Corp. The remaining authors declare that the research was conducted in the absence of any commercial or financial relationships that could be construed as a potential conflict of interest.

Abbreviations

The following abbreviations are used in this manuscript:

AP	Access point
ANH	Average number of handover
ALT	Average lasting time
BAPS	Based AP selection
COLH	Collaborative online learning-based handover
CBA	Clustering of bandits approach
CC	Central controller
CCI	Co-channel interference
FHO	Frequent handovers
FBS	Feedback sharing
LiFi	Light fidelity
MAB	Multi-armed bandit
NCOLH	Non-collaborative online learning-based handover
VLC/RF	Visible light communication/radio frequency
VLC	Visible light communication
RF	Radio frequency
RWP	Random waypoint mobility
RFH	Rate-first handover
WiFi	Wireless fidelity

References

1. Arshad, R.; Lampe, L. Stochastic Geometry Analysis of User Mobility in RF/VLC Hybrid Networks. *IEEE Trans. Wirel. Commun.* **2021**, *20*, 7404–7419. [CrossRef]
2. Huang, S.; Chuai, G.; Gao, W. Two-Way Selection Handover Algorithm for Load Balancing in Hybrid VLC-RF Networks. In Proceedings of the 2021 IEEE/CIC International Conference on Communications in China (ICCC), Xiamen, China, 28–30 July 2021; pp. 1065–1070.
3. Basnayaka, D.A.; Haas, H. Hybrid RF and VLC Systems: Improving User Data Rate Performance of VLC Systems. In Proceedings of the 2015 IEEE 81st Vehicular Technology Conference (VTC Spring), Glasgow, UK, 11–14 May 2015; pp. 1–5.
4. Sun, L.; Hou, J.; Shu, T. Spatial and Temporal Contextual Multi-Armed Bandit Handovers in Ultra-Dense mmWave Cellular Networks. *IEEE Trans. Mob. Comput.* **2021**, *20*, 3423–3438. [CrossRef]
5. Bao, X.; Okine, A.; Shi, L.; Bao, N.; Adjardjah, W. Channel Adaptive Dwell Timer for Vertical Handoff in Hybrid VLC and Wi-Fi Networks. In Proceedings of the 2018 IEEE/CIC International Conference on Communications in China (ICCC), Beijing, China, 16–18 August 2018; pp. 609–613.
6. Liu, R.; Zhang, C. Dynamic dwell timer for vertical handover in VLC-WLAN heterogeneous networks. In Proceedings of the 2017 13th International Wireless Communications and Mobile Computing Conference (IWCMC), Valencia, Spain, 26–30 June 2017; pp. 1256–1260.
7. Liang, S.; Zhang, Y.; Fan, B.; Tian, H. Multi-Attribute Vertical Handover Decision-Making Algorithm in a Hybrid VLC-Femto System. *IEEE Commun. Lett.* **2017**, *21*, 1521–1524. [CrossRef]
8. Camporez, H.; Costa, W.; Segatto, M.; Silva, J.; Deters, J.K.; Wörtche, H. AI-Driven Enhancements for Handover in Visible Light Communication Systems. *J. Light. Technol.* **2024**, *42*, 8191–8202. [CrossRef]
9. Wu, X.; O'Brien, D.C.; Deng, X.; Linnartz, J.-P.M.G. Smart Handover for Hybrid LiFi and WiFi Networks. *IEEE Trans. Wirel. Commun.* **2020**, *19*, 8211–8219. [CrossRef]
10. Wu, X.; Haas, H. Handover skipping for LiFi. *IEEE Access* **2019**, *7*, 38369–38378. [CrossRef]

11. Wu, X.; O'Brien, D.C. A Novel Machine Learning-Based Handover Scheme for Hybrid LiFi and WiFi Networks. In Proceedings of the 2020 IEEE Globecom Workshops (GC Wkshps), Taipei, Taiwan, 7–11 December 2020; IEEE: Piscataway, NJ, USA, 2020; pp. 1–5.
12. Arfaoui, M.A.; Ghrayeb, A.; Assi, C. Cascaded Artificial Neural Networks for Proactive Power Allocation in Indoor LiFi Systems. In Proceedings of the ICC 2021-IEEE International Conference on Communications, Montreal, QC, Canada, 14–23 June 2021; pp. 1–6.
13. Wu, Z.-Y.; Ismail, M.; Serpedin, E.; Wang, J. Efficient Prediction of Link Outage in Mobile Optical Wireless Communications. *IEEE Trans. Wirel. Commun.* **2021**, *20*, 882–896. [CrossRef]
14. Senaratne, H.; Mueller, M.; Behrisch, M.; Lalanne, F.; Bustos-Jiménez, J.; Schneidewind, J.; Keim, D.; Schreck, T. Urban Mobility Analysis With Mobile Network Data: A Visual Analytics Approach. *IEEE Trans. Intell. Transp. Syst.* **2018**, *19*, 1537–1546. [CrossRef]
15. Peng, Y.; Zhou, Y.; Liu, L.; Li, J.; Pan, Z.; Sun, G. Intelligent Recommendation-Based User Plane Handover With Enhanced TCP Throughput in Ultra-Dense Cellular Networks. *IEEE Trans. Veh. Technol.* **2022**, *71*, 595–610. [CrossRef]
16. Fonseca, D.F.; Guzman, B.G.; Martena, G.L.; Bian, R.; Haas, H.; Giustiniano, D. Prediction-model-assisted reinforcement learning algorithm for handover decision-making in hybrid LiFi and WiFi networks. *J. Opt. Commun. Netw.* **2024**, *16*, 159–170. [CrossRef]
17. Ma, G.; Parthiban, R.; Karmakar, N. An artificial neural network-based handover scheme for hybrid LiFi networks. *IEEE Access* **2022**, *10*, 130350–130358. [CrossRef]
18. Gentile, C.; Li, S.; Kar, P.; Karatzoglou, A.; Zappella, G.; Etrue, E. On context-dependent clustering of bandits. *Proc. Int. Conf. Mach. Learn.* **2017**, *70*, 1253C1262.
19. Sun, Y.; Feng, G.; Qin, S.; Liang, Y.-C.; Yum, T.-S.P. The SMART Handoff Policy for Millimeter Wave Heterogeneous Cellular Networks. *IEEE Trans. Mob. Comput.* **2018**, *17*, 1456–1468. [CrossRef]
20. Soltani, M.D.; Arfaoui, M.A.; Tavakkolnia, I.; Ghrayeb, A.; Safari, M.; Assi, C.M.; Hasna, M.O.; Haas, H. Bidirectional Optical Spatial Modulation for Mobile Users: Toward a Practical Design for LiFi Systems. *IEEE J. Sel. Areas Commun.* **2019**, *37*, 2069–2086. [CrossRef]
21. Chen, C.; Basnayaka, D.A.; Purwita, A.A.; Wu, X.; Haas, H. Wireless Infrared-Based LiFi Uplink Transmission With Link Blockage and Random Device Orientation. *IEEE Trans. Commun.* **2021**, *69*, 1175–1188. [CrossRef]
22. Demir, M.S.; Uysal, M. A Cross-Layer Design for Dynamic Resource Management of VLC Networks. *IEEE Trans. Commun.* **2021**, *69*, 1858–1867. [CrossRef]
23. Perahia, E.; Stacey, R. *Next Generation Wireless LAN: 802.11n and 802.11ac*; Cambridge University Press: Cambridge, UK, 2013.

electronics

MDPI

Article

Towards Failure-Aware Inference in Harsh Operating Conditions: Robust Mobile Offloading of Pre-Trained Neural Networks

Wenjing Liu [1,2], Zhongmin Chen [3,*] and Yunzhan Gong [1]

1 State Key Laboratory of Networking and Switching Technology, Beijing University of Posts and Telecommunications, Beijing 100876, China; liuwenjing2015@bupt.edu.cn (W.L.); gongyz@bupt.edu.cn (Y.G.)
2 College of Data Science and Application, Inner Mongolia University of Technology, Hohhot 010080, China
3 Weihai Wenlong Power (Group) Co., Ltd., State Grid Corporation of China, Weihai 264423, China
* Correspondence: zhongmin.chen@foxmail.com

Abstract: Pre-trained neural networks like GPT-4 and Llama2 have revolutionized intelligent information processing, but their deployment in industrial applications faces challenges, particularly in harsh environments. To address these related issues, model offloading, which involves distributing the computational load of pre-trained models across edge devices, has emerged as a promising solution. While this approach enables the utilization of more powerful models, it faces significant challenges in harsh environments, where reliability, connectivity, and resilience are critical. This paper introduces failure-resilient inference in mobile networks (FRIM), a framework that ensures robust offloading and inference without the need for model retraining or reconstruction. FRIM leverages graph theory to optimize partition redundancy and incorporates an adaptive failure detection mechanism for mobile inference with efficient fault tolerance. Experimental results on DNN models (AlexNet, ResNet, VGG-16) show that FRIM improves inference performance and resilience, enabling more reliable mobile applications in harsh operating environments.

Keywords: smart environment; edge intelligence; distributed neural networks; mobile inference; failure-resilient offloading

1. Introduction

The emerging pre-trained neural networks, e.g., GPT-4, Llama2, etc., have revolutionized the field of intelligent information processing with a transformative impact on AI, science, and society. These neural networks have been used as backbone models for enabling efficient mobile inference, which benefits improved model generalization and supports more intelligent industrial applications [1]. For such an intelligent industrial application, deploying the learning model in the cloud may be impractical. Instead, collaborative local devices are preferred, as continuously transmitting large volumes of raw data from end devices to the cloud model can result in high transmission latency, ultimately degrading the performance of the industrial application [2]. Compared with the rapid and remarkable progress in pre-trained neural networks, the computation and storage resources of devices in an operating condition always remain extremely limited and become a bottleneck for deploying large neural network models [3]. To address the computation limitation of end devices in processing pre-trained neural networks, model offloading [4] is proposed as a promising approach. It is to divide the computation of pre-trained neural networks and offload the obtained partitions to edge devices along the path from the edge to the cloud [5]. Specifically, although industrial devices increasingly utilize the offloading of more powerful models for complex inference, such approaches face significant challenges in harsh operating conditions.

Existing systems in harsh operating conditions face multiple environmental and connectivity challenges, which results in limited functionality, high costs, and difficult deployment. Mobile inference solutions for harsh and hazardous areas must be more resilient to withstand extreme conditions, and designing such equipment requires specialized knowledge to meet stringent safety standards. As a result, these solutions are more expensive to produce, limiting the options available on the market. Connectivity is another common issue faced by industries in remote, harsh, and hazardous areas, as many systems rely on specific connectivity requirements that may not be feasible in these environments.

Robust offloading of the pre-trained models, as well as inference on these models, is vital for failure-resilient inference on mobile devices in harsh operating conditions. In recent years, failure resilience problems have been studied in DNN-based inference processes [6–10]. Hadidi et al. [6] provide robustness by coding-based distributed inference. However, this coding-based method, which increases computational complexity and communication overhead, also affects inference efficiency. In [7,8], Yousef et al., introduced the concept of skip hyper-connections in distributed DNNs, which provides failure resilience for inferencing based on distributed DNNs. By building hyper-connections, intermediate layers of the distributed DNN can be skipped without significant loss of inference accuracy. These hyper-connections between non-contiguous devices with model partitions help make distributed DNNs more resilient to physical failures. They provide an alternative inference path for DNNs when one of the devices with model partitions fails. However, this method requires a total change in the structure of the DNN model, which will make the structure of the DNN model more complicated. Even worse, after the skip hyper-connections are added, the DNN model needs to be retrained, which is infeasible for large neural models with billions of tokens. Ref. [9] proposes Conflict-resilient Incremental Offloading of Deep Neural Networks at Edge (CIODE) for improving the efficiency of DNN inference in the edge smart environment. Ref. [10] implements replicas of model partitions, but no redundancy adaptation is considered. CONTINUER [11] models trade-offs in accuracy, end-to-end latency, and downtime thresholds to handle a device failure but cannot adapt various inference scenarios. But, this approach increase the costs and complexity of the inference process. Khan F M et al. [12] proposed a resilient DNN with an adaptive architecture to reduce resource consumption. They present an empirical method that identifies the connections in ResNet that can be dropped without significant impact on the model's performance. How to provide failure resilience quickly and accurately without redesigning the pre-trained model structure is an urgent challenge.

To address the aforementioned problems, we present failure-resilient inference in mobile networks (FRIM), with robust offloading of DNN partitions, which is a promising paradigm to guarantee the failure resilience of DNN inference on mobile devices without additional model reconstruction and retraining (see Figure 1). Specifically, we propose theoretical analysis for adaptive offloading of DNN partitions to optimize partition redundancy, which models the offloading of DNN partitions based on graph theory and ensures that redundant partitions are deployed to maintain inference continuity in the face of device failures. On the other hand, these redundant partitions can perform inference in parallel and thus improve inference efficiency. In contrast to state-of-the-art methods, our proposed solution does not need model reconstruction and retraining and improves the failure resilience of mobile inference, as well as its inference performance improvement.

The primary contributions are as follows:

1. We model the offloading of DNN partitions by graph theory, and adapt offloading redundancy to guarantee failure resilience and enhance inference performance as well.
2. As a part of FRIM, we design an adaptive failure detection mechanism to locate partition failures. By incorporating a detection mechanism into the mobile inference process, FRIM can detect and mitigate failures efficiently and accurately.
3. We implement FRIM and other baselines in a mobile computing environment, and evaluate FRIM on three well-known DNN models (Alex-Net, Res-Net, and VGG-16). Experimental results demonstrate FRIM can adapt to different scales of device failures while enhancing inference efficiency and thus intelligence-empowered mobile applications in harsh operating conditions.

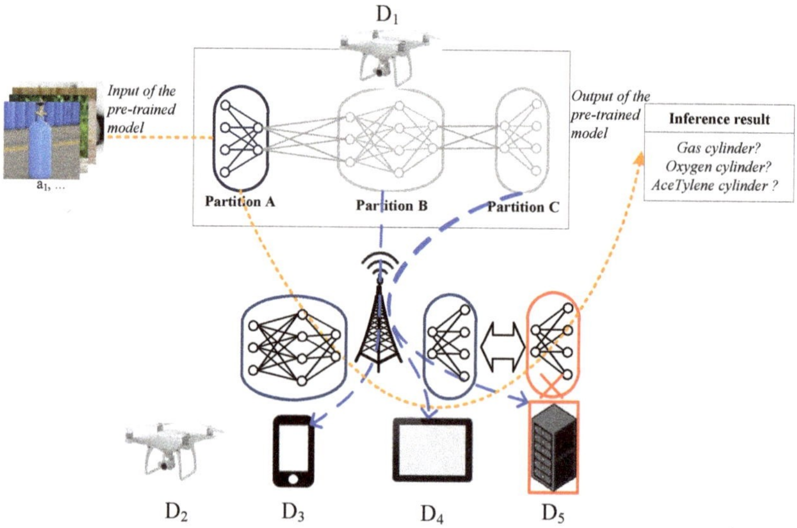

Figure 1. A pre-trained model-based mobile inference with redundancy.

The rest of this paper is summarized as follows. We review the related works in Section 2. Some preliminary works are introduced in Section 3. In Section 4, we propose FRIM, including adaptive model partition offloading and and a failure-resilient inference scheme. In Section 5, we implement our experiments and discuss experimental results. Conclusions are drawn in Section 6.

2. Related Work

2.1. DNN Computation Offloading

Computation offloading is a paradigm that allows multiple clients to run neural network models collaboratively. Mohammed [13] proposes a technique to divide a DNN into multiple partitions that can be processed locally by end devices or distributed to one or multiple powerful nodes, such as in fog networks. In order to minimize the execution delay between the client and the edge server, PerDNN [14] uses the server's GPU statistics to distribute DNN models. Xu et al. [15] focus on distributing DNNs based on one or more cloudlets to minimize the energy consumption or maximize the inference requests. A tensor-based Lyapunov DNN Offloading Control strategy [16] is proposed, aiming to offload DNN computational tasks to cloud–fog–edge from an overall perspective. To optimize the partition process, Wang et al. [17] presented an adaptive DNN partition scheme for inference acceleration. Almeida [18] proposes a distributed reasoning framework that can jointly adjust the partition deployment and the transferred data to the environment. Y Duan et al. [19] further proposed an optimal partition algorithm for tree-structure DNNs. Although multiple DNNs are considered, concurrent inference on these models is not discussed. Liu K et al. [20] formally defined the Cooperative Partitioning and Offloading (CPO) problem, with the objective of minimizing average inference latency. Liao Z et al. [21] proposed a Partition Point Retain algorithm, which is used to exclude layers unsuitable as partition points. Then, the Optimal Partition Point algorithm is employed to find the partition point with a minimal cost for each Mobile DNN deployment. Kakolyris et al. [22] formulates a range of Pareto optimal DNN partitioning strategies for a balance between performance and energy consumption. Duan Y et al. [23] addressed the challenge of jointly optimizing DNN partitioning and task offloading scheduling, to achieve a layer-level scheduling algorithm to manage heterogeneous DNN inference jobs.

Among state-of-the-art solutions, adaptive methods are the ultimate solution for more advanced DNN offloading in a heterogeneous environment. CIODE [9] can dynamically select collaborative targets among trusted edge clusters and collaborate with multiple targets for inference. Zhou et al. [24] leverage the Particle Swarm Optimization (PSO) algorithm to dynamically update the fused-layer path length, intercepting the fused layer's size and path offloading strategy to explore the optimal solution. In [25], the offloading sequential DNN task is formulated as an infinite-horizon Markov decision process and the Bellman equation for optimal conditions is provided, aiming to minimize the average latency of DNN tasks. DistrEdge [26] uses deep reinforcement learning techniques to adapt the heterogeneity of devices, network conditions, and nonlinear features of DNNs. Wei et al. [27] propose a mobility-aware computation offloading and task migration approach (MCOTM) based on trajectory and resource prediction. Younis et al. [28] introduce the Energy-Latency-aware Task Offloading and Approximate Computing (ETORS) problem to utilize the Dual-Decomposition Method (DDM) to decompose it into sub-problems. Na et al. [29] introduce a deep deterministic policy based on a greedy strategy (DDPGG) that employs a greedy strategy to simultaneously optimize dynamic scheduling, device association, and task allocation for UAVs. Xiaotian Guo et al. [30] introduce a novel methodology, called EASTER, designed to learn robust distribution strategies for transformer models against device failures that considers the tradeoff between robustness (i.e., maintaining model functionality against failures) and resource utilization (considering memory usage and computations). Xiaotian Guo et al. also [31] present a novel partitioning method, called RobustDiCE, for robust distribution and inference of CNN models over multiple edge devices. In [32], an end-edge collaborative inference framework of CFNNs for big data-driven IoT, named DisCFNN, is proposed.

When a DNN model is partitioned and deployed among mobile devices, the failure of any device will make the model partitions placed on this device invalid and thus result in catastrophic outage. Although DNN computation offloading has been studied extensively, the concerns about failure resilience should be taken into account for the various deployment of DNNs in harsh operating conditions.

2.2. Failure-Resilient DNN Computation Offloading and Distributed Inference

Among the failure-resilient approaches of neural network computation offloading, the work of Hadidi et al. [6] first concerns the robustness of DNN-based inference by optimizing the offloading of DNNs. However, this program-based approach is too complex to facilitate improvement of inference efficiency in practice.

DeepFogGuard [7] uses skip hyper-connections to achieve the failure resilience of distributed DNN inference. It is similar to its follow-up works, ResiliNet [8], approaching failure resilience capability through redesigning the neural network model and modifying the training procedures of DNN models. However, both DeepFogGuard and ResiliNet need to redesign the neural network model. It is not feasible to redesign and retrain every model in practice. A failure-resilience paradigm without model modification is highly desired. Hou et al. [33] proposed an edge-computing-aided IoV architecture to traverse potential failures of subtasks. Whaiduzzaman [34] adapted a fog-based fault-tolerant framework. This framework of microservices can effectively recover from any single failure. By incorporating an advanced lock mechanism into computation offloading, CIODE [9] can handle concurrency conflicts and improve the robustness of DNN applications. P. Li et al. [35] propose ResPipe, a novel resilient model-distributed DNN training mechanism against delayed or failed devices. CONTINUER [11] can leverage trade-offs in accuracy, end-to-end latency and downtime thresholds to handle a device failure. However, these two approaches increase the costs and complexity of the inference process. Khan F M et al. [12] proposed a resilient DNN with an adaptive architecture to reduce resource consumption. This paper presents an empirical study that identifies the connections in ResNet that can be dropped without significant impact on the model's performance in case of resource shortage. However, these existing studies only consider offloading the inference model, while the scheduling of robust model partition copies is not discussed. In [10], a preliminary scheme to use replicas of model partitions is implemented, but no redundancy adaptation is considered. A study on robust inference with rational redundancy is highly desired.

3. Problem Statement and Analysis

In this section, the typical offloading and inference strategy is formulated and analyzed. We focus on the problem caused by the failures of partitions (layers) of pre-trained neural network models after these partitions are offloaded to edge devices.

3.1. Formulation

The purpose of the partition offloading of the pre-trained models is to support distributed inference based on large neural network models and balance the overhead of inference tasks [36,37]. In this paper, we consider a distributed collaborative inference in a harsh industrial environment. In our system model, each edge device can request collaborative inference with each other. In addition to requesting collaborative inference from other edge nodes, the edge device also monitors the others at regular intervals to detect whether they meet a failure. If a failure is detected, the edge device needs to offload copies of the model partitions deployed on the failed device to another device. This would inevitably involve recovery time for inference tasks. To alleviate the impact of failed devices, we need to minimize the recovery time of inference tasks. DNN partitioning follows a popular method [13], which can partition the DNN model adaptively.

An execution graph of the pre-trained neural network (see Figure 2) is generated to guide the inference task on the neural network distributed on edge devices, which indicates the inference process and overhead of the collaborative inference among various devices in a wireless industrial network. For this execution graph, a neural network is divided into three partitions, partition A, B and C. Partition A, B and C of the pre-trained model, as well as the corresponding computational load, are transferred between an edge device and a central server to collaboratively complete the inference task. An inference task consists of several states, which are indicated by yellow cycles, i.e., $S_1, S_2, ..., S_{11}$. Each line between cycles has a weight to describe the corresponding time delay. Among them, the line between two adjacent states of a device related to the same model partition represents the partition execution delay of this device. The line between adjacent states of different devices indicates transmission delay between these two devices. Note that only the states in the inference process are marked with the color yellow, but the states that are not be included in the run-time inference are marked by the color blue instead. At first, partition A and B are deployed at the edge device, whereas partition C is deployed at the central server, represented by partition distribution [A B], [C] . In the 2nd round of this inference process, partition B is additionally offloaded to the central server to improve the inference performance while state S_5 transmits to S_6 and is performed at the central server by state S_7. The partition distribution becomes [A B], [B C]. An edge device will keep partition B offloaded to it as a redundant copy of partition B. Here, the redundant copy of Partition B is a necessary redundancy for an inference task in a harsh operating condition. In this way, this dynamic partition offloading would balance lower cost and failure-resilient inference in harsh operating conditions.

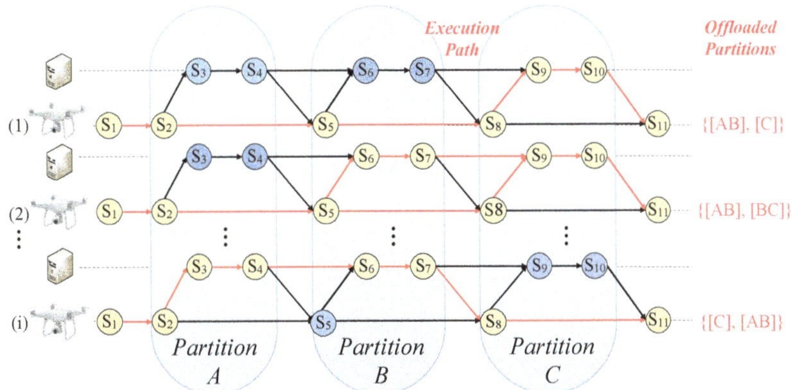

Figure 2. An execution graph of neural network models with redundant offloading.

3.2. Redundancy Modeling for Efficient Failure Resilience

Necessary redundancy in intentional offloaded duplication of the model partitions is highly desired to achieve failure-resilient inference, especially in harsh operation conditions. That means the redundant copies of model partitions are offloaded to edge devices before any of them fail. Furthermore, how to maintain the balance of the computational and communication cost with intentional redundancy is a crucial problem for robust mobile offloading of pre-trained neural networks. To model and optimize this process, we take a directed graph to represent the offloaded partition copies of a pre-trained neural network model (see the graph of the collaborative devices in Figure 3).

In this case, only if all of the copies of a partition become unavailable, this inference task is canceled. As depicted in Figure 3, each cycle represents a partition copy offloaded to a device, and we take a directed graph to depict this failure-resilient inference. In a harsh environment, some devices may fail at the same time. All devices covered by the communication have links with other devices. Considering devices usually communicate through mesh networking or MANET (mobile ad hoc network), the link between every two devices becomes unstable in a harsh operating condition, which is affected by the factors such as the distance between devices, antenna types to establish a reliable and low-latency communication network, etc. Hence, we analyze the impact of device failure or offline devices by formulating the above system in a harsh operating condition.

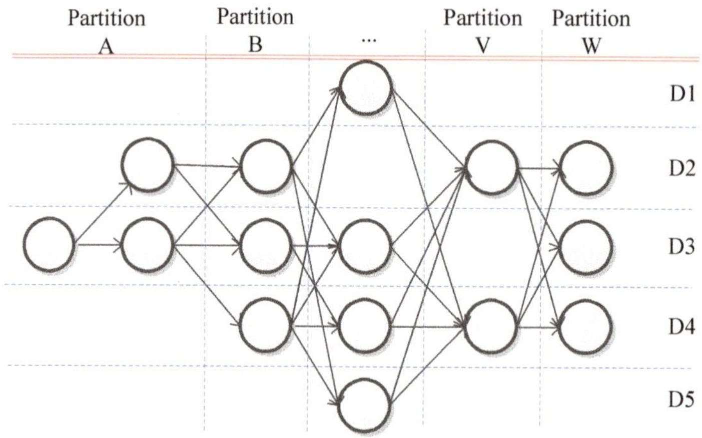

Figure 3. An example for partition offloading with redundancy.

Let m be the total number of devices with offloaded partition copies. Note that some devices cannot link to each other due to their limited wireless communication range. While we separate a pre-trained neural network into partitions, two adjacent partitions comprise a bipartite graph G_0. The copies of the former partition are represented by a set V_1 of size n_1, while the copies of the subsequent partition are V_2 of size n_2. Note that t represents the relative index of elements within V_2, not their absolute values. Let

$$\begin{aligned} &V_1 = \{1, 2, ..., n_1\}, \\ &V_2 = \{n_1 + 1, n_1 + 2, ..., n_1 + n_2\}, \\ &1 \leq s \leq n_1, 1 \leq t \leq n_2 \end{aligned} \tag{1}$$

and the possible links between V_1 and V_2,

$$E = \{ij : i \in V_1, j \in V_2\} \tag{2}$$

Considering the impact of device failure or offline devices for a specific time slot, the $\binom{|E|}{Q}$ candidate graphs with vertex set $V = V_1 \cup V_2$ having exactly Q edges from E and none outside E. Let $K_{s,t}$ be the subgraphs contained in the bipartite graph, and include s vertices with the former partitions and t vertices with the subsequent partitions. The expected number of $K_{s,t}$ is

$$\mathbb{E}(K_{s,t}) = \binom{n_1}{s}\binom{n_2}{t}\binom{|E| - st}{Q - st}\binom{|E|}{Q}^{-1} \tag{3}$$

where the first part of the formula is the number of ways the copies of the first partition of $K_{s,t}$ can be chosen, the second part is the number of ways the copies of the second partition can be chosen. Take $K_{s,t}$ as a whole component and the third part is the number of choices for such a component, i.e., the ways that the $Q - st$ edges outside a $K_{s,t}$ can be chosen. Here,

$$\begin{aligned} \binom{|E| - st}{Q - st}\binom{|E|}{Q}^{-1} &= \prod_{i=0}^{st-1} \frac{Q - i}{n_1 n_2 - i} \\ &< (\frac{Q}{n_1 n_2})^{st} \end{aligned} \tag{4}$$

Hence,

$$\mathbb{E}(K_{s,t}) < \frac{1}{s!t!} n_1^s n_2^t (\frac{Q}{n_1 n_2})^{st} \tag{5}$$

Therefore, when s copies of the former partition and t copies of the subsequent partition fail, the probability that the inference would not be interrupted after the former partition (partition i) is executed is

$$P_i^A > \frac{n_1^s n_2^t - \frac{1}{s!t!} n_1^s n_2^t (\frac{Q}{n_1 n_2})^{st}}{n_1^s n_2^t} = 1 - \frac{1}{s!t!}(\frac{Q}{n_1 n_2})^{st} \tag{6}$$

Here, we name P_i^A as *partition-availability* to identify the availability of partition i.

As for a special case that there is no failed copy of the former partition, whereas t copies of the subsequent partition fail,

$$P_i^A = \frac{n_1 - t}{n_1} \tag{7}$$

On the other hand, in the case that no copy of the former partition but t copies of the subsequent partition fail,

$$P_i^A = \frac{n_2 - s}{n_2} \tag{8}$$

To achieve robust mobile offloading under harsh operating conditions, the key objective is to reduce redundant offloading while ensuring the failure resilience of all DNN partitions. We take *partition-availability* of different partitions to guide mobile offloading of pre-trained neural networks in adaptive failure-aware offloading and inference.

4. Adaptive Failure-Aware Offloading and Inference

In practical industrial scenarios, adverse conditions in harsh and hazardous areas will interfere with inference tasks based on pre-trained neural network models. Once any edge device crashes, the related execution path of the inference task will fail, and then the corresponding inference tasks will be delayed. Considering the wireless environment of edge devices in practical industrial scenarios, network congestion or jitters will exacerbate this problem. To guarantee the effectiveness and efficiency of inference tasks in harsh operating conditions, a failure-resilience strategy should be taken into account.

The state-of-the-art failure-resilience strategies exploit some redundancy to counterbalance the effects of partition failures. Usually, redundancy mainly refers to extra partition copy deployment [38]. The edge devices are monitored to identify failures during the mobile inference process and leverage redundant model partitions to compensate failures. The failure of an edge device leads to the failure of the neural network partition offloaded on the device. We offload copies of neural network partitions to edge devices as redundancy. Here, offload refers to the process of transferring computation or data from one device to another. Due to the heterogeneity of edge devices, different devices require specific failure-resilience configurations. In order to optimize redundancy for each edge device, we add partition copies on demand of the inference and continue to adjust the amount in an adaptive way. In this way, we propose failure-resilient inference in mobile networks (FRIM) in order to guarantee inference performance in scenarios with failed devices. We take three phases to detect and alleviate the impact of partition failures:

1. We divide a pre-trained model into partitions and offload their copies to edge devices. Specifically, extra copies of partitions are offloaded to available edge devices to provide failure-resilience.
2. Once the detection scheme identifies failure of the offloaded partitions, we adapt the number of partition copies according to the difference between statistical dependability.
3. Finally, we use a random scheduling strategy to execute distributed inference tasks.

4.1. Failure Detection

To discover device failure and adapt model partition offloading, we incorporate a heartbeat mechanism into a statistic model and detect failures in time. In the learning stage, the heartbeat packets are sent among devices periodically, and the delay in the response packets indicates the statements of the corresponding devices [39]. Furthermore, considering that the Monte Carlo hypothesis test can take fewer samples to estimate the potential distribution [40], we reuse the detection results in terms of heartbeat response delay in a hypothesis test to determine a threshold for the regular response delay of heartbeat packets. In its failure detection stage, a failure is identified once the average response delay of successive heartbeat packets exceeds this threshold. The whole detection process includes six steps:

1. Periodically, a device sends heartbeat packets to each device and the average response time of the device accumulates;
2. Repeat step 1 k times, and we can obtain k records of average delay;
3. To perform a Monte Carlo hypothesis test, we randomly select a delay record from the above k average delay, record its value, and put it back without replacement. Repeat this k times, and a new group of delay records is attained, whose size is k.
4. Repeat step 3 $g - 1$ times in total, and we can obtain g groups of delay records;
5. In this way, we can obtain the confidence interval of response delay according to the distribution of the above g record groups;
6. Finally, calculate the confidence intervals to achieve a confidence rate where the response delay ought to be larger than the value that is used as a threshold for failure detection.

In this way, our failure detection mechanism can detect and locate failures during runtime. With the support of our detection mechanism, we can adapt the copy of the same partition of the failure device to compensate for the failure.

4.2. Adaptive Redundancy of Failure-Resilient Model Offloading

Compared with conventional methods of computation offloading for pre-trained neural networks, our scheme is tailored to harsh scenarios where devices may fail. We leverage redundancy to counterbalance the impact of device failures. More specifically, if some devices fail in harsh operation conditions, our scheme can adapt collaborative computing across multiple devices with redundant partitions of neural networks and perform inference efficiently. It is essential to note that for this design, partition copies are not offloaded randomly. Upon a device failure being detected, the partitions offloaded on this device cannot support model inference, and the redundant copy of these partitions will be used instead. Here, we need to maintain necessary redundant copy of the partitions; otherwise, we must initiate the process of offloading a new copy of the same partitions to other devices and delay the inference process. Note that, the unnecessary redundancy for specific partitions will occupy the limited resources on devices and degrade inference efficiency. Therefore, we offload the copy of partitions in an adaptive way, achieving efficient and failure-resilient inference. Specifically, for model partitions with copies, we treat each original partition and its copies as a unit. After a device fails, the partition copies on this device, as well as their connected partition copies, cannot be used any more. In this case, we need to calculate the number of copies for each partition and adapt the offloading of the partition copies with Formulas (6)–(8). For the example illustrated in Figure 4, after device D4 fails, not only do the partition copies on D4 become unavailable, but also some successors or precursors of these partition copies become unavailable according to the logic described in lines 10–23 of Algorithm 1. In this algorithm, when a device fails, it triggers a series of checks regarding the connectivity and the availability of related partition copies. For instance, when D4 fails, the system checks if there are any successor or precursor relationships between the partition copies on D4 and those on other devices. Due to the absence of an alternative execution path as defined in the algorithm, some related partition copies on other devices become unavailable. Specifically, in this case, the copy of partition B on D5 is also unavailable after D4 fails. This is because, based on the algorithm, D5 might be considered as a successor or precursor in a certain relation to the partition copies on D4, and when D4 fails, the lack of a proper execution path makes the copy of partition B on D5 unable to be used for inference any more.

More specifically, we implement an algorithm to adapt the offloading of the redundant copy of the partitions (see Algorithm 1).

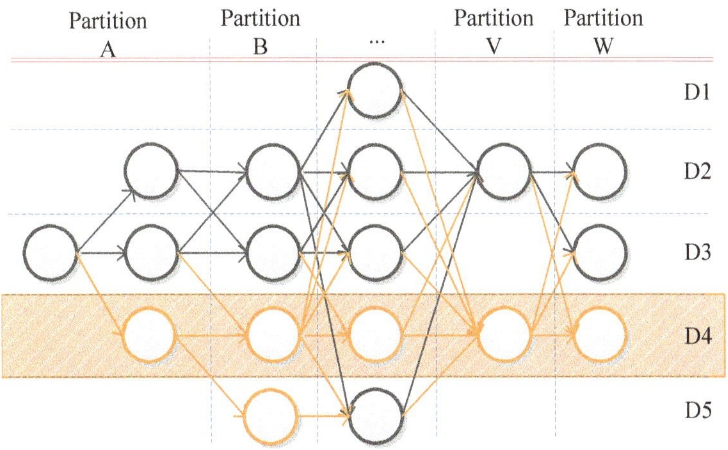

Figure 4. An example for adapting redundancy.

Algorithm 1 Adaptive failure-resilient offloading

Require:
$d[]$: The set of the available devices.
ϵ : The threshold to offload new copy of the partition i to next device with available resource.
if Device d_j detected to be failed **then**
  for Each i in $PSet_j$ $//PSet_j$ is the set of Partition copies in d_j. **do**
    Update(P_i^A);
    if $P_i^A < \epsilon$ $//\epsilon$ is a threshold for offloading new partition copies. **then**
      Announce(d_j, Partition i);$//d_j$ announces its failed copy of Partition i.
      Offload(Partition i, $d[]$);//Offload a copy of Partition i to another available device.
    end if
  end for
end if
for Each d_k in $d[]$ **do**
  if RAnnounce(d_k,d_j,Partition i)&&Contain(d_k,Partition i)
  Check if d_k received an announce and contains Partition i. **then**
    if HasLink(d_k,d_j) **then**
      $l = i - 1;$
      if !HasSuccessor(d_k,Partition l) **then**
        Remove(d_k,Partition l);//Remove isolated precursors.
      end if
      $l = i + 1;$
      if !HasPrecursor(d_k,Partition l) **then**
        Remove(d_k,Partition l);//Remove isolated successors.
      end if
    end if
  end if
end for

The threshold ϵ for offloading new partition copies in Algorithm 1 is an empirical threshold configured according to the failure probabilities of the devices. Different devices have different failure probabilities and thus different empirical thresholds.

4.3. Distributed Robust Inference with Duplicated Partition Copies

The execution delay of the partition copies changes by time. As depicted by the execution graph in Figure 5, each edge between two different states is associated with a specific delay. After a copy of the i_{th} model partition is offloaded to an edge device, we can take this device to execute the offloaded partition copy without any transmission delay, and the delay $\mathcal{T}_i$ for the copy of partition i is equal to the local execution delay $\mathcal{T}_i^{exe}$. Otherwise, a copy of this partition will be offloaded to another high-performance device, and the total delay, $\mathcal{T}_i$, includes the transmission time of input, $\mathcal{T}_i^{in}$; the transmission time of output, $\mathcal{T}_i^{out}$; and the execution delay, $\mathcal{T}_i^{exe}$ on the new device. Hence, the inference delay with the i_{th} partition is

$$\mathcal{T}_i = \mathcal{T}_i^{in} + \mathcal{T}_i^{exe} + \mathcal{T}_i^{out} \tag{9}$$

Considering significant resource consumption on the edge device, the device usually cannot perform multiple partition copies simultaneously. To schedule the offloaded partition copies and facilitate robust inference in a rational way, we design a protocol for distributed inference with duplicated partition copies and execution pathes. The detailed design is present as follows:

1. **Execution Graph Update for Devices with Copies of the i_{th} Partition.** We take each device containing the copies of the i_{th} partition to update its execution graph, including the devices containing the copies of the $i - 1_{th}$ partition and the devices containing copies of the $i + 1_{th}$ partitions.
2. **Shortest Path Calculation for i_{th} Partition Execution.** After a device completes the computation of the i_{th} partition, it calculates the first and second shortest paths on its execution graph to identify two copies of the $i + 1_{th}$ partition and the corresponding devices and then confirms the available computation resources on the above devices by exchanging messages.
    - If the computation resources on any of the aforementioned devices are not enough for executing the $i + 1_{th}$ partition, another device on the next shortest path of the execution graph will be checked to confirm whether it has enough resources to perform the $i + 1_{th}$ partition.
    - This process continues until two devices, D_x and D_y, are selected for executing the $(i+1)_{th}$ partition.
    - Finally, two devices are confirmed for executing the $i + 1_{th}$ partition, namely, D_x and D_y, and then the parameters of the i_{th} model partition are sent to D_x and D_y.
3. **Handling Execution Delays.** For the device to complete its computation of the $i + 1_{th}$ partition earlier, it will broadcast a message to announce its execution delay of the $i + 1_{th}$ partition. Without loss of generalization, we assume D_x first completes its computation. Once the other device, D_y, receives such a message from D_x, D_y stops its computation of the $i + 1_{th}$ partition.
4. **Updating Execution Graph for Other Devices.** Any other devices containing the copies of the i_{th} partition or the $i + 2_{th}$ partition update its execution graph according to the received massage.

In this way, the overall inference delay in this collaborative environment can be calculated using Formula (10):

$$\mathcal{T} = \sum_{i \in I} \min \mathcal{T}_i + \sum_{j \in J} \min \mathcal{T}_j^{exe} \tag{10}$$

where I is the set of partitions executed on local devices, and J is the set of partitions offloaded to other devices.

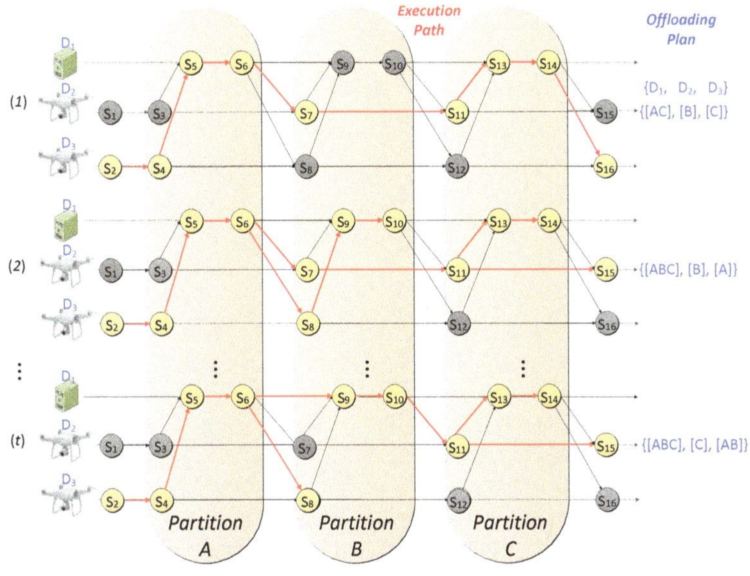

Figure 5. Execution graph with redundant model partitions.

For example, consider the execution sequence along the red path (from S_2 to S_{16}) shown in Figure 5. Initially, we switch to device D_1 and execute partition A. Subsequently, the output of partition A is transmitted to device D_2 for collaborative execution of partition B, and then the output of partition B is sent back to D_1 to continue the execution of partition C. The total sum of weights along the red path represents the overall delay when collaboratively executing this inference. As for the second inference task, D_2 and D_3 are selected to perform partition B. Since D_2 completes the computation of partition B earlier, D_2 broadcasts a message to announce its execution delay of partition B. After D_1 and D_3 receive the message from D_2, D_1 updates the execution delay of partition B in its execution graph, while D_3 stops its computation of partition B. Finally, D_1 and D_2 are selected to perform the copies of partition C, among them, D_2 the first one that completes the computation of partition C. The second inference task has been completed. In this way, this approach allows us to capitalize on performance improvements promptly and minimize the cold start time of interrupted inference in harsh operating conditions.

5. Evaluation

5.1. Experimental Setup

5.1.1. Testbed

We implement FRIM on *Caffe* [41] based on Ubuntu 16.04 LTS and Android 13 systems. Three moto X40 mobile phones with Android 13 are used, namely D1, D2, and D3. These mobile devices are used within a building and connected with a wireless router TP-LINK

AX1800M and communicate with each other by using a network library *boost.asio*. On the other hand, a remote edge server, D4, is deployed in another sub-net, which is used to initiate inference requests in a random way. The detailed information for these devices is listed in Table 1.

Table 1. Detailed information for deployed devices.

ID		**D1, D2, D3**	**D4**
CPU		Kryo 3.2 GHz	i7-9700 (3.00 GHz)
RAM		12 GB	16 GB
GPU		Adreno 740 680 MHz	NVIDIA GeForce RTX 3090
Wireless network		802.11ac (2.4/5 GHz), Bluetooth 5.0	802.11ac (2.4/5 GHz), Bluetooth 5.0
Wired network		Gigabit Ethernet	Gigabit Ethernet
Power	Idle power	4 W	95 W
	Full load power	6 W	120 W
	Average power	5 W	100 W

5.1.2. Implementation

To evaluate the performance of the proposed failure-resilient inference solution with mobile offloading (FRIM), three pre-trained neural networks popular in industrial IoT networks are used as the payloads to be offloaded to mobile devices, including Alex-Net [42], Res-Net [43], and VGG-16 [44]. All of these DNN models are pre-trained on the ImageNet dataset [45], the most popular and authoritative dataset in the field of image classification and object detection. The ImageNet dataset contains 14,197,122 annotated images of 21,841 classes. The proposed scheme (FRIM) and five baselines are implemented as follows:

- No-config: Offloading DNN models with no failure resilience.
- CIODE [9]: Robust offloading strategy of DNN models on multiple end devices. It is robust to deadlock and network jitter through an advanced lock mechanism.
- DFG [7]: It takes additional skip hyper-connections for failure resiliency of distributed DNN inference.
- Early exit [11]: When a partition fails at an early-exit point, the inference task will be terminated before this partition.
- EDGESER [46]: A follow-up work incorporates skip connections and early-exit technology into pre-trained-neural network-based inference tasks.
- FRIM: FRIM can adapt to DNN models of various topologies to offload and enhance the failure resilience of distributed DNN inference.

With human-guided supervision, we make the mobile devices perform inference tasks of object recognition in practical operating conditions, and the inference accuracy and efficiency of different strategies with or without device failures are evaluated. Specifically, we evaluate failure resilience of FRIM and baselines in different scenarios in Section 5.2. Finally, the impact of different failed devices on inference performance is evaluated (in Section 5.3).

5.2. Resilience Evaluation of Inference Tasks

We compare FRIM with No-config (pre-trained-model-based inference without failure resilience), CIODE, DFG, EDGESER, and early exit to evaluate the failure awareness and resilience of FRIM. In detail, the inference accuracy of these schemes is compared under different numbers of failures.

As depicted in Figure 6, for all of the three pre-trained models, FRIM maintains high accuracy. When a random failure occurs, the accuracy of No-config and CIODE decreases to about 7–9% due to their design without failure-resilience configuration. In contrast, DFG, early exit, EDGESER, and FRIM are implemented with failure resilience design. When the number of failures increases, the inference accuracy of DFG, early exit, and EDGESER drops sharply, whereas FRIM can maintain accurate inference very well. This is because DFG has a limited number of skip hyper-connections, where skip hyper-connections are only added between every two neural network layers. Once successive neural network layers fail, the intermediate data of DFG will be lost. The accuracy of early exit and EDGESER will drop more than 57%. In contrast, FRIM offloads the copies of the pre-trained models to the candidate nodes before detecting a failure. Taking advantage of optional execution paths, the intermediate data of FRIM will not be lost, thereby ensuring the accuracy of inference.

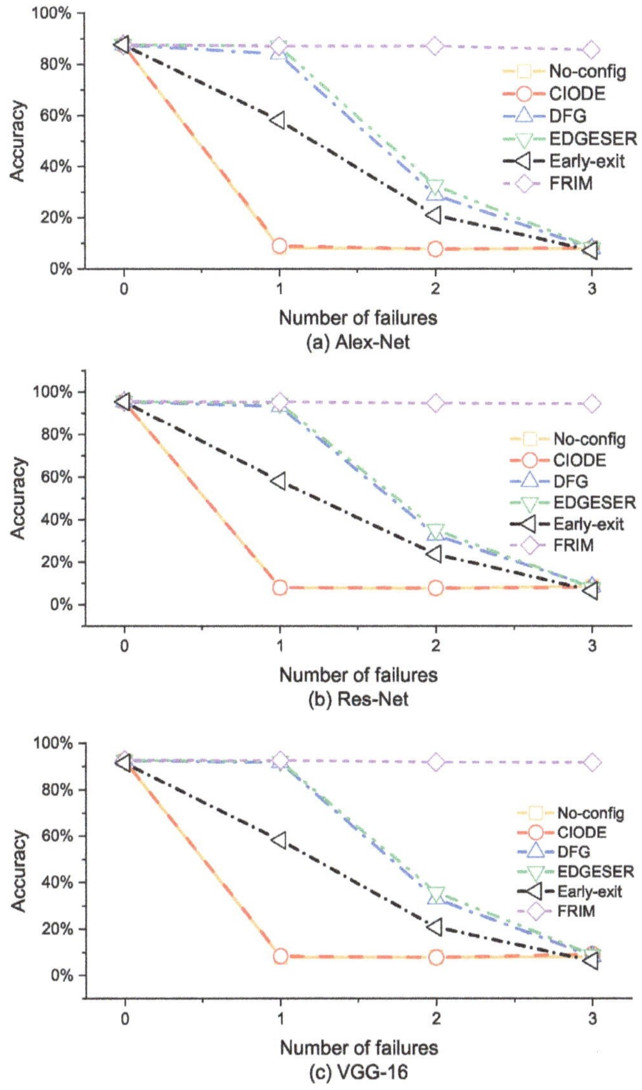

Figure 6. Average accuracy of FRIM and other strategies under different numbers of failures.

FRIM has been experimentally proven to improve the failure resilience of pre-trained-model-based inference tasks. We now comprehensively evaluate the impact of different failures on the inference performance of FRIM. To evaluate that, we first perform inference with D1 failure, D2 failure, or D3 failure. Then, to evaluate the impact of the failure of two nodes, we let $\{D1, D2\}$, $\{D2, D3\}$, or $\{D1, D3\}$ fail. As shown in Table 2, when a failure occurs, the accuracy of No-config and CIODE drops significantly, no matter whether D1, D2, or D3 fails. If two nodes fail, the accuracy of the others except for FRIM, DFG, early exit, and EDGESER, also drops to varying extents. This is because the failure resilience of DFG and EDGESER relies on skip hyper-connections between several neural network layers. When two nodes with consecutive layers fail, there may be no complete execution path for DFG, early exit, and EDGESER, and the loss of intermediate data seems inevitable. Meanwhile, the early exit strategy may result in incomplete or inaccurate inference results. On the contrary, FRIM can avoid these types of potential problems. FRIM offloads the copies of pre-trained models to the candidate nodes before detecting a failure. There is always at least a complete execution path, and the intermediate data of FRIM will not be lost, thereby ensuring the accuracy of inference.

Table 2. Accuracy degradation under various failure scenarios.

Failure Devices		Accuracy (%)					
		No-Config	CIODE	DFG	Early Exit	EDGESER	FRIM
Alex-Net	D1	8.59	9.01	85.24	75.36	87.71	87.66
	D2	8.01	9.22	82.50	72.23	86.50	87.55
	D3	7.99	8.85	84.42	73.86	87.43	86.31
	D1, D2	7.92	7.82	7.98	7.54	8.07	87.42
	D2, D3	7.79	7.85	7.64	7.43	7.79	86.59
	D1, D3	7.88	7.61	71.13	60.36	82.11	87.55
Res-Net	D1	8.33	7.73	93.10	84.20	94.67	95.47
	D2	8.14	8.21	93.65	81.56	94.50	94.75
	D3	7.26	8.03	92.83	80.36	95.03	95.64
	D1, D2	8.07	7.16	8.01	7.96	8.17	94.67
	D2, D3	7.84	8.07	8.18	7.82	7.59	94.81
	D1, D3	7.13	7.94	82.19	71.34	90.23	94.61
VGG-16	D1	8.41	8.69	91.46	82.42	91.74	92.67
	D2	7.36	7.79	92.32	80.23	92.61	92.71
	D3	8.20	8.71	91.55	83.56	92.60	92.65
	D1, D2	7.12	8.26	8.31	8.28	9.03	92.16
	D2, D3	8.55	7.36	8.41	8.32	8.49	91.56
	D1, D3	8.13	8.07	82.12	71.24	89.71	91.69

5.3. *Inference Efficiency Analysis*

To demonstrate the enhanced inference efficiency of FRIM, we compare the inference efficiency of FRIM with that of CIODE, DFG, DGESER, and early exit. Similar to the experiential implementation for impact evaluation of different failures on inference performance, we deploy the partitions of the pre-trained model and schedule the failure of the devices in a random way. Figure 7 illustrates the latency of ten inferences for FRIM and the other baselines for the considered benchmarks (Alexnet, Res-Net32 and VGG16). Each point represents the latency of an inference task. Due to adverse conditions like network jitter, the inference latency of FRIM, CIODE, DFG, EDGESER, and Early-exit exhibits a fluctuating trend of initially increasing and then decreasing over their average latency. FRIM achieve the shortest latency comapred with the others, since the other schemes cannot complete inference tasks without any interruption except for FRIM. The inference latency of EDGESER is longer than that of DFG and early exit due to EDGESER taking too much time to support more redundant failure resilience. Benefiting from neural network partitions and their copies offloaded to candidate nodes, the inference tasks are performed continuously without any interference. On the other hand, the total latency for Alexnet is higher but still lower than VGG16, which happens as Alexnet has two independent paths that come to be efficiently parallelized by all schemes. ResNet32 achieves the best evaluation results in terms of inference efficiency due to its enhanced residual computation.

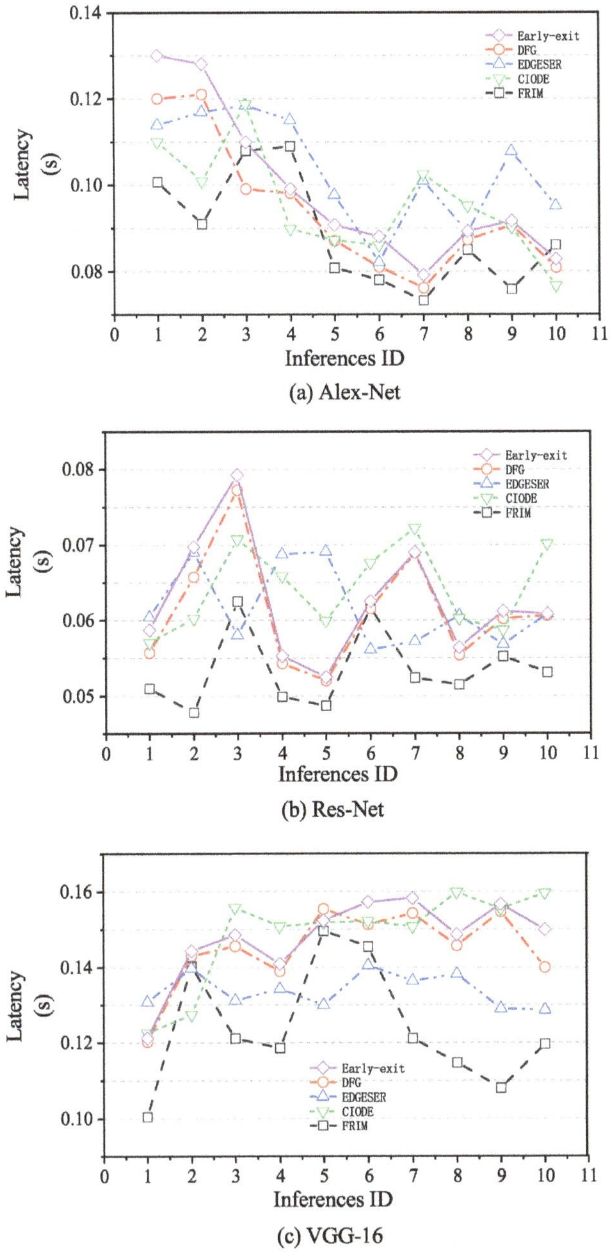

Figure 7. Latency for ten inference queries on FRIM and other strategies.

6. Conclusions

In this paper, we introduce failure-resilient inference in mobile networks (FRIM), a new design method that can improve the failure resilience of distributed DNN inference in edge environments. In contrast to state-of-the-art methods, our proposed solution does not need additional model redesign and retraining while improving the failure resilience of distributed neural networks. In this work, we add copies to DNN partitions as redundancy. We add redundancy on demand and adjust the amount of redundancy adaptively to optimize redundancy. As a part of FRIM, we design a failure detection mechanism to detect and locate failures. In order to select the optimal deployment node for DNN partitions, we propose a DNN partition offloading strategy based on a delay improvement matrix and a deployment matrix. Moreover, we propose two guidelines for adaptively adjusting the number of DNN partitions based on the availability of each DNN partition to optimize redundancy. Finally, we implement FRIM and other baselines in a real edge computing environment composed of edge devices with different hardware configurations. Our experiments show that FRIM can ensure performance and execution efficiency while adapting to varying numbers of failures. In addition, we prove that FRIM is suitable for various failure scenarios through ablation experiments. FRIM is not only applicable to edge computing environments but also has broad potential for deployment in other resource-constrained, failure-prone intelligent systems, such as autonomous vehicles, IoT networks, and remote healthcare systems. Its adaptive redundancy and failure resilience make it particularly suitable for environments where reliability, low latency, and efficient resource usage are critical. Therefore, FRIM opens up new possibilities for robust, real-time, distributed inference in a wide range of industrial applications, achieving future advances in fault-tolerant systems.

Author Contributions: Conceptualization, W.L.; methodology, W.L.; validation, Z.C.; investigation, W.L.; data curation, Z.C.; writing—original draft preparation, W.L.; writing—review and editing, Z.C.; supervision, Y.G. All authors have read and agreed to the published version of the manuscript.

Funding: This work was funded by the National Science Foundation of China (61962045, 61502255, 61650205), the Program for Young Talents of Science and Technology in Universities of Inner Mongolia Autonomous Region (NJYT23104), the Natural Science Foundation of Inner Mongolia Autonomous Region (2023LHMS06023), and the Basic Scientific Research Expenses Program of Universities directly under Inner Mongolia Autonomous Region (JY20220273, JY20240002, JY20240061).

Data Availability Statement: The raw data supporting the conclusions of this article will be made available by the authors on request.

Conflicts of Interest: Author Zhongmin Chen was employed by the company State Grid Corporation of China, Weihai Wenlong Power (Group) Co., Ltd. The remaining authors declare that the research was conducted in the absence of any commercial or financial relationships that could be construed as a potential conflict of interest.

References

1. Tang, S.; Chen, L.; He, K.; Xia, J.; Fan, L.; Nallanathan, A. Computational intelligence and deep learning for next-generation edge-enabled industrial IoT. *IEEE Trans. Netw. Sci. Eng.* **2022**, *10*, 2881–2893. [CrossRef]
2. Huang, Y.; Qiao, X.; Dustdar, S.; Zhang, J.; Li, J. Toward decentralized and collaborative deep learning inference for intelligent iot devices. *IEEE Netw.* **2022**, *36*, 59–68. [CrossRef]
3. Shuvo, M.M.H. Edge AI: Leveraging the Full Potential of Deep Learning. In *Recent Innovations in Artificial Intelligence and Smart Applications*; Springer: Berlin/Heidelberg, Germany, 2022; pp. 27–46.
4. Wu, Y.; Wu, J.; Chen, L.; Liu, B.; Yao, M.; Lam, S.K. Share-Aware Joint Model Deployment and Task Offloading for Multi-Task Inference. *IEEE Trans. Intell. Transp. Syst.* **2024**, *25*, 5674–5687. [CrossRef]
5. Xu, Y.; Mohammed, T.; Di Francesco, M.; Fischione, C. Distributed Assignment with Load Balancing for DNN Inference at the Edge. *IEEE Internet Things J.* **2022**, *10*, 1053–1065. [CrossRef]

6. Hadidi, R.; Cao, J.; Ryoo, M.S.; Kim, H. Robustly executing DNNs in IoT systems using coded distributed computing. In Proceedings of the 56th Annual Design Automation Conference 2019, Las Vegas, NV, USA, 2–6 June 2019; pp. 1–2.
7. Yousefpour, A.; Devic, S.; Nguyen, B.Q.; Kreidieh, A.; Liao, A.; Bayen, A.M.; Jue, J.P. Guardians of the deep fog: Failure-resilient dnn inference from edge to cloud. In Proceedings of the First International Workshop on Challenges in Artificial Intelligence and Machine Learning for Internet of Things, New York, NY, USA, 10–13 November 2019; pp. 25–31.
8. Yousefpour, A.; Nguyen, B.Q.; Devic, S.; Wang, G.; Kreidieh, A.; Lobel, H.; Bayen, A.M.; Jue, J.P. ResiliNet: Failure-Resilient Inference in Distributed Neural Networks. *arXiv* **2020**, arXiv:2002.07386.
9. Chen, Z.; Xu, Z.; Wan, J.; Tian, J.; Liu, L.; Zhang, Y. Conflict-Resilient Incremental Offloading of Deep Neural Networks to the Edge of Smart Environment. *Math. Probl. Eng.* **2021**, *2021*, 1–12. [CrossRef]
10. Sen, T.; Shen, H. Fault Tolerant Data and Model Parallel Deep Learning in Edge Computing Networks. In Proceedings of the 2024 IEEE 21st International Conference on Mobile Ad-Hoc and Smart Systems (MASS), Seoul, Republic of Korea, 23–25 September 2024; pp. 460–468. [CrossRef]
11. Majeed, A.A.; Kilpatrick, P.; Spence, I.; Varghese, B. CONTINUER: Maintaining Distributed DNN Services During Edge Failures. In Proceedings of the 2022 IEEE International Conference on Edge Computing and Communications (EDGE), Barcelona, Spain, 10–16 July 2022; pp. 143–152. [CrossRef]
12. Khan, F.M.; Baccour, E.; Erbad, A.; Hamdi, M. Adaptive ResNet Architecture for Distributed Inference in Resource-Constrained IoT Systems. In Proceedings of the 2023 International Wireless Communications and Mobile Computing (IWCMC), Marrakesh, Morocco, 19–23 June 2023; pp. 1543–1549.
13. Mohammed, T.; Joe-Wong, C.; Babbar, R.; Di Francesco, M. Distributed inference acceleration with adaptive DNN partitioning and offloading. In Proceedings of the IEEE INFOCOM 2020-IEEE Conference on Computer Communications, Toronto, ON, Canada, 6–9 July 2020; pp. 854–863.
14. Jeong, H.J.; Lee, H.J.; Shin, K.Y.; Yoo, Y.H.; Moon, S.M. Perdnn: Offloading deep neural network computations to pervasive edge servers. In Proceedings of the 2020 IEEE 40th International Conference on Distributed Computing Systems (ICDCS), Singapore, 29 November–1 December 2020; pp. 1055–1066.
15. Xu, Z.; Zhao, L.; Liang, W.; Rana, O.F.; Zhou, P.; Xia, Q.; Xu, W.; Wu, G. Energy-aware inference offloading for DNN-driven applications in mobile edge clouds. *IEEE Trans. Parallel Distrib. Syst.* **2020**, *32*, 799–814. [CrossRef]
16. Chen, Y.; Yang, L.T.; Cui, Z. Tensor-Based Lyapunov Deep Neural Networks Offloading Control Strategy with Cloud-Fog-Edge Orchestration. *IEEE Trans. Ind. Inform.* 2023, *early access*.
17. Wang, N.; Duan, Y.; Wu, J. Accelerate cooperative deep inference via layer-wise processing schedule optimization. In Proceedings of the 2021 International Conference on Computer Communications and Networks (ICCCN), Athens, Greece, 19–22 July 2021; pp. 1–9.
18. Almeida, M.; Laskaridis, S.; Venieris, S.I.; Leontiadis, I.; Lane, N.D. Dyno: Dynamic onloading of deep neural networks from cloud to device. *ACM Trans. Embed. Comput. Syst.* **2022**, *21*, 1–24. [CrossRef]
19. Duan, Y.; Wu, J. Computation offloading scheduling for deep neural network inference in mobile computing. In Proceedings of the 2021 IEEE/ACM 29th International Symposium on Quality of Service (IWQOS), Tokyo, Japan, 25–28 June 2021; pp. 1–10.
20. Liu, K.; Liu, C.; Yan, G.; Lee, V.C.; Cao, J. Accelerating DNN Inference With Reliability Guarantee in Vehicular Edge Computing. *IEEE/ACM Trans. Netw.* **2023**, *31*, 3238–3253. [CrossRef]
21. Liao, Z.; Hu, W.; Huang, J.; Wang, J. Joint multi-user DNN partitioning and task offloading in mobile edge computing. *Ad Hoc Netw.* **2023**, *144*, 103156. [CrossRef]
22. Kakolyris, A.K.; Katsaragakis, M.; Masouros, D.; Soudris, D. RoaD-RuNNer: Collaborative DNN partitioning and offloading on heterogeneous edge systems. In Proceedings of the 2023 Design, Automation & Test in Europe Conference & Exhibition (DATE), Antwerp, Belgium, 17–19 April 2023; pp. 1–6.
23. Duan, Y.; Wu, J. Optimizing Job Offloading Schedule for Collaborative DNN Inference. *IEEE Trans. Mob. Comput.* **2023**, *23*, 3436–3451. [CrossRef]
24. Zhou, H.; Li, M.; Wang, N.; Min, G.; Wu, J. Accelerating Deep Learning Inference via Model Parallelism and Partial Computation Offloading. *IEEE Trans. Parallel Distrib. Syst.* **2022**, *34*, 475–488. [CrossRef]
25. Wang, F.; Cai, S.; Lau, V.K. Sequential offloading for distributed dnn computation in multiuser mec systems. *IEEE Internet Things J.* **2023**, *10*, 18315–18329. [CrossRef]
26. Hou, X.; Guan, Y.; Han, T.; Zhang, N. Distredge: Speeding up convolutional neural network inference on distributed edge devices. In Proceedings of the 2022 IEEE International Parallel and Distributed Processing Symposium (IPDPS), Lyon, France, 30 May–3 June 2022; pp. 1097–1107.
27. Qin, W.; Chen, H.; Wang, L.; Xia, Y.; Nascita, A.; Pescapè, A. MCOTM: Mobility-aware computation offloading and task migration for edge computing in industrial IoT. *Future Gener. Comput. Syst.* **2024**, *151*, 232–241. [CrossRef]
28. Younis, A.; Maheshwari, S.; Pompili, D. Energy-Latency Computation Offloading and Approximate Computing in Mobile-Edge Computing Networks. *IEEE Trans. Netw. Serv. Manag.* **2024**, *21*, 3401–3415. [CrossRef]

29. Lin, N.; Bai, L.; Hawbani, A.; Guan, Y.; Mao, C.; Liu, Z.; Zhao, L. Deep Reinforcement Learning-Based Computation Offloading for Servicing Dynamic Demand in Multi-UAV-Assisted IoT Network. *IEEE Internet Things J.* **2024**, *11*, 17249–17263. [CrossRef]
30. Guo, X.; Jiang, Q.; Shen, Y.; Pimentel, A.D.; Stefanov, T. EASTER: Learning to Split Transformers at the Edge Robustly. *IEEE Trans. Comput.-Aided Des. Integr. Circuits Syst.* **2024**, *43*, 3626–3637. [CrossRef]
31. Guo, X.; Jiang, Q.; Pimentel, A.D.; Stefanov, T. RobustDiCE: Robust and Distributed CNN Inference at the Edge. In Proceedings of the 2024 29th Asia and South Pacific Design Automation Conference (ASP-DAC), Incheon, Republic of Korea, 22–25 January 2024; pp. 26–31. [CrossRef]
32. Hu, Y.; Xu, X.; Duan, L.; Bilal, M.; Wang, Q.; Dou, W. End-Edge Collaborative Inference of Convolutional Fuzzy Neural Networks for Big Data-Driven Internet of Things. *IEEE Trans. Fuzzy Syst.* **2024**, *33*, 203–217. [CrossRef]
33. Hou, X.; Ren, Z.; Wang, J.; Cheng, W.; Ren, Y.; Chen, K.C.; Zhang, H. Reliable Computation Offloading for Edge-Computing-Enabled Software-Defined IoV. *IEEE Internet Things J.* **2020**, *7*, 7097–7111. [CrossRef]
34. Whaiduzzaman, M.; Barros, A.; Shovon, A.R.; Hossain, M.R.; Fidge, C. A resilient fog-IoT framework for seamless microservice execution. In Proceedings of the 2021 IEEE International Conference on Services Computing (SCC), Chicago, IL, USA, 5–10 September 2021; pp. 213–221.
35. Li, P.; Koyuncu, E.; Seferoglu, H. Respipe: Resilient model-distributed dnn training at edge networks. In Proceedings of the ICASSP 2021–2021 IEEE International Conference on Acoustics, Speech and Signal Processing (ICASSP), Toronto, ON, Canada, 6–11 June 2021; pp. 3660–3664.
36. Jeong, H.J.; Lee, H.J.; Shin, C.H.; Moon, S.M. IONN: Incremental offloading of neural network computations from mobile devices to edge servers. In Proceedings of the ACM Symposium on Cloud Computing, Carlsbad, CA, USA, 11–13 October 2018; pp. 401–411.
37. Shin, K.Y.; Jeong, H.J.; Moon, S.M. Enhanced Partitioning of DNN Layers for Uploading from Mobile Devices to Edge Servers. In Proceedings of the 3rd International Workshop on Deep Learning for Mobile Systems and Applications, Seoul, Republic of Korea, 21 June 2019; pp. 35–40.
38. Peercy, M.; Banerjee, P. Fault tolerant VLSI systems. *Proc. IEEE* **1993**, *81*, 745–758. [CrossRef]
39. Banerjee, M.; Borges, C.; Choo, K.K.R.; Lee, J.; Nicopoulos, C. A hardware-assisted heartbeat mechanism for fault identification in large-scale iot systems. *IEEE Trans. Dependable Secur. Comput.* **2020**, *19*, 1254–1265. [CrossRef]
40. Xu, Z.; Chen, B.; Wang, N.; Zhang, Y.; Li, Z. Elda: Towards efficient and lightweight detection of cache pollution attacks in ndn. In Proceedings of the 2015 IEEE 40th Conference on Local Computer Networks (LCN), Clearwater Beach, FL, USA, 26–29 October 2015; pp. 82–90.
41. Guo, T. Cloud-based or on-device: An empirical study of mobile deep inference. In Proceedings of the 2018 IEEE International Conference on Cloud Engineering (IC2E), Orlando, FL, USA, 17–20 April 2018; pp. 184–190.
42. Krizhevsky, A.; Sutskever, I.; Hinton, G.E. Imagenet classification with deep convolutional neural networks. *Adv. Neural Inf. Process. Syst.* **2012**, *25*, 1097–1105. [CrossRef]
43. He, K.; Zhang, X.; Ren, S.; Sun, J. Identity mappings in deep residual networks. In Proceedings of the European Conference on Computer Vision, Amsterdam, The Netherlands, 11–14 October 2016; Springer: Berlin/Heidelberg, Germany, 2016; pp. 630–645.
44. Simonyan, K.; Zisserman, A. Very deep convolutional networks for large-scale image recognition. *arXiv* **2014**, arXiv:1409.1556.
45. Russakovsky, O.; Deng, J.; Su, H.; Krause, J.; Satheesh, S.; Ma, S.; Huang, Z.; Karpathy, A.; Khosla, A.; Bernstein, M.; et al. Imagenet large scale visual recognition challenge. *Int. J. Comput. Vis.* **2015**, *115*, 211–252. [CrossRef]
46. Majeed, A.A. Strategies for Maintaining Efficiency of Edge Services. Ph.D. Thesis, Queen's University Belfast, Belfast, UK, 2023.

electronics

MDPI

Article

Enhanced In-Network Caching for Deep Learning in Edge Networks

Jiaqi Zhang [1,2], Wenjing Liu [3,4,*], Li Zhang [1,5] and Jie Tian [6]

[1] Department of Computer Education, Baicheng Medical College, Baicheng 137701, China; 20191100104@imut.edu.cn (J.Z.); zhangli@bcmc.edu.cn (L.Z.)
[2] College of Information Engineering, Inner Mongolia University of Technology, Hohhot 010051, China
[3] College of Data Science and Application, Inner Mongolia University of Technology, Hohhot 010051, China
[4] State Key Laboratory of Networking and Switching Technology, Beijing University of Posts and Telecommunications, Beijing 100876, China
[5] College of Computer and Technology, Jilin University, Changchun 130015, China
[6] Department of Computer Science, New Jersey Institute of Technology, Newark, NJ 07102, USA; jt66@njit.edu
* Correspondence: liuwenjing2015@bupt.edu.cn

Abstract: With the deep integration of communication technology and Internet of Things technology, the edge network structure is becoming increasingly dense and heterogeneous. At the same time, in the edge network environment, characteristics such as wide-area differentiated services, decentralized deployment of computing and network resources, and highly dynamic network environment lead to the deployment of redundant or insufficient edge cache nodes, which restricts the efficiency of network service caching and resource allocation. In response to the above problems, research on the joint optimization of service caching and resources in the decentralized edge network scenario is carried out. Therefore, we have conducted research on the collaborative caching of training data among multiple edge nodes and optimized the number of collaborative caching nodes. Firstly, we use a multi-queue model to model the collaborative caching process. This model can be used to simulate the in-network cache replacement process on collaborative caching nodes. In this way, we can describe the data flow and storage changes during the caching process more clearly. Secondly, considering the limitation of storage space of edge nodes and the demand for training data within a training epoch, we propose a stochastic gradient descent algorithm to obtain the optimal number of caching nodes. This algorithm entirely takes into account the resource constraints in practical applications and provides an effective way to optimize the number of caching nodes. Finally, the simulation results clearly show that the optimized number of caching nodes can significantly improve the adequacy rate and hit rate of the training data, with the adequacy rate reaching 84% and the hit rate reaching 100%.

Keywords: deep learning in edge networks; in-network caching; optimization configuration; queuing theory

1. Introduction

Industry 5.0 has favored edge computing and AI technologies more frequently in recent years. The driving forces behind this decision are the expansion of Industrial IoT connected manufacturing, Industrial IoT resources, data analysis techniques that require less power-consuming computing equipment, and the demand for real-time decision-making in Industry 5.0 [1]. With the extension and expansion of the network center, edge computing technology is another major network construction change. The traditional cloud computing method is to pass all the data to the remote data center for processing through the core network, which will not only cause the network center to face enormous communication pressure, but also cause a significant delay due to long-distance data transmission. Compared with cloud computing, edge computing can not only relieve bandwidth pressure but also ensure real-time data transmission by deploying the network, storage, and computing resources in a distributed manner at the edge of the network and in processing the request tasks submitted by terminal devices [2,3]. Edge computing technology has the following characteristics: First, it can reduce the load pressure of network bandwidth and sink request tasks to edge cache nodes. Second, it can process request tasks at edge cache nodes, thereby reducing transmission delay and satisfying delay-sensitive applications. Third, it can effectively protect private data by taking the authorized entity as the trust center and integrating multi-trust domain sharing. In general, edge computing sinks some essential services to edge cache nodes for caching. It provides services to users through distributed deep learning on edge servers, which is an intermediate stage between cloud computing centers and personal computing centers [4]. The distributed deep learning framework in the network is shown in Figure 1.

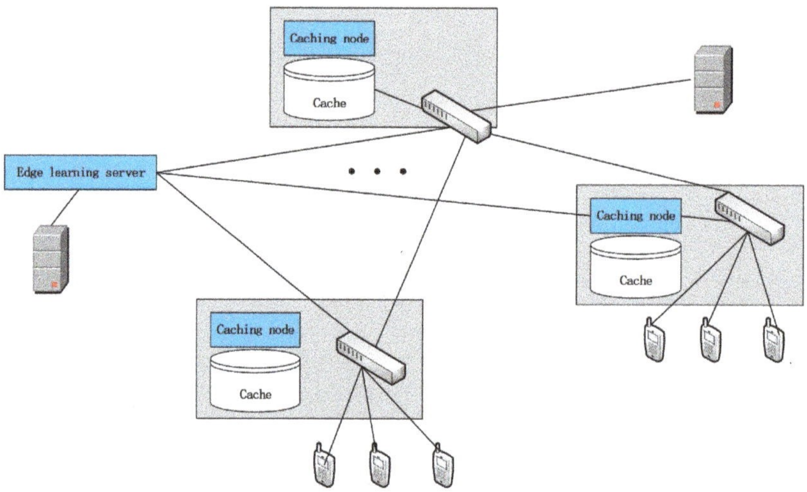

Figure 1. In-network caching for distributed deep learning.

At present, edge computing combined with neural network models is mainly used in the following five aspects, and these applications have significant implications for cache adequacy rate and hit rate within the system: (1) The application of edge deep learning [5,6]: In this context, edge deep learning is often employed in scenarios where real-time data processing is crucial. For instance, in Industrial Internet of Things (IIoT) applications, sensors constantly generate massive amounts of data. When using edge deep learning for tasks like predictive maintenance, a high cache adequacy rate is essential. This ensures that the necessary historical data and model parameters related to equipment operation are readily available in the cache. The hit rate also plays a vital role as it determines the efficiency of accessing the cached data during the decision-making process of the deep learning model. If the cache hit rate is low, it may lead to delays in analyzing sensor data and identifying potential equipment failures. (2) The reasoning of edge deep learning [7–10]: Edge deep-learning reasoning requires quick access to relevant data and models stored in the cache. Consider an intelligent surveillance system in an urban environment. The deep learning model needs to rapidly retrieve cached data related to object recognition patterns and previous surveillance events. A sufficient cache adequacy rate guarantees that the model has all the necessary information for accurate reasoning. Meanwhile, a high hit rate ensures that the data retrieval process is seamless, enabling the system to quickly make inferences about potential security threats or abnormal situations based on the real-time video feed. (3) The training of edge deep learning [11,12]: During edge deep learning training, a large amount of data is required to optimize the model. In applications such as autonomous vehicles, where edge computing is used to train the vehicle's decision-making system, the cache adequacy rate directly affects the availability of training data. If the cache can store sufficient data related to different driving scenarios, road conditions, and traffic patterns, the training process will be more effective. Additionally, a high cache hit rate reduces the time spent on data fetching from other sources, accelerating the training process and improving the overall performance of the deep learning model for better decision-making in complex driving situations. (4) The application of edge deep learning deployment [13–15]: When deploying edge deep learning applications, ensuring a proper cache environment is crucial. For example, in a distributed healthcare system where edge devices are used for patient monitoring and diagnosis, the cache adequacy rate determines whether the deep learning models on these devices have access to comprehensive patient data, including a history of vital signs and previous diagnosis records. A high hit rate allows for quick access to these data during the deployment of diagnostic models, enabling timely and accurate medical decisions. This is especially important in emergency situations where every second counts. (5) Deep learning for edge computing optimization [16–18]: Edge computing optimization using deep learning aims to improve the overall efficiency of the system. In scenarios like intelligent grid management, where numerous edge nodes handle power consumption data and grid status information, a high cache adequacy rate ensures that the deep learning models have sufficient data for optimizing power distribution and predicting demand. The cache hit rate affects the speed at which these models can access and process the data, enabling a more efficient control of the power grid and reducing energy waste. Overall, optimizing cache adequacy rate and hit rate in these applications can significantly enhance the performance of edge computing combined with neural network models. Usually, after the neural network model is deployed on the edge server, to ensure the hit rate and adequate rate of the cached training data and improve the efficiency of model training and update, it is necessary to analyze the distribution of training data in the edge cache nodes. Based on this, edge computing needs to use multiple edge cache nodes to perform the distributed processing of computing tasks through operations such as caching [19,20]. Due to the unbalanced resource allocation of edge nodes and the small number of resources, edge caching still faces challenges [21]. It is necessary to analyze the impact of the number of nodes caching data on model training and configure a reasonable number of edge cache nodes for the cached data. When the configured number of edge cache nodes is too large, there will be idle edge cache nodes, resulting in a waste of resource allocation; on the contrary, when the configured number of edge cache nodes is too small, the pre-cached data will be inadequate, and it is difficult to support the neural network in the edge server. The model training of the network will thus be inadequate, thereby reducing the performance of the network cache. Therefore, configuring the optimal number of edge cache nodes for different Internet tasks is a critical issue in improving the performance of in-network caches.

To improve the performance of in-network caching, this paper establishes a multi-edge node training data collaborative caching model to simulate the in-network cache replacement process of edge caching nodes. In the period of model training, based on the constraints of maximizing cache utilization, a stochastic gradient descent algorithm is designed to solve the optimal number of edge cache nodes. The main contributions of this paper are as follows:

1. Based on the multi-queue model, an in-network collaborative caching model of multi-edge cache nodes is established to simulate the in-network cache replacement process of edge cache nodes.
2. In the period of model training, based on the constraints of maximizing cache utilization, a stochastic gradient descent algorithm is designed to find the optimal number of edge cache nodes.
3. The sim4DistrDL-based simulation results demonstrate that the hit rate of cached training data can be improved and the proposed scheme can efficiently support the training process of deep learning models at the edge.

Section 2 introduces related work on caching; Section 3 describes the in-network caching model for multiple-edge-node collaborative deep learning; Section 4 evaluates the effectiveness of the enhanced in-network caching scheme for multiple-edge-node collaborative deep learning through simulation; and Section 5 concludes the whole article.

2. Related Work

To improve the caching performance and the efficiency of neural network training in edge networks, researchers at home and abroad have conducted extensive and in-depth studies. They start from different angles to explore new caching strategies and optimization algorithms, with the aim of reducing data transmission latency and improving cache hit rate. At the same time, they improve the training methods of neural networks to adapt to the resource constraints and real-time requirements of edge computing environments. Among the various research efforts, Zahra Aghapour et al. proposed a method based on deep reinforcement learning. This method divides offloading and resource allocation into two sub-problems: the algorithm updates the offloading policy according to environmental information, and it optimizes resource allocation with the Salp SwarmAlgorithm [22]. Qianlin Liang et al. designed analytic models to capture the performance of DNN inference workloads on shared edge accelerators, such as GPU and edgeTPU, under different multiplexing and concurrency behaviors [23]. Zhiyuan Wang et al. designed and implemented an FL system called CoopFL, which trains DNNs through the cooperation between devices and edge servers [24]. Zhenyang Shu et al. modeled a relay-assisted multi-access edge computing (MEC) framework, employing multi-hop transmission to enable cross-domain service coverage [25]. Avilia Kusumaputeri Nugroho et al. presented NAFEOS, a proposed solution formulated as a two-stage algorithm that can effectively integrate association optimization with vertical and horizontal scaling. The Stage-1 problem optimizes the user–base station association and federation assignment so that the edge servers can be utilized in a balanced manner. The following Stage-2 dynamically schedules both vertical and horizontal scaling so that the fluctuating task offloading demands from users are fulfilled [26]. Zheng Lin et al. advocated for the integration of the edge computing paradigm and parallel split learning (PSL), allowing multiple edge devices to offload substantial training workloads to an edge server via layer-wise model splitting [27]. Yonglin Pu et al. drew on the domino effect and the combined impact of task migration. A dynamic node-growing algorithm (DNGA) and a dynamic node-shrinking algorithm (DNSA), both of which are grounded in the task migration strategy, are put forward [28]. Yishan Chen et al. built a flexible and generic DAG task model to support the associative task offloading process with complex data dependencies in IoT edge computing environments. Additionally, a priority-based DAG task offloading algorithm and a secondary resource allocation algorithm are proposed to minimize the response delay and improve the resource utilization of edge servers [29]. Linbo Liao et al. proposed an online algorithm, namely, the double reinforcement learning computation offloading (DRLCO) algorithm, which jointly decides the offloading decision; the CPU frequency; and transmit power for computation offloading [30]. Binbin Huang et al. adopted the graph convolution neural network to transform multiple workflow instances with different shapes and sizes into embeddings and formulate the online multiple workflow scheduling problem as a finite Markov decision process. Furthermore, they proposed a policy gradient learning-based online multiple-workflow scheduling scheme (PG-OMWS) to optimize the average completion time of all workflow instances [31]. Xingwang Wang et al. presented EHCI, an on-edge high-throughput collaborative inference framework for real-time video analytics. On the mobile device, EHCI crops the critical regions from the current video frame based on the local detection cache and offloads these regions to the edge server, which can significantly reduce bandwidth consumption and computation costs [32]. The above literature studies present issues such as the joint optimization of task offloading and resource allocation for different MEC scenarios. However, the above research ignores the impact of the relationship between the deployment number of edge nodes and service caching on performance. At the same time, centralized control management schemes make it difficult to meet the application requirements of ultra-large capacity and ultra-low latency in edge networks, which also brings challenges to the integration and scheduling of multi-dimensional network resources. Therefore, a more flexibly distributed resource management scheme is needed.

Deep learning methods learn low-dimensional codes from high-dimensional input vectors and are widely used in many fields, such as image recognition, and achieve remarkable results. In addition, the queuing theory is a well-known method that can be applied to analyze and optimize systems. Although it is not a traditional supervised feature learning method, in the context of deep learning, it has been explored to find concise and high-level representations of complex data and has been widely studied to realize deep learning. Based on previous studies, this paper proposes an enhanced in-network caching scheme for deep learning in edge networks. Its purpose is to analyze and evaluate the optimal configuration number of edge cache nodes. This is achieved by establishing a multi-queue model that simulates the cache in the network, aiming to effectively improve the cache performance in the edge network.

3. In-Network Cache Modeling for Deep Learning in Edge Networks

In order to study the multi-edge node training data collaborative caching modeling, this section first presents the notation and problem definition. Table 1 describes the symbols used in this article.

Table 1. Description of symbols.

Symbol	Description
D	the maximum capacity of a single edge node
λ	average arrival speed
ϖ	average response time
π	steady-state probability
π_i	the steady-state probability of the i-th node
c	the number of deployed edge nodes
ρ	replacement strength of an edge cache node
W_s	average sojourn time
L_s	average queue length
h	awaiting the limiting value of the average queue length

Currently, the Least Recently Used (LRU) [33,34] algorithm is the most widely used in caching. The idea of the algorithm is that when there is a referenced page in memory, the content of the list needs to be separated, and the page is moved to the head of the cache queue; on the contrary, it is directly cached. Therefore, the execution process of the algorithm in the multi-edge cache node is as follows: When there is a new data request, first, it is judged whether the data exist in the cache queue of the multi-edge cache node. Second, if data exist, move them to the head of the multi-edge cache node's cache queue; otherwise, insert them directly into the head of the queue. Since the request probability of each datum is the same and has no aftereffect, the LRU cache queue of multiple edge cache nodes can be abstracted into a Markov chain model.

3.1. Cached Data Replacement Model for Edge Nodes

In order to identify and analyze the relationship between the sojourn time of data caching and the queue length of data caching in multi-edge nodes, a multi-queue hierarchical collaboration model that simulates in-network caching is established. Since the data caching process is memoryless and follows a Markov chain, queuing theory algorithms can be adopted. To facilitate the calculation, it is first assumed that the cached data of the edge cache nodes obey a discrete probability distribution. Secondly, due to the limited cache capacity of a single edge node, according to the limited algorithm of queuing theory, the multi-queue hierarchical collaboration model should satisfy M1/M2/c/D, where M1 represents the distribution of the data request interval; M2 represents the distribution of the response time; c represents the number of deployed edge nodes; and D represents the maximum capacity of a single edge node. Finally, a model for simulating the replacement of cached data in the edge network is established to discover and analyze the relationship between the sojourn time of the cached data in the node and the queue length. The difference equation for this model is expressed as follows:

$$\begin{cases} \lambda\pi_{n-1} - [\lambda + n(\varpi)]\pi_n + (n+1)(\varpi)\pi_{n+1} = 0 \\ \lambda\pi_{n-1} - [\lambda + c(\varpi)]\pi_n + c(\varpi)\pi_{n+1} = 0 \\ \lambda\pi_{D-1} - c(\varpi)\pi_D = 0 \\ \lambda\pi_0 - (\varpi)\pi_1 = 0 \end{cases} \quad (1)$$

Among them, n represents the number of data that need to be cached, and π_D represents the steady state of the node cache capacity (that is, the speed of data caching and releasing is balanced and does not exceed the node capacity limit). According to the queuing theory model, the replacement strength ρ of an edge cache node is

$$\rho = \frac{\lambda}{\varpi} \quad (2)$$

The steady-state probabilities of the node caching data and releasing data are

$$\pi_0 = \left[\sum_{i=0}^{c-1}\frac{\rho^n}{n!} + \frac{\rho^c(1-\rho_c^{D-c+1})}{c!(1-\rho_c)}\right]^{-1} \quad 0 < \rho_c < 1 \quad (3)$$

The replacement strength ρ_c of c edge cache nodes is

$$\rho_c = \frac{c\lambda}{\varpi} \quad (4)$$

The steady-state probabilities of caching and releasing pieces of data in the node are

$$\pi_n = \frac{\rho^n}{c!c^{n-c}}\pi_0 \quad (5)$$

The average queue length L_s of c edge cache nodes is

$$L_s = \sum_{n=1}^{c}(n-1)\pi_n \quad (6)$$

The average sojourn time W_s of c edge cache nodes is

$$W_s = \frac{L_S}{\lambda(1-\pi_D)} \quad (7)$$

In the multi-edge node data cache replacement model based on the queuing theory, fewer edge cache nodes need to be deployed when the cache queue length of each node is constant, the training data remain for a long time, the required cache space is large, and more edge cache nodes need to be deployed. Both cases will affect the performance of training data caching within the edge network, thereby affecting the training results of the model. Therefore, when the cache space (queue) of each node is determined based on the multi-queue cooperative cache model, the configuration number of edge cache nodes can be effectively optimized.

3.2. Cache Deployment Optimization for In-Network Caching

In order to optimize the configuration number of edge cache nodes, this paper proposes a configuration algorithm based on stochastic gradient descent (enhanced stochastic gradient descent algorithm, ESGD) [35–37]. The idea of the algorithm is that when the maximum capacity of a single edge node is limited, the optimal relationship between the sojourn time and queue length in the multi-queue cooperative cache model is taken as the solution goal, and the idea of stochastic gradient descent is used to solve for the optimal node quantity.

For the convenience of calculation, the algorithm first assumes that the training period is T. Second, input parameters such as the stochastic gradient descent model, dataset, etc., are considered to find edge cache nodes where the data sojourn time and data queue length meet the requirements of the minimum time and adequacy for training data. Finally, within the period of model training, the optimal number of node configurations c is returned based on the constraint of maximizing the cache utilization. Among the parameters, when looking for an edge cache node that can meet the minimum time and adequate training data for the sojourn time and data queue length in the node, according to the limit theorem, there is ϵ, such that

$$\log \sum \mathrm{L}_s \otimes \mathrm{W}_s - \mathrm{h} < \varepsilon \tag{8}$$

The queue length limit h is expressed as

$$\mathrm{h} = \frac{d \log \sum \mathrm{L_S} \otimes \mathrm{W_S}}{dc_i} \tag{9}$$

This Algorithm 1 takes the dataset, learning rate, average arrival speed, average response speed, training period, replacement strength of an edge cache node, edge cache node-set, and maximum capacity of a single edge node as inputs, and the output is the optimal number of nodes. First, initialize the variables (Line 1), and calculate the steady-state probability that each edge cache node maintains a balanced storage space in the data caching process (Line 2). Then, calculate the average queue length, steady-state probability, average sojourn time, and length limit of the collaborative cache of n edge cache nodes (Lines 3–11). Next, traverse the n nodes in the edge cache node-set to determine the sojourn time and amount of data (queue length) in the edge cache node, and check whether the minimum time and adequacy of training data for the neural network are met (Line 12). If the conditions are met, update the optimal number of nodes; otherwise, return and break the loop. When all the nodes in the edge cache node-set have been traversed, jump out of the loop (Lines 13–17). Finally, return the value of c, which is the optimal number of nodes (Line 18). The convergence rate of the algorithm is related to the learning rate α. A higher learning rate α enables the model to converge faster, but it may also lead to under-fitting problems.

Algorithm 1 ESGD algorithm

Input:

Stochastic gradient descent model, dataset, learning rate α, average arrival speed λ, average response speed ϖ, training period T, replacement strength ρ of an edge cache node, edge cache node-set ($n_0, n_1, \dots, n_c$), D;

Output:

c;

Initialization parameters $c, \rho, L_s, W_s, c_i, b_i, n, D$;

$\pi_0 = \left[\sum_{i=0}^{c-1} \frac{\rho^n}{n!} + \frac{\rho^c\left(1-\rho_c^{D-c+1}\right)}{c!(1-\rho_c)} \right]^{-1}$;

t = 0;

while (t $\leq$ T) **do**

  t++;

  for i in range(n) **do**

    $\mathrm{L_s} = \sum_{\mathrm{n}=1}^{\mathrm{c}} (\mathrm{n}-1)\pi_{\mathrm{n}}$;

    $\pi_{\mathrm{n}} = \frac{\rho^n}{c!c^{n-c}}$;

    $\mathrm{W_s} = \frac{\mathrm{L_S}}{\lambda(1-\pi_{\mathrm{D}})}$;

    $\mathrm{h} = \frac{d \log \sum \mathrm{L_S} \otimes \mathrm{W_S}}{dc_i}$;

  end for

  if $\log \sum W_s \otimes L_s - h < \varepsilon$ **then**

    $c = c_i$;

    break;

  end if

  $c_{i+1} = c_i - \alpha * h$;

end while

return c

End

4. Simulation and Results Analysis

4.1. Simulation Environment

Hardware environment: Leno i7, 3.4G CPU, and 16G RAM. Software environment: Ubuntu 16.04, sim4DistrDL with kernel version 3.29, and C++ language. On the sim4DistrDL [38–40] simulation platform, the multi-edge node training data collaborative cache modeling was simulated and evaluated, and five edge network typologies were built. Five types of edge networks were constructed. As shown in Figure 2, Figure 2a illustrates that one edge server obtains training data from two edge cache nodes via one router. Figure 2b shows that one edge server acquires training data from three edge cache nodes via one router. Figure 2c indicates that one edge server obtains training data from four edge cache nodes via one router. Figure 2d demonstrates that one edge server fetches training data from five edge cache nodes via two routers. Figure 2e presents that one edge server retrieves training data from six edge cache nodes via three routers. In the real network, we observed the training process of popular deep learning models (MLP, AlexNet, VGG) on OpenNN and correspondingly set the simulation parameters according to the observation. Let the maximum cache capacity of each edge cache node be $D = 1024$ MB, the average speed of cached data be 1.36 KB/s, and the average speed of responding to server requests be 0.94 KB/s. In the entire edge network environment, the sending frequency of background traffic packets is set to 0.4 KB/s.

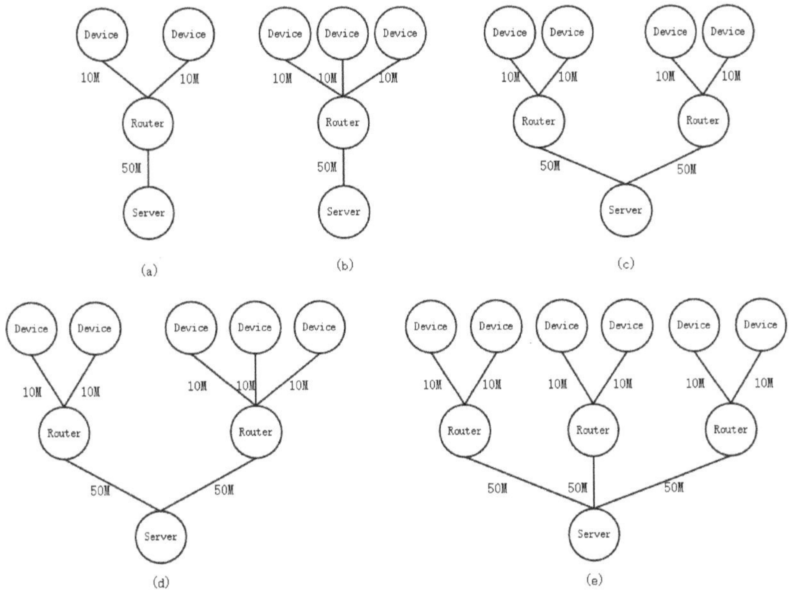

Figure 2. Topology diagrams.

4.2. Simulation Dataset

A dataset of twenty newsgroups [41] was used, which was published by Ken Lang in the Proceedings of the 12th International Conference on Machine Learning in 1995 and is one of the international standard datasets currently used for text classification, text mining, and information retrieval research. The dataset consists of 20,000 documents, approximately equally divided into 20 groups. In order to effectively evaluate the impact of the optimal configuration number of edge cache nodes on the cache performance in the edge network (data cache hit rate and adequate rate), 10 groups were used; each group contained 400 documents, corresponding to a topic number (documents with the same category of feature words were divided into the same group of topics). For example, the group number for alt. stheism is topic No. 0; the group number for comp. graphics is topic No.1; the comp.windows.x group is numbered as topic 2, etc., until the 10 groups are numbered sequentially. Since each file consists of text data and labels, it has typical characteristics. Therefore, the dataset can effectively simulate the hit rate and adequate rate of the neural network training model cache in the edge network under different hierarchical network typologies. A total of 4000 files were then cached in different hierarchical network topology nodes. The specific information of the dataset is shown in Table 2.

Table 2. The information of the dataset.

Topic	Topic Number	Number of Files
comp. graphics	1	400
comp. windows.x	2	400
misc. forsale	3	400
rec. autos	4	400
rec. sport. baseball	5	400
sci. electronic	6	400
sci. space	7	400
talk. politics. guns	8	400
talk. religion. misc	9	400

4.3. Evaluation Index

The effectiveness of the multi-edge node training data collaborative caching model is evaluated using the hit rate and the adequate rate. The hit rate is expressed as the number of hit packets divided by the number of cached data. The adequate rate is expressed as the amount of data requested for model training divided by the amount of cached data.

The hit rate formula is

$$\text{Hit rate} = \frac{N_r}{N} \tag{10}$$

The adequate rate formula is

$$\text{Adequate rate} = \frac{N_r^{\text{training}}}{N} \tag{11}$$

where N_r is the amount of data needed to satisfy the received request (number of hit packets), $\mathrm{N_r^{training}}$ is the amount of data requested for model training, and N is the amount of cached data.

4.4. Simulation Competition Scheme

In different hierarchical network topologies, the comparison schemes include the enhanced stochastic gradient descent algorithm (ESGD), maximum popularity cache (MPC), and uniform cache (UC). The performance of these schemes in terms of hit rate and adequate rate is compared. Among them, MPC first ranks the popularity of the content, and then the ranking node caches the most popular content. UC is to cache content evenly across nodes. The scheme comparison is shown in Table 3.

Table 3. The steps of the scheme.

Scheme	Step
MPC	1. Rank the popularity of content 2. Sorter caches the most popular content 3. Cache content in nodes
UC	1. Ignore differences in content popularity 2.The caching probability of content is uniformly distributed 3. Cache content in nodes

4.5. Simulation Results

Ten groups of news data were adopted to analyze and compare the impact of the number of deployed nodes on data caching and model training in the edge network environment with different numbers of deployed nodes. As shown in Figure 3, when only two or three cache nodes are deployed in the edge network environment, the adequacy rates of ESGD, MPC, and UC are all relatively low. The reason for this phenomenon is that with a small number of deployed nodes, the nodes cannot cache sufficient data, resulting in the cached data being insufficient to support model training. When four cache nodes are deployed in the edge network environment, the adequacy rates of ESGD, MPC, and UC can all meet the minimum adequacy rate requirement of 70%. The minimum adequacy rate is determined based on the empirical rule, that is, it is based on the number of observed training samples and the performance of the training model, and it represents the minimum amount of data used for model training. When five or six cache nodes are deployed and when using the ESGD and MPC models, the data cached in the nodes are relatively sufficient to support model training. However, when using the UC model to cache data, it fails to meet the minimum adequacy rate requirement for model training. The reason for this phenomenon is that the ESGD model has restrictions on the cache queue length and the data residence time in the nodes. The MPC model caches and replaces stale data based on the popularity of the data, while the UC model adopts uniform caching and cannot cache data according to user preferences. Moreover, the data cached in the nodes have no characteristics, and there is a large amount of redundant data.

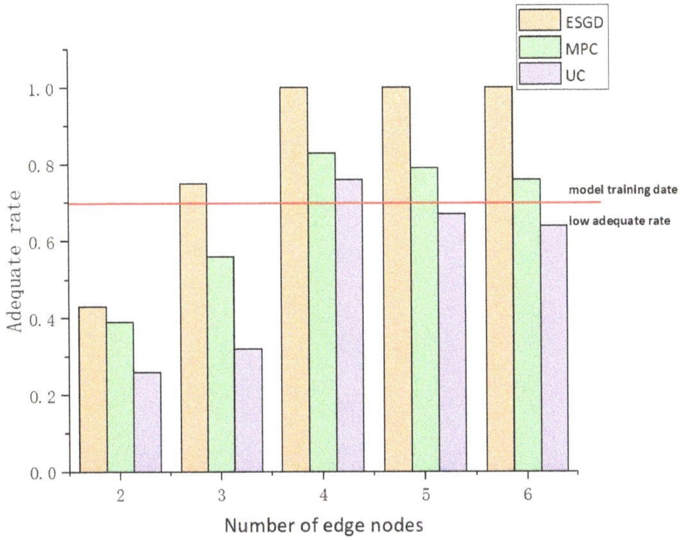

Figure 3. The result of adequate rate.

We conducted a more in-depth analysis and comparison of how the number of deployed nodes affects the cache hit rate via simulation. Under ideal circumstances, the cache hit rate is usually positively correlated with the number of deployed nodes, that is, the more nodes are deployed, the higher the hit rate. However, in practical scenarios, the redundant deployment of nodes can bring many problems. On the one hand, it will increase costs and cause a waste of resources; on the other hand, it will lead to performance degradation, and a large amount of data of no value for model training will be stored in the nodes. As shown in Figure 4, when only two or three nodes are deployed in the edge network environment for data caching and model training, the hit rates of the ESGD, MPC, and UC are all relatively low. The reason for this is that too few nodes result in limited cache capacity, and the data required by the neural network training model may not be fully stored. When data requests are made, a large number of requests cannot be satisfied in the cache, which requires data to be retrieved from other storage locations or may even fail to obtain accurate data, thereby negatively affecting the accuracy of model training and ultimately leading to a reduction in the cache hit rate. When four nodes are deployed in the edge network environment for data caching and model training, the cache hit rates of ESGD, MPC, and UC all increase. However, when five or six edge cache nodes are deployed, the cache hit rates decrease again. The reason for this phenomenon is that there are redundant edge cache nodes in the edge network, and at the same time, there are a large number of background traffic packets in the nodes, such as system updates, network monitoring data transmissions, etc. These traffic flows will occupy cache resources. In the edge network environment, such background traffic may frequently replace the valid data in the cache. Even if there are a large number of edge cache nodes, when background traffic packets keep pouring in, the cache nodes will be busy processing these non-critical data, thus squeezing out the data truly used for user requests from the cache. This will cause the neural network training model to deviate, thereby leading to a further decrease in the cache hit rate.

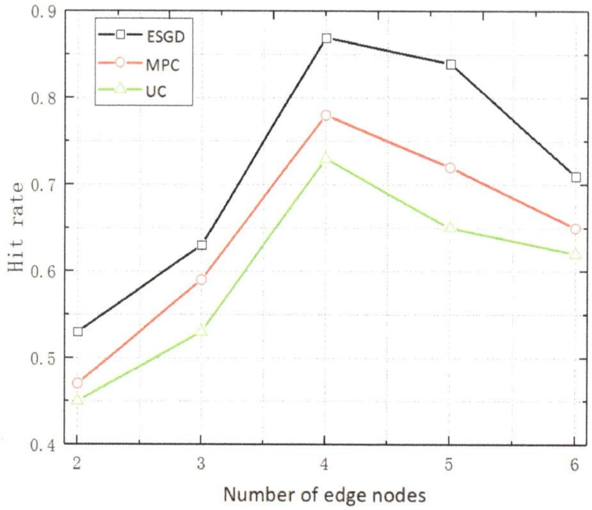

Figure 4. The result of hit rate.

As shown in Figures 3 and 4, both the adequacy rate and the hit rate of the ESGD model are higher than those of the MPC and UC models. The reason for this is that the ESGD scheme takes the optimization relationship between the data cache residence time and the cache space in the multi-queue collaborative caching model as the solution goal, and uses the stochastic gradient descent idea to search for the optimal number of nodes for data caching. Specifically, this model ensures that the data in the cache are those that are likely to be accessed in the near future by reasonably setting the maximum residence time of data in the node. As shown in Table 4, after the edge nodes are optimally deployed, the adequacy rate of the training data required by the ESGD model can reach 87%, and the cache hit rate can reach 100%. This is mainly attributed to the high emphasis of the ESGD model on the balance between cache space and data residence time. The ESGD model adjusts the residence time of data in the cache according to the access frequency and timeliness of the data. For example, for real-time data frequently used in model training, their residence time will be correspondingly extended. Through the optimization of edge node deployment, the cache space of each node can be more reasonably allocated so that this balance reaches an optimal state, thereby ensuring that the key training data will not be replaced prematurely, and thus ensuring the adequacy rate of the training data. In addition, the ESGD uses the stochastic gradient descent algorithm to determine the optimal number of edge nodes. In this process, it comprehensively considers various factors such as network bandwidth, data flow volume, and data update frequency. During the optimization process, it can accurately calculate the required number of nodes based on the actual conditions of the edge network, including network coverage range, user density, etc. In this way, each node can effectively store training data, thereby increasing the cache hit rate.

Table 4. The impact of node quantity on adequate rate and hit rate.

Number of Nodes	Adequate Rate	Hit Rate
2	53%	43%
3	63%	75%
4	87%	100%
5	84%	100%
6	71%	100%

5. Conclusions

This chapter presents an enhanced in-network cache for edge deep learning. A multi-edge-node data cache replacement model based on the queuing theory is established, and the optimal number of data collaborative cache nodes is determined based on this model. Through a comparison with other cache mechanisms, it can be proven that the ESGD strategy proposed in this study can effectively guarantee the cache performance in the edge network. Moreover, in scenarios such as the industrial Internet, intelligent manufacturing, and intelligent vehicle management, the number of node services to be deployed in the relevant edge network environments is often huge. Therefore, when simulating the scenarios, a large amount of actual data is required to simulate the large-scale service deployment scenarios. If experiments and simulations can be conducted using the actual big data and relevant platforms, it will be more conducive to the adjustment and improvement of the existing scheduling schemes and will also be more instructive. However, due to the limitations of simulation, in the case of a maneuvering network, since there are different input variables that will affect the optimal number of edge nodes, deep learning technology will exhibit better performance and achieve better edge node cache performance.

Author Contributions: Conceptualization, J.Z. and W.L.; methodology, L.Z.; validation, J.Z.; resources, W.L.; writing—original draft preparation, J.Z.; writing—review and editing, W.L.; supervision, J.T. All authors have read and agreed to the published version of the manuscript.

Funding: This work was supported by the National Science Foundation of China (61962045), Program for Young Talents of Science and Technology in Universities of Inner Mongolia Autonomous Region (NJYT23104), Basic Scientific Research Expenses Program of Universities directly under Inner Mongolia Autonomous Region (JY20220273, JY20240002), and the Natural Science Foundation of Inner Mongolia Autonomous Region (2023LHMS06023, JY20240061).

Data Availability Statement: Data are contained within the article.

Conflicts of Interest: The authors declare no conflicts of interest.

References

1. Hazra, A.; Rana, P.; Adhikari, M.; Amgoth, T. Fog computing for next-generation internet of things: Fundamental, state-of-the-art and research challenges. *Comput. Sci. Rev.* **2023**, *48*, 100549. [CrossRef]
2. Chi, H.R.; Wu, C.K.; Huang, N.-F.; Tsang, K.-F.; Radwan, A. A survey of network automation for industrial internet-of-things towards industry 5.0. *IEEE Trans. Ind. Inform.* **2023**, *19*, 2065–2077. [CrossRef]
3. Cherukuri, B.R. Edge computing vs. cloud computing: A comparative analysis for real-time ai applications. *Int. J. Multidiscip. Res.* **2024**, *6*, 1–17. [CrossRef]
4. Mahbub, M.; Shubair, R.M. Contemporary advances in multi-access edge computing: A survey of fundamentals, architecture, technologies, deployment cases, security, challenges, and directions. *J. Netw. Comput. Appl.* **2023**, *219*, 103726. [CrossRef]
5. Men, J.; Feng, L.; Chen, X.; Tian, L. Atmospheric correction under cloud edge effects for geostationary ocean color imager through deep learning. *ISPRS J. Photogramm. Remote Sens.* **2023**, *201*, 38–53. [CrossRef]
6. Lu, Y.; Lin, Q.; Chi, H.; Chen, J.-Y. Automatic incident detection using edge-cloud collaboration based deep learning scheme for intelligent transportation systems. *Appl. Intell.* **2023**, *53*, 24864–24875. [CrossRef]
7. Liu, G.; Dai, F.; Xu, X.; Fu, X.; Dou, W.; Kumar, N.; Bilal, M. An adaptive dnn inference acceleration framework with end–edge–cloud collaborative computing. *Future Gener. Comput. Syst.* **2023**, *140*, 422–435. [CrossRef]
8. Li, R.; Ouyang, T.; Zeng, L.; Liao, G.; Zhou, Z.; Chen, X. Online optimization of dnn inference network utility in collaborative edge computing. *IEEE/ACM Trans. Netw.* **2024**, *32*, 4414–4426. [CrossRef]
9. Geng, H.; Zeng, D.; Li, Y.; Gu, L.; Chen, Q.; Li, P. Plays: Minimizing dnn inference latency in serverless edge cloud for artificial intelligence-of-things. *IEEE Internet Things J.* **2024**, *11*, 37731–37740. [CrossRef]
10. Sada, A.B.; Khelloufi, A.; Naouri, A.; Ning, H.; Aung, N.; Dhelim, S. Multi-agent deep reinforcement learning-based inference task scheduling and offloading for maximum inference accuracy under time and energy constraints. *Electronics* **2024**, *13*, 2580. [CrossRef]
11. Yang, L.; Gan, Y.; Chen, J.; Cao, J. Autosf: Adaptive distributed model training in dynamic edge computing. *IEEE Trans. Mob. Comput.* **2024**, *23*, 6549–6562. [CrossRef]
12. Hua, H.; Li, Y.; Wang, T.; Dong, N.; Li, W.; Cao, J. Edge computing with artificial intelligence: A machine learning perspective. *ACM Comput. Surv.* **2023**, *55*, 1–35. [CrossRef]

13. Wu, C.; Peng, Q.; Xia, Y.; Jin, Y.; Hu, Z. Towards cost-effective and robust ai microservice deployment in edge computing environments. *Future Gener. Comput. Syst.* **2023**, *141*, 129–142. [CrossRef]
14. Pandey, R.; Uziel, S.; Hutschenreuther, T.; Krug, S. Towards deploying dnn models on edge for predictive maintenance applications. *Electronics* **2023**, *12*, 639. [CrossRef]
15. Heidari, A.; Navimipour, N.J.; Unal, M.; Zhang, G. Machine learning applications in internet-of-drones: Systematic review, recent deployments, and open issues. *ACM Comput. Surv.* **2023**, *55*, 1–45. [CrossRef]
16. Jiang, X.; Hou, P.; Zhu, H.; Li, B.; Wang, Z.; Ding, H. Dynamic and intelligent edge server placement based on deep reinforcement learning in mobile edge computing. *Ad Hoc Netw.* **2023**, *145*, 103172. [CrossRef]
17. Abdulazeez, D.H.; Askar, S.K. Offloading mechanisms based on reinforcement learning and deep learning algorithms in the fog computing environment. *IEEE Access* **2023**, *11*, 12555–12586. [CrossRef]
18. Yu, H.; Yu, D.; Wang, C.; Hu, Y.; Li, Y. Edge intelligence-driven digital twin of cnc system: Architecture and deployment. *Robot. Comput.-Integr. Manuf.* **2023**, *79*, 102418. [CrossRef]
19. Nie, Q.; Tang, D.; Liu, C.; Wang, L.; Song, J. A multi-agent and cloud-edge orchestration framework of digital twin for distributed production control. *Robot. Comput.-Integr. Manuf.* **2023**, *82*, 102543. [CrossRef]
20. Liu, C.; Liu, K.; Ren, H.; Xu, X.; Xie, R.; Cao, J. Rtds: Real-time distributed strategy for multi-period task offloading in vehicular edge computing environment. *Neural Comput. Appl.* **2023**, *35*, 12373–12387. [CrossRef]
21. Raeisi-Varzaneh, M.; Dakkak, O.; Habbal, A.; Kim, B.-S. Resource scheduling in edge computing: Architecture, taxonomy, open issues and future research directions. *IEEE Access* **2023**, *11*, 25329–25350. [CrossRef]
22. Aghapour, Z.; Sharifian, S.; Taheri, H. Task offloading and resource allocation algorithm based on deep reinforcement learning for distributed ai execution tasks in iot edge computing environments. *Comput. Netw.* **2023**, *223*, 109577. [CrossRef]
23. Liang, Q.; Hanafy, W.A.; Ali-Eldin, A.; Shenoy, P. Model-driven cluster resource management for ai workloads in edge clouds. *ACM Trans. Auton. Adapt. Syst.* **2023**, *18*, 1–26. [CrossRef]
24. Wang, Z.; Xu, H.; Xu, Y.; Jiang, Z.; Liu, J. Coopfl: Accelerating federated learning with dnn partitioning and offloading in heterogeneous edge computing. *Comput. Netw.* **2023**, *220*, 109490. [CrossRef]
25. Shu, Z.; Deng, X.; Wang, L.; Gui, J.; Wan, S.; Zhang, H.; Min, G. Relay-assisted edge computing framework for dynamic resource allocation and multiple-access tasks processing in digital divide regions. *IEEE Internet Things J.* **2024**, *11*, 35724–35741. [CrossRef]
26. Nugroho, A.K.; Shioda, S.; Kim, T. Optimal resource provisioning and task offloading for network-aware and federated edge computing. *Sensors* **2023**, *23*, 9200. [CrossRef]
27. Lin, Z.; Zhu, G.; Deng, Y.; Chen, X.; Gao, Y.; Huang, K.; Fang, Y. Efficient parallel split learning over resource-constrained wireless edge networks. *IEEE Trans. Mob. Comput.* **2024**, *23*, 9224–9239. [CrossRef]
28. Pu, Y.; Li, Z.; Yu, J.; Lu, L.; Guo, B. An elastic framework construction method based on task migration in edge computing. *Softw. Pract. Exp.* **2024**, *54*, 1811–1830. [CrossRef]
29. Chen, Y.; Luo, X.; Liang, P.; Han, J.; Xu, Z. Priority-based dag task offloading and secondary resource allocation in iot edge computing environments. *Computing* **2024**, *106*, 3229–3254. [CrossRef]
30. Liao, L.; Lai, Y.; Yang, F.; Zeng, W. Online computation offloading with double reinforcement learning algorithm in mobile edge computing. *J. Parallel Distrib. Comput.* **2023**, *171*, 28–39. [CrossRef]
31. Huang, B.; Wang, L.; Liu, X.; Huang, Z.; Yin, Y.; Zhu, F.; Wang, S.; Deng, S. Reinforcement learning based online scheduling of multiple workflows in edge environment. *IEEE Trans. Netw. Serv. Manag.* **2024**, *21*, 5691–5706. [CrossRef]
32. Wang, X.; Shen, M.; Yang, K. On-edge high-throughput collaborative inference for real-time video analytics. *IEEE Internet Things J.* **2024**, *11*, 33097–33109. [CrossRef]
33. Albonesi, D.H. Selective cache ways: On-demand cache resource allocation. In Proceedings of the MICRO-32. Proceedings of the 32nd Annual ACM/IEEE International Symposium on Microarchitecture, Haifa, Israel, 16–18 November 1999; pp. 248–259.
34. Suh, G.E.; Devadas, S.; Rudolph, L. Analytical cache models with applications to cache partitioning. In Proceedings of the ACM International Conference on Supercomputing 25th Anniversary Volume, Munich, Germany, 10–13 June 2014; pp. 323–334.
35. Kennedy, R.K.; Khoshgoftaar, T.M.; Villanustre, F.; Humphrey, T. A parallel and distributed stochastic gradient descent implementation using commodity clusters. *J. Big Data* **2019**, *6*, 16. [CrossRef]
36. Bottou, L. Large-scale machine learning with stochastic gradient descent. In Proceedings of the COMPSTAT'2010: 19th International Conference on Computational Statistics, Paris, France, 22–27 August 2010; Keynote, Invited and Contributed Papers; Springer: Berlin/Heidelberg, Germany, 2010; pp. 177–186.
37. Chih-Chung, C. Libsvm: A library for support vector machines. *ACM Trans. Intell. Syst. Technol.* **2011**, *2*, 1–27. [CrossRef]
38. Liu, X.; Xu, Z.; Qin, Y.; Tian, J. A discrete-event-based simulator for distributed deep learning. In Proceedings of the 2022 IEEE Symposium on Computers and Communications (ISCC), Rhodes, Greece, 30 June–3 July 2022; pp. 1–7.
39. Liu, S.; Liu, Z.; Xu, Z.; Liu, W.; Tian, J. Hierarchical decentralized federated learning framework with adaptive clustering: Bloom-filter-based companions choice for learning non-iid data in iov. *Electronics* **2023**, *12*, 3811. [CrossRef]

40. Liu, X.; Dong, Z.; Xu, Z.; Liu, S.; Tian, J. Enhanced decentralized federated learning based on consensus in connected vehicles. *arXiv* **2022**, arXiv:2209.10722.
41. Lang, K. Newsweeder: Learning to filter netnews. In *Machine Learning Proceedings 1995*; Prieditis, A., Russell, S., Eds.; Morgan Kaufmann: San Francisco, CA, USA, 1995; pp. 331–339.

electronics

MDPI

Article

Traffic-Aware Intelligent Association and Task Offloading for Multi-Access Edge Computing

Avilia Kusumaputeri Nugroho and Taewoon Kim *

School of Computer Science and Engineering, Pusan National University, Busan 46241, Republic of Korea; avilia22@pusan.ac.kr

* Correspondence: taewoon@pusan.ac.kr

Abstract: Edge computing is a promising technology, especially for offloading users' computationally heavy tasks. The close proximity of edge computing units to users minimizes network latency, thereby enabling delay-sensitive applications. Although optimal resource provisioning and task offloading in edge computing are widely studied in the literature, there are still some critical research gaps. In this study, we propose a traffic-aware optimal association and task-offloading approach. The proposed method does not rely solely on the average rate of offloading requests, which can differ from actual values in real time. Instead, it uses an intelligent, high-precision prediction model to forecast future offloading requests, allowing resource provisioning to be based on future sequences of requests rather than average values. Additionally, we propose an optimization-based approach that can meet task deadlines, which is crucial for mission-critical applications. Finally, the proposed approach distributes the computing load over multiple time steps, ensuring future resource scheduling and task-offloading decisions can be made with a certain level of flexibility. The proposed approach is extensively evaluated under various scenarios and configurations to validate its effectiveness. As a result, the proposed deep learning model has resulted in a request prediction error of 0.0338 (RMSE). In addition, compared to the greedy approach, the proposed approach has reduced the use of local and cloud computing from 0.02 and 18.26 to 0.00 and 0.62, respectively, while increasing edge computing usage from 1.31 to 16.98, which can effectively prolong the lifetime of user devices and reduce network latency.

Keywords: multi-access edge computing; task offloading; traffic-awareness; optimization; time-series forecasting

1. Introduction

The proliferation of mobile devices is unmistakably pervasive, by recent statistics. According to the Pew Research Center, as of 2021, 97% of Americans own a cellphone, with 85% owning smartphones specifically, showcasing their ubiquitous presence in daily life [1]. Globally, there are over 6.4 billion smartphone users as of 2023, with projections indicating this number will surpass 7 billion by 2026 [2]. Furthermore, smartphone shipments totaled 1.35 billion units in 2021 alone [3], underscoring the continuous growth and adoption of mobile technology worldwide. These figures illustrate the widespread integration of mobile devices into personal and professional spheres, driving digital connectivity and innovation across various sectors.

In the meantime, mobile applications are evolving rapidly, becoming increasingly complex to meet the growing demands of users and advancements in technology. Today's mobile apps integrate sophisticated features such as real-time data processing [4], augmented reality (AR) [5], virtual reality (VR) [6], artificial intelligence (AI) [7], and complex backend integrations [8]. Despite advancements in computation and battery capacity, the complexity of mobile applications increases response time while decreasing battery life. Mobile/multi-access edge computing (MEC) holds significant promise by bringing computational capabilities closer to end-users, reducing latency, and improving mobile network efficiency [9–12]. By leveraging MEC, applications can offload processing tasks from mobile devices to nearby edge servers (ESs), leading to faster response times for real-time applications such as AR, VR, and autonomous vehicles.

Task offloading in MEC addresses mobile computing challenges, including battery constraints, limited processing capacity, and delays in conventional cloud architectures [13]. This approach optimizes task execution, thereby reducing data travel distances and minimizing latency. MEC utilizes edge servers with a resource allocation system that dynamically allocates CPU, memory, and storage resources for fluctuating task offloading demands. Sophisticated algorithms optimize resource consumption, avoid conflicts over shared resources, maximize user experience (QoS), and enhance overall system efficiency. Additionally, load balancing distributes workloads among edge servers, ensuring none are overloaded and optimizing network utilization.

Moreover, user-base station (BS) association in task offloading involves strategic device connection to nearby BSs for optimal edge server utilization. Devices dynamically associate with BSs based on signal strength, available resources, and proximity to edge servers, ensuring efficient processing of offloaded tasks with minimal latency.

Extensive research has been conducted on the most effective strategies for provisioning and offloading tasks in MEC. A method was suggested to achieve optimal resource provisioning and task offloading in federated edge computing, involving the partitioning of edge servers into groups [14]. Another approach introduced a low-complexity task offloading solution through task routing [15]. Despite the technical progress the previous studies have successfully made, there are still some research gaps, including the following three. First, previous studies optimized resource provisioning and/or task offloading by assuming the average rate of task generation. However, the actual amount of tasks received at a particular moment may be different from the assumed average, which may cause resource under-/over-provisioning. Second, most studies assume that the received tasks can be completely processed right away or in the current time step (e.g., tasks are small enough). However, it may not be the case if the task is highly complex, requires sequential execution, or takes a long time. Lastly, some studies do not consider the fact that some applications are deadline-sensitive, which is especially important for mission-critical applications.

In this paper, we propose optimal resource provisioning and task offloading for MEC. By using a deep learning approach, the proposed method can predict future offloading requests with high precision by analyzing the network traffic history. The proposed approach optimizes multiple tasks for multiple future time steps to yield optimal scheduling decisions while guaranteeing deadline constraints. The summary of the contributions we make in this paper is given below.

- To avoid the mismatch between the average and actual offloading requests, we propose a deep learning-based multi-step offloading request prediction approach by learning from the past traffic, which includes the offloading requests.
- We propose a computing load balancing scheme over the time horizon so that each ES can make some resources available for accommodating unpredictable requests. This is particularly useful when the prediction of future requests is not perfect, as is the case in general.
- To maximize the offloading performance and fulfill the deadline constraints, we propose a multi-step optimization technique. That is, the proposed method optimizes both resource provisioning and task offloading for multiple future time steps.
- To maximize resource utilization and prevent excessive resource allocations, we propose an optimal network association solution that leads to the efficient use of edge servers.
- To validate the effectiveness of the proposed solution, we implement a time-slotted simulation environment and carry out extensive evaluations along with performance comparisons.

The remainder of this paper is structured as follows. The following Section 2 provides a comprehensive summary of related studies. In Section 3, the proposed approach is described in detail. In Section 4, the evaluation and comparison results are provided. Finally, Section 5 concludes this paper. The abbreviations and acronyms that frequently appear in this paper are summarized in Table 1.

Table 1. Abbreviations and acronyms used in this paper.

Abbreviation	Definition
BS	Base Station
CC	Cloud Computing
EC	Edge Computing
ES	Edge Server
MEC	Mobile/Multi-access Edge Computing
QoS	Quality of Service

2. Related Work

This section comprehensively reviews the optimization of resource provisioning and/or task offloading in MEC. For resource provisioning in MEC, the study in [16] optimizes MEC resource provisioning in IoT networks to meet performance requirements considering limited device resources and high data generation. Their method frames the provisioning of MEC resources and assignment of workloads as a mixed-integer program, utilizing a decomposition strategy to effectively manage workload variations. While this paper addresses workload assignment for immediate processing to achieve required response times, it assumes average user requests and does not consider delays for particularly heavy tasks. Xiang et al. [17] explore optimizing computing power allocation and traffic scheduling to minimize service response time in MEC, particularly for urgent or popular services. Their study introduces PCA-CATS, an online algorithm that effectively reduces service response time and expenses by optimizing resource allocation and traffic scheduling. However, the approach assumes immediate processing of received requests and does not address strict deadlines or time-sensitive tasks.

From the perspective of task offloading in MEC, various approaches have been proposed to enhance the efficiency of determining which tasks should be offloaded to edge servers or cloud data centers by considering aspects such as compute demands, network conditions, and device capabilities. Jiang et al. [18] proposed the Joint Offloading and Resource Allocation (JORA) framework, which employs Lyapunov optimization to maximize Quality of Experience (QoE) while considering long-term MEC energy constraints. JORA provides both centralized and distributed online approaches that distribute near-optimal performance. However, the immediate processing of received requests, which ignores task delay constraints such as processing deadlines, can result in prolonged processing times for heavy workloads. Apostolopoulos et al. [19] introduce an approach for optimizing data offloading in a multi-MEC server environment, focusing on users' risk-seeking tendencies rooted in Prospect Theory. Their research investigates the complexities of user decision-making in the face of uncertainty, placing it within a non-cooperative game framework aimed at achieving optimal offloading strategies. However, the study overlooks the task delay constraints, assumes average user request patterns, and employs immediate processing capabilities for all user requests. Han et al. [20] study impatience-driven user behaviors in MEC queue management, proposing an adaptive decision-making mechanism to balance latency outage risk and energy consumption. Their approach optimizes the allocation of tasks between local computing and MEC based on dynamic user demands and server conditions, with the goal of enhancing the QoE for applications that are sensitive to latency. However, they assume average user requests, which may differ from the actual values in real time.

An ES is, in general, co-located with a BS, and thus, making an optimal user-BS or user-edge association is important to further enhance the performance of MEC. Song et al. [21]

employ a genetic algorithm to optimize server deployment and user offloading in wireless edge networks with the objective of minimizing service latency. Feng et al. [22] concentrate on the optimization of task partitioning and user association in MEC systems to reduce the average latency. However, their approach depends on average requests and does not consider delay constraints for delay-sensitive tasks. In contrast, Charatsaris et al. [23] introduce Hierarchical Federated Learning (HFL) for wireless networks, focusing on user-to-edge association and power allocation to balance accuracy, energy, and time. However, they do not consider delay constraints for tasks. Wang et al. [24] introduced an optimization approach for associations, focusing on minimizing system delay and enhancing Quality of Service (QoS) through efficient user-BS pairing. However, they assume average user requests and that user requests are always processed immediately.

Traffic-aware task offloading strategies, introduced by Qi et al. [25] for vehicular edge computing, optimize task and wireless bandwidth ratios to minimize response time. Their algorithm efficiently handles this optimization, particularly with limited wireless capacity. Wang et al. [26] propose a method for IoV task offloading and content caching using traffic stream forecasting. However, their approach lacks explicit consideration of task processing deadlines and user demand variations. Oza et al. [27] introduce deadline-aware task offloading, which integrates traffic light data to optimize task scheduling. Their method ensures timely task processing by considering static and dynamic deadlines influenced by traffic conditions, yet immediate processing without queuing considerations may face challenges for longer tasks.

Intelligent approaches, such as those utilizing machine learning and deep learning, have also been proposed to enhance MEC systems. Guo et al. [28] introduce an intelligent task offloading scheme at the edge using supervised decision trees, improving prediction accuracy and processing delay in IoT scenarios. However, their method does not optimize resource provisioning and task offloading for multiple future time steps. Kim et al. [29] propose prediction-based sub-task offloading in MEC, employing linear regression to predict processing times across multiple nodes simultaneously. Their approach aims to enhance resource utilization efficiency and reduce application execution time on MEC servers but does not consider multiple future time forecasting for optimization. Zeng et al. [30] present a prediction-based task-offloading strategy for vehicular edge computing using deep-learning models. Their approach predicts task-offloading performance, including success/failure and service delay, yet does not optimize resource provisioning for multiple future time steps.

To summarize, Table 2 provides a comparative analysis of previous studies, highlighting their approaches to real value optimization, deadline-awareness, offloading planning, and resource provisioning over multiple time steps, and while many studies focus on individual aspects, our proposed work addresses all four points comprehensively. This makes our approach distinct in its ability to handle task prediction-based multi-step optimization of resource provisioning and task offloading, effectively overcoming the limitations in previous work.

The aforementioned studies commonly optimize for average user request rates under constant conditions. However, real-time fluctuations in request rates can lead to inefficient resource allocation (e.g., under- or over-utilization) at specific times, thereby decreasing system efficiency. Moreover, they often prioritize the immediate processing of requests within the current time step without considering deadline awareness, which is similar to a greedy algorithm and may not be feasible in some cases. This overlooks the overall dynamics of the queue and may result in longer processing times, particularly for complex tasks such as deep learning. Furthermore, effective resource provisioning or task offloading should differentiate treatment based on application deadline sensitivity, which varies between those that require timely completion and those with flexible or no strict time constraints. In this study, we propose a task prediction-based multi-step optimization of resource provisioning and task offloading that effectively overcomes the aforementioned limitations.

Table 2. Comparison of selected previous studies under four critical aspects in edge computing research.

Reference	Real Value-Based Optimization	Deadline Awareness	Multi-Step Offloading Planning	Multi-Steps Resource Provisioning
Kheraf et al. [16]				
Xiang et al. [17]	✓			
Jiang et al. [18]	✓			
Apostolopoulus et al. [19]				
Han et al. [20]		✓		
Song et al. [21]	✓	✓		
Feng et al. [22]				
Charatsaris et al. [23]	✓			
Wang et al. [24]		✓		
Qi et al. [25]	✓	✓		
Wang et al. [26]			✓	✓
Oza et al. [27]	✓	✓		
Guo et al. [28]	✓	✓		
Kim et al. [29]	✓			
Zeng et al. [30]	✓	✓	✓	
our work	✓	✓	✓	✓

3. Proposed Idea

In this section, we provide a description of the assumed system and the proposed approach in detail. The notations that frequently appear in this section are summarized in Table 3.

Table 3. Summary of the mathematical notations used in this study.

Notation	Definition
t	Index of time step whose length is Δ_t
$\mathbf{A}^{(t)}$	BS-user accessibility matrix at t
AC_b	Association capacity of BS b
$\mathbf{c}_{local}^{(t)}$	Normalized, available computing capacity of users at t
$\mathbf{c}_{bs}^{(t)}$	Normalized, available computing capacity of ESs at t
$\mathbf{c}_{cloud}$	Normalized, available computing capacity of cloud at t
$\mathbf{d}^{(t)}$	Deadlines of users' requests at t
$\mathbf{f}_{local}^{(t)}$	Portion of tasks to be processed locally at t
$\mathbf{F}_{es}^{(t)}$	Portion of tasks to be offloaded to ESs at t
$\mathbf{f}_{cloud}^{(t)}$	Portion of tasks to be offloaded to cloud at t
h_u	User u's task-offloading request history
$\mathbf{I}^{(t)}$	BS-user association indication matrix at t
l_{bs}	Scalar determining round-trip latency to the BS (ES), being $l_{bs} \times \Delta_t$
l_{cloud}	Scalar determining round-trip latency to cloud, being $l_{cloud} \times \Delta_t$
N_{bs}	Number of BSs
N_{es}	Number of ESs
N_{fh}	Forecasting horizon length
N_{lw}	Lookback window length
N_{sh}	Number of time steps over which an optimal resource scheduling is carried out
N_{user}	Number of users
$\mathbf{o}_{local}^{(t)}$	Binary task offloading decision vector for local processing at t
$\mathbf{O}_{es}^{(t)}$	Binary task offloading decision matrix between an ES and user at t
$\mathbf{o}_{cloud}^{(t)}$	Binary task offloading decision vector for cloud processing at t
$q_u^{(t)}$	Task-offloading requests of users at t

We assume a hierarchical networked system, as shown in Figure 1. A mobile user is connected to the access network via a BS, and each BS is connected to an ES with a dedicated, high-speed link. The BS is connected to the Internet, as is the cloud data center. From the computing perspective, the assumed system is composed of three layers. At the lowest level is the local computing layer, enabling mobile users to process tasks directly on their devices. In the middle layer lies edge computing, facilitating task offloading to nearby edge servers with minimal network latency. Finally, the top layer is the cloud computing infrastructure, where abundant computing resources are available with a relatively large network latency. In this work, we assume that both mobile devices and edge servers are resource-limited, while cloud computing is not.

If a mobile user is near the edge of the base station (BS) with which it is currently associated, and begins to move away, a handover event will occur. This handover allows the user to connect to a different BS, referred to as $BS_{b'}$. Consequently, this may involve either migrating virtual resources from the edge server (ES) at BS_b or allocating new resources on the ES at $BS_{b'}$. However, this study does not account for the effects of user mobility. Given that the average walking speed of individuals ranges from 94.3 cm/s to 143.4 cm/s [31], and considering the random deployment of users and the coverage area of the BS, it is reasonable to assume that the accessibility matrix will remain nearly static over the period considered for resource and offloading optimization.

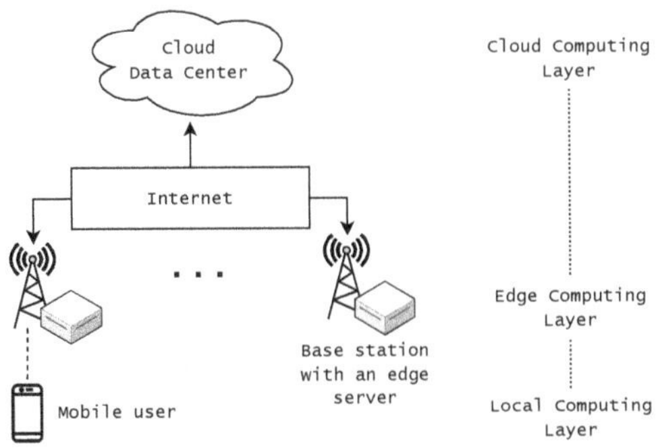

Figure 1. Illustration of the considered 3-layer computing system in this study where an edge server is co-located with a base station.

The overview of the proposed traffic-aware intelligent association and task offloading scheme is illustrated in Figure 2, which has both offline and online components. The offline operation includes training a prediction model given each user u's offloading request history (h_u). Then, by using the predicted future requests, the online logic iteratively performs the optimal scheduling subsystem that optimizes both resource provisioning and task offloading. In the figure, N_{lw} and N_{fh} refer to the lookback window and forecasting horizon size, determining the input and output length of the prediction model, respectively.

3.1. Multi-Step Task-Offloading Prediction

The development of the deep learning-based sequence-to-sequence prediction is a well-known problem [32,33]. The available approaches range from conventional statistical approaches, e.g., ARIMA (Auto Regressive Integrated Moving Average) and ETS (Error Trend and Seasonality, or exponential smoothing) [34], to state-of-the-art deep learning models, e.g., one-dimensional convolutional network (1DCNN), long short-term memory (LSTM) [35], and Transformer [36]. In this study, 1DCNN, LSTM, and Transformer are taken for predicting future task-offloading requests. The performance comparison among the three models are presented in Section 4.1.

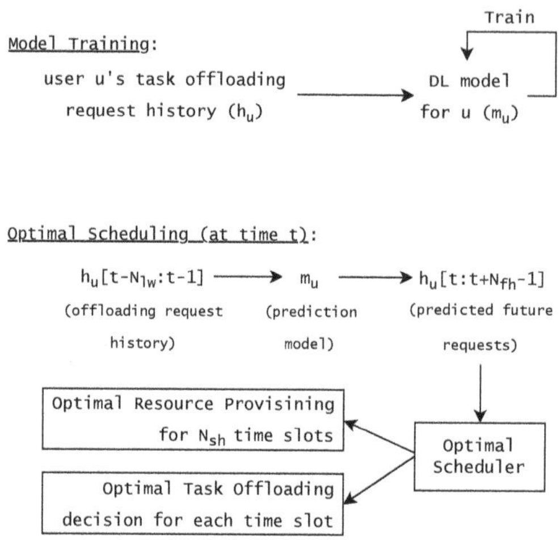

Figure 2. Overall workflow of the proposed idea where the model training and optimal scheduling is carried out offline and online, respectively.

The 1DCNN is particularly effective for processing and predicting time series data. The 1DCNN takes a sequence of time series data as input, and the convolutional layers therein apply convolution operations using filters (kernels) that slide over the input data to extract local patterns or features. In a 1DCNN, the filters move along one dimension (time). The major advantages of 1DCNN include the following three: (i) Feature extraction: The convolutional layers learn to automatically extract important features from the input time series data. Early layers capture simple patterns, while deeper layers capture more complex structures; (ii) Temporal dependencies: By applying convolutions across the time dimension, the model can capture temporal dependencies and correlations between different time points; (iii) Down-sampling: Pooling layers reduce the size of the data representation, helping to summarize the learned features and make the model more robust.

LSTM is a type of recurrent neural network (RNN) model designed to effectively learn temporal sequences and long-range dependencies by using three distinctive features, i.e., memory cells, forget/input/output gates, and recurrent architecture. The key features and advantages of LSTM include the following three: (i) Long-term dependency handling: LSTMs are designed to remember information over long periods of time, which is useful for tasks where context is important; (ii) Mitigation of the vanishing gradient problem: The design of LSTM gates helps in propagating gradients throughout the network, thus addressing the vanishing gradient problem that traditional RNNs face; (iii) Stateful processing: LSTMs can maintain a state across different sequences, which is valuable in applications like continuous speech recognition and video analysis.

The Transformer model was first introduced to handle tasks involving natural language processing, and is now widely used for analyzing and predicting time series datasets. Transformers bring various advantages, as listed below, from its features such as self-attention mechanisms, positional encoding, and encoder-decoder architecture: (i) Parallelization: Unlike RNN-type networks, Transformers allow for parallel processing of input sequences, leading to significantly faster training times; (ii) Handling Long-Range Dependencies: The self-attention mechanism allows the model to capture dependencies between tokens regardless of their distance in the sequence; (iii) Reduced Vanishing Gradient Problem: Since Transformers rely on attention mechanisms rather than sequential processing, they are less susceptible to the vanishing gradient problem that plagues RNNs and LSTMs.

3.2. Optimal Association and Task Offloading

In this work, we assume a time-slotted system where each equal-length time step is indexed by t. Given the user u's task-offloading request history, h_u, a deep learning model is trained to make precise predictions on future offloading requests. In contrast to most previous studies utilizing only the average request rates, we propose to make predictions on the future offloading requests for N_{fh} time steps. This is because the actual offloading request each time step can be different from the average. Thus, the optimal resource provisioning and offloading decisions made upon the average offloading rate may experience resource under-/over-provisioning, reducing resource utilization or QoS. Once the prediction model is trained, it is used to make predictions on future offloading requests, with which the optimal decision on resource provisioning and task offloading will be made. It is worth noting that in this study the optimal offloading decision is made each time step, while the optimal resource provisioning is made for the future N_{sh} time steps. The reason for making such multi-step provisioning decisions is that some procedures that are tightly related to resource provisioning, e.g., horizontal scaling, migration, and starting/stopping virtual machines, are time-consuming [37], and thus, it is impractical to carry out resource scheduling on every time step.

Upon generating the future offloading requests, the proposed resource provisioning and task offloading algorithms will operate periodically and on each time step, respectively, to process the users' offloading requests without violating the deadline constraints while evenly distributing the computing load of edge servers over time. The reasons for distributing the load are to make a certain amount of computing resources available on each edge server each time step so that future resource scheduling and task offloading can be optimized with a certain level of flexibility. To achieve an optimal load balancing, it is also important to optimize the association between BSs and users as well, since BS-user association leads to the association between the user and the ES which is co-located with the BS.

In this work, each user can offload their task to an ES and/or the cloud, in addition to processing tasks locally on their device. Such diverse access options for task offloading enhance flexibility in resource optimization but also increase the complexity of the optimization which will be effectively managed in what follows. This multi-access capability allows for more adaptable resource management, addressing varying load conditions and user demands.

To address these needs, the optimal resource provisioning shown in Figure 2 includes the following two components, i.e., user-BS association and computing resource provisioning. Once the decisions are made, the optimal task offloading will be carried out at each time step. Next, we present the formulated problem of optimal resource provisioning and task offloading as proposed. We first formulate a greedy optimization problem that schedules both resource provisioning and task offloading only for the current time step. Then, we extend the problem so that optimal decisions spanning multiple time steps can be made while guaranteeing the deadlines.

Let N_{bs}, N_{es}, and N_{user} be the number of BSs, ESs, and users in the system, respectively. In this work, we assume a cellular communication technology for its wide coverage [38], though others, such as WiFi, can be applied with little modification. In general, BSs periodically broadcast beacon signals to notify their presence [39]. Upon receiving the signal, a user can enumerate the accessible BSs. In this work, accessibility is guaranteed if the measured signal-to-interference plus noise ratio (SINR) exceeds the predefined threshold. By collecting the accessible BS lists from users, the central scheduler can configure an accessibility matrix $\mathbf{A}^{(t)} \in \{0,1\}^{N_{bs} \times N_{user}}$ at time t where the (b,u)-th element therein is denoted by $a_{bu}^{(t)}$. Here, b is the integer-valued index of BSs and ESs ranging from 1 to N_{bs} or N_{es}, and u is the integer-valued user index ranging from 1 to N_{user}.

A single scheduler is assumed responsible for configuring the accessibility matrix and solving the proposed optimization problem while having a single central entity can introduce a risk of failure affecting overall system reliability, we assumed that the scheduler operates within a cloud infrastructure equipped with high-availability clusters and redundancy features [40,41]. In this configuration, if the primary scheduler fails, a standby scheduler is available to assume its responsibilities without delay.

Let the decision variable $\mathbf{I}^{(t)} \in \{0,1\}^{N_{bs} \times N_{user}}$ be the association indication matrix. Each (b,u)-th element $i_{bu}^{(t)}$ in $\mathbf{I}^{(t)}$ takes a value of either 0 or 1, indicating that the association between BS b and user u is to be made or not, respectively. Then, the following constraint Equation (1) forces that an association can only be made if a user is accessible to a BS.

$$\forall b, u : i_{bu}^{(t)} \leq a_{bu}^{(t)} \tag{1}$$

In this work, a mobile device is assumed to have a single antenna, and thus, for a time step, a user can access only a single BS.

$$\forall u : \sum_{\forall b} i_{bu}^{(t)} = 1 \tag{2}$$

Ingeneral, at each time step, a BS b can associate with a predefined number, AC_b, of users due to its limited resource [38,39], where AC_b stands for the association capacity of a BS b.

$$\forall b : \sum_{\forall i} i_{bu}^{(t)} \leq AC_b \tag{3}$$

Once the BS-user association is made, the user can utilize the ES connected to the BS for task offloading. Let $\mathbf{o}_{local}^{(t)} \in \{0,1\}^{N_{user}}$ be the task offloading decision vector for local processing at time t, where $o_{local,u}^{(t)}$ being 1 or 0 indicates that the user u has decided to process (some) tasks locally or not, respectively. In the same manner, $\mathbf{O}_{es}^{(t)} \in \{0,1\}^{N_{es} \times N_{user}}$ is the task offloading decision matrix between the ES b and user u at time t. Since a BS b has a dedicated ES by assumption, the same index notation b is used to indicate the ES connected to the BS b. Furthermore, $\mathbf{o}_{cloud}^{(t)}$ is the task offloading decision vector to cloud at time t. Regardless of which BS a user is connected to at the moment, the user can choose to offload locally or to the cloud. However, offloading to a particular BS b is possible only when the user is associated with the BS b, which is formulated as a constraint as below.

$$\forall b, u : o_{es,bu}^{(t)} \leq i_{bu}^{(t)} \tag{4}$$

The decision variables $\mathbf{o}_{local}^{(t)}$, $\mathbf{O}_{es}^{(t)}$, and $\mathbf{o}_{cloud}^{(t)}$ indicate whether or not to offload tasks, and the specific amount of task to offload is determined by the following decision variables. Let $\mathbf{f}_{local}^{(t)} \in \mathcal{R}_{[0,1]}^{N_{users}}$ be the normalized decision variable determining the number of tasks to be offloaded locally. The subscript indicates that each $f_{local,u}^{(t)} \in \mathbf{f}_{local}^{(t)}$ takes a value from the range $[0,1]$. Similarly, $\mathbf{F}_{es}^{(t)} \in \mathcal{R}_{[0,1]}^{N_{es} \times N_{user}}$ is a matrix determining the offloading portion between ESs and users, whereas $\mathbf{f}_{cloud}^{(t)} \in \mathcal{R}_{+}^{N_{users}}$ is for offloading to cloud. Since decisions regarding the amount of tasks to be offloaded can only be made when the corresponding offloading is allowed, the following constraints are formulated. Here the scaling constant κ_{cloud} is multiplied to the right-hand side of Equation (7) so that the decision variable determining the actual amount of cloud offloading can take values without being limited to the $[0,1]$ range.

$$\forall u : f_{local,u}^{(t)} \leq o_{local,u}^{(t)} \tag{5}$$

$$\forall b, u : f_{es,bu}^{(t)} \leq o_{es,bu}^{(t)} \tag{6}$$

$$\forall u : f_{cloud,u}^{(t)} \leq \kappa_{cloud} \times o_{cloud,u}^{(t)} \tag{7}$$

The amount of requests to be offloaded is also limited by the available computing capacity. Let $\mathbf{c}^{(t)}_{local} \in \mathcal{R}^{N_{user}}_{[0,1]}$ be the normalized, available local computing capacity of users at time t, where the subscript indicates that each $c^{(t)}_{local,u} \in \mathbf{c}^{(t)}_{local}$ takes a value from the range $[0,1]$. The superscript t does not indicate that the physical capacity changes over time. However, if a mobile device has some tasks to process at the moment, its computing capacity should be reduced, which necessitates the time step notation. In the same manner, the computing capacity of ESs and CC is defined as $\mathbf{c}^{(t)}_{es} \in \mathcal{R}^{N_{es}}_{[0,1]}$ and $\mathbf{c}_{cloud} \in \mathcal{R}^{N_{user}}_{+}$, respectively. The CC resource is large enough by assumption, and thus, the notation t is omitted from the CC capacity. As a result, the following constraints are formulated to limit the amount of offloading to the available capacity.

$$\forall u : f^{(t)}_{local,u} \leq c^{(t)}_{local,u} \tag{8}$$

$$\forall b : \sum_{\forall u} f^{(t)}_{es,bu} \leq c^{(t)}_{es,b} \tag{9}$$

The resource provisioning and task offloading scheduling problems should maximize the QoS by fulfilling the user's offloading demand. Let a vector $\mathbf{q}^{(t)} \in \mathcal{R}^{N_{user}}_{+}$ be the offloading request of users, where the subscript $+$ indicates that each element $q^{(t)}_u \in \mathbf{q}^{(t)}$ is non-negative. To guarantee the completion of task offloading for each user, the total amount of tasks offloaded to the local device, ES, and cloud should be equal to the request. As a result, the following constraint is formulated as follows:

$$\forall b : f^{(t)}_{local,u} + \sum_{\forall b} f^{(t)}_{es,bu} + f^{(t)}_{cloud,u} = q^{(t)}_u \tag{10}$$

Finally, the objective function is formulated to minimize the response time for the user's request. In this problem formulation, each task is assumed to be completely processed within the current time step. Thus, the factor impacting the response time is which computing resource the user has utilized. It is assumed in this work that the network latency for local processing is zero and the latency for accessing a BS is much smaller than that for accessing the cloud. Let l_{bs} and l_{cloud} be the integer scalar determining the round-trip network latency to the BS/ES (i.e., $l_{bs} \times \Delta_t$) and cloud (i.e., $l_{cloud} \times \Delta_t$), respectively. Then, the response time $L^{(t)}_u$ that user u experiences for task offloading can be written as below:

$$\forall u : L^{(t)}_u = \Delta_t \times l_{bs} \sum_{\forall b} o^{(t)}_{es,bu} + l_{cloud} \times \Delta_t \times o^{(t)}_{cloud,u} + \Delta_t, \tag{11}$$

where the first term is the latency for accessing the BS (ES), the second term is the latency for accessing the cloud, and the last term is the time spent on the current time step. Finally, the objective function is formulated as below using Equation (11). The main objective here is to minimize the total response time, and in addition to that, the second term in the objective function minimizes the use of local processing, as shown below.

$$\min.\ (1-\alpha) \sum_{\forall u} L^{(t)}_u + \alpha \times \sum_{\forall u} f^{(t)}_{local,u} \tag{12}$$

The $\alpha \in [0,1]$ represents the service provider's preference to prolonging the lifetime of mobile users by minimizing the amount of local processing. As expected when $\alpha = 0$, the local processing on the user devices will be carried out as much as possible to minimize the response time. On the other hand, as α increases, the use of local processing will be minimized and the use of ESs will increase. Still, the offloading to the cloud will not be heavily exercised for causing high response time.

Although the above optimization problem, called OPT(1), can produce an effective scheduling solution for the current time step, it has the following drawbacks. In general, the length of a time step Δ_t is short, and resource provisioning may consume computing resources and take time, as discussed earlier. Thus, carrying out resource provisioning every time step may not be practical, especially for real-time scheduling. Thus, in this work, we propose to perform resource provisioning for $N_{sh} > 1$ time steps, within which both the network association and computing resource allocation decisions remain the same. OPT(1) optimizes only a single time step at a time and thus, what it can do as to the deadline constraint is process as many tasks as possible at the current time step, operating as a greedy solution. In the following multi-time step approach, we propose an optimization formulation that guarantees the deadline requirements of tasks by scheduling over multiple time steps. In addition, we propose to distribute the offloading requests over multiple time steps so that future resource provisioning and task offloading can be made with a certain level of flexibility. Furthermore, it helps to effectively adapt to the case of misprediction on future requests.

It is assumed in this work that on each time step, a user can generate up to one offloading request. However, this can be extended to various scenarios where a user generates multiple requests. Since the amount of the offloading request can be any arbitrary number, the scenario where a user generates multiple requests can be treated as a single request with the request amount being the sum of all simultaneous requests. Let $\mathbf{d}^{(t)}$ be the deadlines of the tasks generated by users at t. The deadline is application-specific and that of each request is assumed to be known when the request arrives. Each value is represented by a strongly positive integer if the user has generated a task, indicating the number of time steps from t the deadline is not violated. After collecting the deadlines, the scheduler computes the largest deadline which becomes the number of time steps to optimize the computing resource and the offloading decision. Let $\sigma^{(t)}$ be the largest deadline among the offloading requests to be scheduled together at t, which is defined as follows.

$$\sigma^{(t)} = \max\{d_u^{(t)} : \forall u\} \tag{13}$$

It is worth noting that the value of $\sigma^{(t)}$ is an integer value and thus the actual timespan of it can be derived, if needed, by multiplying the length of each time step, Δ_t.

The following optimization problem addresses resource provisioning and task offloading over $\sigma^{(t)} = N_{sh}$ time steps for offloading requests generated at time t. The entire time horizon is indexed by $t = \tau_1, \tau_2, \cdots, \tau_{\sigma^{(t)}}$. The length of each time step is determined by system-specific parameters. In this study, the duration of each time step is set to 1 ms. However, the proposed method is designed to be flexible and can be adapted to accommodate time step lengths of varying sizes.

The optimization model, OPT(N_{sh}), aims to minimize a weighted sum of three components: the overall system cost, local device processing cost, and cloud processing cost. The weights α and β control the relative importance of local and cloud processing costs. This allows for flexible adjustment based on system requirements. The deadline-constrained OPT(N_{sh}), multiple-time step resource provisioning and task offloading problem is formulated as follows:

$$\min.\ (1-\alpha-\beta)\phi + \alpha \times \sum_{\forall t}\sum_{\forall u} f_{local,u}^{(t)} + \beta \times \sum_{\forall t}\sum_{\forall u} f_{cloud,u}^{(t)} \tag{14a}$$

$$\text{s.t.}\quad \forall b,u : i_{bu}^{(\tau_1)} \le a_{bu}^{(\tau_1)} \tag{14b}$$

$$\forall u : \sum_{\forall b} i_{bu}^{(\tau_1)} = 1 \tag{14c}$$

$$\forall b : \sum_{\forall i} i_{bu}^{(\tau_1)} \le AC_b \tag{14d}$$

$$\forall b,u,t : o_{es,bu}^{(t)} \le i_{bu}^{(\tau_1)} \tag{14e}$$

$$\forall u,t : f_{local,u}^{(t)} \le o_{local,u}^{(t)} \tag{14f}$$

$$\forall b, u, t : f_{es,bu}^{(t)} \leq o_{es,bu}^{(t)} \tag{14g}$$

$$\forall u, t : f_{cloud,u}^{(t)} \leq \kappa_{cloud} \times o_{cloud,u}^{(t)} \tag{14h}$$

$$\forall u, t : f_{local,u}^{(t)} \leq c_{local,u}^{(t)} \tag{14i}$$

$$\forall b, t : \sum_{\forall u} f_{es,bu}^{(t)} \leq c_{es,b}^{(t)} \tag{14j}$$

$$\forall b, t : \sum_{t} (f_{local,u}^{(t)} + \sum_{\forall b} f_{es,bu}^{(t)} + f_{cloud,u}^{(t)}) = q_u^{(\tau_1)} \tag{14k}$$

$$\forall u : \sum_{t=d_u^{(\tau_1)}+1}^{\tau_{\sigma^{(t)}}} o_{local,u}^{(t)} \leq 0 \tag{14l}$$

$$\forall u : \sum_{t=d_u^{(\tau_1)}+1-l_{bs}}^{\tau_{\sigma^{(t)}}} \sum_{\forall b} o_{bs,bu}^{(t)} \leq 0 \tag{14m}$$

$$\forall u : \sum_{t=d_u^{(\tau_1)}+1-l_{cloud}}^{\tau_{\sigma^{(t)}}} o_{cloud,u}^{(t)} \leq 0 \tag{14n}$$

$$\forall t, b : \sum_{\forall u} f_{es,bu}^{(t)} \leq \phi \tag{14o}$$

$$\forall b, u, t : o_{local,u}^{(t-1)} \geq o_{local,u}^{(t)}, o_{es,bu}^{(t-1)} \geq o_{es,bu}^{(t)}, o_{cloud,u}^{(t-1)} \geq o_{cloud,u}^{(t)} \tag{14p}$$

The OPT(N_{sh}) is similar to OPT(1) except for the following major differences: (i) OPT(N_{sh}) performs optimization over multiple time steps, while OPT(1) does only for a single time step; (ii) OPT(N_{sh}) guarantees the deadline of each task, while OPT(1) minimizes the response time only; (iii) OPT(N_{sh}) distributes the computing load over multiple time steps, while OPT(1) cannot.

The constraints in Equations (14b)–(14k) for OPT(N_{sh}) are similar to those in OPT(1), but they differ in that they apply across multiple time steps rather than a single time step. Constraints in Equations (14b)–(14d) ensure that each user is associated with exactly one BS and that no BS exceeds its capacity. This requirement is extended to cover all time steps in OPT(N_{sh}). On the other hand, constraints in Equations (14e)–(14k) handle offloading decisions by ensuring that offloading is only permitted if a user is associated with a BS, that local device and edge server processing limits are not exceeded, and that user task requirements are satisfied. These constraints are applied over multiple time steps, accommodating the dynamic nature of the system.

Key differences in OPT(N_{sh}) are introduced with constraints Equations (14l)–(14n), which enforce deadlines. Constraint Equation (14l) prevents offloading if a task's deadline has passed, thus avoiding offloading beyond the deadline. Constraint Equation (14m) applies this rule to edge server offloading, while constraint Equation (14n) applies it to cloud offloading. Finally, constraint Equation (14o) and the term ϕ in the objective function Equation (14a) are used to balance computing load over multiple time steps. Constraint Equation (14o) ensures that the total load on edge servers does not exceed ϕ at any time step, while the term ϕ in the objective function penalizes uneven load distribution, encouraging balanced resource allocation.

The objective function also raises some penalties for the use of local resources and the cloud for prolonging the lifetime of mobile devices and reducing network latency, respectively. The objective function has two preference parameters, $\alpha \in [0,1]$ and $\beta \in [0,1]$, highlighting the importance of reducing local processing and cloud offloading, respectively.

It is assumed in this work that users are stationary for a small number of time steps, thereby causing no changes in the accessibility matrix, $\mathbf{A}^{(t)}$, over $\sigma^{(t)}$ time steps. In addition, as mentioned earlier, frequent rescheduling of resources (e.g., association, horizontal scaling, and migration) causes computational overhead and delays. Thus, we propose to make optimal associations and resource provisioning for multiple time steps, which is possible by making accurate predictions on future requests. As in Equations (14b)–(14e), the optimal decision on BS-user association remains the same over $\sigma^{(t)}$ time steps. Furthermore, if offloading is to happen, the related resources should be allocated in advance. For example, a containerized virtual environment should be created and started in advance. The constraint Equation (14p) states that if offloading is to be enabled at some t, it should be enabled in advance. On the other hand, the actual allocated computing portion determined by $\mathbf{f}^{(t)}_{local}$, $\mathbf{F}^{(t)}_{es}$, and $\mathbf{f}^{(t)}_{cloud}$ changes over time steps. In the widely used Docker platform [42], for example, the change in CPU/MEM resources (i.e., vertical scaling) can be performed in real time by using Docker's built-in runtime options [43], enabling frequent scheduling.

It is worth noting that in both OPT(1) and OPT(N_{sh}), we intentionally omitted the constraints for limiting the feasible value ranges of the decision variables since they are already stated in the manuscript. Additionally, the greedy version of the proposed approach, OPT(1), processes all tasks within the current time step without considering deadline constraints. In contrast, OPT(N_{sh}) optimizes resource allocation and task offloading decisions over multiple time steps while ensuring that deadlines are consistently met by incorporating these constraints.

4. Evaluation

For evaluation, we have configured networks as shown in Figure 3. On a 300 m-by-300 m area, there are nine BSs and ESs located in a planned manner with 100 m spacing vertically and horizontally, while mobile users are randomly placed. The transmit/receive range is set to 150 m. Each mobile device has a computing budget that is randomly drawn from Uniform [0.05, 0.20], while the available computing resources at each ES are randomly drawn from Uniform [0.40, 0.80]. Each user generates an offloading request, which requires computing resources drawn from Distribution [0.00, 1.00] $\times \eta$, where $\eta \in \mathcal{R}_{++}$ is a scaling factor to make low or high request rate scenarios. During the evaluation, the *Distribution* is configured to one of the following: sine-, triangle-, and sawtooth-shaped patterns or uniform random. Regarding the network latency, l_{bs} and l_{cloud} are set to 1 and 2, resulting in $1 \times \Delta_t$ and $2 \times \Delta_t$, respectively. The simulation and evaluation are carried out on a high-performance workstation with an Intel Core i9 10940X CPU, 128 GB of memory, and NVIDIA GeForce RTX 3090 graphics card, and the reported values in this section are the average of 10 evaluations.

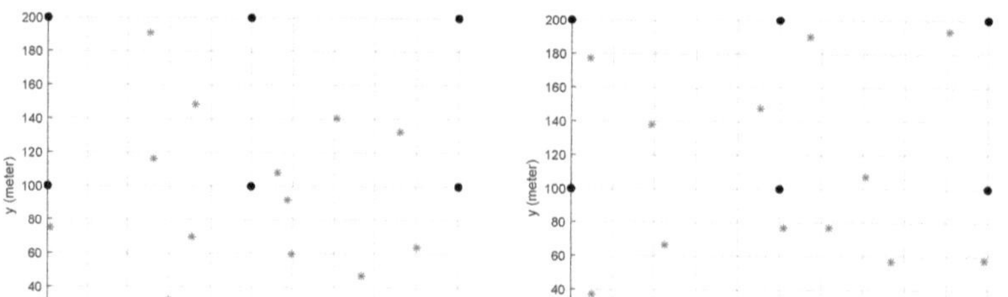

(**a**) (**b**)

Figure 3. Some randomly sampled layouts of the assumed 300 m-by-300 m area where the nine red stars and fifteen black dots are the locations of users and BSs, respectively. (**a**) Example layout 1. (**b**) Example layout 2.

4.1. *Traffic Offloading Dataset and Prediction Model*

Task offloading patterns (or traffic patterns) we assume in this study include sine-, triangle-, and sawtooth-shaped patterns and a random pattern as shown in Figure 4. The values are generated at 1000 Hz for $T = 50$ s, yielding 50,000 data samples. We used an 80:10:10 split for training, validation, and testing. As a pre-processing step, the dataset is normalized. The input/output length of the model is configured to $l_{lb} = 128$ and $l_{fh} = 5$. The deep learning models are implemented with Tensorflow and Keras framework. The Adam optimizer is used with a learning rate of 0.001, and the number of epochs and the batch size are configured to 10 and 128, respectively.

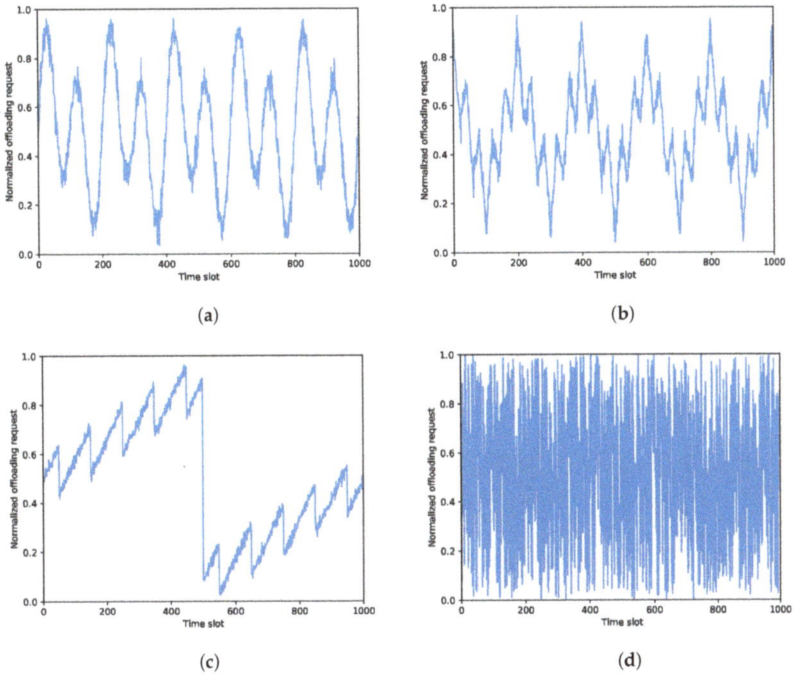

Figure 4. The task-offloading request patterns assumed in this study where the x-axis shows only up to the first 1000 samples out of 50,000. (**a**) Sine pattern. (**b**) Triangle pattern. (**c**) Sawtooth pattern. (**d**) Random.

Real patterns can often be decomposed into multiple primitive patterns. This implies that the sum of one, two, or three basic patterns can result in a realistic pattern. Therefore, by studying these fundamental shapes, we can gain insights into more complex and realistic traffic patterns. According to a study analyzing mobile traffic using a real dataset collected from over 150,000 users [44], such decomposition is a valid approach for capturing the variability in real-world traffic patterns. This view is further supported by techniques such as Fourier analysis and other effective methods, which can decompose compound signals into multiple basic, primitive signals [45–48]. In this study, we demonstrate that the proposed prediction model can accurately forecast these compound signals using the generated composite signals. Furthermore, if the given offloading pattern exhibits high complexity, it can be decomposed into simpler, more manageable components.

The measured accuracy of the considered neural network models is reported in Table 4, where the reported values therein are the root mean square errors (RMSE). Overall, the 1DCNN model outperformed the rest with respect to mean accuracy, and thus, it is used for evaluation as the offloading request prediction model in what follows.

Table 4. Prediction accuracy performance (RMSE) of the three neural networks with respect to different request patterns.

Request Pattern	1DCNN	LSTM	Transformer
Sine	0.0350	0.0337	0.0350
Triangle	0.0336	0.0337	0.0347
Sawtooth	0.0328	0.0575	0.0349
Random	0.2874	0.2869	0.2868
mean (total)	0.0972	0.1030	0.0979
mean (except Random)	0.0338	0.0416	0.0349

The predicted results of 1DCNN are shown in Figure 5, where Figure 5a is for sine-shaped requests, Figure 5b is for triangle-shaped requests, Figure 5c is for sawtooth-shaped requests, and Figure 5d is for randomly generated requests. As can be seen from the figures, requests exhibiting a certain pattern are predicted with high precision. However, in the case of the randomly generated requests, it is impossible to learn the underlying patterns that do not exist, and thus, the model outputs the mean values all the time.

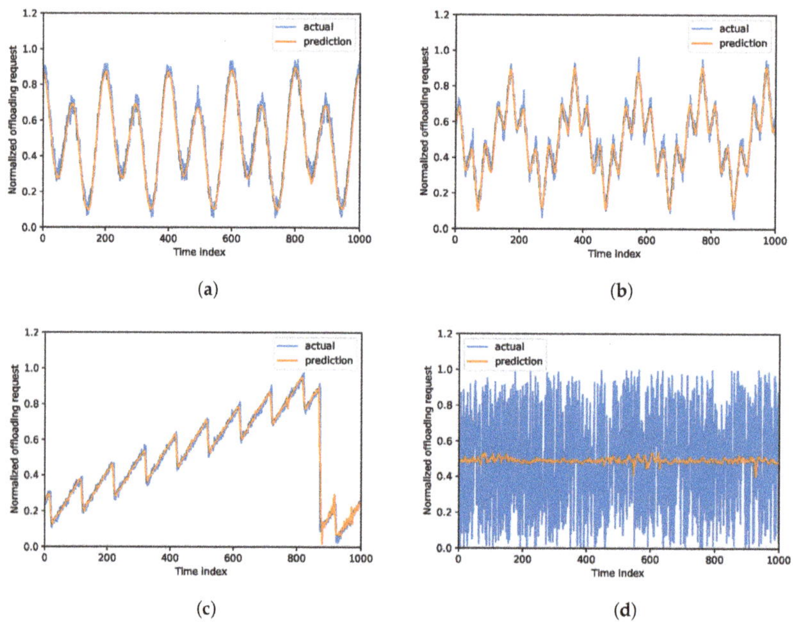

Figure 5. Task-offloading prediction results with 1DCNN for the four different shapes or patterns. (**a**) Sine pattern. (**b**) Triangle pattern. (**c**) Sawtooth pattern. (**d**) Random.

The predicted requests are then used in the following subsection for optimizing resource provisioning and task offloading. By carrying out extensive evaluations, we found that the results from using sine-, triangle-, and sawtooth-shaped requests are very similar to each other for making highly accurate predictions. On the other hand, the evaluations with random tasks showed different outcomes. Thus, in the following sections, we report the cases with the sine-, triangle-, and sawtooth-shaped requests as a single result after taking the average of all three. In addition, such requests will be called *pattern requests*.

4.2. Multi-Step Optimal Resource Provisioning and Task Offloading

We implemented the proposed algorithm and a discrete-time simulation environment on MATLAB R2020b [49]. To implement and solve the proposed optimization problem, we used CVX 2.1 [50] and Gurobi 11.0 [51]. To evaluate the performance of the proposed approach and to make a comparison analysis, we implemented the following algorithms:

- OPT(N_{sh}): the optimal method OPT(N_{sh}) proposed in this paper, which optimizes resources and offloads over multiple time steps with deadline constraints.
- OPT(N_{sh})/SSF: the proposed OPT(N_{sh}) without optimal BS-user association; the conventional strongest signal first (SSF) association rule [52] is used instead.
- OPT(1): The optimal method OPT(1) proposed in this paper, which optimizes resources and offloading for the current time step only in a greedy manner.

It is important to note that the greedy version of the proposed approach, OPT(1), reflects the methodologies discussed in previous studies. However, unlike earlier methods, OPT(1) includes advanced features such as optimization of BS-user associations and minimization of delays. Additionally, by comparing OPT(1) with OPT(N_{sh})/SSF, we can highlight the benefits of BS-user association optimization, which is also an important aspect of the proposed approach.

The design parameters or preference values are set as follows, and the most suitable values are found empirically. To be specific, for OPT(1), the value of α is set to 0.1. On the other hand, for both OPT(N_{sh}) and OPT(N_{sh})/SSF, the following configurations for the two parameters are used: $\alpha = 0.2$ and $\beta = 0.15$.

4.2.1. Effects of Multi-Time Step Optimization: Comparison between OPT(N_{sh}) and OPT(1)

We first carry out an evaluation to show the advantages of OPT(N_{sh}) over OPT(1). That is, the benefits of optimizing the resources over multiple time steps will be evaluated. For this evaluation, we assume that both OPT(1) and OPT(N_{sh}) can perfectly predict the future requests. The reported values are the average over the three different traffic patterns and the random traffic. During evaluations, OPT(N_{sh}) has successfully satisfied the deadline constraints, which is the case in the following evaluations as well. The following Figures 6 and 7 depict the amount of computing resource used for task offloading when the users' offloading requests are small and large, respectively. In the small request rate scenario (see Figure 6), the overall computing resource usage is quite similar to each other in that most computations are carried out on ESs. The notable difference is that OPT(1) offloaded tasks as much as possible to an ES to minimize the response time and to minimize the local processing according to its objective function Equation (12). On the other hand, OPT(N_{sh}) optimizes over multiple time steps, and thus, excessive use of ESs does not occur. Rather, OPT(N_{sh}) evenly distributes the computing resource allocations on ESs, and a small portion of the tasks are offloaded to the cloud. This is because, as long as the deadline is not violated, the use of the cloud is not penalized much. The fair distribution of the load is desired in this study. It is worth noting that for OPT(N_{sh}), the use of ESs can exceed the ES's capacity as shown in Figure 6c. This is because the ES capacity in the figure is the capacity for each time step, while the resource use is the accumulation over multiple time steps.

In the large request rate scenario (see Figure 7), the two methods show quite different results. The OPT(1) takes an extreme approach in that each user offloads their tasks completely to either the cloud or ES, and most tasks are offloaded to cloud for not having enough capacity in an ES to process all within a single time step. As a result, users with relatively small requests offload their tasks to ESs completely. On the other hand, users with large amounts of requests completely offload their traffic to the cloud. However, OPT(N_{sh}) can utilize ESs over multiple time steps, and thus, it has decided to offload much of the user's tasks to ESs while maintaining the balance of the ES resources. To be specific, the use of ESs in OPT(1) and OPT(N_{sh}) has been 1.31 and 16.98, respectively. On the other hand, the use of local and cloud computing in OPT(1) are 0.02 and 18.26, respectively, while those of OPT(N_{sh}) are 0.00 and 0.62, respectively. This demonstrates that optimizing across multiple time steps can effectively distribute the workload over time, thereby minimizing reliance on both local and cloud resources.

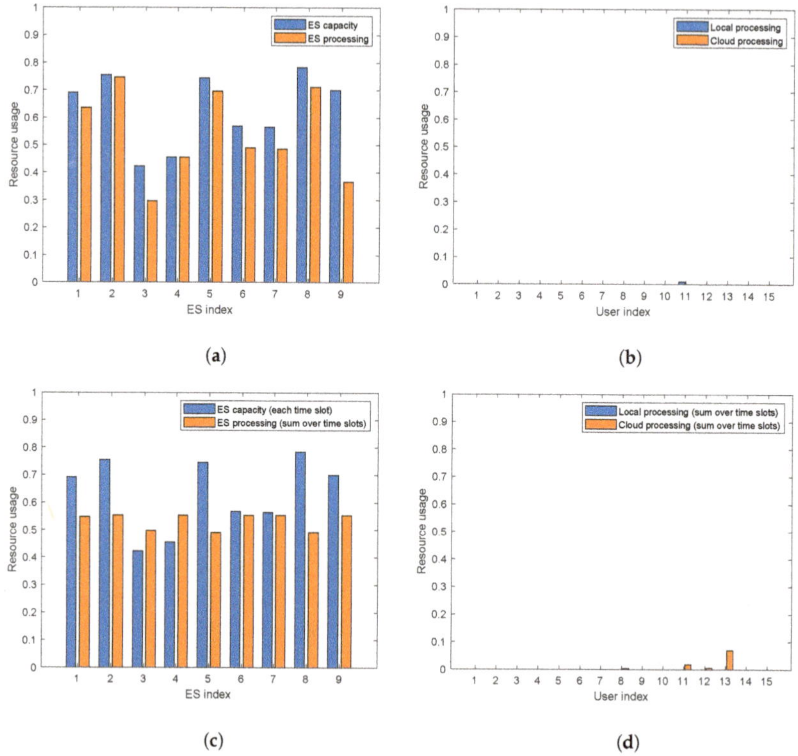

Figure 6. Comparison of computing resource usage between OPT(1) and OPT(N_{sh}) under a low request rate ($\eta = 0.5$). Subfigures (**a**,**c**) show edge server (ES) usage, while subfigures (**b**,**d**) display the combined usage of local devices and cloud resources. (**a**) ES usage of OPT(1). (**b**) Local device and cloud usage of OPT(1). (**c**) ES usage of OPT(N_{sh}). (**d**) Local device and cloud usage of OPT(N_{sh}).

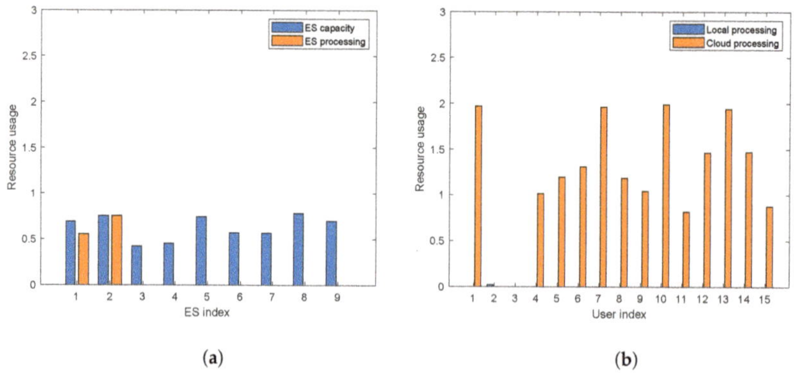

Figure 7. *Cont.*

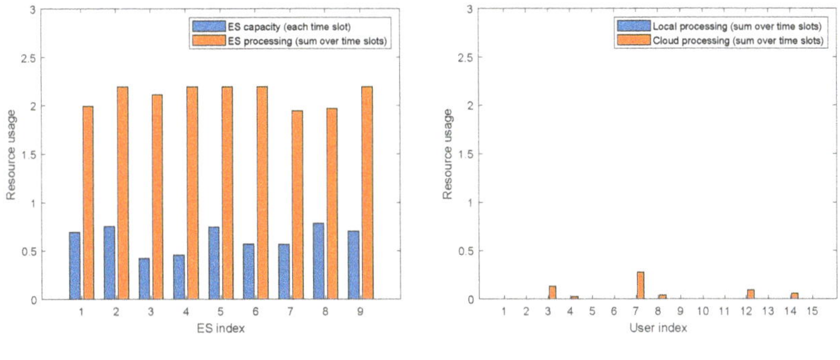

(c) (d)

Figure 7. Comparison of computing resource usage for OPT(1) and OPT(N_{sh}) at a high request rate ($\eta = 2.0$). Subfigures (**a**,**c**) show edge server usage, while (**b**,**d**) display local device and cloud resource usage. (**a**) ES usage of OPT(1). (**b**) Local device and cloud usage of OPT(1). (**c**) ES usage of OPT(N_{sh}). (**d**) Local device and cloud usage of OPT(N_{sh}).

4.2.2. Effects of Optimal Association: Comparison between OPT(N_{sh}) and OPT(N_{sh})/SSF

To validate the importance and effectiveness of the proposed optimal association approach, we make a comparison between OPT(N_{sh}) and one variant of it, called OPT(1)/SSF. As similar to the previous subsection, we assumed the case where the future request rates can be perfectly predicted in this evaluation. It is the same as OPT(N_{sh}) except that the BS-user association is made based on the strongest signal first rule. For SSH, we assume a free space path loss model [53] where the distance between the transceiver and receiver dominates the path loss: $P_L dB = -10 \times log_{10} G_l \lambda^2/(4\pi d)^2$ with d being the distance.

When the mean request rates are small (i.e., $\eta = 0.5$), there was not much difference between OPT(N_{sh}) and OPT(1)/SSF. However, when the mean rate increased (i.e., $\eta = 0.5$), OPT(1)/SSF is much outperformed by OPT(N_{sh}) as shown in Figure 8. Despite the optimal computing resource provisioning and task offloading, OPT(1)/SSF has failed to make balanced use of ES computing resources, as shown in Figure 8a. On the other hand, OPT(1) has achieved better load balancing among ESs, as shown in Figure 8c. In addition, compared to OPT(1)/SSF which has utilized the cloud resource much (see Figure 8b), OPT(1) has used much less (see Figure 8d). Such performance difference arises from the optimal association strategy. The BS-user association determines the ES-user association as well. Thus, poor association may result in the case where many users associate with a small number of BSs, which prevents fair load distribution.

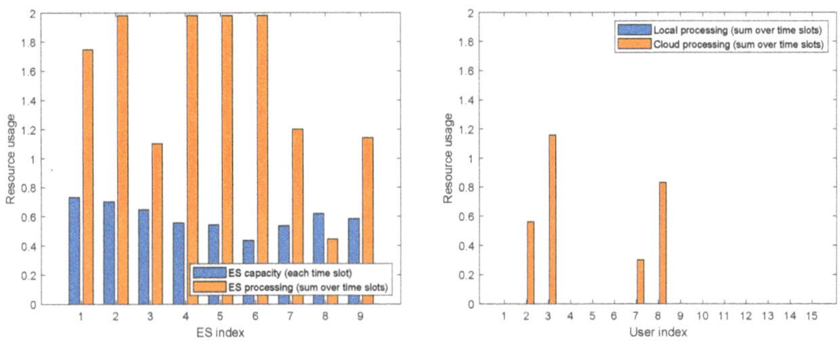

(a) (b)

Figure 8. *Cont.*

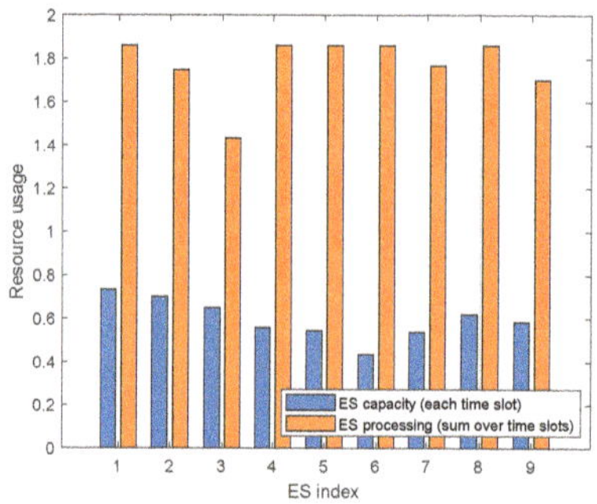

(c)

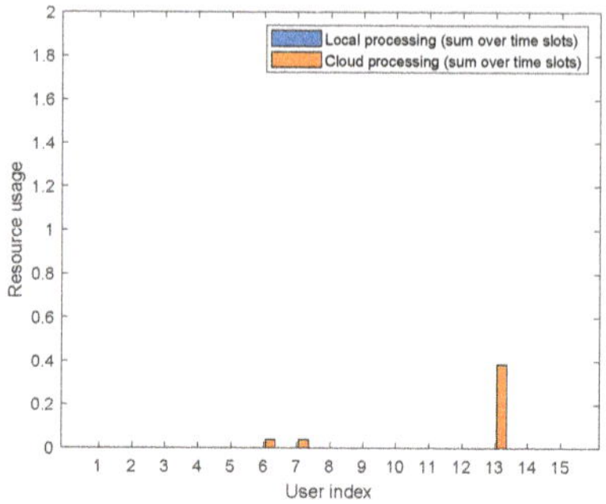

(d)

Figure 8. Computing resource usage comparison between OPT(N_{sh}) and OPT(N_{sh})/SSF with a large request rate (η = 2.0). (**a**) ES usage of OPT(N_{sh})/SSH. (**b**) Local device and cloud usage of OPT(N_{sh})/SSH. (**c**) ES usage of OPT(N_{sh}). (**d**) Local device and cloud usage of OPT(N_{sh}).

4.2.3. Effects of Request Prediction Accuracy on OPT(N_{sh})

Lastly, we conduct evaluations to examine how errors in predicting future offloading requests impact resource utilization. As aforementioned, the proposed 1DCNN-based prediction model can make highly accurate predictions for the three patterns, and thus, the resource usage outcomes are similar to each other. In this regard, we configured two scenarios in the following manner. In one scenario, during the simulation, each user generates requests by using one of the sine-, triangle-, and sawtooth-shaped patterns. In the other scenario, all users will generate requests randomly. The difference between the two is the level of precision in predicting future requests. As a result, we configured the three scenarios as follows: (i) users' requests can be perfectly predicted; (ii) users' requests can be predicted with high accuracy (i.e., each user is generating requests by using sine-, triangle-, and sawtooth-shaped pattern); (iii) users' requests cannot be predicted accurately (i.e., each user is generating requests at uniform random). When the users' request rates are small with η = 0.5, the results among the above three cases are not much different, while the more accurate scenario has yielded better performance in terms of the fair distribution among ESs and less use of local and cloud computing resource. Thus, we present only the results when the users' request rates are large with η = 0.5, as shown in Figure 9.

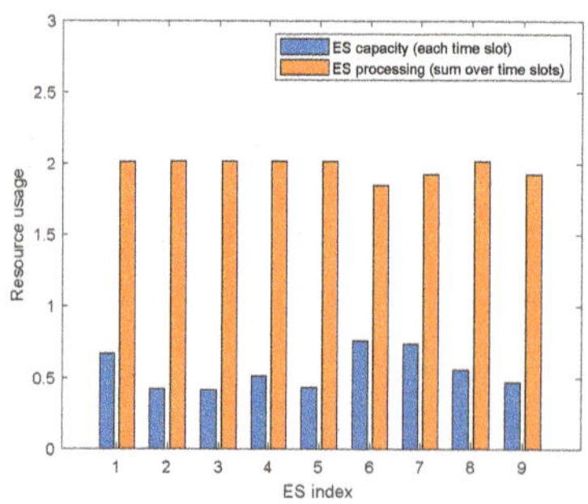

(a)

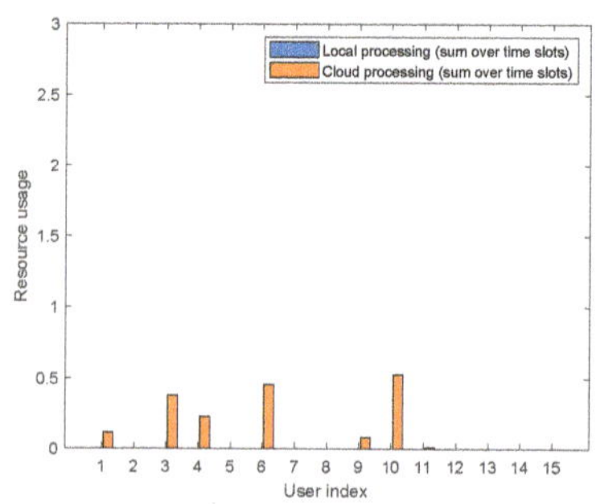

(b)

Figure 9. *Cont.*

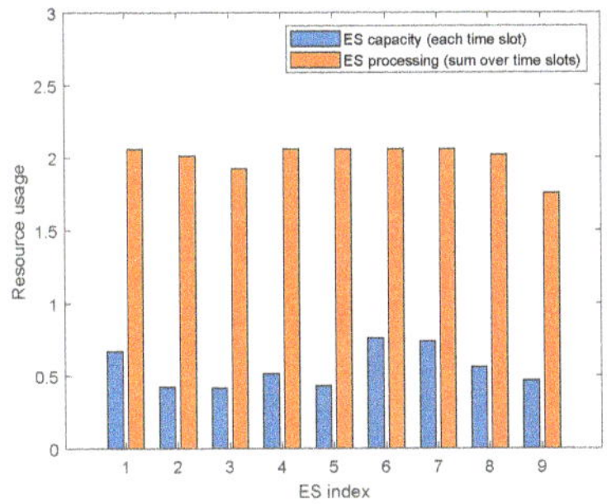

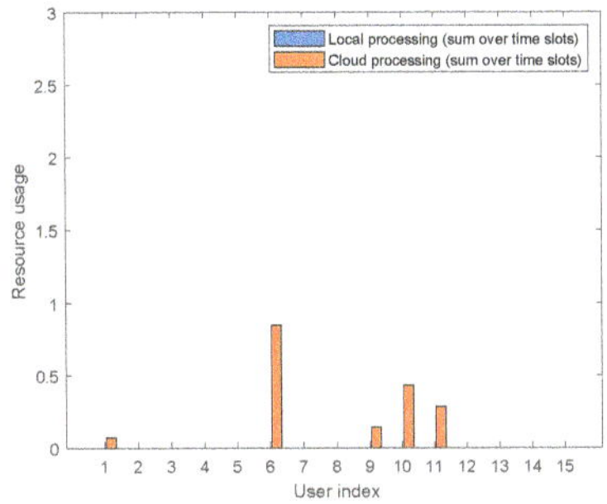

(c) (d)

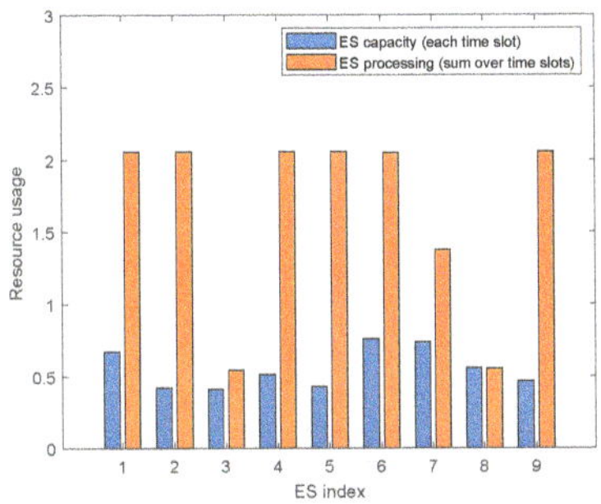

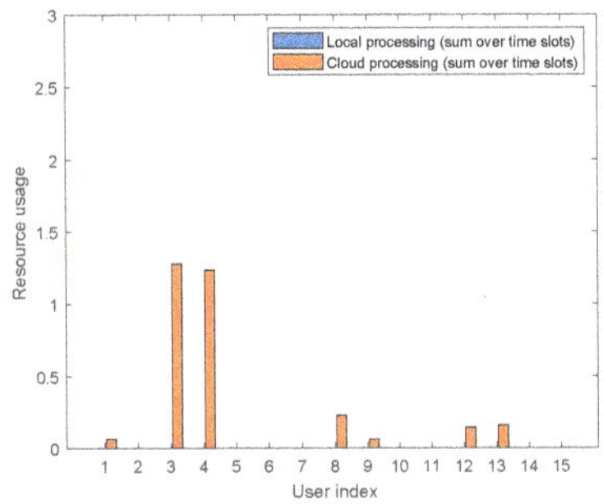

(e) (f)

Figure 9. Computing resource usage comparison of OPT(N_{sh}) between the cases with different levels of prediction accuracy with a large request rate ($\eta = 2.0$). (**a**) ES usage of OPT(N_{sh}) when the request prediction is perfect. (**b**) Local device and cloud usage of OPT(N_{sh}) when the request prediction is perfect. (**c**) ES usage of OPT(N_{sh}) when the request prediction is highly accurate. (**d**) Local device and cloud usage of OPT(N_{sh}) when the request prediction is highly accurate. (**e**) ES usage of OPT(N_{sh}) when the request prediction is inaccurate. (**f**) Local device and cloud usage of OPT(N_{sh}) when the request prediction is inaccurate.

When the future task requests can be predicted with high accuracy, the resource use in ESs and user/cloud (see Figure 9c and Figure 9d, respectively) is quite similar to that of optimum (see Figure 9a and Figure 9b, respectively). Such little differences is mainly because the future requests have been predicted with high accuracy. In addition, OPT(N_{sh}) makes some resources available by fairly distributing the load over time. Thus, in the case of under-provisioning, it can allocate additional computing resources on ESs without accessing cloud or local device. As a result, the use of ESs can still be balanced, and the use of cloud can be minimized. Yet, in scenarios where all users generate offloading requests uniformly at random, accurately predicting future requests becomes impossible. Thus, OPT(N_{sh}) suffers much from under-/over-provisioning problems. Still, OPT(N_{sh}) distributes the load on ESs over time, but the level of load balancing is worse than the rest. In addition, the use of the cloud has increased much, which is not preferred under the current objective function (see Equation (14a)). This result shows the importance of highly accurate predictions on the future request. However, random traffic cannot be captured, and the proposed approach has shown that under the random scenario, it has a certain level of load balancing and the use of cloud has been successfully controlled.

We have also carried out additional experiments to evaluate the effect of misprediction on the performance of OPT(1) and OPT(N_{sh})/SSF, whereas the performance of the two with perfect prediction is presented in Section 4.2.1 and Section 4.2.2, respectively. In the case of

OPT(1) with a low request rate ($\eta = 0.5$), when the prediction is highly accurate, the use of local, ES, and cloud computing has been similar to the case when the prediction is perfect. When the user request is generated uniformly at random, on the other hand, the use of computing resources has been less efficient. The most notable difference is, compared to the perfect prediction case, the use of local computing resources increased from 0.0095 to 0.1010, on average. This is because most users have closed their access to the cloud during the optimization, which considers the average rate only. This is clearly against the goal we programmed in the objective function since it will shorten the battery lifetime of the user device.

In the case of OPT(1) with a high request rate ($\eta = 2.0$), we have observed the following. Similar to the case with low request rates, when the prediction is highly accurate, the use of local, ESs, and cloud computing has been similar to that of the perfect prediction case. When the user request is generated uniformly at random, the offloading scheduling has become infeasible frequently. As can be seen in Figure 7b, both users 2 and 3 do not allocate resources on the cloud. It might be the desired outcome under the average request rates. However, in real time, the offloading request can be much larger than the average, but the closed access to the cloud for both users causes failure in fulfilling the user's request.

Lastly, in the case of OPT(N_{sh})/SSF with a high request rate ($\eta = 2.0$), we have learned the following. Similar to the above cases, when the prediction is highly accurate, the use of local, ESs, and cloud computing has been similar to that of the perfect prediction case. When the user request is generated uniformly at random, the use of cloud resources is increased from 2.8482 to 3.7279, on average. Due to the non-optimal approach taken for user-BS association, OPT(N_{sh})/SSF can result in a few BSs with a large number of associations. When the real-time requests exceed the average for the users associated with such busy BSs, part of the excessive amount of requests are forwarded to the cloud, resulting in a longer response time.

4.2.4. Discussions

Enhanced resource utilization and reduced task offloading latency significantly improve service quality for applications such as real-time streaming and gaming. Efficient resource usage reduces costs for providers, particularly in large-scale deployments, while improved load distribution enhances network scalability, allowing for the accommodation of more users and devices. However, average-based optimization has limitations, as real-time offloading request amounts can deviate from the average. Consequently, this work employs real-value-based optimization to better address these variations, making it more suitable for delay-constrained or sensitive applications.

However, some limitations exist. The framework's effectiveness relies on the accuracy of predicting future offloading requests; unpredictable traffic can reduce performance. Implementing multi-time step optimization adds computational overhead, which may be challenging in resource-constrained or large-scale networks. Stable evaluation conditions may not reflect real-world scenarios where dynamic network changes, such as user mobility and signal variations, can affect performance.

Finally, the summary of findings regarding the feasibility and practical challenges of implementing the proposed approach is as follows. The proposed deep learning model is implemented by using the widely used combination of Keras and Tensorflow frameworks [54] and thus, the resulting trained model can be easily ported or migrated to different operating systems and CPU architectures. The iterative inference step takes a negligible amount of time, making it applicable for real-time operations. On the other hand, each training epoch during the training process takes approximately two seconds on the aforementioned computing machine, but the training process is supposed to be carried out offline before the deployment of the proposed approach. As aforementioned, the proposed optimal approach as well as its variants are implemented by using the widely available computer solver. Although the proposed OPT(N_{sh}) utilizes binary variables, by leveraging advanced algorithms for handling binary/integer variables such as branch-and-bound, cutting planes, and parallelism [55], the proposed optimization problem is solved in at most tens of milliseconds which is applicable for real-time scheduling since the proposed method can plan in advance by using the predicted future requests. In addition, by leveraging advanced techniques such as Lagrangian relaxation and problem decomposition [15] or gradual one-by-one removal [39] the computation time can be further reduced.

5. Conclusions

In this study, we proposed a multi-step request prediction and optimization scheme for MEC. The proposed scheme first forecasts the multi-step task-offloading requests. Then, using the predictions, the proposed approach called OPT(N_{sh}) optimizes network association, computing resource provisioning, and task offloading so that users' tasks are efficiently processed with reduced battery consumption, guaranteed deadlines, and reduced cloud use which causes larger delays. The proposed multi-time step optimization framework can schedule the computing resources and task offloading over multiple time steps, and thus, the deadline-constrained optimization problem can effectively be implemented while making a balanced use of ESs over time. Extensive evaluations have been carried out to show that the proposed approach can effectively predict future offloading requests with a pattern, and with these predictions, edge computing resources can be optimally utilized without violating deadlines. Even under the cases where the requests cannot be predicted for randomness, the proposed scheme has shown its effectiveness in not exploding the use of local and cloud computing resources and for making balanced use of ESs to some extent.

Author Contributions: Conceptualization, A.K.N. and T.K.; methodology, A.K.N. and T.K.; software, A.K.N.; validation, A.K.N. and T.K.; formal analysis, T.K.; investigation, A.K.N.; resources, T.K.; data curation, A.K.N.; writing—original draft preparation, A.K.N. and T.K.; writing—review and editing, T.K.; visualization, A.K.N.; supervision, T.K.; project administration, T.K.; funding acquisition, T.K. All authors have read and agreed to the published version of the manuscript.

Funding: This work was supported by a 2-Year Research Grant of Pusan National University.

Data Availability Statement: The data presented in this study along with the related code are available at the following GitHub repository: https://github.com/CISLAB-PNU/Traffic-Aware-Intelligent-Association-and-Task-Offloading-for-Multi-Access-Edge-Computing.git (accessed on 29 July 2024).

Conflicts of Interest: The authors declare no conflicts of interest.

References

1. Pew Research Center. Mobile Fact Sheet. 2021. Available online: https://www.pewresearch.org/internet/fact-sheet/mobile/ (accessed on 6 July 2024).
2. Statista. Number of Smartphone Users Worldwide from 2016 to 2023. 2023. Available online: https://www.statista.com/statistics/330695/number-of-smartphone-users-worldwide/ (accessed on 6 July 2024).
3. International Data Corporation (IDC). Smartphone Shipments Totaled 1.35 Billion Units in 2021, According to IDC. 2022. Available online: https://www.idc.com/getdoc.jsp?containerId=prUS52032524 (accessed on 6 July 2024).
4. Yew, H.T.; Ng, M.F.; Ping, S.Z.; Chung, S.K.; Chekima, A.; Dargham, J.A. Iot Based Real-Time Remote Patient Monitoring System. In Proceedings of the 2020 16th IEEE International Colloquium on Signal Processing & Its Applications (CSPA), Langkawi, Malaysia, 28–29 February 2020; IEEE: Piscataway, NJ, USA, 2020; pp. 176–179.
5. Herskovitz, J.; Wu, J.; White, S.; Pavel, A.; Reyes, G.; Guo, A.; Bigham, J.P. Making mobile augmented reality applications accessible. In Proceedings of the 22nd International ACM SIGACCESS Conference on Computers and Accessibility, Virtual Event, Greece, 26–28 October 2020; pp. 1–14.
6. Chen, Y.L.; Hsu, C.C. Self-regulated mobile game-based English learning in a virtual reality environment. *Comput. Educ.* **2020**, *154*, 103910. [CrossRef]
7. Imran, A.; Posokhova, I.; Qureshi, H.N.; Masood, U.; Riaz, M.S.; Ali, K.; John, C.N.; Hussain, M.I.; Nabeel, M. AI4COVID-19: AI enabled preliminary diagnosis for COVID-19 from cough samples via an app. *Inform. Med. Unlocked* **2020**, *20*, 100378. [CrossRef] [PubMed]
8. Vaz, D.; Matos, D.R.; Pardal, M.L.; Correia, M. MIRES: Intrusion Recovery for Applications Based on Backend-As-a-Service. *IEEE Trans. Cloud Comput.* **2023**, *11*, 2011–2027. [CrossRef]

9. Mach, P.; Becvar, Z. Mobile edge computing: A survey on architecture and computation offloading. *IEEE Commun. Surv. Tutor.* **2017**, *19*, 1628–1656. [CrossRef]
10. Mao, Y.; You, C.; Zhang, J.; Huang, K.; Letaief, K.B. A survey on mobile edge computing: The communication perspective. *IEEE Commun. Surv. Tutor.* **2017**, *19*, 2322–2358. [CrossRef]
11. Chen, C.L.; Brinton, C.G.; Aggarwal, V. Latency minimization for mobile edge computing networks. *IEEE Trans. Mob. Comput.* **2021**, *22*, 2233–2247. [CrossRef]
12. Hu, H.; Song, W.; Wang, Q.; Hu, R.Q.; Zhu, H. Energy Efficiency and Delay Tradeoff in an MEC-Enabled Mobile IoT Network. *IEEE Internet Things J.* **2022**, *9*, 15942–15956. [CrossRef]
13. Antonopoulos, N.; Gillam, L. *Cloud Computing*; Springer: Berlin/Heidelberg, Germany, 2010; Volume 51.
14. Nugroho, A.K.; Shioda, S.; Kim, T. Optimal Resource Provisioning and Task Offloading for Network-Aware and Federated Edge Computing. *Sensors* **2023**, *23*, 9200. [CrossRef] [PubMed]
15. Kim, T.; Lin, J.W.; Hsieh, C.T. Delay and QoS Aware Low Complex Optimal Service Provisioning for Edge Computing. *IEEE Trans. Veh. Technol.* **2023**, *72*, 1169–1183. [CrossRef]
16. Kherraf, N.; Alameddine, H.A.; Sharafeddine, S.; Assi, C.M.; Ghrayeb, A. Optimized provisioning of edge computing resources with heterogeneous workload in IoT networks. *IEEE Trans. Netw. Serv. Manag.* **2019**, *16*, 459–474. [CrossRef]
17. Xiang, Z.; Deng, S.; Jiang, F.; Gao, H.; Tehari, J.; Yin, J. Computing power allocation and traffic scheduling for edge service provisioning. In Proceedings of the 2020 IEEE International Conference on Web Services (ICWS), Beijing, China, 18–24 October 2020; IEEE: Piscataway, NJ, USA, 2020; pp. 394–403.
18. Jiang, H.; Dai, X.; Xiao, Z.; Iyengar, A. Joint task offloading and resource allocation for energy-constrained mobile edge computing. *IEEE Trans. Mob. Comput.* **2022**, *22*, 4000–4015. [CrossRef]
19. Apostolopoulos, P.A.; Tsiropoulou, E.E.; Papavassiliou, S. Risk-aware data offloading in multi-server multi-access edge computing environment. *IEEE/ACM Trans. Netw.* **2020**, *28*, 1405–1418. [CrossRef]
20. Han, B.; Sciancalepore, V.; Xu, Y.; Feng, D.; Schotten, H.D. Impatient queuing for intelligent task offloading in multiaccess edge computing. *IEEE Trans. Wirel. Commun.* **2022**, *22*, 59–72. [CrossRef]
21. Șong, H.; Gu, B.; Son, K.; Choi, W. Joint optimization of edge computing server deployment and user offloading associations in wireless edge network via a genetic algorithm. *IEEE Trans. Netw. Sci. Eng.* **2022**, *9*, 2535–2548. [CrossRef]
22. Feng, M.; Krunz, M.; Zhang, W. Joint task partitioning and user association for latency minimization in mobile edge computing networks. *IEEE Trans. Veh. Technol.* **2021**, *70*, 8108–8121. [CrossRef]
23. Charatsaris, P.; Diamanti, M.; Papavassiliou, S. Joint User Association and Resource Allocation for Hierarchical Federated Learning Based on Games in Satisfaction Form. *IEEE Open J. Commun. Soc.* **2023**, *5*, 457–471. [CrossRef]
24. Wang, H.; Wang, Y.; Sun, R.; Su, R.; Liu, B. Joint user association and power allocation for minimizing multi-bitrate video transmission delay in mobile-edge computing networks. In *Innovative Mobile and Internet Services in Ubiquitous Computing: Proceedings of the 12th International Conference on Innovative Mobile and Internet Services in Ubiquitous Computing (IMIS-2018), Sydney, NSW, Australia, 3–5 July 2019*; Springer: Berlin/Heidelberg, Germany, 2019; pp. 467–478.
25. Qi, Y.; Zhou, Y.; Liu, Y.F.; Liu, L.; Pan, Z. Traffic-aware task offloading based on convergence of communication and sensing in vehicular edge computing. *IEEE Internet Things J.* **2021**, *8*, 17762–17777. [CrossRef]
26. Wang, P.; Wang, Y.; Qiao, J.; Hu, Z. Traffic-Aware Optimization of Task Offloading and Content Caching in the Internet of Vehicles. *Appl. Sci.* **2023**, *13*, 13069. [CrossRef]
27. Oza, P.; Hudson, N.; Chantem, T.; Khamfroush, H. Deadline-aware task offloading for vehicular edge computing networks using traffic light data. *ACM Trans. Embed. Comput. Syst.* **2024**, *23*, 1–25. [CrossRef]
28. Guo, H.; Liu, J.; Lv, J. Toward intelligent task offloading at the edge. *IEEE Netw.* **2019**, *34*, 128–134. [CrossRef]
29. Kim, K.; Lynskey, J.; Kang, S.; Hong, C.S. Prediction based sub-task offloading in mobile edge computing. In Proceedings of the 2019 International Conference on Information Networking (ICOIN), Kuala Lumpur, Malaysia, 9–11 January 2019; IEEE: Piscataway, NJ, USA, 2019; pp. 448–452.
30. Zeng, F.; Tang, J.; Liu, C.; Deng, X.; Li, W. Task-offloading strategy based on performance prediction in vehicular edge computing. *Mathematics* **2022**, *10*, 1010. [CrossRef]
31. Bohannon, R.W.; Andrews, A.W. Normal walking speed: A descriptive meta-analysis. *Physiotherapy* **2011**, *97*, 182–189. [CrossRef] [PubMed]
32. Benidis, K.; Rangapuram, S.S.; Flunkert, V.; Wang, Y.; Maddix, D.; Turkmen, C.; Gasthaus, J.; Bohlke-Schneider, M.; Salinas, D.; Stella, L.; et al. Deep learning for time series forecasting: Tutorial and literature survey. *ACM Comput. Surv.* **2022**, *55*, 1–36. [CrossRef]
33. Kim, N.; Balaraman, A.; Lee, K.; Kim, T. Multi-Step Peak Power Forecasting with Constrained Conditional Transformer for a Large-Scale Manufacturing Plant. *IEEE Access* **2023**, *11*, 136692–136705. [CrossRef]
34. Brownlee, J. *Deep Learning for Time Series Forecasting: Predict the Future with MLPs, CNNs and LSTMs in Python*; Machine Learning Mastery: Vermont, Australia, 2018.
35. Hochreiter, S.; Schmidhuber, J. Long short-term memory. *Neural Comput.* **1997**, *9*, 1735–1780. [CrossRef] [PubMed]
36. Vaswani, A.; Shazeer, N.; Parmar, N.; Uszkoreit, J.; Jones, L.; Gomez, A.N.; Kaiser, Ł.; Polosukhin, I. Attention is all you need. *Adv. Neural Inf. Process. Syst.* **2017**, *30*, 6000–6010.

37. Kim, T.; Al-Tarazi, M.; Lin, J.W.; Choi, W. Optimal container migration for mobile edge computing: Algorithm, system design and implementation. *IEEE Access* **2021**, *9*, 158074–158090. [CrossRef]
38. Kim, T.; Chang, J.M. Profitable and energy-efficient resource optimization for heterogeneous cloud-based radio access networks. *IEEE Access* **2019**, *7*, 34719–34737. [CrossRef]
39. Kim, T.; Chang, J.M. QoS-aware energy-efficient association and resource scheduling for HetNets. *IEEE Trans. Veh. Technol.* **2017**, *67*, 650–664. [CrossRef]
40. Amazon Web Services, High Availability and Scalability on AWS—Real-Time Communication on AWS, Amazon Web Services. 2024. Available online: https://docs.aws.amazon.com/whitepapers/latest/real-time-communication-on-aws/high-availability-and-scalability-on-aws.html (accessed on 26 July 2024).
41. Microsoft Azure, Azure Availability Zones—High Availability at Scale. Available online: https://azure.microsoft.com/en-us/explore/global-infrastructure/availability-zones#features (accessed on 25 July 2024).
42. Docker Inc. Docker. Available online: https://www.docker.com/ (accessed on 6 July 2024).
43. Docker Inc. Runtime Options with Memory, CPUs, and GPUs. Available online: https://docs.docker.com/config/containers/resource_constraints/ (accessed on 6 July 2024).
44. Wang, H.; Xu, F.; Li, Y.; Zhang, P.; Jin, D. Understanding mobile traffic patterns of large scale cellular towers in urban environment. In Proceedings of the 2015 Internet Measurement Conference, Tokyo, Japan, 28–30 October 2015; pp. 225–238.
45. James, J.F. *A Student's Guide to Fourier Transforms with Applications in Physics and Engineering*; Cambridge University Press: Cambridge, UK, 2011.
46. Roonizi, A.K.; Sassi, R. ECG signal decomposition using Fourier analysis. *EURASIP J. Adv. Signal Process.* **2024**, *2024*, 79. [CrossRef]
47. Huang, H.; Chen, J.; Sun, R.; Wang, S. Short-term traffic prediction based on time series decomposition. *Phys. A Stat. Mech. Its Appl.* **2022**, *585*, 126441. [CrossRef]
48. Shi, J.; Leau, Y.-B.; Li, K.; Park, Y.-J.; Yan, Z. Optimization and Decomposition Methods in Network Traffic Prediction Model: A Review and Discussion. *IEEE Access* **2020**, *8*, 202858–202871. [CrossRef]
49. The MathWorks Inc. *MATLAB*, Version: 9.13.0 (R2022b); The MathWorks Inc.: Portola Valley, CA, USA, 2022.
50. Grant, M.; Boyd, S. *CVX: Matlab Software for Disciplined Convex Programming*, Version 2.1; CVX Research, Inc.: Austin, TX, USA, 2014.
51. Gurobi Optimization, LLC. *Gurobi Optimizer Reference Manual*, Version 11.0; Gurobi Optimization, LLC: Beaverton, OR, USA, 2024.
52. Khan, M.A.; Hamila, R.; Gastli, A.; Kiranyaz, S.; Al-Emadi, N.A. ML-based handover prediction and AP selection in cognitive Wi-Fi networks. *J. Netw. Syst. Manag.* **2022**, *30*, 72. [CrossRef]
53. Goldsmith, A. *Wireless Communications*; Cambridge University Press: Cambridge, UK, 2005.
54. Tensorflow, Keras: The High-Level API for TensorFlow, Tensorflow. Available online: https://www.tensorflow.org/guide/keras (accessed on 15 June 2024).
55. Gurobi Optimization, Mixed-Integer Programming (MIP)—A Primer on the Basics, Gurobi Optimization. Available online: https://www.gurobi.com/resources/mixed-integer-programming-mip-a-primer-on-the-basics (accessed on 15 June 2024).

electronics

Article

A Distributed Non-Intrusive Load Monitoring Method Using Karhunen–Loeve Feature Extraction and an Improved Deep Dictionary

Siqi Liu, Zhiyuan Xie * and Zhengwei Hu

School of Electrical and Electronic Engineering, North China Electric Power University, Baoding 071003, China; liusiqi@ncepu.edu.cn (S.L.); hzwwizard@ncepu.edu.cn (Z.H.)
* Correspondence: zhiyuanxie@ncepu.edu.cn

Abstract: In recent years, the non-invasive load monitoring (NILM) method based on sparse coding has shown promising research prospects. This type of method learns a sparse dictionary for each monitoring target device, and it expresses load decomposition as a problem of signal reconstruction using dictionaries and sparse vectors. The existing NILM methods based on sparse coding have problems such as inability to be applied to multi-state and time-varying devices, single-load characteristics, and poor recognition ability for similar devices in distributed manners. Using the analysis above, this paper focuses on devices with similar features in households and proposes a distributed non-invasive load monitoring method using Karhunen–Loeve (KL) feature extraction and an improved deep dictionary. Firstly, Karhunen–Loeve expansion (KLE) is used to perform subspace expansion on the power waveform of the target device, and a new load feature is extracted by combining singular value decomposition (SVD) dimensionality reduction. Afterwards, the states of all the target devices are modeled as super states, and an improved deep dictionary based on the distance separability measure function (DSM-DDL) is learned for each super state. Among them, the state transition probability matrix and observation probability matrix in the hidden Markov model (HMM) are introduced as the basis for selecting the dictionary order during load decomposition. The KL feature matrix of power observation values and improved depth dictionary are used to discriminate the current super state based on the minimum reconstruction error criterion. The test results based on the UK-DALE dataset show that the KL feature matrix can effectively reduce the load similarity of devices. Combined with DSM-DDL, KL has a certain information acquisition ability and acceptable computational complexity, which can effectively improve the load decomposition accuracy of similar devices, quickly and accurately estimating the working status and power demand of household appliances.

Keywords: load decomposition; distributed non-invasive load monitoring; sparse coding technology; deep dictionary learning; Karhunen–Loeve

1. Introduction

NILM technology is one of the key technologies for implementing load management, which can monitor the usage of electrical equipment in buildings online. Through NILM, users can understand their own electricity usage characteristics, and power companies can also have a detailed understanding of their electricity usage behavior. This can improve the planning, operation, and management capabilities of the power grid, providing services for two-way interaction and intelligent electricity consumption between both parties [1]. NILM mainly monitors household and commercial appliances. According to their working modes, these electrical appliances can be divided into three categories [2]: on-off-state devices, multi-state devices, and time-varying-state devices.

The earliest NILM technology was proposed by Hart in 1992, which used load characteristics such as power, voltage, and reactive power measured by household electricity meters to model devices as finite state machines [3]. This method is relatively successful in decomposing simple switch-state devices, but its effect is not good for multi-state and time-varying-state devices. At present, one development direction of the NILM system is achieving non-invasive load monitoring. Specifically, it relies on the existing data collection equipment and communication network of the power information collection system, adopts advanced data communication technology to obtain fine user power load data, and then uses the powerful data processing capabilities of the power cloud platform to run more complex and accurate load decomposition algorithms [4–6], such as kNN clustering and Fisher discrimination [7], FCM fuzzy clustering [8], subtraction clustering [9], quadratic linear programming [10], deep learning methods based on seq2seq and attention mechanisms [11], etc. Reference [4] designed an AdaBoost sample selection algorithm that simplifies the load feature library by analyzing the distribution of load samples in the feature space. It combines the k-nearest neighbors (k-NN) classification algorithm and kernel Fisher discriminant algorithm to identify loads by controlling the risk of misclassification. In Reference [7], for low-power electrical appliances, the most obvious harmonic amplitude in the frequency domain is selected as a new feature, and a new NILM method is proposed. This method uses incremental feature extraction to obtain changes in load characteristics and uses information entropy to determine the optimal number of clusters and load similarity by calculating inter-cluster entropy. Then, the fuzzy clustering method is used to monitor the number and types of electrical appliances. Reference [8] proposed a low-sampling-rate, non-invasive device load monitoring (NIALM) method, which is based on subtraction clustering and maximum likelihood classifiers. Compared with the NIALM method based on K-means, this method has lower sensitivity to power grid noise.

Load characteristics are an important basis for load decomposition, and the load characteristics of equipment can be roughly divided into steady-state characteristics and transient characteristics [12]. Steady state characteristics mainly include parameters such as steady-state voltage, steady-state power, and reactive power, while transient characteristics mainly include transient voltage, transient power, and power at the moment of equipment switching. Due to the high requirement for device sampling accuracy in obtaining transient data (sampling frequencies greater than 10 kHz), it is difficult to use it for large-scale residential or commercial electricity monitoring. Therefore, the use of steady-state characteristics is more widespread in practical applications.

NILM that utilizes steady-state characteristics mostly relies on analyzing historical operating data of individual devices and inferring the current state of the device by combining observation data. Reference [9] proposed a new NILM method called Linear Chain Conditional Random Fields (CRFs), which combines the characteristics of current signal and real power. This method relaxes the independent assumption, avoids label bias issues, and can effectively identify and detect polymorphic household appliances. Reference [10] first introduces sparse coding and dictionary learning methods into NILM, proposing a discriminative decomposition sparse coding method suitable for low-sampling-rate data load decomposition. Although the decomposition effect is not satisfactory, it brings new ideas to NILM research. Subsequently, the load decomposition technique based on dictionary learning has received increasing attention. Reference [11] combines dictionary learning with time-based prior probabilities and proposes the use of power-let technology to learn load features. Reference [13] combines sparse coding techniques with deep learning concepts and uses deep sparse coding for load decomposition. This method learns a multi-layer dictionary (also called a deep dictionary) for each device in the scene and then obtains a corresponding sparse matrix through the deep dictionary and measurement data as the basis for judging the device status. Deep dictionary learning effectively improves the accuracy of load decomposition, but there are also some shortcomings: devices can only be assumed to be simple switch-state devices, and dictionaries are learned separately for each device, which not only breaks the interconnection between devices but also accumulates recognition errors of individual devices, affecting the judgment of the overall state. In addition, due to the limitations of the dictionary learning framework used, existing load decomposition methods based on sparse coding cannot simultaneously recognize devices based on multiple load features. Using only a specific load feature is highly susceptible to interference from device feature aliasing, resulting in poor recognition ability for devices with similar features. With the advancement of technology and science, the types of household electrical equipment are constantly increasing, and the load characteristics are gradually converging, making the existing steady-state load characteristics unable to effectively distinguish and identify equipment. It is necessary to further explore the load characteristics of equipment to meet the needs of NILM [12].

This paper proposes a non-invasive load monitoring method that combines the KLE load feature matrix with improved deep dictionary learning based on distance separability measure to address the problems of existing NILM methods based on sparse coding, such as inability to apply to multi-state and time-varying devices, single-load features, and poor recognition ability for similar devices. This method first quantifies the states of multi-state devices and time-varying-state devices in the training sample set and aggregates the target device states into super states. With a method based on KL expansion and singular value decomposition for dimensionality reduction, a new feature, i.e., the KLE feature matrix, is extracted from the total power of the target device, and a hyper-state feature library is established based on it. Using the KL feature matrix of the super state as the learning sample, a distance-based class separability measure function is used to improve the objective function of deep dictionary learning for super states with similar load characteristics and high risk of misjudgment. The spatial sparsity of the super state is utilized to reduce the computational complexity of load decomposition, the current super state is identified, and the state and power of each device are estimated based on the minimum reconstruction error criterion. Through testing on the UK-DALE [14] power dataset, it was verified that the proposed load decomposition method based on the KLE feature matrix and improved deep dictionary learning has the advantages of low similarity of equipment load features, fast load decomposition speed, and improved recognition accuracy of appliances with similar features.

2. Establishment of a Super-State Feature Library

A hyper-state is an aggregation of all target device states and each hyper-state uniquely corresponding to a combination of internal states within a single device. The super state preserves the correlation between device operations, and the state of all devices can be directly inferred from the super state during load decomposition, which can reduce the impact of device feature aliasing. The establishment process of the hyper-state feature library is shown in Figure 1, which will be introduced in detail in Section 2.1 of this paper.

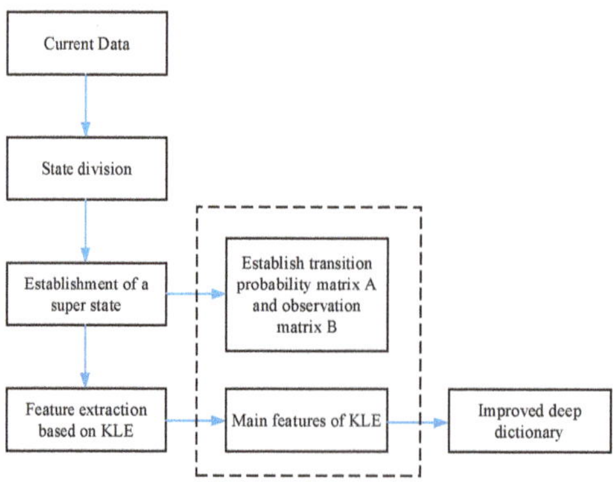

Figure 1. Flowchart of KLE feature extraction.

2.1. Equipment State Division and Hyper-State Modeling

Most existing NILM methods simply assume devices are switch-state electrical appliances; however, in practical applications, most devices have multiple states or time-varying states. The power difference between different gears and functions of electrical equipment can be significant, and recording the status changes in the equipment while recording electrical data can also create a heavy workload. Therefore, this paper first uses the peak-binning method to partition the states of devices in the dataset and then models the devices. Assuming the distribution of power values of device m$P = \{P_1, P_2, \ldots P_n\}$ is as shown in Table 1, we first calculate the number of power values P_n and their proportion $PY_m(P_n)$. Then, we search for the peak power $y_{peak}^{(m)}$ from low to high according to P, and the peak value must meet the requirements of Equation (1).

$$\begin{cases} PY_m(P_n) - PY_m(P_{n-1}) > 0 \\ PY_m(P_{n+1}) - PY_m(P_n) < 0 \end{cases}, PY_m(P) > 0.002 \tag{1}$$

Table 1. Example of state quantization.

P (W)	0	100	200	300	400	500
Count (n)	900	80	100	620	200	100
$PY_m(I)$	0.45	0.04	0.05	0.31	0.10	0.05
$\frown{X}^{(m)}, y_{peak}^{(m)}$	0.0			1.3		

A threshold 0.002 is set for the peak value in the formula to filter out background noise, that is, to filter out smaller peaks. After the search is completed, the peak values are numbered, with each peak representing a quantized state of the device. The power value corresponding to the peak value is used as the quantized power value for that state, and non-peak power is included in the state where the nearest peak is located. As shown in Table 1, there are six power values for the equipment, with only two peak values $y_{peak}^{m}[0] = 0$ and $y_{peak}^{m}[1] = 300$ W. Therefore, the power values will be divided into two quantization states: $Q^{(m)} \in \{0, 1\}$, with quantization powers of $y[Q^{(m)} = 0] = 0$ and $y[Q^{(m)} = 1] = 300$ W, respectively. At the same time, the quantified states corresponding to each power of device m in the dataset can also be obtained, such as $Q[y^{(m)} = 200] = 1$ and $Q[y^{(m)} = 100] = 0$.

Next, according to Reference [15], the states of all devices in the house are aggregated into super states. Assuming there are M target devices in the scene, the super state S_t at time t can be directly represented as $\frown{S}_t = (\frown{X}^{(1)}, \frown{X}^{(2)}, \ldots, \frown{X}^{(M)})$ by the quantified states of each appliance, where $\frown{X}^{(m)}$ represents the quantified state of device m in S_t.

After establishing a super state for all target devices, the super state corresponding to the total power at each moment in the training set can be determined. Based on the super state, the state transition probability matrix and observation probability matrix can be established. If the number of total power observations in the scene is N and the number of super states is L, then A is a transition probability matrix of size $L \times L$ and B is an observation probability matrix of size $K \times N$. The elements in matrices A and B are defined by Equations (2) and (3), respectively.

$$\mathrm{A}[i, j] = P_a(i.j) = P[S_t = j | S_{t-1} = i] \tag{2}$$

$$\mathrm{B}[j, n] = P_b(y_t, j) = P[y_t = n | S_t = j] \tag{3}$$

where S_t is the super state of time t, y_t is the observed value of S_t, and S_{t-1} is the super state of time $t-1$. In this paper, the observed value of the super state refers to the total power data in the test dataset.

2.2. Spatial Distribution of Load Characteristics

Decomposing the load into super states requires a substantial amount of training and testing samples. A super-state load sample, represented by a high-dimensional feature vector, corresponds to a point in the load feature space. Consequently, all samples of a super state within a dataset form a cluster in the load feature space, referred to as the class domain of the super state. This class domain encompasses all possible load feature values for that super state. If the load features of two super states differ significantly, their respective class domains are well separated, with no overlap. However, when the features of two super states are highly similar, their class domains overlap, as illustrated in Figure 2. In such cases, it becomes challenging to accurately determine the category of a test sample located within the overlapping region.

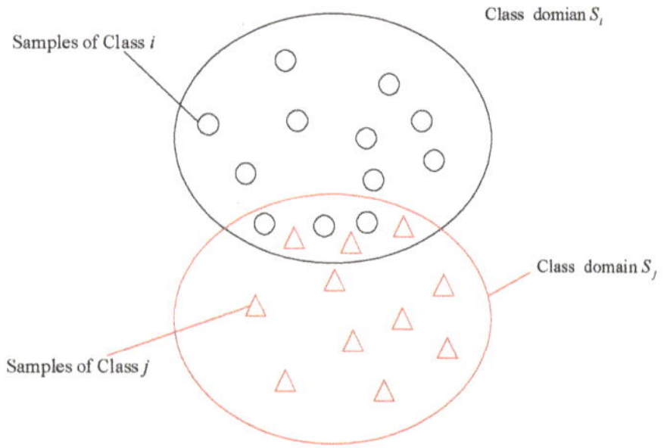

Figure 2. Overlapping-region graph of super-state class clusters.

The recognition ability of the samples in the overlapping area directly affects the accuracy of the NILM system. In order to reduce the overlapping region of the hyper-state class domain, on the one hand, the load feature with low similarity should be selected, on the other hand, the overlapping region can be reduced in the load decomposition algorithm. In these two directions, this paper proposes a load feature extraction method based on KLE and an improved depth dictionary based on the distance separability measure function. These two methods are described in detail in Sections 2.3 and 3.2 later.

2.3. Load Feature Extraction Based on KLE

$X = [X(0)X(1)\dots X(N)]^T$ is set to represent the power sequence of a particular electrical appliance, and its autocorrelation matrix Φ_{XX} is of size $\widetilde{N} \times \widetilde{N}$. By performing eigenvalue decomposition on Φ_{XX}, we obtain $\widetilde{N}$ orthogonal eigenvectors $q_0, q_1, \dots q_{\widetilde{N}-1}$, and the Karhunen-Loeve (KL) transformation of the sample X is expressed as follows:

$$\widetilde{x} = Q^T X \quad (4)$$

In Equation (4), $\widetilde{x}$ represents the KL-transformed signal, and $Q = [q_0, q_1, \dots, q_{\widetilde{N}-1}]$ is a unitary matrix, ensuring $Q^T Q = QQ^T = I$. Hence, the original signal X can be perfectly reconstructed using the inverse KL transformation. The process of reconstructing the original signal X using the KL-transformed signal is expressed as follows:

$$X = Q\widetilde{x} = \sum_{i=0}^{\widetilde{N}-1} q_i^T X q_i \quad (5)$$

From Equation (5), it can be seen that the signal X can be decomposed into $\widetilde{N}$ uncorrelated spectral components $x_0, x_1, \ldots, x_{\widetilde{N}-1}$, in which $x_i = q_i^T X q_i$. These unrelated spectral components are called subspace components (subspace component, SC) of signal X. These SCs expand the $N \times 1$ dimensional sampled power vector into an $\widetilde{N} \times \widetilde{N}$ size SC matrix $X_{SC} = [x_0, x_1, \ldots x_{\widetilde{N}-1}]$. The KL expansion decomposes X into multiple subspaces with minimal-truncation mean-square errors. By applying dimensionality reduction to the SC matrix and retaining only the elements within each SC that best represent the original signal characteristics, the similarity between signals can be reduced to some extent. Therefore, this paper utilizes a dimensionality reduction method based on singular value decomposition (SVD) to analyze the subspace matrix and extract deeper information hidden in the power data.

Singular value decomposition (SVD) is a widely used mathematical technique in the field of signal processing. By applying SVD to the subspace matrix for dimensionality reduction, noise and correlated components within the signal can be removed, leaving only the primary features of the samples. Additionally, SVD provides some degree of filtering for outliers caused by data acquisition equipment or equipment malfunctions. During the dimensionality reduction process, it is necessary to do singular value decomposition of the covariance matrix $X_{SC}X_{SC}^T$ of X_{SC} to obtain the eigenvalue matrix and the left singular matrix U of the covariance matrix.

The eigenvalue matrix is used to determine the row number k of the reduced matrix, and the square method is expressed as Formula (6):

$$\mathrm{k} = \min_{\mathrm{k}}\left(1 - \frac{\sum_1^k \lambda_i}{\sum_1^{\widetilde{N}} \lambda_i} \leq 0.05\right) \tag{6}$$

In the formula, λ_i is the i eigenvalue of the covariance matrix $X_{SC}X_{SC}^T$. The purpose of Formula (6) is to select the minimum k value which can retain more than 95% of the information of the original matrix. After the k value is determined, the first k column of the matrix U is taken to form a reduced-dimension matrix U_k, and a matrix Z of $\widetilde{N} \times k$ value is calculated by using Formula (7), which is called the KLE load characteristic matrix of the equipment.

$$Z = U_k^T X_{SC} \tag{7}$$

To achieve a relatively stable subspace, the length of a sampling sequence should be much smaller than the total length of the device state power signal, and it should be determined based on the data sampling frequency. In the UK-DALE dataset, the total length of the device state power signals ranges between 60 and 80 samples. Therefore, this paper selects five samples as the length of a sampling sequence, resulting in a 5×5 autocorrelation matrix, that is, $N = \widetilde{N} = 5$.

In actual measurement data, the power value of each super state is not unique. Even if the internal state of the appliance does not change, small power fluctuations can still occur within the super state. The approach used in this paper is to sequentially obtain five total power samples from the current super state each time a super-state transition occurs in the training set. If the super state i appears r times in the dataset, then r power vectors of size 5 can be obtained. The KL feature matrices of these vectors constitute the KLE feature class domain for super state i. The mean vector of the r power vectors is calculated, and the KLE feature matrix of the mean vector is taken as the KLE central feature matrix for the super state i. This central feature matrix is then used as the training sample for dictionary learning.

3. Improved In-Depth Dictionary Learning

This paper proposes an improvement to the objective function of deep dictionary learning by incorporating a distance-based class separability measure function and applying it to load decomposition. Section 3 provides a detailed introduction to the optimization method of DSM-DDL and outlines the specific process for performing load decomposition using this approach.

3.1. Deep Dictionary Learning

Reference [10] was the first to introduce the method of sparse coding and dictionary learning into NILM. Sparse coding is essentially a modeling approach, where a signal matrix can be linearly represented by a subset of elements from a dictionary. One of the key aspects of classification methods based on sparse representation is dictionary learning. The learning process primarily involves optimizing the dictionary through training samples and minimizing an objective function.

Assume that the target device's power has been time-sampled using a smart meter, represented as a column vector X. This vector can be represented by a dictionary D and a sparse matrix Z as follows:

$$X = DZ \tag{8}$$

This is a typical sparse dictionary learning problem, and the objective function can be obtained by L_1 regularization of sparse matrix Z.

$$\min_{D,Z} \|X - DZ\|_F^2 + \lambda \|Z\|_1 \tag{9}$$

In the case where X is known, the device dictionary D can be obtained by optimizing Formula (9) using the KSVD method [16]. If there are multiple devices in the scene, load characteristics such as power are used, and it is assumed that the total reading X of the smart meter is the sum of the readings X_m of M devices. Total power is modeled as

$$X = \sum_M X_m = \sum_M D_m Z_m \tag{10}$$

The objective function is

$$\min_{z_1,\ldots,z_M} \left\| X - [D_1|\ldots|D_M] \begin{bmatrix} Z_1 \\ \vdots \\ Z_M \end{bmatrix} \right\|_F^2 + \lambda \left\| \begin{matrix} Z_1 \\ \vdots \\ Z_M \end{matrix} \right\|_1 \tag{11}$$

In-depth dictionary learning extends the single-layer dictionary of Formula (8) to multiple layers, as follows:

$$X = D^1 D^2 \ldots D^l Z,\ l = 1,2,3\ldots \tag{12}$$

The corresponding objective function is

$$\min_{D_1,D_2,D_3,Z} \|X_i - D_1 D_2 D_3 \ldots D_l Z\|_F^2 + \lambda \|Z\|_1 \tag{13}$$

3.2. Improved Objective Function Based on Distance Separability Measure

As seen from Equation (10), methods based on deep dictionary learning can only utilize additive load features, modeling the total load as the sum of the power from individual devices. This approach assumes that the devices being monitored are simple on–off-state devices, which makes it challenging to accurately identify devices with overlapping features. Furthermore, modeling the total load as the sum of the power from all appliances in the scenario can lead to the accumulation of decomposition errors from individual devices into the total load. As the number of appliances increases, the total state error will rapidly escalate.

To address these issues, this paper proposes an improved deep dictionary learning method based on a distance separability measure function. The objective function of deep dictionary learning, as shown in Equation (13), is enhanced using a distance-based measure function to reduce the overlapping regions of load feature class domains for similar super states. The solution method for the improved objective function is also provided. The number of layers in the dictionary involves a trade-off between learning depth and overfitting, with most medium-sized problems using a three-layer architecture. The three-layer objective function for the improved deep dictionary learning proposed in this paper is formulated as follows:

$$\begin{aligned}\min_{D_1,D_2,D_3,Z}\|K_i - D_1D_2D_3Z\|_F^2 + \frac{1}{n_i}\Big(\sum_{K_c^i\in C_{ij}}\|K_c^i - D_1D_2D_3Z\|_F^2 \\ -n_i\|D_1D_2D_3Z - K_j\|_F^2\Big) + \lambda\|Z\|_1\end{aligned} \tag{14}$$

where K_i is the KL central eigenmatrix of the hyper-state i, D shows the multi-layer dictionary matrix, Z is the sparse representation matrix of K_i, and λ is the regularization parameter greater than 0. K_j is another KL characteristic matrix of hyper-state j which overlaps with class domain K_i, C_{ij} is the KL matrix set of super state i and j overlapping-region samples, and n_i is the number of KL matrix K_c belonging to hyper-state i in C_{ij}. This paper stipulates that the number of K_c^i does not exceed $1/10$ of K_i. The method of determining C_{ij} and K_c is as follows: After determining the KL feature class domain of each hyper-state in Section 2.2, the Adaboost-based method in Reference [4] is used to find the hyper-state j which has the highest similarity with the class domain of hyper-state i, the KL feature matrix K_c^i, and K_c^j with high similarity in the two class domains, and these matrices are placed into the set C_{ij}.

In this method, the concepts of intra-class distance and inter-class distance are introduced to optimize the target function. In Formula (14), $\sum_{K_c^i\in C_{ij}}\|K_c^i - D_1D_2D_3Z\|_F^2$ and $n_i\|D_1D_2D_3Z - K_j\|_F^2$ are F norm forms of intra-class dispersion and inter-class dispersion, respectively, and they are subtracted and multiplied by $\frac{1}{n_i}$ as the optimization function of similar hyper-state discrimination. The F-norm form is used here to facilitate the measurement of the distance among matrices and can also be synchronized with the original objective function during optimization iterations. On the one hand, the optimization function can make the distance between the learned dictionary and the same kind of samples in the overlapping area closer; on the other hand, it can increase the distance between different kinds of dictionaries. Combining the load characteristics of KLE proposed beforehand can reduce the number of samples in the overlapping area and enhance the ability of NILM system to distinguish the super state of feature similarity.

It is not easy to optimize Equation (14). In this paper, the split Bragman method [17] is used to decompose the objective function. By making $Y_1 = D_2D_3Z$ and introducing Bragman relaxation coefficient B_1, we can obtain

$$\begin{aligned}\min_{D_1,D_2,D_3,z}\|K_i - D_1Y_1\|_F^2 + \frac{1}{n_i}\Big(\sum_{K_c^i\in C_{ij}}\|K_c^i - D_1Y_1\|_F^2 - n_i\|D_1Y_1 \\ - K_j\|_F^2\Big) + \mu_1\|Y_1 - D_2D_3Z - B_1\| + \lambda\|Z\|_1\end{aligned} \tag{15}$$

The objective function of the improved deep dictionary learning for $Y_2 = D_3Z$ is as follows:

$$\begin{aligned}\min_{D_1,D_2,D_3,Z,Y_1,Y_2}\|K_i - D_1Y_1\|_F^2 + \frac{1}{n_i}\Big(\sum_{K_c^i\in C_{ij}}\|K_c^i - D_1Y_1\|_F^2 \\ -n_i\|D_1Y_1 - K_j\|_F^2\Big) + \mu_1\|Y_1 - D_2Y_2 - B_1\|_F^2 \\ +\mu_2\|Y_2 - D_3Z - B_2\| + \lambda\|Z\|_1\end{aligned} \tag{16}$$

In Formula (16), μ_1 and μ_2 are weight coefficients, and the function is to determine the weight of each part in the optimization of the objective function. In this paper, $\mu_1 = \mu_2 = 1$.

Using the alternating direction method, Formula (16) is decomposed into six sub-problems:

$$1.\min_{D_1} \|K_i - D_1 Y_1\|_F^2 + \frac{1}{n_i}\Big(\sum_{K_c^i \in C_{ij}} \|K_c^i - D_1 Y_1\|_F^2 - n_i \|D_1 Y_1 - K_j\|_F^2\Big)$$

$$2.\min_{Y_1} \|K_i - D_1 Y_1\|_F^2 + \mu_1 \|Y_1 - D_2 Y_2 - B_1\|_2^2 + \frac{1}{n_i}\Big(\sum_{K_c^i \in C_{ij}} \|K_c^i - D_1 Y_1\|_F^2 - n_i \|D_1 Y_1 - K_j\|_F^2\Big)$$

$$3.\min_{D_2} \|Y_1 - B_1 - D_2 Y_2\|_F^2$$

$$4.\min_{Y_2} \mu_1 \|Y_1 - B_1 - D_2 Y_2\|_F^2 + \mu_2 \|Y_2 - D_3 Z - B_2\|_F^2$$

$$5.\min_{D_3} \|Y_2 - B_2 - D_3 Z\|_F^2$$

$$6.\min_{Z} \mu_3 \|Y_2 - B_2 - D_3 Z\|_F^2 + \lambda \|Z\|_1$$

Sub-problem 1 to 5 are convex problems and are least-square problems with closed solutions, which can be optimized block by block by using the least-square method. The partial derivative of D_1 can be obtained using sub-problem 1.

$$D_1 = \Big[(K_i - n_i K_j) Y_1^T + \frac{1}{n_i} \sum_{K_c^i \in C_{ij}} K_c^i Y_1^T\Big] (3 Y_1 Y_1^T)^{-1} \tag{17}$$

In the same way, the optimization formulas of sub-equations 2 to 5 can be obtained, which will not be repeated in this paper.

Sub-problem 6 is a single-objective L1 regular sparse problem, which can be optimized by the orthogonal matching pursuit algorithm [18]. In each iteration, the update formula of relaxation coefficient B is as follows:

$$B_1^{k+1} = -B_1^k + D_2 Y_2 - Y_1 \tag{18}$$

$$B_2^{K+1} = -B_2^k + D_3 Z - Y_2 \tag{19}$$

When learning the improved depth dictionary according to the training samples, we first initialize the three sub-dictionaries randomly. In this paper, we make them an n-order unit matrix, and n is the number of rows of the KL characteristic matrix. On this basis, use the following:

$$\min_{Z} \|K_i - D_1 D_2 D_3 Z\|_F^2 + \frac{1}{n_i}\Big(\sum_{K_c^i \in C_{ij}} \|K_c^i - D_1 D_2 D_3 Z\|_F^2 - n_i \|D_1 D_2 D_3 Z - K_j\|_F^2\Big) \tag{20}$$

Initialize Z, then initialize $Y_1 = D_2 D_3 Z$, $Y_2 = D_3 Z$.

In dictionary learning, the reconstruction error d is obtained by Formula (21) after each iteration optimization.

$$d = \|K_i - D_1 D_2 D_3 Z\|_F^2 + \frac{1}{n_i}\Big(\sum_{K_c^i \in C_{ij}} \|K_c^i - D_1 D_2 D_3 Z\|_F^2 - n_i \|D_1 D_2 D_3 Z - K_j\|_F^2\Big) \tag{21}$$

In this paper, two termination conditions are set for the algorithm: when the reconstruction error d converges to the local minimum or reaches the maximum number of iterations. The local minimum is defined as five consecutive iterations without a smaller d, and the maximum number of iterations is set to 50. After terminating the algorithm, the three-layer dictionary D_1, D_2, D_3 of hyper-state i can be obtained.

3.3. Load Decomposition Based on Prior Probability Matrix and Minimum Reconstruction Error

In load decomposition, super-state estimation and power consumption prediction need to be carried out according to the power samples in the test set and the previously acquired dictionary. Assuming that the KL characteristic matrix of the t-time test sample is K_t, the objective function of load decomposition using the depth dictionary of super state j is as follows (22):

$$\begin{aligned}\min_{Z}\left\|K_t - D_1^{(i)}D_2^{(i)}D_3^{(i)}Z\right\|_F^2 + \tfrac{1}{n_i}\Big(\sum_{K_c^{(i)}\in C_{ij}} \left\|x_k - D_1^{(i)}D_2^{(i)}D_3^{(i)}Z\right\|_{\mathrm{F}}^2 \\ -n_i\|D_1^{(i)}D_2^{(i)}D_3^{(i)}Z - X_j\|_{\mathrm{F}}^2\Big) + \lambda\|Z\|_1\end{aligned} \tag{22}$$

The optimization method of Formula (22) is the same as the termination condition and Formula (16).

If the sparse matrices corresponding to all hyper-states are solved every time during load decomposition, the amount of calculation will be very large. In order to reduce the computational complexity, the concepts of state transition probability matrix and observation probability matrix in the hidden Markov model are introduced, and a dictionary screening method based on a posteriori probability is proposed. In this method, the transition probability between super states and the observation probability of total power are used as the basis for dictionary selection in load decomposition.

The load decomposition process is shown in Figure 3. In the load decomposition stage, the event detection of the power signal in the test set is carried out firstly, and the event detection uses the edge detection method in Reference [18]. After a change in the overstate is detected, five consecutive power samples are taken as load decomposition samples. Assuming that the total power value of the moment before the event is y_{t-1} and the observed value of the event time is y_t, according to the matrices An and B constructed in Section 2.1, a posteriori probability P_{post} is obtained by using the following formula:

$$P_{post} = P_b(y_{t-1}, i) \times P_a(i, j) \times P_b(y_t, j) \tag{23}$$

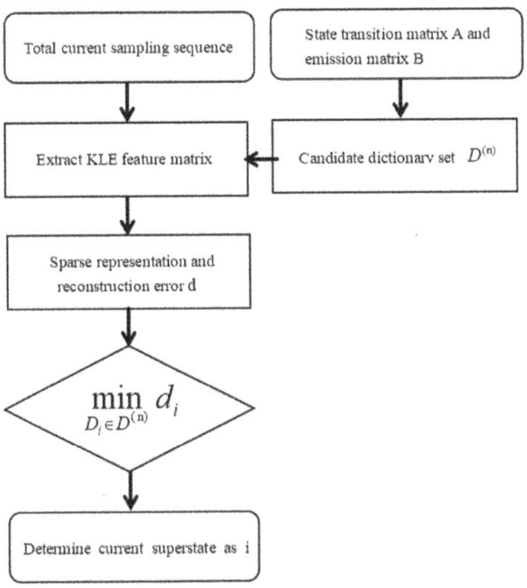

Figure 3. Flowchart of energy disaggregation.

Select the hyper-state dictionary whose P_{post} is not zero to form an alternative hyper-state dictionary $\Psi_D = [D_i, \ldots D_k]$, where D_i represents the improved depth dictionary of hyper-state i. Select $D_i, \ldots, D_k$ in Ψ_D and then use Formula (7) to extract KL features from load decomposition samples, obtain KLE feature matrix K_t with the same order as the depth dictionary, calculate sparse matrix Z and reconstruction error d_i, and use Formula (24) to select the hyper-state corresponding to depth dictionary with minimum reconstruction error.

$$j = \arg\min_{D_i \in \Psi_D} d_i \tag{24}$$

It is stipulated that the quantized state of each equipment in the super state is the state-estimated value of each target equipment at the current time, and the quantized power of each equipment state is the power-estimated value of each piece of equipment. The quantized status and quantized power values within a single equipment have been determined according to the box-splitting method in Section 2.1. So far, the DSM-DDL algorithm has completed a device state and power estimation.

4. Experimental Results and Analysis

The proposed method in this paper was validated and analyzed using a real-world dataset. The software platform utilized the Anaconda3 compiler with Python 3.6. The hardware platform consisted of a desktop computer with an Intel i7-8700 CPU and 16 GB of RAM. The experimental data used in this study were sourced from the UK-DALE dataset, specifically the sampling data from House 1 published by Imperial College London. This dataset provides device-level and total power data for 50 appliances in a single UK household over 385 days, along with records of state-change events for each device. The sampling interval is 6 s.

4.1. Comparison of Similarity of Load Characteristics

The accuracy of NILM load identification largely depends on the selected load features. In this paper, the super states are formed by aggregating the internal states of all target devices. If the target devices include appliances or combinations of appliances with similar power values and change patterns, super states with similar observed values and patterns of change may be generated, which can adversely affect the accuracy of load decomposition.

To validate the ability of the KLE feature matrix to reduce the similarity of load features, we first identified appliances and appliance combinations with high-power feature similarity. By comparing the power waveforms of appliances in the dataset, three devices were selected: a television (TV), a refrigerator (fridge, FRE), and a desktop computer (office_PC, OP). Among these, the power curves of the television and refrigerator exhibit high similarity, and the power curve of the television–refrigerator combination has a high similarity to that of the desktop computer. For each device and device combination, a representative portion of power samples was selected, with the sample waveforms shown in the following figure.

It can be seen that the power values of the refrigerator and TV are mainly distributed in the range of 80 W to 120 W, and there are very similar waves near 90 W. Compared with the power waveform of the combination of the computer and TV machine–refrigerator, it can also be found that the power value and waveform change law have a high similarity. For these devices and equipment combinations, it is difficult to distinguish effectively by using traditional steady-state characteristics such as power and current.

The binning method was used to quantify the internal states of the super states for the television, refrigerator, computer, and television–refrigerator combination. The power curves in Figure 4 were converted into the corresponding quantized-state sequence diagrams, with the results shown in Figure 5. For simplicity in labeling, the quantized states of the television, computer, refrigerator, and television–refrigerator combination are denoted as TV, OP, FR, and TV-FRE, respectively.

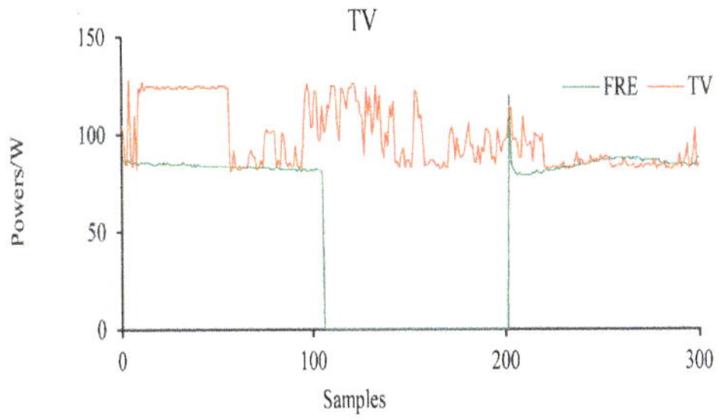

(**a**)

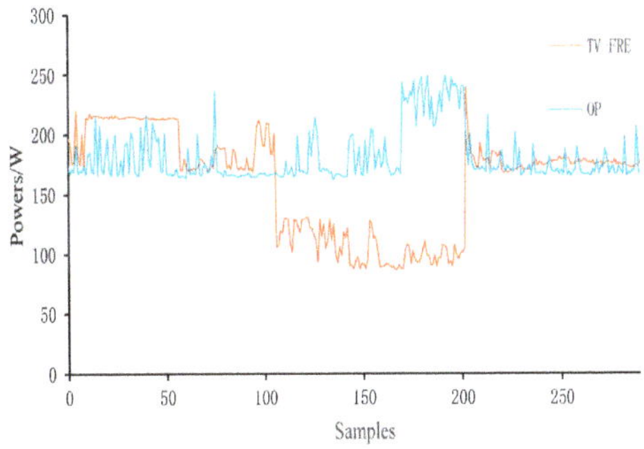

(**b**)

Figure 4. Current diagram of three appliances. (**a**) Power curve of TV and refrigerator; (**b**) Power curve of refrigerator and computer.

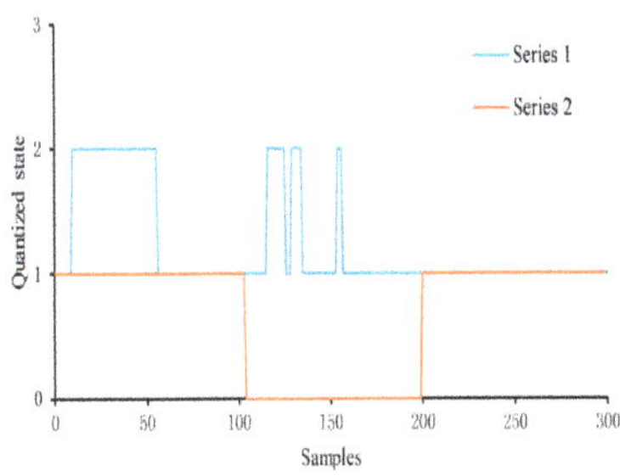

(**a**)

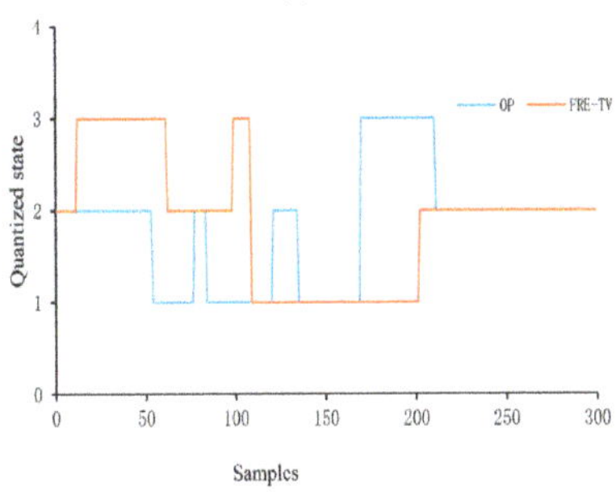

(**b**)

Figure 5. Quantitative feature diagram of three kinds of equipment. (**a**) Quantitative characteristic curve of TV and refrigerator; (**b**) Quantitative characteristic curves of desktop computer and refrigerator–TV set.

By examining Figures 4 and 5, it can be observed that the states of the television and refrigerator have a high degree of similarity. This implies that if these devices or combinations are included in a super state, and other device states remain the same, the power magnitude and waveform of the super states where the television is on and the refrigerator is off, or the refrigerator is on and the television is off, will be very similar. Similarly, the computer's state has a high similarity to the state of the television–refrigerator super state, which can also lead to misclassification during load decomposition. The experiment will use these states as examples to demonstrate the ability of the KL feature extraction method to reduce the similarity of load feature curves with close values and change patterns.

To quantitatively compare the impact of different load feature selections on the similarity of various device states or super states, the similarity index in Formula (25) is used to represent the degree of similarity between the load features of two states.

$$R^{j}_{(a,b)} = \frac{\left\|y_{f,a}\right\|_2}{\left\|y_{f,a}\right\|_2 + \left\|y_{f,a} - y_{f,b}\right\|_2} \tag{25}$$

In Equation (25), a, b represent any two device states or super states, f denotes the load feature currently being compared, and y represents the sample vectors of a and b. By calculating the similarity index for a specific type of load feature using the similarity function, the similarity and identifiability of appliances under that load feature can be quantitatively compared. The higher the similarity, the more challenging it is to distinguish between the states.

Based on the analysis of Figures 4 and 5, the following states were selected for comparison: TV(1) and REF(1), PC(2) and TV-REF(2), PC(2) and TV-REF(3). Equation (25) was used to calculate the similarity indices for both the power features and KLE features of these device states.

The power and corresponding KLE feature matrices of TV(1), PC(2) and REF(1) are shown in Figure 6. In the experiment, $N = \widetilde{N} = 5$.

	0	1	2	3	4
0	-7.0371×10^{-18}	-6.37773×10^{-17}	-3.01822	-1.65236×10^{-18}	5.29148×10^{-18}
1	4.04107×10^{-16}	0.836752	-4.8591×10^{-18}	$-4.070433 \times 10^{-18}$	3.30683×10^{-17}

(a)

	0	1	2	3	4
0	-9.24416×10^{-17}	-1.34303×10^{-16}	-1.45655×10^{-18}	6.38952×10^{-15}	−2.14498
1	-1.77484×10^{-17}	-3.9147×10^{-17}	-1.45089×10^{-17}	1.77967	5.50981×10^{-15}

(b)

	0	1	2	3	4
0	5.98985×10^{-17}	-6.39728×10^{-16}	-2.89352	5.23415×10^{-18}	4.1364×10^{-18}
1	-3.89539×10^{-17}	-0.786203	-6.73047×10^{-17}	-8.7475×10^{-17}	-2.6067×10^{-17}

(c)

Figure 6. KL characteristic matrix of three appliances. (**a**) KL characteristic matrix of TV(1); (**b**) KL characteristic matrix of PC(2); (**c**) KL characteristic matrix of REF(1).

Figure 7 compares the similarity indices of the three state groups under different load features. It can be observed that when using power states, the similarity indices of all three comparison groups are above 0.8, indicating a high degree of similarity. In contrast, the similarity indices for the KLE feature matrices show a significant reduction, all falling between 0.3 and 0.4. This indicates that KLE features can reduce the similarity between device states and super states with similar power curves, which is beneficial for load decomposition and state detection.

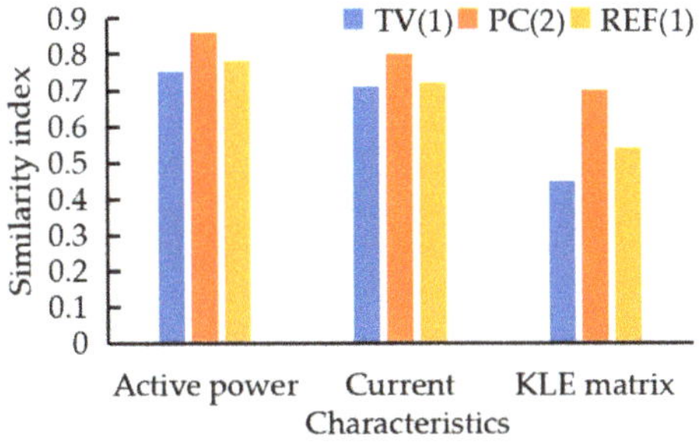

Figure 7. Similarity index comparison.

The similarity index experiment confirms that KLE features can increase the distinction between load features at the feature level. The DSM-DDL algorithm further enhances the ability to identify devices with similar features at the algorithmic level.

4.2. Definition and Handling of Noise in the Dataset

Before conducting the load decomposition tests, it is essential to define the noise in the experimental dataset. In the actual monitoring of household electricity usage, monitoring all devices would make the model extremely cumbersome and negatively impact load detection efficiency. Low-power appliances, such as lamps and chargers, consume very little electricity, and their state changes have minimal impact on the total load, making them of little monitoring value. On the other hand, changes in the total power due to the addition or removal of appliances can also affect the performance of the load monitoring system. How non-target appliances should be handled is a practical issue in the design of NILM systems. Most existing studies only use the sampling data of the appliances of interest as the training and test sets. Although this approach yields good load identification results, it considers actual application scenarios insufficiently.

In this paper, the power data outside the target equipment are set as noise, and the size of noise is defined as the total power minus the power value of non-target equipment.

$$noise = y_t - \sum_{m=1}^{M} y_t^{(m)} \tag{26}$$

In Formula (26), y_t is the total power value of the equipment at t time, which is obtained by adding the power of the target device and the non-target device in the scene, and $y_t^{(m)}$ is the measured value of device m at time t.

Define the percentage of noise in the experiment as follows:

$$\mathrm{NM} = \frac{\sum_{t=1}^{T} \left| y_t - \sum_{t=1}^{M} y_t^{(m)} \right|}{\sum_{t=1}^{T} y_t} \times 100\% \tag{27}$$

4.3. Accuracy Testing Criteria

Firstly, three parameters are defined. For hyper-state j, the load decomposition results are as follows: TP is true positive (recognition result is j), FP is false positive (identification result is not j), and FN is false negative (other hyper-states are identified as j).

Compared with the classical f-score criterion, the finite state FS-f score method [19] with local penalty measures can transform the binary attributes of true positive (TP) into the measurement of discrete values and is more suitable for measuring the accuracy of non-binary classification such as state classification and power estimation.

The FS-F score is defined as follows:

The inaccurate portion of true positives (inacc) is defined as follows:

$$inacc = \sum_{t=1}^{T} \frac{\left|\widehat{y}_t - y_t\right|}{K} \tag{28}$$

where T is the length of the time series, $\widehat{y}_t$ duration is the estimated power value of the super state at t time, and y_t is the power observation value at t time. K is the total number of super states. The method punishes according to the error between the estimated state and the real state. The precision and recall rate of FS-f score are defined as

$$precision = \frac{tp - inacc}{tp + fp}, \; recall = \frac{tp - inacc}{tp + fn} \tag{29}$$

The FS-f score is the harmonic mean of precision and recall:

$$FS\text{-}fscore = \frac{2 \cdot precision \cdot recall}{precision + recall} \tag{30}$$

Considering the power consumption estimation error of the algorithm, it is defined as follows:

$$EST.Acc = (1 - \frac{\sum_{t=1}^{T}\left|\widehat{y}_t - y_t\right|}{2 \cdot \sum_{t=1}^{T} y_t}) \times 100\% \tag{31}$$

The higher the $EST.ACC$, the more accurate the algorithm's energy consumption estimation.

4.4. Analysis of Algorithm Efficiency

The super state includes all possible combinations of the internal states of the target devices. Same as the state space of multi-agents, the number of super states grows exponentially [20] with the number of devices increases. For example, if two devices with three internal states each form a super state, the number of possible super states would be $3^2 = 9$, and for three devices, it increases to $3^3 = 27$. However, this is only the theoretical count. An analysis of datasets such as AMpds [21] and UK-DALE reveals that if we only consider the super states that actually appear in the dataset, they are highly sparse. This sparsity is determined by household electricity usage patterns and the operating principles of the appliances. For instance, a washing machine's state sequence might be wash–rinse–spin, but it is unlikely to follow the sequence spin–wash–rinse. Additionally, some appliances are only used at specific times of the day, such as lights and kitchen appliances. These factors lead to the actual number of super states being far lower than the theoretical number.

In the UK-DALE dataset, the relationship between the theoretical number of super states and the actual number of super states as the number of devices increases is illustrated in Figure 8. Even when simultaneously decomposing 15 devices, only about 6500 super states are observed. The sparsity of the super states not only prevents the number of improved deep dictionaries that need to be learned from growing exponentially but also results in the state transition probability matrix **A** and the observation probability matrix **B** having high sparsity. By only considering the super states that actually occur when learning dictionaries and constructing matrices, storage requirements and computational complexity can be significantly reduced.

Figure 9 illustrates the relationship between the time required for a complete super-state estimation using the KL feature extraction and DSM-DDL load disaggregation method and the actual number of super states [22]. As shown, the algorithm's execution time increases in a piecewise linear fashion as the number of super states increases. The impact of the number of super states on load disaggregation time primarily affects the selection of the candidate super-state set, which requires traversing the state transition matrix **A** and the observation probability matrix **B** to calculate P_{post}. The greater the number of super states, the more dictionaries are included in the candidate super-state set. By examining Figures 8 and 9, it can be observed that even with as many as 10^6 super states, the load disaggregation time is only around 7 s. For common scales of load monitoring target devices, where the number of appliances ranges from 5 to 15, the actual number of super states is below 10,000, and the algorithm's runtime is less than 1.3 s, meeting the requirements for practical applications.

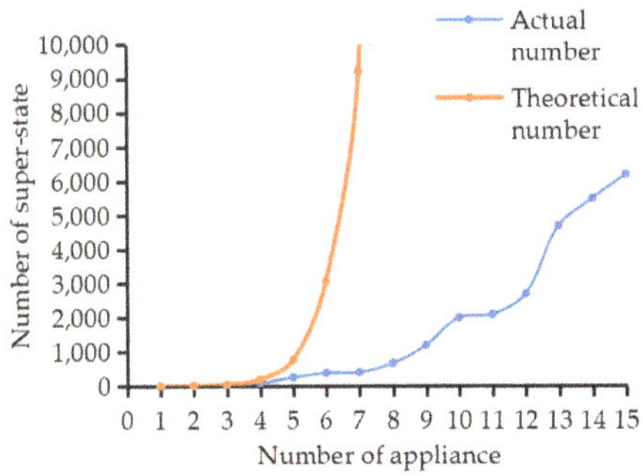

Figure 8. The relationship between the number of super states and the number of appliances.

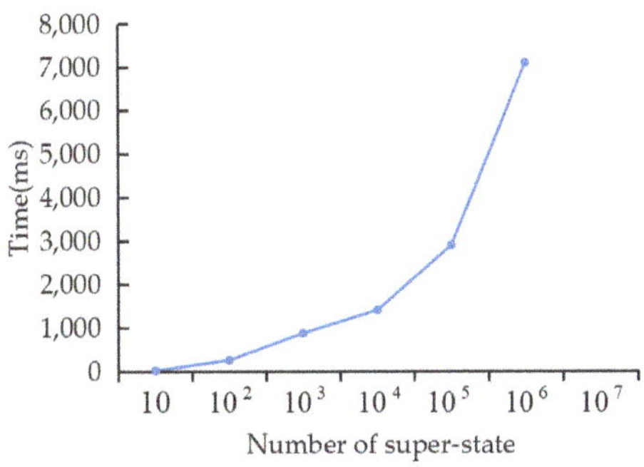

Figure 9. Effect of super-state number on load decomposition time.

4.5. Load Disaggregation Accuracy Experiment

We selected 10 days of sampling data from seven commonly used and highly similar devices in the UK-DALE dataset as the experimental data. The seven devices are kitchen lights (KILs), refrigerators (FRs), televisions (TVs), computers (PCs), dishwashers (DWs), hoovers (HOs), washing machines (WMs), hair dryers (HDs), and toasters (TOs). The appliances involved in the experiment were divided into two groups. The first group consists of devices with high similarity, including DWs, WMs, TOs, and HOs. Among them, HOs and WMs, as well as TOs and HDs, have a high degree of similarity, as shown in the power curve graphs in Figure 4. The second group consists of devices with lower similarity, including KILs, TVs, PCs, DWs, and FRs.

In addition to the target devices involved in the super-state modeling, data from non-modeled devices were added to the total power data of each group as noise, resulting in an approximately 6% NM for both groups. Sampling data from non-operating periods (where the power remains at 0 for an extended duration) were partially removed to refine the dataset. For each group of devices, the load disaggregation experiments were designed for the following two scenarios [22]:

No Noise: Only the power data of the devices of interest are used in both the training and test sets, representing an ideal scenario.

With Noise: The power data of non-participating devices are retained in both the training and test sets, making this scenario more aligned with real-world conditions.

First, the deep dictionary optimization function defined in Equation (13) is used for dictionary learning and load disaggregation. The current, power, and KLE feature matrices are separately used as load features to aggregate the target devices into super states. The KL features of the target devices are extracted from the power sampling data, while the KL feature matrices of the super states are extracted from the total power sampling data. Experiments are conducted on the first group of devices under both noise scenarios, following the iteration stopping criteria established in Section 2.3. The results are as follows:

The average number of dictionaries within the load disaggregation candidate dictionary set is 4.7.

It is clear that, in the absence of noise, all three methods achieve the best results. Among the three load features, experiments using power features exhibit the lowest accuracy due to the high similarity between the power characteristics of the devices, while current features perform slightly better than power features. In all scenarios, the KLE features achieve the best results, demonstrating that this feature effectively reduces the similarity between similar devices' characteristics and, when applied to load disaggregation, can significantly improve the algorithm's accuracy.

Next, the proposed DSM-DDL algorithm is applied. The optimization objective is given by Equation (14). The threshold in Equation (6) is set to 0.1, and both the dimension of the power column vector and the order of the autocorrelation matrix are set to 5. Parameters $\mu_1 = \mu_2 = 1$ and $\lambda = 0.05$ in Equation (16) are configured accordingly. The algorithm is then tested using current, KLE feature matrices, and power as load features to verify whether the improved deep dictionary method can further enhance the NILM system's ability to disaggregate similar devices.

The experimental results of the improved depth dictionary in three scenarios are as follows.

The average number of dictionaries within the load disaggregation candidate dictionary set Ψ_D to 4.7.

Based on the results of both experiments, it can be observed that using state transition probabilities and observation probabilities as criteria for selecting the super-state dictionary resulted in an average of 4.7 algorithm runs per disaggregation, significantly less than the total 268 super states. This approach effectively reduces computation time and hardware overhead while maintaining accuracy, thereby ensuring efficient load disaggregation.

When comparing the results of the two experiments, it is evident that the proposed DSM-DDL algorithm outperforms deep dictionary learning in all aspects, especially when disaggregating highly similar devices. Interestingly, the accuracy improvement was more pronounced when using power features compared to KLE features. This is because KLE features already exhibit low similarity, resulting in minimal overlap between super-state domains. Consequently, the effect of reducing overlap using the improved deep dictionary was more significant for the power features, which originally had higher similarity.

Comparing Tables 2 and 3 as well as Tables 4 and 5, it is evident that noise has a more significant negative impact on the deep dictionary method than on the improved deep dictionary method. After incorporating the distance-based optimization into the dictionary learning objective function, the elements within the super-state domains are more closely aligned, and the position of the KL feature matrix within the domains is more optimal. Consequently, the overlap between similar super-state domains is reduced, making the disaggregation process less susceptible to noise-induced measurement deviations.

Table 2. Comparison of load decomposition results of denoised data.

Without Noise	Precision	Recall	FS-fscore	EST.Acc
Current	87.3%	89.8%	87%	90.2%
Power	84.7%	84.3%	84.5%	88.1%
KLE features	91.2%	90.5%	90.8%	91.6%

Table 3. Comparison of load decomposition results of noisy data.

With Noise	Precision	Recall	FS-fscore	EST.Acc
Current	79.6%	76.4%	79.1%	78.8%
Power	77%	75.2%	75.2%	77.3%
KLE features	82.9%	81.7%	82.3%	82.4%

Table 4. Comparison of load decomposition results of denoised data.

Without Noise	Precision	Recall	FS-fscore	EST.Acc
Current	90.7%	91.1%	90.9%	90.2%
Power	87.6%	89.3%	86.4%	88.5%
KLE features	93.2%	93.5%	93.4%	96.1%

Table 5. Comparison of load decomposition results of noisy data.

With Noise	Precision	Recall	FS-fscore	EST.Acc
Current	83.1%	82.7%	82.9%	84.8%
Power	85.3%	81.5%	82.1%	83.7%
KLE features	88.4%	86.5%	86.4%	90.2%

In both sets of experiments, the overall accuracy of noise modeling is lower than in the noise-free scenarios, which is expected given the complexity of real-world applications. However, when compared to scenarios where noise is retained but not addressed, noise modeling demonstrates a higher disaggregation accuracy, highlighting its effectiveness in practical applications.

In the noise modeling scenario, the accuracy metrics for the load disaggregation method using current load features and deep dictionary learning (DDL) are compared against the method using the KL feature matrix and the proposed DSM-DDL algorithm. As shown in Figure 10 and Table 6, the NILM method combining the KL feature matrix with the improved deep dictionary learning significantly outperforms the method using current features and DDL. Specifically, there is an approximately 8% improvement in both the FS-f score and EST.ACC accuracy metrics.

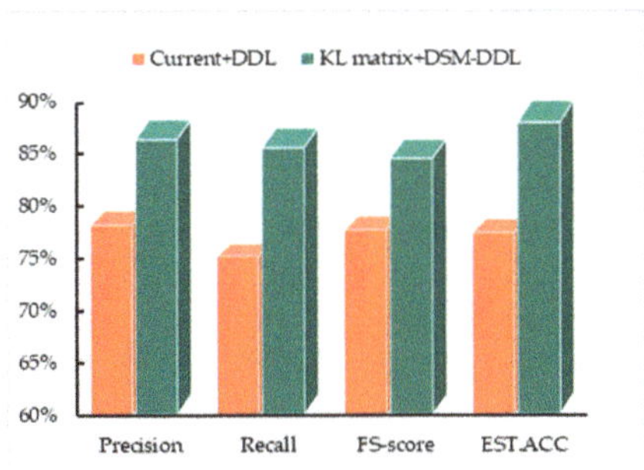

Figure 10. Comparison of accuracy between DDL and DSM-DDL.

Table 6. Comparison of load decomposition results of modeled noisy data.

	Current + DDL		KL Matrix + DSM-DDL	
	FSscore	**EST.ACC**	**FSscore**	**EST.ACC**
Aggregated data	83.24%	85.82%	86.4%	90.2%
FR	87.05%	90.77%	90.2%	93.04%
DW	80.63%	84.21%	86.71%	89.46%
HO	81.26%	83.95%	85.02%	87.25%
HD	88.74%	90.14%	90.83%	92.42%

The above experiments tested the algorithm's accuracy on super states aggregated from devices with partially similar features. It can be observed that even in the noise modeling scenario, where KL features and the improved deep dictionary are used, the power estimation accuracy only reaches 73.4%. Based on the feature similarity experiments in Section 3.1 and experimental data from References [10,14], this is likely due to the high similarity among devices in the scenario. In fact, similar devices only make up a portion of the entire dataset, while most devices have significantly different load characteristics.

As a comparison, four devices with generally lower similarity—refrigerators, dishwashers, hair dryers, and vacuum cleaners—were selected for aggregation into super states for the load disaggregation experiment. In the noise modeling scenario, load disaggregation was performed using current features combined with DDL and KL feature matrices combined with DSM-DDL, respectively. The results are shown in Table 6. It can be observed that device similarity significantly impacts the accuracy of load disaggregation. The disaggregation accuracy for the highly similar dishwasher and vacuum cleaner is noticeably lower than that for the other two devices. However, the overall accuracy of the aggregated data improves substantially compared to previous experiments as the overall similarity among target devices decreases. Furthermore, combining the results from Figure 10 and Table 6, it can be seen that the refrigerator has low similarity in power consumption with other devices. However, its small power consumption means that its power variation has little impact on the overall power variation, leading to high similarity between super states where only the refrigerator's state differs, thus affecting accuracy. Table 6 also shows that the accuracy parameters of the aggregated data are closer to those of dishwashers and vacuum cleaners, indicating that the larger the proportion of a device in the total power, the greater its influence on the final power estimation. Improving the estimation accuracy of similar high-power devices can effectively enhance the performance of the load disaggregation method.

The load disaggregation accuracy experiments demonstrate that the use of KLE features and super-state modeling with improved deep dictionary learning significantly enhances the ability to identify similar devices. When combined with noise modeling techniques, the accuracy and robustness of the NILM system are effectively improved.

5. Conclusions

This paper addresses the low-frequency sampling NILM system by employing KL expansion and singular value decomposition (SVD) to extract the KL load feature matrix from device power data. It aggregates the states of all target electrical appliances into super states and applies an improved deep dictionary learning method, combined with distance-based measures, to learn the KL feature matrix of the super states for household appliance load identification. The method demonstrates strong performance on low-sampling-rate datasets like UK-DALE. The empirical results show that the KLE feature matrix has the advantage of lower load feature similarity, and the improved deep dictionary learning algorithm, based on distance separability metrics, outperforms standard deep dictionary methods in recognizing similar devices. While maintaining the accuracy of the NILM system, the use of posterior probability matrices reduces the computational complexity and time consumption of the load disaggregation algorithm. Additionally, noise modeling enhances the system's robustness against noise, ensuring a certain level of load identification accuracy and information retrieval capability. This provides a solid foundation for further analyzing household energy consumption behavior, formulating optimized energy strategies, and facilitating precise power scheduling and load peak shaving for power suppliers.

Author Contributions: Conceptualization, S.L. and Z.H.; methodology, S.L.; software, S.L.; validation, S.L.; formal analysis, S.L.; writing—original draft preparation, Z.X.; writing—review and editing, Z.X. and Z.H.; supervision, Z.H. All authors have read and agreed to the published version of the manuscript.

Funding: This work was funded by the General Program of National Natural Science Foundation of China (Grant No. 52177083).

Data Availability Statement: Data are contained within the article.

Conflicts of Interest: The authors declare no conflicts of interest.

References

1. Bonfigli, R.; Principi, E.; Squartini, S.; Fagiani, M.; Severini, M.; Piazza, F. User-aided footprint extraction for appliance modelling in Non-Intrusive Load Monitoring. In Proceedings of the 2016 IEEE Symposium Series on Computational Intelligence (SSCI), Athens, Greece, 6–9 December 2016; pp. 1–8.
2. Dong, W.X.M.; Meira, M.C.M.; Freitas, W. An event window based load monitoring technique for smart meters. *IEEE Trans. Smart Grid* **2012**, *3*, 782–796. [CrossRef]
3. Hart, G.W. Nonintrusive appliance load monitoring. *Proc. IEEE* **1993**, *80*, 1870–1891. [CrossRef]
4. Song, X.; Zhou, M.; Tu, J.; Li, G. Non-intrusive Load Monitoring Method based on k-NN and Kernel Fisher Discriminant. *Autom. Electr. Power Syst.* **2018**, *42*, 73–80. [CrossRef]
5. Jia, D.; Cao, M.; Sun, J.; Wang, F.; Xu, W.; Wang, Y. Interval Constrained Multi-Objective Optimization Scheduling Method for Island-Integrated Energy Systems Based on Meta-Learning and Enhanced Proximal Policy Optimization. *Electronics* **2024**, *13*, 3579. [CrossRef]
6. Meng, X.; Hu, G.; Liu, Z.; Wang, H.; Zhang, G.; Lin, H.; Sadabadi, M.S. Neural Network-Based Impedance Identification and Stability Analysis for Double-Sided Feeding Railway Systems. *IEEE Trans. Transp. Electrif.* **2024**. [CrossRef]
7. Sun, Y.; Cui, C.; Lu, J.; Hao, J.; Liu, X. Non-intusive Load Monitoring Based on Delta Feature Extraction and Fuzzy Clustering. *Autom. Electr. Power Syst.* **2017**, *41*, 86–91. [CrossRef]
8. Henao, N.; Agbossou, K.; Kelouwani, S.; Dubé, Y.; Fournier, M. Approach in Nonintrusive Type I Load Monitoring Using Subtractive Clustering. *IEEE Trans. Smart Grid* **2015**, *8*, 812–821. [CrossRef]
9. Kong, W.; Dong, Z.Y.; Ma, J.; Hill, D.J.; Zhao, J.; Luo, F. An Extensible Approach for Non-Intrusive Load Disaggregation with Smart Meter Data. *IEEE Trans. Smart Grid* **2023**, *7*, 3362–3372. [CrossRef]
10. Kolter, J.Z.; Batra, S.; Ng, A.Y. Energy Disaggregation via Discriminative Sparse Coding. In Proceedings of the Advances in Neural Information Processing Systems 23: 24th Annual Conference on Neural Information Processing Systems 2010, Vancouver, BC, Canada, 6–9 December 2010.
11. Elhamifar, E.; Sastry, S. Energy Disaggregation via Learning 'Powerlets' and Sparse Coding. In Proceedings of the AAAI Conference on Artificial Intelligence, Austin, TX, USA, 25–30 January 2015.
12. Cheng, X.; Li, L.; Wu, H.; Ding, Y.; Song, Y.; Sun, W. A Survey of the Research on Non-intrusive Load Monitoring and Disaggregation. *Power Syst. Technol.* **2016**, *40*, 3108–3117.
13. Singh, S.; Majumdar, A. Deep Sparse Coding for Non-Intrusive Load Monitoring. *IEEE Trans. Smart Grid* **2017**, *9*, 4669–4678. [CrossRef]
14. Kelly, J.; Knottenbelt, W. The UK-DALE dataset, domestic appliance-level electricity demand and whole-house demand from five UK homes. *Sci. Data* **2015**, *2*, 150007. [CrossRef] [PubMed]
15. Makonin, S.; Popowich, F.; Bajić, I.V.; Gill, B.; Bartram, L. Exploiting HMM Sparsity to Perform Online Real-Time Nonintrusive Load Monitoring. *IEEE Trans. Smart Grid* **2016**, *7*, 2575–2585. [CrossRef]
16. Aharon, M.; Elad, E.; Bruckstein, A. K-SVD:and algorithm for designing over-complete dictionaries for sparse representations. *IEEE Trans. Signal Process.* **2006**, *54*, 4311–4322. [CrossRef]
17. Goldstein, T.; Osher, S. The Split Bregman Method for L1-Regularized Problems. *SIAM J. Imaging Sci.* **2009**, *2*, 323–343. [CrossRef]
18. Li, C. Research on the Original Sinal Reconstruction Algorithm of Compressed Sensing. Master's Thesis, Xidian University, Xi'an, China, 2015.
19. Lu, T.; Xu, Z.; Huang, B. An Event-Based Nonintrusive Load Monitoring Approach: Using the Simplified Viterbi Algorithm. *IEEE Pervasive Comput.* **2017**, *16*, 54–61. [CrossRef]
20. Liu, X.; Chuai, G.; Wang, X.; Xu, Z.; Gao, W.; Zhang, K.; Liu, Q.; Maimaiti, S.; Zuo, P. QoE-driven antenna tuning in cellular networks with cooperative multi-agent reinforcement learning. *IEEE Trans. Mob. Comput.* **2022**, *23*, 1186–1199. [CrossRef]

21. Makonin, S.; Popowich, F.; Bartram, L.; Gill, B.; Bajić, I.V. AMPds: A public dataset for load disaggregation and eco-feed back research. In Proceedings of the 2013 IEEE Electrical Power & Energy Conference, Halifax, NS, Canada, 21–23 August 2013; IEEE: Piscataway, NJ, USA, 2014.
22. Ming, L.I.; Peng, X.; Yan, W.A. Facial Expression Recognition Based on Improved Dictionary Learning and Sparse Representation. *J. Syst. Simul.* **2018**, *30*, 28–36.

electronics

MDPI

Article

Hierarchical Decentralized Federated Learning Framework with Adaptive Clustering: Bloom-Filter-Based Companions Choice for Learning Non-IID Data in IoV

Siyuan Liu [1], Zhiqiang Liu [1,*], Zhiwei Xu [2,3], Wenjing Liu [4] and Jie Tian [5]

1 College of Information Engineering, Inner Mongolia University of Technology, Hohhot 010051, China; siyuan_liu2022@foxmail.com
2 Haihe Laboratory of Information Technology Application Innovation, Tianjin 300350, China; xuzhiwei2001@ict.ac.cn
3 Institute of Computing Technology, Chinese Academy of Sciences, Beijing 100086, China
4 College of Data Science and Application, Inner Mongolia University of Technology, Hohhot 010051, China; liuwenjing2015@bupt.edu.cn
5 Department of Computer Science, New Jersey Institute of Technology, Newark, NJ 07102, USA; jt66@njit.edu
* Correspondence: liuzq@imut.edu.cn

Abstract: The accelerating progress of the Internet of Vehicles (IoV) has put forward a higher demand for distributed model training and data sharing in vehicular networks. Traditional centralized approaches are no longer applicable in the face of drivers' concerns about data privacy, while Decentralized Federated Learning (DFL) provides new possibilities to address this issue. However, DFL still faces challenges regarding the non-IID data of passing vehicles. To tackle this challenge, a novel DFL framework, Hierarchical Decentralized Federated Learning (H-DFL), is proposed to achieve qualified distributed training among vehicles by considering data complementarity. We include vehicles, base stations, and data center servers in this framework. Firstly, a novel vehicle-clustering paradigm is designed to group passing vehicles based on the Bloom-filter-based compact representation of data complementarity. In this way, vehicles train their models based on local data, exchange model parameters in each group, and achieve a qualified local model without the interference of imbalanced data. On a higher level, a local model trained by each group is submitted to the data center to obtain a model covering global features. Base stations maintain the local models of different groups and judge whether the local models need to be updated according to the global model. The experimental results based on real-world data demonstrate that H-DFL dose not only reduces communication latency with different participants but also addresses the challenges of non-IID data in vehicles.

Keywords: Internet of Vehicles; hierarchical decentralized federated learning; in-network compact representation; vehicle clustering

1. Introduction

Advanced Internet of Vehicles (IoV) facilitates vehicle-to-everything (V2X) communications in a smart transportation environment, especially improving the efficiency of data transmission among autonomous vehicles [1,2]. For instance, recent research by Ngo et al. [3] has highlighted the effectiveness of cooperative vehicle communication in improving data transmission efficiency among autonomous vehicles. This complements autonomous vehicles beyond their sensors' sight and makes them cooperate with each other to boost road safety, traffic efficiency, and overall driving experience, thereby shaping the future of urban mobility [4,5]. Considering the fact that IoV is a type of open network, the data exchanged among vehicles are vulnerable without ensuring vehicles behave as per the norms. Therefore, data sharing in IoV becomes scarce [6]. Although advance learning models for smart transportation have been studied extensively, these models cannot be applied in practice due to lack of data available for model training. Even worse, the vehicles in IoV always seem to involve significant dynamics and driver concerns regarding privacy [7]. Traditional centralized methods for model training and data analysis in vehicular networks face significant challenges in addressing data privacy concerns, as they necessitate the aggregation of sensitive data from multiple vehicles in a single location, exposing individuals to security risks and legal complexities [8]. Moreover, such approaches can compromise data trustworthiness, introduce communication latency, and struggle with scalability. Ultimately, traditional centralized training methods are no longer sufficient to meet the requirements of model training and applications in V2X [9,10]. Those node-centric learning frameworks become ill-fit in IoV.

As a type of federated learning (FL) [11], Decentralized federated learning (DFL) provides a decentralized learning approach for model training while maintaining data at a local level. DFL allows models to be trained on local participants, and they only share model parameters with each other. The shared parameters are also aggregated in each participant [12]. DFL has been widely applied in the industrial Internet of Things (IoT) environment, particularly in the context of vehicular networking [13]. With the advent of autonomous and semi-autonomous vehicles, the need for fast response and real-time decision-making has become more pressing. As emphasized by Soto et al. [14], V2X interactions are instrumental in coordinating vehicles and managing traffic flow, vital components in achieving efficient urban transportation. This dynamic landscape underscores the significance of communication and collaboration among vehicles, especially underlining the importance of DFL. Through DFL, vehicles can conduct model training and inference locally, reducing communication latency with centralized servers and improving responsiveness and real-time capability [15]. However, due to differences in vehicle types and features, the distribution of the training data of passing vehicles may vary greatly. The varying and imbalanced distribution of data among vehicles introduces biases, compromises accurate insights, increases communication overhead, fosters unfair resource allocation, and diminishes real-time performance. This skewed data distribution challenges traditional learning methods and hinders their ability to generalize and adapt effectively [16]. The fluctuating distribution of training data held by passing vehicles hinders traditional learning methods from achieving optimal performance. It is a significant challenge to achieve qualified learning on the non-IID data of vehicles by decentralized federated learning [17].

Addressing the challenges posed by the diverse distribution of vehicle data, a prospective strategy is to leverage the clustering of vehicles based on their complementary data and subsequently implement balanced learning by aggregating model updates within each cluster. While this intra-cluster aggregation ensures learning quality, it may lead to model convergence only with a part of features. To cover all valuable features, a global level of aggregation becomes indispensable. In this way, it is necessary to develop a hierarchical aggregation strategy that leverages vehicle data for distributed model training. In this work, we propose Hierarchical Decentralized Federated Learning (H-DFL), a new framework that incorporates vehicle clustering and hierarchical federated learning through a consideration of data balancing (See Figure 1). The proposed H-DFL approach aims to bridge the gaps left by conventional methods by strategically leveraging vehicle clustering, hierarchical aggregation, and data complementarity. The main contributions are as follows:

1. To accommodate the evolving intelligent transportation scenarios, we introduce a Hierarchical Decentralized Federated Learning framework, H-DFL, for the distributed training of vehicles in IoV.
2. We explore a novel paradigm of vehicle clustering according to the data complementarity of vehicles. We take merge-CBF [18] to represent local data in a compact way, in order to support exchange compact representations and judge the data complementarity of other vehicles. Finally, we cluster vehicles with complementary data into one group and train local models with the group.

3. On a higher level, base stations maintain the local models of different groups, while submitting them to a data center to obtain a global aggregation to cover more features. In an asynchronous manner, base stations judge whether the local models need to be updated according to the global model.
4. We evaluate our proposed method and baselines using two real-world datasets on the Sim4DistrDL simulation platform. The simulation results validate the effectiveness and superiority of our approach against existing baselines.

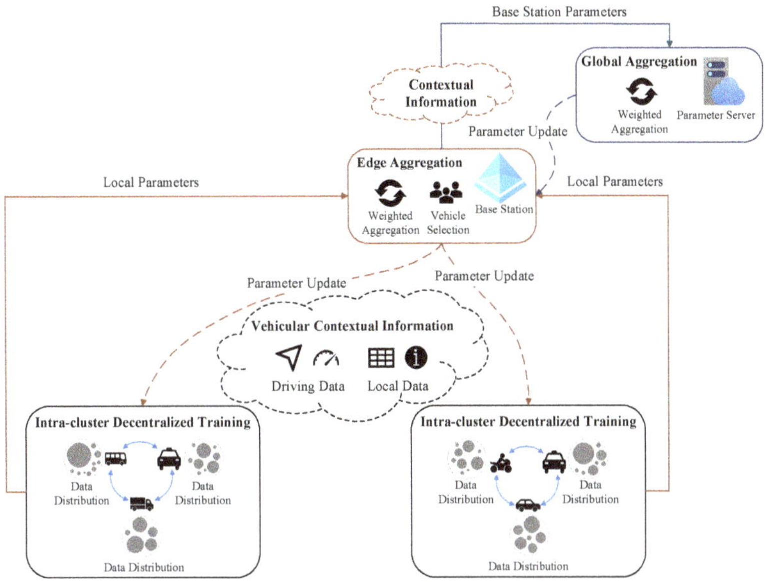

Figure 1. Hierarchical decentralized federated learning.

The organizational structure of this paper is as follows. Section 2 reviews the relevant literature on participant selection strategies in federated learning. Section 3 provides a detailed introduction to the relevant theoretical methods. In Section 4, a Hierarchical Decentralized Federated Learning framework is proposed, which adopts a novel paradigm of local clustering to mitigate the impact of imbalanced data. In Section 5, two real-world datasets are utilized to demonstrate the superiority of the proposed framework in the V2X scenario compared to the current state-of-the-art techniques. Finally, a summary of this work is presented in Section 6.

2. Related Work

In recent years, Federated Learning (FL) has emerged as a distributed optimization paradigm that enables collaboration in model training among a large number of client nodes with limited resources, without sharing data. However, FL faces several challenges, such as heterogeneity among clients, label noise, and biased client selection. To address these challenges, researchers have conducted a series of explorations.

In reference [19], Lim et al. presents a framework that addresses communication inefficiency challenges in the FL network. This approach leverages a Hierarchical Federated Learning (HFL) framework with cluster heads to facilitate data aggregation and model training on heterogeneous distributed devices. In reference [20], Lim et al. focus on addressing node failures and device dropouts through a Hierarchical Federated Learning (HFL) framework, introducing a two-level resource allocation and incentive mechanism involving cluster selection dynamics modeled by evolutionary game theory and a deep-learning-based auction mechanism, ultimately demonstrating the effectiveness of these mechanisms in terms of uniqueness, stability, and revenue optimization. Considering the problem of malicious node behaviors, Li et al. [21] present a novel DFL framework, Trustiness-based Hierarchical Decentralized Federated Learning (TH-DFL), which incorporates a trust mechanism through Security Robust Aggregation (SRA) to enhance privacy protection and robustness against malicious nodes, while also reducing communication overhead.

In reference [22], Cho et al. introduced a client selection method based on discriminative weights. This strategy reduces the number of transmitted models by selecting clients with significant weight updates, thereby reducing communication overhead. In reference [23], Ribero and Vikalo proposed an optimal sampling strategy based on weight updates. This strategy models the progress of model weights and selects clients with significant weight updates, reducing the number of transmitted models and improving communication efficiency. Cho et al. presented an adaptive client selection strategy in reference [24] to adapt to FL on mobile participants. This strategy selects participating clients based on activity status and mobility, achieving smooth model updates when participants join or leave. Ruan et al. extended the traditional FL paradigm to allow flexible participant participation in reference [25]. They proposed a novel joint aggregation scheme that can adapt to different participant states, achieving model convergence even when participants may be inactive or provide incomplete updates. Ji et al. explored the client selection problem in privacy-preserving settings in [26]. They proposed a random selection strategy that takes privacy requirements into account, thus protecting client data privacy. Liu et al. presented FedEraser [27], which efficiently removes specific training data from a trained FL model. They reconstruct the unlearning model by leveraging historical parameter updates preserved on the central server during the FL training process.

In actual edge application scenarios, the data of edge participants is heterogeneous. Several studies focus on formulating client selection strategies based on client data. In reference [16], Nishio et al. proposed a client selection method based on diversity and representativeness. This strategy involves selecting clients with diverse and representative data to participate in model updates, aiming to achieve better global model performance. In reference [28], Goetz et al. considered scenarios where clients have different data distributions. By designing appropriate client selection strategies and combining methods for handling non-iid data, they achieved model updates and convergence in such non-iid environments. Cho et al. investigated biased client selection in FL [29] and found that biasing client selection towards clients with higher local losses can accelerate error convergence. Based on this observation, they proposed Power-of-Choice, a communication- and computation-efficient client selection framework that offers flexible trade-offs between convergence speed and solution bias. Tan et al. proposed a novel FL framework called FedProto in reference [30], which enhances tolerance to heterogeneity by aggregating knowledge among clients through a communication abstract prototype instead of gradients. Fang and Ye [31] addressed robust FL problems with noise and heterogeneous clients. They proposed the RHFL framework, which effectively mitigates the negative impact under different noise levels/types by directly aligning model feedback using public data, applying robust noise-tolerant loss functions, and designing client confidence reweighting schemes.

These research works have made valuable explorations in addressing heterogeneity, unlearning, bias, and noise-related issues in FL. They have demonstrated the effectiveness of corresponding methods on various datasets and tasks. However, further research is still needed to continue promoting the development of FL technology and addressing various challenges in practical V2X applications.

3. Preliminary

3.1. Federated Averaging

Federated averaging is a widely adopted parameter aggregation technique that entails averaging the local model parameters of individual participants to derive the global model parameters. This approach offers several benefits, including efficiency, scalability, decentralization, and applicability to large-scale distributed systems and privacy-sensitive scenarios. This section presents an overview of the fundamental principles underlying federated averaging.

The Federated Average Algorithm (FedAvg) [11] is commonly utilized in both centralized and hierarchical federated learning. The algorithm assumes the existence of K clients and a central server, with the former conducting local training and the latter responsible for parameter aggregation. FedAvg comprises the following steps:

Step 1: Initialization phase. The central server initializes the model and distributes the model parameters to all participating clients.

Step 2: Local update phase. Each client employs the received model parameters as the starting point for the current iteration and trains on their local dataset using optimization algorithms, such as gradient descent, with the aim of minimizing the loss function. After several iterations, if the client is selected by the central server, the model parameters (e.g., parameters, gradients, etc.) are uploaded to the central server.

Step 3: Global aggregation phase. The central server aggregates the model parameters uploaded by selected clients using a weighted average method to obtain the global model:

$$w_{t+1} \leftarrow \sum_{k=1}^{K} \frac{n_k}{n} w_{t+1}^{k}, \tag{1}$$

as depicted in Equation (1), where n refers to the size of the dataset owned by the selected client, n_k denotes the size of the local dataset of the k-th client, and w_{t+1}^{k} refers to the parameters of the model of the k-th client after $t+1$ rounds of training. Following parameter aggregation by the central server, the updated model parameters are disseminated to the clients. The client then proceeds to a new round of training according to Step 2. This federated learning process is repeated iteratively until the model converges or reaches the maximum number of training rounds.

3.2. Consensus Learning

Consensus learning is a decentralized collaborative algorithm that addresses the parameter aggregation challenge in federated learning by enabling participants to reach a consensus through information exchange without the need for a central server. Consensus learning can enhance the efficiency and security of federated learning, and mitigate potential threats such as malicious attacks and data breaches. In a federated learning system with N distributed participants, each node updates its local learning based on local data and information exchanged with neighboring nodes, and repeats the process until all nodes converge to a consensus estimate. In the average consensus algorithm, the i-th node updates its parameters in the $k+1$-th round based on its local training results and those of its neighbors, as follows:

$$\hat{\boldsymbol{\theta}}_i(k+1) = \hat{\boldsymbol{\theta}}_i(k) + \varepsilon \sum_{j \in \mathcal{N}_i} \left(\hat{\boldsymbol{\theta}}_j(k) - \hat{\boldsymbol{\theta}}_i(k) \right) \tag{2}$$

Here, i denotes the node to be updated locally, k denotes the result of the previous round of iterations, $\mathcal{N}_i$ denotes the set of nodes i and its neighbors, ε denotes the step size, $\hat{\boldsymbol{\theta}}_j(k)$ denotes the model parameters of the neighbor node j at the end of the k-th round of learning, and $\hat{\boldsymbol{\theta}}_i(k)$ denotes the model parameters of node i at the end of the k-th round of learning.

To approach the global performance of federated learning, the weighted average consensus method introduces a weight in the update rule of the average consensus method. The weighted average consensus update rule is given by:

$$\hat{\boldsymbol{\theta}}_i(k+1) = \hat{\boldsymbol{\theta}}_i(k) + \varepsilon \mathbf{W}_i^{-1} \sum_{j \in \mathcal{N}_i} \left(\hat{\boldsymbol{\theta}}_j(k) - \hat{\boldsymbol{\theta}}_i(k) \right), \tag{3}$$

where $\mathbf{W}_i^{-1}$ represents the weighting coefficient.

3.3. Mergeable Counting Bloom Filter

The Bloom Filter [32] is a widely adopted compact data representation structure that provides an efficient solution for data aggregation by saving space. The Counting Bloom Filter (CBF) [33] is a variation of the Bloom Filter that not only determines the presence of elements in a set but also keeps track of the frequency of each element's occurrence. CBF achieves this functionality by leveraging bit array counters instead of binary values alone. Nonetheless, directly merging CBFs is not possible due to the potential risk of overflow issues when combining the bit array counters. To overcome this limitation and aggregate data compact representation of each participant, we use a mergeable CBF called mergeCBF [18] here.

The design overview of mergeCBF is illustrated in Figure 2. In mergeCBF, the counter array of CBF is expanded into a set of bit arrays $barr_1, \ldots, barr_g$, where each bit array has M bits. Following the principles of cuckoo hashing, these bit arrays are scheduled in a fixed order to record the inserted items. When obtaining the hash result for an item, mergeCBF selects one bit array and sets the corresponding cell to "1". This process is repeated h times using different hash functions $Hash_1, \ldots, Hash_h$. After setting h cells based on the h hash results, all the "1" bits in the different bit arrays of mergeCBF's filters are utilized to record the inserted item's information. In this way, by querying these bit arrays, we can determine whether an item exists in mergeCBF and estimate its frequency of occurrence. When multiple mergeCBF instances need to be merged, an efficient way to support the merge is by performing bitwise OR operations on the bit arrays. For the merged result, an additional array is included to record the bitwise OR result of all cells in each column, which is used to query the existence of items. This design facilitates the evaluation of the data distribution of each participant, and groups the participants with complementary data into a group. In this way, the features learned by the group can cover the domain knowledge more comprehensively.

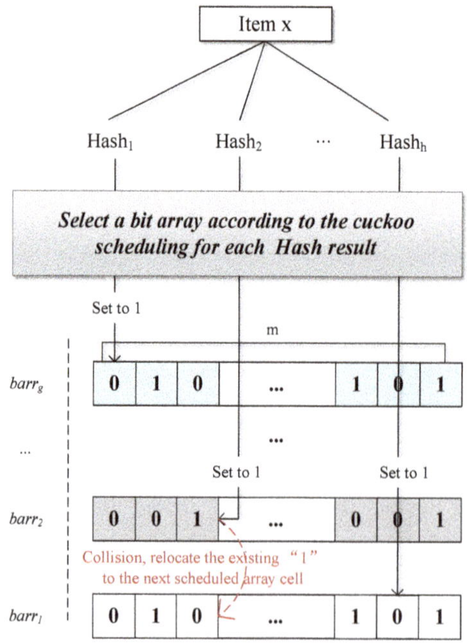

Figure 2. Overview of mergeCBF.

4. Adaptive Hierarchical Decentralized Federated Learning

4.1. Framework

In this subsection, we propose H-DFL, a Hierarchical Decentralized Federated Learning framework with a novel participants clustering approach to mitigate the impact of imbalanced data among participants in the global model. Specifically, we first explore a new scheme for clustering participants, mapping the data into a compact representation to serve as a record of local data distribution, and then clustering participants based on this compact representation to achieve a more uniform distribution of data within each cluster. In Section 4.3, we further present the Hierarchical Decentralized Federated Learning framework, H-DFL, for the distributed training of vehicles within the network.

The algorithm maps the data into a compact representation as a record of local data distribution. By exchanging this type of compact representation, participants are clustered into several clusters with evenly distributed data, thereby reducing the bias in the global model caused by uneven data distribution. After several rounds of decentralized federated learning in each cluster, a representative is randomly selected to perform centralized federated aggregation with the edge server. At a higher level, edge servers perform the federated averaging of parameters with parameter servers to correct for bias. The H-DFL algorithm consists of two main components: participant clustering and global model aggregation. Subsequently, in Sections 4.2 and 4.3, we provide detailed explanations of participant clustering and global model training, respectively.

4.2. Vehicle-Side Clustering and Cooperation Based on mergeCBF Filters

In practice, a vast amount of data will be generated in V2X networks. The data collected by vehicles are often influenced by various factors, such as vehicle type, driving conditions, and geographical location. Consequently, the data collected by different vehicles exhibit certain characteristics and variances. These characteristics and variances may lead to biases in the distribution of data labels within the vehicle's dataset, thus affecting the efficiency and accuracy of model training. To address this issue, we propose a Data Distribution Statistics Algorithm (DDSA), a method for clustering vehicles to achieve a uniform distribution of data in a cluster.

MergeCBF is a compact and mergeable data structure that can be used to represent the data distribution of vehicles. Specifically, the parameters such as the size of the bit arrays and the number of hash functions used in mergeCBF are initialized. To represent the sparsity and density of the data distribution, we employ locally sensitive hash functions in mergeCBF. Next, each data from vehicles k is inserted into $mergeCBF_k$. For each data, multiple hash calculations are performed using the specified locally sensitive hash functions, and the corresponding cells in the bit arrays are set to "1" according to the cuckoo scheduling. Finally, the bit array $mergeCBF_k$ recording the data distribution of the vehicles is transmitted to nearby vehicles.

After receiving the bit array of data distribution from neighboring vehicles, vehicles with complementary data will be clustered together. We measure the level of data complementarity among them by merging the mergeCBFs of vehicles. Specifically, to represent the data complementarity, as shown Figure 3, we perform bitwise OR operations on the cells of each column when merging the mergeCBFs. As we employ locally sensitive hash functions, similar data will have similar positions in the array. Therefore, after the bitwise OR operation, the count of "1" in each column can indicate the level of complementarity for the corresponding data. We use an additional array, named $sumBar$, to record the count of "1" in each column.

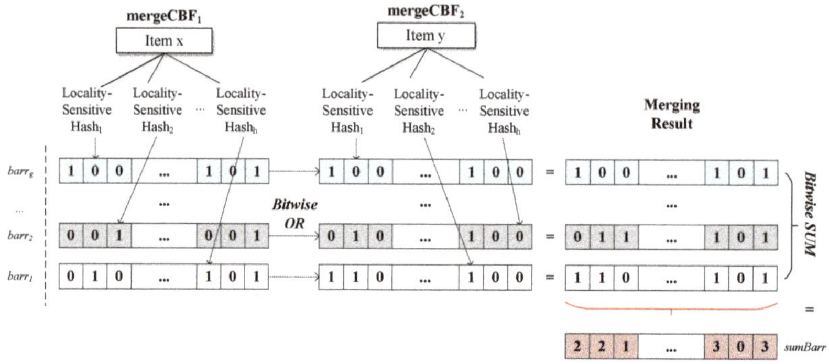

Figure 3. Merging CBF.

Clustering is performed to achieve a more uniform distribution of data within groups, and it is essential for the bits of $sumBar$ to be closely similar in order to guarantee such uniform distribution. Therefore, we introduce the concept of variance to measure the similarity of each bit in the merged bit array $sumBar$. The formula for calculating the variance Var is as follows:

$$Var = \frac{\sum_{m=1}^{M} (sumbarr[m] - \overline{sumbarr})^2}{M}, \tag{4}$$

where $m(1, \ldots, M)$ represents the number of cells in $sumbarr$. Ultimately, clustering is carried out based on the magnitude of the variance, and the clustering results are sent back to other neighboring vehicles. Specifically, initially, each vehicle is treated as an individual cluster. By calculating the variance of the merged $sumBar$ between each pair of clusters, the complementarity of the distribution between two clusters is determined. The two clusters with the minimum variance are selected, and they are merged to form a new cluster. This process of merging the most similar clusters is repeated until all base stations are clustered. The specific DDSA is shown in Algorithm 1.

Algorithm 1 Data Distribution Statistics

Input: item, number of clusters $n_{cluster}$;
Output: Base station set $Cluster_l$;
$barrset_k = mergeCBF.insert(\text{item}_k)$ ▷Insert each data item of vehicle k into mergeCBF.
receive $barrset_{p\{p \in N_k\}}$
for each $barrset$ in $barrset_{c\{c \in N_k\}}$ **do**
    create $Cluster_l$
end for
while the number of $Cluster_c \geq n_{cluster}$ **do**
    for each $Cluster_i$, $Cluster_j$ in $Cluster_c$ **do**
        $sumbarr_{ij} = mergeCBF.merge(Cluster_i, Cluster_j)$ ▷Merge the mergeCBF arrays.
        $Var_{ij} = Variance(sumbarr_{ij})$ ▷Calculate the variance of $sumbarr$.
    end for
    Find the minist Var_{ij}
    merge $Cluster_i$ and $Cluster_j$
end while

Algorithm 1 takes the training data of vehicle k and the number of clusters $n_{cluster}$ as inputs, and outputs the clustering of vehicles $Cluster_{c\{c \in N_k\}}$, where N_k represents all neighboring vehicles. Firstly, mergeCBF is used to count the data distribution of vehicle k, resulting in $barrset_k$ (line 3). Then, $barrset_{p\{p\in N_{\bar{k}}\}}$, where $N_{\bar{k}}$ represents the neighboring vehicles except for k, is received. Next, each neighboring vehicle is initialized as an initial cluster $Cluster_l$ (lines 5–7). To ensure an even distribution of data in each cluster, the variance of the merged $sumbarr_{ij}$ for each cluster is calculated using Equation (4) (lines 9–12). Finally, the clusters are clustered based on the magnitude of variance, merging the two clusters with the smallest variance until the desired number of clusters is achieved. The resulting grouping is then sent to other vehicles.

4.3. Global Aggregation Based on Gradient Difference

In this subsection, we introduce and propose a Hierarchical Decentralized Federated Learning (H-DFL) algorithm. Firstly, neighboring vehicles are clustered based on the data distribution of each vehicle, aiming to achieve an even distribution of data within each cluster. Then, decentralized federated learning is applied to form weak learners within each cluster. Each base station randomly selects a vehicle from each neighboring cluster and averages the learning results of vehicles in different clusters to form a strong learner. At the base station, we evaluate the unevenness of data within each cluster and perform weighted averaging based on the evaluation results and send them to both the vehicles and the parameter server. The parameter server performs a weighted averaging of the received parameters and sends the averaged result back to the base station. During the parameter averaging process, network instability may result in delayed parameter transmission for some base stations. Therefore, we adopt an incremental federated averaging aggregation strategy. Due to the typically long transmission distance to the parameter server, the base station does not wait for the averaged result before proceeding to the next training round. Upon receiving the global parameters from the parameter server, the base station compares them with the current parameters. If there is a significant difference, the base station replaces its current parameters with the received global parameters.

The proposed communication framework follows a three-layer communication flow, as follows:

(1) The parameter transmission between base stations and neighboring vehicles

After clustering, decentralized federated learning is conducted within each cluster for a certain number of rounds. The base station randomly selects a vehicle from each neighboring cluster, and the vehicles upload their trained model parameters and the data distribution arrays of all vehicles within the cluster to the base station. We propose an evaluation metric D_l to assess the unevenness of data distribution within each cluster, which is calculated as follows:

$$D_{l\{l\in N_G\}} = 1 \setminus \left(\sum_{m=1}^{M} s_l[m] \cdot \log_2 \frac{s_l[m]}{1 \setminus m} \right), s_l[m] = \frac{sumbarr_l[m]}{\sum_{m=1}^{M} sumbarr_l[m]}. \tag{5}$$

Here, N_G represents the set of vehicles randomly selected by the base station from each cluster, $sumbarr_l$ denotes the data distribution of base station l within its respective cluster, and $m(1,\ldots,M)$ represents the length of the $sumbarr_l$ array. We can measure whether data distribution within each cluster is balanced. Let D indicate a more balanced data distribution within the cluster. Based on the value of D, we perform a weighted average at the base station as follows:

$$w_{t+1} \leftarrow \sum_{l=1}^{L} \frac{n_l}{n} \cdot \frac{D_l}{\sum_{l=1}^{L} D_l} w_{t+1}^{l}. \tag{6}$$

where L represents the number of vehicles participating in global aggregation, n_l denotes the size of the dataset owned by the l-th vehicle in its respective cluster, n represents the size of the cluster dataset participating in global aggregation, and w_{t+1}^{l} represents the parameters of the model after $t+1$ rounds of training for vehicle l.

(2) The parameter transmission between the parameter server and base stations.

After each round of the locally weighted aggregation of nearby vehicle parameters, the base station not only sends the result back to the vehicle cluster, but also sends the result to the parameter server. Since the parameter server is generally far away and the transmission is delayed, the base station does not wait for the global aggregation result returned by the parameter server. An incremental parameter aggregation strategy is employed on the parameter server, and the aggregated parameter results are transmitted back to all base stations. After receiving the global aggregation result w_{e+1}^{G} sent by the parameter server, the base station compares it with the current local weighted aggregation result:

$$w_{e+1}^{G} - w_{t+1}, \tag{7}$$

and replaces the current parameter with the global parameter if the difference is larger than threshold β.

(3) The parameter transmission between vehicles.

There are two types of parameters transmitted between vehicles: the distribution of vehicles data and the model training parameters. The first parameter is used for clustering vehicles to address the issue of class imbalance. Firstly, Algorithm 1 is employed to compute the data distribution for each vehicle. Then, the computed data distribution results are broadcasted to nearby vehicles in the form of bitmaps. Upon receiving the bit arrays, the vehicles merge the bit arrays and form clusters based on the variance of the merged bit array.

Regarding the second parameter, after each vehicle in a cluster undergoes a certain level of local learning, the parameters are transferred to neighboring nodes. The neighboring nodes converge the parameters based on their local training results and the training results of their neighbors. This process repeats until a consensus is reached within the cluster.

The detailed design of the algorithm and a description of the model parameters are shown in Algorithm 2.

In Algorithm 2, the base station utilizes a random sampling algorithm to select one vehicle from each cluster for centralized federated learning. The set of selected vehicles is denoted as N_G, and the participating vehicles in training are represented by l. The aggregated parameters from the base station are sent to the parameter server for global aggregation according to Equation (1), where N_b denotes the set of base stations. Upon receiving the globally aggregated parameters from the parameter server, the base station compares them with its current parameters using a threshold value, denoted as β. If the difference exceeds the threshold value, the base station updates its parameters to the received global parameters. Within each cluster, vehicles engage in decentralized federated learning based on weighted average consensus, where the learning rate is denoted as η_t and the weights are represented by γ_t. Each vehicle locally trains its model using mini-batch gradient descent, with the size of the local mini-batch for participating vehicles denoted as B.

The algorithm proposed in this paper is based on vehicle clustering, where vehicles are clustered according to their data distribution. Due to the influence of geographical locations, the overall uniformity of data distribution differs among vehicle clusters. Therefore, we evaluate the uniformity of data within each cluster at the base station and perform a weighted average, as shown in Equation (6). Additionally, the distance between base stations and the parameter server negatively affects the effectiveness of global aggregation. The time interval for each iteration at the parameter server is influenced by the base station with the longest transmission time, leading to a bottleneck effect. Thus, during the global aggregation process, we adopt an incremental parameter update method. Firstly, a global aggregation based on averaging is performed using the received parameters. Once the parameter server completes the aggregation, the result is sent back to the base stations. If there are new base stations sending data at that time, they will be added to the aggregation process and the parameters will be updated according to Equation (6) (lines 8–18). For intra-cluster aggregation, a decentralized method, as described in Equation (3) (lines 19–28), is employed. Prior to consensus learning within the cluster, multiple local stochastic gradient descents are executed locally to ensure a certain level of accuracy in each base station's local model (lines 29–35).

Algorithm 2 Hierarchical Decentralized Federated Learning Algorithm

1: Parameter Server side:
2: **for** each global round $e = 1, 2, \ldots, E$ **do**
3:     **for** each base station $b \in N_B$ **do**
4:         $w_{e+1}^{b} \leftarrow GroupUpdate(b, w)$
5:     **end for**
6:     $w_{e+1}^{G} \leftarrow \sum_{b=1}^{B} \frac{n_b}{n} w_{e+1}^{b}$
7: **end for**
8: Base Station side:
9: **for** each round $t = 1, 2, \ldots, T$ **do**
10:     $N_G \leftarrow$ (Each group randomly selects one)
11:     **for** each vehicle $l \in N_G$ **do**
12:         $w_{t+1}^{l}, sumbarr_{t+1}^{l} \leftarrow GroupUpdate(l, w, sumbarr)$
13:     **end for**
14:     $w_{t+1} \leftarrow \sum_{l=1}^{L} \frac{n_l}{n} \cdot \frac{D_l}{\sum_{l=1}^{L} D_l} w_{t+1}^{l}$ ▷ Perform global weighted average aggregation.
15:     **if** $w_{e+1}^{G} - w_{t+1} \geq \beta$ **then**
16:         $w_{t+1} \leftarrow w_{e+1}^{G}$ ▷ Update the parameters of base station.
17:     **end if**
18: **end for**
19: Intra-cluster aggregation:
20: **for** each vehicle $k \in N_k$ in parallel **do**
21:     receive $w_{t,i}\{i \in N_{\bar{k}}\}$
22:     $\varphi_{t,k} \leftarrow w_{t,k}$ ▷The local parameters are updated by receiving the aggregated parameters of the base station.
23:     **for** all vehicles $i \in N_{\bar{k}}$ **do**
24:         $\varphi_{t,k} \leftarrow \varphi_{t,k} + \gamma_t \eta_{t,i}(w_{t,i} - w_{t,k})$ ▷Update parameters by the weighted average consensus method.
25:     **end for**
26:     $w_{t+1,k} = ModelUpdate(\varphi_{t,k})$
27:     Send $(w_{t+1,k})$
28: **end for**
29: Vehicle gradient update:
30: $VehicleUpdate(\varphi_{t,k})$
31: B $mini - batches$ of size B
32: **for** batch $b \in B$ **do**
33:     $\phi_{t,k} \leftarrow \varphi_{t,k} - \eta_t \nabla L_{t,k}(\varphi_{t,k})$
34:     $w_{t,k} \leftarrow \phi_{t,k}$
35: **end for**

Informed by the research of El-Ghamrawy [34], we draw upon a novel clustering strategy grounded in Bloom filter techniques to effectively address the challenge of data imbalance within clusters. Inspired by this approach, our proposal capitalizes on the inherent capabilities of Bloom filters to achieve data balance, contributing to more equitable data representations within each cluster. Moving beyond this local level, we extend the concepts of common federated averaging strategies, thereby enabling the amalgamation of high-level parameters to attain a comprehensive global model. By merging the strengths of Bloom-filter-based clustering with established federated learning principles, our proposal seeks to offer a robust and balanced framework for hierarchical decentralized federated learning.

5. Experiments

We conducted experiments on the Sim4DistrDL [35], with a three-layer network topology, in order to validate the convergence speed and accuracy of our proposed H-DFL method.

5.1. Experimental Details

In this subsection, we present the experimental details of IoV, encompassing comprehensive information regarding the simulation setup and training tasks.

5.1.1. Simulation Setup

In order to construct a environment for IoV that closely resembles a real-world scenario, we conducted simulations using Sim4DistrDL [35]. The simulation environment consists of a parameter server, four base stations, and four neighboring vehicles for each base station. Wireless communication base stations serve as roadside participants to facilitate communication within the IoV network. Neighboring vehicles collaborate by using local data to train deep neural network (DNN) models and communicate with the base stations. Simultaneously, the four base stations send parameters to the parameter server and receive updated global parameters in return. Each base station is connected to four vehicles via V2X communication, and the clusters of vehicles change over time in response to fluctuations in local data. Figure 4 illustrates the initial clustering scenario.

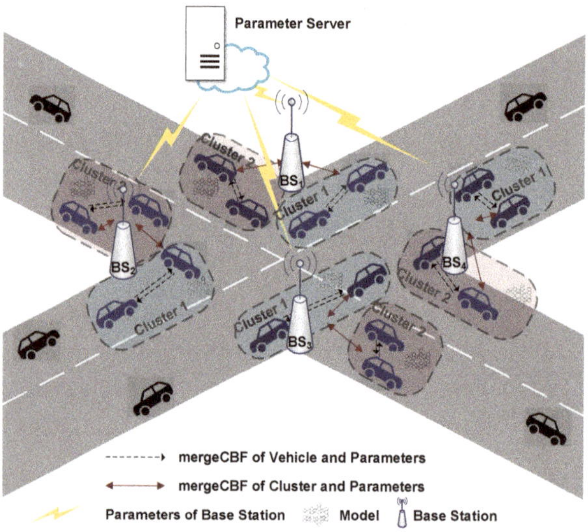

Figure 4. The topology structure of the H-DFL vehicle scenario.

5.1.2. Training Tasks and Data Redistribution

In order to validate the efficiency of H-DFL, we considered two types of machine learning tasks related to image classification, VGG-16 [36] and Multi-Layer Perceptron(MLP) [37]. The image classification tasks were based on two different datasets, namely the Belgian Traffic Sign Classification Benchmark (BelgiumTSC) [38] and CIFAR-10 [39].

BelgiumTSC consists of more than 7000 high-resolution color images captured from different angles and under various environmental conditions. It provides precise annotation in the form of bounding boxes for each traffic sign present in the images. These bounding boxes indicate the exact location and extent of the traffic signs. In total, there are 11,219 annotated bounding boxes, which correspond to more than 2000 individual traffic sign instances. CIFAR-10 is a popular image classification dataset widely used in the field of computer vision and machine learning. It consists of a collection of 60,000 small color images and is divided into 10 different classes.

Given that federated learning must account for the heterogeneity in data distributions among participants, it was necessary to create imbalanced datasets among the participants. For this purpose, we selected five classes from the BelgiumTSC, and Figure 5a illustrates the initial data distribution for the four vehicles at each base station during training. Similarly, when using the CIFAR-10 dataset, Figure 5b displays the initial data distribution for the four vehicles at each base station.

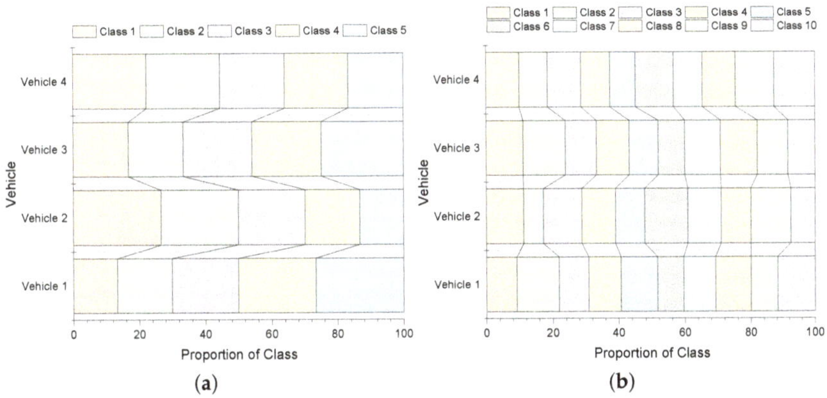

Figure 5. The initial data distribution of vehicles. (**a**) The initial data distribution of BelgiumTSC. (**b**) The initial data distribution of CIFAR-10.

5.1.3. Baselines

To evaluate the convergence speed and accuracy of H-DFL, we compared three classical algorithms, comparing H-DFL with other three FL protocols: FedAvg [11], Consensus-based FA (CFA) [12], and Cooperative Decentralized Federated Averaging (CDFA) [40].

FedAvg is a distributed machine learning algorithm with a network topology consisting of two layers: participants and parameter servers. After completing local learning on each participant, the parameter server randomly selects a subset of participants to upload their learned model parameters to the server. The parameter server aggregates the model parameters received and sends back the aggregated result to the participants. This process iterates until the model converges.

CFA is a consensus-based decentralized federated learning strategy. It leverages decentralized networks, enabling devices to perform collaborative training steps using local data and consensus-based methods, ensuring convergence efficiency across varying connectivity graphs and network sizes, particularly within industrial IoT settings.

CDFA addresses privacy concerns in smart healthcare, employing real-time distributed networking via MQTT protocol and validating its efficacy through brain tumor segmentation on physically separated machines with varying operational conditions.

5.1.4. Evaluation Metrics

To evaluate the performance of the proposed algorithm in this paper, two metrics are used: loss and accuracy. The loss of model training on the dataset is defined as follows:

$$H(y,q) = -\frac{1}{N}\sum_{i=1}^{n} y_i^{(c)} \log\left(q_i^{(c)}\right), \tag{8}$$

where N is the number of iterations required to complete a round of training, n is the total number of categories in the classification, $y_i^{(c)}$ is the value of whether the i-th item belongs to class c, and $q_i^{(c)}$ is the predicted probability that the i-th item belongs to class c.

The test accuracy (Acc) of the model on the data set is defined as follows:

$$Acc = \frac{1}{N} \frac{\sum_{i=1}^{n} T_i}{\sum_{i=1}^{n} (T_i + F_i)}, \tag{9}$$

where n is the total number of classes, T_i is the number of correctly classified items in the i-th class, and F_i is the number of misclassified items in the i-th class.

5.2. Performance in Different Training Tasks

In this subsection, we primarily analyze the results of H-DFL and two other Federated Learning algorithms on the two training tasks, focusing on two aspects: convergence speed and accuracy.

For the FedAvg, communication rounds refer to the rounds of communication between participants and the parameter server. Due to the typically large communication distances, significant communication overhead is incurred. In the case of the CFA, the number of communication rounds is calculated based on the communication rounds with neighboring nodes. As for H-DFL, communication rounds encompass both rounds of communication with neighbors and rounds of communication with the base stations. In the experiments, for each vehicle, batch size, learning rate, and the number of epochs for local training were set to 10, 0.01, and 1, respectively.

The convergence speed of the VGG model under different distributed learning algorithms based on the BelgiumTSC dataset is presented in Figure 6. The results indicate that the H-DFL algorithm (black curve) exhibits the fastest convergence, typically starting to converge after around 10 communication rounds. The second fastest convergence is observed in the CFA algorithm (red curve), while the FedAvg (green curve) and CDFA (blue curve) algorithms demonstrate slower convergence rates. Figure 7 displays the loss values' variation of the MLP model on the non-uniform CIFAR-10 dataset. The results suggest that the H-DFL algorithm achieves the fastest convergence, followed by the CFA algorithm and CDFA algorithm, while the FedAvg algorithm exhibits a slower convergence rate. Real-time responsiveness is a critical factor for vehicular networks or IoV applications, and H-DFL appears to be better suited for the IoV environment.

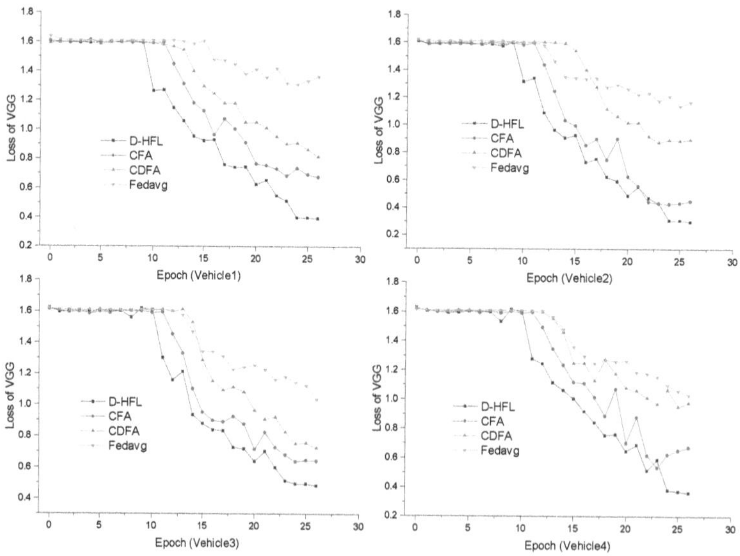

Figure 6. Loss of VGG.

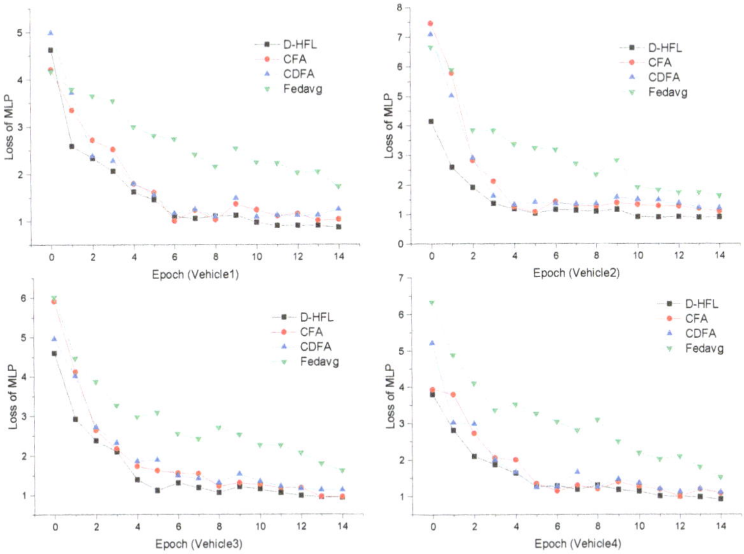

Figure 7. Loss of MLP.

We further analyze the accuracy of the models. As shown in Figure 8, all methods achieve an accuracy of over 65%, indicating that each method is capable of making correct predictions to a certain extent. This demonstrates the feasibility of modern machine learning approaches in advancing autonomous driving. Figure 8a displays the training accuracy of the VGG model under different distributed learning algorithms. As shown in the graph, the H-DFL algorithm achieves approximately a 9% improvement in accuracy compared to the CFA algorithm. Moreover, the improvement is more significant when compared to the FedAvg and CDFA algorithms. Similarly, Figure 8b illustrates the training accuracy of the MLP model under different distributed learning algorithms. The H-DFL algorithm also achieves higher accuracy performance.

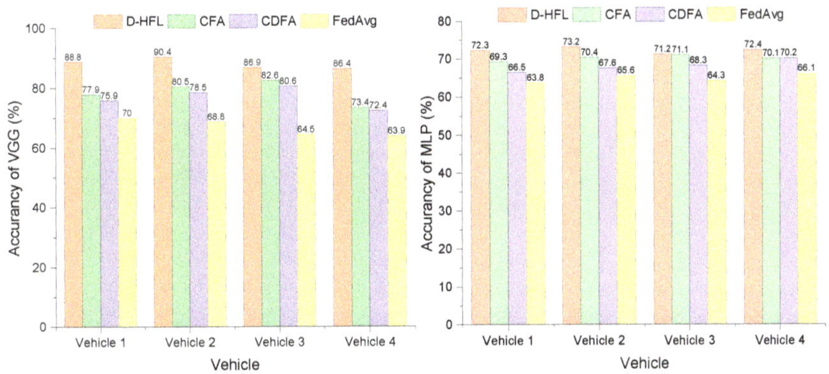

(**a**) Accurancy of VGG. (**b**) Accurancy of MLP.

Figure 8. Test accuracy (%) comparison of H-CFL to CFA, CDFA, and FedAvg.

In addressing non-IID data challenges, our framework's grouping strategy, based on Bloom filter, demonstrated remarkable capabilities in achieving data balance within clusters. The results showcased a significant improvement in the convergence of local models. This outcome underscores the potential of Bloom-filter-based clustering to enhance the utilization of diverse data, leading to more robust and unbiased local models. Analyzing the trade-offs between accuracy and convergence speed revealed an interesting interplay. While the hierarchical decentralized federated learning approach achieved faster convergence due to the efficient cluster-level aggregation, there were subtle accuracy trade-offs compared to traditional methods that relied on central parameter updates. In some scenarios, the initial convergence speed of our framework was marginally slower, particularly when clusters contained fewer vehicles or when data distribution was extremely skewed. However, as training iterations progressed, our framework demonstrated an ability to catch up with and, in certain cases, surpass the accuracy of traditional methods. This suggests that, while there might be minor trade-offs in initial accuracy, our approach achieves competitive accuracy levels while benefiting from faster convergence in the long run.

The reason for these results is that the algorithm we proposed utilizes clustering based on data distribution, which mitigates the issue of data imbalance within clusters. On the other hand, CFA and CDFA algorithms only collaborate with neighboring vehicles, limiting their performance due to lower imbalance. The FedAvg algorithm involves training with all participants, resulting in a significant impact from data distribution imbalance, thereby reducing the efficiency of model learning.

6. Conclusions

By capitalizing on participant grouping and decentralized learning paradigms, H-DFL navigates the intricacies of data imbalances, accelerating convergence and enhancing model accuracy across various distributed learning algorithms. Moreover, the adaptable nature of H-DFL lends itself to diverse IoV scenarios. Its potential applicability in varied contexts, from urban to rural environments, differing vehicle densities, and contrasting data characteristics, underscores its versatility. As a clustering adaptive algorithm, H-DFL exhibits scalability and adaptability, poised to cater to the unique demands of different environments. By effectively addressing the challenges of model training and data sharing in vehicular networks, our framework has far-reaching implications for IoV applications, such as intelligent traffic management, collaborative safety measures, and dynamic decision-making. While the journey from theory to practice comes with its set of challenges, we are committed to addressing the potential barriers and aligning our framework with the practical nuances of real-world infrastructure.

Author Contributions: Conceptualization, S.L. and Z.L.; methodology, Z.X.; validation, W.L.; resources, J.T.; writing—original draft preparation, S.L.; writing—review and editing, Z.X.; supervision, Z.L. All authors have read and agreed to the published version of the manuscript.

Funding: This research was funded by the National Natural Science Foundation of China (61962044, 61962045), the Program for Young Talents of Science and Technology in Universities of Inner Mongolia Autonomous Region (NJYT23104), the Inner Mongolia Science and Technology Plan Project (2021GG0250), the Natural Science Foundation of Inner Mongolia Autonomous Region (2021MS06029), the Basic scientific research business fund project of universities directly under the autonomous region (JY20220324), and the Inner Mongolia Autonomous Region Higher Education Scientific Research Project (NJZZ22428).

Data Availability Statement: The data are available in a publicly accessible repository. The data presented in this study are openly available in BelgiumTSC at https://doi.org/10.1007/s00138-011-0391-3 (accessed on 2011), reference number [29] and CIFAR-10 at http://www.cs.toronto.edu/kriz/cifar.html (accessed on 2009), reference number [30].

Conflicts of Interest: The authors declare no conflict of interest.

References

1. Tsaramirsis, G.; Kantaros, A.; Al-Darraji, I.; Piromalis, D.; Apostolopoulos, C.; Pavlopoulou, A.; Alrammal, M.; Ismail, Z.; Buhari, S.M.; Stojmenovic, M.; et al. A modern approach towards an industry 4.0 model: From driving technologies to management. *J. Sens.* **2022**, *2022*, 5023011. [CrossRef]
2. Khattak, S.B.A.; Nasralla, M.M.; Farman, H.; Choudhury, N. Performance Evaluation of an IEEE 802.15. 4-Based Thread Network for Efficient Internet of Things Communications in Smart Cities. *Appl. Sci.* **2023**, *13*, 7745. [CrossRef]
3. Ngo, H.; Fang, H.; Wang, H. Cooperative Perception With V2V Communication for Autonomous Vehicles. *IEEE Trans. Veh. Technol.* **2023**, 1–10. [CrossRef]
4. Ali, Y.; Haque, M.M.; Mannering, F. Assessing traffic conflict/crash relationships with extreme value theory: Recent developments and future directions for connected and autonomous vehicle and highway safety research. *Anal. Methods Accid. Res.* **2023**, *39*, 100276. [CrossRef]
5. Piromalis, D.; Kantaros, A. Digital twins in the automotive industry: The road toward physical-digital convergence. *Appl. Syst. Innov.* **2022**, *5*, 65. [CrossRef]
6. Taslimasa, H.; Dadkhah, S.; Neto, E.C.P.; Xiong, P.; Ray, S.; Ghorbani, A.A. Security issues in Internet of Vehicles (IoV): A comprehensive survey. *Internet Things* **2023**, *22*, 100809. [CrossRef]
7. Wang, Y.; Su, Z.; Guo, S.; Dai, M.; Luan, T.H.; Liu, Y. A survey on digital twins: Architecture, enabling technologies, security and privacy, and future prospects. *IEEE Internet Things J.* **2023**, *10*, 14965–14987. [CrossRef]
8. Lim, W.Y.B.; Luong, N.C.; Hoang, D.T.; Jiao, Y.; Liang, Y.C.; Yang, Q.; Niyato, D.; Miao, C. Federated learning in mobile edge networks: A comprehensive survey. *IEEE Commun. Surv. Tutor.* **2020**, *22*, 2031–2063. [CrossRef]
9. Liu, R.; Pan, J. CRS: A Privacy-preserving Two-layered Distributed Machine Learning Framework for IoV. *IEEE Internet Things J.* **2023**. [CrossRef]
10. Choudhury, N.; Nasralla, M.M. A proposed resource-aware time-constrained scheduling mechanism for dsme based iov networks. In Proceedings of the 2021 IEEE 94th Vehicular Technology Conference (VTC2021-Fall), Norman, OK, USA, 27–30 September 2021; IEEE: Piscataway, NJ, USA, 2021; pp. 1–7.
11. McMahan, B.; Moore, E.; Ramage, D.; Hampson, S.; y Arcas, B.A. Communication-efficient learning of deep networks from decentralized data. In Proceedings of the Artificial Intelligence and Statistics, PMLR, Fort Lauderdale, FL, USA, 20–22 April 2017; pp. 1273–1282.
12. Savazzi, S.; Nicoli, M.; Rampa, V. Federated learning with cooperating devices: A consensus approach for massive IoT networks. *IEEE Internet Things J.* **2020**, *7*, 4641–4654. [CrossRef]
13. Pokhrel, S.R.; Choi, J. A decentralized federated learning approach for connected autonomous vehicles. In Proceedings of the 2020 IEEE Wireless Communications and Networking Conference Workshops (WCNCW), Seoul, Republic of Korea, 6–9 April 2020; IEEE: Piscataway, NJ, USA, 2020; pp. 1–6.
14. Soto, I.; Calderon, M.; Amador, O.; Urueña, M. A survey on road safety and traffic efficiency vehicular applications based on C-V2X technologies. *Veh. Commun.* **2022**, *33*, 100428. [CrossRef]
15. Barbieri, L.; Savazzi, S.; Brambilla, M.; Nicoli, M. Decentralized federated learning for extended sensing in 6G connected vehicles. *Veh. Commun.* **2022**, *33*, 100396. [CrossRef]
16. Nishio, T.; Yonetani, R. Client selection for federated learning with heterogeneous resources in mobile edge. In Proceedings of the ICC 2019–2019 IEEE International Conference on Communications (ICC), Shanghai, China, 20–24 May 2019; IEEE: Piscataway, NJ, USA, 2019; pp. 1–7.
17. Li, B.; Jiang, Y.; Pei, Q.; Li, T.; Liu, L.; Lu, R. Feel: Federated end-to-end learning with non-iid data for vehicular ad hoc networks. *IEEE Trans. Intell. Transp. Syst.* **2022**, *23*, 16728–16740. [CrossRef]
18. Liu, W.; Xu, Z.; Tian, J.; Zhang, Y. Towards In-Network Compact Representation: Mergeable Counting Bloom Filter Vis Cuckoo Scheduling. *IEEE Access* **2021**, *9*, 55329–55339. [CrossRef]
19. Lim, W.Y.B.; Ng, J.S.; Xiong, Z.; Jin, J.; Zhang, Y.; Niyato, D.; Leung, C.; Miao, C. Decentralized edge intelligence: A dynamic resource allocation framework for hierarchical federated learning. *IEEE Trans. Parallel Distrib. Syst.* **2021**, *33*, 536–550. [CrossRef]
20. Lim, W.Y.B.; Ng, J.S.; Xiong, Z.; Niyato, D.; Miao, C. Evolutionary edge association and auction in hierarchical federated learning. In *Federated Learning over Wireless Edge Networks*; Springer: Berlin/Heidelberg, Germany, 2022; pp. 117–145.
21. Li, Y.; Wang, X.; Sun, R.; Xie, X.; Ying, S.; Ren, S. Trustiness-based hierarchical decentralized federated learning. *Knowl.-Based Syst.* **2023**, *276*, 110763. [CrossRef]
22. Cho, Y.J.; Gupta, S.; Joshi, G.; Yağan, O. Bandit-based communication-efficient client selection strategies for federated learning. In Proceedings of the 2020 54th Asilomar Conference on Signals, Systems, and Computers, Pacific Grove, CA, USA, 1–4 November 2020; IEEE: Piscataway, NJ, USA, 2020; pp. 1066–1069.
23. Ribero, M.; Vikalo, H. Communication-efficient federated learning via optimal client sampling. *arXiv* **2020**, arXiv:2007.15197.
24. Cho, Y.J.; Wang, J.; Joshi, G. Client selection in federated learning: Convergence analysis and power-of-choice selection strategies. *arXiv* **2020**, arXiv:2010.01243.
25. Ruan, Y.; Zhang, X.; Liang, S.C.; Joe-Wong, C. Towards flexible device participation in federated learning. In Proceedings of the International Conference on Artificial Intelligence and Statistics, PMLR, Virtual, 13–15 April 2021; pp. 3403–3411.
26. Ji, S.; Jiang, W.; Walid, A.; Li, X. Dynamic sampling and selective masking for communication-efficient federated learning. *IEEE Intell. Syst.* **2021**, *37*, 27–34. [CrossRef]

27. Liu, G.; Ma, X.; Yang, Y.; Wang, C.; Liu, J. Federaser: Enabling efficient client-level data removal from federated learning models. In Proceedings of the 2021 IEEE/ACM 29th International Symposium on Quality of Service (IWQOS), Tokyo, Japan, 25–28 June 2021; IEEE: Piscataway, NJ, USA, 2021; pp. 1–10.
28. Goetz, J.; Malik, K.; Bui, D.; Moon, S.; Liu, H.; Kumar, A. Active federated learning. *arXiv* **2019**, arXiv:1909.12641.
29. Cho, Y.J.; Wang, J.; Joshi, G. Towards understanding biased client selection in federated learning. In Proceedings of the International Conference on Artificial Intelligence and Statistics, PMLR, Virtual, 28–30 March 2022; pp. 10351–10375.
30. Tan, Y.; Long, G.; Liu, L.; Zhou, T.; Lu, Q.; Jiang, J.; Zhang, C. Fedproto: Federated prototype learning across heterogeneous clients. In Proceedings of the AAAI Conference on Artificial Intelligence, Virtual, 22 February–1 March 2022; Volume 36, pp. 8432–8440.
31. Fang, X.; Ye, M. Robust federated learning with noisy and heterogeneous clients. In Proceedings of the IEEE/CVF Conference on Computer Vision and Pattern Recognition, New Orleans, LA, USA, 18–24 June 2022; pp. 10072–10081.
32. Bloom, B.H. Space/time trade-offs in hash coding with allowable errors. *Commun. ACM* **1970**, *13*, 422–426. [CrossRef]
33. Fan, L.; Cao, P.; Almeida, J.; Broder, A.Z. Summary cache: A scalable wide-area web cache sharing protocol. *IEEE/ACM Trans. Netw.* **2000**, *8*, 281–293. [CrossRef]
34. El-Ghamrawy, S.M. A knowledge management framework for imbalanced data using frequent pattern mining based on bloom filter. In Proceedings of the 2016 11th International Conference on Computer Engineering & Systems (ICCES), Cairo, Egypt, 20–21 December 2016; IEEE: Piscataway, NJ, USA, 2016; pp. 226–231.
35. Liu, X.; Xu, Z.; Qin, Y.; Tian, J. A discrete-event-based simulator for distributed deep learning. In Proceedings of the 2022 IEEE Symposium on Computers and Communications (ISCC), Rhodes, Greece, 30 June–3 July 2022; IEEE: Piscataway, NJ, USA, 2022; pp. 1–7.
36. Simonyan, K.; Zisserman, A. Very deep convolutional networks for large-scale image recognition. *arXiv* **2014**, arXiv:1409.1556.
37. LeCun, Y.; Bengio, Y.; Hinton, G. Deep learning. *Nature* **2015**, *521*, 436–444. [CrossRef]
38. Timofte, R.; Zimmermann, K.; Van Gool, L. Multi-view traffic sign detection, recognition, and 3D localisation. *Mach. Vis. Appl.* **2014**, *25*, 633–647. [CrossRef]
39. Krizhevsky, A.; Nair, V.; Hinton, G. The CIFAR-10 Dataset. 2014; Volume 55. Available online: http://www.cs.toronto.edu/kriz/cifar.html (accessed on 13 August 2009).
40. Tedeschini, B.C.; Savazzi, S.; Stoklasa, R.; Barbieri, L.; Stathopoulos, I.; Nicoli, M.; Serio, L. Decentralized federated learning for healthcare networks: A case study on tumor segmentation. *IEEE Access* **2022**, *10*, 8693–8708. [CrossRef]

electronics

MDPI

Article

An Efficient Path Planning Method for the Unmanned Aerial Vehicle in Highway Inspection Scenarios

Yuanlong Li [1], Shang Gao [2], Xuewen Liu [2], Peiliang Zuo [2,*] and Haoliang Li [2]

1 Certification Management Office of the Ministry of Information and Cybersecurity, National Information Center, Beijing 100045, China; lyl@sic.gov.cn
2 Beijing Institute of Electronic Science and Technology (BESTI), Beijing 100070, China; gaoshangnoble@mail.besti.edu.cn (S.G.); xuewen_liu1990@bupt.edu.cn (X.L.); lhl2018@bupt.edu.cn (H.L.)
* Correspondence: zplzpl88@bupt.cn

Abstract: Unmanned aerial vehicles (UAVs) have received widespread attention due to their flexible deployment characteristics. Automated airports equipped with UAVs are expected to become important equipment for improving quality and reducing costs in many inspection scenarios. This paper focuses on the automated inspection business of UAVs dispatched by automated airports in highway scenarios. On the basis of considering the shape of highway curves, inspection targets, and the energy consumption characteristics of UAVs, planning the flight parameters of UAVs is of great significance for ensuring the effectiveness of the inspection process. This paper first sets the inspection path points for the UAV based on highway curves, and then proposes an efficient heuristic method for the nonlinear non-convex parameter optimization problem, through which the parameters of the UAV's inspection altitude, hovering altitude, and flight speed are planned. Simulation and analysis show that the proposed method possesses good parameter planning efficiency. By combining several existing trajectory planning methods, e.g., the traversal method, the deep Q-network based method, and the genetic method, it can be concluded that the proposed method in this paper has better overall planning performance including planning efficiency and inspection effectiveness.

Keywords: UAV; highway inspection; path planning; inspection quality; automatic airport

1. Introduction

In recent years, the development of information technology has greatly promoted the application of UAVs (also know as drones) in many fields [1,2], such as public safety, environmental monitoring, military strikes, etc. The application of UAV platforms can significantly improve the efficiency of traditional business operations, reduce business costs, or enhance the security capabilities of business operations [3,4]. The task planning and trajectory setting for integrating the main body of UAVs and their many characteristics is of great significance for the operational efficiency of UAV platforms [5,6].

Data collection through UAV systems generally requires the prediction of energy consumption, endurance, etc., based on environmental conditions and UAV performance parameters. By optimizing the flight altitude, speed, and route parameters of the UAV, the coverage or quality of inspections can be improved [7–10]. At present, there are difficulties in the inspection process of highways, such as low inspection efficiency, poor safety assurance, high economic costs, and many blind spots in inspection.

The intelligent inspection system based on UAVs is expected to provide key support for three-dimensional, flexible, and rapid response of highway management and services. Specifically, there are two issues with route planning in the UAV inspection process for highway scenarios: Firstly, the matching between the inspection path and the geographic curve of the highway is not perfect, and the density of inspection path points is sparse compared to the highway, which limits the detection opportunities and inspection effects of the inspection process; secondly, during the inspection process, the flight parameters of the drone were not optimized to match the scene, resulting in excessive energy consumption or limited inspection coverage radius.

1.1. Related Work

Targeting different application scenarios and business objectives, conducting path planning and task planning is of great significance for improving the coverage of UAVs, reducing energy consumption, or ensuring their own safety. Referring to the application of artificial intelligence (AI) technology, planning methods can be generally divided into two categories, namely non-AI methods and AI-based methods.

Non-AI programming methods mainly include biological evolution methods and mathematical programming. As a method of biological evolution, genetic algorithms (GA) are often used in complex and time rich planning scenarios due to their significantly better computational efficiency compared to traversal methods [11–14]. In order to minimize the energy consumption of the UAV for completing a task, a genetic algorithm was proposed in [11], and its simulation performance is significantly superior to the greedy method. For inventory counting scenarios, ref. [12] proposed a path planning model with a genetic algorithm to determine the access routes of a swarm of drones. To achieve 3D path planning for disaster rescue, the adaptive genetic algorithm and sine–cosine particle swarm optimization (PSO) were combined in [13], and the simulation showed that the method can sometimes achieve the global optimization. In [14], a hybrid algorithm integrating the genetic algorithm and the estimation of distribution algorithm was presented for cooperative path planning of UAVs and unmanned ground vehicles.

Mathematical programming is often used for the rapid setting of drone flight parameters to match the dynamics of the considered scene. A dynamic group reconstruction algorithm on the basis of a fourth-order motif was proposed in [15] for UAV swarm dynamic reconstruction. A planning framework of the drone swarm missions was proposed in [16], where the mixed integer linear programming methods were adopted. K. Kuru et al. [17] forged the Hungarian and cross-entropy Monte Carlo techniques together to assign tasks and plan 3D routes dynamically in logistics. In order to generate trajectories in real-time for multiple robots, a distributed model predictive control method on the basis of an on-demand collision avoidance algorithm was proposed in [18], which showed a high success rate in transition tasks with a high density of agents. For handling complex spatial, temporal and reactive requirements, a method that satisfies a given signal temporal logic requirement was presented in [19] to generate trajectories for multiple drones. To achieve efficient coverage path planning of the UAV, a rural postman problem was formulated and solved in [20] by two steps, i.e., optimization of the visiting order and optimization of the flight lines orientation. In [21], an edge computing D* lite algorithm with distributed characteristics was proposed to autonomously plan the flight path, fly in formation, and avoid obstacles for the UAV swarm.

Thanks to the rapid development of computing technology, AI technology can effectively empower drone trajectory and mission planning [22–29]. In [22], a half random Q-Learning-based task assignment method was raised for multi-UAV cooperation. A novel sequential deep model integrating proximal policy optimization and long short-term memory (LSTM) was proposed in [23] for assigning tasks and planning the route of UAVs to achieve good energy efficiency, data collection ratio, and geographic fairness. To save energy consumption of the UAV in sea-farming scenarios, a deep Q-network (DQN)-based path planning method was presented in [24], and the performance of the proposed method was verified through simulation in a virtual environment. A double deep Q-network was adopted in [25] for UAV path planning in wireless data harvesting process, and the method achieved good performance in flight efficiency and collision avoidance. A multi-task regression-based learning method, which is capable of defining flight commands in unstructured outdoor environments, was proposed in [26], and the simulation showed that the approach could perform sufficient exploration within the target search perimeter.

In [27], a deep reinforcement learning (DRL) method that integrates three main components, i.e., optimization, learning, and prediction, for generating reliable and efficient routes for swarms of UAVs was presented. A. Loquercio et al. [28] explored a data-driven approach using convolutional neural network (CNN) for UAV swarm in highly dynamic scenarios to keep the navigating process as well as to avoid obstacles. In order to provide long-term coverage for the ground communication, the deep reinforcement learning technology was adopted in [29] to navigate a group of UAVs with the function of the base station.

1.2. Contributions of This Paper

Currently, there are few UAV mission or path planning methods that combine the characteristics of highway scenes, while transferring existing methods directly to the highway scenario is likely to greatly reduce the inspection effectiveness. In this case, to improve the inspection performance of UAV systems in highway scenes, this paper optimizes the flight parameters of the UAV, and the key contributions of this paper are threefold:

- By analyzing the highway scene inspection business, this paper summarizes the UAV flight parameter planning problem with the goal of optimizing inspection quality. The problem is limited by practical requirements such as UAV available energy and data transmission quality.
- By presenting an efficient approach, we supplement the patrol points of drones in order to improve the matching degree of UAV flight routes with highway curves.
- We propose an effective heuristic method that combines the characteristics of the business scenario to address the nonlinear and non-convex optimization problem, and the method has low operational complexity.
- Finally, we verify the performance of the proposed method and the comparative methods. The multi-dimensional simulation results indicate that the proposed method in this paper has significant advantages in terms of comprehensive planning effectiveness and operational efficiency.

This paper is organized as follows. The system model and problem formulation are introduced in Section 2. Section 3 covers the proposed operational planning method. Section 4 provides the experimental results and performance analysis, and Section 5 presents the conclusions.

Notation: In this paper, scalars are expressed by a non-boldface type, while matrices as well as vectors are expressed by a boldface type. $(\cdot)^T$ and $E\{\cdot\}$ denote the matrix transpose and statistical expectation respectively. Finally, ω_i represents the *i*th entry of the vector $\boldsymbol{\omega}$.

2. System Model and Problem Formulation

In this section, we first introduce the model of using UAV for highway inspection, and then summarize the drone inspection planning issues that need to be optimized.

2.1. System Model

Using UAVs based on automated airports to patrol the highway environment can greatly reduce the cost of manual inspection processes, and due to their broad field of vision (see Figure 1), their inspection effectiveness is more advantageous compared to the ground inspection. Thanks to the development of mobile communication systems, the visual content (the inspection data) of the drone's flight process can be wirelessly transmitted back to the unmanned airport and the management platform behind it. Therefore, multiple inspection targets on highways must be covered during drone flight, and in order to ensure inspection quality, the signal transmission quality of the UAV needs to be guaranteed in order to meet the clarity requirements of returning video and other data. The field of view of UAV mounted camera should be able to cover the inspection targets and highway curves well, to ensure that the content of concern can be inspected.

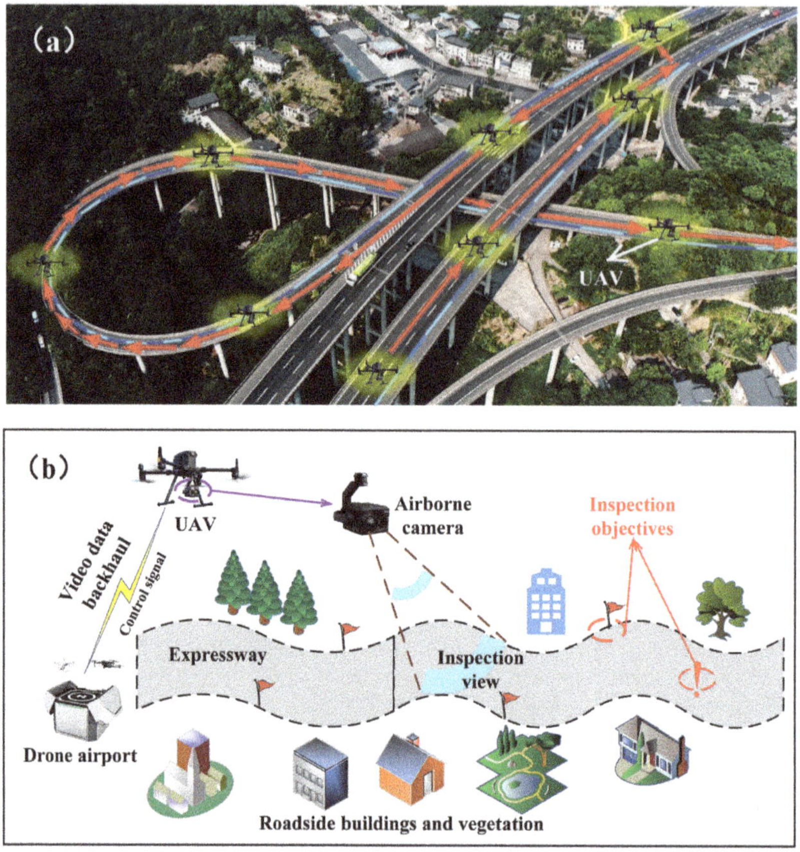

Figure 1. Schematic diagram of UAV inspection process for highway scenes. (**a**) Patrol trajectory of UAV in highway scenes. (**b**) System model for UAV inspection on the highway.

The inspection process of the UAV is set from the starting point S to the destination point D, which includes N inspection targets. Considering the curve characteristics of highways themselves, this paper assumes that the inspection sequence of targets is determined. This setting is reasonable, as for safety reasons, the UAV needs to patrol on the periphery of both sides of the highway, and the order in which the UAV flies through inspection points can be ensured by dividing inspection targets (inspection points) onto both sides of the highway. The total number of inspection sections for the UAV is $N + 1$, and their corresponding interval lengths are represented as $L_0, L_1, \ldots, L_N$. For convenience, this paper sets the flight altitude of the UAV to be fixed within each inspection section. The flying heights corresponding to multiple inspection sections are represented as $h_0, h_1, \ldots, h_N$. Without loss of generality, this paper sets each patrol target in the expressway scene as a circle, and their space radii are expressed as $r_1, r_2, \ldots, r_N$. The UAV takes photos or records the inspection targets by hovering around them, and the hovering time for each inspection target is represented as $t_1, t_2, \ldots, t_N$. The hovering heights of the UAV for inspection of each target are $h_1^H, h_2^H, \ldots h_N^H$.

To ensure the spatial integrity of the UAV's onboard camera for the inspection section and inspection target, the minimum flight altitude of the UAV can be calculated as $h_{\min} = \frac{f \times r}{R_{CCD}}$, where f represents the focal length of the airborne camera, R_{CCD} denotes the lens radius size of the airborne camera equivalent to the CCD camera, and r signifies the radius size of the inspection object [30,31].

In highway scenarios, the patrol process of the UAV may frequently encounter non-line of sight (NLOS) transmission of signals, and the probability of line of sight (LOS) transmission of the UAV is expressed as [32]

$$P_{LOS} = \frac{1}{1 + a\exp(-b[\theta - a])}, \tag{1}$$

where $\theta = \arctan\frac{h}{L}$, a and b represent parameters related to the transmission environment, h and L represent the flight altitude of the UAV and the distance interval between the UAV's vertical projection on the ground and the ground signal transceiver, respectively. Correspondingly, the expected received power of the signal of the UAV at its current position is $\bar{P}(h) = P_{LOS}\beta\delta_{LOS} + (1 - P_{LOS})\beta\delta_{NLOS}$, where β, δ_{LOS}, and δ_{NLOS}, respectively, represent the transmission power of the signal, the corresponding path loss in LOS environment, and the corresponding path loss in NLOS environment.

Taking into account the starting and ending points, inspection sections, and inspection targets of the UAV, the inspection height of the UAV in the entire highway scene can be summarized as $\underbrace{h_S, h_0, h_1^H, h_1, h_2^H, h_2, \ldots h_N^H, h_N, h_D}_{2N+3}$, where h_S and h_D denote the altitude of the starting and ending unmanned airports, respectively. And if the starting and ending points are the same unmanned airport, then $h_S = h_D$. For the convenience of representation, this paper re-expresses the sequence as $\tau_0, \tau_1, \tau_2, \ldots \tau_M$, with $M = 2N + 2$.

For the rotorcraft drone, its power consumption during the hovering process can be expressed as [33,34]

$$P_h = \frac{\delta}{8}\rho s A \Omega^3 R^3 + (1 + \chi)\frac{W^{3/2}}{\sqrt{2\rho A}}, \tag{2}$$

where δ denotes the profile drag coefficient, ρ represents air density, while A, s, R, Ω, χ and W, respectively, signify rotor disc area, rotor solidity, rotor radius, blade angular velocity, incremental correction factor to induced power and aircraft weight. The power consumption of the UAV during flight is expressed as

$$P(V) = P_0\left(1 + \frac{3V^2}{U_{\text{tip}}^2}\right) + P_i\left(\sqrt{1 + \frac{V^4}{4v_0^4}} - \frac{V^2}{2v_0^2}\right)^{1/2} + \frac{1}{2}d_0\rho s A V^3, \tag{3}$$

in which P_0 and P_i correspond to the first and second terms in Equation (2), respectively. V represents the flight speed of the UAV, U_{tip} represents the speed of the rotor blades, v_0 represents the average rotor speed generated during hovering, and d_0 represents the fuselage drag ratio. Furthermore, the power consumption of the UAV during ascent and descent can be written as

$$P(V, \tilde{\kappa}) = P_0\left(1 + \frac{3V^2}{\Omega^2 R^2}\right) + P_i\tilde{\kappa}\left(\sqrt{\tilde{\kappa}^2 + \frac{V^4}{4v_0^4}} - \frac{V^2}{2v_0^2}\right)^{1/2} + \frac{1}{2}d_0\rho s A V^3, \tag{4}$$

where $\tilde{\kappa}$ represents the thrust to weight ratio, we have $\tilde{\kappa} > 1$ when the UAV rises, otherwise $\tilde{\kappa} < 1$ when the UAV descends. For simplicity, this paper sets the speed of the UAV's ascent and descent processes to be constant at V_{UD}, and the thrust to weight ratio is fixed at $\tilde{\kappa}_U$ and $\tilde{\kappa}_D$, respectively. Therefore, the power consumption of the corresponding processes can be expressed as $P(V_{UD}, \tilde{\kappa}_U)$ and $P(V_{UD}, \tilde{\kappa}_D)$.

2.2. Problem Formulation

The effectiveness of the UAV inspection process is crucial. By referring to the minimum flight altitude of the UAV, this pair sets the inspection effect coefficient as $e^{\sqrt{h_{\min}/h_x}-1}$ with e denoting the Euler number and h_x representing the current flight altitude of the UAV.

Let Ψ represent the overall effect of the inspection process, which can be calculated using the following equation:

$$\Psi = \sum_{i=0}^{N} \left(e^{\sqrt{h_{\min}/h_i} - 1} \right) \times L_i + \sum_{j=1}^{N} \left(e^{\sqrt{h_{\min}/h_j^H} - 1} \right) \times M_j, \tag{5}$$

in which $M_j, j = 1, 2, \ldots, N$ represents the importance of the j-th inspection target.

Due to the relatively small communication power of UAVs compared to flight power consumption, this paper ignores the former and aims to optimize the inspection effect for highway scenarios. With the available energy of the UAV supporting the inspection process, inspection altitude and speed, as well as signal transmission quality as constraints, the optimization problem of UAV inspection process can be summarized as follows:

$$\max_{h_i, h_j^H, v_i^f, i=0,1,\ldots,N, j=1,2,\ldots,N} \quad (\Psi) \tag{6a}$$

$$\text{s.t.} \sum_{k=0}^{M-1} |(\tau_{k+1} - \tau_k) \times P(V_{UD}, \tilde{\kappa}_U) or P(V_{UD}, \tilde{\kappa}_D)| \times \frac{|(\tau_{k+1} - \tau_k)|}{V_{UD}} +$$

$$\sum_{i=0}^{N} \left(P(v_i^f) \times \frac{L_i}{v_i^f} \right) + \sum_{i=1}^{N} (P_h \times t_i) \leq E \tag{6b}$$

$$\frac{1}{2N+1} \left(\sum_{i=0}^{N} \bar{P}(h_i) + \sum_{i=0}^{N+1} \bar{P}\left(h_i^H\right) \right) \geq \Phi \tag{6c}$$

$$\frac{f \times r_{way}}{R_{CCD}} \leq h_i \leq h_{\max}, i = 0, 1, \ldots N \tag{6d}$$

$$\frac{f \times r_i}{R_{CCD}} \leq h_i^H \leq h_{\max}, i = 1, 2, \ldots N \tag{6e}$$

$$0 \leq v_i^f \leq v_{\max}, i = 0, 1, \ldots N, \tag{6f}$$

where r_{way} represents the equivalent radius of the highway, $h_{\max}$ represents the upper limit of the UAV's cruising altitude, $v_{\max}$ represents the upper limit of the UAV's cruising speed, and Φ represents the threshold requirement for the expected average received power of the UAV's signal.

We can observe that problem (6) belongs to a mixed integer nonlinear programming problem. This paper will propose an effective heuristic method in the next section to improve the effectiveness of planning.

3. Proposed Path Planning Method

In this section, we first provide a method for supplementing the cruise points of the unmanned aerial vehicle, and then introduce the proposed drone inspection planning for highways (DIPH) method.

3.1. Selection of Supplementary Inspection Points

We have noticed that the density of patrol points can greatly affect the quality of drone inspections on highways, as (1) the highway management department does not recommend drones to fly directly over highways, but rather over both sides of the road to prevent drones from falling to the ground and posing risks to the operation of highways; (2) if the drone's patrol points are too sparse, the drone's straight-line flight between points will significantly affect the correlation between the camera mounted on it and the highway road surface. Therefore, we first briefly provide a method for selecting patrol points for highways before introducing the unmanned aerial vehicle path planning method proposed in this paper.

As a feasible method, we believe that the acquisition of patrol points can be briefly divided into four steps, i.e., data acquisition, center point selection, side delineation and patrol points selection. We now introduce these four steps separately.

3.1.1. Data Acquisition

In order to obtain the patrol points of the highway area, it is first necessary to obtain the longitude and latitude information of the area. Generally, this information can be obtained from geographic information system (GIS) data. Figure 2a illustrates the longitude and latitude value points of Guiyang section of the highway (Guizhou Province, China).

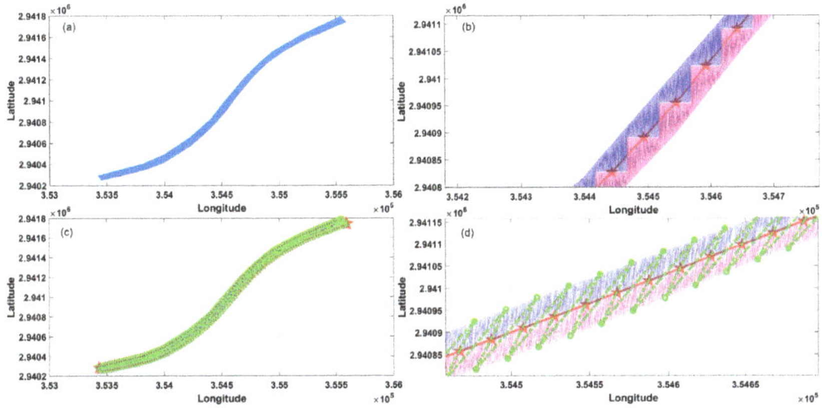

Figure 2. Schematic diagram of the selection process of patrol points for highways. (**a**) The longitude and latitude value points corresponding to the highway area of concern, this paper takes the Guiyang section of the highway (Guizhou Province, China) as an example. (**b**) Divide the area into several sub-segments, select the center of each sub-segment, and divide each sub-segment into two sub-regions. (**c**) Select one point in each sub-segment's two sub-regions as the patrol point. (**d**) An enlarged display of part areas of (**c**).

3.1.2. Center Point Selection

The goal of this method is to obtain dense points on both sides of the highway as patrol points for UAVs. Therefore, we divide the focus area into multiple sub-road sections based on the range of longitude and latitude values, and obtain the center of each sub-road section by averaging the longitude and latitude values (see Figure 2b). Note that the selected density of sub-road sections corresponds to the density of patrol points. By relying on these selected centers, we can further divide the edges and select inspection points.

3.1.3. Side Delineation

For the deployment of a single automatic airport on a highway, the drone's patrol process needs to cover both sides of the highway, and this inspection perspective and content are more diverse compared to unilateral inspections on highways. On this condition, the selection of patrol points needs to be on both sides of the highway, and we then divide the sub-section into two parts based on the latitude of the points in the sub-section compared to the latitude of the center point (see Figure 2b).

3.1.4. Patrol Points Selection

In this step, we select one point on each side of each sub-section as the patrol point. Since each sub-section is divided into two parts, we only need to select one point located at the edge of the highway in each part. For simplicity, we select the point farthest from the center point in each part as the patrol point (see Figure 2c,d).

By performing the above four steps and finally sorting all selected patrol points by the highway side, we can obtain the drone's patrol points, which are spatially fitted to the highway curve. It should be noted that the patrol points in this section are not completely equivalent to the patrol target points mentioned earlier. The patrol target points can be integrated into the drone's patrol points, such as by replacing some close points in the patrol points or directly adding them to the set of patrol points. For the convenience of understanding, we use patrol points as a general term in the following text, which includes the target points to be inspected and the path points to improve the effectiveness of drone patrols, considering that patrol points can also be considered as inspection target points.

3.2. *Summary of the Proposed DIPH Method*

3.2.1. Method Preliminary

We notice that the solution to problem (6) includes three types of parameters, namely, the hovering heights of the drone facing the inspection targets, the patrol heights of the drone between the inspection targets, and the patrol speeds. Additionally, through observation, we can find that the goal of the problem is to maximize the effectiveness of cruising, while the cruising speed of drones is only a parameter of the energy consumption condition (i.e., (6b)). Therefore, by referring to Equation (3), the speed of cruising can be calculated from the perspective of minimizing energy consumption, and this speed has the least impact on the energy consumption condition.

Regarding the cruising altitude of the UAV between cruising points, this paper sets the flight altitude of the UAV to be consistent within each segment, considering that the selection of patrol points has already matched the highway curve and the distance between adjacent patrol points is short. The selection of UAV patrol altitude and the selection of UAV suspension altitude towards patrol targets have similarities in ideas. Both of which have the same relationship with patrol effectiveness, signal quality, and the energy consumption. By referring to Equation (1), it can be observed that the higher the flying (hovering) altitude of the UAV, the greater the probability of LOS in the communication link between the UAV and the airport. Specifically, as the flight altitude increases, the strength of the communication signal first increases and then decreases. However, the flight altitude of the drone used in this paper cannot reach the altitude corresponding to the maximum communication signal strength (see Figure 6 in [32]). In other words, we can assume that the higher the flight altitude of the drone, the stronger its communication signal strength, and we can obtain the flight altitude that matches the signal strength through one-dimensional search.

Considering that the UAV inspection process needs to meet the requirements of inspection field of view quality, and the higher the drone's flight altitude, the greater the energy consumed during its ascent, the preliminary selected drone inspection (hovering) altitude in this paper corresponds to the higher values of the altitude corresponding to the inspection field of view quality and the signal strength threshold corresponding to the altitude. At this point, we can preliminarily obtain solutions for three types of parameters. Considering that the currently selected parameters may not meet condition (6b), this paper reduces the energy consumption of the UAV by smoothing out the differences between the cruising heights of the UAV on certain road sections and the hovering heights of adjacent cruising points.

3.2.2. Method Summary

We summarize the proposed DIPH method and its process in Algorithm 1 and Figure 3, respectively. In the method, we first calculate the hovering height of the corresponding drone for each inspection target, combined with the transmission requirements of signal quality. Meanwhile, considering the requirements for inspection quality, we obtain the suspension height of the drone by taking a larger value in Step 5. We then determine whether each obtained drone's hovering height exceeds the drone's ceiling, and if so, it is determined that a feasible solution to the parameters cannot be obtained.

Algorithm 1: The drone inspection planning for highways (DIPH) method.

1: **Input**: $\delta, \rho, A, s, R, \Omega, \chi, W, d_0, v_0, U_{\text{tip}}, V_{UD}, \tilde{\kappa}_U, \tilde{\kappa}_D, a, b, R_{CCD}, L_0, L_1, \ldots, L_N, f, r_1, r_2, \ldots, r_N, t_1, t_2, \ldots, t_N, \beta, M_j, j = 1,2,\ldots,N$.
2: **Output**: $h_i, h_j^H, v_i^f, i = 0,1,\ldots,N, j = 1,2,\ldots,N$.
3: **Initialize**: $r_{way}, h_{max}, v_{max}, \Phi$.

4: Let $\bar{P}(h_i^H) = \Phi, i = 1,2,\ldots,N$, and obtain $h_{i,1}^H$ by using the dichotomy algorithm.
5: Calculate $h_{i,2}^H = \max\left(h_{i,1}^H, \frac{f \times r_i}{R_{CCD}}\right), i = 1,2,\ldots,N$.
6: **If** $\exists i, h_{i,2}^H > h_{\max}, i = 1,2,\ldots,N$ **Do**
7:     Break, there is no feasible solution.
8: **Else**
9:     Let $\bar{P}(h_i) = \Phi, i = 0,1,\ldots,N$, and obtain $h_{i,1}$ by using the dichotomy algorithm.
10:     Calculate $h_{i,2} = \max\left(h_{i,1}, \frac{f \times r_{way}}{R_{CCD}}\right)$.
11:     If $\exists i, h_{i,2} > h_{\max}, i = 0,1,\ldots,N$ **Do**
12:         Break, there is no feasible solution.
13:     Else
14:         Combine (3) and use the dichotomy method to obtain $v = \min(P(V))$, and set $v_i^f = v, i = 0,1,\ldots,N$.
15:         If $v_i^f, h_{i,2}^H, h_{i,2}$ satisfy (6b) **Do**
16:             Output $v_i^f, h_{i,2}^H, h_{i,2}$.
17:         Else
18:             Search for $\max_i\left(\left|h_{i,2} - h_{i-1,2}^H\right|\right)$ in the current results, and let $h_{i,2} = h_{i-1,2}^H = \max\left(h_{i,2}, h_{i-1,2}^H\right)$.
19:             Perform Step 15.
20:         End If
21:     End If
22: **End If**

Next, we calculate the cruising altitude of the drone on each road section (corresponding to the road section between adjacent inspection points) through a process similar to the above, and make conditional judgments on the obtained altitudes. Considering that the cruising energy consumption of drones decreases first and then increases with their flight speed, this paper uses the dichotomy method to obtain the cruising speed corresponding to the minimum energy consumption during the drone cruising process.

Finally, based on obtaining three types of parameters to be solved, this paper evaluates the availability of the parameters in Step 15. If the parameters cannot meet condition (6b), we search to find the maximum difference in height between the adjacent patrol section and patrol point, and reduce the energy consumption of the drone by making the two heights equal (take the larger of the two). The height adjustment and condition judgment loop execution until the parameters meet condition (6b).

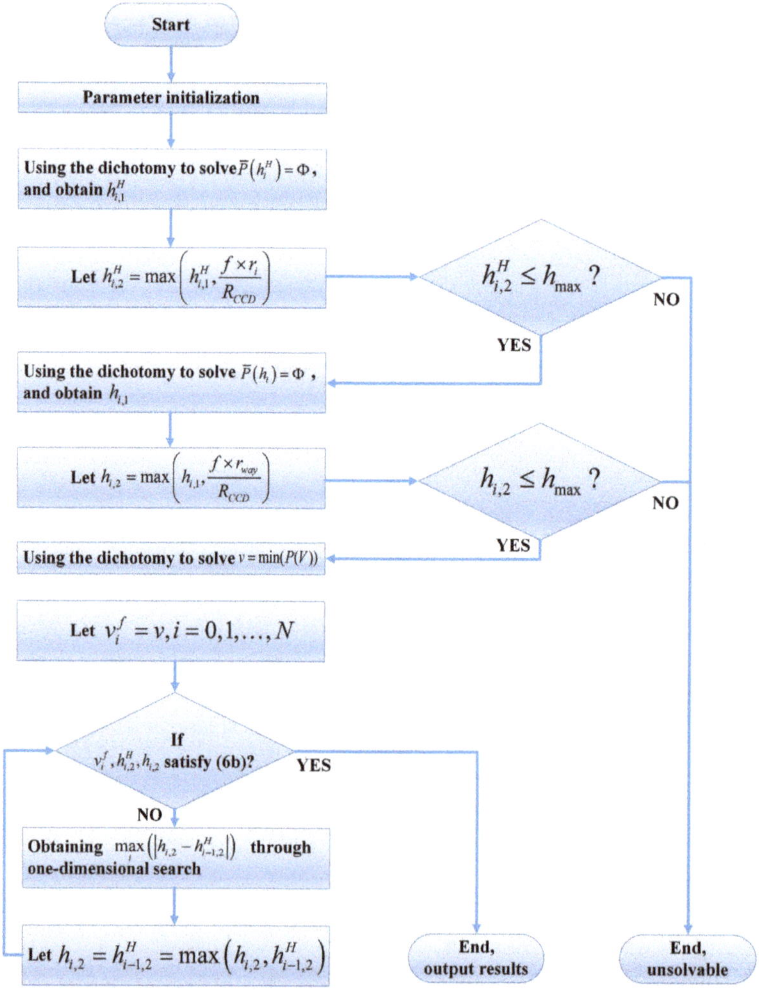

Figure 3. Flowchart of the proposed DIPH method.

3.2.3. Complexity Analysis

We now analyze the complexity of the proposed DIPH method. We assume that the number of optional heights and speeds for the UAV is Λ and Υ discrete values, respectively. Then, the complexity of Steps 4, 9 and 14 is $O(\log_2\Lambda)$, $O(\log_2\Lambda)$, and $O(\log_2\Upsilon)$, respectively. Additionally, the complexity of Steps 5, 6, 10 and 11 is $O(N)$. The complexity of the loop from Steps 18 to 19 is $O(\varpi N)$ with ϖ denoting the number of times the loop is executed. Therefore, the complexity of the DIPH method proposed in this paper can be expressed as $O(4N + \varpi N + 2\log_2\Lambda + \log_2\Upsilon)$. Considering that ϖ is almost zero in the simulation and we have $N > \Lambda, N > \Upsilon$, the complexity can be further simplified as $O(N)$.

4. Simulation and Performance Analysis

4.1. Simulation Settings

To verify the effectiveness of the method proposed in this paper, we generate a rectangle 5 km long and 30 m wide to simulate a highway, and generate 20 to 200 patrol points using the method in Section 3.1, where 20% of the patrol points are considered as inspection targets for the UAV. This paper sets the drone's hovering observation time for patrol points to be randomly generated with equal probability between 0 and 30 s. The transmission bandwidth and power of the drone's return data are set to 20 MHz and 20 dBm, respectively, while the threshold requirement for the expected average received power of the UAV's signal Φ is set as -160 dBm/Hz. The fuselage drag ratio d_0, average rotor speed v_0, speed of the rotor blades U_{tip}, profile drag coefficient δ, air density ρ, rotor solidity s, rotor disc area A, rotor radius R, blade angular velocity Ω, incremental correction factor to induced power χ are, respectively, set as 0.6, 1.44∼7.19, 48 m/s, 0.012, 1.225 kg/m^3, 0.05, 0.79 m^2, 0.12 m, 400 rads/s and 0.1. We randomly generate the importance coefficient of the inspection target (i.e., M_j) between 1 and 100.

To demonstrate the performance of the proposed method under parameter changes, we set the weight variation range of the as 5 to 50 Newton, while the available energy of the UAV is set to 100∼500 Wh. Parameters related to the transmission environment (i.e., a and b) are set as 0.5 and 1.2, respectively. Meanwhile, the focal length of the airborne camera f and the lens radius size of the airborne camera equivalent to the CCD camera R_{CCD} are separately set as 105 mm and 25 mm. The simulation parameters are summarized in Table 1, and all simulations are carried out in Matlab R2016a on a PC with Windows 10 and an Intel i7-12700 CPU. The results shown in this paper are averaged over 200 trials.

Table 1. Simulation parameters.

Parameter	Value
The width and length of the highway	30 m, 5 km
Number of patrol points	20∼200
Transmit power of the signal β	20 dBm (i.e., 100 mW)
The fuselage drag ratio d_0	0.6
The average rotor speed v_0	1.44∼7.19
The speed of the rotor blades U_{tip}	48 m/s
Profile drag coefficient δ	0.012
Air density ρ, Rotor solidity s	1.225 kg/m^3, 0.05
Rotor disc area A, Rotor radius R	0.79 m^2, 0.12 m
Blade angular velocity Ω	400 rads/s
Incremental correction factor to induced power χ	0.1
Weight of UAV W	5∼50 Newton
Available energy of UAV E	100∼500 Wh
Φ, Noise power σ^2	-160 dBm/Hz, -174 dBm/Hz
V_{UD}, $\tilde{\kappa}_U$, $\tilde{\kappa}_D$	1 m/s, 1.2, 0.8
a, b, R_{CCD}, f	0.5, 1.2, 25 mm, 105 mm
r_{way}, h_{max}, v_{max}	20 m, 1000 m, 30 m/s
$t_i, i = 1, 2, \ldots, N$	0∼30 s
$M_j, j = 1, 2, \ldots, N$	1∼100

To comprehensively demonstrate the path planning efficiency and planning effectiveness of the proposed DIPH method, the following five additional methods are adopted for performance comparison:

- GA, the genetic algorithm [11], in the simulation, we set the three parameters of cruising altitude, cruising speed, and hovering altitude as gene sequences and solve them with objective (6a) as the optimization value.

- DQN, method based on deep Q-network [25], this paper takes the parameters of the UAV and patrol points as the state inputs of the method, and takes the patrol altitude, patrol speed, and hovering altitude as the model's actions step by step. The model is trained with the patrol quality as the reward.
- FH, the DIPH method with fixed height, on the basis of using the DIPH method to obtain the various cruising heights and hovering heights of the UAV, this method directly takes the maximum value of all heights as the cruising and hovering heights.
- RanG, method of randomly generating relevant parameters, this method randomly generates the three types of parameters for the UAV within the feasible range.
- TA, the traversal method, this method determines all possible combination solutions through traversal, and selects the solution that can achieve target (6a) as the output of the method.

4.2. Performance and Analysis

We first verify the energy consumption of the drone and the quality of the patrol process under different patrol points using the method proposed in this paper. Figure 4 shows the results. We set $W = 10$ Newton, $E = 400$ Wh, and the number of inspection targets and corresponding inspection time are fixed in the current simulation. For ease of presentation, we have normalized the two performance values. As can be seen, the energy consumption and inspection effectiveness of the UAV gradually improve with the increase in inspection points. This is because the increase in the number of patrol points means that there are more adjustments to the cruising altitude of the drone, which requires additional energy consumption. However, this adjustment process is beneficial for improving the cruising quality of the drone, as the patrol route that matches the shape of the highway and the patrol height that matches the highway section can improve the inspection effect in terms of inspection field of view and return signal quality.

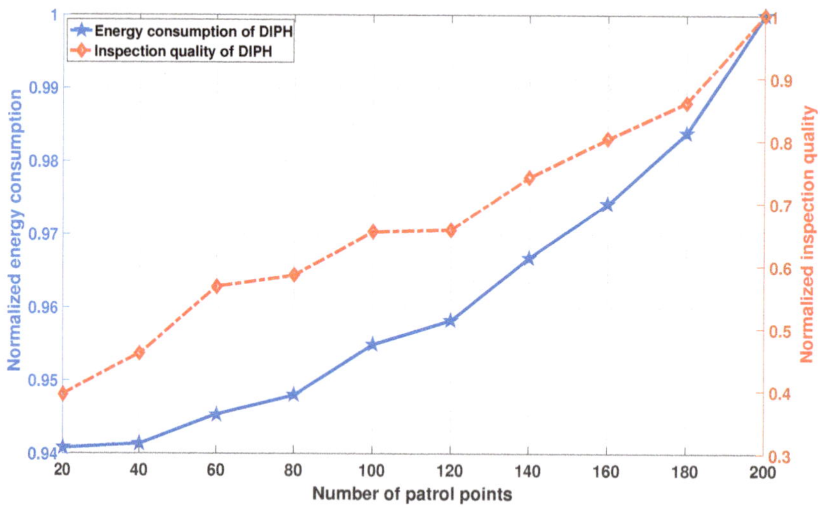

Figure 4. Energy consumption and inspection effectiveness of the proposed DIPH method under changes in inspection points.

Secondly, the planning performance of each comparison method under different number of patrol points is shown in Figure 5. We set $W = 10$ Newton and $E = 500$ Wh, which ensures that the energy required for the drone inspection process is sufficient. The number of inspection targets and corresponding inspection time are fixed in the current simulation. We can observe that all six methods increase with the number of patrol points, which is attributed to the gradual improvement of shooting results achieved by drone mounted camera. GA and DQN methods have some interleaving in performance, but overall, GA performs better than DQN. The TA method performs best among all methods because it compares all possible solutions. Compared to the highly complex TA method, although there is a significant gap, the DIPH method proposed in this paper has better performance than the other four methods.

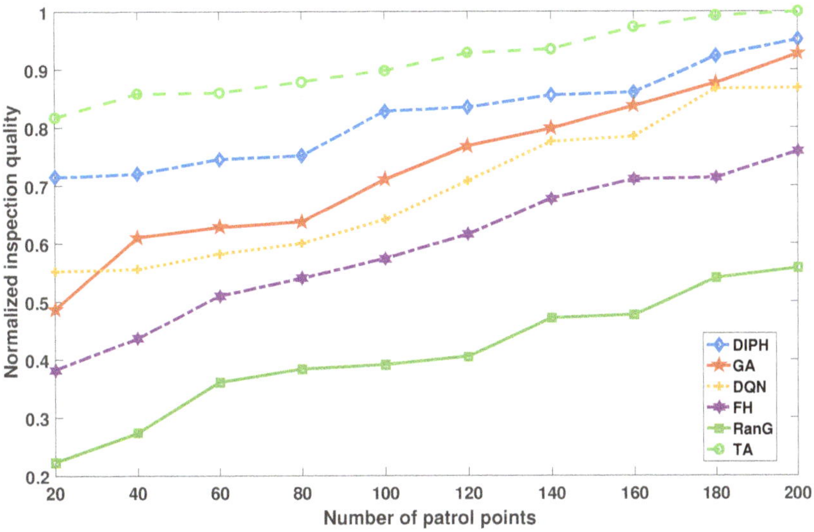

Figure 5. Planning performance of various comparison methods under different number of patrol points.

We then compare and verify the performance of six methods under the condition of changes in available energy of the UAV, and the results are shown in Figure 6. We set $W = 10$ Newton, and the number of patrol points is set as 50. The number of inspection targets and corresponding inspection time are fixed in the current simulation. A value of 0 for inspection quality means that the current method cannot obtain a valid solution. It can be seen that when the available energy of the UAV is low, FH method and RanG method cannot obtain feasible solutions, this is because the flight altitude of the FH method is too high, making the required energy higher than the available energy of the drone, while the RanG method cannot obtain a feasible solution under harsh conditions due to the randomness of solution selection. An interesting phenomenon can be seen from Figure 6, which is that when the energy of the UAV exceeds 200 Wh, the FH method is feasible, and as the energy increases, the inspection effect of this method remains fixed. This is because the results of the FH method do not change with the energy of the UAV, and the output solution is a fixed value. Meanwhile, we can conclude from the figure that the overall ranking of the performance of the six methods is successively TA, DIPH, GA, DQN, FH and RanG.

Fourthly, we validate the performance of the methods in response to changes in drone weight, and the results are illustrated in Figure 7. We set $E = 400$ Wh, and the number of patrol points is set as 60. The number of inspection targets and corresponding inspection time are fixed in the current simulation. It can be observed that except for the FH method with special characteristics, the inspection quality of other methods gradually decreases with the increase in UAV weight. Due to the fact that the fixed flight altitude selected by the FH method does not change with the weight of the drone, the inspection quality of this method remains constant during the initial increase in UAV weight, and in the later stages of increase, the planning becomes ineffective due to insufficient available energy. Among the remaining five methods, the DIPH method proposed in this paper is second only to the TA method in terms of performance, and sequentially superior to GA, DQN, and RanG methods.

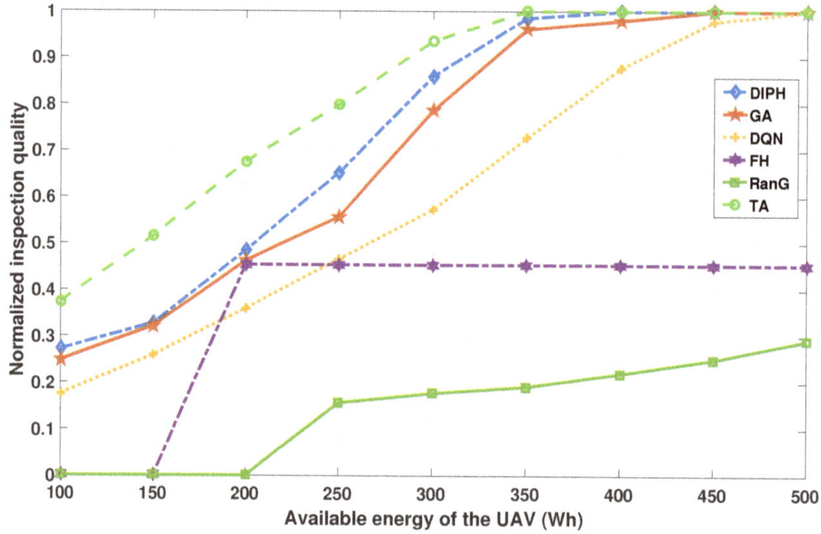

Figure 6. Performance of the method under the condition of changes in available energy of the UAV.

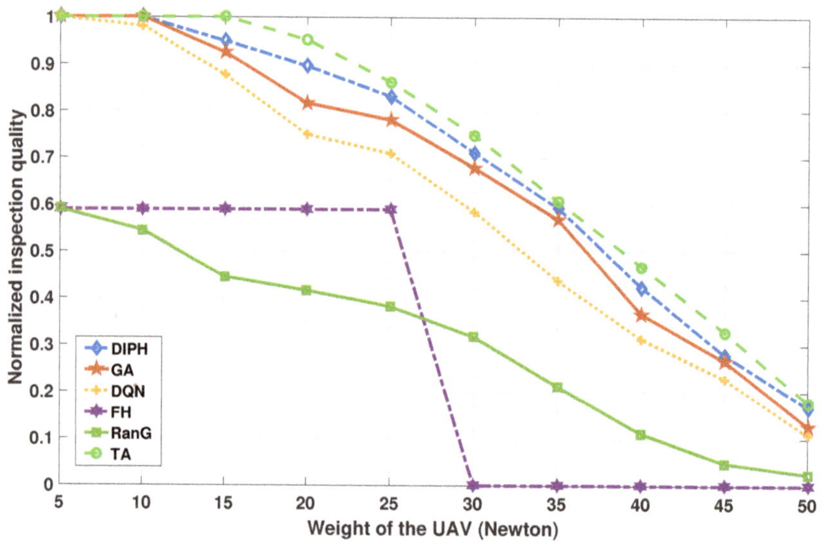

Figure 7. The inspection quality of methods under changes in drone weight.

We finally summarize the time consumption of each method in Table 2. It should be noted that the DQN method requires pre-training of the model, therefore it requires training time. Although the training process can be carried out before the DQN method is applied, compared to methods that do not require training, this time cannot be directly ignored. From the table, we can see that among the six methods, the TA method takes the longest time, surpassing the DIPH method by 5000 times, and this is unacceptable in certain situations (such as the need to dispatch the UAV for emergency patrols in a timely manner). The average time spent on DIPH, GA, FH, and RanG is 15.7 ms, 2168.2 ms,

10.5 ms, and 1.2 ms, respectively. It can be considered that the DIPH method does not have disadvantages compared to other methods in terms of computational efficiency.

Table 2. Time consumed by methods.

Method	Average Execution Time
DIPH	15.7 ms
GA	2168.2 ms
DQN	3.6 ms (Average training time: 52,815.1 ms)
FH	10.5 ms
RanG	1.2 ms
TA	89,436.7 ms

4.3. Discussion

In order to clearly observe the performance of the methods, this paper sorts and summarizes the performance of the methods in Table 3. Due to the long training time required, the DQN method is not taken into account in the efficiency entry therein. It can be seen that the DIPH proposed in this paper ranks third in terms of operational efficiency, and its performance in other aspects is only second to the TA method which has very low operational efficiency and cannot be used in practical scenarios. Taking into account the overall performance (i.e., inspection quality and execution efficiency) of methods, we can conclude that the DIPH method proposed in this paper has better performance compared to other methods.

Table 3. Summary of methods' performance.

Performance Category	Performance Sorting
Inspection quality vs. Number of inspection points	TA > DIPH > GA > DQN > FH > RanG
Inspection quality vs. Available energy of the UAV	TA > DIPH > GA > DQN > FH > RanG
Inspection quality vs. Weight of the UAV	TA > DIPH > GA > DQN > FH ≈ RanG
Operational efficiency	RanG > FH > DIPH ≫ GA ≫ TA

5. Conclusions

This paper considered the path planning problem of unmanned aerial vehicles for highway scenarios. In response to the mismatch between the drone patrol path and the shape of the highway, as well as the urgent need to improve the quality of drone inspection, this paper proposed an efficient path planning method for the unmanned aerial vehicle, aiming to improve the quality of the UAV inspection process by quickly setting parameters including the UAV's inspection altitudes, suspension altitudes towards inspection targets, and inspection speeds. The simulation results with multiple feasible comparison methods indicate that the proposed method has advantages in terms of overall performance of operational efficiency and planning effectiveness.

Author Contributions: Conceptualization, Y.L. and P.Z.; investigation, S.G. and X.L.; methodology, P.Z. and X.L.; project administration, P.Z. and H.L.; validation, S.G., Y.L. and H.L.; writing—original draft, Y.L. and P.Z.; writing—review and editing, S.G. and X.L. All authors have read and agreed to the published version of the manuscript.

Funding: This work was supported in part by 2023 Guizhou Provincial Science and Technology Support Plan Project (No. 282), in part by the Fundamental Research Funds for the Central Universities (No. 328202206, No. 328202232 and No. 3282023034), the Beijing Natural Science Foundation (No. L192002), and in part by the "Advanced and sophisticated" discipline construction project of universities in Beijing (No. 20210013Z0401), the China National Key R&D Program (No. 2020YF-B1808000).

Data Availability Statement: Not applicable.

Conflicts of Interest: The authors declare no conflict of interest.

Abbreviations

The following abbreviations are used in this manuscript:

IoT	Internet of Things
DRL	deep reinforcement learning
DQN	deep Q-Network
UAV	unmanned aerial vehicle
AI	artificial intelligence
LOS	line of sight
NLOS	non line of sight
DIPH	drone inspection planning for highways
GIS	geographic information system
PSO	particle swarm optimization
GA	genetic algorithm
LSTM	long short-term memory
CNN	convolutional neural networks

References

1. McEnroe, P.; Wang, S.; Liyanage, M. A Survey on the Convergence of Edge Computing and AI for UAVs: Opportunities and Challenges. *IEEE Internet Things J.* **2022**, *9*, 15435–15459. [CrossRef]
2. Lyu, M.; Zhao, Y.; Huang, C.; Huang, H. Unmanned Aerial Vehicles for Search and Rescue: A Survey. *Remote Sens.* **2023**, *15*, 3266. [CrossRef]
3. Mugnai, M.; Teppati Losé, M.; Herrera-Alarcón, E.P.; Baris, G.; Satler, M.; Avizzano, C.A. An Efficient Framework for Autonomous UAV Missions in Partially-Unknown GNSS-Denied Environments. *Drones* **2023**, *7*, 471. [CrossRef]
4. Zhou, Y.; Rao, B.; Wang, W. UAV Swarm Intelligence: Recent Advances and Future Trends. *IEEE Access* **2020**, *8*, 183856–183878. [CrossRef]
5. Motlagh, N.H.; Bagaa, M.; Taleb, T. Energy and Delay Aware Task Assignment Mechanism for UAV-Based IoT Platform. *IEEE Internet Things J.* **2019**, *6*, 6523–6536. [CrossRef]
6. Zhao, Y.; Yan, L.; Dai, J.; Hu, X.; Wei, P.; Xie, H. Robust Planning System for Fast Autonomous Flight in Complex Unknown Environment Using Sparse Directed Frontier Points. *Drones* **2023**, *7*, 219. [CrossRef]
7. Baek, D.; Chen, Y.; Bocca, A.; Bottaccioli, L.; Di Cataldo, S.; Gatteschi, V.; Pagliari, D.J.; Patti, E.; Urgese, G.; Chang, N.; et al. Battery-Aware Operation Range Estimation for Terrestrial and Aerial Electric Vehicles. *IEEE Trans. Veh. Technol.* **2019**, *68*, 5471–5482. [CrossRef]
8. Piao, S.; Ba, Z.; Su, L.; Koutsonikolas, D.; Li, S.; Ren, K. Automating CSI Measurement with UAVs: From Problem Formulation to Energy-Optimal Solution. In Proceedings of the IEEE INFOCOM 2019—IEEE Conference on Computer Communications, Paris, France, 29 April–2 May 2019; pp. 2404–2412. [CrossRef]
9. Krajewski, R.; Moers, T.; Bock, J.; Vater, L.; Eckstein, L. The rounD Dataset: A Drone Dataset of Road User Trajectories at Roundabouts in Germany. In Proceedings of the 2020 IEEE 23rd International Conference on Intelligent Transportation Systems (ITSC), Rhodes, Greece, 20–23 September 2020; pp. 1–6. [CrossRef]
10. Liu, H.; Chen, Q.; Pan, N.; Sun, Y.; An, Y.; Pan, D. UAV Stocktaking Task-Planning for Industrial Warehouses Based on the Improved Hybrid Differential Evolution Algorithm. *IEEE Trans. Ind. Inform.* **2022**, *18*, 582–591. [CrossRef]
11. Shivgan, R.; Dong, Z. Energy-Efficient Drone Coverage Path Planning using Genetic Algorithm. In Proceedings of the 2020 IEEE 21st International Conference on High Performance Switching and Routing (HPSR), Newark, NJ, USA,11–14 May 2020; pp. 1–6. [CrossRef]
12. Gubán, M.; Udvaros, J. A Path Planning Model with a Genetic Algorithm for Stock Inventory Using a Swarm of Drones. *Drones* **2022**, *6*, 364. [CrossRef]
13. Xiong, T.; Liu, F.; Liu, H.; Ge, J.; Li, H.; Ding, K.; Li, Q. Multi-Drone Optimal Mission Assignment and 3D Path Planning for Disaster Rescue. *Drones* **2023**, *7*, 394. [CrossRef]

14. Wu, Y.; Wu, S.; Hu, X. Cooperative Path Planning of UAVs & UGVs for a Persistent Surveillance Task in Urban Environments. *IEEE Internet Things J.* **2021**, *8*, 4906–4919. [CrossRef]
15. Duan, T.; Wang, W.; Wang, T.; Huang, M.; Zhou, X. A Task Planning Method for UAV Swarm Dynamic Reconstruction Based on a Fourth-Order Motif. *Electronics* **2023**, *12*, 692. [CrossRef]
16. Siemiatkowska, B.; Stecz, W. A Framework for Planning and Execution of Drone Swarm Missions in a Hostile Environment. *Sensors* **2021**, *21*, 4150. [CrossRef] [PubMed]
17. Kuru, K.; Ansell, D.; Khan, W.; Yetgin, H. Analysis and Optimization of Unmanned Aerial Vehicle Swarms in Logistics: An Intelligent Delivery Platform. *IEEE Access* **2019**, *7*, 15804–15831. [CrossRef]
18. Luis, C.E.; Vukosavljev, M.; Schoellig, A.P. Online Trajectory Generation with Distributed Model Predictive Control for Multi-Robot Motion Planning. *IEEE Robot. Autom. Lett.* **2020**, *5*, 604–611. [CrossRef]
19. Pant, Y.V.; Abbas, H.; Quaye, R.A.; Mangharam, R. Fly-by-Logic: Control of Multi-Drone Fleets with Temporal Logic Objectives. In Proceedings of the 2018 ACM/IEEE 9th International Conference on Cyber-Physical Systems (ICCPS), Porto, Portugal, 11–13 April 2018; pp. 186–197. [CrossRef]
20. Vasquez-Gomez, J.I.; Herrera-Lozada, J.-C.; Olguin-Carbajal, M. Coverage Path Planning for Surveying Disjoint Areas. In Proceedings of the 2018 International Conference on Unmanned Aircraft Systems (ICUAS), Dallas, TX, USA, 12–15 June 2018; pp. 899–904. [CrossRef]
21. Lee, M.-T.; Chuang, M.-L.; Kuo, S.-T.; Chen, Y.-R. UAV Swarm Real-Time Rerouting by Edge Computing D* Lite Algorithm. *Appl. Sci.* **2022**, *12*, 1056. [CrossRef]
22. Zhu, P.; Fang, X. Multi-UAV Cooperative Task Assignment Based on Half Random Q-Learning. *Symmetry* **2021**, *13*, 2417. [CrossRef]
23. Piao, C.; Liu, C.H. Energy-Efficient Mobile Crowdsensing by Unmanned Vehicles: A Sequential Deep Reinforcement Learning Approach. *IEEE Internet Things J.* **2020**, *7*, 6312–6324. [CrossRef]
24. Tu, G.-T.; Juang, J.-G. UAV Path Planning and Obstacle Avoidance Based on Reinforcement Learning in 3D Environments. *Actuators* **2023**, *12*, 57. [CrossRef]
25. Bayerlein, H.; Theile, M.; Caccamo, M.; Gesbert, D. UAV Path Planning for Wireless Data Harvesting: A Deep Reinforcement Learning Approach. In Proceedings of the GLOBECOM 2020—2020 IEEE Global Communications Conference, Taipei, Taiwan, 7–11 December 2020; pp. 1–6. [CrossRef]
26. Maciel-Pearson, B.G.; Akçay, S.; Atapour-Abarghouei, A.; Holder, C.; Breckon, T.P. Multi-Task Regression-Based Learning for Autonomous Unmanned Aerial Vehicle Flight Control Within Unstructured Outdoor Environments. *IEEE Robot. Autom. Lett.* **2019**, *4*, 4116–4123. [CrossRef]
27. Majd, A.; Ashraf, A.; Troubitsyna, E.; Daneshtalab, M. Integrating Learning, Optimization, and Prediction for Efficient Navigation of Swarms of Drones. In Proceedings of the 2018 26th Euromicro International Conference on Parallel, Distributed and Network-based Processing (PDP), Cambridge, UK, 21–23 March 2018; pp. 101–108. [CrossRef]
28. Loquercio, A.; Maqueda, A.I.; del-Blanco, C.R.; Scaramuzza, D. DroNet: Learning to Fly by Driving. *IEEE Robot. Autom. Lett.* **2018**, *3*, 1088–1095. [CrossRef]
29. Liu, C.H.; Ma, X.; Gao, X.; Tang, J. Distributed Energy-Efficient Multi-UAV Navigation for Long-Term Communication Coverage by Deep Reinforcement Learning. *IEEE Trans. Mob. Comput.* **2020**, *19*, 1274–1285. [CrossRef]
30. Benkhoui, Y.; Korchi, T.E.; Reinhold, L. UAS-Based Crack Detection Using Stereo Cameras: A Comparative Study. In Proceedings of the 2019 International Conference on Unmanned Aircraft Systems (ICUAS), Atlanta, GA, USA, 11–14 June 2019; pp. 1031–1035. [CrossRef]
31. Yang, L.; Li, B.; Li, W.; Brand, H.; Jiang, B.; Xiao, J. Concrete defects inspection and 3D mapping using CityFlyer quadrotor robot. *IEEE/CAA J. Autom. Sin.* **2020**, *7*, 991–1002. [CrossRef]
32. Al-Hourani, A.; Kandeepan, S.; Lardner, S. Optimal LAP Altitude for Maximum Coverage. *IEEE Wirel. Commun. Lett.* **2014**, *3*, 569–572. [CrossRef]
33. Zeng, Y.; Zhang, R. Energy-Efficient UAV Communication With Trajectory Optimization. *IEEE Trans. Wirel. Commun.* **2017**, *16*, 3747–3760. [CrossRef]
34. Yang, D.; Wu, Q.; Zeng, Y.; Zhang, R. Energy Tradeoff in Ground-to-UAV Communication via Trajectory Design. *IEEE Trans. Veh. Technol.* **2018**, *67*, 6721–6726. [CrossRef]

electronics

MDPI

Article

Research on Distributed Smart Home Energy Management Strategies Based on Non-Intrusive Load Monitoring (NILM)

Siqi Liu *, Zhiyuan Xie and Zhengwei Hu

School of Electrical and Electronic Engineering, North China Electric Power University, Beijing 102206, China; zhiyuanxie@ncepu.edu.cn (Z.X.); hzwwizard@ncepu.edu.cn (Z.H.)
* Correspondence: liusiqi@ncepu.edu.cn

Abstract: Home energy optimization management improves energy utilization efficiency and reduces electricity costs through intelligent load control, strategic utilization of time-of-use pricing, and optimized integration of energy storage and distributed energy systems. Simultaneously, it enhances energy autonomy, lowers carbon emissions, and promotes sustainable low-carbon lifestyles. By coordinating demand response programs with flexible load scheduling strategies, this approach effectively reduces peak loads and improves grid stability, thereby advancing smart grid development. This paper investigates the optimized scheduling problem in smart home energy management systems, focusing on achieving integrated optimization of multiple factors, including load balancing, cost control, carbon emission reduction, user comfort, and demand response. Considering the diverse load characteristics of residential energy systems, we propose a novel optimization framework incorporating dynamic pricing mechanisms and intelligent scheduling algorithms, which is rigorously validated through simulation experiments. Results demonstrate that the proposed scheduling strategy successfully balances economic efficiency, load management, and environmental sustainability while maintaining acceptable user comfort levels—providing a comprehensive solution for intelligent home energy management systems.

Keywords: home energy management; load balancing; cost control; carbon emissions; user comfort

1. Introduction

As global energy shortages and environmental pollution issues become increasingly severe, the efficient use of energy has become a focal point of societal concern. Smart home energy management (SHEM), as a critical component of smart energy systems, aims to utilize advanced technological means to achieve optimized scheduling of residential energy resources, improve energy utilization efficiency, reduce user electricity costs, and promote renewable energy integration. In recent years, with advancements in the Internet of Things (IoT), artificial intelligence (AI), and big data analytics, SHEM has emerged as a prominent research frontier [1].

SHEM employs intelligent scheduling technologies to optimize the control of household electrical devices, energy storage systems, renewable energy generation units (e.g., photovoltaics and wind turbines), and distributed energy systems, thereby improving energy efficiency, lowering electricity expenses, and enhancing energy autonomy. Its core mechanism involves rational allocation and dynamic adjustment of residential energy flows through time-of-use pricing, demand response programs, and intelligent control strategies [2]. This optimization framework not only reduces user energy expenditures and improves comfort but also facilitates renewable energy adoption, minimizes carbon emissions, and fosters sustainable low-carbon lifestyles. Furthermore, it supports power grid stability by flattening demand peaks and adapting to grid requirements, advancing the development of smart grids and integrated energy systems.

In recent years, global researchers have extensively explored smart home energy management strategies, focusing primarily on optimization algorithm-based scheduling, artificial intelligence/machine learning applications, and demand response mechanisms. Numerous studies leverage mixed-integer linear programming (MILP) [3], heuristic algorithms (e.g., genetic algorithms [4], particle swarm optimization [5], and ant colony algorithms [6]), and hybrid optimization methods [7,8] to optimize household energy distribution and maximize renewable energy utilization. These algorithms provide optimal solutions for complex scheduling problems, effectively reducing energy waste and enhancing grid efficiency. Researchers have further proposed enhanced heuristic approaches [9] and game-theoretic models [10] to improve the economic efficiency of residential energy use. Notably, intelligent scheduling strategies aligned with peak/off-peak pricing guide users to shift high-energy activities to low-cost periods, significantly reducing overall electricity expenditures.

Artificial intelligence techniques enable precise energy management solutions through deep learning and historical data analysis, enhancing system adaptability in dynamic environments. With advancements in reinforcement learning, these methods are increasingly integrated into home energy management. For instance, Wei et al. [11] applied deep reinforcement learning to optimize energy allocation, while Ye et al. [12] developed a long short-term memory (LSTM)-based load forecasting model to improve scheduling accuracy. Ma et al. [13] proposed a Markov decision process (MDP)-driven strategy accounting for user behavior uncertainty and price fluctuations, achieving intelligent device scheduling. Research on distributed renewable energy integration has also investigated coordinated scheduling of photovoltaics, energy storage, and electric vehicles in SHEM systems to maximize renewable utilization [3].

Scholars have examined user participation mechanisms in electricity markets, including real-time pricing (RTP) and incentive-based demand-side management strategies. Navesi et al. [14] analyzed demand response strategies under RTP to enhance smart distribution network reliability, demonstrating how dynamic pricing guides consumption pattern adjustments for grid stability and economic efficiency. Hu et al. [15] designed a reinforcement learning-driven incentive model addressing demand-side coupling factors (e.g., inter-load correlations) to optimize management efficiency. Dey et al. [16] developed a microgrid-focused incentive scheme integrating carbon emissions, renewable penetration, and economic constraints, evaluating various strategies' operational impacts. These studies confirm that tailored pricing and incentive mechanisms effectively reshape household consumption patterns, optimizing grid load distribution and energy efficiency.

Amid global efforts toward climate change mitigation, "carbon neutrality" and "peak carbon" have become central objectives in energy transitions. As a vital element of smart energy ecosystems, SHEM plays a pivotal role in carbon reduction and efficiency enhancement. By integrating distributed energy resources (e.g., photovoltaics, energy storage, and EVs) via intelligent scheduling algorithms, SHEM reduces fossil fuel dependence and enables low-carbon smart energy consumption. Ikram A. I. et al. [17] proposed a load scheduling strategy balancing user demand and price fluctuations to minimize peak consumption. Akram A. et al. [18] combined machine learning with SHEM to predict consumption patterns and optimize scheduling for cost and emission reduction. Youssef H. et al. [19] employed an enhanced Northern Goshawk Optimizer (NGO) to jointly optimize comfort, energy costs, and renewable utilization, while Youssef H. et al. [20] developed a modified bald eagle search (BES) algorithm for dynamic pricing-constrained energy scheduling.

In summary, significant progress has been made in smart home energy management research, with optimization algorithms, AI, and demand response strategies forming core research pillars. However, as residential energy demands diversify, achieving multi-objective coordination among load balancing, cost control, carbon reduction, user comfort, and demand response remains challenging. Developing advanced scheduling strategies is essential for improving energy efficiency, user experience, grid stability, and renewable energy integration.

MILP has become a cornerstone of residential energy scheduling due to its ability to handle discrete variables (e.g., device on/off states) and continuous variables (e.g., power allocation). With advantages in global optimality, rigorous constraint modeling, and transparent decision logic, MILP outperforms deep learning's opacity and heuristic algorithms' approximations, providing verifiable solutions for small-to-medium-scale problems. The branch and bound (B&B) method systematically identifies global optima by decomposing solution spaces and iteratively narrowing feasible regions. However, B&B suffers from exponential complexity, slow bound convergence, and high computational costs. In contrast, genetic algorithms (GA) enhance MILP-solving efficiency through dynamic feasible solution generation and global search optimization. This paper proposes a hybrid genetic branch and bound algorithm that embeds GA within B&B to rapidly generate integer-feasible solutions, update bounds, and accelerate pruning. This approach addresses the co-optimization of load balancing, cost control, carbon emissions, user comfort, and demand response in household energy management. For the convenience, we have listed all abbreviations used in the paper in Table 1.

Table 1. All abbreviations used in the paper.

Abbreviations	Meanings
SHEM	Smart home energy management
NILM	Non-intrusive load monitoring
AI	Artificial intelligence
IoT	Internet of Things
MILP	Mixed-integer linear programming
GA	Genetic algorithm
DR	Demand response
TOU	Time-of-use pricing
SOC	State of charge
PV	Photovoltaic
RTP	Real-time pricing
EV	Electric vehicle
B&B	Branch and bound
LP	Linear programming
MDP	Markov decision process
LSTM	Long short-term memory
HVAC	Heating, ventilation, and air conditioning
CNY	Chinese yuan

2. Smart Home Energy Management

2.1. Home Energy Management

Home energy management refers to the coordinated control and optimization of residential energy devices through advanced scheduling technologies, aiming to maximize efficiency, minimize costs, and promote renewable energy utilization. With the advancement of distributed energy systems, smart grids, and IoT infrastructure, SHEM has evolved into a critical component of modern intelligent households.

As illustrated in Figure 1, a typical SHEM system comprises smart meters, energy management controllers, renewable energy generation units (e.g., photovoltaic panels and wind turbines), energy storage systems (e.g., batteries), and smart appliances. By integrating real-time data collection and intelligent scheduling algorithms, SHEM dynamically monitors energy consumption, forecasts load demands, and generates optimal energy allocation plans based on grid pricing signals, user preferences, and environmental conditions. For instance, during periods of low electricity prices or high renewable energy availability, SHEM prioritizes local power generation and stored energy usage. Conversely, it suppresses high-power device operation during peak pricing intervals to reduce energy expenditures.

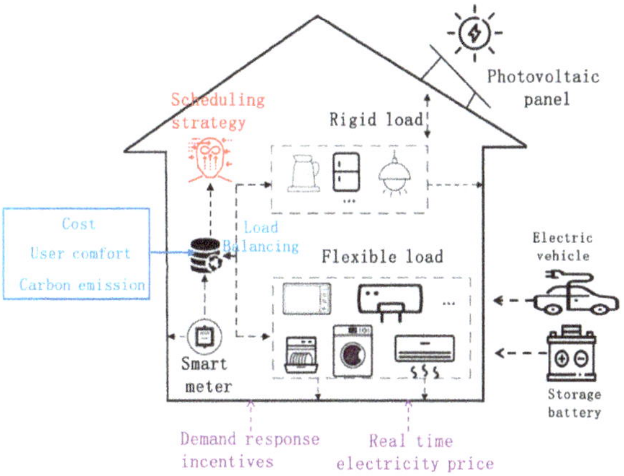

Figure 1. Schematic diagram of the SHEM system.

The core objectives of home energy management include load balancing, cost optimization, carbon reduction, and user comfort preservation. Load balancing involves rational scheduling of appliances and storage systems to avoid grid stress caused by excessive peak demand. Cost optimization focuses on strategic energy procurement and usage to minimize household expenses. Carbon reduction is achieved by increasing renewable energy penetration and decreasing fossil fuel reliance, while user comfort ensures that energy-saving measures do not compromise basic living standards—such as maintaining thermal comfort, adequate lighting, and habitual appliance usage patterns.

2.2. Household Load Model

In home energy management, rigid loads refer to appliances that must operate and cannot be easily adjusted or reduced, such as lighting, refrigerators, and medical devices. These loads have low scheduling flexibility and typically form the household's baseline electricity demand. Their operating times are nearly fixed since they are essential for users. The modeling of rigid loads usually considers factors such as time dimensions, power characteristics, and uncertainty. For loads with relatively stable power demand and operating times, such as refrigerators and lighting, a common mathematical expression is

$$P_{rigid}(t) = P_{rated}(t) \tag{1}$$

where $P_{rigid}(t)$ represents the power of the rigid load at time t and $P_{rated}(t)$ is the rated power of the load at time t.

Flexible loads can be scheduled and adjusted within a certain range based on grid demand or economic incentives. Unlike rigid loads, flexible loads can be shifted in time or have their operational power reduced according to scheduling strategies to optimize overall energy use. Based on load scheduling, flexible loads can be classified into three categories: power-adjustable loads, time-adjustable loads, and power-time adjustable loads.

- Power-adjustable load: These loads have adjustable power output through step control, such as air conditioners, water heaters, and lighting. The energy consumption of these devices can be controlled by adjusting their power levels. The model is expressed as

$$P_{adjustable}(t) = P_i \tag{2}$$

where $P_{adjustable}(t)$ is the power-adjustable load at time t, P_i is the power value for the i-th power level, and t represents a specific moment.

- Time-adjustable load: These loads, such as washing machines and dishwashers, can have their operating times adjusted. Once started, they must complete their entire work cycle without interruption. The model is

$$P_{adjustable}(t) = \left\{ \begin{matrix} P_{rated}(t), & t \in \left((n-1) * T_{cycle}, n * T_{cycle}\right) \\ & 0 \end{matrix} \right\}, \tag{3}$$

where $P_{rated}(t)$ is the rated power of the load at time t and T_{cycle} is the operating cycle of the equipment.

- Power-time adjustable load: Power-time loads are time-variable and interruptible loads, such as electric vehicles and other new energy transportation tools. Due to their flexible adjustability, they are a primary target for demand-side response scheduling. In a sense, they can be considered a form of energy storage without the discharge process. Power-time loads can be modeled using a power-time function, where both the power and time of operation are adjustable and can be interrupted within a certain time period. Charging an electric vehicle or a battery is a common example, where the charging power can be adjusted or interrupted during a time period, and the charging process is considered a variable time window. The model can be expressed as follows:

$$P_{flexible}(t) = \left\{ \begin{matrix} P_{rated}(t), & t \in (T_{start}, T_{end}) \\ & 0 \end{matrix} \right\}, \tag{4}$$

where $P_{flexible}(t)$ is the power-time adjustable load at time t, $P_{rated}(t)$ is the rated power of the load, T_{cycle} is the operating cycle of the equipment, and T_{start} and T_{end} are the start time and end time, respectively.

Batteries, as the most common power-time adjustable load, can be modeled as [21]

$$\begin{aligned}
&SOC(t) = C_{net}(t)/C_{bat} \\
&SOC(t+1) = SOC(t) + P_{ch}(t)\cdot\Delta t\cdot\eta_{ch}/C_{bat} \\
&SOC(t+1) = SOC(t) - P_{disch}(t)\cdot\Delta t/(C_{bat}\cdot\eta_{disch}) \\
&0 \le P_{ch}(t) \le P_{ch,max} \\
&0 \le P_{disch}(t) \le P_{disch,max} \\
&SOC_{min} \le SOC(t) \le SOC_{max} \\
&P_{ch}(t)\cdot P_{disch}(t) = 0
\end{aligned} \tag{5}$$

where $SOC(t)$ represents the state of charge of the battery at time t; $C_{net}(t)$ and C_{bat} represent the remaining energy and rated capacity of the battery at time t; P_{ch} and P_{disch} represent the charging and discharging power, respectively; η_{ch} and η_{disch} are the charging and discharging efficiencies; $P_{ch,max}$ and $P_{disch,max}$ are the maximum charging and discharging powers, respectively; and SOC_{max} is the maximum state of charge.

- Temperature-controlled adjustable load: These are loads whose operation is influenced by temperature constraints, with their operating status depending on indoor and outdoor temperatures, set temperature values, and the thermal properties of the building. The indoor temperature setting is determined based on user demand within a given time period. When required, the indoor temperature should remain within the upper and lower bounds of the specified value. The mathematical model for air conditioners and water heaters is typically represented by a discrete thermal dynamic model as shown:

$$T_{in}(t+1) = e^{-\Delta t/RC_{room}}T_{\text{in}}(t) + R\cdot(e^{-\Delta t/RC_{room}} - 1)\cdot P_{\text{AC}} + (1 - e^{-\Delta t/RC_{room}})\cdot T_{\text{out}}(t), \tag{6}$$

where $T_{in}(t)$ is the indoor temperature at time t, R is the room thermal resistance (°C/kW), C_{room} is the room thermal capacity (kWh/°C), $P_{rated}(t)$ is the rated power of the air conditioner or water heater, and $T_{out}(t)$ is the outdoor temperature at time t.

2.3. DR Incentives

DR is a load management strategy in power systems that encourages users to adjust their electricity consumption behavior during high load periods or when electricity prices are high in order to improve the stability and economy of the power system. To attract users to participate in demand response, economic incentives are usually designed to provide subsidies to users. Economic incentives mainly encourage users to adjust their consumption behavior through price signals or direct compensation.

- Time-of-Use Pricing

The time-of-use (TOU) pricing mechanism encourages users to consume electricity when prices are lower and reduce consumption when prices are higher, based on fluctuations in the electricity market. Different electricity rates are set according to the load conditions at different times of the day, typically categorized into peak, mid-peak, and off-peak periods. During extreme peak load periods, temporary price increases incentivize users to reduce electricity consumption.

- DR Compensation

DR compensation is an economic reward provided by grid operators or power supply companies to users participating in DR programs. It encourages users to adjust their electricity consumption behavior during peak periods to enhance grid stability and improve energy utilization efficiency. DR compensation can be implemented through load reduction rewards and load shift compensation. Users receive compensation based on the amount of load they reduce during DR events, incentivizing electricity consumption during off-peak periods and providing corresponding subsidies.

In home energy management, to encourage users to adjust consumption during off-peak hours, a dynamic incentive subsidy mechanism is employed, adjusting the incentive based on real-time electricity prices. Specifically, when the electricity price is below 0.3 CNY/kWh (off-peak period), the subsidy is issued at twice the base rate; when the price is above 0.6 CNY/kWh (peak period), no subsidy is issued; during the intermediate periods, the base subsidy is issued. 1 CNY ≈ 0.14 USD. The total *incentive*(*t*) subsidy for period *t* is calculated as

$$incentive(t) = \begin{cases} m(t) \times incentive\_rate \times 2, & Low\ valley\ period \\ m(t) \times incentive\_rate, & Off\ peak\ period \\ 0, & Peak\ hours \end{cases} \tag{7}$$

where *m(t)* represents the adjustment amount or response scale for period t and *incentive_rate* is the base incentive rate. The total incentive subsidy is the sum of the incentives for all periods.

$$T = \sum_{t=1}^{N} incentive(t). \tag{8}$$

2.4. *User Comfort*

In home energy management, user comfort refers to the level of electricity consumption adjustment that users can tolerate when accepting optimized scheduling or DR without significantly affecting their quality of life and satisfaction. Comfort is a subjective metric that typically involves factors such as temperature, appliance usage habits, tolerance for delays, and lifestyle impacts. Proper comfort modeling ensures user satisfaction while achieving energy-saving optimization. User comfort generally falls into two categories: time comfort and temperature comfort.

- Time Comfort

Time comfort refers to the extent to which the operating time of home appliances aligns with the user's expectations. For example, a user may prefer the washing machine to operate between 8:00 and 10:00 p.m., but if the system schedules it at 7:00 or 11:00 p.m., the user may be dissatisfied. Similarly, an electric vehicle owner may expect the vehicle to be fully charged between 12:00 AM and 6:00 a.m. If the system schedules charging between 6:00 and 8:00 a.m., it could disrupt the user's travel plans. To quantify time comfort, the user's expected time window is defined, and a time deviation metric is introduced

$$\begin{aligned} U^i_{\text{time}}(t) &= 1 - \frac{|T_{\text{start}} - T_{\text{opt}}|}{T_{\text{max}} - T_{\text{min}}}, \\ U_{time}(t) &= \frac{\sum_{i=0}^{M} U^i_{time}(t)}{M}, \end{aligned} \tag{9}$$

where M is the number of devices, T_{start} is the actual start time of the device, and T_{opt} is the user's preferred start time. $[T_{min}, T_{max}]$ is the acceptable time window.

- Temperature Comfort

Temperature comfort refers to the user's satisfaction with indoor temperatures, which are typically regulated by HVAC systems (e.g., air conditioners and heaters). Key influencing factors include the target temperature and acceptable temperature fluctuations. A comfortable temperature range is defined, within which the user feels comfortable. If the indoor temperature deviates beyond this range, comfort decreases.

The temperature comfort function is given by

$$U^i_{\text{thermal}}(t) = \begin{cases} 1, & T_{\min} \le T_{indoor} \le T_{\max} \\ 1 - \frac{|T_{indoor} - T_{opt\_temp}|}{T_{\max} - T_{\min}}, & \text{otherwise} \end{cases},$$
$$U_{\text{thermal}}(t) = \frac{\sum_{i=0}^{M} U^i_{\text{thermal}}(t)}{M}, \quad (10)$$

where T_{indoor} is the indoor temperature at time t, T_{opt_temp} is the user's preferred temperature (e.g., 26 °C), and the acceptable range is the range of temperatures the user finds comfortable (e.g., 22–28 °C). If the temperature exceeds this range, comfort decreases progressively.

2.5. Carbon Emissions and Carbon Consumption

Carbon emissions generally refer to the total amount of carbon dioxide (CO_2) and other greenhouse gases produced from energy consumption (e.g., electricity, natural gas, oil, etc.). For households, the primary sources include household electricity use, heating, and cooking with gas, which result in both direct and indirect emissions. Carbon consumption refers to the amount of carbon emissions "consumed" during energy usage, i.e., the cost of energy consumption expressed in terms of carbon emissions. It can be understood as the carbon quota "used" by a household over a given period due to its energy consumption. Changes in carbon pricing can affect users' willingness to adjust their electricity consumption behavior. The tiered carbon trading mechanism establishes multiple emission tiers, where carbon pricing increases progressively with emission levels, penalizing excess emissions through incremental cost escalation.

Assuming the household's electricity consumption in period t is $E(t)$ (in kWh), with a corresponding carbon emission factor $\alpha(t)$ (in $kgCO_2/kWh$) [22], the carbon emissions (or carbon consumption) for that period can be expressed as

$$C(t) = \alpha(t) \cdot E(t). \quad (11)$$

For tiered carbon trading, α(t) may vary over time, reflecting the proportion of different energy sources (e.g., thermal power, wind, or solar) in the grid during different time periods. The total carbon consumption C_{total} for the entire period (such as a day or month) is

$$C_{total} = \sum_t C(t). \quad (12)$$

2.6. Load Balancing

In home energy management, load balancing refers to the process of maintaining a stable household power demand over a specified time period, avoiding significant fluctuations or peak loads. A stable load curve helps not only in reducing electricity costs but also in alleviating grid pressure, improving energy efficiency, and promoting the effective integration of renewable energy sources. Typically, load balancing is expressed in terms of the net load curve flatness. The net load is the remaining electricity demand after subtracting the electricity generated by the household's distributed energy systems (e.g., solar PV). The flatness of the net load curve can be quantified in various ways, with common methods including the peak-to-valley difference, standard deviation, and maximum adjacent difference. This paper comprehensively considers system load fluctuations (e.g., standard deviation or dispersion), the magnitude range of loads, and the matching degree between control variables and load fluctuations to quantify the flatness of the net load curve. The calculation is as follows:

1. Let S_i represent the system load at the i-th moment and $\mu_S = \frac{1}{N}\sum_{i=1}^{N} S_i$ represent the average system load over N time periods. The system load dispersion can be defined as the standard deviation of the system load.

$$h_{\text{sfsys}} = -\sqrt{\sum_{i=1}^{N} (S_i - \mu_S)^2} \tag{13}$$

2. The baseline flatness calculation is calculated as

$$h_{\text{sfbase}} = \frac{h_{\text{sfsys}}}{max(S_i) - min(S_i)}. \tag{14}$$

3. Let X_i represent the flexible load in the i-th period. The correlation or matching degree between the control variable X and system load fluctuations can be calculated as

$$h_{\text{sftotal}} = \frac{\sum_{i=1}^{N} [(X_i - \mu_X)(S_i - \mu_S)]}{\sqrt{\sum_{i=1}^{N} (S_i - \mu_S)^2}}. \tag{15}$$

4. Finally, the flatness index can be calculated as

$$h = \left|\frac{h_{\text{sftotal}}}{h_{\text{sfbase}}}\right|. \tag{16}$$

3. SHEM Based on Mixed-Integer Linear Programming

3.1. Objective Function

For the optimization scheduling problem of household or small commercial building loads, this paper aims to comprehensively consider electricity costs, user comfort, carbon emission costs, and dynamic incentive subsidies to develop a reasonable electricity optimization strategy. The model, based on photovoltaic generation, electricity price information, external temperature, rigid loads, and flexible loads, optimizes the usage schedule of various electrical appliances to reduce electricity costs, enhance load balance, and improve user satisfaction. Based on the linear weighting method, the home energy management optimization objective is as follows:

$$\begin{gathered}
\min f = \alpha \cdot Z - \beta \cdot U - \gamma \cdot H - \delta \cdot T + \varepsilon \cdot C_{total}, \\
Z = \sum_{t=1}^{N} P_{\text{ele}}(t) \cdot \left(m(t) - 0.8P_{\text{pho}}(t)\right), \\
U = \sum_{t=1}^{N} U(t) = U_{\text{thermal}} + U_{\text{time}}, \\
H = \sum_{t=1}^{N} H(t) = h = \alpha \times \frac{h_{\text{sftotal}}}{h_{\text{sfbase}}}, \\
T = \sum_{t=1}^{N} incentive(t) C_{total} = \sum_{t=1}^{N} \alpha(t) \cdot E(t),
\end{gathered} \tag{17}$$

where $\alpha, \beta, \gamma, \delta, \varepsilon$ are the weight coefficients; N is the total number of time intervals in the cycle; Z is the electricity cost of the load, excluding photovoltaic output; $P_{ele}(t)$ is the electricity price at time t; and $P_{pho}(t)$ is the photovoltaic power generation, with a degradation coefficient of 0.8 to account for generation quality losses. The lower the load electricity cost, the smaller the objective function. $U_{thermal}$ and U_{time} represent temperature and time comfort, respectively. The higher the total comfort level, the smaller the objective function. H represents the quantified flatness of the net load curve, which is used to measure load balance. The higher the flatness, the smaller the objective function. T is the total incentive subsidy from demand response. The higher the subsidy, the smaller the objective function. C_{total} is the total carbon emission cost. The smaller the carbon emission cost, the smaller the objective function.

3.2. Calculation of Efficacy Coefficients

Considering that the five optimization objectives above have different units of measurement, this paper designs a comprehensive evaluation index based on the efficacy coefficient method to balance the impacts of economic efficiency, comfort, and flatness (load balancing) on scheduling results. The core idea of the efficacy coefficient method is to normalize each optimization objective into an efficacy coefficient within the range [0, 1], where 1 represents the best performance and 0 the worst. The geometric mean of all efficacy coefficients serves as the total efficacy coefficient.

(1) For the economic optimization objective Z, T, C_{total}, the calculation method for its efficacy coefficient is

$$G_i = \frac{\max F_i - F_i}{\max F_i - \min F_i} \tag{18}$$

where F_i represents any of the three economic objectives, i.e., electricity cost (Z), incentive subsidy (T), or carbon emission cost (C_{total}). Max F_i and min F_i denote the maximum and minimum values of these objectives across all scheduling schemes.

(2) For the comfort optimization objective U, which consists of time comfort and temperature comfort, the efficiency coefficient calculation method is

$$\begin{aligned} U^i_{\text{time}} &= \frac{\sum_{t=1}^{N} U^i_{\text{time}}(t)}{N}, \\ U^i_{\text{thermal}} &= \frac{\sum_{t=1}^{N} U^i_{\text{thermal}}(t)}{N}, \\ K^i_{time} &= 1 - \frac{e^{U^i_{\text{time}}} - 1}{e-1}, \\ K^i_{\text{thermal}} &= 1 - \frac{e^{U^i_{\text{thermal}}} - 1}{e-1}, \\ U &= \sqrt[M]{\prod_{i=1}^{M} K^i_{time} \times K^i_{\text{thermal}}}. \end{aligned} \tag{19}$$

(3) The calculation method for the efficiency coefficient of the flatness optimization objective H is

$$H = 1 - e^{-h} \tag{20}$$

Based on the calculation process of the five optimization objectives mentioned above, using the power coefficient calculation method, the optimization objective for household energy management is transformed into

$$\max f = \sqrt[5]{G_1 \cdot G_2 \cdot G_3 \cdot U \cdot H} \tag{21}$$

3.3. Mixed-Integer Linear Programming

Mixed-integer linear programming (MILP) is a mathematical programming method that involves both continuous and integer variables in optimization problems. It is widely used in logistics scheduling, supply chain management, production planning, and other fields. The standard form of MILP is as follows:

$$\begin{aligned} & min\mathbf{c}^T\mathbf{x} + \mathbf{d}^T\mathbf{y} \\ & \text{s.t.} A\mathbf{x} + D\mathbf{y} \leq \mathbf{b} \\ & \mathbf{x} \in \mathbb{Z}_+^n, \mathbf{y} \in \mathbb{R}_+^m \end{aligned} \tag{22}$$

where $\mathbf{x}$ is the integer variable and $\mathbf{y}$ is the continuous variable, and both the objective function and constraints are linear. $\mathbf{c}^T$ is cost vector associated with the integer variables $\mathbf{x}$. $\mathbf{d}^T$ is cost vector associated with the continuous variables $\mathbf{y}$. $\mathbb{Z}_+^n$ represents non-negative integers $(0, 1, 2, \cdots)$. $\mathbb{R}_+^m$ denotes non-negative real numbers $(x \geq 0)$.

Due to the presence of integer variables, MILP problems are typically NP-hard, and branch and bound methods are commonly used to solve these types of problems. The branch and bound method is an exact algorithm for solving MILP problems, and its core idea is to systematically decompose the problem space, progressively narrowing the feasible solution space to eventually find the global optimum. The algorithm combines two key operations: "branching" and "bounding":

- **Branching**: The original problem is decomposed into several subproblems (subnodes); each subproblem reduces the solution space by adding additional constraints (e.g., fixing the integer values of variables).
- **Bounding**: By solving the relaxed version of the subproblem (e.g., linear programming relaxation), upper and lower bounds are calculated. These bounds are used to prune branches that cannot contain the optimal solution, thereby reducing the computational effort.

The detailed implementation process of the branch and bound method is as follows:

Step 1: Initialization

- Create the root node corresponding to the original MILP problem.
- Set the global upper bound (UB) and the lower bound (LB).

Step 2: Relaxation Solution

- Perform linear programming relaxation on the current node (ignoring integer constraints) to solve the relaxed problem:

$$\min\mathbf{c}^T\mathbf{x} + \mathbf{d}^T\mathbf{y} \ \ \text{s.t.} A\mathbf{x} + D\mathbf{y} \leq \mathbf{b}, \mathbf{x} \in \mathbb{R}_+^n, \mathbf{y} \in \mathbb{R}_+^m \tag{23}$$

- If the relaxed problem has no feasible solution, prune this branch; otherwise, obtain the relaxed solution x_{LP} and its objective value $f(x_{LP})$.

Step 3: Pruning Conditions

- **Optimality Pruning**: If the relaxed solution satisfies the integer constraints, update the global upper bound as min $(f(x_{LP}), UB)$ and record this solution.
- **Bounding Pruning**: If $f(x_{LP}) \geq UB$, it means that this branch cannot produce a better solution, so prune this branch. Otherwise, update LB = max $(LB,\ f(x_{LP}))$.

Step 4: Branching Operation

If there are non-integer integer variables x_i in the relaxed solution, select this variable for branching. Create two subproblems:

- Subproblem 1: $x_i \leq \lfloor x_i^* \rfloor$
- Subproblem 2: $x_i \geq \lceil x_i^* \rceil$

Then, add these subproblems to the queue of nodes to be processed.

Step 5: Node Selection Strategy

- Use depth-first search (DFS) to select the next node to process from the queue. DFS is a tree/graph traversal or search strategy that prioritizes exploring along one branch as deeply as possible until a leaf node is reached or no further progress is possible. In branch and bound, DFS processes the most recently generated subnodes first, quickly delving deeper into the tree, potentially finding feasible solutions early, which can update the global upper bound and trigger pruning, thus reducing the exploration of subsequent invalid branches.

Step 6: Termination Condition

The algorithm terminates when one of the following conditions is met:

- All branches have been pruned or processed.
- The difference between the global *UB* and *LB* is smaller than the preset threshold $\epsilon = 10^{-4}$.

3.4. Hybrid Genetic Branch-and-Bound Algorithm

GA is an optimization algorithm based on natural selection and Darwin's theory of evolution. It simulates the process of biological evolution, iteratively optimizes, and seeks the optimal solution. The algorithm first randomly generates an initial population, with each individual representing a potential solution. In each generation, individuals' strengths and weaknesses are evaluated according to the fitness function, and individuals with higher fitness are selected for inheritance based on the principle of "survival of the fittest". Subsequently, new individuals are generated through crossover and mutation operations, allowing the population to continuously evolve. After multiple iterations, the algorithm ultimately converges to the optimal or approximate optimal solution.

This paper uses a hybrid genetic branch and bound algorithm to embed genetic algorithms in the branching process to quickly generate integer feasible solutions, update upper bounds, and accelerate pruning. The detailed implementation process of the hybrid genetic branch and bound algorithm is as follows:

Step 1: Initialization

- Encode the integer variables of MILP into gene sequences.
- Randomly generate *O* individuals (*O* = 50), calculate the fitness value of each individual, and record the optimal solution x_{ga}.
- Let the global upper bound be the initial optimal solution $UB = f(x_{ga})$ and the lower bound $LB = -\infty$.
- Add the original MILP problem as the root node to the active node queue, and prioritize the queue by LP relaxation value.

Step 2: Relaxation Solution

- Perform linear programming relaxation on the current node (ignoring integer constraints) to solve the relaxed problem.

$$\min \mathbf{c}^T\mathbf{x} + \mathbf{d}^T\mathbf{y} \text{ s.t.} A\mathbf{x} + D\mathbf{y} \le \mathbf{b}, \mathbf{x} \in \mathbb{R}_+^n, \mathbf{y} \in \mathbb{R}_+^m \tag{24}$$

- If the relaxed problem has no feasible solution, prune this branch; otherwise, obtain the relaxed solution x_{LP} and its objective value $f(x_{LP})$.

Step 3: Pruning Conditions

- **Optimality Pruning**: If the relaxed solution satisfies the integer constraints, update the global upper bound as min $(f(x_{LP}), UB)$, and record this solution.
- **Bounding Pruning**: If $f(x_{LP}) \ge UB$, it means that this branch cannot produce a better solution, so prune this branch. Otherwise, update LB = max $(LB, f(x_{LP}))$.

Step 4: Branching Operation

If there are non-integer integer variables x_i in the relaxed solution, select this variable for branching. Create two subproblems:

- Subproblem 1: $x_i \leq \lfloor x_i^* \rfloor$
- Subproblem 2: $x_i \geq \lceil x_i^* \rceil$

Then, add these subproblems to the queue of nodes to be processed.

Step 5: Dynamic Feasible Solution Generation via Genetic Algorithm

- Trigger Conditions:
  - Process $K = 50$ branch and bound nodes;
  - No update to the global UB for $T = 10$ consecutive iterations;
  - LP relaxation solution is close to integrality (e.g., fractional variables have values near 0 or 1).
- Genetic Operations:
  - **Crossover**: Combine the current best solution x_i with the rounded integer solution x_{LP} to round(x_{LP}) to generate offspring.
  - **Mutation**: Apply random perturbations (e.g., flipping binary variables or adjusting integer values) to offspring while ensuring constraint satisfaction.
  - **Selection**: Retain the top $p = 20$ individuals with the highest fitness (i.e., lowest objective value $f(x)$).
- Update Upper Bound:

  If the new population's best solution x_{ga_new} satisfies $f\left(x_{ga}\right) < UB$, then update $UB = f\left(x_{ga\_new}\right)$ and set $x_i^* = x_{ga\_new}$.

- Dynamic Pruning:

  Remove all nodes from the active queue where the LP relaxation value $f_{LP} > UB$.

Step 6: Termination Condition

The algorithm terminates when one of the following conditions is met:

- All branches have been pruned or processed.
- The difference between the global UB and LB is smaller than the preset threshold $\epsilon = 10^{-4}$.

3.5. Constraints

SHEM typically includes various constraints, which can be divided into power balance constraints and load operation constraints.

3.5.1. Balance Constraints

In each scheduling period, power balance must be maintained, i.e.,

$$P_{load}(t) - P_{pho}(t) - P_{disch}(t) = P_{grid}(t) \tag{25}$$

where $P_{load}(t)$ is the total household load power (kW) at time t,$P_{pho}(t)$ is the photovoltaic output power (kW) at time t, $P_{disch}(t)$ is the discharging power of the energy storage device (kW) at time t, and $P_{grid}(t)$ is the total interaction power between the household and the grid at time t, which includes both rigid and flexible loads (kW).

3.5.2. Load Operation Constraints

For power-adjustable loads: These loads, such as smart lighting, air conditioning, and water heaters, can adjust their power output within certain limits. The operating power must be within the rated power range of the device and must avoid instantaneous overload to ensure grid stability and equipment safety.

For time-adjustable loads: These loads can adjust their operation time, but their power output remains largely fixed, such as washing machines, dishwashers, and dryers. Constraints for time-adjustable loads include:

- Operating Time Range: The device must start within the allowed operating time window, for example, prioritizing operation during off-peak hours with lower electricity rates.
- Optimal Comfort Time Window: The load should operate primarily within the user's desired time window, such as having the dishwasher automatically run after dinner.

For power-duration adjustable loads: These loads can adjust both their power output and operation duration, such as electric vehicle charging and energy storage devices. Constraints for these loads include:

- Minimum/Maximum Power Limits:

$$P_{ch,min} \leqslant P_{ch}(t) \leqslant P_{ch,max} \quad P_{disch,min} \leqslant P_{ch}(t) \leqslant P_{disch,max}, \tag{26}$$

where $P_{ch}(t)$ and $P_{disch}(t)$ are the charging and discharging power at time t and $P_{ch,min}$, $P_{ch,max}$, $P_{disch,min}$, $P_{disch,\ max}$ are the respective minimum and maximum power limits.

- Minimum/Maximum Capacity Limits:

$$SOC_{min} \leqslant SOC(t) \leqslant SOC_{max}, \tag{27}$$

where $SOC(t)$ is the state of charge of the storage device at time t and SOC_{min} and SOC_{max} are the minimum and maximum allowable charge levels.

- Load Distribution Balance: These loads should operate primarily during periods with low electricity rates and low grid load to flatten the peak demand and fill the valley periods.

For temperature-controlled adjustable loads: These loads are subject to temperature constraints, such as air conditioners and water heaters, whose operation is controlled by temperature. Constraints for temperature-controlled loads include:

- Temperature range for adjustment: For air conditioning, the cooling temperature cannot fall below a set lower limit, and in heating mode, it cannot exceed a set upper limit. For water heaters, the minimum water temperature must meet household needs.
- Optimal temperature comfort range: The temperature should ideally be maintained within the user's most comfortable range, such as keeping air conditioning between 24–26 °C and water heaters between 45–55 °C, balancing both comfort and energy efficiency.
- Dynamic adjustment mechanism: The system adjusts the operation strategy based on environmental temperature, load status, and electricity prices. For example, the air conditioning temperature setpoint can be raised during peak times to reduce energy consumption.

4. Example Analysis

4.1. Parameter Settings

In this study, the distributed power source is primarily photovoltaic (PV) generation. The charging and discharging efficiencies of the battery, denoted as η_{ch} and $\eta_{disch,}$, are 0.9 and 0.8, respectively. The maximum charging and discharging power, $P_{ch,max}$ and $P_{disch,max}$, are 2 kW and 1.8 kW, respectively. The minimum and maximum state of charge (SOC),

SOC_{min} and SOC_{max}, are 0.2 and 1, respectively. The real-time electricity prices, rigid load, and photovoltaic output in each period are shown in Figure 2. The flexible load parameters are provided in Table 2. Table 3 lists the symbol definitions.

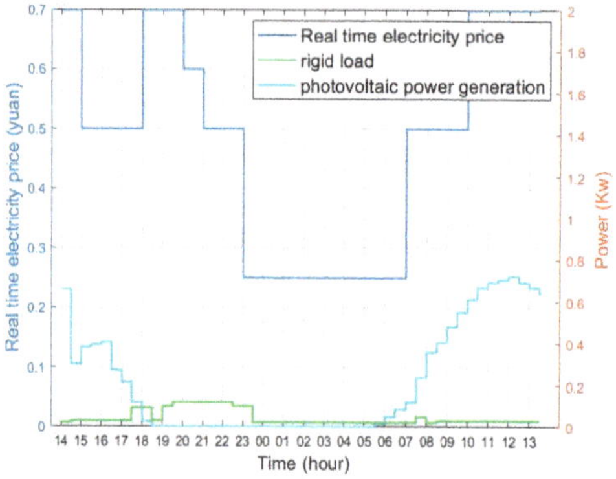

Figure 2. Rigid load, photovoltaic output power, and real-time electricity price.

Table 2. Flexible load parameters.

Appliance Name	Power (kW)	Operating Window	Required Operating Duration (h)	Minimum Continuous Operating Duration (h)
Washing Machine	0.5	12:00–22:00	1	1
Kettle	1.5	18:00–07:00	0.5	0.5
Vacuum Cleaner	1.0	08:00–12:00	1	1
Dishwasher	0.5	19:00–02:00	1	1
Disinfection Cabinet	0.3	19:00–07:00	0.5	0.5
Tumble Dryer	1.5	19:00–07:00	1	1
Electric Car	3.0	18:00–06:00	3	1
Computer	0.15	19:00–24:00	1.5	1
Air Conditioner	2.0	All day	-	-
Water Heater	2.5	07:00–00:00	-	-

Table 3. Symbol definitions.

Symbols	Meanings
$P_{rigid}(t)$	Power of the rigid load at time t
$P_{rated}(t)$	Rated power of the load at time t
$P_{adjustable}(t)$	Power-adjustable load
$P_{flexible}(t)$	Power-time adjustable load
$SOC(t)$	State of charge of the battery at time t
$U^{i}_{\text{time}}(t)$	Time comfort of device i at time t
$U^{i}_{\text{thermal}}(t)$	Temperature comfort of device i at time t
$\alpha(t)$	Carbon emission factor
Z	Electricity cost of the load excluding photovoltaic output
$P_{ele}(t)$	Electricity price at time t
$P_{pho}(t)$	Photovoltaic power generation

Table 3. *Cont.*

Symbols	Meanings
H	Quantified flatness of the net load curve
T	Total incentive subsidy from demand response
C_{total}	Total carbon emission cost for one period
$C(t)$	Carbon emissions (or carbon consumption) at period t
C_{room}	Room thermal capacity (kWh/°C)
x_{LP}	Relaxed solution
UB	Upper bound
LB	Lower bound
DR	Demand response
η_{ch}	Charging efficiencies
η_{disch}	Discharging efficiencies

4.2. Simulation and Result Analysis

The load optimization scheduling results in the home energy management system are shown in Figure 3. Figure 3a presents the optimized scheduling results for the washing machine, kettle, computer, and electric vehicle. In the case setup, the operating time window for the washing machine includes the low, peak, and off-peak pricing periods. After optimization, the model selects the low-price period from 23:00 to 24:00 for the washing machine operation. Similarly, the operating windows for the kettle and computer also include these three periods. After optimization, the kettle is scheduled to operate from 21:00 to 21:30, and the computer from 21:00 to 22:30, both during the off-peak pricing period. The energy storage device, the electric vehicle, is scheduled for charging from 01:00 to 04:00, following the low-price strategy, effectively reducing electricity costs.

Figure 3b shows the optimized scheduling results for the dishwasher, sterilizer, dryer, and vacuum cleaner. In the case study, the dishwasher's operational time range includes three periods: off-peak, peak, and mid-peak hours. After optimization, the model schedules the dishwasher to run during the mid-peak period from 20:00 to 21:00. Similarly, the sterilizer and dryer are scheduled to operate during the off-peak periods from 21:00 to 21:30 and 22:00 to 23:00, respectively. The vacuum cleaner is scheduled to run during the off-peak period from 09:00 to 10:00.

Figure 3c presents the optimized scheduling results for temperature-controlled loads, such as air conditioners and water heaters. As seen in the figure, the water heater's operating time spans multiple periods but is always within mid-peak or off-peak times. The use of the water heater is closely linked with other household appliance usage, such as the 20:00–21:30 period, which overlaps with the dishwasher's operating time. The 22:00–23:30 period also includes part of the washing machine's operation and is a peak time for household members taking showers. Additionally, 07:30–08:00 is the peak time for morning washing, leading to a significant increase in hot water demand. The air conditioner maintains a temperature of around 26°C, ensuring maximum comfort for the user. The case study results show that this temperature-controlled load optimization strategy efficiently schedules the air conditioner and water heater, ensuring comfort while avoiding unnecessary energy waste and reducing overall electricity costs by optimizing based on real-time electricity prices.

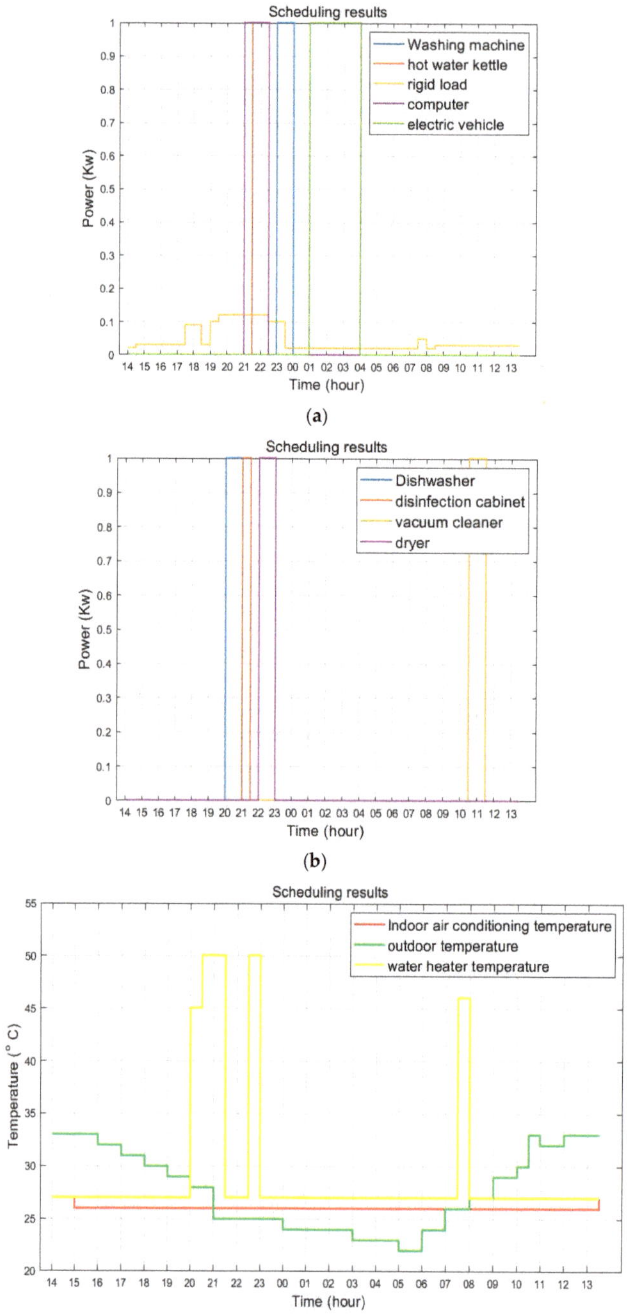

(c)

Figure 3. Household load scheduling results. (**a**) Optimized scheduling results for the washing machine, kettle, computer, and electric vehicle. (**b**) Optimized scheduling results for the dishwasher, disinfection cabinet, vacuum cleaner, and dryer. (**c**) Optimized scheduling results for temperature-controlled loads.

Figure 4 illustrates the model's control of battery charging and discharging, showing the comparison between time-of-use electricity prices and the SOC of the battery. The purpose of using the battery is to store energy during low-price periods and release it during high-price periods to reduce electricity costs. From the figure, it is clear that during the off-peak period (23:00–06:30), the battery charges from 23:30 to 01:30. Between 01:30 and 06:30, the SOC reaches its maximum value. During the mid-peak period (06:30–09:30), the battery neither charges nor discharges. During the peak period (10:00–14:30), the battery first discharges, reaching the minimum SOC value of 0.2 at 13:00, and then charges again, reaching 0.4. During other mid-peak periods (15:00–17:30 and 21:00–22:30), the battery continuously charges. During the evening peak (18:00–20:30), the battery discharges to reduce the load.

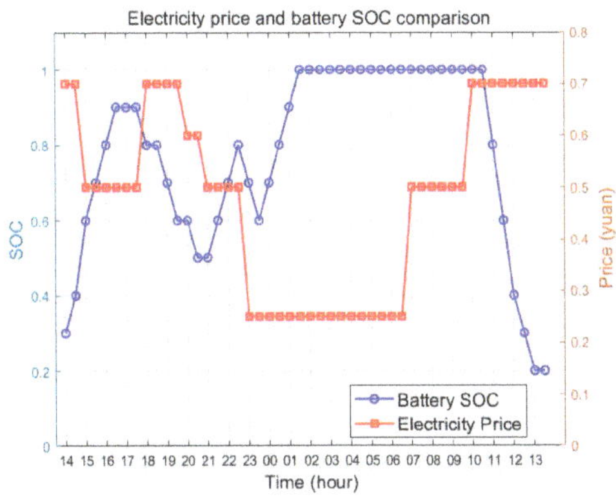

Figure 4. Battery charging and discharging.

To further verify the effectiveness of the model proposed in this paper for demand response, Figure 5 shows the dynamic incentive subsidy in relation to electricity price fluctuations. From the figure, it can be seen that during the off-peak price period, the subsidy is higher, encouraging users to use electricity at night; during the mid-peak price period, the subsidy decreases to avoid further increasing the grid load; during the peak price period, the subsidy is zero, guiding users to shift their electricity usage.

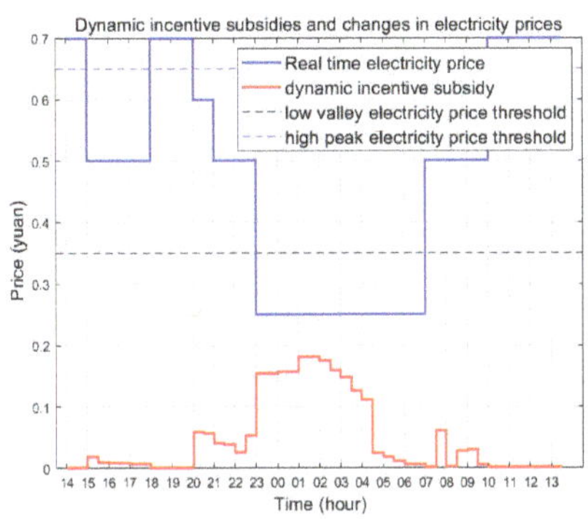

Figure 5. Dynamic incentive subsidy and electricity price fluctuations.

Figure 6 shows the variation of different types of loads in the household energy system under the dynamic pricing mechanism. As can be seen from the results, flexible loads are mostly intelligently scheduled to operate during off-peak or mid-peak hours, reducing overall electricity costs and improving energy efficiency. The scheduling optimization of these loads fully takes advantage of electricity price fluctuations, running them during periods of lower prices to alleviate the grid load during peak hours. In contrast, rigid loads generally have higher electricity demand during morning and evening peak periods. This is because the usage of these devices is often constrained by users' daily routines and habits, making it difficult to adjust their operation time flexibly.

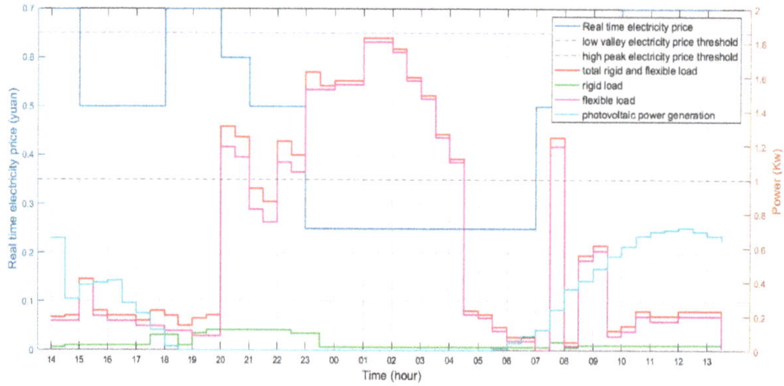

Figure 6. Power variation of different types of loads with changes in electricity prices.

Overall, the intelligent scheduling of flexible loads can effectively reduce household energy costs and ease the burden on the grid to some extent, while rigid loads are more driven by user demand and are still concentrated during peak hours. This study enhances the intelligence of household energy management by reasonably configuring flexible load scheduling strategies, combined with the collaborative optimization of energy storage systems and distributed energy sources (e.g., photovoltaic generation), achieving a balance between economic and reliability goals.

To validate the effectiveness of the proposed model in reducing household electricity costs, optimizing load curve flatness, reducing carbon emissions, and ensuring user comfort, Table 3 presents the simulation results before and after optimization using the linear weighting method and the efficacy coefficient method for constructing the objective function. This further evaluates the model's applicability and optimization performance.

From the comparative data in Table 4, it is evident that for the objective functions constructed using both methods, the proposed scheduling approach achieves significant improvements in reducing electricity costs, optimizing load balance, and decreasing carbon emissions. Specifically, after optimization with the efficacy coefficient method, in terms of economic efficiency, the flexible load electricity cost decreased from 3.94 to 2.776, a reduction of approximately 29.6%, demonstrating that the scheduling method effectively reduces users' electricity expenses. Regarding load balance, the load curve flatness increased from 1.23 to 1.84, an improvement of approximately 49.6%, indicating that the optimized load curve is smoother, achieving better peak shaving and valley filling effects, thereby alleviating grid pressure and enhancing energy utilization efficiency. In terms of carbon emissions, carbon consumption costs dropped from 1.418 to 0.994, a decrease of about 29.9%, demonstrating that the optimization approach effectively reduces carbon emissions and enhances the environmental friendliness of household energy use. In terms of user comfort, there was a slight decline after optimization, from 1 to 0.95, but it remained at a relatively high level, indicating that the optimization method balances electricity cost reduction and load balancing while maintaining a good user experience, preventing excessive disruption to users' daily electricity usage.

Table 4. Comparison before and after optimization.

Metrics	Methods of Efficacy Coefficients		Linear Weighting Method	
	Before Optimization	After Optimization	Before Optimization	After Optimization
Flexible load electricity fee	3.94	2.776	3.94	2.481
Flatness of load curve	1.23	1.84	1.23	1.46
Carbon consumption	1.418	0.994	1.418	0.883
User comfort	1	0.95	1	0.61

By comparing the simulation results before and after optimization using the linear weighting method and the efficacy coefficient method for constructing the objective function, it is found that the efficacy coefficient method better balances the impact of differences in dimensional scales among different optimization objectives. Although optimization with the efficacy coefficient method resulted in an 11.89% increase in flexible load electricity costs and a 12.5% increase in carbon consumption, the load curve flatness and user comfort improved by 26.02% and 55.73%, respectively.

In summary, the proposed scheduling method performs excellently in economic efficiency, load balance, and carbon emission reduction while also considering user comfort, proving its effectiveness and practical value in household energy management.

To verify the effectiveness of the proposed algorithm in multi-objective balancing, this study compares multiple indicators under different scenarios and algorithms.

- **Scenario 1**: Only electricity cost is considered, while user comfort is not taken into account.
- **Scenario 2**: A comprehensive consideration of electricity cost, user comfort, load curve flatness, and carbon consumption.

Table 5 presents the comparison results of different metrics under various scenarios and algorithms. It can be observed that in Scenario 1, where only electricity cost is considered without accounting for user comfort, all three algorithms effectively reduce electricity costs; however, user comfort also decreases significantly.

Table 5. Comparison results of different metrics under various scenarios and algorithms.

Metrics	Scenario 1			Scenario 2		
	GA	MILP	MILP +GA	GA	MILP	MILP +GA
Flexible load electricity fee	1.904	1.316	1.422	3.446	2.912	2.776
Flatness of load curve	1.049	1.274	1.315	1.54	1.71	1.84
Carbon consumption	0.669	0.571	0.476	1.214	1.133	0.994
User comfort	0.149	0.207	0.243	0.78	0.87	0.95
Time (s)	3346.8	139.74	3547.6	3538.1	141.54	3661.3

Comparing the optimization results of the three algorithms in Scenario 1 and Scenario 2, it is evident that the MILP algorithm achieves better optimization than the GA algorithm but is still inferior to the proposed MILP + GA algorithm. However, the MILP algorithm has a significant advantage in solving time compared to the proposed MILP + GA algorithm. The proposed MILP + GA algorithm achieves a trade-off between performance and computation time, making it better suited for real-world applications.

5. Conclusions

This paper investigates the optimization scheduling problem in smart home energy management, focusing on how to achieve coordinated optimization across multiple factors such as load balancing, cost control, carbon emissions, user comfort, and demand-side response. For various load characteristics in home energy systems, this paper proposes an optimization method based on dynamic electricity pricing and intelligent scheduling strategies, and its effectiveness is verified through simulation. The simulation results show that the proposed method can effectively reduce household electricity costs, optimize load curve flatness, and reduce carbon emissions. Economically, the cost of flexible loads decreases by approximately 29.6%, indicating that the optimized scheduling strategy makes full use of off-peak electricity prices, effectively reducing electricity expenses. In terms of load balancing, the load curve flatness improves by about 49.6%, which helps to reduce peak loads and fill valleys, thus alleviating grid stress and improving energy efficiency. Regarding carbon emissions, carbon consumption costs decrease by 29.9%, suggesting that the optimization method contributes to reducing the carbon footprint of the household energy system and promotes green and low-carbon development. Furthermore, user comfort remains at a relatively high level, with a slight decrease of 5% in the comfort index, indicating that the optimization strategy maintains a good balance between improving economy and environmental performance while ensuring user experience. Overall, the proposed optimization scheduling strategy achieves a good balance between economic efficiency, load balancing, and carbon emissions optimization while also ensuring user comfort. This provides an effective solution for smart home energy management. Future research will further integrate artificial intelligence and deep learning technologies to enhance the intelligence of scheduling models and explore more flexible demand-side response strategies to meet increasingly complex home energy management needs.

Author Contributions: Conceptualization, S.L. and Z.H.; methodology, S.L.; software, S.L.; validation, S.L.; formal analysis, S.L.; writing—original draft preparation, Z.X.; writing—review and editing, Z.X. and Z.H.; supervision, Z.H. All authors have read and agreed to the published version of the manuscript.

Funding: This work was funded by the General Program of National Natural Science Foundation of China (Grant No. 52177083 and 62001166) and by Major Science and Technology Projects in Hebei Province (Grant No. 23281701Z).

Data Availability Statement: Data are contained within the article.

Conflicts of Interest: The authors declare no conflicts of interest.

References

1. Mischos, S.; Dalagdi, E.; Vrakas, D. Intelligent energy management systems: A review. *Artif. Intell. Rev.* **2023**, *56*, 11635–11674. [CrossRef]
2. Li, J.; Zhou, Z. Distributed energy management and optimization analysis in smart grids. *Electron. Technol.* **2024**, *53*, 286–287.
3. Ajao, A.; Luo, J.; Liang, Z.; Alsafasfeh, Q.H.; Su, W. Intelligent home energy management system for distributed renewable generators, dispatchable residential loads, and distributed energy storage devices. In Proceedings of the 8th International Renewable Energy Congress (IREC), Amman, Jordan, 21–23 March 2017; pp. 1–6. [CrossRef]
4. Kwon, K.; Lee, S.; Kim, S. AI-Based Home Energy Management System Considering Energy Efficiency and Resident Satisfaction. *IEEE Internet Things J.* **2022**, *9*, 1608–1621. [CrossRef]
5. Yang, Q.; Wang, H. Privacy-Preserving Transactive Energy Management for IoT-Aided Smart Homes via Blockchain. *arXiv* **2021**, arXiv:2101.03840. [CrossRef]

6. Dong, X.; Shao, X.; Guan, R. Cost optimization problem of home energy management system based on particle swarm algorithm. *Comput. Knowl. Technol.* **2021**, *17*, 122–124. [CrossRef]
7. Ruan, B.J. Energy Optimization Scheduling Method for Home Hybrid Power Supply System Considering Real-Time Electricity Prices. Ph.D. Thesis, Zhejiang University, Hangzhou, China, 2015.
8. Yin, Z.D.; Lin, Z.; Li, D.Z. Intelligent home energy management strategy based on hybrid particle swarm optimization algorithm. *J. North China Electr. Power Univ. (Nat. Sci. Ed.)* **2018**, *45*, 25–33.
9. Zhang, T.; Zhao, Q.; Chen, Z.; Wang, R.; Xing, Q.; Tian, J. Hierarchical optimization strategy for home energy management based on deep reinforcement learning. *Autom. Electr. Power Syst.* **2021**, *45*, 149–158.
10. Zhang, K.J.; Ding, G.F.; Wen, M.; Hui, H.; Ding, Y.; He, M. Optimization scheduling technology and market mechanism design of virtual power plants: A review. *Compr. Smart Energy* **2022**, *44*, 60–72.
11. Wei, G.; Chi, M.; Liu, Z.W.; Ge, M.; Li, C.; Liu, X. Deep reinforcement learning for real-time energy management in smart home. *IEEE Syst. J.* **2023**, *17*, 2489–2499. [CrossRef]
12. Ye, Y.J.; Wang, H.Y.; Tang, Y. Optimal autonomous energy management strategy for residents based on deep reinforcement learning. *Autom. Electr. Power Syst.* **2022**, *46*, 110–119.
13. Ma, Y.; Chen, X.; Wang, L.; Yang, J. Study on smart home energy management system based on artificial intelligence. *J. Sens.* **2021**, *2021*, 9101453. [CrossRef]
14. Navesi, R.B.; Naghibi, A.F.; Zafarani, H.; Tahami, H.; Pirouzi, S. Reliable operation of reconfigurable smart distribution network with real-time pricing-based demand response. *Electr. Power Syst. Res.* **2025**, *241*, 111341. [CrossRef]
15. Hu, R.; Zhou, K.; Yin, H. Reinforcement learning model for incentive-based integrated demand response considering demand-side coupling. *Energy* **2024**, *308*, 132997. [CrossRef]
16. Dey, B.; Sharma, G.; Bokoro, P.N.; Dutta, S. An intelligent incentive-based demand response program for exhaustive environment-constrained techno-economic analysis of microgrid systems. *Sci. Rep.* **2025**, *15*, 894. [CrossRef] [PubMed]
17. Ikram, A.I.; Ullah, A.; Datta, D.; Islam, A.; Ahmed, T. Optimizing energy consumption in smart homes: Load scheduling approaches. *IET Power Electron.* **2024**, *17*, 2656–2668. [CrossRef]
18. Akram, A.; Abbas, S.; Khan, M.; Athar, A.; Ghazal, T.; Al Hamadi, H. Smart energy management system using machine learning. *Comput. Mater. Contin.* **2024**, *78*, 959–973. [CrossRef]
19. Youssef, H.; Kamel, S.; Hassan, M.H.; Yu, J.; Safaraliev, M. A smart home energy management approach incorporating an enhanced northern goshawk optimizer to enhance user comfort, minimize costs, and promote efficient energy consumption. *Int. J. Hydrogen Energy* **2024**, *49*, 644–658. [CrossRef]
20. Youssef, H.; Kamel, S.; Hassan, M.H.; Nasrat, L.; Jurado, F. An improved bald eagle search optimization algorithm for optimal home energy management systems. *Soft Comput.* **2024**, *28*, 1367–1390. [CrossRef]
21. Wu, H.C.; Wang, C.; Zuo, Y.L.; Chen, Y.J.; Liu, K. Home energy system optimization based on time-of-use pricing and real-time control strategy for batteries. *Power Syst. Prot. Control.* **2019**, *47*, 23–30. [CrossRef]
22. Yang, Y. A review of the carbon emission factor method's application to power system accounting. *Appl. Comput. Eng.* **2023**, *26*, 120–125. [CrossRef]

electronics

MDPI

Article

Oversea Cross-Lingual Summarization Service in Multilanguage Pre-Trained Model through Knowledge Distillation

Xiwei Yang, Jing Yun *, Bofei Zheng, Limin Liu and Qi Ban

School of Data Science and Applications, Inner Mongol University of Technology, Hohhot 010080, China; 20211800677@imut.edu.com (X.Y.); ax979710378@126.com (B.Z.); liulimin@imut.edu.com (L.L.); 20221800740@imut.edu.com (Q.B.)

* Correspondence: yunjing@imut.edu.cn

Abstract: Cross-lingual text summarization is a highly desired service for overseas report editing tasks and is formulated in a distributed application to facilitate the cooperation of editors. The multilanguage pre-trained language model (MPLM) can generate high-quality cross-lingual text summaries with simple fine-tuning. However, the MPLM does not adapt to complex variations, like the word order and tense in different languages. When the model performs on these languages with separate syntactic structures and vocabulary morphologies, it will lead to the low-level quality of the cross-lingual summary. The matter worsens when the cross-lingual summarization datasets are low-resource. We use a knowledge distillation framework for the cross-lingual summarization task to address the above issues. By learning the monolingual teacher model, the cross-lingual student model can effectively capture the differences between languages. Since the teacher and student models generate summaries in two languages, their representations lie on different vector spaces. In order to construct representation relationships across languages, we further propose a similarity metric, which is based on bidirectional semantic alignment, to map different language representations to the same space. In order to improve the quality of cross-lingual summaries further, we use contrastive learning to make the student model focus on the differentials among languages. Contrastive learning can enhance the ability of the similarity metric for bidirectional semantic alignment. Our experiments show that our approach is competitive in low-resource scenarios on cross-language summarization datasets in pairs of distant languages.

Keywords: multilingual pre-trained language model; cross-lingual summary; knowledge distillation; similarity metric

1. Introduction

The cross-lingual summarization (CLS) task emerged to convert documents from one language to a summary in another. It is a highly desired service in foreign report editing and formulated in a distributed application to facilitate the cooperation of editors. This service plays a crucial role in report writing on a global scale, facilitating collaboration and communication among editorial teams through concise summaries and multilingual translations.

MPLMs, such as mBART [1] and mT5 [2], have led to significant breakthroughs in the cross-lingual summarization task. In particular, ref. [3] discovers that the mBART (mbart.cc25) model outperforms many multitask models on large-scale cross-lingual summary datasets through simple fine-tuning. However, ref. [4] proposes that the syntactic structure of the language will still influence the relevance of cross-linguistic representations of models trained on multilingual corpora. Therefore, for the mBART model, learning feature relationships between two languages with separate syntactic structures and vocabulary morphologies is challenging. Specifically, the mBART model will be pre-trained in multiple languages. When generating a cross-lingual summary of two languages, the model may mistake the lingual features in the pre-trained corpus for features of two languages. Constructing cross-lingual relationships between two languages with separate syntactic structures and vocabulary morphologies is more challenging. Significantly, the matter worsens in low-resource scenarios where the cross-lingual summary dataset contains only a few languages and a limited number of samples for each language.

To address the above issues, we propose a knowledge distillation framework to mitigate cross-linguistic interference that can improve the quality of the generated target language summaries. Our model consists of a monolingual teacher model and a cross-lingual student model. By distilling the attention weight and word distribution of the fine-tuned teacher model into the student model, the student model can effectively construct cross-lingual relationships in low-resource scenarios. To improve the quality of the cross-lingual summary, we propose a text similarity metric to evaluate the similarity of the summaries in two languages. As the linguistic representations of the two summaries lie on different vector spaces, we adopt the UMH in [5] to map the linguistic representations into a unified vector space. Then, we view the bidirectional semantic alignment of summaries as an optimal transmission problem. Additionally, we use contrast learning to capture the semantic similarity between two summaries. It helps the student model focus on differentials among languages and extract critical information from the text.

Our main contributions can be described as follows:

- We propose a knowledge distillation framework for the cross-lingual summarization task. The student model constructs strong relationships between two languages by learning the attention weight and word distribution of the teacher model.
- We propose a text similarity metric that maps texts from different languages into a unified similarity space for comparison. Furthermore, we introduce contrastive learning to push similar text vectors toward each other, combined with the text similarity metric to compute the bidirectional semantics of two summaries.
- We validate our model by training on datasets of language pairs with separate syntactic structures and vocabulary morphologies in a low-resource scenario. We find that our approach outperforms other baselines in most cases.

2. Related Work

Early cross-lingual summary generation mainly focused on pipe-lined approaches [6–8], which suffered from error propagation problems. Since [9] first proposed that end-to-end methods are significantly better than pipe-lined methods, such methods are gradually becoming the mainstream methods for generating cross-lingual text summaries [3,10].

Since cross-lingual summarization still lacks large-scale, high-quality supervised datasets [11], methods that can be pre-trained from large-scale unsupervised corpora have been extensively investigated. Applying a pre-trained model to the cross-lingual summarization task involves pre-training and fine-tuning. In the former, the model uses many unlabeled data to learn generic linguistic knowledge; the latter uses the labeled data to fine-tune the cross-lingual summarization task. However, early pre-training models were trained in only one language [12–15]. It is difficult for models to learn general knowledge of another language in a cross-lingual task.

Then, multilanguage pre-trained models started to be pre-trained in multiple languages [1,2,16], which allowed them to learn syntactic, lexical, and semantic similarities between languages. Overall, the application of pre-training methods in cross-lingual summarization has been widely explored and studied [17–19] and achieved good performances in different languages. For instance, ref. [20] proposes an mBERT-based knowledge distillation framework that improves the summarization performance for remote languages by aligning cross-language summaries with monolingual summaries. Ref. [21] propose a many-to-one summarization model using the mT5 model combined with a contrastive learning approach to unify cross-lingual and monolingual representations to enrich low-resource data.

In contrast to the former study, we introduce contrastive learning into the knowledge distillation framework to construct strong correlations between languages. Moreover, we introduce the attention weight and word distribution of the teacher model to form adequate alignment supervision information.

3. Methods

The MPLM will be pre-trained in multiple languages. When generating a cross-lingual summary of two languages, the model may mistake the lingual features in the pre-trained corpus for features of two languages, thus interfering with the quality of the summary. We propose a knowledge distillation framework and a similarity metric based on contrast learning to address the problem that the cross-lingual summarization model suffers from data interference in low-resource settings.

We construct cross-lingual supervision by linking a monolingual teacher model with a cross-lingual student model. Then, we use a bidirectional semantic alignment of the similarity metric to construct strong correlations among languages. Finally, we use contrast learning to enhance the ability of the similarity metric for bidirectional semantic alignment. The overall model framework is shown in Figure 1. In this way, we can improve the performance of the model on languages with separate syntactic structures and vocabulary morphologies.

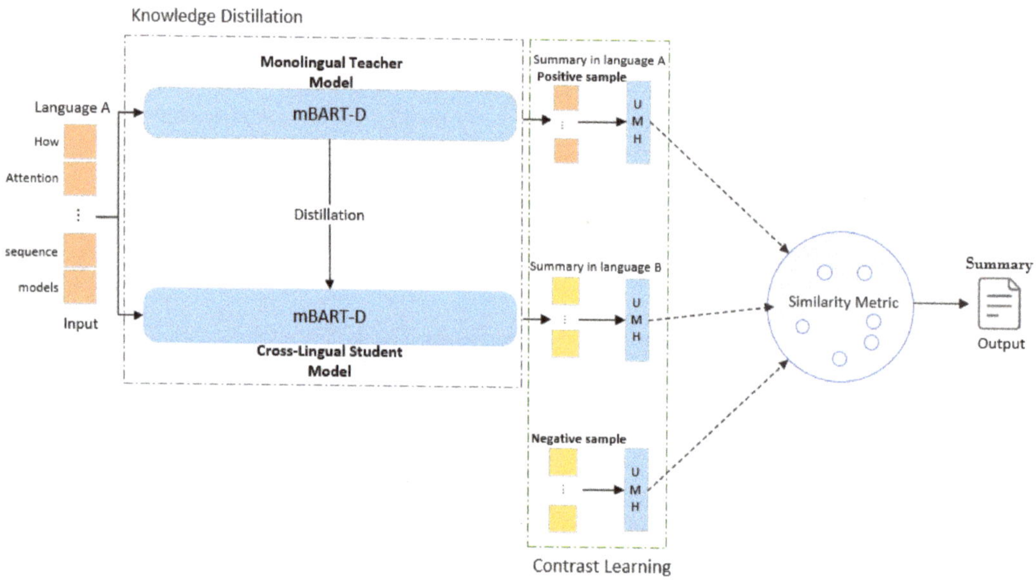

Figure 1. Diagram of knowledge distillation framework for cross-lingual summary.

3.1. Knowledge Distillation

The knowledge distillation framework transfers knowledge from a teacher model trained on a specific corpus to a student model. While preserving the effective encoding of the source language by the multilingual pre-trained model, this framework alleviates interference among different languages in the pre-training corpus during the generation of target language summaries by the decoder. In particular, we use a new model named the mBART-D model to construct teacher and student models. The architecture diagram of the mBART-D model is shown in Figure 2. In addition, the cross-lingual summary model requires understanding both the source and target languages and constructing the relationship between the two languages. To make the student model have the same ability to generate summaries as the teacher model, we transfer the attention weights and word distributions from the teacher model to the student model. The specific distillation is shown in Figure 3.

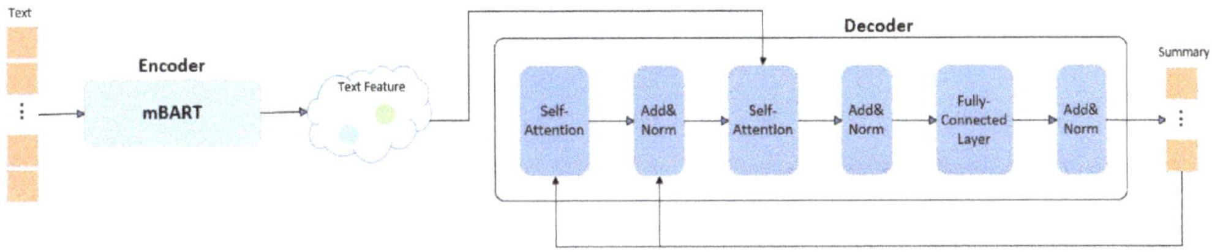

Figure 2. Overview of the proposed mBART-D model. The encoder of the mBART model extracts the text features of the source text and then inputs the text features into an additionally constructed decoder to generate the final summary.

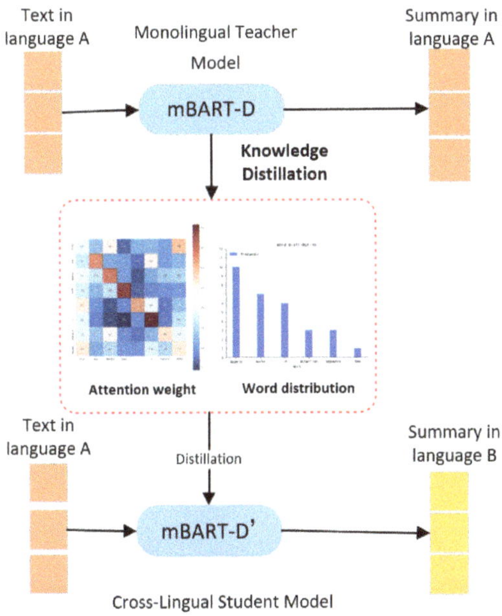

Figure 3. Framework for the refinement process. Both the monolingual teacher and the cross-language student models use mBART-D (for better differentiation, we set the student model to mBART-D'). The aim is to refine the attentional weights and word distributions from the monolingual teacher model into the cross-language student model. The teacher and student models generate monolingual and cross-lingual summaries, respectively.

3.1.1. mBART-D Model

Since the mBART model is a multilingual pre-trained model, many datasets are needed to fine-tune it for cross-language text summary generation tasks. However, when the mBART model is used in low-resource scenarios, the model may mistake linguistic features in the pre-trained corpus as features in both languages during text summary generation. It will affect the quality of the final generated text summaries.

To address the above issues, we construct an mBART-D model consisting of the mBART encoder and the decoder initialized by Xavier [22]. Specifically, the mBART-D model performs text feature extraction using the mBART encoder to obtain contextual and semantic information then employs the Xavier initialization method to initialize the weight values of the decoder, which inputs the text features into the decoder. Compared to generating summaries using the mBART model in low-resource scenarios, the mBART-D model inherits the encoding capabilities of the mBART model. At the same time, the initialized decoder is not affected by other linguistic features. We use the mBART-D model to mitigate the problem that the model may misidentify linguistic features in the pre-trained corpus as two linguistic features when outputting summaries.

3.1.2. Teacher Model

We utilize the mBART-D model as the teacher model to generate the monolingual summary. In detail, given the text input $T^A = \{X_1^A, X_2^A, X_3^A, \ldots, X_n^A\}$ in language A, the teacher model uses the maximum likelihood function with cross-entropy loss to generate the monolingual summary $S^A = \{Y_1^A, Y_2^A, Y_3^A, \ldots, Y_m^A\}$, where the m and n are the lengths of the input text and the monolingual summary and $m < n$. The formula is as follows:

$$S_{mls} = -\sum_{j=1}^{m} logP(Y_j^A | Y_{<j}^A, X) \tag{1}$$

We use a monolingual summary dataset to train the mBART-D model as a teacher model. Adequate training samples allow the mBART-D model to capture source language semantic information and generate accurate summaries efficiently.

3.1.3. Student Model

We train the student model using the mBART-D model and a cross-lingual summary corpus. In detail, given the text input $T^A = \{X_1^A, X_2^A, X_3^A, \ldots, X_n^A\}$, also using the maximum likelihood function with cross-entropy loss, it finally generates cross-linguistic text summaries $S^B = \{Y_1^B, Y_2^B, Y_3^B, \ldots, Y_l^B\}$, where the m and l are the lengths of the input text and the cross-lingual summary and $l < n$. The task form is as follows:

$$S_{cls} = -\sum_{j=1}^{l} logP(Y_j^B | Y_{<j}^B, X) \tag{2}$$

After fine-tuning the teacher model, we trained the student model on a cross-lingual summary dataset. Such training enabled the student model to inherit the same encoding capabilities as the teacher model and the ability to decode in the target language.

3.1.4. Attention Weight

The summary model generates summaries by automatically assigning weights to each word in each input sentence. These weights are the importance of each word in the summary generation process. In the teacher model, the encoder processes the source language input X^A, while the decoder receives the source language summary Y^A, thereby facilitating the provision of attention alignment information from X^A to Y^A. In the student model, the encoder also takes the source language X^A as input, allowing the teacher model to furnish direct and effective supervisory information. Ref. [10] defined the attention weight distribution matrix in a cross-lingual sentence summarization model as A_j. During training, it is desired that the attention weight B_j of the student model approximates the attention weight A_j of the teacher model. Therefore, we use the attention relay approach and Euclidean distance to encourage the consistency of the attention weights of the student model and the teacher models' attention weights. The formula is as follows:

$$L_{att} = -\sqrt{\sum_j (A_j - B_j)^2} \tag{3}$$

where j represents the location of the attention weight. Through Equation (3), the student model can learn the attention weights from the teacher model to better understand the semantics of the input sentences.

Note that the teacher and student models use a Transformer architecture that contains multiple attention heads but omits self-attention in the Transformer. Therefore, we use the average attention method, which averages all attention heads' weights in the same layer.

3.1.5. Word Distribution

The word distribution reflects the ability of the teacher model to understand and summarize the input text. To better understand the associations and similarities between different words, the student model learns the word distribution of the teacher model. This can improve the accuracy and coherence of the cross-lingual summaries. Therefore, we use the cross-entropy loss to encourage the similarity of the probability distributions of the summary words generated by the two models. The formula is as follows:

$$L_{word} = -P(Y_i^A|Y_{<i-1}^A, X)logP(Y_i^B|Y_{<i-1}^B, X) \quad (4)$$

where $P(Y_i^A|Y_{<i-1}^A, X)$ denotes the summary word distribution of the teacher model and $P(Y_i^B|Y_{<i-1}^B, X)$ denotes the summary word distribution of the student model.

3.2. Similarity Metric

To understand the relationships between texts that are context-rich and cross-linguistic, we propose a similarity metric based on bidirectional semantic alignment inspired by [23]. The approach uses bidirectional semantic alignment, allowing the model to capture more contextual information at different locations in the text and making the metric more focused on the overall context of the text. The process is shown in Figure 4.

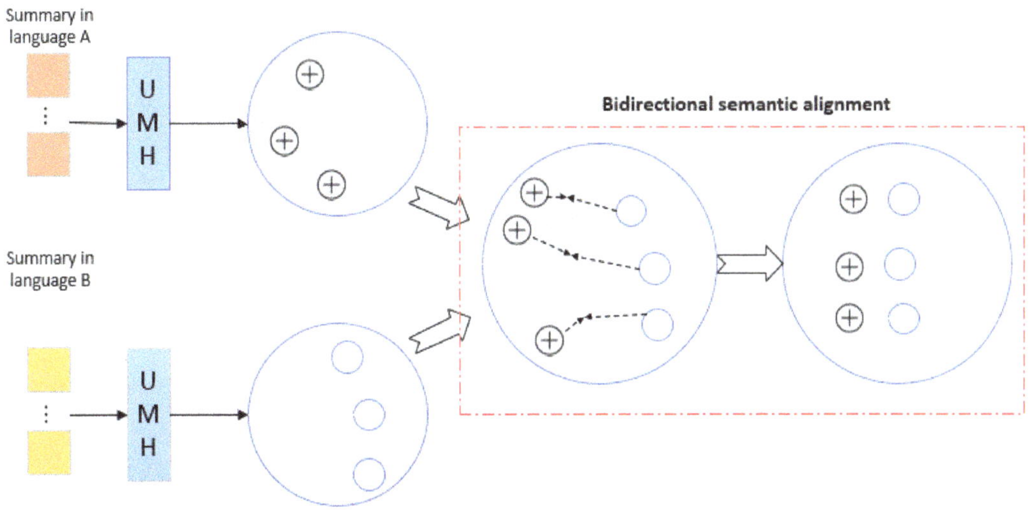

Figure 4. The similarity metric is based on bidirectional semantic alignment. The summaries in language A and language B are mapped to the same vector space by the UMH. Then, the distance between the vectors is measured using the similarity metric through bidirectional semantic alignment.

The teacher and student models generate summaries in two languages. Their linguistic representations lie on different vector spaces. So, the similarity of the two summaries cannot be calculated directly. We use UMH, an unsupervised hyper-alignment for multilingual word embeddings, to map the word vectors of summaries in different languages to a unified vector space. The formula is as follows:

$$\min_{Q_i, P_{i,j}} \sum_{i,j} \alpha_{i,j} l(X_i Q_i, P_{ij} X_j Q_j) \quad (5)$$

where α is the weighting coefficient and X_i, X_j represent different languages. P and Q denote the allocation and mapping matrices, respectively.

Then, we apply optimal transport in a contextual embedding space. It uses the optimal solution of a relaxed transport problem as a distance metric and converts the distance metric to the corresponding similarity measure with the following equation:

$$Sim_{s1}(s^1, s^2) = \frac{1}{L_1} \sum_{i=1}^{L_1} \underset{j}{max}\, cos(x_i^1, x_j^2) \tag{6}$$

$$Sim_{s2}(s^2, s^1) = \frac{1}{L_2} \sum_{j=1}^{L_2} \underset{i}{max}\, cos(x_i^2, x_j^1) \tag{7}$$

where *s1* and *s2* represent the summaries in two different languages and L_1 and L_2 represent the lengths of the summaries in the two languages. x_i^1 represents the sentence token of the summary in language 1, and x_j^2 represents the sentence token of the summary in language 2, where i and j represent the positions of the tokens. x_j^1 and x_i^2 mean the same as x_i^1 and x_j^2.

By comparing the word vectors in the two sentences one by one and choosing the maximum cosine similarity value, we can obtain two scores that measure the similarity of the sentences. These scores were averaged to obtain a combined bidirectional semantic alignment metric between the two summary sentences. The formula is as follows:

$$Sim(s^1, s^2) = \frac{1}{2}(Sim_{s1}(s^1, s^2) + Sim_{s2}(s^2, s^1)) \tag{8}$$

3.3. Contrastive Learning

We use contrastive learning to enhance the ability of the similarity metric for bidirectional semantic alignment. We consider the monolingual summaries generated by the teacher model as positive samples. Moreover, following the idea of [24], we use the other sentences in the batch as negative pairs. We then calculate the similarity metrics of the cross-lingual summaries to the positive and negative samples separately so that the cross-lingual summaries are close to the predicted values for the positive samples and far from a certain threshold for the negative samples. The process is shown in Figure 5. This enables the final generated cross-language text summaries to express the same content as the positive samples. So, the contrast learning for sentence i in the batch is defined as follows.

For the above distillation process, we define our distillation loss as follows:

$$L_{KD} = \lambda_1 L_{att} + \lambda_2 L_{word} + \lambda_3 L_{sim} \tag{9}$$

where L_{att} comes from Equation (3), L_{word} comes from Equation (4), and L_{sim} comes from Equation (8). λ_1, λ_2, and λ_3 are the weighted hyper-parameters.

$$L_{sim} = -log \frac{exp(\frac{Sim(s^i, S_+^i)}{\tau})}{\sum_{j=1}^{B}(exp(\frac{Sim(s^i, S_+^j)}{\tau}) + exp(\frac{Sim(s^i, S_-^j)}{\tau}))} \tag{10}$$

where τ is the temperature parameter, B is the batch size, and s_+ and s_- represent positive and negative samples, respectively.

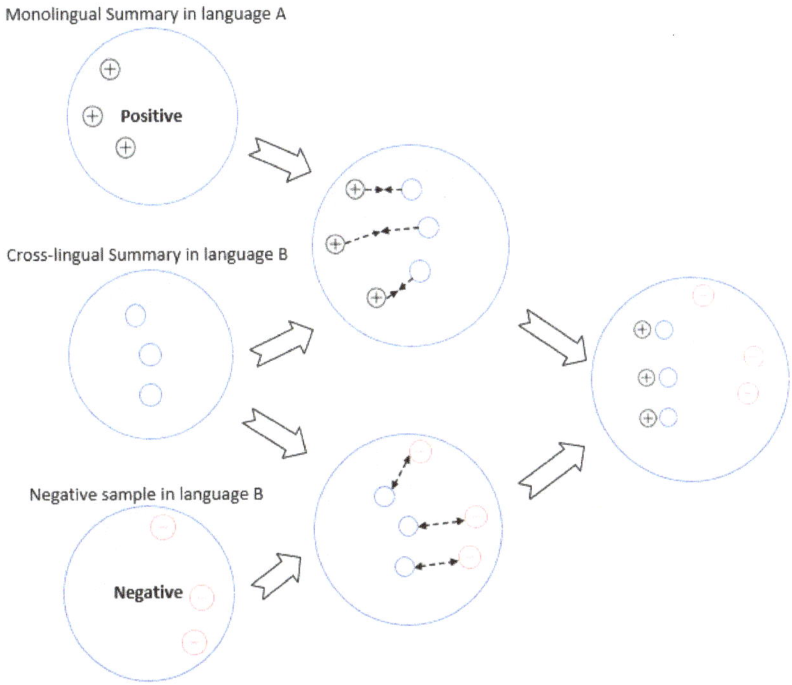

Figure 5. Contrast learning. We used the monolingual summary in language A as a positive sample. Following the idea of [24], we used other sentences in language B in the batch as negative sentence pairs. Then, the positive and negative samples and the cross-lingual summary are aligned using the similarity measure.

3.4. Training Objective

We propose a cross-lingual summary model based on knowledge distillation. Its overall model framework is shown in Figure 4. Our total training loss is computed as follows for each input:

$$L = S_{cls} + \delta L_{KD} \tag{11}$$

where S_{cls} comes from Equation (2) and L_{KD} comes from Equation (10). δ is a weighted hyper-parameter that balances the weights between S_{cls} and L_{KD}.

4. Experiments

4.1. Datasets and Evaluation

To validate the effectiveness of our method on the languages with separate syntactic structures and vocabulary morphologies in low-resource settings, we processed the Wikilingua [25] dataset. Inspired by [20], we use a back-translation pre-processing strategy to convert each sample into a document consisting of three parts: a document, a monolingual summary, and a cross-language summary.

For the evaluation, we specifically chose four linguistic variants that exhibited variations in either structure or morphology. These variants include En2ArSum (summary from English to Arabic), En2ViSum (summary from English to Vietnamese), and En2JaSum (summary from English to Japanese). Moreover, to validate the performance of the model in cross-language summarization tasks where the source language is not English, we also introduce Ja2EnSum (summary from Japanese to English) with the same content as En2JaSum. The selected dataset encompasses diverse syntactic structures and character sets across several languages. The En2ViSum dataset presents a low-resource scenario with a mere 7500 samples. The average lengths of the source texts, monolingual summaries, and cross-lingual summaries for each dataset and the size of each dataset are shown in Table 1.

Table 1. Statistics for the Wikilingua variant datasets.

Dataset	Len_{Source}	Len_{MLS}	Len_{CLS}	Size
En2ArSum	1589	227	133	12,500
En2JaSum	1463	212	133	10,000
Ja2EnSum	2103	133	212	10,000
En2ViSum	1657	175	135	7500

After [26], most studies have used the standard ROUGE method to assess the performance of models. Therefore, we used the ROUGE method to evaluate the ROUGE-1, ROUGE-2, and ROUGE-L scores of our model on the Wikilingua variant dataset.

4.2. Implementation Details

We use mBART model to initialize our encoder and Xavier to initialize the decoder. The encoder and decoder have dimensions of 1024, and the model contains 1,277,437,076 parameters. The encoder and decoder use separate Adam optimizers, with learning rates of 0.002 and 0.2, respectively. The model is trained on a Tesla V100S-PCIE-32 GB with a training phase of 15,000 steps and gradient accumulation every five steps. To estimate the text similarity, we set the temperature parameter τ to 0.05 and the batch size to 128. The weighted hyper-parameters in the loss function are set to 1. In addition, the teacher model in the knowledge distillation framework has the same structure and parameters as the student model. In the training phase, the monolingual summary teacher model is first trained. Then, the cross-lingual summary student model learns the knowledge of the teacher model. In the inference phase, the student model is fed with textual content and undergoes three hours of inference to generate a summary.

4.3. Baseline

For performance comparison, we select several baselines that have better performances in the current study, comparing our proposed model architecture with the following baselines:

- mBART(mbart.cc25): Here, we fine-tune the mBART [1] model for a cross-lingual specific text summarization task, and we apply grid search to update hyper-parameters, such as the learning rate and batch size in the model, as a way to obtain the best performance of mBART in the downstream task.
- mBART + $MADP_D$: Inspired by [27], we use parallel data and connect each parallel instance of the two languages. Then, we combine these data with masking and noise reduction targets to train mBART further.
- MCLAS: The model in [28] is a strong baseline model that uses a unified decoder to generate sequential links between monolingual and cross-lingual summaries, making the monolingual summary task a prerequisite for the cross-lingual summarization task.
- Ref. [20] proposed a knowledge distillation framework based on the mBERT model. Furthermore, Sinkhorn scattering is utilized to bring the representation distance of summaries in two languages closer to generate high-quality cross-language text summaries.

4.4. Contrast Experiment

The experiments are validated on the En2ArSum, En2ViSum, En2JaSum, and Ja2EnSum datasets in the low-resource scenario, and the experimental results correspond to Tables 2, 3, 4 and 5, respectively.

Table 2. The ROUGE score on the En2ArSum dataset for cross-lingual summarization.

Model	ROUGE-1	ROUGE-2	ROUGE-L
mBART	30.13	13.58	22.47
mBART + $MADP_D$	30.58	13.97	22.63
MCLAS	36.28	17.27	27.56
[20]	36.89	20.28	32.38
Our model	35.89	16.20	25.21

Table 3. The ROUGE score on the En2ViSum dataset for cross-lingual summarization.

Model	ROUGE-1	ROUGE-2	ROUGE-L
mBART	31.46	9.69	18.32
mBART + $MADP_D$	31.81	10.05	19.09
MCLAS	36.31	15.91	28.62
[20]	37.38	16.20	28.97
Our model	37.79	15.27	25.83

Table 4. The ROUGE score on the En2JaSum dataset for cross-lingual summarization.

Model	ROUGE-1	ROUGE-2	ROUGE-3
mBART	26.17	10.01	17.94
mBART + $MADP_D$	25.41	10.27	18.26
MCLAS	29.60	16.08	23.20
[20]	30.21	16.27	23.90
Our model	30.12	14.23	21.52

Table 5. The ROUGE score on the Ja2EnSum dataset for cross-lingual summarization.

Model	ROUGE-1	ROUGE-2	ROUGE-3
mBART	27.93	8.19	18.09
mBART + $MADP_D$	28.22	9.57	19.04
MCLAS	33.20	12.57	27.27
[20]	34.21	13.08	27.63
Our model	31.74	14.01	24.47

In Table 2 on the En2ArSum dataset, our model outperforms the mBART model by 5.76 points for ROUGE-1, 2.62 points for ROUGE-2, and 2.74 points for ROUGE-L. Similarly, in Table 3, on the En2ViSum dataset, which has slightly similar syntactic structures and semantic information, the ROUGE-1, ROUGE-2, and ROUGE-L scores of our model improve by 6.33, 5.58, and 7.51 points compared to the mBART model. In addition, we use two reverse datasets, the En2JaSum dataset and the Ja2EnSum dataset, to validate our model. For the En2JaSum dataset in Table 4, the ROUGE-1, ROUGE-2, and ROUGE-L scores of our model improve by 3.95, 4.22, and 3.58 points compared to the mBART model. For the reverse dataset Ja2EnSum in Table 5, our model outperforms the mBART model by 3.81 points for ROUGE-1, 5.82 points for ROUGE-2, and 6.38 points for ROUGE-L. There is a significant improvement in the performance of our model compared to the mBART model. This shows that our model can build a strong correlation between two languages by adopting the knowledge distillation framework, and it has improved in semantic and context understanding.

Compared to the strong baseline MCLAS model, in Table 2, on the En2ArSum dataset, we see that our model is just 0.39, 1.07, and 2.35 points lower on ROUGE-1, ROUGE-2, and ROUGE-L. Similarly, in Table 3, on the En2ViSum dataset, the ROUGE-1 scores of our model improve by 1.438 points. For the En2JaSum dataset in Table 4, the ROUGE-1 scores of our model improve by 0.52 points. It shows that our model can capture and retain critical information in the generated summaries. For the reverse dataset Ja2EnSum in Table 5, our model outperforms the MCLAS model 1.44 points for ROUGE-2. Compared to [20], the partial ROUGE values of our model on the En2ViSum dataset and the Ja2EnSum dataset increased. In particular, the ROUGE-1 score on the low-resource dataset En2ViSum improved by 0.41. In contrast, the partial ROUGE values on the other datasets decreased only slightly. This demonstrates that our model can correctly capture the contextual relationships between words in a summary, generating a more coherent cross-linguistic summary. We can see that our model performance has some improvement on some datasets. It shows that our model is competitive.

In conclusion, our approach can improve the quality of cross-lingual summaries on language pairs with separate syntactic structures and vocabulary morphologies in low-resource scenarios.

4.5. Ablation Experiment

We conduct the following ablation experiments on our model to investigate the importance of different model components for improving the quality of cross-lingual summaries.

4.5.1. Attention Weight and Word Distribution

We adopt a knowledge distillation to distill the attention weight and word distribution of the monolingual teacher model into the cross-lingual student model. To verify the rationality of distilled content, we set the following variables on the En2ArSum dataset: (1) no distilled content (non-KD), (2) no distilled attention weight (our model—attention weight), and (3) no distillation word distribution (our model—word distribution), (4) simultaneous distillation attention weight and word distribution (our model). The ablation experiments results of knowledge distillation are shown in Table 6.

Table 6. Results of ablation tests of attention weight and word distribution.

Method	ROUGE-1	ROUGE-2	ROUGE-3
Non-KD	31.41	14.27	22.98
Our model—attention weight	32.59	14.31	23.75
Our model—word distribution	32.74	14.28	23.92
Our model	35.89	16.20	25.21

The analysis of the experimental results in Table 6 shows that distilling only the attention weights or word distribution improves the performance of the model compared to no distilled content. This is because distilling the attention weights of the teacher model can help the student model better understand the critical information in the original text, thus improving the accuracy of the generated summaries. The distillation of word distribution can better guide the student model to learn the content and structure of the text, thus improving the readability of the generated summaries. Our model distills both attention weights and word distributions, resulting in the cross-lingual model having significant performance improvements and the cross-lingual summaries becoming more accurate and fluent.

4.5.2. Similarity Metric

We use a similarity metric via optimal transport-based contrastive learning, constructing a bidirectional semantic alignment between two different language summaries. To verify the rationality of the similarity metric, we set the following variables on the En2ArSum dataset: (1) no similarity metric (non-Sim), (2) average pooling (average pooling), (3) bidirectional semantic alignment of similarity metric (Bid-Sim), (4) Bid-Sim with contrast learning (our model). The experimental results are shown in Table 7.

Table 7. Results of ablation tests in text similarity.

Method	ROUGE-1	ROUGE-2	ROUGE-3
Non-Sim	32.31	14.79	23.74
Average pooling	32.43	14.80	23.78
Bid-Sim	33.16	14.92	24.05
Our model	35.89	16.20	25.21

The analysis of the experimental results in Table 7 shows that the quality of cross-lingual summaries can be improved using only the average pooling. Compared with the average pooling, Bid-Sim captures the bidirectional semantic similarity between two texts and mitigates the influence of language differences, improving the ROUGE score. As seen from lines 3 and 4, our model further improves the quality of the generated cross-lingual summaries. We think that because contrast learning helps the model to focus on the differences between languages it can better capture text bidirectional semantics.

4.5.3. Vector Space Mapping

Since the teacher and student models generate summaries in different languages, the representation of two summaries lies on different vector spaces. To verify the rationality of the vector space mapping method, we set the following variables on the En2ArSum dataset: (1) GeoMM [29], (2) Gromov–Wasserstein (GW) [30],(3) ICP [31],(4) UMH (our model). The experimental results are shown in Table 8.

Table 8. Results of ablation tests in vector space mapping.

Method	ROUGE-1	ROUGE-2	ROUGE-3
GeoMM	34.72	15.48	23.07
GW	34.91	15.75	23.66
ICP	35.14	16.03	24.54
Our model	35.89	16.20	25.21

The analysis of the experimental results in Table 8 shows that the UMH method maps vectors from different spaces to the same vector space better than other space vector mapping methods. This is because the UMH method can maximize the quality of word translation between languages when mapping each language into a common space.

4.6. *Case Study*

We take the example of a cross-lingual summary from English to Arabic. We compare our model with three models. The results of the summaries generated by each model are shown in Figure 6.

In Table 2, on the En2ArSum dataset, we choose two samples of high-quality summaries generated by the baseline model. As can be seen, except for the MCLAS model and [20], the other baseline models are missing keywords, e.g., "cooperation" in sample 1 and "traffic control" and "temporary" in sample 2. Our model and MCLAS can extract most of the keywords. However, in sample 1, MCLAS generates the wrong person's name. Our model and [20] can extract keywords from text and generate text summaries with complete semantics. Therefore, the quality of the summaries generated by our model is competitive, even sometimes better than MCLAS regarding summary readability.

Sample 1

Source: Former US Secretary of State Henry Kissinger and Clinton Secretary of State Madeleine Albright stressed the importance of the US-China relationship in New York City on Monday night, expressing optimism about the two countries' cooperation with the US in the direction of the transition to the Trump administration.
(**Translation:** 前美国国务卿亨利·基辛格和克林顿国务卿马德琳·奥尔布赖特周一晚上在纽约市强调了美中关系的重要性，对两国与美国向特朗普政府过渡方向的合作表示乐观。)

mBART: وزيرا خارجية أمريكيان يؤكدان على أهمية العلاقات مع الصين. (**Translation**: Two US Secretary of State emphasized the importance of relations with China.)

mBART+MADP_D: اثنين من وزراء الخارجية السابقين : أهمية أمريكا الوسطى والتفاؤل بشأن ولاية ترامب. (**Translation:** Two former secretaries of state: The importance of Central America and optimism about the Trump presidency.)

MCLAS: كيسنجر أولبرايت التأكيد على أهمية العلاقات بين الولايات المتحدة والصين ، متفائل بشأن التعاون خلال الفترة الانتقالية من حكومة ترامب. (**Translation:** Kissinger Albright emphasized the importance of China US relations and expressed optimism about cooperation during the Trump administration's transitional period.)

Nguyen, T et al.(2021): كيسنجر أولبرايت شدد على أهمية العلاقات بين الولايات المتحدة والصين ، وأعرب عن تفاؤله بشأن التعاون مع حكومة ترامب خلال الفترة الانتقالية. (**Translation:** Kissinger and Albright emphasized the importance of China US relations and expressed optimism about cooperation with the Trump administration during the transitional period.)

Our Model: **كيسنجر أولبرايت** على أهمية العلاقات بين الولايات المتحدة والصين ، متفائل بشأن **التعاون** مع حكومة ترامب. (**Translation:** Kissinger and Albright emphasized the importance of China US relations and expressed optimism about cooperation with the Trump administration.)

Monolingual summary: Kissinger and Albright emphasized the importance of US-China relations and expressed optimism for cooperation in the transition to the Trump administration.

Reference: كيسنجر أولبرايت على أهمية العلاقات بين الولايات المتحدة والصين ، وأعرب عن تفاؤله بشأن التعاون خلال الفترة الانتقالية إلى حكومة ترامب .

Sample 2

Source: On Monday morning, a group of nearly 50 Tibetan antelopes was seen gathering by the side of the road at a section of the Qinghai-Tibet Highway. As a precautionary measure, the staff of the nature reserve implemented temporary traffic control to ensure safety.
(**Translation:** 周一早上，在青藏公路的一个路段，看到一群近 50 只藏羚羊聚集在路边。作为预防措施，自然保护区的工作人员实施了临时交通管制，以确保安全。)

mBART: الموظفين في التبت الظباء الأغنام بالقرب من الطريق السريع لتنفيذ الرقابة. (**Translation**: Xizang staff are monitoring near the expressway.)

mBART+MADP_D: الظباء التبتية تجمعوا على طول الطريق السريع تشينغهاى التبت ، مما دفع الموظفين لمراقبة حركة المرور. (**Translation:** Xizang antelopes gathered along the Qinghai Tibet Expressway, prompting staff to monitor traffic.)

MCLAS: الظباء التبتية يتجمعون في تشينغهاى التبت السريع ، محمية طبيعية مؤقتة لمراقبة حركة المرور لحماية الموظفين (**Translation:** Tibetan antelopes gather in the fast-paced Shanghai of Qinghai Tibet, a temporary traffic controlled nature reserve to protect employees)

Nguyen, T et al.(2021): التبت الظباء على طول الطريق السريع بين تشينغهاى والتبت ، حيث الموظفين في المناطق المحمية المؤقتة لمراقبة حركة المرور. (**Translation:** Tibetan antelopes along the Qinghai Tibet Highway are being monitored for traffic by staff in temporary protected areas.)

Our Model: الظباء التبتيين تجمعوا على طول الطريق السريع ، والموظفين في المناطق المحمية المؤقتة لمراقبة حركة المرور السريع. (**Translation:** Tibetan antelope gather along the highway, and reserve staff conducts temporary traffic control.)

Monolingual summary: Tibetan antelopes gathered by the Qinghai-Tibet Highway, prompting temporary traffic control from nature reserve staff.

Reference: الظباء التبتية تجمعوا على طول الطريق السريع تشينغهاى التبت ، مما دفع موظفي المحميات الطبيعية المؤقتة لمراقبة حركة المرور .

Figure 6. Case studies of English-to-Arabic summarization (Nguyen, T et al. (2021) from the [20]).

5. Conclusions

This paper proposes a knowledge distillation model to construct strong correlations between two languages with separate syntactic structures and vocabulary morphologies in low-resource settings. We construct a monolingual teacher model and a cross-lingual student model, respectively. The attention weight and word distribution from the teacher model are transferred to the student model. Furthermore, we propose a similarity metric based on contrast learning to estimate cross-lingual differences effectively. Extensive experiments show that our approach has an improved accuracy and performance in low-resource settings for languages with separate syntactic structures and vocabulary morphologies.

Our research addresses the challenges of cross-linguistic associations, especially by enhancing the collaboration of editors in editing overseas reports. By providing relevant experimental results demonstrating the effectiveness of our model in low-resource environments, we aim to emphasize the great strides our approach has made in facilitating effective multilingual collaboration. However, one potential weakness of our work is that it may not perform as well in languages with more complex syntaxes and vocabularies. We plan to attempt to address this issue in future research endeavors.

Author Contributions: Conceptualization, X.Y. and J.Y.; methodology, X.Y.; software, X.Y.; validation, X.Y.; formal analysis, X.Y., J.Y. and B.Z.; investigation, X.Y. and B.Z.; resources, J.Y. and L.L.; data curation, X.Y. and Q.B.; writing—original draft preparation, X.Y.; writing—review and editing, X.Y.,

B.Z. and J.Y.; visualization, X.Y.; supervision, J.Y. and L.L.; project administration, J.Y. All authors have read and agreed to the published version of this manuscript.

Funding: The work was supported by the National Natural Science Foundation of China (62062055); Basic Scientific Research Expenses Program of Universities directly under Inner Mongolia Autonomous Region (JY20220249); and Teaching Reform Project for Postgraduate Education under the Inner Mongolia University of Technology (YJG2021016).

Data Availability Statement: Data are contained within the article.

Conflicts of Interest: The authors declare no conflict of interest.

References

1. Liu, Y.; Gu, J.; Goyal, N.; Li, X.; Edunov, S.; Ghazvininejad, M.; Zettlemoyer, L. Multilingual denoising pre-training for neural machine translation. *Trans. Assoc. Comput. Linguist.* **2020**, *8*, 726–742. Available online: https://arxiv.org/pdf/2001.08210v2.pdf (accessed on 13 August 2022). [CrossRef]
2. Xue, L.; Constant, N.; Roberts, A.; Kale, M.; Al-Rfou, R.; Siddhant, A.; Raffel, C. mT5: A massively multilingual pre-trained text-to-text transformer. *arXiv* **2020**, arXiv:2010.11934.
3. Liang, Y.; Meng, F.; Zhou, C.; Xu, J.; Chen, Y.; Su, J.; Zhou, J. A variational hierarchical model for neural cross-lingual summarization. *arXiv* **2022**, arXiv:2203.03820.
4. Bjerva, J.; Östling, R.; Veiga, M.H.; Tiedemann, J.; Augenstein, I. What do language representations really represent? *Comput. Linguist.* **2019**, *45*, 381–389. [CrossRef]
5. Alaux, J.; Grave, E.; Cuturi, M.; Joulin, A. Unsupervised hyperalignment for multilingual word embeddings. *arXiv* **2018**, arXiv:1811.01124.
6. Wan, X.; Li, H.; Xiao, J. Cross-language document summarization based on machine translation quality prediction. In Proceedings of the 48th Annual Meeting of the Association for Computational Linguistics, Uppsala, Sweden, 11–16 July 2010.
7. Zhang, J.; Zhou, Y.; Zong, C. Abstractive cross-language summarization via translation model enhanced predicate argument structure fusing. *IEEE/ACM Trans. Audio Speech Lang. Process.* **2016**, *24*, 1842–1853. [CrossRef]
8. Linhares Pontes, E.; Huet, S.; Torres-Moreno, J.M.; Linhares, A.C. Cross-language text summarization using sentence and multi-sentence compression. In Proceedings of the Natural Language Processing and Information Systems: 23rd International Conference on Applications of Natural Language to Information Systems, NLDB 2018, Paris, France, 13–15 June 2018.
9. Zhu, J.; Wang, Q.; Wang, Y.; Zhou, Y.; Zhang, J.; Wang, S.; Zong, C. NCLS: Neural cross-lingual summarization. *arXiv* **2019**, arXiv:1909.00156.
10. Duan, X.; Yin, M.; Zhang, M.; Chen, B.; Luo, W. Zero-shot cross-lingual abstractive sentence summarization through teaching generation and attention. In Proceedings of the 57th Annual Meeting of the Association for Computational Linguistics, Florence, Italy, 28 July–2 August 2019.
11. Cheng, J.; Lapata, M. Neural summarization by extracting sentences and words. *arXiv* **2016**, arXiv:1603.07252.
12. Radford, A.; Narasimhan, K.; Salimans, T.; Sutskever, I. Improving Language Understanding by Generative Pre-Training. 2018. Available online: https://www.mikecaptain.com/resources/pdf/GPT-1.pdf (accessed on 7 March 2023).
13. Devlin, J.; Chang, M.W.; Lee, K.; Toutanova, K. Bert: Pre-training of deep bidirectional transformers for language understanding. *arXiv* **2018**, arXiv:1810.04805.
14. Liu, Y.; Ott, M.; Goyal, N.; Du, J.; Joshi, M.; Chen, D.; Stoyanov, V. Roberta: A robustly optimized bert pretraining approach. *arXiv* **2019**, arXiv:1907.11692.
15. Lewis, M.; Liu, Y.; Goyal, N.; Ghazvininejad, M.; Mohamed, A.; Levy, O.; Zettlemoyer, L. Bart: Denoising sequence-to-sequence pre-training for natural language generation, translation, and comprehension. *arXiv* **2019**, arXiv:1910.13461.
16. Lample, G.; Conneau, A. Cross-lingual language model pretraining. *arXiv* **2019**, arXiv:1901.07291.
17. Huot, F.; Maynez, J.; Alberti, C.; Amplayo, R.K.; Agrawal, P.; Fierro, C.; Lapata, M. μ PLAN: Summarizing using a Content Plan as Cross-Lingual Bridge. *arXiv* **2023**, arXiv:2305.14205.
18. Wang, J.; Meng, F.; Zheng, D.; Liang, Y.; Li, Z.; Qu, J.; Zhou, J. Towards Unifying Multi-Lingual and Cross-Lingual Summarization. *arXiv* **2023**, arXiv:2305.09220.
19. Wang, J.; Meng, F.; Lu, Z.; Zheng, D.; Li, Z.; Qu, J.; Zhou, J. Clidsum: A benchmark dataset for cross-lingual dialogue summarization. *arXiv* **2022**, arXiv:2202.05599.
20. Nguyen, T.; Tuan, L.A. Improving neural cross-lingual summarization via employing optimal transport distance for knowledge distillation. *arXiv* **2021**, arXiv:2112.03473.
21. Li, P.; Zhang, Z.; Wang, J.; Li, L.; Jatowt, A.; Yang, Z. ACROSS: An Alignment-based Framework for Low-Resource Many-to-One Cross-Lingual Summarization. In *Findings of the Association for Computational Linguistics: ACL 2023*; Association for Computational Linguistics: Cedarville, OH, USA, 2023; pp. 2458–2472.
22. Glorot, X.; Bengio, Y. Understanding the difficulty of training deep feedforward neural networks. In Proceedings of the Thirteenth International Conference on Artificial Intelligence and Statistics, JMLR Workshop and Conference Proceedings, Sardinia, Italy, 13–15 May 2010; pp. 249–256.

23. Lee, S.; Lee, D.; Jang, S.; Yu, H. Toward interpretable semantic textual similarity via optimal transport-based contrastive sentence learning. *arXiv* **2022**, arXiv:2202.13196.
24. Gao, T.; Yao, X.; Chen, D. Simcse: Simple contrastive learning of sentence embeddings. *arXiv* **2021**, arXiv:2104.08821.
25. Ladhak, F.; Durmus, E.; Cardie, C.; McKeown, K. WikiLingua: A new benchmark dataset for cross-lingual abstractive summarization. *arXiv* **2020**, arXiv:2010.03093.
26. Zhu, J.; Zhou, Y.; Zhang, J.; Zong, C. Attend, translate and summarize: An efficient method for neural cross-lingual summarization. In Proceedings of the 58th Annual Meeting of the Association for Computational Linguistics, Online, 5–10 July 2020.
27. Chi, Z.; Dong, L.; Wei, F.; Wang, W.; Mao, X.L.; Huang, H. Cross-lingual natural language generation via pre-training. In Proceedings of the AAAI Conference on Artificial Intelligence, New York, NY, USA, 7–12 February 2020.
28. Bai, Y.; Gao, Y.; Huang, H. Cross-lingual abstractive summarization with limited parallel resources. *arXiv* **2021**, arXiv:2105.13648.
29. Jawanpuria, P.; Balgovind, A.; Kunchukuttan, A.; Mishra, B. Learning multilingual word embeddings in latent metric space: A geometric approach. *Trans. Assoc. Comput. Linguist.* **2019**, 7, 107–120. [CrossRef]
30. Alvarez-Melis, D.; Jaakkola, T.S. Gromov-Wasserstein alignment of word embedding spaces. *arXiv* **2018**, arXiv:1809.00013.
31. Hoshen, Y.; Wolf, L. An iterative closest point method for unsupervised word translation. *arXiv* **2018**, arXiv:1801.06126.

electronics

MDPI

Article

Dynamic Artificial Bee Colony Algorithm Based on Permutation Solution

Yongkang Gong [1], Donglin Zhu [2], Chengtian Ouyang [3], Hongjie Guo [2,*] and Changjun Zhou [2]

[1] Institute of Future Technology, Jiangxi University of Applied Science and Technology, Nanchang 330006, China
[2] School of Computer Science and Technology, Zhejiang Normal University, Jinhua 321004, China
[3] School of Information Engineering, Jiangxi University of Science and Technology, Ganzhou 341000, China
* Correspondence: guohongjie@zjnu.edu.cn

Abstract: The artificial bee colony algorithm (ABC), as a classic swarm intelligence algorithm, has advantages such as fewer parameters and clear logic. However, ABC cannot balance the exploration and development stages well in the iterative process, and is easily affected by local optimal solutions in the final optimization stage, which affects the final optimal solution. To effectively compensate for the shortcomings of the algorithm, a neighbor learning artificial bee colony algorithm based on permutation solutions (CNABC) is proposed. In CNABC, a dynamic neighbor learning strategy is proposed to improve the search ability and optimal selection ability of the algorithm in the exploration phase. To solve the problem of lack of balance between exploration and development, the local optimal solution is used to guide the update of the surrounding difference. After the three stages of the algorithm are completed, a substitution mechanism is introduced, which replaces the worst solution by introducing external candidate solutions as feasible solutions, thereby improving the algorithm's ability to escape from local optima. Finally, comparative algorithm experiments are conducted on the CEC2022 test set, and compared with the TOP algorithm in the CEC competition on the CEC2022 test set. According to the experimental results, CNABC has good competitiveness in the comparative algorithm, which verifies the novelty and optimization ability of CNABC.

Keywords: intelligent optimization; artificial bee colony algorithm; dynamic neighbor learning; exchange mechanism; CEC function test set

1. Introduction

In the 21st century, the development of science and technology has made a qualitative leap. The ensuing meta-heuristic algorithms and optimization problems are gradually coming to the public's vision. An optimization problem refers to finding the smallest, best, or most efficient target solution in a complex problem. Optimization is increasingly being seen in biology [1], engineering optimization [2,3], production scheduling [4], feature selection [5,6], image processing [7], and network planning [8]. At present, with the complexity, diversification, and multi-quantification of optimization problems, traditional optimization methods, such as gradient descent method and Newton's method, fail to solve the problem in terms of time efficiency and target accuracy. Therefore, there is an increasing demand for efficient, stable, and robust optimization algorithms. Therefore, the emergence of swarm intelligent optimization algorithms brings good news to this phenomenon. Swarm intelligence optimization algorithms, inspired by cooperation, competition, or symbiosis among natural organisms, have been applied to computational intelligence by many scholars. Eberhart et al. [9] proposed a novel particle swarm optimization (PSO) algorithm in 1995, which attracted the attention of many researchers to swarm intelligence optimization; in 1991, Dorigo M et al. [10] designed and proposed the ant colony optimization (ACO) algorithm, inspired by the pheromones generated by the communication of ant communities when foraging outside; Yang et al. [11] proposed the cuckoo algorithm based on the living habits of cuckoo birds; Seyedali Mirjalili et al. [12] were inspired by the hunting method of wolves in 2014 and proposed the grey wolf optimizer (GWO) with reasonable logic and simple parameters; Xue et al. [13] proposed the sparrow search algorithm (SSA) in 2020 with simple parameters and population classification based on the cooperative competition relationship during the foraging division of sparrows; Zhu et al. [14] developed a new human memory optimization algorithm (HMO) by simulating human memory behavior. The aforesaid algorithms, such as the particle swarm optimization algorithm, merely employ the information of the global optimum and individual optimum within the swarm, thereby resulting in a relatively lower precision of the outcome. The ant colony algorithm is characterized by complex parameter adjustment, and the inherent positive feedback mechanism of the algorithm itself is prone to being trapped in local optima. The Levy flight strategy of the cuckoo algorithm during the random walk stage makes it arduous to set the step size when updating the candidate solutions. The gray wolf algorithm is highly reliant on parameter settings during optimization and its capacity for global search is unstable. The sparrow search algorithm has a comparatively slow convergence rate during optimization and its parameter settings are rather intricate. The human memory algorithm lacks some dynamic adaptability and is incapable of fully simulating the human memory mechanism. But, compared with traditional optimization methods, swarm intelligence optimization algorithms have the advantages of simple implementation, fewer parameters, strong exploration ability, and strong logical structure, and are widely used in many fields by many researchers [15–18].

Inspired by the division of labor and behavior of the bee population in nectar collection, Karaboga et al. [19] proposed an artificial bee colony algorithm (ABC) in 2005. The algorithm divides the process of honey collection into three stages: the hiring stage, the following stage, and the reconnaissance stage. As part of the swarm intelligence algorithm, the artificial bee colony algorithm has the characteristics of clear logic, complete and easy to understand structure, fast convergence speed, and strong optimization ability. At present, it has certain advantages compared with existing particle swarm optimization algorithms, grey wolf algorithms, etc. ABC has also been applied in many fields, such as parameter optimization supporting SVM models [20], predictive coding based on biological RNA sequences [21], predictive analysis of photovoltaic energy storage models [22], and flight scheduling during adverse weather conditions [23], among other practical problems.

However, as a swarm intelligence algorithm, ABC cannot escape the no free lunch (NFL) law [24], it cannot show the outstanding side in all fields, and will always show the unsatisfactory side in some problems. During the process of search optimization, ABC depends on random population individuals, disregarding the benefits of information exchange. Due to the alternation of information and the mechanism of random search, the convergence efficiency of the algorithm is slowed down. For complex problems, the ABC algorithm may encounter problems such as slow solution updates, slightly insufficient optimization ability, and randomness in target solution search.

Therefore, in order to comprehensively improve the problems of ABC mentioned above, many researchers have improved ABC to make the original ABC more capable of solving complex optimization problems, and finally applied the improved ABC variant to different field projects. Wang et al. [25] proposed a novel binary optimization cross artificial bee colony algorithm applied to the problem of location selection for incompetent facilities (nABC). Based on the fusion of binary ABC, a cross strategy and a new disturbance frequency were proposed to improve the efficiency of information exchange between bees, while eliminating the random disturbance caused by the update strategy in the original ABC. Gürcan Yavuz et al. [26] proposed an artificial bee colony algorithm (SSEABC) based on an adaptive search equation and a competitive local search strategy. This feature eliminates inappropriate search equation groups through adaptive strategies, and then adds new food sources to the optimal food source location through competitive local search strategies and incremental population size strategies to ensure the convergence efficiency of SSEABC. Zhou et al. [27] improved the artificial bee colony algorithm by combining deep Q-learning strategy and introducing adaptive strategy. The improved ABC more reasonably selects domain search operators, while expanding the search range of the population. At the same time, it minimizes energy allocation and consumption in milk truck scheduling projects and has a good improvement on the inherent Nphard problem. Ye et al. [28] applied the depth-first search strategy to the newly proposed stochastic domain structure strategy, which improved the search ability and solution accuracy of ABC, and to some extent helped the ABC algorithm jump out of local extremum. Zhou et al. [29] proposed a strategy for online fitness value analysis to improve the artificial bee colony algorithm. By identifying the structure of the problem to be solved and selecting the appropriate fitness value problem strategy, the online FLA technology was finally designed to improve the computational power of ABC and improve the efficiency of the algorithm at low cost. Zhou et al. [30] proposed an adaptive domain topology strategy to enhance the population diversity of ABC, enhance the transmission of valuable information, and improve the reconnaissance bee stage, while incorporating a random selection strategy at the end. It is used to reduce computational waste, improve the search efficiency of the algorithm, and jump out of local optima, greatly improving the accuracy of the original ABC. Indadul et al. [31] combined eight different rules with the roulette wheel to improve the accuracy of understanding. At the same time, a fixed number of perturbation techniques are added during the reconnaissance bee stage, so that the points trapped in the local optimum can jump out of the local optimum. Finally, the improved ABC is applied to solve the traveling salesman problem with good results. Zheng et al. [32] proposed an ABC algorithm based on population umbrella layering, which layers the historical information carried by the population and allows information exchange between levels. The above strategy improves the search ability of ABC and delays the convergence efficiency of the algorithm, improving the accuracy of the solution. Finally, the solution can jump out of the local optimum when trapped in a local optimum state. Song et al. [33] adjusted two solution update strategies applied in the exploration and development stages through adaptive mechanisms, and introduced the optimal solution to adjust the exploration and development stages. The algorithm ultimately achieved good results in solution accuracy and success rate. Guan et al. [34] proposed a self-regulating artificial bee colony algorithm (RCABC) based on random grouping, and improved the algorithm by proposing a dynamic random grouping strategy that has the opportunity to allocate the true solution set to subsets for optimization. At the same time, a self-regulating artificial bee colony strategy is used to improve the convergence of the algorithm and detect interaction features in subsets. The improved algorithm has shown good performance on both synthetic and real biological datasets. Wang et al. [35] fully utilized the professional performance advantages of individual bees, combined with the three stages of bee population, to combine behavior-based bee development and achieve individual professional division of labor. Finally, they achieved good results in testing functions and circular packaging problems. Tao et al. [36] combined two-dimensional vectors with adaptive perturbation and local search to generate a multi-strategy combined adaptive artificial bee colony algorithm, which increased the search ability of the algorithm. Finally, the effectiveness of the improved algorithm was verified on a randomly generated dataset combined with an actual workshop scheduling system. Yang et al. [37] proposed a discrete artificial bee colony algorithm (DABC) with a variable domain structure and four domain structures, and selectively applied them to the three stages of ABC. The improved algorithm achieved good results in solving distributed permutation flow shop problems with sequence dependent installation time. All of the above have proposed excellent and constructive enhancements based on ABC; however, certain deficiencies remain. (a) The majority of ABCs employ random or chaotic selection strategies in relation to search factors. Nevertheless, such random or chaotic approaches possess uncertainties and, thus, should not be overly selected or relied upon. (b) Multi-strategy combinations or fusions with other algorithms are implemented without considering whether the improved algorithm after fusion elevates the computational complexity or time complexity of the algorithm. (c) The aforementioned algorithms give less consideration to the issue of convergence efficiency caused by information exchange.

Numerous scholars have attained remarkable outcomes in the study of ABC, but it is imperative to improve the stability and limitations of the algorithm. Therefore, while conducting a comprehensive analysis and improvement of the ABC literature, this article proposes a dynamic neighbor learning artificial bee colony algorithm based on commutative solutions. Combining the characteristics of ABC solution updates, candidate solutions are introduced from outside, and the combination of introducing candidate competition habits and solution updates is adopted to achieve solutions stopping at different stages due to optimal stagnation. To achieve more comprehensive searches and higher accuracy in different stages to the greatest extent possible, existing uncertainty and instability is eliminated, and ultimately the performance of ABC is further optimized. At the same time, considering the convergence efficiency problem caused by ABC information exchange and addressing the randomness of the hiring bee stage, a dynamic neighbor learning strategy is proposed to improve convergence efficiency while reducing the randomness of selecting bee individuals as hiring bees by learning the characteristics of multiple neighbors. The main novelty and work of CNABC are as follows:

- Based on the ABC solution update model, a novel strategy is proposed to improve the performance of the algorithm by introducing candidate solution schemes externally.
- By using dynamic neighbor learning strategies to stimulate the enthusiasm of local bee populations and create better search efficiency, the optimization performance of the algorithm can be improved.
- The stability and effectiveness of CNABC on the CEC2022 function test set and the TOP competition algorithm is verified.

This paragraph elaborates on the writing style of CNABC, and its paragraph structure is described as follows: In Section 1, we introduce the relevant work of ABC algorithm. In Section 2, we briefly introduce the ideas and related processes of the original ABC. Section 3 provides a detailed introduction to the CNABC proposed in this article. In Section 4, CNABC is compared with different algorithms and improved algorithms to verify its effectiveness and superior performance. In Section 5, we compare it with the TOP algorithm to understand its advantages and limitations in some aspects. Section 6 provides a general summary of the writing CNABC and looks forward to future research directions.

2. Artificial Bee Colony Algorithm

The artificial bee colony algorithm (ABC) is a novel population-based swarm intelligence optimization algorithm proposed by Karaboga [13] based on the foraging behavior of bee colonies in nature. In the algorithm model, three types of bees in nature were emulated, namely hired bees, follower bees, and scout bees, and the algorithm was partitioned into three stages based on this. Based on the corresponding behaviors and division of labor, a positional update formula model for the three types of bees was generated, and, subsequently, the acquisition of the maximum honey source for the three types of bees was accomplished.

Similar to other swarm intelligence optimization algorithms, food sources (SNs) are generated during the population initialization phase. Herein, SN represents the number of populations and is also a candidate solution for the current iteration. The population commences with random sampling, undergoes the stages of hiring bees, following bees, and reconnaissance bees, and exits the cycle when it reaches the predetermined maximal function evaluations (FESmax) for the stopping conditions.

During the honeybee hiring phase, the hired bees use their previous stored information to search for food around the honey source, while recording relevant honey source information (honey source quantity) and transmitting information on the location of food sources within the dance area to recruit onlookers. At this stage, the behavior of hiring bees is to generate new food sources F_i near the candidate solution x_i. The mathematical model is as follows:

$$F_{i,j} = x_{i,j} + \varphi_{i,j} \cdot (x_{i,j} - x_{r,j}) \tag{1}$$

where φ is a number between [−1, 1] and is the object that hired bees choose to learn from SN honey sources, $i \in \{1, 2, \ldots, SN\}$ and $j \in \{1, 2, \ldots, D\}$ are integers within the defined domain. The last new honey source F_i and x_i choose between i using a greedy strategy, if x_i is poor, then the newly generated F_i will replace.

During the bee-following stage, the following bees lack a certain degree of subjective initiative and tend to follow elite bees to learn the way to find high-quality honey sources. However, the probability P_i of following bees to choose honey sources depends on the fitness value of the amount of nectar, and the elite bees selected by the following bees are determined based on the roulette wheel strategy. The probability formula is as follows:

$$P_i = fit_i / \sum_{i=1}^{SN} fit_i \tag{2}$$

$$F_{i,j} = x_{rand} + \varphi_{i,j} \cdot (x_{i,j} - x_{r,j}) \tag{3}$$

where fit_i is the fitness value of the i-th food source in the current iteration. From Formula (2), it can be seen that the probability P_i is directly proportional to fit_i. The better the fitness value of the food source, the higher the probability of being selected. In Formula (3), x_{rand} is a random bee in the population.

In the final reconnaissance stage, when the food source is limited to the defined range without numerical updates, we determine that the source of the thing does not meet the honey gathering requirements of bees and needs to be discarded. At this point, the reconnaissance bee needs to randomly search for new food sources within the defined global range and the formula is updated as follows:

$$x_{i,j} = lb + rand \cdot (ub - lb) \tag{4}$$

rand is a random number defined as uniformly distributed between [0, 1], while *lb* and *ub* are upper and lower bounds on the source of food.

3. A Neighbor Learning Artificial Bee Colony Algorithm with Exchange Elements

This paragraph introduces the strategy of substitution and introduces the habit of competitive learning through candidate solutions, with the aim of comparing the advantages and disadvantages of bee populations with candidate solutions and eliminating inferior solutions. Bees are no exception; thus, in artificial bee colony algorithms, individuals (solutions) with poor performance in the bee population are replaced, and their positions are updated through past optimal solutions. Therefore, for this approach, we propose a method to construct candidate solutions by creating new solutions externally. By introducing new and excellent bees to eliminate poorer individuals in the population, the excellent bees are encouraged to seek higher quality honey sources. This idea is evidently in line with the competitive habits of organisms. The strategy of the new solution updating method is based on a candidate solution of the bee population, so there is also a certain interaction between the candidate solutions, which fully utilizes the population-based information through cooperation, competition, and other means. At the same time, due to the cooperative relationship between bee colonies, a dynamic neighbor learning strategy is proposed in the recruitment stage. This strategy, combined with dynamic group discussion, guides poor solutions to a position update through good and excellent solutions, and locks the location of bee sources.

3.1. Exchange Solution Mechanism

Next, before the new candidate solution X_{in} is added to the population, a representative set of solutions $\{X_{best}, X_{avg}, X_{worst}^{rep}, X_{best}^{rep}, X_{rand}\}$ is created externally or selected based on past bee population information, collectively referred to as candidate solutions. The final substitution solution is solved through the above candidate solutions.

$$\begin{bmatrix} 0 & dist(X_1, X_2) & \cdots & dist(X_1, X_n) \\ dist(X_2, X_1) & 0 & \cdots & dist(X_2, X_n) \\ \cdots & \cdots & \cdots & \cdots \\ dist(X_n, X_1) & dist(X_n, X_2) & \cdots & 0 \end{bmatrix}$$

where $dist()$ represents the Euclidean distance between the bee individual i created in the similarity matrix and the remaining $N-1$ bee individuals. Next, the average Euclidean distance from the i-th bee individual to the remaining bee individuals is represented as follows. The candidate solution with the smallest S_i represents X_{best}^{rep}, the solution with the largest S_i represents X_{worst}^{rep}. $X_{avg} = 1/n\sum_{i=1}^{n} X_i$. X_{avg}, is calculated. Then, X_{in} is obtained by X_{best} and the formula is as follows:

$$S_i = 1/n\sum_{j=1}^{n} Dist_{ij}, i = 1 \cdots n \tag{5}$$

$$X_{in} = X_{best} + N(0, (1 - iter/Maxiter)) * (X_{best} - X_{avg}) \tag{6}$$

In Formula (6), $iter$ is the current number of iterations. $Maxiter$ is the maximum number of iterations, and N represents the standard deviation of a normal distribution with a mean of 0 and an expected value of $(1 - iter/Maxiter)$. Because the standard deviation is largely influenced by the optimization progress, the worst solution replaced by X_{in} in the early iterations is located further away from the optimal solution in the current iteration. As optimization continues, X_{in} will also become closer to the optimal solution in the current iteration. Then, considering that the positional relationship between the current optimal solution X_{best} and the average X_{avg} cannot represent a more comprehensive search space, there may be insufficient exploration of the region where X_{in} reaches the point. Therefore, the new candidate solutions X_{h1} and X_{h2} will be obtained by X_{best}^{rep}, X_{worst}^{rep}, and X_{rand}. The formula is as follows:

$$X_{h1} = X_{best} + N(0, (1 - iter/Maxiter)) * \left(X_{best} - X_{best}^{rep}\right) \tag{7}$$

$$X_{h2} = X_{best} + N(0, (1 - iter/Maxiter)) * \left(X_{best} - X_{worst}^{rep}\right) \tag{8}$$

Next, the final representative solution X_{rand} is created to avoid the possibility of generating candidate solutions far from the region of interest of the algorithm in future iterations when creating random solutions. Considering that the candidate solutions are externally created, the decision upper and lower bounds of X_{rand} will not use the algorithm's own upper and lower bounds, but instead use X_{min} and X_{max} from the generated similarity matrix as the boundaries of X_{rand}. The formula is as follows:

$$X_{rand} = X_{min} + rand(X_{max} - X_{min}) \tag{9}$$

In Formula (9), $rand$ is a random vector from 0 to 1.

Finally, X_{in} is updated based on the created or selected candidate solutions. The above operation will only be performed when the probability p meets the requirements and $p \leq 0.67$ is generally selected. In order to distinguish new candidate solutions, the obtained candidate solutions are numbered according to their order. The formula for updating candidate solutions is as follows:

$$X_{in}^{2} = rand * X_{in} + (1 - rand) * X_{rand} + R, rand \leq 0.5 \tag{10}$$

$$X_{in}^{3} = rand * X_{best} + (1 - rand) * X_{rand} + R, rand > 0.5 \tag{11}$$

In the formula, *rand* is a uniform random number in [0, 1]. It combines X_{rand} and X_{h1} as a random weight in X_{best}. The calculation of R is shown in Equation (12).

$$R = N(0, (1 - iter/Maxiter)) * (X_{h1} - X_{h2}) \tag{12}$$

This part of the equation uses the differences between auxiliary solutions to modify the results and moves the solutions to a new area. In the proposed hybrid algorithm, the worst candidate solution is replaced by the solution generated by the replacement solution update strategy.

$$X_{worst} = \begin{cases} X_{in}, rand > 0.67 \\ X_{in}^{2}, \ rand < 0.5 \\ X_{in}^{3}, else \end{cases} \tag{13}$$

The model diagram of the exchange element solution mechanism (EESM) is shown in Figure 1, and the pseudocode is shown in Algorithm 1:

Algorithm 1: Pseudocode for ESM

Input
SN: The number of current iteration populations
K: The number of candidate solutions is generally taken as 10% of the population size
X_{best}: *The optimal representative solution in the current iteration number*
X_{avg}: *The average solution of SN population solutions in the current iteration*
X_{worst}^{rep}: *Based on the similarity matrix, determine the average Euclidean distance from the individual to the remaining individuals, with the worst difference*
X_{best}^{rep}: *Obtain the optimal average Euclidean distance from an individual to the remaining individuals based on the similarity matrix*
X_{rand}: *Random solution created*
Output
X_{new}: *In the current iteration, the solution that ultimately replaces the difference in value*
1: ***For*** *i = 1 : K*
2: *Create new solution () based on and Created, (6)*
3: *Create solutions, and, (7)–(9)*
4: ***If*** *rand < 0.67 then*
5: ***If*** *rand < 0.5*
6: *Create* X_{in}^{2}, $X_{new} = X_{in}^{2}$, *(10)*
7: ***Else***
8: *Create* X_{in}^{3}, $X_{new} = X_{in}^{3}$, *(11)*
9: ***End If***
10: ***End If***
11: *Replace the* X_{new} *with Preyin*
12: ***End***
13: *Return* X_{new}

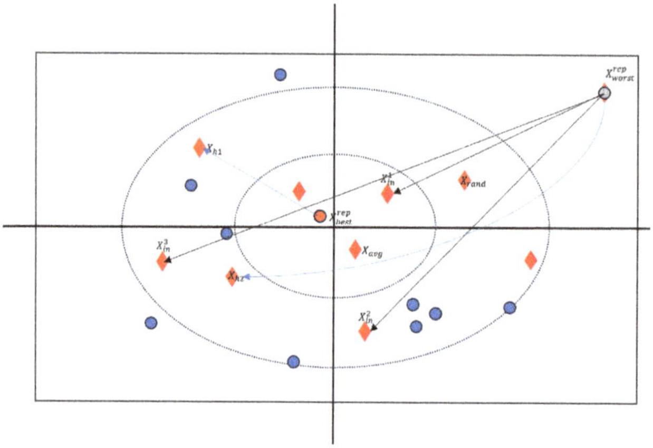

Figure 1. Schematic diagram of the exchange solution mechanism.

3.2. Dynamic Local Optimal Neighbor Learning

The optimization of primitive ABC involves extracting learning information from randomly selected individuals based on food sources and utilizing it as a medium for the optimization process. The original ABC optimization Formula (1) encapsulates this approach, demonstrating commendable performance in optimizing search processes by leveraging random food sources as learning objects, as indicated in [36]. However, the uniform probability associated with the quality of these randomly selected food sources significantly limits their effectiveness in developing and identifying optimal solutions. The current challenge lies in enhancing both the search efficiency and developmental capability of algorithms while achieving a balance between exploration and exploitation. In response to this challenge, this article proposes a dynamic local optimal neighbor learning strategy.

The bee dynamically selects N neighbors from the current iterated population and selects the best learning object among N neighbors for learning, ensuring the algorithm's global and local search capabilities. According to reference [38], the closer the N value is to SN, the closer the candidate solution is to the global optimal solution; on the contrary, it is a local optimal solution. Therefore, the N value in this article is determined to be 5. The updated formula is as follows:

$$F_{i,j} = x_{best}^{n,j} + \varphi_{i,j} \cdot \left(x_{best}^{n,j} - x_{i,j} \right) \tag{14}$$

X is the optimal value among the N neighbors of Xi currently.

The pseudocode for dynamic neighbor learning (DNL) is shown in Algorithm 2:

Algorithm 2: Pseudocode of DNL

Input
SN: *The number of current iteration populations*
$x_{best}^{n,j}$: *The optimal value within N neighbors in the current iteration.*
N: *N bee neighbors selected in the current iteration*
Output
$F_{i,j}$: *Generate new bee positions based on dynamic neighbor strategy in the current iteration*
1: ***For*** *i = 1:SN*
2: Use Formula (14) to update the position of bees
3: ***End for***
4: Return new position $F_{i,j}$

3.3. CNABC Process and Pseudocode

The process of learning artificial bee colony algorithm with swapped neighbors is as follows, with the pseudocode shown in Algorithm 3:

Algorithm 3: Pseudocode of CNABC

Input:
SN: *The number of populations*
N: *Update dynamically selected bee neighbors in iterations*
FESmax: *Maximum number of fitness value evaluations*
Dim: *Dimension of the problem*
K: *Number of candidate solutions*
Output:
$Fitness_{best}$: *The optimal fitness value output at the end of the loop condition*
X_{best}: *At the end of the loop condition, the optimal position corresponding to the optimal value*
1: Generate x_1, x_2, x_3, $\cdots x_n$ *food sources (SN) during population initialization stage*
2: Set the maximum fitness value evaluation frequency FESmax, problem dimension Dim, dynamic bee neighbors N, and K candidate solutions
3: FESmax = Dim × 10,000
4: ***While*** *FES < FESmax do*
*5: * Hiring Bee Stage **
6: ***For*** *i = 1 : SN*
7: Execute a dynamic neighbor learning strategy according to Equation (14) to generate a new bee position $X_{i(new)}$
8: ***If*** $f(X_i) > f(X_{i(new)})$ *then*
9: $X_i = X_{i(new)}$
10: trail = 0
11: ***Else***
12: trail = trail + 1
13: ***End if***
14: FES = FES + 1
15: ***End for***
*16: * Reconnaissance Bee Stage **
17: Calculate the probability p of the selected bee using Formula (2)
18: ***For*** *i = 1 : SN do*
19: Calculate the probability p according to Formula (2) to select the food source X_j,
20: Execute a dynamic neighbor guided search strategy according to Equation (14). Generate new candidate solution $X_{j(new)}$
21: ***If*** $f(X_j) > f(X_{j(new)})$ *then*
22: $X_j = X_{j(new)}$
23: trial = 0
24: ***else***
25: trial = trial + 1
26: ***End if***
27: FES = FES + 1
28: ***End For***
*29: *Scout bee phase**
30: ***For*** *i = 1 : SN do*
31: ***If*** *triali > limit then*
32: trial = 0
33: Execute global neighbor search strategy according to Equation (3) to generate a new solution $X_{i,j}$

Algorithm 3: Cont.

$X_{i,j} = V_{i,j}$
FES = FES + 1
End if
End for
***For** i = 1 : K*
Create new solution (X_{new}) based on X_{best}^{rep} and the created X_{avg}, (5)
Create solutions X_{h1}, X_{h2} and X_{rand}, (7)–(9)
***If** rand < 0.67 then*
***If** rand <0.5*
Create X_{in}^{2}, $X_{new} = X_{in}^{2}$, (10)
Else
Create X_{in}^{3}, $X_{new} = X_{in}^{3}$, (11)
End If
End if
Replace the X_{new} with Preyin
End For
End while
Return X_{best} & $Fitness_{best}$

3.4. Analysis of Algorithm Time Complexity

Time complexity is the ability to comprehensively consider the efficiency, performance, and computational cost of an algorithm. Therefore, in order to demonstrate that CNABC does not increase the time complexity of the algorithm, this article conducts macro- and micro-analyses on CNABC and ABC. In the macro analysis, during the operation of ABC, assuming the number of food sources is M, the time required to initialize the consumption of each honey source is O(t1), and the time required to calculate the objective function of the Dim dimension problem is O(D). Therefore, the total time consumed to complete the initialization of the honey source is O(M × (t1)). Entering an iteration, the time consumed to calculate the fitness value in the D dimension is O(M × (D + t)). According to Formula (1), the time required to generate a new position during the hiring phase is O(M × (D + t2)). The time O(M*(D + t3) consumed to generate a new position according to Formulas (2) and (3) is during the following bee phase. In the final reconnaissance bee stage, the time required to generate a new position according to Formula (4) is O(M × (D + t4)). Therefore, assuming ABC is iterated T times, the algorithm time complexity is O(ABC) = O(M × (D + t)) + O(M × (t1)) + T × (O(M × (D + t2)) + O (M × (D + t3)) + O(M × (D + t4)), because O(M × (D + t)) and O(M × (t1)) are single finite, and the t2, t3, and t4 time periods are in a parallel order structure. The final algorithm time complexity is O(T × M(D + t2 + t3 + t4)) = O(T × M(D + t). Regarding the time complexity analysis of CBABC, although dynamic neighbor learning and substitution update mechanisms have been added, dynamic neighbor learning has not changed the algorithm structure and is only an operation for updating the population position. Therefore, the algorithm time complexity is not increased, so this period is still the same as ABC. The time complexity of the added swapping update mechanism is O(K × (t5)) = O (M × (0.1 × t5)), where K is the number of candidate solutions (usually 10% of M). So, the total time complexity O(CNABC) is O(M × (D + t)) + O(M × (t1)) + T × (O(M × (D + t2)) + O(M × (D + t3)) + O(M × (D + t4)) + O(M × (0.1 × t5))). Therefore, the final analysis shows that O (CNABC) = O(T × M(D + t)), which is consistent with the time complexity of ABC.

In micro-analysis, dynamic population learning is introduced in the hiring bee stage, and the time required to select the optimal neighbor from N populations is t1. If the calculation time is t2, the time complexity is O(M × t1 + M × (D × t2)), and the time analysis in the same stage as ABC is O(M × (D × t3)). In the final stage, the substitution update mechanism added is analyzed as O(M × (0.1 × t5)), which is used to adjust the position of the worst solution. However, the above strategies all increase the number of algorithms for CNABC, so the time complexity of CNABC and ABC is the same, namely O(T × M (D + t)).

4. Experimental Analysis

4.1. Experimental Setting and Analysis

In order to test the comprehensive performance of the improved algorithm CNABC, this study conducted experiments in both 10-dimensional and 20-dimensional spaces using CNABC alongside 10 other algorithms on the CEC2022 test set. The parameter settings for each algorithm were consistent with those outlined in the original literature. CEC 2022 is also a test set containing unimodal, multimodal, mixed, and combination functions. In the CEC2022 test set, F1 is a unimodal function, F2–F5 is a multimodal function based on F2–F5, F6–F8 are mixed functions, and F9–F12 are combination functions. These two test sets encompass identical function type, thereby facilitating an evaluation of both the search capability and overall robustness of the algorithms employed. The relevant information of CEC 2022 is shown in Table 1.

Table 1. CEC 2022 test function information.

Type	No.	Function Name	F^*
Unimodal	C1	Shifted and Full Rotated Zakharov Function	300
Basic Functions	C2	Shifted and Full Rotated Rosenbrocks Function	400
	C3	Shifted and Full Rotated Expanded Scaffers F6 Function	600
	C4	Shifted and Full Rotated Non-Continuous Rastrigins Function	800
	C5	Shifted and Full Rotated Levy Function	900
Hybrid Functions	C6	Hybrid Function 1 (N = 3)	1800
	C7	Hybrid Function 2 (N = 6)	2000
	C8	Hybrid Function 3 (N = 5)	2200
Composition Functions	C9	Composition Function 1 (N = 5)	2300
	C10	Composition Function 2 (N = 4)	2400
	C11	Composition Function 3 (N = 5)	2600
	C12	Composition Function 4 (N = 6)	2700

To consider the principle of controlling variables and achieve fairness as much as possible should be considered. During the experiment, the population size of all algorithms was set to 100, and the maximum fitness value was calculated Dim × 10,000 times. Each algorithm participating in the test ran independently thirty times, and the average and standard deviations of the data after each algorithm ran independently thirty times were calculated. This was to clarify that the optimal values in the table were subtracted from the theoretical optimal values of the corresponding functions. The optimal value was marked in bold. The experimental results for the 10 and 20 dimensions of the CEC2022 test set are presented in Tables 2 and 3, respectively. The Friedman tests for each algorithm on the test set are at the end of Tables 2 and 3, and the rank sum test results for each algorithm are shown in Tables 4 and 5, respectively. The convergence and box plots indicate the analysis results for the 10 and 20 dimensions of the CEC2022 test set. The 10-dimensional convergence diagram, box plot, and radar plot of CEC2022 are shown in Figures 2–4. The 20-dimensional convergence diagram, box plot, and radar plot of CEC2022 are shown in Figures 5–7.

Table 2. Comparison of results for various functions in CEC2022 test set (dim = 10).

Function	Index	ABC	GWO	AGWO	PSO	VPPSO	WOA	SBWOA	SSA	QMESSA	NABC	CNABC
C01	Mean	8.2546E+03	4.9346E+02	1.9544E+03	3.0289E-02	1.5906E+01	9.9112E+03	8.3029E+03	1.3895E+02	4.9348E+01	1.8785E+03	**1.1973E-03**
	Std	1.8719E+03	1.0539E+03	1.7793E+03	7.0860E-02	2.9497E+01	5.4077E+03	4.8247E+03	3.3065E+02	5.5672E+01	8.7899E+02	**4.3849E-03**
C02	Mean	8.9340E-01	1.5132E+01	4.2507E+01	1.6844E+01	6.7331E+00	1.4244E+01	2.4366E+01	1.3054E+01	6.4125E+00	**5.2521E-01**	7.7435E+00
	Std	**9.2956E-01**	1.3983E+01	2.4314E+01	2.5592E+01	1.2669E+01	2.1196E+01	3.0260E+01	2.3171E+01	1.1854E+01	1.3779E+00	1.7176E+01
C03	Mean	1.6938E-02	6.0941E-01	8.6122E+00	5.8107E+01	4.7492E+00	3.2522E+01	2.7624E+01	6.9257E+00	1.3457E+01	3.6038E-09	**9.8529E-14**
	Std	6.5686E-03	9.1018E-01	5.5624E+00	1.5289E+00	3.7150E+00	1.3220E+01	1.1424E+01	6.7689E+00	9.6438E+00	3.3372E-09	**3.8646E-14**
C04	Mean	2.2731E+01	1.1440E+01	2.0022E+01	3.2436E+01	1.5356E+01	3.4056E+01	3.5387E+01	2.6393E+01	3.4326E+01	**5.9157E+00**	1.0911E+01
	Std	4.7129E+00	6.0415E+00	6.3683E+00	**4.8742E-01**	6.0340E+00	1.3720E+01	1.3062E+01	9.3352E+00	6.7126E+00	1.8201E+00	3.9254E+00
C05	Mean	2.3155E+02	4.0714E+00	5.6884E+01	5.6262E+02	5.0028E+00	4.0786E+02	3.8922E+02	4.3461E+02	4.4084E+02	1.0178E+00	**6.3937E-02**
	Std	1.2641E+02	1.0352E+01	6.3290E+01	2.9178E+01	6.1317E+00	3.1262E+02	2.7645E+02	1.9820E+02	1.7761E+02	6.2615E-01	**1.9356E-01**
C06	Mean	1.8419E+03	3.4077E+03	6.9263E+03	**1.0786E+02**	1.9803E+03	2.6490E+03	2.3237E+03	2.1067E+03	5.0388E+02	2.5580E+02	8.3687E+02
	Std	1.1742E+03	2.2306E+03	4.4139E+03	**9.2902E+01**	1.9824E+03	1.8867E+03	2.0229E+03	2.0572E+03	7.4311E+02	2.3720E+02	1.2552E+03
C07	Mean	5.6068E+00	2.2183E+01	4.0080E+01	3.4922E+02	3.6430E+01	5.7282E+01	5.0860E+01	2.7469E+01	3.3215E+01	**5.5491E-01**	1.8372E+00
	Std	1.9832E+00	1.0368E+01	1.2716E+01	1.2822E+01	1.1143E+01	2.1742E+01	1.8563E+01	1.1009E+01	1.3814E+01	**8.7477E-01**	4.9007E+00
C08	Mean	1.6429E+01	1.9684E+01	2.5943E+01	2.6477E+02	2.3180E+01	3.0538E+01	3.0001E+01	2.1540E+01	2.0810E+01	**1.1323E+01**	1.3731E+01
	Std	2.4709E+03	8.6649E+00	3.9720E+00	9.6430E+01	6.8472E+00	6.6605E+00	4.9137E+00	**2.7324E+00**	3.5512E+00	4.0116E+00	9.3017E+00
C09	Mean	**1.8472E+02**	2.4027E+02	2.7729E+02	2.7338E+02	2.2996E+02	2.4752E+02	2.4913E+02	2.3908E+02	2.2928E+02	2.3432E+02	2.2928E+02
	Std	3.3988E+01	1.9514E+01	2.2971E+01	6.7321E+01	7.5628E-01	3.9621E+01	3.3409E+01	3.6651E+01	1.4211E-13	3.9308E+00	**1.4211E-13**
C10	Mean	**3.9832E+00**	1.4081E+02	1.4821E+02	1.1379E+03	1.0434E+02	1.1843E+02	1.2292E+02	1.4832E+02	1.5707E+02	8.6611E+01	1.0022E+02
	Std	3.2375E+00	5.3259E+01	5.8618E+01	1.7744E+02	2.0022E+01	4.5104E+01	4.9923E+01	6.2871E+01	9.3835E+01	2.9139E+01	**5.5811E-02**
C11	Mean	4.2985E+01	1.0097E+02	1.8766E+02	1.9187E+02	4.3772E+01	2.3244E+02	2.1397E+02	9.8054E+01	2.3013E+02	4.6344E-03	**4.0927E-13**
	Std	2.2436E+01	1.3104E+02	1.4393E+02	1.4834E+02	1.0572E+02	2.0025E+02	1.5753E+02	1.3564E+02	1.0761E+02	2.4957E-02	**1.3642E-13**
C12	Mean	**1.4825E+02**	1.6397E+02	1.7952E+02	3.9439E+02	1.6336E+02	1.7802E+02	1.7983E+02	1.6673E+02	1.6774E+02	1.6598E+02	1.6292E+02
	Std	**6.2750E-01**	4.4185E+00	1.7683E+01	4.4916E+01	1.8335E+00	2.6114E+01	2.1621E+01	5.1859E+00	2.3001E+00	1.0712E+00	1.9242E+00
F-test		3.5833	5.5000	8.1667	8.6667	4.5833	8.8333	8.9167	6.4167	6.5417	2.5833	2.2083

Table 3. Comparison of results for various functions in CEC2022 test set (dim = 20).

Function	Index	ABC	GWO	AGWO	PSO	VPPSO	WOA	SBWOA	SSA	QMESSA	NABC	CNABC
C01	Mean	8.2546E+03	4.9346E+02	1.9544E+03	3.0289E-02	1.5906E+01	9.9112E+03	8.3029E+03	1.3895E+02	4.9348E+01	1.8785E+03	**1.1973E-03**
	Std	1.8719E+03	1.0539E+03	1.7793E+03	7.0860E-02	2.9497E+01	5.4077E+03	4.8247E+03	3.3065E+02	5.5672E+01	8.7899E+02	**4.3849E-03**
C02	Mean	8.9340E-01	1.5132E+01	4.2507E+01	1.6844E+01	6.7331E+00	1.4244E+01	2.4366E+01	1.3054E+01	6.4125E+00	**5.2521E-01**	7.7435E+00
	Std	**9.2956E-01**	1.3983E+01	2.4314E+01	2.5592E+01	1.2669E+01	2.1196E+01	3.0260E+01	2.3171E+01	1.1854E+01	1.3779E+00	1.7176E+01
C03	Mean	1.6938E-02	6.0941E-01	8.6122E+00	5.8107E+01	4.7492E+00	3.2522E+01	2.7624E+01	6.9257E+00	1.3457E+01	3.6038E-09	**9.8529E-14**
	Std	6.5686E-03	9.1018E-01	5.5624E+00	1.5289E+00	3.7150E+00	1.3220E+01	1.1424E+01	6.7689E+00	9.6438E+00	3.3372E-09	**3.8646E-14**
C04	Mean	2.2731E+01	1.1440E+01	2.0022E+01	3.2436E+01	1.5356E+01	3.4056E+01	3.5387E+01	2.6393E+01	3.4326E+01	**5.9157E+00**	1.0911E+01
	Std	4.7129E+00	6.0415E+00	6.3683E+00	**4.8742E-01**	6.0340E+00	1.3720E+01	1.3062E+01	9.3352E+00	6.7126E+00	1.8201E+00	3.9254E+00
C05	Mean	2.3155E+02	4.0714E+00	5.6884E+01	5.6262E+02	5.0028E+00	4.0786E+02	3.8922E+02	4.3461E+02	4.4084E+02	1.0178E+00	**6.3937E-02**
	Std	1.2641E+02	1.0352E+01	6.3290E+01	2.9178E+01	6.1317E+00	3.1262E+02	2.7645E+02	1.9820E+02	1.7761E+02	6.2615E-01	**1.9356E-01**
C06	Mean	1.8419E+03	3.4077E+03	6.9263E+03	**1.0786E+02**	1.9803E+03	2.6490E+03	2.3237E+03	2.1067E+03	5.0388E+02	2.5580E+02	8.3687E+02
	Std	1.1742E+03	2.2306E+03	4.4139E+03	**9.2902E+01**	1.9824E+03	1.8867E+03	2.0229E+03	2.0572E+03	7.4311E+02	2.3720E+02	1.2552E+03
C07	Mean	5.6068E+00	2.2183E+01	4.0080E+01	3.4922E+02	3.6430E+01	5.7282E+01	5.0860E+01	2.7469E+01	3.3215E+01	**5.5491E-01**	1.8372E+00
	Std	1.9832E+00	1.0368E+01	1.2716E+01	1.2822E+01	1.1143E+01	2.1742E+01	1.8563E+01	1.1009E+01	1.3814E+01	**8.7477E-01**	4.9007E+00
C08	Mean	1.6429E+01	1.9684E+01	2.5943E+01	2.6477E+02	2.3180E+01	3.0538E+01	3.0001E+01	2.1540E+01	2.0810E+01	**1.1323E+01**	1.3731E+01
	Std	2.4709E+03	8.6649E+00	3.9720E+00	9.6430E+01	6.8472E+00	6.6605E+00	4.9137E+00	**2.7324E+00**	3.5512E+00	4.0116E+00	9.3017E+00
C09	Mean	**1.8472E+02**	2.4027E+02	2.7729E+02	2.7338E+02	2.2996E+02	2.4752E+02	2.4913E+02	2.3908E+02	2.2928E+02	2.3432E+02	2.2928E+02
	Std	3.3988E+01	1.9514E+01	2.2971E+01	6.7321E+01	7.5628E-01	3.9621E+01	3.3409E+01	3.6651E+01	1.4211E-13	3.9308E+00	**1.4211E-13**
C10	Mean	**3.9832E+00**	1.4081E+02	1.4821E+02	1.1379E+03	1.0434E+02	1.1843E+02	1.2292E+02	1.4832E+02	1.5707E+02	8.6611E+01	1.0022E+02
	Std	3.2375E+00	5.3259E+01	5.8618E+01	1.7744E+02	2.0022E+01	4.5104E+01	4.9923E+01	6.2871E+01	9.3835E+01	2.9139E+01	**5.5811E-02**
C11	Mean	4.2985E+01	1.0097E+02	1.8766E+02	1.9187E+02	4.3772E+01	2.3244E+02	2.1397E+02	9.8054E+01	2.3013E+02	4.6344E-03	**4.0927E-13**
	Std	2.2436E+01	1.3104E+02	1.4393E+02	1.4834E+02	1.0572E+02	2.0025E+02	1.5753E+02	1.3564E+02	1.0761E+02	2.4957E-02	**1.3642E-13**
C12	Mean	**1.4825E+02**	1.6397E+02	1.7952E+02	3.9439E+02	1.6336E+02	1.7802E+02	1.7983E+02	1.6673E+02	1.6774E+02	1.6598E+02	1.6292E+02
	Std	**6.2750E-01**	4.4185E+00	1.7683E+01	4.4916E+01	1.8335E+00	2.6114E+01	2.1621E+01	5.1859E+00	2.3001E+00	1.0712E+00	1.9242E+00
F-test		4.7500	5.6667	8.5833	7.8333	4.7500	8.7500	8.1667	6.4167	5.5000	3.2500	2.3333

Table 4. *p*-values of the Wilcoxon rank sum tests on CEC 2022 functions (Dim = 10).

Function	ABC	GWO	AGWO	PSO	VPPSO	WOA	SBWOA	SSA	QMESSA	NABC
C01	3.02E-11	3.02E-11	3.02E-11	4.08E-05	7.66E-05	3.02E-11	3.02E-11	3.02E-11	3.02E-11	3.02E-11
C02	4.55E-01	4.41E-07	5.43E-06	4.50E-01	3.91E-02	1.24E-04	8.11E-05	2.62E-03	1.05E-01	1.54E-01
C03	4.08E-12	4.08E-12	4.08E-12	4.05E-12	4.08E-12	4.08E-12	4.08E-12	4.08E-12	4.08E-12	4.08E-12
C04	6.06E-10	9.82E-01	5.57E-07	2.99E-11	1.11E-03	4.46E-11	2.35E-10	1.53E-09	2.99E-11	5.83E-06
C05	1.96E-11	4.20E-10	1.96E-11	1.96E-11	5.38E-11	1.96E-11	1.96E-11	1.96E-11	1.96E-11	2.86E-10
C06	2.60E-05	8.20E-07	6.12E-10	1.38E-02	4.23E-03	1.25E-05	7.30E-04	2.62E-03	7.62E-01	2.34E-01
C07	8.48E-09	5.07E-10	3.69E-11	3.02E-11	3.69E-11	3.02E-11	3.02E-11	3.69E-11	6.07E-11	6.00E-01
C08	3.63E-01	9.51E-06	2.67E-09	3.02E-11	7.09E-08	2.15E-10	2.15E-10	1.07E-09	7.09E-08	5.55E-02
C09	1.21E-12	1.21E-12	1.21E-12	6.61E-04	1.21E-12	1.21E-12	1.21E-12	4.57E-12	1.21E-12	1.21E-12
C10	3.02E-11	3.82E-09	3.02E-11	3.02E-11	3.02E-11	3.02E-11	3.02E-11	3.02E-11	3.79E-01	6.35E-02
C11	3.15E-12	3.15E-12	3.15E-12	3.15E-12	3.15E-12	3.15E-12	3.15E-12	3.15E-12	3.15E-12	3.12E-12
C12	2.98E-11	1.33E-01	6.00E-11	2.98E-11	3.79E-01	9.66E-10	1.76E-10	8.11E-05	6.06E-10	5.91E-09

Table 5. *p*-values of the Wilcoxon rank sum tests on CEC 2022 functions (Dim = 20).

Function	ABC	GWO	AGWO	PSO	VPPSO	WOA	SBWOA	SSA	QMESSA	NABC
C01	3.02E-11	1.33E-10	3.02E-11	2.23E-09	7.29E-03	5.87E-04	6.20E-04	4.98E-11	1.09E-10	3.02E-11
C02	6.36E-05	6.74E-06	3.02E-11	2.77E-01	2.61E-02	1.29E-06	6.36E-05	1.91E-01	2.84E-01	2.12E-01
C03	3.02E-11	3.02E-11	3.02E-11	3.02E-11	3.02E-11	3.02E-11	3.02E-11	3.02E-11	3.02E-11	3.02E-11
C04	3.02E-11	3.26E-01	4.98E-11	3.02E-11	1.73E-06	3.02E-11	3.02E-11	3.02E-11	3.02E-11	5.09E-08
C05	3.02E-11	6.05E-07	7.09E-08	3.02E-11	7.73E-02	3.69E-11	3.69E-11	4.50E-11	4.08E-11	4.84E-02
C06	4.08E-11	2.71E-02	3.02E-11	8.65E-01	5.59E-01	4.42E-06	2.53E-04	1.37E-01	9.35E-01	4.42E-06
C07	3.02E-11	1.25E-07	3.02E-11	3.02E-11	1.33E-10	3.02E-11	3.02E-11	3.02E-11	3.02E-11	4.20E-01
C08	5.57E-10	4.62E-10	3.16E-10	3.02E-11	2.87E-10	5.49E-11	9.92E-11	1.61E-10	2.87E-10	5.57E-10
C09	3.02E-11	3.02E-11	3.02E-11	3.02E-11	3.02E-11	3.02E-11	3.02E-11	3.02E-11	3.02E-11	3.02E-11
C10	7.77E-09	1.09E-10	6.07E-11	3.02E-11	4.62E-10	8.99E-11	7.39E-11	6.70E-11	6.53E-07	1.46E-10
C11	2.60E-10	1.69E-08	3.01E-11	2.37E-07	2.25E-04	1.99E-05	6.20E-04	9.20E-05	8.66E-05	2.50E-03
C12	3.02E-11	6.35E-02	7.12E-09	3.02E-11	3.92E-02	2.15E-06	5.09E-08	1.70E-02	9.51E-06	2.78E-07

It should be noted that the experimental environment used for this test was provided by MATLAB 2020b, the operating system was Windows 11, the main frequency was 3.20 GHz, and the memory was 16 GB. The comparative algorithms were ABC [19], GWO [12], AGWO [3], PSO [9], VPPSO [39], WOA [40], SBWOA [41], SSA [13], QMESSA [42], and NABC [38].

In the analysis of the 10-dimensional problem of the CEC2022 test set function, CNABC ranked first in the test function with 4. The test data of all four functions were bright spots, far ahead of the comparison algorithms in terms of magnitude. The C03 and C11 test functions were able to find the optimal values. As shown in Figure 2, in terms of the convergence curves of each algorithm in each function, CNABC achieved good results in C01, C03, C05, and C11 under 10 dimensions, indicating that CNABC exhibited good performance in unimodal functions, simple multimodal functions, and combination functions. Although CNABC did not achieve first place in the hybrid function, it was able to maintain the same order of magnitude as the final result of the top ranked algorithm, with C06 in fourth place and C07 and C08 in second place, all on the same order of magnitude as the current best. Overall, CNABC had strong performance in both pre-optimization and post-optimization search. On the combination function, the values of C09, C10, and C12 were slightly worse than ABC, and the overall optimization values were not significantly different.

$$CD = Q\alpha_{0.05}\sqrt{\left(\frac{K(K+1)}{6N}\right)} \tag{15}$$

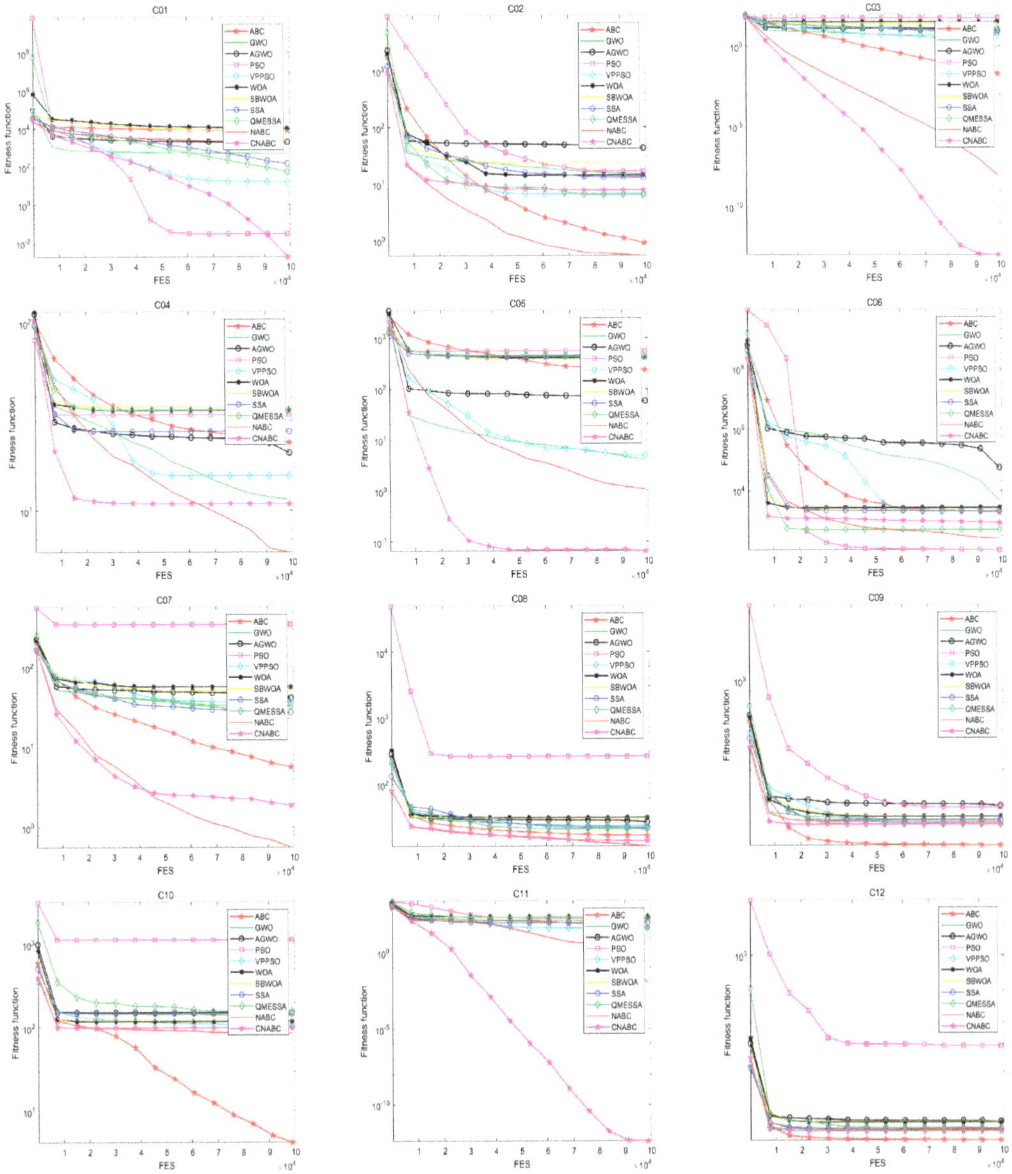

Figure 2. CEC2022 convergence graph (10 dim).

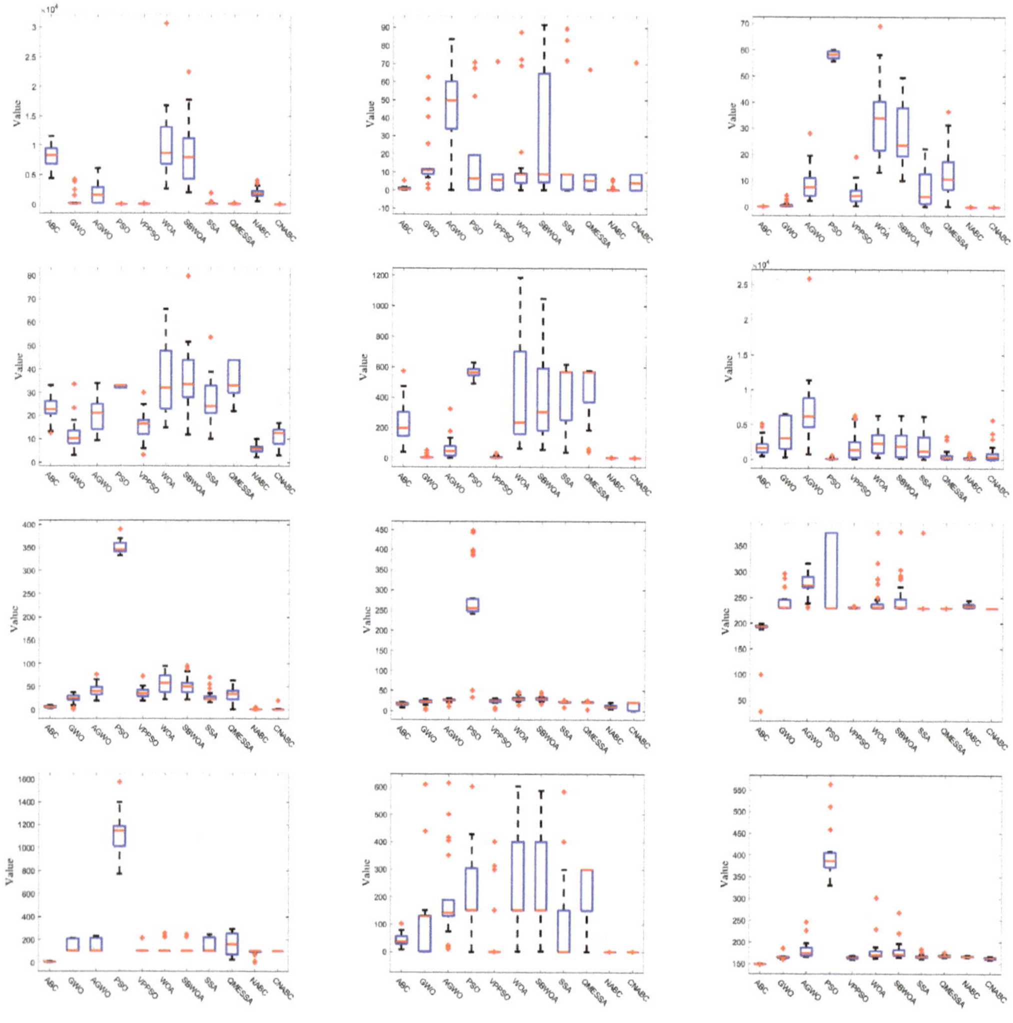

Figure 3. CEC2022 box diagram (10 dim).

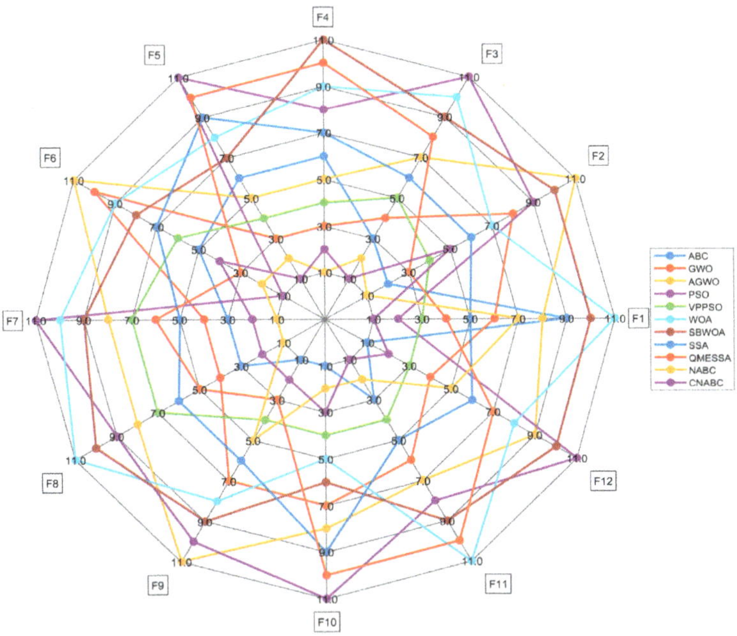

Figure 4. Radar ranking chart of CEC2022 test set for each algorithm (10 dim).

From the results of the Friedman test, the rank ranking of CNABC was 2.2100. According to Formula (15) and by looking up the table [43], the critical CD value of the algorithm was 4.3585. The CD line value obtained by adding the rank ranking to the critical CD value was 6.5685. It can be concluded that there were significant differences between CNABC and AGWO, PSO, WOA, and SBWOA, while the differences between the remaining comparison algorithms were relatively small. Furthermore, as shown in Figure 3, CNABC had smaller optimal, median, and worst values on functions C01, C03, C05, C09, and C11. On the C06, C11, and C12 functions, although the optimal, median, and worst values of CNABC algorithm were not the best, it can be seen that they tended to stabilize in the interval, ranking second or third in the ranking, and were at the forefront of the comparison algorithms. Overall, it can be concluded that CNABC has good comprehensive performance in 10 dimensions.

As shown in Figure 7, a specific analysis was conducted on the 20-dimensional problem of the CEC2022 test set function. CNABC ranked first in the test function with four numbers, namely C03, C04, C07, and C08. From this perspective, CNABC had a good effect on higher dimensional unimodal functions, simple multimodal functions, and mixed functions. In the analysis of the combination function, although it did not achieve the first ranking, all rankings in the combination function were in the top three positions, still ranking among the top in the comparison algorithm. From the convergence curve graph, it can be seen that CNABC had good search performance in both the early and late stages of iteration, and when dealing with local optima, it can adjust the worst solution through EESM. There was also a downward trend in exploration on C01, C03, C04, and C07.

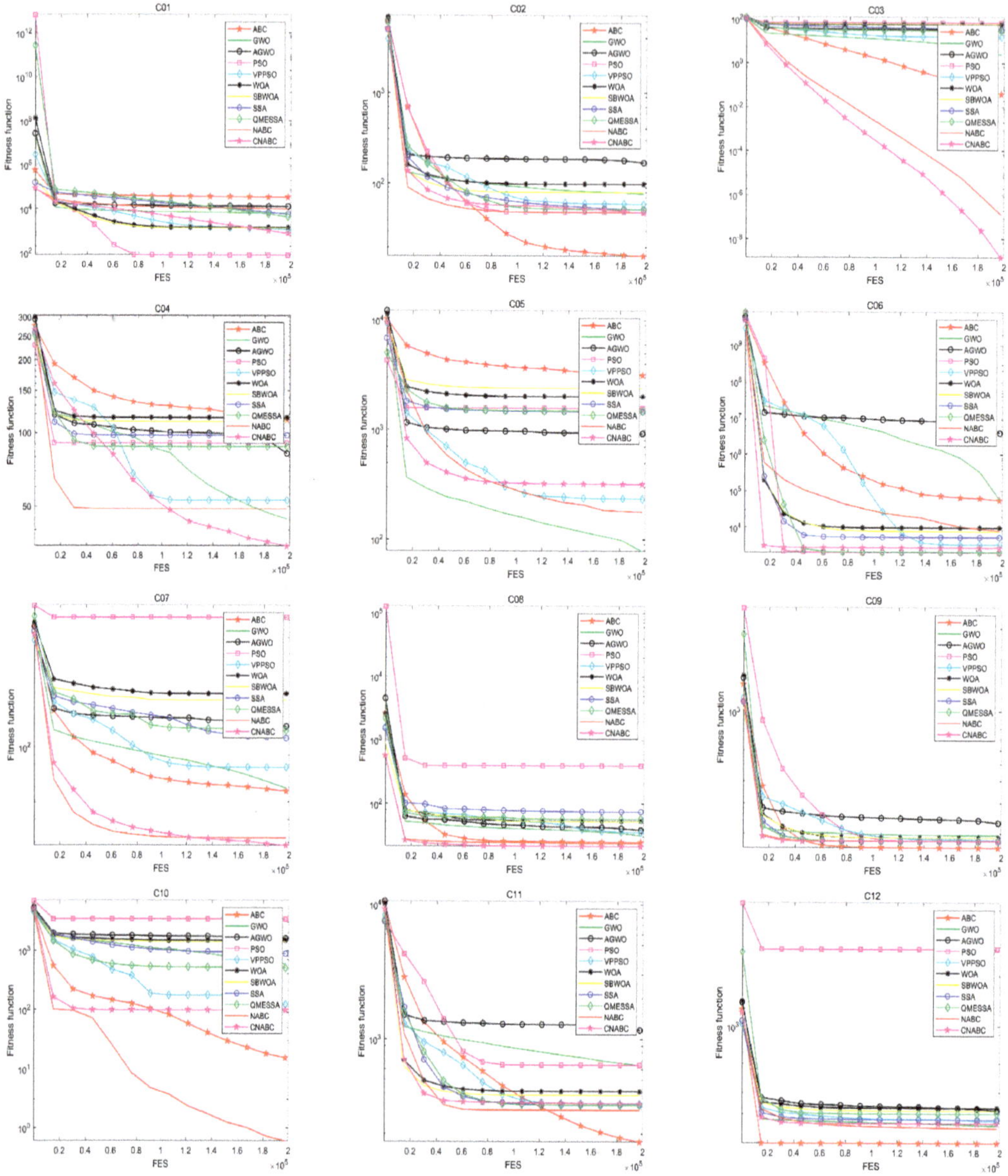

Figure 5. CEC2022 convergence graph (20 dim).

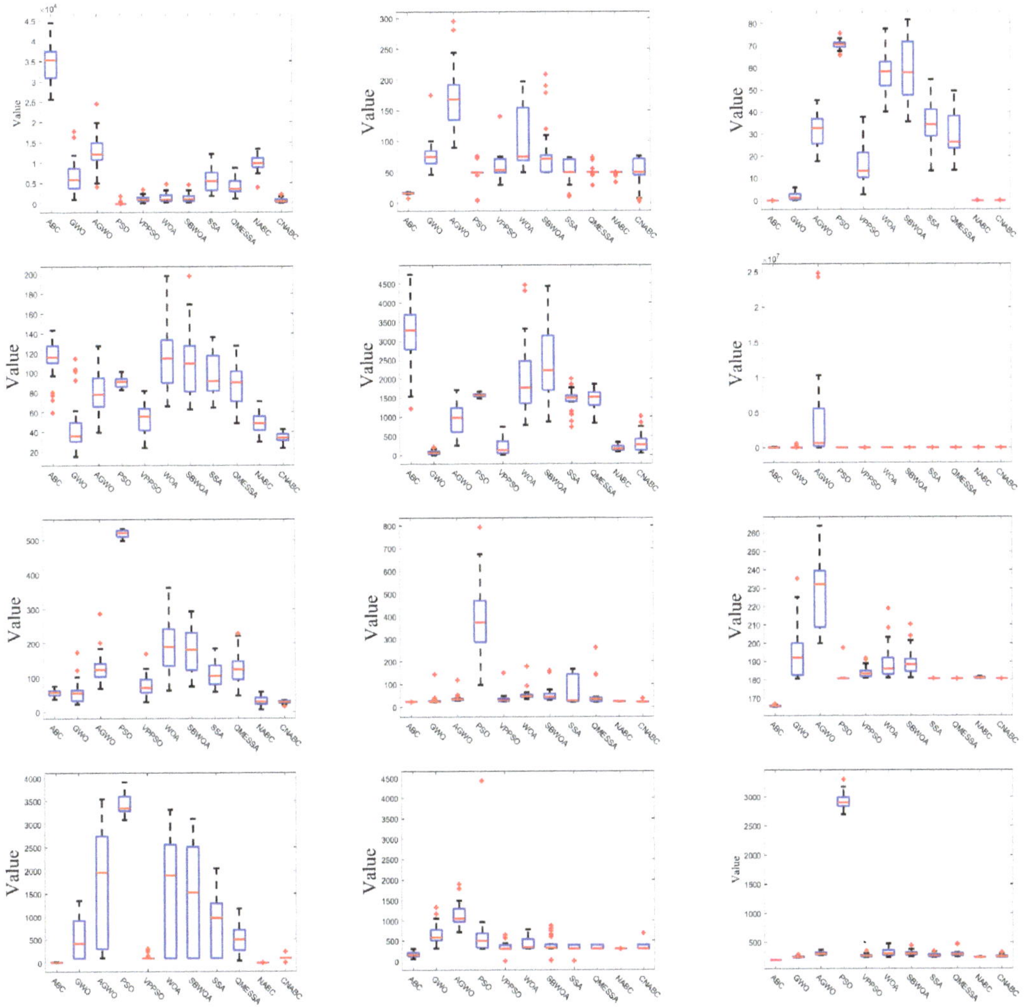

Figure 6. CEC2022 box diagram (20 dim).

From the Friedman test results, it can be seen that CNABC had some advantages in comparison algorithms. Its average rank value was 2.333, which was a good performance compared with the second highest ranking. Although there were only four ranked as first in the 20 dimensions, it can reflect the fact that it can still maintain its position before the exam without ranking first in other functions compared with the algorithm, and the optimal value, variance, and other factors were similar. For example, the above situation can be reflected on functions C02, C06, and C09. Next, according to the 10-dimensional analysis, the critical value CD was 4.3585, so the CD line value can be calculated as 6.6918. Therefore, it can be concluded that there was a significant difference between CNABC and AGWO, PSO, WOA, and SBWOA algorithms, and there was no significant difference compared with the remaining algorithms. Finally, from Figure 6, the box plot analysis of the 20 dimensions shows that the top ranked functions C03, C04, C07, and C08 were superior to other comparison algorithms in terms of optimal value, median, and worst value. Although the performance on C05, C09, and C10 was somewhat unsatisfactory, it can still be accepted that CNABC ranked around third place without the free lunch rule.

Based on the above two points, analyzing the data from the 20 dimensions can reflect some advantages of CNABC in handling this test set function, and also demonstrates that the algorithm is at an average leading level among the selected comparative algorithms.

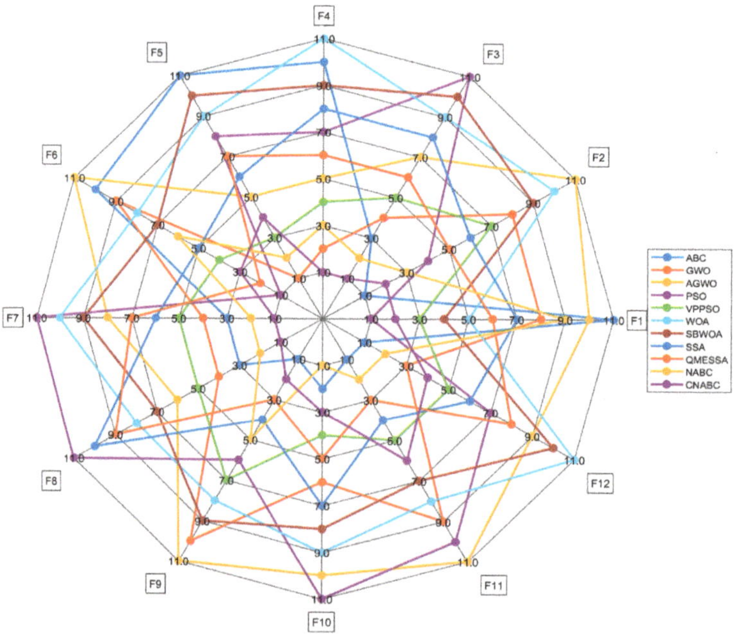

Figure 7. Radar ranking chart of CEC2022 test set for each algorithm (20 dim).

The data analysis of CNABC were compared with other comparative algorithms in different dimensions on two different test sets. Overall, the improved algorithm in this article had good optimization performance and good competitiveness. However, we can see that on both test sets, as the problem dimension increased, the comprehensive advantage of CNABC also slightly decreased. Therefore, further research is needed to enhance the search performance of CNABC in high-dimensional problems.

In the above analysis, the convergence graphs of each algorithm in 10 dimensions are recorded, as shown in Figure 2; the box plot is shown in Figure 3; and the radar chart of algorithm ranking is shown in Figure 4. The convergence graph of the 20 dimensional algorithm is recorded here, as shown in Figure 5; the box plot, as shown in Figure 6; and the radar chart of the algorithm ranking, as shown in Figure 7. From the convergence chart of 10 dimensions, C01, C03, and C011 demonstrated excellent performance; however, it can also be observed that C06 and C10 performed inadequately. From the convergence chart of 20 dimensions, C01, C03, C04, and C07 exhibited outstanding performance, but it was evident that C05, C11, and C12 showed insufficient performance. This further substantiates that CNABC is in line with the NFL theorem, which stipulates that an algorithm cannot have exceptional performance on all issues. From the data of algorithm testing, the average value, variance, box plot, and convergence plot of the algorithm demonstrated the performance of CNABC in algorithm iteration, the stability of algorithm optimization, and the search ability of the algorithm during iteration. The Friedman rank sum test analysis of algorithm differences reflected the difference between CNABC and comparison algorithms, but it was still difficult to judge the poor habits of some comparison algorithms. Therefore, this article also added the Wilcoxon rank sum test to further analyze and compare the significant differences in the algorithm. The population size was 100, and each algorithm ran independently 30 times under D $\times$ 10,000 maximum evaluation times. Tables 4 and 5 show the test results of each algorithm at the p = 5% significance level under different dimensions of the two test set functions. When p < 5%, it is considered that there is a significant difference in algorithm time. When p > 5%, it is considered that the difference between the two algorithms is not significant, NaN indicates that the difference in results between the two algorithms cannot be compared, and the underlined data indicate that p > 5%.

As can be seen from Tables 4 and 5, the number of occurrences of NaN in both tables is 0, and there is less underlined data in the functions of the two test sets. This implies that CNABC and the comparison algorithm had lower similarity in search results in different dimensions of the CEC2022 test set, and there was a significant difference in optimization results. Therefore, it can be seen that there was still a significant difference in optimization performance between CNABC and the comparison algorithm. Therefore, based on the comprehensive analysis of the test set function results, rank ranking, convergence function graph, and box plot in Tables 2 and 3, we can see that the comprehensive performance of CNABC was the most outstanding among many algorithms. Therefore, it can be verified that CNABC has certain core competitiveness and better optimization performance compared with other algorithms.

In addition, to evaluate the effectiveness of the proposed strategy for problem solving, this paper designed four algorithms: CNABC, ABC, and ABC-1, which utilize only a commutative solution mechanism in their search processes; and ABC-2, which employs solely dynamic neighbor learning during the search. During the experiment, variables were rigorously controlled with a population size set at 100 and a maximum evaluation budget of Dim × 10,000. Each algorithm was executed independently for 30 iterations, from which the average and variance of the results were computed. The test outcomes for dimensions 10 and 20 are presented in Tables 6 and 7.

Table 6. Contribution experiments of each strategy in CEC2022 (10 dim).

Function	Index	ABC	CNABC-1	CNABC-2	CNABC
C01	Mean	8.2546E+03	8.6449E+03	6.6300E+03	**1.1973E-03**
	Std	1.8719E+03	2.4694E+03	1.7684E+03	**4.3849E-03**
C02	Mean	8.9340E-01	**6.1016E-01**	1.0583E+00	7.7435E+00
	Std	9.2956E-01	**4.0496E-01**	1.6864E+00	1.7176E+01
C03	Mean	1.6938E-02	1.7948E-02	2.3692E-09	**9.8529E-14**
	Std	6.5686E-03	7.1088E-03	2.0757E-09	**3.8646E-14**
C04	Mean	2.2731E+01	2.3656E+01	1.3585E+01	**1.0911E+01**
	Std	4.7129E+00	5.2725E+00	**3.2801E+00**	3.9254E+00
C05	Mean	2.3155E+02	2.0214E+02	2.9538E+01	**6.3937E-02**
	Std	1.2641E+02	1.1178E+02	1.8018E+01	**1.9356E-01**
C06	Mean	1.8419E+03	1.2539E+03	**4.1614E+02**	8.3687E+02
	Std	1.1742E+03	7.5952E+02	**3.2035E+02**	1.2552E+03
C07	Mean	5.6068E+00	5.4867E+00	**5.2867E-01**	1.8372E+00
	Std	1.9832E+00	2.2070E+00	**5.1254E-01**	4.9007E+00
C08	Mean	1.6429E+01	1.5061E+01	1.5199E+01	**1.3731E+01**
	Std	2.4709E+03	4.9502E+00	**3.9161E+00**	9.3017E+00
C09	Mean	**1.8472E+02**	1.8788E+02	2.3500E+02	2.2928E+02
	Std	3.3988E+01	2.0674E+01	3.0032E+00	**1.4211E-13**
C10	Mean	**3.9832E+00**	3.2194E+00	1.6798E+01	1.0022E+02
	Std	3.2375E+00	3.2337E+00	2.6190E+01	**5.5811E-02**
C11	Mean	4.2985E+01	4.1253E+01	4.8308E+00	**4.0927E-13**
	Std	2.2436E+01	2.3979E+01	2.4598E+01	**1.3642E-13**
C12	Mean	1.4825E+02	**1.4802E+02**	1.6575E+02	1.6292E+02
	Std	**6.2750E-01**	6.7384E-01	7.2086E-01	1.9242E+00

Table 7. Contribution experiments of each strategy in CEC2022 (20 dim).

Function	Index	ABC	CNABC-1	CNABC-2	CNABC
C01	Mean	3.4642E+04	3.4690E+04	2.6389E+04	**6.9833E+02**
	Std	4.2200E+03	5.4458E+03	3.6725E+03	**5.6114E+02**
C02	Mean	**1.5929E+01**	1.6771E+01	4.9083E+01	4.7313E+01
	Std	**1.8484E+00**	8.9264E-01	9.5493E-02	2.4233E+01
C03	Mean	3.4459E-02	3.3505E-02	7.7464E-08	**5.5911E-10**
	Std	1.1165E-02	8.8402E-03	3.4143E-08	**7.2191E-10**
C04	Mean	1.1296E+02	1.1210E+02	8.1940E+01	**3.4144E+01**
	Std	1.9159E+01	2.1172E+01	1.2208E+01	**4.8546E+00**
C05	Mean	3.1665E+03	3.2314E+03	1.5164E+03	**3.2107E+02**
	Std	7.5259E+02	6.8987E+02	4.4258E+02	**2.4450E+02**
C06	Mean	5.0428E+04	5.1701E+04	2.3538E+04	**2.7414E+03**
	Std	2.9475E+04	2.4541E+04	1.5881E+04	**2.9384E+03**
C07	Mean	5.6819E+01	5.4296E+01	3.2103E+01	**2.8564E+01**
	Std	8.5524E+00	8.5808E+00	4.2517E+00	**3.5577E+00**
C08	Mean	2.5000E+01	2.5078E+01	2.4429E+01	**2.1493E+01**
	Std	7.6912E-01	**7.1254E-01**	5.6114E-01	3.0215E+00
C09	Mean	1.6597E+02	**1.6589E+02**	1.8112E+02	1.8078E+02
	Std	3.8039E-01	3.2523E-01	2.1197E-01	**2.8422E-14**
C10	Mean	1.4781E+01	1.4277E+01	**3.5878E-01**	9.8298E+01
	Std	5.8370E+00	6.9522E+00	**4.4507E-01**	3.5593E+01
C11	Mean	**1.7419E+02**	1.6484E+02	3.0000E+02	3.3640E+02
	Std	5.6744E+01	5.3780E+01	**0.0000E+00**	7.8303E+01
C12	Mean	**2.0000E+02**	**2.0000E+02**	2.4599E+02	2.6224E+02
	Std	**7.9512E-05**	9.2856E-05	3.7484E+00	2.0616E+01

From Table 6, it can be seen that CNABC had the most bold individuals, ranking first in the number of optimal values. It can be seen that CNABC exhibited excellent optimization performance on multiple types of test functions. Looking at the comprehensive data of ABC-1 and ABC-2, it can be seen that both improved compared with ABC. However, the overall improvement of ABC-1 was relatively small compared with ABC-2. However, the comprehensive data of ABC-2 was worse than CNABC, indicating that the substitution mechanism can compensate for the shortcomings of dynamic neighbor learning when trapped in local optima. Therefore, it can be concluded that the strategy proposed in the 10 dimensions has good performance.

From Table 7, it can be seen that CNABC had the best overall results with the most bold font, and ABC-1 and ABC-2 were not significantly different from the 10 dimensional analysis compared with ABC. At 20 dimensions, ABC-1 can better maintain the advantages of ABC and had an improvement compared with ABC, while ABC-2 had a good effect on C03, C08, and C10 compared with ABC. Although ABC-1 and ABC-2 showed good improvements in other functions, overall, CNABC, which combined the advantages of both strategies, still outperformed. Overall, CNABC performed better than single strategy ABC in both the 10 and 20 dimensions.

4.2. Analysis of the Running Time of Each Algorithm

The time complexity of the algorithm was analyzed to prove that the time complexity of CNABC remained unchanged. In this section, the time complexity analysis of CNABC and the comparison algorithm is included. Compared with the original ABC, CNABC is of the same order of magnitude in terms of time consumption, with a minor difference. Compared with the time consumption of other comparison algorithms, the time consumed by CNABC is in the upper-middle position, which takes less time and is more efficient. The time consumption chart is presented in Table 8.

Table 8. Time consumption table of each algorithm.

Function	dim	ABC	GWO	AGWO	PSO	VPPSO	WOA	SBWOA	SSA	QMESSA	NABC	CNABC
C01	10	6.66E-01	7.67E-01	1.30E+00	1.09E+00	6.40E-01	6.86E-01	6.57E-01	6.00E-01	5.69E-01	8.63E-01	7.88E-01
	20	1.38E+00	1.76E+00	3.92E+00	1.98E+00	1.53E+00	1.37E+00	1.40E+00	5.79E-01	8.30E-01	1.75E+00	1.70E+00
C02	10	6.61E-01	7.46E-01	1.30E+00	9.48E-01	6.46E-01	6.60E-01	6.58E-01	5.64E-01	4.27E-01	8.67E-01	7.79E-01
	20	1.38E+00	1.75E+00	3.82E+00	1.95E+00	1.42E+00	1.37E+00	1.42E+00	5.79E-01	8.28E-01	1.75E+00	1.64E+00
C03	10	8.40E-01	9.19E-01	1.47E+00	1.13E+00	7.40E-01	8.32E-01	8.25E-01	6.71E-01	4.81E-01	9.84E-01	9.54E-01
	20	2.10E+00	2.46E+00	4.52E+00	2.67E+00	1.81E+00	2.07E+00	2.09E+00	8.01E-01	9.38E-01	2.22E+00	2.37E+00
C04	10	7.04E-01	7.86E-01	1.33E+00	9.86E-01	6.47E-01	7.02E-01	6.92E-01	5.84E-01	4.34E-01	8.88E-01	8.18E-01
	20	1.53E+00	1.95E+00	3.99E+00	2.09E+00	1.45E+00	1.52E+00	1.58E+00	6.34E-01	8.59E-01	1.86E+00	1.80E+00
C05	10	7.21E-01	8.06E-01	1.35E+00	1.08E+00	6.63E-01	7.26E-01	7.08E-01	6.00E-01	4.53E-01	8.96E-01	8.33E-01
	20	1.56E+00	2.00E+00	4.04E+00	2.18E+00	1.48E+00	1.57E+00	1.58E+00	6.45E-01	8.75E-01	1.89E+00	1.85E+00
C06	10	6.77E-01	7.61E-01	1.32E+00	9.64E-01	6.49E-01	6.74E-01	6.69E-01	5.73E-01	4.23E-01	8.71E-01	8.07E-01
	20	1.43E+00	1.82E+00	3.87E+00	2.03E+00	1.38E+00	1.42E+00	1.43E+00	6.00E-01	8.41E-01	1.80E+00	1.68E+00
C07	10	8.81E-01	9.63E-01	1.52E+00	1.16E+00	7.70E-01	8.79E-01	8.76E-01	6.98E-01	4.93E-01	1.00E+00	1.01E+00
	20	2.22E+00	2.59E+00	4.63E+00	2.78E+00	1.85E+00	2.20E+00	2.21E+00	8.33E-01	9.68E-01	2.35E+00	2.49E+00
C08	10	9.36E-01	1.01E+00	1.57E+00	1.22E+00	7.97E-01	9.37E-01	9.19E-01	7.26E-01	4.98E-01	1.04E+00	1.07E+00
	20	2.36E+00	2.74E+00	4.80E+00	2.93E+00	1.96E+00	2.35E+00	2.32E+00	8.77E-01	9.92E-01	2.44E+00	2.64E+00
C09	10	8.51E-01	9.47E-01	1.50E+00	1.14E+00	7.87E-01	8.56E-01	8.54E-01	6.98E-01	4.78E-01	9.75E-01	9.75E-01
	20	2.25E+00	2.65E+00	4.80E+00	2.84E+00	2.00E+00	2.25E+00	2.25E+00	8.78E-01	9.65E-01	2.36E+00	2.52E+00
C10	10	8.34E-01	9.17E-01	1.47E+00	1.11E+00	7.44E-01	8.23E-01	8.08E-01	6.60E-01	4.69E-01	9.63E-01	9.54E-01
	20	2.00E+00	2.37E+00	4.45E+00	2.54E+00	1.75E+00	2.00E+00	1.96E+00	7.87E-01	9.42E-01	2.20E+00	2.27E+00
C11	10	9.44E-01	1.03E+00	1.59E+00	1.27E+00	8.04E-01	9.40E-01	9.29E-01	7.38E-01	5.03E-01	1.04E+00	1.07E+00
	20	2.49E+00	2.87E+00	4.89E+00	3.02E+00	2.00E+00	2.47E+00	2.48E+00	9.30E-01	1.01E+00	2.50E+00	2.77E+00
C12	10	9.87E-01	1.07E+00	1.63E+00	1.26E+00	9.72E-01	9.85E-01	9.72E-01	7.84E-01	5.21E-01	1.07E+00	1.17E+00
	20	2.73E+00	3.06E+00	5.15E+00	3.21E+00	2.48E+00	2.66E+00	2.66E+00	9.97E-01	1.03E+00	2.67E+00	3.02E+00

4.3. *Effectiveness Analysis of Neighbor Population*

A new parameter, namely the size of the neighbor population N, was incorporated into the DNL strategy in CNABC. To comprehend what the most suitable size of N was in the new algorithm, we added parameter analysis experiments for parameter N in this section to better determine the value of N for the optimal algorithm performance, where N is selected from the set {2, 3,. . .15}. Finally, we set the identical parameters as per Section 4.1; the test function was CEC2022; the dimension was 10; and a Friedman test was conducted to select the most appropriate N from a statistical perspective.

It can be observed from the results that, for CNABC, the value of N influenced the algorithm's outcomes. We analyzed that, when the value of N was small, the small learning population reduced the diversity of the population, leading to the decline of its search ability. When the value of N was large, the value was more similar to the global search, and the development ability of CNABC was diminished. The results of Friedman's test are similar. It indicates that the value of N had a negligible impact on the overall optimization result. Therefore, we chose N with a higher ranking as the most appropriate value, that is, when N = 5. In conclusion, when N = 5, the development ability and population diversity of the algorithm will not be affected by an overly large or small N. The experimental results of different N values under CEC2022 are shown in Table 9.

Table 9. Experimental result data with different N values (dim = 10).

Function	Index	2	3	4	5	6	7	8
C01	Mean	4.89E-04	8.89E-04	**3.41E-05**	1.20E-03	3.12E-03	1.24E-03	2.14E-04
	Std	3.58E-04	2.22E-03	5.40E-05	4.38E-03	8.83E-03	3.86E-03	6.62E-04
C02	Mean	8.71E+00	6.52E+00	2.89E+00	7.74E+00	**2.62E+00**	3.42E+00	1.75E+00
	Std	2.03E+01	3.92E+00	1.97E+00	1.72E+01	3.01E+00	3.47E+00	3.03E+00
C03	Mean	1.14E-13	1.14E-13	1.42E-07	**9.85E-14**	1.14E-13	1.14E-13	1.20E-06
	Std	0.00E+00	0.00E+00	4.49E-07	3.86E-14	0.00E+00	0.00E+00	3.79E-06
C04	Mean	**7.96E+00**	1.13E+01	8.26E+00	1.09E+01	9.35E+00	1.28E+01	1.09E+01
	Std	2.77E+00	4.35E+00	2.85E+00	3.93E+00	5.27E+00	4.44E+00	4.40E+00
C05	Mean	1.36E-01	**5.68E-14**	9.98E-02	6.39E-02	9.09E-02	4.54E-02	1.36E-01
	Std	8.00E+00	5.99E-14	2.11E-01	1.94E-01	1.92E-01	1.44E-01	3.07E-01
C06	Mean	1.17E+03	1.33E+03	1.41E+03	**8.37E+02**	1.30E+03	1.35E+03	1.26E+03
	Std	4.95E+02	1.06E+03	1.54E+03	1.26E+03	1.48E+03	1.95E+03	1.56E+03
C07	Mean	2.30E+00	3.62E-01	4.24E-01	1.84E+00	4.61E-01	**2.62E-01**	2.46E+00
	Std	6.23E+00	6.05E-01	4.66E-01	4.90E+00	4.98E-01	4.33E-01	6.19E+00
C08	Mean	1.16E+01	1.04E+01	1.06E+01	1.37E+01	**1.29E+01**	1.23E+01	1.66E+01
	Std	9.63E+00	1.04E+01	1.02E+01	9.30E+00	9.56E+00	1.03E+01	7.70E+00
C09	Mean	**2.29E+02**	**2.29E+02**	**2.29E+02**	**2.29E+02**	**2.29E+02**	**2.29E+02**	**2.29E+02**
	Std	0.00E+00	0.00E+00	0.00E+00	1.42E-13	0.00E+00	0.00E+00	0.00E+00
C10	Mean	**1.00E+02**	**1.00E+02**	**1.00E+02**	**1.00E+02**	**1.00E+02**	1.11E+02	**1.00E+02**
	Std	4.17E-02	4.89E-02	6.67E-02	5.58E-02	3.95E-02	3.44E+01	7.21E-02
C11	Mean	5.46E-13	4.55E-13	4.55E-13	**4.09E-13**	1.50E+01	5.00E-13	**4.09E-13**
	Std	1.92E-13	0.00E+00	2.14E-13	1.36E-13	4.76E+01	1.44E-13	1.44E-13
C12	Mean	1.62E+02	1.63E+02	1.63E+02	1.63E+02	1.64E+02	1.63E+02	1.63E+02
	Std	1.75E+00	1.51E+00	1.88E+00	1.92E+00	1.43E+00	1.69E+00	2.02E+00
Optimal number		3	3	3	5	4	2	3

Function	Index	9	10	11	12	13	14	15
C01	Mean	1.17E-04	2.71E-04	1.67E-04	3.25E-04	4.40E-03	1.41E-03	2.93E-04
	Std	2.68E-04	4.59E-04	4.90E-04	4.74E-04	4.61E-03	1.04E-03	3.01E-04
C02	Mean	3.74E+00	3.90E+00	9.72E+00	3.35E+00	1.09E+01	2.66E+00	5.52E+00
	Std	2.47E+00	3.26E+00	2.18E+01	2.69E+00	2.12E+01	3.72E+00	2.47E+00
C03	Mean	1.02E-13	1.14E-13	1.13E-06	1.14E-13	2.02E-05	2.83E-07	2.83E-07
	Std	3.60E-14	0.00E+00	3.58E-06	0.00E+00	6.38E-05	8.96E-07	8.96E-07
C04	Mean	9.95E+00	1.22E+01	1.11E+01	1.36E+01	1.01E+01	1.17E+01	1.02E+01
	Std	3.35E+00	6.28E+00	4.14E+00	6.68E+00	3.53E+00	4.11E+00	5.12E+00
C05	Mean	9.09E-14	1.18E-01	4.48E-02	9.09E-02	6.33E-02	1.79E-02	4.38E-01
	Std	4.79E-14	2.26E-01	4.62E-02	1.92E-01	1.48E-01	5.66E-02	1.23E+00
C06	Mean	1.26E+03	1.47E+03	1.11E+03	8.68E+02	1.12E+03	1.27E+03	1.03E+03
	Std	1.50E+03	1.86E+03	1.15E+03	1.10E+03	1.15E+03	1.71E+03	1.34E+03
C07	Mean	2.86E+00	6.22E-01	7.47E-01	1.23E+00	5.97E-01	4.52E+00	6.30E+00
	Std	6.20E+00	5.87E-01	6.15E-01	5.67E-01	5.14E-01	8.17E+00	9.46E+00
C08	Mean	1.23E+01	**9.55E+00**	1.42E+01	1.63E+01	1.73E+01	1.22E+01	1.76E+01
	Std	1.03E+01	9.96E+00	9.50E+00	8.19E+00	6.44E+00	9.48E+00	6.97E+00
C09	Mean	**2.29E+02**	**2.29E+02**	**2.29E+02**	**2.29E+02**	**2.29E+02**	**2.29E+02**	**2.29E+02**
	Std	0.00E+00	0.00E+00	0.00E+00	0.00E+00	0.00E+00	0.00E+00	0.00E+00
C10	Mean	**1.00E+02**	**1.00E+02**	**1.00E+02**	**1.00E+02**	**1.00E+02**	1.12E+02	**1.00E+02**
	Std	4.75E-02	6.00E-02	4.77E-02	3.85E-02	7.49E-02	3.58E+01	6.36E-02
C11	Mean	1.50E+01	4.55E-13	1.50E+01	1.50E+01	**4.09E-13**	1.50E+01	1.50E+01
	Std	4.76E+01	0.00E+00	4.76E+01	4.76E+01	1.44E-13	4.76E+01	4.76E+01
C12	Mean	**1.62E+02**	1.63E+02	1.63E+02	1.63E+02	1.64E+02	1.63E+02	1.63E+02
	Std	1.50E+00	2.00E+00	1.06E+00	2.18E+00	1.39E+00	2.16E+00	1.74E+00
Optimal number		3	2	2	2	3	1	2

5. Comparative Experiment with TOP Algorithm

Based on the experimental analysis in the previous section, CNABC has certain core competitiveness and better optimization performance compared with other algorithms. In order to further demonstrate the competitiveness of CNABC, this section will conduct experimental comparisons between CNABC and the TOP algorithm proposed in recent years in the CEC competition, in order to demonstrate CNABC's optimization ability and look forward to future work directions that need to be supplemented. The algorithms include IMODE [44], AGSK [45], AGSKIMODE [46], and EA4eig [47]. IMODE is the top ranked algorithm in CEC2020, AGSK is the second ranked algorithm, AGSK-IMODE is the fourth ranked algorithm in CEC 2021, and EA4eig is the first ranked algorithm in CEC 2022. The parameters of each algorithm are shown in the original text, and while the experimental parameters remain unchanged, the maximum evaluation frequency FES is still Dim × 10,000. The specific optimization results are shown in Tables 10 and 11, and the radar charts for the 10 and 20 dimensions are shown in Figures 8 and 9. The rank sum test value is p, and data results less than E-10 are considered 0.

Table 10. Comparison of experimental results with TOP algorithm (10 dim).

Function	Index	AGSK	APGSK-IMODE	EA4eig	IMODE	CNABC
C01	Mean	0.0000E+00	0.0000E+00	0.0000E+00	0.0000E+00	1.1973E-03
	Std	0.0000E+00	0.0000E+00	0.0000E+00	0.0000E+00	4.3849E-03
	Rank	1	1	1	1	2
	P	7.57E-12	1.77E-11	1.21E-12	1.21E-12	
C02	Mean	4.3152E+00	1.6766E-06	6.6443E-01	0.0000E+00	7.7435E+00
	Std	1.2296E+00	6.4403E-06	1.4857E+00	0.0000E+00	1.7176E+01
	Rank	4	2	3	1	5
	P	5.29E-01	2.92E-11	3.52E-09	1.19E-12	
C03	Mean	2.1819E-04	0.0000E+00	0.0000E+00	2.2624E-06	0.0000E+00
	Std	2.4169E-04	0.0000E+00	0.0000E+00	2.2078E-06	0.0000E+00
	Rank	3	1	1	2	1
	P	4.08E-12	2.25E-04	1.97E-11	4.08E-12	
C04	Mean	9.4244E+00	4.8590E+00	1.0281E+00	8.8883E+00	1.0911E+01
	Std	1.9325E+00	1.4671E+00	9.4332E-01	2.1483E+00	3.9254E+00
	Rank	4	2	1	3	5
	P	5.55E-02	3.48E-07	2.28E-11	3.14E-02	
C05	Mean	0.0000E+00	0.0000E+00	0.0000E+00	1.8424E+00	6.3937E-02
	Std	0.0000E+00	0.0000E+00	0.0000E+00	3.0732E+00	1.9356E-01
	Rank	1	1	1	3	2
	P	8.39E-03	1.20E-05	1.20E-05	8.41E-09	
C06	Mean	3.2980E-01	4.0670E-01	4.4834E-02	1.6979E+00	8.3687E+02
	Std	1.1129E-01	1.1401E-01	9.0058E-02	1.4846E+00	1.2552E+03
	Rank	2	3	1	4	5
	P	3.02E-11	3.01E-11	3.02E-11	3.02E-11	
C07	Mean	3.8735E-01	4.3631E-04	2.0934E-10	5.4350E-04	1.8372E+00
	Std	5.5332E-01	9.4390E-04	6.7468E-10	5.7188E-04	4.9007E+00
	Rank	4	2	1	3	5
	P	7.84E-01	4.45E-04	2.11E-11	4.51E-02	
C08	Mean	3.8053E+00	1.1567E+00	3.3965E-01	2.3765E+00	1.3731E+01
	Std	2.4133E+00	1.1865E+00	2.1644E-01	1.9064E+00	9.3017E+00
	Rank	4	2	1	3	5
	P	1.44E-02	1.86E-03	1.87E-05	4.23E-03	
C09	Mean	2.2928E+02	2.2928E+02	1.8550E+02	2.1400E+02	2.2928E+02
	Std	8.5265E-14	8.5265E-14	3.4654E-13	5.7194E+01	1.4211E-13
	Rank	3	3	1	2	3
	P	1.69E-14	1.69E-14	8.64E-14	6.91E-10	
C10	Mean	1.0029E+02	1.0026E+02	1.0019E+02	8.2928E+01	1.0022E+02
	Std	3.1802E-02	4.6911E-02	4.0734E-02	3.4986E+01	5.5811E-02
	Rank	5	4	2	1	3
	P	7.22E-06	6.10E-03	7.01E-02	3.85E-03	
C11	Mean	0.0000E+00	0.0000E+00	0.0000E+00	3.7651E-08	0.0000E+00
	Std	0.0000E+00	0.0000E+00	0.0000E+00	2.3221E-08	0.0000E+00
	Rank	1	1	1	2	1
	P	2.20E-09	5.35E-07	3.94E-12	1.14E-09	
C12	Mean	1.6101E+02	1.6246E+02	1.4719E+02	1.6384E+02	1.6292E+02
	Std	9.2072E-01	1.0661E+00	3.2503E+00	7.0591E-01	1.9242E+00
	Rank	2	3	1	5	4
	P	1.47E-06	2.40E-01	3.64E-11	3.14E-02	

Table 11. Comparison of experimental results with TOP algorithm (20 dim).

Function	Index	AGSK	APGSK-IMODE	EA4eig	IMODE	CNABC
C01	Mean	2.4887E-09	5.3677E+02	0.0000E+00	0.0000E+00	6.9833E+02
	Std	1.1681E-08	2.6484E+02	0.0000E+00	0.0000E+00	5.6114E+02
	Rank	2	3	1	1	4
	P	2.99E-11	5.59E-01	1.21E-12	1.21E-12	
C02	Mean	4.8945E+01	4.6162E+01	5.2945E+00	3.4493E+01	4.7313E+01
	Std	7.5195E-01	9.2179E+00	2.9091E+00	2.2299E+01	2.4233E+01
	Rank	5	3	1	2	4
	P	9.53E-04	1.59E-03	3.01E-07	3.52E-05	
C03	Mean	6.1868E-03	7.6936E-07	0.0000E+00	1.2810E+00	0.0000E+00
	Std	4.2229E-03	5.8359E-07	0.0000E+00	8.1892E-01	0.0000E+00
	Rank	4	3	1	5	1
	P	3.02E-11	3.01E-11	1.21E-12	3.02E-11	
C04	Mean	3.7751E+01	2.9132E+01	1.1144E+01	6.0063E+01	3.4144E+01
	Std	5.2045E+00	5.5429E+00	4.4228E+00	1.1524E+01	4.8546E+00
	Rank	4	2	1	5	3
	P	2.07E-02	9.02E-04	2.98E-11	5.49E-11	
C05	Mean	4.9963E-01	4.8880E+00	0.0000E+00	7.1216E+02	3.2107E+02
	Std	3.4276E-01	4.5295E+00	0.0000E+00	2.7596E+02	2.4450E+02
	Rank	2	3	1	5	4
	P	3.02E-11	3.01E-11	1.21E-12	2.00E-06	
C06	Mean	3.8645E+01	1.1731E+03	6.7614E-01	2.2384E+01	2.7414E+03
	Std	1.4041E+01	8.9562E+02	5.5963E-01	6.6968E+00	2.9384E+03
	Rank	3	4	1	2	5
	P	3.02E-11	1.26E-01	3.02E-11	3.02E-11	
C07	Mean	2.9975E+01	2.4774E+01	1.2557E+01	3.4001E+01	2.8564E+01
	Std	2.0967E+00	3.1719E+00	8.9337E+00	4.1091E+00	3.5577E+00
	Rank	4	2	1	5	3
	P	1.15E-01	3.59E-05	3.47E-10	5.46E-06	
C08	Mean	2.4295E+01	2.2690E+01	1.9660E+01	2.1835E+01	2.1493E+01
	Std	3.3946E-01	5.9443E-01	4.2501E+00	6.4596E-01	3.0215E+00
	Rank	5	4	1	2	3
	P	5.57E-10	6.11E-10	2.07E-02	2.68E-06	
C09	Mean	1.8078E+02	1.8078E+02	1.6534E+02	1.8078E+02	1.8078E+02
	Std	8.5265E-14	5.0618E-07	3.9794E-09	1.0012E-07	2.8422E-14
	Rank	2	2	1	2	2
	P	1.21E-12	9.75E-10	3.01E-11	6.74E-06	
C10	Mean	1.0040E+02	1.0053E+02	1.0412E+02	1.0062E+02	9.8298E+01
	Std	4.7991E-02	6.8048E-02	2.0291E+01	6.8914E-02	3.5593E+01
	Rank	2	3	5	4	1
	P	3.65E-08	6.12E-10	3.77E-04	5.57E-10	
C11	Mean	3.5000E+02	3.0000E+02	3.3000E+02	2.8046E+02	3.3640E+02
	Std	5.0000E+01	6.4438E-10	4.5826E+01	7.4998E+01	7.8303E+01
	Rank	5	2	3	1	4
	P	7.39E-02	2.05E-03	1.40E-04	1.44E-02	
C12	Mean	2.3987E+02	2.3896E+02	1.9971E+02	2.5429E+02	2.6224E+02
	Std	2.6782E+00	2.6503E+00	1.5617E+00	6.5203E+00	2.0616E+01
	Rank	3	2	1	4	5
	P	4.87E-11	4.97E-11	3.02E-11	3.63E-01	

From the data results in Tables 10 and 11, it can be seen that the competition algorithm in CEC performs significantly better in the same experimental environment, while, in terms of the comprehensive ranking of CNABC, the 20-dimensional algorithm is lower than the 10-dimensional algorithm and is relatively backward.

From Figures 8 and 9, it can be seen that the top three functions of CNABC in the 10-dimensional rank are C01, C03, C05, C09, C10, and C11, while the top three functions in the 20-dimensional rank are C03, CO4, C07, C08, C09, and C11. Among these functions, it can be seen that CNABC's search ability is commendable. The TOP algorithm is not significantly different from C03 and C11 in terms of optimization, but we acknowledge that the search ability of the TOP algorithm is indeed better than that of CNABC. However,

CNABC also has good optimization capabilities in some functions, which is also what we need to see.

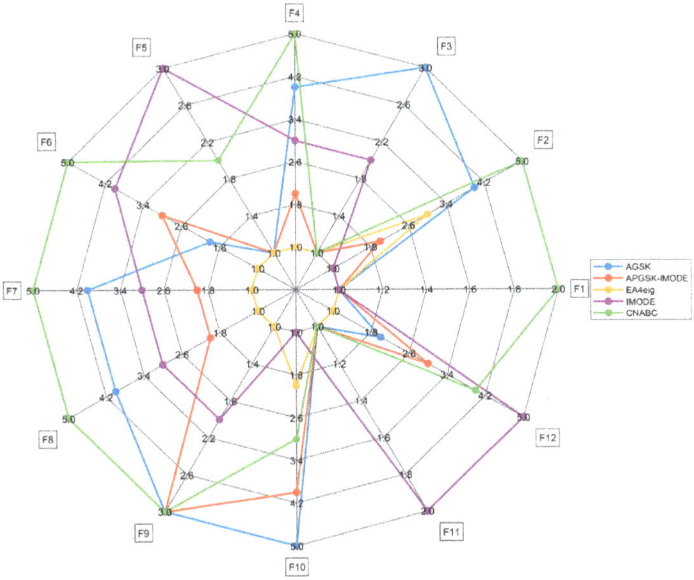

Figure 8. Radar ranking chart of the competition algorithm CEC2022 test set (10 dim).

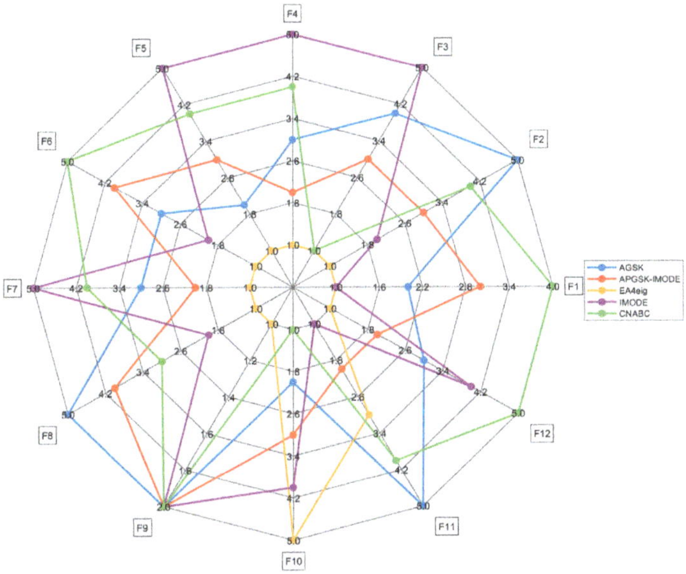

Figure 9. Radar ranking chart of the competition algorithm CEC2022 test set (10dim).

6. Conclusions

To assess the comprehensive performance of the enhanced algorithm CNABC, this study undertook experiments in both 10-dimensional and 20-dimensional spaces using the CEC2022 test set. The CNABC was contrasted with 10 different algorithms, with parameters for each algorithm configured according to their respective original literature. Within the CEC2022 test set, F1 is a unimodal function, F2–F5 is a multimodal function based on F2–F5, F6–F8 is a hybrid function, and F9–F12 is a combination function. The two test sets contain the same function types and can evaluate the algorithm's search ability and overall robustness. This study presents a dynamic neighbor artificial bee colony algorithm (CNABC) based on commutative solutions. In CNABC, bee leaders are updated in the three stages of the original bee population, and the randomness of randomly selected hired bees as leaders is reduced by selecting the optimal individuals in a small population. The best leader in a small range is maintained as a highlight to improve ABC. Secondly, upon the completion of the three stages, a novel approach is introduced to reduce the risk of the worst solution falling into local or global optima by introducing candidate solutions through the exchange solution mechanism. Next, to verify the search ability of the improved CNABC, experiments were conducted on the CEC2022 test sets. Based on the experimental results, it was verified that CNABC possesses excellent search performance and certain competitiveness in an algorithm through mean and standard deviation. The box plot can reflect that CNABC's stability performance in the comparison algorithm is good, and there is no significant unreasonable existence, The Wilcoxon rank sum test and Friedman test show that there is a difference in the optimization results between CNABC and the comparison algorithm, that is, the optimization method has novelty, which comprehensively verifies the effectiveness, novelty, and competitiveness of the improved CNABC.

Although CNABC has shown good performance in the optimization search aspect in the comparison algorithm, it is still possible to know the limitations of CNABC. It satisfies the NFL theorem and cannot show good performance in many problems. This shows the obvious shortcomings of CNABC. First, there is still room for improvement in the convergence speed and optimization accuracy in the 10-dimensional C06 and C10, and the 20-dimensional C05, C11, and C12 in the two test sets. Secondly, there is still a gap compared with the TOP algorithm in the CEC competition, especially in terms of combinatorial functions. Therefore, the focus of future work will be on the following two aspects:

- On the basis of CNABC, let it shine on composite functions, no longer limited to the other three functions, but more on problem functions;
- Explore and design more transformation search mechanisms to further improve the algorithm's optimization ability and the ability to jump out of local optima.

Author Contributions: Conceptualization, C.O. and Y.G.; methodology, C.O. and Y.G.; software, Y.G.; validation, Y.G. and D.Z.; formal analysis, Y.G. and D.Z.; investigation, Y.G. and D.Z.; resources, H.G. and D.Z.; data curation, Y.G. and D.Z.; writing—original draft preparation, Y.G.; writing—review and editing, H.G. and D.Z.; visualization, Y.G. and D.Z.; supervision, H.G. and C.Z.; project administration, C.Z.; funding acquisition, C.O. All authors have read and agreed to the published version of the manuscript.

Funding: This research was funded by the National Natural Science Foundation of China (Nos. 62272418, 62102058), and the basic public welfare research program of Zhejiang Province (No. LGG18E050011).

Data Availability Statement: All data for this study are available from the corresponding author.

Acknowledgments: The authors thank the reviewers and editors for their valuable suggestions, which substantially improve this paper.

Conflicts of Interest: The authors declare no conflicts of interest.

References

1. Zhu, D.; Huang, Z.; Liao, S.; Zhou, C.; Yan, S.; Chen, G. Improved Bare Bones Particle Swarm Optimization for DNA Sequence Design. *IEEE Trans. Nanobiosci.* **2022**, *22*, 603–613. [CrossRef] [PubMed]
2. Sun, G.; Han, R.; Deng, L.; Li, C.; Yang, G. Hierarchical structure-based joint operations algorithm for global optimization. *Swarm Evol. Comput.* **2023**, *79*, 101311. [CrossRef]

3. Ma, C.; Huang, H.; Fan, Q.; Wei, J.; Du, Y.; Gao, W. Grey wolf optimizer based on Aquila exploration method. *Expert Syst. Appl.* **2022**, *205*, 117625. [CrossRef]
4. Hassan, M.H.; Houssein, E.H.; Mahdy, M.A.; Kamel, S. An improved Manta ray foraging optimizer for cost-effective emission dispatch problems. *Eng. Appl. Artif. Intell.* **2021**, *100*, 104155. [CrossRef]
5. Wang, J.; Zhang, Y.; Hong, M.; He, H.; Huang, S. A self-adaptive level-based learning artificial bee colony algorithm for feature selection on high-dimensional classification. *Soft Comput.* **2022**, *26*, 9665–9687. [CrossRef]
6. Yu, W.; Kang, H.; Sun, G.; Liang, S.; Li, J. Bio-Inspired Feature Selection in Brain Disease Detection via an Improved Sparrow Search Algorithm. *IEEE Trans. Instrum. Meas.* **2022**, *72*, 2500515. [CrossRef]
7. Jena, B.; Naik, M.K.; Panda, R.; Abraham, A. Maximum 3D Tsallis entropy based multilevel thresholding of brain MR image using attacking Manta Ray foraging optimization. *Eng. Appl. Artif. Intell.* **2021**, *103*, 104293. [CrossRef]
8. Zhang, J.; Zheng, J.; Xie, X.; Lin, Z.; Li, H. Mayfly sparrow search hybrid algorithm for RFID Network Planning. *IEEE Sens. J.* **2022**, *22*, 16673–16686. [CrossRef]
9. Eberhart, R.; Kennedy, J. A new optimizer using particle swarm theory. In Proceedings of the Mhs95 Sixth International Symposium on Micro Machine & Human Science, Nagoya, Japan, 4–6 October 1995.
10. Dorigo, M. The ant system: An autocatalytic optimizing process. In Proceedings of the First European Conference on Artificial Life, Paris, France, 11–13 December 1991.
11. Yang, X.-S.; Deb, S. Cuckoo Search via Lvy flights. In Proceedings of the 2009 World Congress Nature & Biologically Inspired Computing (NaBIC), Coimbatore, India, 9–11 December 2009; pp. 210–214. [CrossRef]
12. Mirjalili, S.; Mirjalili, S.M.; Lewis, A. Grey Wolf Optimizer. *Adv. Eng. Softw.* **2014**, *69*, 46–61. [CrossRef]
13. Xue, J.; Shen, B. A novel swarm intelligence optimization approach: Sparrow search algorithm. *Syst. Sci. Control. Eng.* **2020**, *8*, 22–34. [CrossRef]
14. Zhu, D.; Wang, S.; Zhou, C.; Yan, S.; Xue, J. Human Memory Optimization Algorithm: A memory-inspired optimizer for Global Optimization Problems. *Expert Syst. Appl.* **2024**, *237*, 121597. [CrossRef]
15. Adhikary, J.; Acharyya, S. Randomized Balanced Grey Wolf Optimizer (RBGWO) for solving real life optimization problems. *Appl. Soft Comput.* **2022**, *117*, 108429. [CrossRef]
16. Precup, R.-E.; David, R.-C.; Roman, R.-C.; Szedlak-Stinean, A.-I.; Petriu, E.M. Optimal tuning of interval type-2 fuzzy controllers for nonlinear servo systems using Slime Mould Algorithm. *Int. J. Syst. Sci.* **2021**, *54*, 2941–2956. [CrossRef]
17. Meng, Z.; Zhong, Y.; Mao, G.; Liang, Y. PSO-sono: A novel PSO variant forsingle-objective numerical optimization. *Inf. Sci.* **2022**, *586*, 176–191. [CrossRef]
18. Zhu, D.; Wang, S.; Shen, J.; Zhou, C.; Li, T.; Yan, S. A multi-strategy particle swarm algorithm with exponential noise and fitness-distance balance method for low-altitude penetration in secure space. *J. Comput. Sci.* **2023**, *74*, 102149. [CrossRef]
19. Karaboga, N.; Latifoglu, F. Adaptive filtering noisy transcranial Doppler signal by using artificial bee colony algorithm. *Eng. Appl. Artif. Intell.* **2013**, *26*, 677–684. [CrossRef]
20. Chiang, H.-S.; Sangaiah, A.K.; Chen, M.-Y.; Liu, J.-Y. A novel artificial bee colony optimization algorithm with SVM for bio-inspired software-defined networking. *Int. J. Parallel Program.* **2020**, *48*, 310–328. [CrossRef]
21. Lalwani, S.; Kumar, R. An efficient three-Level parallel ABC algorithm for secondary structure prediction of complex RNA sequences. *Appl. Soft Comput.* **2021**, *99*, 106848. [CrossRef]
22. Naware, D.; Badigenchala, R.; Mitra, A.; Das, D. Impact of demand response on battery energy storage degradation using gbest-guided artificial bee colony algorithm with forecasted solar insolation. *J. Energy Storage* **2022**, *52*, 104915. [CrossRef]
23. Erdem, E.; Aydın, T.; Erkayman, B. Flight scheduling incorporating bad weather conditions through big data analytics: A comparison of metaheuristics. *Expert Syst.* **2021**, *38*, e12752. [CrossRef]
24. Wolpert, D.H.; Macready, W.G. No free lunch theorems for optimization. *IEEE Trans. Evol. Comput.* **1997**, *1*, 67–82. [CrossRef]
25. Xiang, W.L.; Li, Y.Z.; He, R.C.; An, M.Q. Artificial bee colony algorithm with a pure crossover operation for binary optimization. *Comput. Ind. Eng.* **2021**, *152*, 107011. [CrossRef]
26. Yavuz, G.; Aydın, D. Improved Self-adaptive Search Equation-based Artificial Bee Colony Algorithm with competitive local search strategy. *Swarm Evol. Comput.* **2019**, *51*, 100582. [CrossRef]
27. Zhou, B.; Zhao, Z. An adaptive artificial bee colony algorithm enhanced by Deep Q-Learning for milk-run vehicle scheduling problem based on supply hub. *Knowl.-Based Syst.* **2023**, *264*, 110367. [CrossRef]
28. Ye, T.; Wang, W.; Wang, H.; Cui, Z.; Wang, Y.; Zhao, J.; Hu, M. Artificial bee colony algorithm with efficient search strategy based on random neighborhood structure. *Knowl.-Based Syst.* **2022**, *241*, 108306. [CrossRef]
29. Zhou, X.; Song, J.; Wu, S.; Wang, M. Artificial bee colony algorithm based on online fitness landscape analysis. *Inf. Sci.* **2023**, *619*, 603–629. [CrossRef]
30. Zhou, X.; Wu, Y.; Zhong, M.; Wang, M. Artificial bee colony algorithm based on adaptive neighborhood topologies. *Inf. Sci.* **2022**, *610*, 1078–1101. [CrossRef]
31. Khan, I.; Maiti, M.K. A swap sequence based Artificial Bee Colony algorithm for Traveling Salesman Problem. *Swarm Evol. Comput.* **2019**, *44*, 428–438. [CrossRef]
32. Zheng, T.; Zhang, H.; Zhang, B.; Cai, Z.; Wang, K.; Todo, Y.; Gao, S. Umbrellalike Hierarchical Artificial Bee Colony Algorithm. *IEICE Trans. Inf. Syst.* **2023**, *106*, 410–418. [CrossRef]

33. Song, X.; Zhao, M.; Yan, Q.; Xing, S. A high-efficiency adaptive artificial bee colony algorithm using two strategies for continuous optimization. *Swarm Evol. Comput.* **2019**, *50*, 100549. [CrossRef]
34. Guan, B.; Xu, T.; Zhao, Y.; Li, Y.; Dong, X. A random grouping-based self-regulating artificial bee colony algorithm for interactive feature detection. *Knowl.-Based Syst.* **2022**, *243*, 108434. [CrossRef]
35. Wang, Y.; Jiao, J.; Liu, J.; Xiao, R. A labor division artificial bee colony algorithm based on behavioral development. *Inf. Sci.* **2022**, *606*, 152–172. [CrossRef]
36. Tao, X.R.; Pan, Q.K.; Gao, L. An efficient self-adaptive artificial bee colony algorithm for the distributed resource-constrained hybrid flowshop problem. *Comput. Ind. Eng.* **2022**, *169*, 108200. [CrossRef]
37. Bilal, M.E. COVID-19 detection based on pre-trained deep networks and LSTM model using X-ray images enhanced contrast with artificial bee colony algorithm. *Expert Syst.* **2022**, *40*, e13185.
38. Peng, H.; Deng, C.; Wu, Z. Best neighbor-guided artificial bee colony algorithm for continuous optimization problems. *Soft Comput.* **2019**, *23*, 8723–8740. [CrossRef]
39. Shami, T.M.; Mirjalili, S.; Al-Eryani, Y.; Daoudi, K.; Izadi, S.; Abualigah, L. Velocity pausing particle swarm optimization: A novel variant for global optimization. *Neural Comput. Appl.* **2023**, *35*, 9193–9223. [CrossRef]
40. Mirjalili, S.; Lewis, A. The whale optimization algorithm. *Adv. Eng. Softw.* **2016**, *95*, 51–67. [CrossRef]
41. Too, J.; Mafarja, M.; Mirjalili, S. Spatial bound whale optimization algorithm: An efficient high-dimensional feature selection approach. *Neural Comput. Appl.* **2021**, *33*, 16229–16250. [CrossRef]
42. Wu, R.; Huang, H.; Wei, J.; Ma, C.; Zhu, Y.; Chen, Y.; Fan, Q. An improved sparrow search algorithm based on quantum computations and multi-strategy enhancement. *Expert Syst. Appl.* **2023**, *215*, 119421. [CrossRef]
43. Liu, S.-H.; Mernik, M.; Hrnčič, D.; Črepinšek, M. A parameter control method of evolutionary algorithms using exploration and exploitation measures with a practical application for fitting Sovova's mass transfer model. *Appl. Soft Comput.* **2013**, *13*, 3792–3805. [CrossRef]
44. Sallam, K.M.; Elsayed, S.M.; Chakrabortty, R.K.; Ryan, M.J. Improved multi-operator differential evolution algorithm for solving unconstrained problems. In Proceedings of the 2020 IEEE Congress on Evolutionary Computation (CEC), Glasgow, UK, 9–24 July 2020; pp. 1–8. [CrossRef]
45. Mohamed, A.W.; Hadi, A.A.; Awad, N.H. Evaluating the performance of adaptive gainingsharing knowledge based algorithm on CEC 2020 benchmark problems. In Proceedings of the 2020 IEEE Congress on Evolutionary Computation (CEC), Glasgow, UK, 9–24 July 2020; pp. 1–8. [CrossRef]
46. Mohamed, A.W.; Hadi, A.A.; Agrawal, P.; Sallam, K.M.; Mohamed, A.K. Gaining-sharing knowledge based algorithm with adaptive parameters hybrid with imode algorithm for solving cec 2021 benchmark problems. In Proceedings of the 2021 IEEE Congress on Evolutionary Computation, Kraków, Poland, 28 June–1 July 2021; pp. 841–848. [CrossRef]
47. Bujok, P.; Kolenovsky, P. Eigen crossover in cooperative model of evolutionary algorithms applied to CEC 2022 single objective numerical optimization. In Proceedings of the 2022 IEEE Congress on Evolutionary Computation, Padua, Italy, 18–23 July 2022; pp. 1–8. [CrossRef]

electronics

MDPI

Article

Joint Pricing, Server Orchestration and Network Slice Deployment in Mobile Edge Computing Networks

Yijian Hou [1], Kaisa Zhang [1,*], Gang Chuai [1], Weidong Gao [1], Xiangyu Chen [2] and Siqi Liu [3]

[1] School of Information and Communication Engineering, Beijing University of Posts and Telecommunications, Beijing 100876, China; houyijian@bupt.edu.cn (Y.H.); chuai@bupt.edu.cn (G.C.); gaoweidong@bupt.edu.cn (W.G.)

[2] School of Electronic Engineering, Beiing University of Posts and Telecommunications, Beiing 100876, China; xychen324@bupt.edu.cn

[3] School of Electrical and Electronic Engineering, North China Electric Power University, Baoding 071003, China; liusiqi@ncepu.edu.cn

* Correspondence: kaisa@bupt.edu.cn

Abstract: The integration of mobile edge computing (MEC) and network slicing can provide low-latency and customized services. In such integrated wireless networks, we propose a pricing-driven joint MEC server orchestration and network slice deployment scheme (PD-JSOSD), jointly solving the pricing, MEC server orchestration and network slicing deployment issues. We divide the system into an infrastructure provider layer (IPL), network planning layer (NPL) and resource allocation layer (RAL), and a three-stage Stackelberg game is proposed to describe their relationships. To obtain the Stackelberg equalization, we propose a three-layer deep reinforcement learning (DRL) algorithm. Specifically, the dueling double deep Q-network (D3QN) is used in the IPL, and the DRL with branching dueling Q-network (BDQ) is used in the NPL and the RAL to cope with the large-scale discrete action spaces. Moreover, we propose an innovative illegal action modification algorithm to improve the convergence of the BDQ. Simulations verify the convergence of the three-layer DRL and the superiority of modified-BDQ in dealing with large-scale action spaces, where modified-BDQ can improve the convergence by 21.9% and 28.3%. Furthermore, compared with the benchmark algorithms, JSOSD in the NPL and the RAL can improve system utility by up to 52.1%, proving the superiority of the server orchestration and slice deployment scheme.

Keywords: mobile edge computing (MEC); server orchestration; network slice deployment; pricing; cost; Stackelberg game; deep reinforcement learning (DRL)

1. Introduction

The growing popularity of smart devices has led to diverse applications, driving an urgent demand for services with higher performance, lower delay and more reliable connectivity. Numerous applications, such as smart transportation and healthcare, require real-time response and interaction. Traditional communication methods that rely on central or remote clouds often result in significant delay and network bottlenecks [1]. Mobile edge computing (MEC) brings resources and network functions closer to the network edge, thereby enhancing the responsiveness of services [2]. Network function virtualization (NFV) decouples network functions from dedicated hardware devices, creating virtual network functions (VNFs) that can run on general-purpose hardware. By combining a set of VNFs with virtualized network resources, a virtual network, known as a network slice, is formed [3]. Network slicing has become a key technology for efficiently managing diverse use cases. Recent studies have shown its effectiveness across various domains, including vehicular communication, industrial applications, and mission-critical services. For instance, ref. [4] proposed a network slicing solution for vehicular networks, effectively isolating traffic types such as safety messages and infotainment services. Ref. [5] described a network architecture framework based on network slicing that provides high service quality for data-intensive mission critical tasks. Ref. [6] explored the dynamic resource allocation of network slicing for ultra reliable and low-latency communication and enhanced mobile broadband services. In practical applications, the authors of [7] conducted an experiment at the Hamburg Seaport, demonstrating how network slicing can provide tailored services for various applications. These works highlight the importance of network slicing in meeting the diverse and demanding requirements of modern networks. In MEC networks, MEC servers often have limited computational and storage resources compared with cloud servers [8]. Introducing network slicing technology allows for a more efficient allocation of resources. Each slice can request edge resources and perform targeted optimization, enhancing resource utilization. Moreover, edge resources can be managed through software-defined methods without adding additional hardware deployment. This reduces hardware construction and maintenance costs while increasing network flexibility. Therefore, integrating MEC and network slicing technologies will improve resource utilization, offer personalized services and enhance the configurability of the MEC network. In such integrated wireless networks, the orchestration of MEC servers, the deployment network slices and the pricing schemes all have an impact on network performance. In the following, we will discuss these issues in detail and analyze their interrelationships.

The orchestration of MEC servers involves planning their locations and managing their association with base stations, both of which are critical elements in MEC networks. Because the geographic distribution of services may change over time, the dynamic server placement is desirable. However, the migration of servers will incur unavoidable labor costs and service disruptions [9], which are often ignored in previous studies [10–13]. Transforming the MEC server location optimization problem into a server activation problem is proposed in [8,14], where the locations of MEC servers are fixed but the servers to be activated need to be determined. This would not only avoid the frequent migration of servers but also allow for dynamic change of the number of servers based on demand. Accordingly, we will address the MEC server activation problem in this paper.

With the help of software-defined networking (SDN) and NFV, network slicing can provide customized VNF chains [15]. In the MEC network, VNF chains can be deployed on edge servers based on factors such as delay demand and users' locations [16]. Optimizing the VNF chain deployment can improve resource utilization and reduce network operating costs. In addition to the VNF chains deployed on MEC servers, the access functions of the base station can also be virtualized as VNFs, which are responsible for user access control, signal transmission and reception, data forwarding, radio resource management, etc. Unlike the deployment of VNF chains on edge servers, the deployment of access functions on base stations directly affects the geographical coverage of slices. Providing full coverage for all network slices may lead to cost inefficiencies. Therefore, in the MEC network, slice deployment needs to consider both the deployment of VNF chains on edge servers and the deployment of access functions on base stations [17]. However, most studies have neglected the deployment of access functions [8,14,18]. In addition, while addressing the slice deployment problem, it also requires the allocation schemes for radio, computational and storage resources.

Tenants are entities or organizations that use specific network slices, such as individuals, enterprises, and government agencies [3]. Tenants can submit requests to the InP to create slices based on the demand of theirs subscribers. In response, the InP virtualizes the corresponding network slice and selects network nodes for its deployment. Then, the InP is responsible for the installation, configuration, and ongoing maintenance of the slices. Consequently, the InP charges the tenant for both deployment costs and resource costs [17,19]. The tenant needs to provide services to its users through the network slice and guarantee their QoS requirements. Additionally, the tenant expects to reduce the fees paid to the InP. These two objectives can be achieved by optimizing the orchestration of MEC servers, the deployment of slices and the resource allocation strategies, which were addressed in our previous work [20]. Because the InP needs to bear the construction and maintenance costs of servers [10], the utility of the InP is influenced by the fees paid by tenants and the number of active services. Generally, higher income and fewer servers result in greater utility for the InP. Additionally, the InP's income is affected by pricing schemes. Specifically, low prices may lead to lower revenue, while high prices may discourage tenants from deploying more access functions and VNF chains as well as renting more resources. Therefore, the InP not only needs to optimize MEC server orchestration to reduce costs, but also needs to optimize the prices of resource and deployment to improve income, which was not considered in our previous work [20].

The previous analysis revealed that the pricing strategy affects the network slice deployment strategy. In addition, only if the MEC server is associated with the base station on which the access function of a slice is deployed can the VNF chain associated with the slice be deployed on the server. Thus, the server orchestration, VNF chain deployment, access function deployment and pricing strategy are coupled with each other and need to be considered simultaneously. However, previous studies failed to address this joint problem and instead only focused on one or two aspects [8–14,17,18]. Accordingly, we jointly address the issues of pricing, server orchestration and network slice deployment in this paper. Specifically, the considered system is divided into the InP layer (IPL), network planning layer (NPL) and resource allocation layer (RAL). The IPL achieves the goal of maximizing the average revenue generated by each activated server through pricing optimization. The NPL is responsible for optimizing the server activation and slice deployment, while the RAL is in charge of optimizing the radio, computational and storage resource allocation. The NPL and RAL share the common goal of maximizing the utility of slices, which is correlated with delay and cost. In our scheme, the IPL, NPL and RAL make decisions sequentially, with each layer following the decisions of the previous layer. Their relationship can be modeled as a three-stage Stackelberg game, where players make decisions in a strict order [21]. During the decision-making process, the players who decide first are the leaders, while the players who decide later are the followers. The Stackelberg game provides decision support for both leaders and followers by analyzing their strategies, aiming to find the Stackelberg equilibrium [22].

Backward induction is commonly used to obtain Stackelberg equilibrium solutions [22]. However, the aforementioned three-stage Stackelberg game constitutes a complex combinatorial optimization problem, which is NP-hard, rendering backward induction inapplicable [23]. In contrast, deep reinforcement learning (DRL) works well in solving complex optimization problems. DRL enables self-adaptation and strategy improvement by interacting with the environment. Deep Q-network (DQN) and its variants have been widely applied to DRL problems involving discrete action spaces. Among them, double DQN (DDQN) and dueling DQN (D3QN) are two significant improvements over the standard DQN. DDQN mitigates the overestimation bias in Q-learning by decoupling action selection and evaluation, while D3QN introduces separate value and advantage estimations to improve learning stability [24]. Recent advancements in D3QN-based DRL have demonstrated its effectiveness in wireless communications. For instance, in [25], the authors proposed a D3QN-based path planning solution for unmanned aerial vehicles, incorporating quantum-inspired experience replay to optimize experience sampling and improve training efficiency. This study highlighted the potential of D3QN in solving complex wireless network problems. However, D3QN has limitations in dealing with the problem of exponentially growing discrete action spaces, which exists in our model. In this context, authors in [26] gave a solution with their proposed branching dueling Q-network (BDQ), which is a branching variant of the dueling double deep Q-network (D3QN). BDQ's neural network builds network branches for each action dimension while retaining a shared module. The shared module encodes the latent representation of the state and provides information for each action branch. The number of the network's outputs in BDQ grows linearly with the increase in the action dimension. Currently, many works have verified the superiority of BDQ in solving large-scale discrete action spaces problems [27–29]. In BDQ, because each action branch has an independent network, inter-branch coordination is weakened, potentially resulting in joint actions that fail to meet the requirements. When these kind of illegal actions occur frequently, applying a fixed penalty can hinder the agent's exploration and distort the value function estimation. Thus, it is crucial to develop an effective method for avoiding illegal actions to ensure the convergence of BDQ.

Based on the above context, the main contributions of this paper are summarized as follows:

- We design an innovative wireless network model that integrates MEC networks with network slicing, combining MEC servers and base stations with VNF chains of network slices. This design enhances the configurability and scalability of MEC networks.
- We divide the system into the InP layer, network planning layer, and resource allocation layer, which are responsible for pricing, server orchestration and slice deployment, and resource allocation, respectively. To the best of our knowledge, this is the first work to comprehensively consider these interconnected challenges. Moreover, we build a three-stage Stackelberg game model according to the relationships among these three layers. Then, we prove the existence of a Stackelberg equilibrium.
- We design a three-layer DRL model to obtain the Stackelberg equilibrium. D3QN is used to solve the pricing problem for the IPL, while double-layer BDQ (DBDQ) is used to make decisions for the NPL and RAL to reduce the complexity of the neural network. The joint actions of all branches in BDQ are likely to output illegal actions. Thus, we innovatively proposed an illegal action modification algorithm, successfully enhancing the convergence of the DRL model.
- We perform extensive simulations to evaluate the performance of PD-JSOSD. Numerical results demonstrate the convergence of the algorithm. It is also demonstrated that compared with the benchmark schemes, the proposed method not only achieves a higher utility of slices but also effectively improves the utility of the InP.

2. Related Work

(1) Orchestration of MEC Servers: With the development of MEC, numerous studies have investigated the orchestration of MEC servers. The authors of [11] studied the joint problem of MEC server placement and service placement. They employed a clustering algorithm and nonlinear programming to solve server placement and service placement sequentially. On the downside, this work used a fixed number of servers, which may incur unnecessary maintenance costs. The numbers of servers in [10,13] were dynamically adjusted according to service demand. The authors of [10] proposed a three-layer algorithm to determine server locations, deployed computation units and subscribed computational resource, aiming to maximize the revenue of MEC operators. The authors of [13] used reinforcement learning to place MEC servers with the goal of minimizing the delay and the number of servers. However, the server deployment schemes in [10,13] were "one-shot" decisions. In this case, when the geographic distribution of users shifts, servers need to be migrated to other locations in order to improve resource utilization, which may incur service interruptions, transportation costs, etc. Accordingly, the server activation problem was raised in [8,14]. They both assumed that the locations of the MEC servers were fixed, but decisions need to be made on which servers to be activated. Inspired by [8,14], we study the activation of MEC servers in this paper.

(2) Deployment of Network Slice: Except for the server activation issue, refs. [8,14] also addressed the VNF chain deployment on MEC servers. Ref. [8] studied the deployment of VNF chains and their replicas on MEC servers with the goal of minimizing the cost. Ref. [14] investigated deploying primary and backup VNF chains on servers and presented a multi-objective optimization problem to minimize the number of VNF chains and servers, as well as the response delay. Differently, ref. [14] ignored the propagation delay, which is part of the delay and is related to the distance between the MEC server and the base station, whereas ref. [8] took this into account. However, neither of them took into account the geographic distribution of users and the deployment of access functions. The authors in [18] proposed a method for deploying VNF chains at the network edge, effectively improving resource utilization and latency utility. In [30], a real-time end-to-end VNF deployment and migration method was proposed, successfully increasing the throughput of network slices and reducing the migration cost of VNFs. Although refs. [18,30] considered the physical connections between MEC servers, they did not optimize the placement of the MEC servers. In [19], although the authors considered the selection of remote radio heads (RRHs) to reduce the cost of RRHs, they also did not take into account the geographical distribution of users. In [17], access function deployment and VNF deployment were considered sequentially. However, the authors did not jointly optimize these two issues. In fact, the deployment scheme of access functions and the deployment scheme of VNF chains jointly determine the users' delay and the tenants' cost, and they mutually influence each other. Therefore, optimizing both schemes simultaneously can achieve better system performance. In our previous work [20], we designed a three-stage algorithm to address the above issues. Specifically, DRL was used to determine the number of activated servers, the k-means clustering algorithm was used to determine the server activation scheme and convex optimization was applied to solve the network slice deployment and resource allocation problems. However, the k-means clustering algorithm in [20] only considered the distance between servers and did not take into account factors such as user distribution and available resources, which did not guarantee that the solution is effective.

(3) Pricing and Stackelberg Game: For the problem of MEC server orchestration and network slice deployment, many studies attempted to optimize different objectives, such as delay, deployment cost and number of servers. However, only a few studies have considered the benefit of an InP. For the InP, revenue and energy consumption are more of a concern. For example, ref. [31] optimized resource allocation in a multi-tenant scenario to maximize the InP's revenue and provide satisfactory services. However, just like [31], many works that considered the InP's revenue ignored the impact of pricing. Recently, the Stackelberg game has been widely used to seek the equilibrium between pricing strategies and resource allocation strategies. To illustrate, in [22], the interaction between access service provider (ASP) and users is formulated as a multi-leader, multi-follower Stackelberg game. As the leader, the ASP decides the access price based on users' expected budgets and the pricing strategies of other ASPs. As the follower, users decide the access bandwidth to be purchased based on the prices. Inspired by this, in this paper, we design a three-layer Stackelberg game with the InP as the leader and the NPL as the follower and also with the NPL as the leader and the RAL as the follower.

(4) Reinforcement Learning Approach: Recently, multi-layer reinforcement learning has made significant progress in solving the Stackelberg game problem, which is NP-hard. In [32], the pricing decisions of MEC servers and offloading decisions of users were modeled as a multi-leader multi-follower Stackelberg game. To enhance the applicability of the pricing decisions, this work proposed using a multi-armed bandit (MAB) in the leader layer. However, the MAB solves the problem on a stateless premise, which does not apply to situations where pricing needs to be dynamically adjusted according to the state of the network. Similar to our scheme, in [33,34], a three-layer DRL algorithm was employed to solve the three-layer Stackelberg games. These works have proven that the three-layer DRL was able to reach an equilibrium solution. Although multi-layer DRL has proven to be an effective approach for solving multi-layer Stackelberg games, the current research has yet to explore its applicability in handling multi-layer Stackelberg games with large-scale discrete action spaces. The convergence difficulty of multi-layer DRL is inherently higher than that of single-layer DRL, and this challenge is further exacerbated in scenarios with large-scale action spaces, imposing greater demands on model training efficiency. Therefore, exploring methods to reduce the convergence difficulty of multi-layer DRL is critical. Ref. [26] proposed the BDQ algorithm to enhance the applicability of DRL in large-scale discrete action spaces. Then, ref. [27] applied BDQ to the vehicle association problem and validated its effectiveness. However, existing BDQ-related works have a major limitation: they overlook the fact that the branching structure may weaken the correlation between sub-actions, leading to joint actions that fail to meet constraints, thereby compromising the effectiveness of the strategy. Building on the above context, we propose a three-layer DRL algorithm based on D3QN-DBDQ to solve the three-stage Stackelberg game. At the same time, we innovatively design an illegal action modification algorithm to enhance the convergence of BDQ. To clearly illustrate how our work differs from related works, we summarize the aspects covered in related works in Table 1.

Table 1. Comparison of aspects covered by related works.

Ref.	Server Orchestration	Flexible Server Number	Server Activation	Access Function Deployment	User Geographic Distribution	Pricing	Large-Scale Action Spaces
[8]	Yes	Yes	Yes	No	No	No	No
[10]	Yes	Yes	No	No	No	No	No
[11]	Yes	No	No	No	No	No	No
[13]	Yes	Yes	No	No	No	No	No
[14]	Yes	Yes	Yes	No	No	No	No
[17]	No	No	No	Yes	Yes	No	No
[18]	Yes	No	No	Yes	No	No	No
[19]	No	No	No	Yes	No	No	No
[20]	Yes	Yes	Yes	Yes	Yes	No	No
[22]	No	No	No	No	No	Yes	No
[26]	No	No	No	No	No	No	Yes
[27]	No	No	No	No	No	No	Yes
[30]	Yes	No	No	Yes	No	No	No
[31]	No	No	No	No	No	No	No
[32]	No	No	No	No	No	Yes	No
Our work	Yes	Yes	Yes	Yes	Yes	Yes	Yes

3. System Model

3.1. Infrastructure Model

We consider the network model shown in Figure 1, where the InP owns the infrastructure such as base stations and MEC servers. In the network initialization phase, tenants make requests to the InP to create and deploy slices. The InP leverages SDN and NFV-enabled infrastructure (NFVI), such as base stations and MEC servers, to instantiate a set of VNFs to dynamically deploy slices on demand. As shown in Figure 1, the base stations and MEC servers are connected to the virtual infrastructure manager (VIM), which is responsible for managing the NFVI using SDN [8]. The VIM is connected to the NFV/MEC orchestrator (NFVO/MECO), which orchestrates services and manages the lifecycle of the network slices through the VIM. We use $\mathcal{N} = \{1, \ldots, n, \ldots, N\}$ to represent the set of slices. There is a set of base stations $\mathcal{M} = \{1, \ldots, m, \ldots, M\}$ within the region. They possess only the fundamental capabilities of communicating and receiving service requests. In this paper, we only consider downlink transmissions, and each base station has a downlink bandwidth capacity of W_m^{max}. The InP is required to select base stations (in 5G NR, the specific applications of the access functions, such as access control, signal transmission and reception, data forwarding and radio resource management, are performed by the remote radio unit (RRU), distributed unit (DU), and centralized unit (CU). Here, we collectively refer to these three functional modules as the base station) for each slice to deploy access functions, with radio bandwidth resources being allocated accordingly. We use $x = [x_{m,n}]_{M \times N}$ to denote the deployment indication of the access functions, where $x_{m,n} = 1$ means that the access function of slice n is deployed on base station m, and $x_{m,n} = 0$ otherwise.

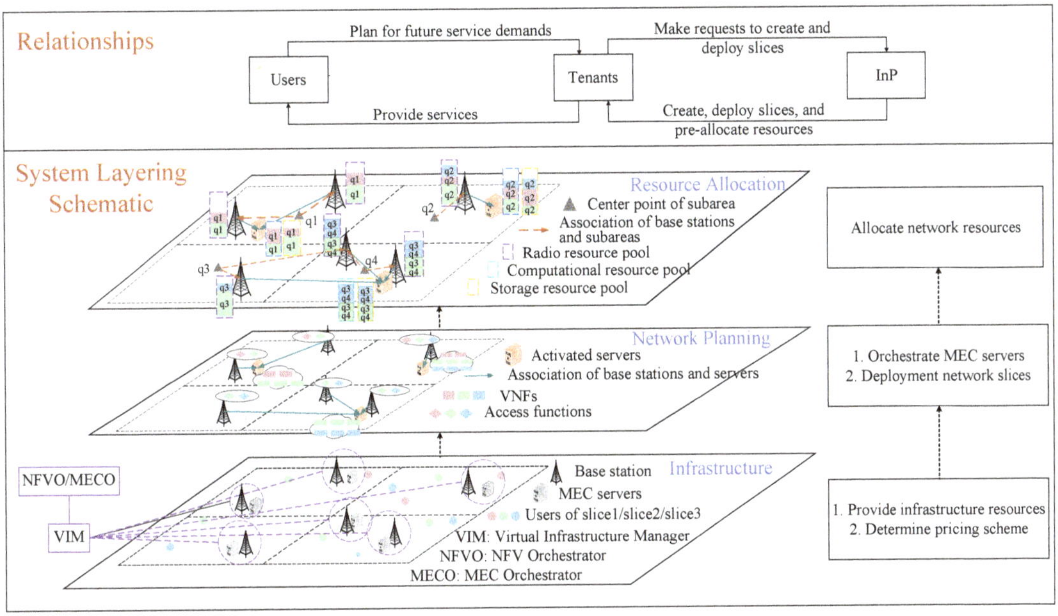

Figure 1. System model.

We assume that each base station is equipped with one MEC server (actually, the number of equipped MEC servers can be less than or equal to the number of base stations, which does not affect our problem modeling. The exact number of MEC servers to be equipped can be decided by the InP, and here we just give an example). Due to factors such as energy consumption, only a subset of servers can be activated simultaneously [8,14].

For the sake of illustration, we denote the set of MEC servers by $\mathcal{V} = \{1, \ldots, v, \ldots, V\}$, where $V = M$. Furthermore, $\boldsymbol{p} = [p_v]_{1\times V}$ represents the server activation indication, where $p_v = 1$ means that server v is activated, and $p_v = 0$ otherwise. A base station can only forward service requests to its associated MEC server. The association between base stations and servers is denoted by $\boldsymbol{a} = [a_{v,m}]_{V\times M}$, where $a_{v,m} = 1$ means that base station m is associated with server v, and $a_{v,m} = 0$ otherwise. The computational and storage capacities of server v are E_v^{max} and S_v^{max}, respectively. The InP is required to select MEC servers for slices to deploy VNF chains and allocate computational and storage resources to them. Let $\boldsymbol{k} = [k_{v,n}]_{V\times N}$ be the VNF chain deployment indication, where $k_{v,n} = 1$ means that the VNF chain of slice n is deployed on server v, and $k_{v,n} = 0$ otherwise.

3.2. Delay Model

When performing slice deployment, the precise location of each user is unknown. The tenants and InP can only know the number of users expected to be served in the region. To address this, ref. [17] employed a subarea partitioning technique where the region is divided into Q convex subareas. When performing slice deployment, resources are allocated to each subarea. The region may be divided into rectangles of equal area or into subareas with an equal average number of users. For example, in Figure 1, we divide a service region into four rectangular parts of equal area with dashed lines. We use $\mathcal{Q} = \{1, \ldots, q, \ldots, Q\}$ to represent the set of subareas. Let $u_{n,q}$ represent the number of users that slice n plans to serve in subarea q. We denote the slice n in subarea q by (n, q). Moreover, $w_{n,q}^m$, $e_{n,q}^v$ and $s_{n,q}^v$ are used to represent the radio, computational and storage resources allocated to (n, q) by base station m and server v. Note that the distribution of these resources within (n, q) is a matter addressed by intra-slice resource management, which is beyond the scope of this paper.

The total data rate of (n, q) can be expressed as [17]:

$$R_{n,q} = \sum_{m=1}^{M} w_{n,q}^m \log_2(1 + SNR_{m,q}), \tag{1}$$

where $SNR_{m,q} = \frac{P_{m,q}^{tx} + G_{m,q}^{tx} + G_{m,q}^{rx} - PL(D_{m,q})}{\sigma^2}$ is the signal-to-noise ratio (SNR). $P_{m,q}^{tx}$, $G_{m,q}^{tx}$, $G_{m,q}^{rx}$, $PL(D_{m,q})$ and σ^2 are the transmitted power, antenna gain of the transmitter and receiver, path loss and noise power, respectively [17]. $D_{m,q}$ denotes the distance between base station m and the center point of subarea q. Because this paper deals with the problems faced in the network planning phase, does not involve real-time resource scheduling and does not address the association of specific users with sub-channels, we do not consider the co-channel interference in the wireless network.

The transmission delay $d_{n,q}^{tran}$ can be calculated by [35]

$$d_{n,q}^{tran} = \frac{l_n u_{n,q}}{R_{n,q}}, \tag{2}$$

where l_n is the size of the computational task for the users of slice n. The propagation delay $d_{n,q}^{prop}$ is positively correlated with the distance between the base station and the server [36], which can be denoted as

$$d_{n,q}^{prop} = \frac{1}{\sum_{m=1}^{M} y_{n,q}^m} \sum_{m=1}^{M} y_{n,q}^m \sum_{v=1}^{V} a_{v,m} D_{v,m} t_0, \tag{3}$$

where $y_{n,q}^m$ indicates whether (n, q) has any users associated with base station m. $D_{m,v}$ is the distance between base station m and server v. t_0 is the propagation delay generated per unit distance. Furthermore, the computational delay can be expressed as [35]

$$d_{n,q}^{comp} = \frac{l_n b_n u_{n,q}}{\sum_{v=1}^{V} e_{n,q}^{v}}, \tag{4}$$

where b_n is the computational demand to process each bit (CPU cycles/bit). The total delay can be expressed as $d_{n,q} = d_{n,q}^{tran} + d_{n,q}^{prop} + d_{n,q}^{comp}$ [12].

3.3. *Cost and Revenue Model*

When a slice deploys its access function on base stations and deploys a VNF chain on MEC servers, the InP will charge deployment fees for the installation of VNFs and subsequent maintenance [17,19]. Hence, the cost of each slice comprises deployment costs and resource costs. We denote the prices of access function deployment, VNF chain deployment, and radio and computational resources as c_a, c_v, c_r and c_e. Note that once the number of users is determined, the user demand on storage resources will not adapt based on price. In this context, we can ignore storage resource cost. The ranges of c_a, c_v, c_r and c_e are denoted as $[c_a^{min}, c_a^{max}]$, $[c_v^{min}, c_v^{max}]$, $[c_r^{min}, c_r^{max}]$ and $[c_e^{min}, c_e^{max}]$, respectively. We quantize the value of prices into L discrete levels, and the c_a with level l_a is denoted as:

$$c_a(l_a) = c_a^{min} + \frac{l_a(c_a^{max} - c_a^{min})}{L-1}, \; l_a = 0, 1, \ldots, L-1. \tag{5}$$

We denote the cost of each slice as:

$$c_n = c_a \sum_{m=1}^{M} x_{m,n} + c_v \sum_{v=1}^{V} k_{v,n} + c_r \sum_{m=1}^{M} \sum_{q=1}^{Q} w_{n,q}^{m} + c_e \sum_{v=1}^{V} \sum_{q=1}^{Q} e_{n,q}^{v}. \tag{6}$$

Thus, the revenue of the InP is expressed as $r^{InP} = \sum_{n=1}^{N} c_n$.

4. The Three-Stage Stackelberg Game

Based on the responsibilities, we divide the proposed system into three layers, i.e., the IPL, NPL, and RAL. We use the three-stage Stackelberg game to describe the interactions among the three layers. In the following, we will introduce the responsibilities of these three layers, give the problem formulation for each layer, construct the Stackelberg game model and prove the existence of a Stackelberg equilibrium.

4.1. *Responsibility Description and Problem Formulation*

4.1.1. InP Layer (Stage I)

The IPL sets deployment and resource prices with the goal of maximizing the average revenue generated by each activated server

$$P1: \; \underset{\mathcal{L}}{\text{maximize}} \; U^{InP} = \frac{r^{InP}}{p^{sum}} \tag{7a}$$

$$\text{s.t. } l_a, l_v, l_r, l_e \in \{0, 1, \ldots, L-1\}, \tag{7b}$$

where $\mathcal{L} = (l_a, l_v, l_r, l_e)$ denotes the set of price levels and $p^{sum} = \sum_{v=1}^{V} p_v$ denotes the number of activated servers.

4.1.2. Network Planning Layer (Stage II)

According to the pricing scheme of the IPL, the NPL determines MEC server orchestration and network slice deployment schemes with the goal of minimizing the weighting of average delay proportion and average user cost of all slices. We denote the average delay proportion of each slice as:

$$d_n^{aver} = \frac{1}{d_n^{max}} \sum_{q=1}^{Q} \frac{d_{n,q} u_{n,q}}{\sum_{q=1}^{Q} u_{n,q}}, \tag{8}$$

where d_n^{max} denote the maximum tolerated delay. The average user cost of each slice is denoted as:

$$c_n^{aver} = \frac{c_n}{\sum_{q=1}^{Q} u_{n,q}}. \tag{9}$$

The objective of the NPL is expressed as:

$$P2: \underset{p,a,x,k}{\text{maximize}}\ U^{NP} = -\sum_{n=1}^{N} (w_d d_n^{aver} + w_c c_n^{aver}) \tag{10a}$$

$$\text{s.t. } p_v, a_{v,m}, x_{m,n}, k_{v,n} \in \{0,1\}, \forall v \in \mathcal{V}, m \in \mathcal{M}, n \in \mathcal{N} \tag{10b}$$

$$\begin{cases} p_v = 1, & \text{if } \sum_{m=1}^{M} a_{v,m} \geq 1 \\ p_v = 0, & \text{otherwise,} \end{cases} \tag{10c}$$

$$\sum_{v=1}^{V} a_{v,m} = 1, \forall m \in \mathcal{M} \tag{10d}$$

$$\begin{cases} k_{v,n} = 1, & \text{if } \sum_{m=1}^{M} x_{m,n} a_{v,m} \geq 1 \\ k_{v,n} = 0, & \text{otherwise,} \end{cases} \tag{10e}$$

where w_d and w_c are the weights of delay and cost, respectively. The types of the variables are specified by (10b). Expression (10c) presents the relationship between the MEC server association scheme and the activation scheme. Expression (10d) restricts a base station to only be associated with one server. Expression (10e) indicates that the VNF chain of slice n is deployed on server v if and only if the slice n deploys its access function on the base station associated with the server v.

4.1.3. Resource Allocation Layer (Stage III)

According to the pricing scheme of the IPL and the server orchestration and slice deployment schemes of the NPL, the RAL determines the radio, computational and storage resource allocation scheme, sharing the same goal as the NPL:

$$P3: \underset{y,w,e,s}{\text{maximize}}\ U^{RA} = -\sum_{n=1}^{N} (w_d d_n^{aver} + w_c c_n^{aver}) \tag{11a}$$

$$\text{s.t. } y_{n,q}^{m} \in \{0,1\},. \forall m \in \mathcal{M}, n \in \mathcal{N}, q \in \mathcal{Q} \tag{11b}$$

$$w_{n,q}^{m}, e_{n,q}^{v}, s_{n,q}^{v} \in [0, +\infty), \forall m \in \mathcal{M}, v \in \mathcal{V}, n \in \mathcal{N}, q \in \mathcal{Q} \tag{11c}$$

$$y_{n,q}^{m} \leq x_{m,n}, \forall m \in \mathcal{M}, n \in \mathcal{N}, q \in \mathcal{Q} \tag{11d}$$

$$w_{n,q}^{m} \leq W_m^{max} y_{n,q}^{m}, \forall m \in \mathcal{M}, n \in \mathcal{N}, q \in \mathcal{Q} \tag{11e}$$

$$e_{n,q}^{v} \leq min(E_v^{max} \sum_{m=1}^{M} y_{n,q}^{m} a_{v,m}, E_v^{max}), \forall v \in \mathcal{V}, n \in \mathcal{N}, q \in \mathcal{Q} \tag{11f}$$

$$s_{n,q}^{v} \leq min(S_v^{max} \sum_{m=1}^{M} y_{n,q}^{m} a_{v,m}, S_v^{max}), \forall v \in \mathcal{V}, n \in \mathcal{N}, q \in \mathcal{Q} \tag{11g}$$

$$\sum_{n=1}^{N} \sum_{q=1}^{Q} w_{n,q}^{m} \leq W_m^{max}, \forall\ m \in \mathcal{M} \tag{11h}$$

$$\sum_{n=1}^{N} \sum_{q=1}^{Q} e_{n,q}^{v} \leq E_v^{max}, \forall\ v \in \mathcal{V} \tag{11i}$$

$$\sum_{n=1}^{N} \sum_{q=1}^{Q} s_{n,q}^{v} \leq S_v^{max}, \forall\ v \in \mathcal{V} \tag{11j}$$

$$\sum_{v=1}^{V} s_{n,q}^{v} = u_{n,q} s_n^{d}, \forall\ n \in \mathcal{N}, q \in \mathcal{Q} \tag{11k}$$

$$d_{n,q} \leq d_n^{max},\ \forall n \in \mathcal{N}, q \in \mathcal{Q} \tag{11l}$$

where (11b) and (11c) specify the type of the variables. Expression (11d) shows that users in (n, q) can connect to base station m only if slice n deploys the access function on the base station. Expressions (11e)–(11g) restrict that a base station or server can allocate resources to users in (n, q) if and only if (n, q) is allowed to be associated with the base station or server. The resource capacity constraints are given in (11h)–(11j). Expression (11k) guarantees that the storage resource allocated to (n, q) is equal to its demand, where s_n^d represents the storage demand for users of slice n. Finally, we present the delay constraints in (11l).

4.2. Construction of the Three-Stage Stackelberg Game

In Figure 2, we present the three-stage Stackelberg game, which can be considered as containing two two-stage Stackelberg games. In the first two-stage Stackelberg game, the IPL is the leader, while the NPL and the RAL are the followers. In the second two-stage Stackelberg game, the NPL is the leader, while the RAL is the follower. Next, we will demonstrate the process of the three-stage Stackelberg game along with Figure 2. In the beginning of each game, the IPL first speculates on the reactions of the NPL and the RAL to decide the prices and thus maximize the objective function of $P1$. Then, the IPL sends the pricing scheme to the NPL and RAL (arrow A in Figure 2). Once the NPL receives the pricing scheme, it first speculates on the reactions of the RAL to determine the server activation and slice deployment scheme with the goal of $P2$. Then, the NPL sends its scheme to the RAL and feeds the number of activated servers back to the IPL (arrow B). Once the RAL receives the IPL's pricing scheme and the NPL's scheme, it decides the resource allocation scheme with the goal of $P3$. Then, the RAL feeds the resource allocation scheme back to the IPL and the NPL, who calculate their own utilities based on the feedback (arrow C). Note that it has been pointed out in [37] that the utility of the leader and follower can be the same in the Stackelberg game. Therefore, using the same utility function for the NPL and RAL is reasonable.

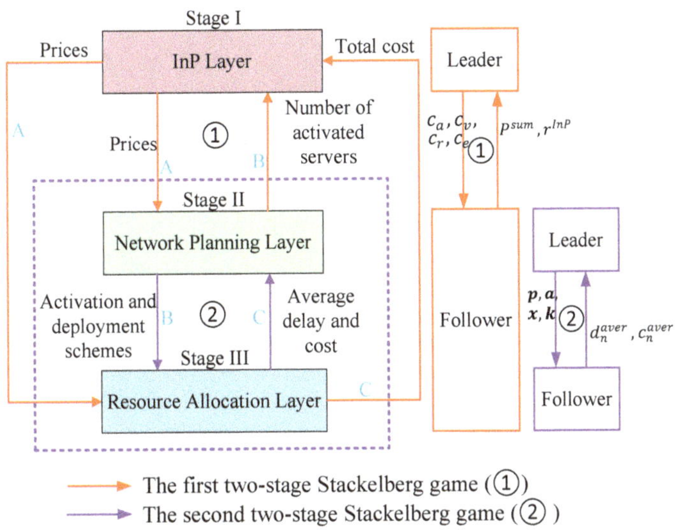

Figure 2. Proposed three-stage Stackelberg game model.

4.3. Analysis of Stackelberg Equilibrium

According to [37], we give the definition of Stackelberg equilibrium as follows:

Definition 1. *Given the strategies of the IPL and NPL, i.e., $\mathcal{L}$ and $(\boldsymbol{p}, \boldsymbol{a}, \boldsymbol{x}, \boldsymbol{k})$, the optimal response of the RAL is denoted as*

$$(\boldsymbol{y}^*, \boldsymbol{w}^*, \boldsymbol{e}^*, \boldsymbol{s}^*) = \arg\max_{\boldsymbol{y},\boldsymbol{w},\boldsymbol{e},\boldsymbol{s}} U^{RA}(\mathcal{L}, (\boldsymbol{p}, \mathbf{a}, \boldsymbol{x}, \boldsymbol{k}), (\boldsymbol{y}, \boldsymbol{w}, \boldsymbol{e}, \boldsymbol{s})). \tag{12}$$

Definition 2. *Given the strategy of the IPL, i.e., $\mathcal{L}$, the optimal response of the NPL is denoted as*

$$(\boldsymbol{p}^*, \boldsymbol{a}^*, \boldsymbol{x}^*, \boldsymbol{k}^*) = \arg\max_{\boldsymbol{p},\boldsymbol{a},\boldsymbol{x},\boldsymbol{k}} U^{NP}(\mathcal{L}, (\boldsymbol{p}, \boldsymbol{a}, \boldsymbol{x}, \boldsymbol{k}), (\boldsymbol{y}^*, \boldsymbol{w}^*, \boldsymbol{e}^*, \boldsymbol{s}^*)), \tag{13}$$

where $(\boldsymbol{y}^*, \boldsymbol{w}^*, \boldsymbol{e}^*, \boldsymbol{s}^*)$ is the optimal response of the RAL reacting to the NPL's strategy.

Definition 3. *$\mathcal{L}^*$ is the Stackelberg equilibrium strategy if and only if*

$$\mathcal{L}^* = \arg\max_{\mathcal{L}} U^{InP}(\mathcal{L}, (\boldsymbol{p}^*, \boldsymbol{a}^*, \boldsymbol{x}^*, \boldsymbol{k}^*), (\boldsymbol{y}^*, \boldsymbol{w}^*, \boldsymbol{e}^*, \boldsymbol{s}^*)), \tag{14}$$

where $(\boldsymbol{p}^*, \boldsymbol{a}^*, \boldsymbol{x}^*, \boldsymbol{k}^*)$ and $(\boldsymbol{y}^*, \boldsymbol{w}^*, \boldsymbol{e}^*, \boldsymbol{s}^*)$ are the optimal responses for the NPL and the RAL reacting to the IPL's strategy.

Theorem 1. *If there exists a set $(\mathcal{L}, (\boldsymbol{p}, \mathbf{a}, \boldsymbol{x}, \boldsymbol{k}), (\boldsymbol{y}, \boldsymbol{w}, \boldsymbol{e}, \boldsymbol{s}))$ such that the constraints of P1, P2 and P3 hold simultaneously, the three-stage stackelberg game must have at least one Stackelberg equilibrium.*

Proof of Theorem 1. *P3* is a mixed-integer nonlinear programming problem. When the integer decision variable $\boldsymbol{y}$ is determined, the problem can be transformed into:

$$\begin{aligned} P4:\ &\underset{\boldsymbol{w},\boldsymbol{e},\boldsymbol{s}}{\text{maximize}}\ U^{RA} = -\sum_{n=1}^{N}(w_d d_n^{aver} + w_c c_n^{aver}) \\ &\text{s.t. constraints (11c), (11e)–(11l).} \end{aligned} \tag{15}$$

It is easy to prove that *P4* is a convex problem, which can be solved by the convex optimization solver. Thus, with the given $\mathcal{L}$ and $(\boldsymbol{p}, \boldsymbol{a}, \boldsymbol{x}, \boldsymbol{k})$, the optimal response of the RAL can be obtained by enumerating all possible values of $\boldsymbol{y}$. Similarly, *P2* is an integer programming problem with finite strategy sets, so the optimal response satisfying (13) can also be obtained by enumerating all possible values of $(\boldsymbol{p}, \boldsymbol{a}, \boldsymbol{x}, \boldsymbol{k})$. It can be seen that the optimal responses of the NPL and RAL can be obtained by exhausting when $\mathcal{L}$ is given. Also, the IPL has a discrete strategy set, so the Stackelberg equilibrium in (14) can also be obtained by enumerating all possible values of $\mathcal{L}$. On the contrary, if there exists no $(\mathcal{L}, (\boldsymbol{p}, \mathbf{a}, \boldsymbol{x}, \boldsymbol{k}), (\boldsymbol{y}, \boldsymbol{w}, \boldsymbol{e}, \boldsymbol{s}))$ such that the constraints in *P1*, *P2* and *P3* hold simultaneously, then the strategy set is empty and there must be no Stackelberg equilibrium. □

The Proof of Theorem 1 refers to [37], which also provides details on how to use the exhaustive search algorithm to obtain the Stackelberg equilibrium. However, although the exhaustive method can yield a Stackelberg equilibrium, its computational complexity is particularly high and it will consume a lot of time. We take the MOSEK solver [38] as an example; the computational complexity of our problem is $O(L^4 2^{(M^2+MNQ)}(MNQ)^{3.5})$, which is unacceptable in the communication system. Therefore, next we will design a three-layer DRL algorithm, which can obtain the Stackelberg equilibrium solution with lower complexity.

5. Three-Layer Deep Reinforcement Learning

DRL utilizes neural networks to learn features from the original data and learn optimal policies by interacting with the environment. Compared with traditional search algorithms, DRL is a better way to escape from local optimal solutions and achieve a global equilibrium. Additionally, once a DRL model is trained, it can be easily deployed, and decisions can be made quickly based on the real-time state [39]. As such, we employ a three-layer DRL to solve the proposed three-layer Stackelberg game.

5.1. The DRL Model for the IPL

The elements of the DRL problem in the IPL are summarized as follows:

- State: $s_t^{InP} = \left[u_{n,q}^t\right]_{N\times Q}$.
- Action: $\hat{a}_t^{InP} = \mathcal{L}_t$.
- Reward: $R_t^{InP} = U_t^{InP}$.

The action space is 4-dimensional and discrete with each dimension taking values in $\{0, 1, \ldots, L-1\}$. The discrete action algorithm D3QN [24] is suitable for solving this problem. D3QN integrates the double deep Q-network (DDQN), prioritized experience replay, and the dueling architecture [40]. D3QN achieves higher data utilization and can obtain good strategies. In the following, we will introduce D3QN in detail.

As shown in Figure 3, D3QN contains two neural networks, which have the same structure but different parameters. The evaluation network with parameter $\boldsymbol{\theta}$ is responsible for action selection, and the target network with parameter $\hat{\boldsymbol{\theta}}$ is used to evaluate the action value [41]. The target network is a copy of the evaluation network, where $\hat{\boldsymbol{\theta}}$ is copied from $\boldsymbol{\theta}$ every ω steps. Each network contains the input layer, the hidden layers and the output layer. The input layer is responsible for receiving environment state information. The hidden layer performs feature extraction and nonlinear transformation, and multiple hidden layers are fully connected to each other. D3QN introduces a dueling architecture with two independent estimators. One is used to estimate the state value $V(s;\boldsymbol{\theta})$, and the other is used to give the action advantage $A(s,\hat{a};\boldsymbol{\theta})$. At the output layer, the outputs of the two estimators are combined to generate the state-action value $\hat{Q}(s_t,\hat{a}_t;\boldsymbol{\theta})$, i.e.,

$$\hat{Q}(s_t,\hat{a}_t;\boldsymbol{\theta}) = V(s_t;\boldsymbol{\theta}) + A(s_t,\hat{a}_t;\boldsymbol{\theta}) - \frac{1}{|\mathcal{A}|}\sum_{\hat{a}\in\mathcal{A}} A(s_t,\hat{a};\boldsymbol{\theta}), \tag{16}$$

where $|\mathcal{A}|$ is the number of all possible actions. The adoption of the dueling architecture ensures that the relative ordering of the advantage function for each action remains unchanged, which improves the algorithmic stability.

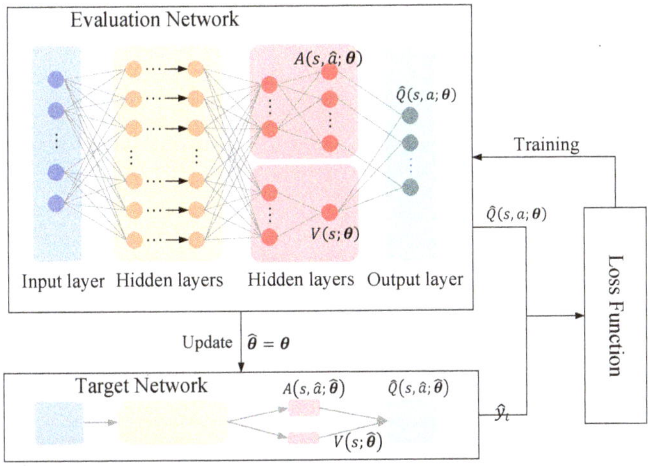

Figure 3. The architecture of D3QN.

During training, we store the transition $(s_t, \hat{a}_t, R_t, s_{t+1})$ in the replay memory buffer and select a mini-batch from the buffer for training. The objective of the training is to minimize the loss function, i.e., $L(\boldsymbol{\theta}) = \mathbb{E}[(\hat{y}_t - \hat{Q}(s_t, \hat{a}_t; \boldsymbol{\theta}))^2]$, where $\hat{Q}(s_t, \hat{a}_t; \boldsymbol{\theta})$ is the state-action value output by the evaluation network. $\hat{y}_t$ is the temporal difference (TD)-target, which is denoted as

$$\hat{y}_t = R_t + \gamma \hat{Q}(s_{t+1}, \arg\max_{\hat{a}_{t+1}} \hat{Q}(s_{t+1}, \hat{a}_{t+1}; \boldsymbol{\theta}); \hat{\boldsymbol{\theta}}), \tag{17}$$

where γ is the discount factor.

It has been proven that experiences with high TD-error are more important because they provide higher learning efficiency. The authors in [42] proposed a framework for prioritized experience replay (PER) to increase the replay probability of transitions with higher TD-error, thus improving the sample efficiency. In D3QN, PER is employed to select samples for training. In PER, the probability that transition i is replayed is denoted as $P(i) = \frac{p_i^{\alpha}}{\sum_j p_j^{\alpha}}$, where α determines the level of prioritization. $p_i = |\delta_i| + \sigma$ and δ_i is the TD-error, which is expressed as

$$\delta_i(s_i, \hat{a}_i, R_i, s_{i+1}) = \hat{y}_i - \hat{Q}(s_i, \hat{a}_i; \boldsymbol{\theta}). \tag{18}$$

σ is a very small positive value used to guarantee the replay probability is not 0 when $\delta_i = 0$. In addition, PER leads to a loss of sample diversity, which can be corrected by introducing the importance sampling weight (ISW) [42], i.e.,

$$w_i = (B \cdot P(i))^{-\beta}, \tag{19}$$

where B is the size of the replay memory buffer and β controls the level of compensation. When performing the gradient descent step, we use the weighted TD-error $w_i \delta_i$ instead of δ_i.

Algorithm 1 shows how D3QN is applied to solve our IPL problem. In each training round, the InP first selects an action based on the greedy strategy (lines 3–4), then executes the pricing scheme and computes rewards based on feedback from the NPL and the RAL (line 5). After that, transition $(s_t^{InP}, \hat{a}_t^{InP}, R_t^{InP}, s_{t+1}^{InP})$ is stored in the replay memory buffer (line 7). Lastly, a mini-batch is sequentially selected from the buffer using PER (lines 8–14). Specifically, we first select a transition based on the replay probability (line 9). Then, we compute the ISW and TD-error and then update its transition priority p_i (line 10–12). Finally, the gradient descent method is employed to update the network parameters (line 13). Moreover, the target network should be updated every fixed number of rounds (line 15).

Algorithm 1 D3QN Algorithm for the IPL

1: **Initialize** the evaluation network with random weights $\boldsymbol{\theta}$ and target network with $\hat{\boldsymbol{\theta}} = \boldsymbol{\theta}$; replay memory buffer $\mathcal{D}$.
2: **for** $t = 1$ to T **do**
3:     Select a random action $\hat{a}_t^{InP}$ with probability ϵ.
4:     Otherwise $\hat{a}_t^{InP} = \arg\max_{\hat{a}_t^{InP}} \hat{Q}(s_t^{InP}, \hat{a}_t^{InP}; \boldsymbol{\theta})$.
5:     Send $\hat{a}_t^{InP}$ to the NPL and RAL and calculate the reward R_t^{InP} according to the feedback.
6:     Obtain the state s_{t+1}^{InP} of the next round based on the number of users the tenants expect to serve.
7:     Store the transition $(s_t^{InP}, \hat{a}_t^{InP}, R_t^{InP}, s_{t+1}^{InP})$ in $\mathcal{D}$.
8:     **for** $i = 1$ to I **do**
9:         Sample a transition $(s_i^{InP}, \hat{a}_i^{InP}, R_i^{InP}, s_{i+1}^{InP})$ with probability $P(i)$.
10:         Compute the ISW according to (19).
11:         Compute the TD-error according to (18).
12:         Update transition priority p_i.
13:         Perform the gradient descent algorithm on the loss function with respect to $\boldsymbol{\theta}$.
14:     **end for**
15:     Set $\hat{\boldsymbol{\theta}} = \boldsymbol{\theta}$ every Ω rounds.
16: **end for**

5.2. The Double-Layer BDQ Model for the NPL and RAL

In line 5 of Algorithm 1, action $\hat{a}_t^{InP}$ is sent as the state to the neural networks of the NPL and RAL. Then, the agents of these two layers select the actions to take and train networks sequentially. Because the NPL and RAL share the same objective, their training processes are synchronized. In this section, we will introduce the DRL models of the NPL and RAL jointly.

5.2.1. The BDQ Model for the NPL

The elements of the DRL problem in the NPL are summarized as follows:

- State: $s_t^{NP} = \{[u_{n,q}^t]_{N\times Q}, \mathcal{L}_t\}$.
- Action: $\hat{a}_t^{NP} = \{[h_m^t]_{M\times 1}, [x_{m,n}^t]_{M\times N}\}$. h_m indicates which server the base station m is associated with. One thing to specify is that once the action $\hat{a}_t^{NP}$ is given, the variables $\boldsymbol{a}$, $\boldsymbol{p}$ and $\boldsymbol{k}$ can be easily derived.
- Reward: $R_t^{NP} = U_t^{NP}$.

The action space is $(M + MN)$-dimensional and discrete. The first M dimensions take values in $\{0, ..., V-1\}$, and the last MN dimensions take values in $\{0,1\}$. Thus, the action space is $V^M 2^{MN}$. The complexity of this neural network grows exponentially with $M + MN$, making it difficult to converge. As such, we introduce the BDQ architecture [26] to solve this DRL problem.

BDQ is a modification on D3QN, and its evaluation network is shown in Figure 4. The input layer, partially hidden layers and state value estimator of BDQ are the same as those of D3QN, i.e., the blue, yellow, and red regions in Figure 4. The difference is that BDQ changes the action advantage estimator into multiple independent branching networks, i.e., the purple region. Each branching network is responsible for evaluating the action advantage value for each action dimension. When the input layer provides environment state information, the hidden layer in the yellow region computes the latent representation, which is used to compute the state values (red region) as well as the factorized action advantages on the subsequent independent branches (purple region). The output layer (green region) is responsible for aggregating the state value and the factorized action advantages to output the state-action value for each action dimension. Then, each action dimension selects the action with the maximum state-action value, which is combined to form the final action. Specifically, suppose that action $\hat{a}$ has F sub-actions, i.e., the action dimension is F. The number of optional actions for each sub-action is $|\mathcal{A}_f|$. $A_f(s, \hat{a}^f; \boldsymbol{\varphi})$ denotes the action advantage of sub-action f and $V(s; \boldsymbol{\varphi})$ denotes the state value; then, the state-action value can be expressed as

$$\hat{Q}_f(s_t, \hat{a}_t^f; \boldsymbol{\varphi}) = V(s_t; \boldsymbol{\varphi}) + A_f(s_t, \hat{a}_t^f; \boldsymbol{\varphi}) - \frac{1}{|\mathcal{A}_f|} \sum_{\hat{a}^f \in \mathcal{A}_f} A_f(s_t, \hat{a}^f; \boldsymbol{\varphi}). \tag{20}$$

BDQ averages the state-action values of all dimensions to compute the TD-target, i.e.,

$$\hat{y}_t = R_t + \gamma \frac{1}{F} \sum_{f=1}^{F} \hat{Q}_f(s_{t+1}, \arg\max_{\hat{a}_{t+1}^f} \hat{Q}_f(s_{t+1}, \hat{a}_{t+1}^f; \boldsymbol{\varphi}); \hat{\boldsymbol{\varphi}}), \tag{21}$$

where $\hat{\boldsymbol{\varphi}}$ is the network parameter of the target network. The loss is defined as the expected value of the TD-error across all the branches:

$$L(\boldsymbol{\varphi}) = \mathbb{E}[\frac{1}{F} \sum_{f=1}^{F} (\hat{y}_t - \hat{Q}_f(s_t, \hat{a}_t^f; \boldsymbol{\varphi}))^2]. \tag{22}$$

When performing the PER, distributed TD-errors need to be aggregated into a uniform form. To preserve the magnitude of the error, the uniform prioritization error is defined as the sum of the absolute value of the TD-error across all the branches. In addition, the BDQ selects an action for each sub-action according to:

$$\hat{a}_t^{f,*} = \arg\max_{\hat{a}_t^f} \hat{Q}_f(s_t, \hat{a}_t^f; \boldsymbol{\varphi}). \tag{23}$$

For the BDQ problem of the NPL, there are $M + MN$ branches, i.e., $F = M + MN$. The first M branches represent $[h_m]_{M\times 1}$, each with V optional actions. The last MN branches represent $[x_{m,n}]_{M\times N}$, each with two optional actions. Thus, the number of network's outputs is reduced to $VM + 2MN$.

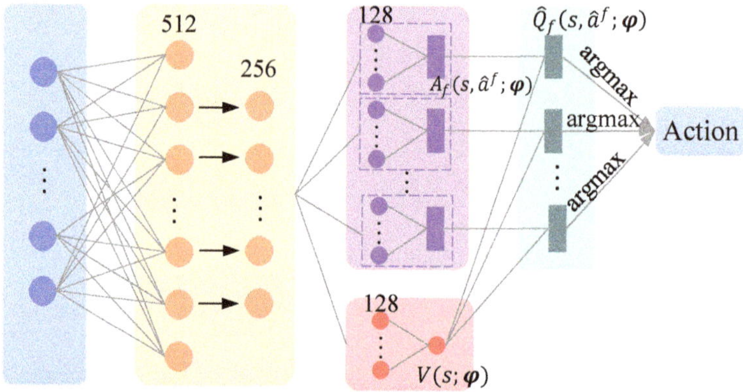

Figure 4. The evaluation network of BDQ.

5.2.2. The BDQ Model for the RAL

The elements of the DRL problem in the RAL are summarized as follows:

- State: s_t^{RA}=$\{[u_{n,q}^t]_{N\times Q}, \mathcal{L}_t, [a_{v,m}^t]_{V\times M}, [x_{m,n}^t]_{M\times N}, [k_{v,n}^t]_{V\times N}\}$.
- Action: As mentioned earlier, once the integer variable $\boldsymbol{y}$ is determined, the optimal $(\boldsymbol{w}, \boldsymbol{e}, \boldsymbol{s})$ can be solved by math tools. Thus, $\hat{a}_t^{RA} = \left[y_{n,q}^{m,t}\right]_{M\times N\times Q}$.
- Reward: $R_t^{RA} = U_t^{RA}$.

With an (MNQ)-dimensional discrete action space consisting of 2^{MNQ} optional actions, the complexity of the neural network grows exponentially with MNQ. To reduce the complexity in finding the solution, we use BDQ to solve the DRL problem for this layer. The number of branches is set to MNQ, and each branch selects action from $\{0, 1\}$. The number of network's outputs is reduced to $2MNQ$. Note that the restriction (11d) specifies that $y_{n,q}^m$ must equal 0 when $x_{m,n} = 0$. Therefore, when we transform the action of the RAL into $\boldsymbol{y}$, we need to process $\boldsymbol{y}$ by

$$y_{n,q}^m = x_{m,n} y_{n,q}^m. \tag{24}$$

5.2.3. The Illegal Action Modification Method

In BDQ, each branching network individually evaluates the action value of all possible sub-actions and outputs the sub-action with the maximum state-action value. The sub-actions from different branches may conflict with each other or be ineffective in combination. We call this an "illegal situation". There are two illegal situations that may occur in our scheme: (1) In the NPL, slice n requires M branches, and the branch corresponding to $x_{m,n}$ determines whether slice n is deployed on base station m or not, which means that the relationship of slice n with each base station is determined by a different branch. Thus, there is a probability that the actions of all the branches corresponding to slice n are 0, i.e., $\sum_{m=1}^{M} x_{m,n} = 0$. In this case, no base station deploys slice n, which is not allowed; (2) Similarly to the NPL, there is a probability in the RAL that the actions of all the branches corresponding to (n,q) are 0, i.e., $\sum_{m=1}^{M} y_{n,q}^{m} = 0$. This is not allowed when there are users in (n,q) who need to be served, i.e., $u_{n,q} > 0$. There may be many illegal actions in the early training stage of BDQ. Merely applying negative penalties would affect the convergence performance. To this end, we design an illegal action modification method based on the branching structure to mask illegal actions in Algorithm 2.

Specifically, in the NPL, suppose there is a slice n that encounters the case where $\sum_{m=1}^{M} x_{m,n} = 0$ (line 2). We need to find all the branches corresponding to $\{x_{m,n} | m \in \mathcal{M}\}$, i.e., F^n. The action of the branch with the largest state-action value is modified to 1 (lines 3–4). In this way, we ensure that at least one base station deploys slice n, and that base station corresponds to the highest state-action value. Similarly, in the RAL, suppose that (n,q) encounters the case where $u_{n,q} > 0$ but $\sum_{m=1}^{M} y_{n,q}^{m} = 0$ (line 8). We need to find all the branches corresponding to $\{y_{n,q}^{m} | m \in \mathcal{M}\}$, i.e., $F^{n,q}$. Then, we set the action of the branch with the largest state-action value to 1 (lines 9–10). For ease of description, we will call the BDQ with illegal action modification as modified-BDQ (MBDQ).

Algorithm 2 The illegal action modification method

The modification method for NPL:
Input: $\hat{a}_t^{NP} = \{[h_m^t]_{M \times 1}, [x_{m,n}^t]_{M \times N}\}$
1: **for all** $n \in \mathcal{N}$ **do**
2:     **if** $\sum_{m=1}^{M} x_{m,n} = 0$ **then**
3:         $\hat{f}_1 = \arg\max_{f \in F^n} \hat{Q}\left(s_t^{NP}, \hat{a}_t^{NP,f}; \varphi\right)$.
4:         $\hat{a}_t^{NP,\hat{f}_1} = 1$.
5:     **end if**
6: **end for**
The modification method for RAL:
Input: $\hat{a}_t^{RA} = \left[y_{n,q}^{m,t}\right]_{M \times N \times Q}$
7: **for all** $(n,q) \in \mathcal{N} \times \mathcal{Q}$ **do**
8:     **if** $u_{n,q} > 0$ and $\sum_{m=1}^{M} y_{n,q}^{m} = 0$ **then**
9:         $\hat{f}_2 = \arg\max_{f \in F^{n,q}} \hat{Q}\left(s_t^{RA}, \hat{a}_t^{RA,f}; \xi\right)$.
10:         $\hat{a}_t^{RA,\hat{f}_2} = 1$.
11:     **end if**
12: **end for**

5.2.4. The Implementation of the Double-Layer MBDQ

We present the training procedure for the double-layer MBDQ (DMBDQ) in Algorithm 3. φ and ξ are set as the network parameters for the NPL and RAL. In each training round, the NPL first selects an action based on the greedy policy (line 5). Then, it needs to judge whether there is an illegal action or not and performs the illegal action modification if it exists (line 6). The RAL receives the NPL's action, obtains the current state and selects an action using greedy policy (lines 7, 13). After that, the RAL performs illegal action judgment and correction (line 14). The resource allocation scheme will be obtained using a math solver (line 15). In this paper, we use the MOSEK solver [38]. If $P4$ is insoluble, we will give a penalty on R_t^{NP} and R_t^{RA}. Once $\hat{a}_t^{NP}$ and $\hat{a}_t^{RA}$ are determined, the rewards are computed and the actions are fed back to the IPL (lines 16–17). We then store transition $(s_t^{NP}, \hat{a}_t^{NP}, R_t^{NP}, s_{t+1}^{NP})$ into the replay memory buffer of the NPL (line 18). After that, we use PER to select a mini-batch from the buffer and update the network parameters of the NPL by gradient descent (lines 19–20). Note that the RAL's state of the next round is determined by the NPL's action in the next round, so the RAL needs to delay storing experience and updating the network to the next round (lines 8–12). Finally, we update the target networks every fixed number of rounds (line 21).

Algorithm 3 DMBDQ algorithm for the NPL and the RAL

1: **Initialize** NPL with random weights $\boldsymbol{\varphi}$ and target network with $\hat{\boldsymbol{\varphi}} = \boldsymbol{\varphi}$; replay memory buffer $\mathcal{D}^{NP}$.
2: **Initialize** RAL with random weights $\boldsymbol{\xi}$ and target network with $\hat{\boldsymbol{\xi}} = \boldsymbol{\xi}$; replay memory buffer $\mathcal{D}^{RA}$.
3: NPL receives pricing information from IPL and gets initial state s_1^{NP}.
4: **for** $t = 1$ to T **do**
5:     Select a random action $\hat{a}_t^{NP}$ with probability ϵ, otherwise get $\hat{a}_t^{NP}$ by (23).
6:     Modify $\hat{a}_t^{NP}$ by **Algorithm 2**.
7:     RAL receives information and gets the state s_t^{RA}.
8:     **if** $t > 1$ **then**
9:         Store transition $(s_{t-1}^{RA}, \hat{a}_{t-1}^{RA}, R_{t-1}^{RA}, s_t^{RA})$ in $\mathcal{D}^{RA}$.
10:         Sample a mini-batch from D^{RA} by PER.
11:         Perform gradient descent with respect to $\boldsymbol{\xi}$.
12:     **end if**
13:     Select a random action $\hat{a}_t^{RA}$ with probability ϵ, otherwise get $\hat{a}_t^{RA}$ by (23).
14:     Modify $\hat{a}_t^{RA}$ by **Algorithm 2** and obtain $\boldsymbol{y}$ by (24).
15:     Use a math solver to solve $P4$ and obtain $\boldsymbol{w}_t, \boldsymbol{e}_t, \boldsymbol{s}_t$.
16:     Calculate rewards R_t^{NP} and R_t^{RA}.
17:     Feedback $\hat{a}_t^{NP}$ and $\hat{a}_t^{RA}$ to the IPL and get s_{t+1}^{NP}.
18:     Store transition $(s_t^{NP}, \hat{a}_t^{NP}, R_t^{NP}, s_{t+1}^{NP})$ in $\mathcal{D}^{NP}$.
19:     Sample a mini-batch from D^{NP} by PER.
20:     Perform gradient descent with respect to $\boldsymbol{\varphi}$.
21:     Set $\hat{\boldsymbol{\varphi}} = \boldsymbol{\varphi}$ and $\hat{\boldsymbol{\xi}} = \boldsymbol{\xi}$ every ω rounds.
22: **end for**

5.3. Computational Complexity and Scalability Analysis

The proposed three-layer deep reinforcement learning algorithm is divided into training and validation phases. We mainly focus on the computational complexity during the training phase, as most of the computation is concentrated in this phase [43]. According to [44], the complexity of the proposed algorithm is expressed as

$$O\left(T_c\left(\sum_{l_{IPL}=0}^{L_{IPL}} f_{l_{IPL}}^{IPL} f_{l_{IPL}+1}^{IPL} + \sum_{l_{NPL}=0}^{L_{NPL}} f_{l_{NPL}}^{NPL} f_{l_{NPL}+1}^{NPL} + \sum_{l_{RAL}=0}^{L_{RAL}} f_{l_{RAL}}^{RAL} f_{l_{RAL}+1}^{RAL} + (MNQ)^{3.5}\right)\right), \tag{25}$$

where T_c represents the number of training steps, which is the same across all three layers. $f_{l_{IPL}}^{IPL}$ represents the number of neurons in the l_{IPL}-th layer of D3QN in the IPL, and $f_{l_{NPL}}^{NPL}$ ($f_{l_{RAL}}^{RAL}$) represents the number of neurons in the l_{NPL}-th (l_{RAL}-th) layer of BDQ in the NPL (RAL). The first three terms are the complexity of the three-layer reinforcement learning, while the last term is the complexity of the MOSEK solver.

It can be seen that the complexity of the proposed solution has a linear time complexity with respect to the number of training steps, the depth of the neural network and the number of neurons in each layer. In Table 2, we compare the complexity of the proposed D3QN-DBDQ with that of the three-layer D3QN, demonstrating the adaptability of D3QN-DBDQ in large-scale networks.

Table 2. Complexity comparison.

Algorithm	Number of Neurons in the Output Layer of the NPL	Number of Neurons in the Output Layer of the RAL	Computational Complexity
D3QN-DBDQ	linear increase	linear increase	linear time complexity
Three-layer D3QN	exponential increase	exponential increase	exponential time complexity

6. Performance Evaluation

The simulations were conducted on a PC equipped with an Intel(R) Core(TM) i5-12500H (12 cores @2.50 GHz) processor and 16 GB of memory, with a 64-bit Windows 11 operating system. We implemented the entire solution using Python 3.6.8 and a TensorFlow 1.0 framework.

6.1. Simulation Settings

We consider an 800 m × 800 m area that is divided into four 400 m × 400 m subareas. Base stations are randomly deployed in the simulation area with a downlink bandwidth of 20 MHz. We set the path loss model as the adapted $\alpha\beta\gamma$-model for 5G mobile networks, i.e., $PL(d) = 10\alpha\log_{10}(d) + \beta + 10\gamma\log_{10}(f_c)$, where $(\alpha, \beta, \gamma) = (3.6, 7.6, 2)$ [17]. Each server has a storage capacity of 300 GB and a computing power of 0.5 GHz. We set the maximum tolerated delay of the users served by each slice to be values randomly selected within $[20, 40]$ ms. The computational task size is 100 bits, and the computational demand for each slice is randomly distributed within $[10, 30]$ cycles/bit. The propagation delay incurred per unit distance is 0.01 ms/m. The range of c_a, c_v, c_r and c_e are set to $[20, 30]$ USD, $[30, 50]$ USD, $[100, 150]$ USD/MHz, $[400, 500]$ USD/GHz, respectively. Prices are classified into three levels, i.e., $L = 3$. The weights of delay and cost are set as $w_d : w_c = 1 : 1$. We use U_{max} to denote the maximum number of users in the considered area. The number of users served by each slice in each subarea is uniformly distributed in the range $[0, U_{max}/(Q \times N)]$.

In D3QN, each neural network is composed of two hidden layers with 512 and 256 units for the shared network module and two hidden layers with 128 units for the state value and action advantage estimators. The BDQs of the NPL and RAL have the same structure, and the shared network modules are the same as that of D3QN. In BDQ, there are 128 units in each branch of the action advantage estimator as well as the state value estimator. The training parameters are the same for these three layers and are shown in Table 3.

Table 3. Simulation parameters.

Parameter	Value
System Model Parameters	
Carrier frequency	2.6 GHz [17]
Transmission power	43 dBm [17]
Noise power	−174 dBm/Hz [17]
Antenna gain of transmitter and receiver	15 dBi [17]
Common Training Parameters for the IPL, NPL and RAL	
Batch size	64
Discount factor	0.45
Size of replay buffer	10^6
Updating frequency of target network	500
PER parameter α, β	0.6, 0.4

6.2. Convergence Performance

Due to the stochasticity of the agent and the inherent uncertainty of the state, the reward curve exhibits notable fluctuations. To visually demonstrate the convergence process, we partitioned the training procedure into epochs, each consisting of 500 episodes. The learning rate balances exploration and convergence and is essential for achieving the global optimal solution. A high learning rate may cause excessive parameter updates, potentially skipping over global or local optima. Meanwhile, a low learning rate may trap the model in local optima, preventing it from escaping and finding the global optimal solution. Because a lower learning rate results in slower convergence, it is preferable to select the largest learning rate within the optimal range. In Figure 5, we illustrate the convergence performance of the IPL, NPL and RAL under different learning rates. The results show that when the learning rate is set to 10^{-4}, it performs best in the IPL, NPL and RAL. Due to the reasons mentioned above, other learning rates fail to achieve better solutions.

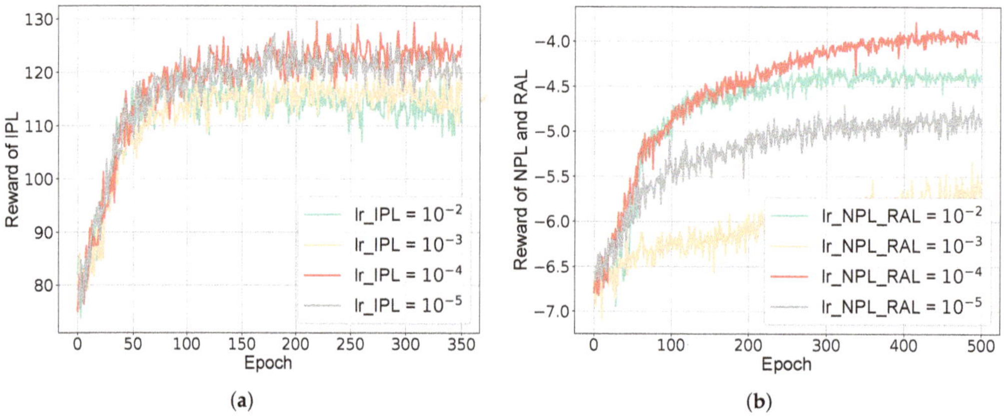

Figure 5. Convergence performance of D3QN-DMBDQ under different learning rates. (**a**) Convergence process of the IPL under different learning rates (lr_NPL_RAL = 10^{-4}); (**b**) convergence process of the NPL and the RAL under different learning rates (stochastic pricing scheme).

With $M = 3$ and $N = 2$, we present the convergence process of D3QN-DMBDQ and compare it with D3QN without dueling architecture (i.e., DDQN) and DMBDQ without dueling architecture (DMBDQ-WOD) in Figure 6. Figure 6a illustrates the convergence process of the IPL, which is the leader of the three-layer structure. Due to the relatively small action space of the IPL and the fact that its decision-making process is mainly based on the current environmental state, it converges rapidly and tends to stabilize after approximately 100 epochs. The rapid convergence of the IPL provides a stable price basis for the NPL and the RAL, reducing the uncertainty in the initial learning stage of the lower layers. Figure 6b shows the convergence process of the NPL and the RAL, whose overall convergence speed is relatively slow. The reason lies in the large action spaces, which makes the learning and policy optimization processes more complex. In addition, the policies of the NPL and the RAL rely on the pricing information provided by the IPL, and the RAL also depends on the server activation and slice deployment schemes of the NPL. In the early stage of training, the strategy of the IPL has not been completely stable, which increases the policy optimization difficulty of the lower layers. As the training process progresses, the synergy among the three layers promotes the convergence of the entire system. That is, the IPL provides a stable pricing scheme, the NPL finds the optimal server activation and slice deployment schemes and the RAL determines the optimal resource allocation scheme. Additionally, it can be seen that D3QN and DMBDQ achieve higher rewards than DDQN and DMBDQ-WOD. Thus, D3QN-DMBDQ is closer to the Stackelberg equilibrium. This is because the dueling architecture can mine valuable states and use them to achieve fast convergence [45]. In addition, the dueling architecture splits the state-action value function into a state value function and an action advantage function, which allows the network to better capture the relationship between states and actions and learn better strategies.

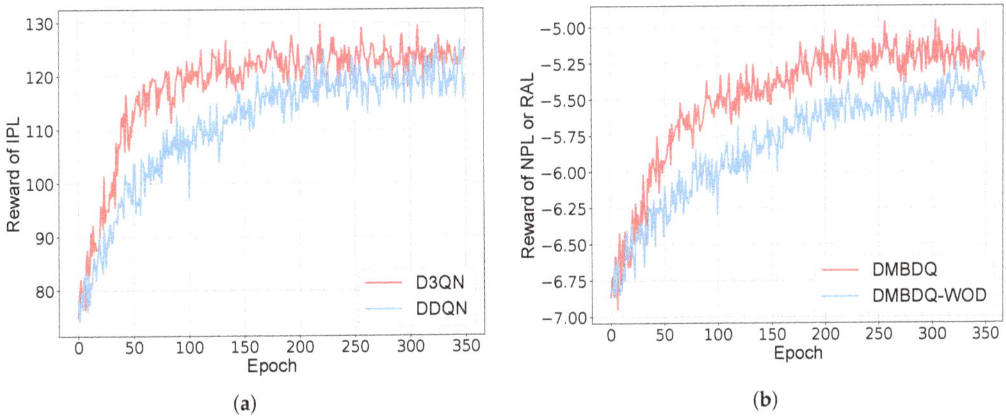

Figure 6. Convergence process of D3QN-DMBDQ. (**a**) Convergence process of the IPL; (**b**) convergence process of the NPL and the RAL.

To demonstrate the superiority of the proposed DMBDQ in dealing with large-scale action spaces, we train the DMBDQ individually by setting the prices in the IPL to random values. The convergence process of DMBDQ under different M and N are shown in Figure 7 and Figure 8, respectively. We compare DMBDQ with (1) DBDQ without modification of the illegal actions, giving a penalty for the illegal actions (DBDQ-WOM); and (2) double-layer D3QN (DD3QN). In DBDQ-WOM, the penalty for illegal actions is set to -5, -10 and -14 when N is equal to 1, 2 and 3.

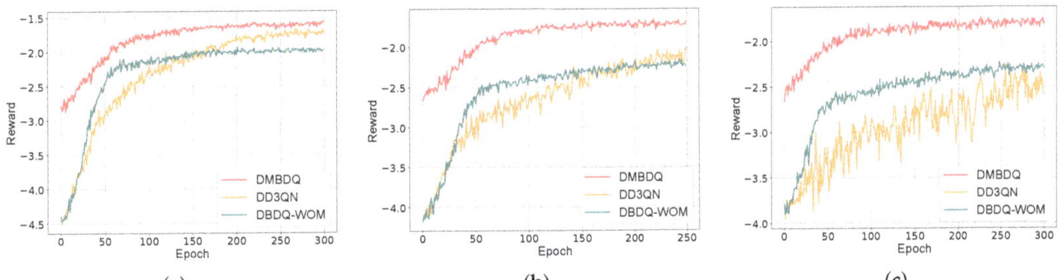

Figure 7. Convergence process of the NPL and RAL with different number of base stations ($N = 1$). (**a**) $M = 3$; (**b**) $M = 4$; (**c**) $M = 5$.

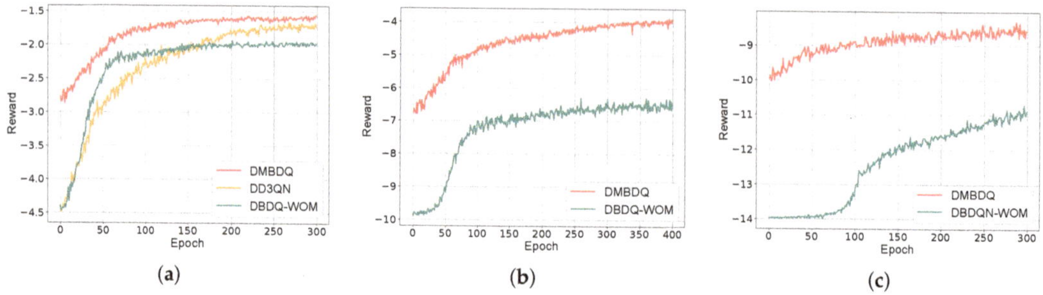

Figure 8. Convergence process of the NPL and RAL with different number of slices ($M = 3$). (**a**) $N = 1$; (**b**) $N = 2$; (**c**) $N = 3$.

We note that as M increases, the convergence of DD3QN becomes slower and less stable. When $N = 2$ and $N = 3$, the output of the RAL's D3QN will be up to 10^7 and 10^{10}, which is beyond the capability of our computer. As for DMBDQ, even as the network scale increases, the efficiency of the algorithm does not decrease significantly, and it can converge between the 150th and 250th epoch. Taking $M = 5$ as an example, the convergence of DMBDQ is improved by 28.3% compared with DD3QN; the reason is that DMBDQ introduces the branching network, which reduces the complexity of the network's outputs, and is more suitable for problems with large-scale action spaces. Meanwhile, the convergence of DMBDQ is improved by 21.9% compared with DBDQ-WOM. The reason is that DMBDQ introduces an illegal action modification method to avoid the agents from incurring a large number of illegal action penalties, which would hinder the exploration of the agents and the estimation of the value functions. The convergence performance of DBDQ-WOM is worse than that of DMBDQ. Reference [46] has pointed out that if we only penalize illegal actions, the agent may explore too many illegal actions during early exploration, requiring excessive time to find rule-compliant actions when the space of illegal actions is large. Taking Figure 7b as an example, DBDQ-WOM takes about 50 epochs to reach the same starting point as that of DMBDQ, because DBDQ-WOM explores lots of illegal actions in the first 50 epochs. In Figure 8, the illegal action space increases as N increases, and the gap between DBDQ-WOM and DMBDQ grows larger. It is worth noting that although DBDQ-WOM uses a branching architecture, its performance is not superior to that of DD3QN. This is because each action advantage branch in BDQ is independent, which leads to a disadvantage for each branch in evaluating joint actions. In contrast, D3QN evaluates the state-action values of all joint actions with a fully connected hidden layer. After incorporating the illegal action modification, DMBDQ performs better than DD3QN, which proves that the proposed DMBDQ is more applicable to our problem.

6.3. Performance Comparison

In this section, we will test the performance of PD-JSOSD under $M = 3$, $N = 2$ and introduce the following schemes as comparisons:

- **WOP-JSOSD**, which is used to highlight the importance of pricing optimization. During the training, the IPL uses a randomized pricing scheme, while the NPL and the RAL use the same algorithms as PD-JSOSD.
- **PD-AAS-SD**, which is used to highlight the importance of optimizing MEC server orchestration. In the NPL, all MEC servers are activated and associated with the base station at their locations. The NPL only needs to decide on the access function deployment variable x. Additionally, the IPL and the RAL use the same algorithms as PD-JSOSD.

- **PD-SO-MSNR**, which is used to highlight the importance of optimizing subareas association. In the RAL, the users in each subarea are associated with the base station with the largest SNR, and accordingly, the access function deployment variable x in the NPL is obtained. Moreover, the IPL and the NPL use the same algorithms as PD-JSOSD.
- **PD-JSP^2** [11], which is used to demonstrate the advantages of the proposed JSOSD. The NPL and the RAL adopt the scheme in [11], which also optimized the server orchestration and the service deployment issues, but there are some shortcomings in the adopted approach. Specifically, ref. [11] fixed the number of activated servers and used the *k-means* clustering to decide which server is activated and its association with base stations. The same scheme as in PD-SO-MSNR is then used to decide the subarea association and access function deployment scheme. Additionally, the IPL uses the same algorithm as PD-JSOSD.

All results are taken as the mean of the results of 1000 experiments. In view of the utility equation of the IPL, we present the revenue of the IPL, the number of activated servers, and the utility of the IPL in Figure 9. The results and analysis are summarized as follows:

- **Number of Activation Servers:** Because PD-AAS-SD activates all servers and PD-JSP^2 fixes the number of activated servers, the numbers of activated servers remain the same for both of them. As the network load rises, WOP-JSOSD, PD-SO-MSNR and PD-JSOSD require more servers to provide service, so the numbers of activated servers in these schemes increase accordingly. It is worth mentioning that when the maximum number of users is small, the changes in WOP-JSOSD, PD-SD-MSNR and PD-JSOSD are not significant. This is because the network load is very low, and one or two servers are enough to cope with all the demands. In terms of results, the access function of each slice in PD-SO-MSNR is deployed in all base stations, so PD-SO-MSNR has enough bandwidth resources as well as low access delay when the network load is low. That means PD-SO-MSNR can activate fewer servers to meet the delay demand, so the number of activated servers in PD-SO-MSNR is lower. However, PD-SO-MSNR adopts the max-SNR principle to determine user associations without load balancing, so as the number of users increases, the competition for resources in PD-SO-MSNR becomes intense. At this point, more servers need to be activated to meet the delay demand, which is why the curve of PD-SO-MSNR rises rapidly in the later part.
- **Revenue of the IPL:** Both PD-JSP^2 and PD-SO-MSNR use the max-SNR principle to determine the deployment scheme of access functions, and thus, the deployment cost is high. In addition, PD-JSP^2 fixes the association between base stations and servers, which implies that the number of deployed VNF chains is fixed, and thus, the variation of PD-JSP^2 is smaller than that of PD-SO-MSNR. Compared with WOP-JSOSD, the IPL has more revenue in JSOSD, which proves that the proposed IPL-dominated Stackelberg game can effectively improve the revenue of the IPL.
- **Utility of the IPL:** The number of activated servers and IPL's revenue together determine the utility of the IPL. PD-AAS-SD has the lowest utility because it activates too many servers. Meanwhile, PD-JSP^2 and PD-SO-MSNR have high revenue, so their utility is higher. Moreover, in comparison with WOP-JSOSD, PD-JSOSD performs better, which highlights that the proposed IPL-dominated pricing game can effectively improve the utility of the IPL.

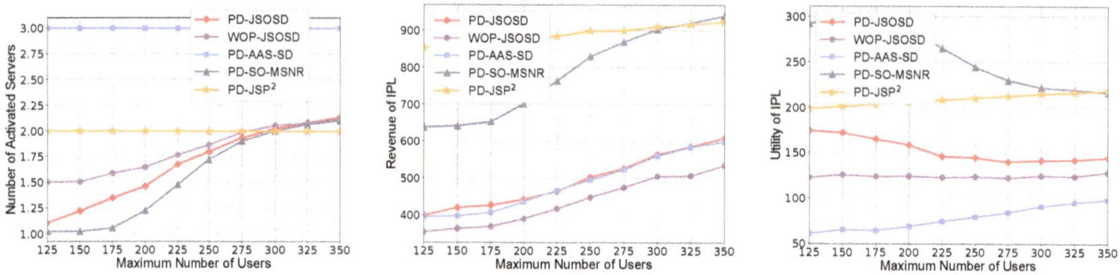

(**a**) (**b**) (**c**)

Figure 9. System performance comparison in terms of (**a**) number of activation servers, (**b**) revenue of the IPL and (**c**) utility of the IPL with different maximum numbers of users.

For the IPL, although both PD-JSP^2 and PD-SO-MSNR could have better utility, these two options are not advantageous for the NPL and the RAL. In order to further analyze the advantages of the proposed JSOSD in the NPL and the RAL, we set all the price levels as fixed to 1 to verify the performance of JSOSD. We present the average user cost, the average delay proportion and the utility of the NPL and the RAL under different maximum numbers of users in Figure 10 and compare JSOSD with AAS-SD, SO-MSNR and JSP^2:

- **Average User Cost:** It is clear that the deployment costs of access functions and VNF chains have a greater impact on the average user cost than the resource cost. At the start, the average user costs of JSOSD and AAS-SD decrease quickly as the number of users increases. The essential reason is that when the number of users is small, there is no need to deploy additional access functions and VNF chains, and an elevated number of users means more users to divide the deployment cost, so the average user cost goes down significantly. As the number of users continues to grow, more access functions and VNF chains are required, so the downward trend in average user cost slows down. A similar phenomenon occurred in SO-MSNR. The difference is that SO-MSNR's access function deployment cost has already been fixed, and as the network load rises, SO-MSNR only needs to deploy more VNF chains, so the downward trend of SO-MSNR is more obvious than that in JSOSD and AAS-SD. Similarly, the deployment costs of access functions and VNF chains in JSP^2 are both fixed values, and thus, JSP^2 has the greatest decline.
- **Average Delay Proportion:** AAS-SD has the lowest delay proportion, which is because servers are associated with base stations one-to-one, and thus, the propagation delay from base stations to servers is zero. In addition, the average delay proportions of AAS-PD and JSP^2 remain stable. We attribute this to the fact that the fixed server activation and association scheme makes the propagation delay less variable. As for JSOSD and SO-MSNR, their server orchestration schemes differ with varying network loads, so their average delay proportion changes significantly. The utility is a weighting of average user cost and average delay proportion, so the changes in the average delay proportion can be influenced by two factors simultaneously. One is that the decrease in average user cost may allow space for more allocated resources and lower delay. The other is that as the network load increases, more users compete for resources, driving the delay higher. In JSOSD, when the number of users is small, the average user cost decreases rapidly, so the average delay proportion decreases. However, as the number of users increases, the average delay proportion is more affected by resource constraints because the decrease in average user cost is not significant, and therefore, the delay tends to increase. This reason can also explain the trend of SO-MSNR.

- **Utility of the NPL and RAL:** When compared with AAS-SD, SO-MSNR and JSP^2, JSOSD has higher utility, which validates the superiority and necessity of the proposed server orchestration scheme and slice deployment scheme. It is worth noting that JSOSD and AAS-SD have almost the same utility when the number of users is low, and the advantage of JSOSD begins to emerge as the number of users rises. The reason is that with a small number of users, JSOSD and AAS-SD only need to deploy one access function and one VNF chain for each slice, so they have almost the same average user cost. Meanwhile, when the network load is heavy, the advantage of JSOSD in reducing the deployment cost of VNF chain starts to appear.

To show the relationships between weights, delay, cost, and utility, we present the performance under different weights in Figure 11. Obviously, as the weight of delay increases, the average delay proportion tends to decrease, while the average user cost tends to increase. This is because a larger w_d means the network prefers to allocate more resources to reduce delay, which may lead to higher costs. In addition, both Figures 10 and 11 show that JSOSD always has the lowest average user cost. Although the delay in JSOSD is higher than that in AAS-SD and JSP^2, the comprehensive utility of JSOSD is still the highest, demonstrating that the proposed JSOSD offers a better trade-off between cost and delay.

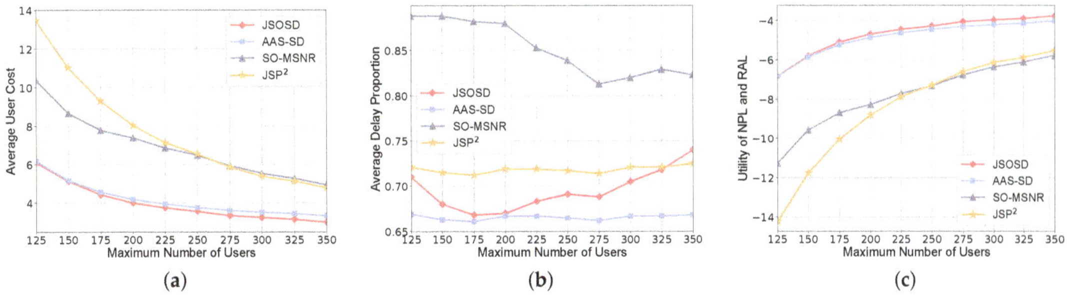

Figure 10. System performance comparison in terms of (**a**) average user cost, (**b**) average delay proportion and (**c**) utility of the NPL and the RAL under different maximum numbers of users with fixed pricing scheme.

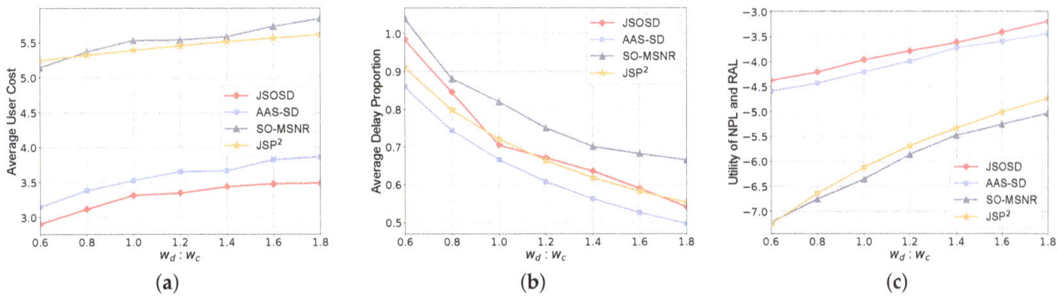

Figure 11. System performance comparison in terms of (**a**) average user cost, (**b**) average delay proportion and (**c**) utility of the NPL and the RAL under different weights with fixed pricing scheme.

To analyze the changes in the pricing scheme under different network scales, we presented the variation in average pricing levels under different numbers of users in Figure 12. It can be seen that as the number of users increases, the average price level shows a downward trend. The reason is that when the number of users is low, tenants only need to deploy a basic number of access functions and VNF chains. At this point, the InP tends to set a higher price to ensure its own profit. Additionally, the higher price limits the number of deployed VNF chains, which in turn reduces the number of activated servers. When the number of users increases, although tenants need to increase their deployments and resource usage, if the InP does not lower the price, tenants may choose to tolerate increased delay to reduce costs, becoming less willing to spend. Therefore, the InP decides to lower the price to encourage tenants' consumption as a trade-off. In conclusion, when tenants have fewer choices, the InP will offer higher prices, while when tenants have more choices, the InP will choose to lower prices to promote tenants' consumption.

We present the impact of price levels on tenant behavior and system utility in Figure 13. Figure 13a illustrates that as prices increase, tenants reduce the number of deployed access functions and VNF chains in response to cost-saving incentives. Similarly, in Figure 13b, as resource prices rise, tenants reduce their resource consumption. Figure 13c,d show the effects of pricing levels on the utility of the IPL and the utility of tenants (the NPL and the RAL), respectively. It is evident that the utility of the IPL does not necessarily increase monotonically with higher pricing. For example, in Figure 13c, the pricing scheme [0 0 1 1] results in higher utility for the IPL compared with [0 0 2 2], as excessively high price leads tenants to reduce their resource purchases, thereby lowering IPL's revenue. This further confirms that the IPL requires pricing optimization to identify the pricing scheme that maximizes its utility. Moreover, the effect of price increases on tenant's utility is complex, as shown in Figure 13d. Higher prices may either reduce or increase tenant utility, as tenant's costs are determined by both pricing and the quantity of access functions, VNF chains, and resources. When price rises, it leads to a reduction in deployment and resource consumption, which may either increase or decrease tenant's costs.

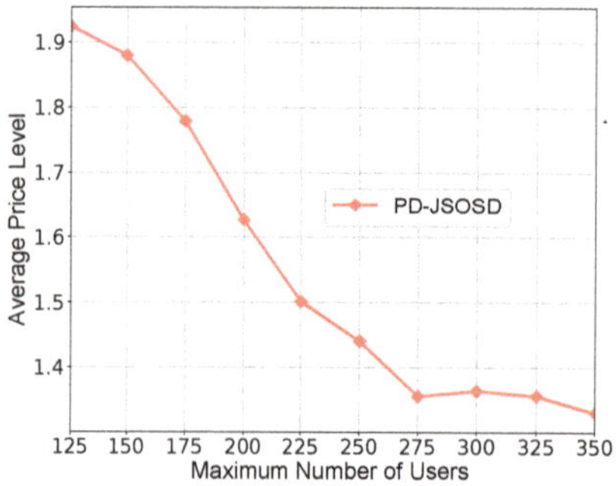

Figure 12. Average price level under different maximum numbers of users.

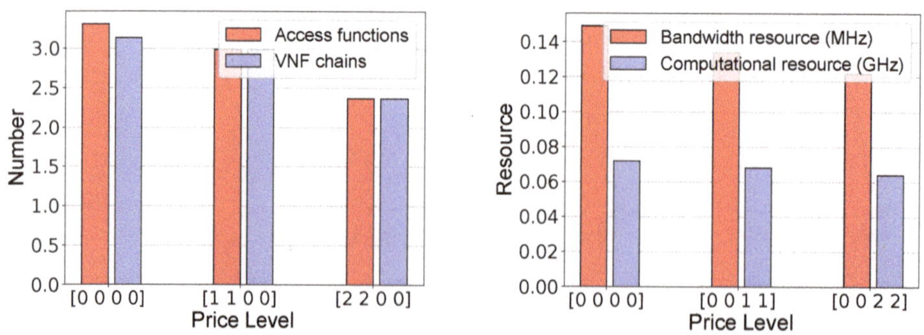

(a) (b)

Figure 13. *Cont.*

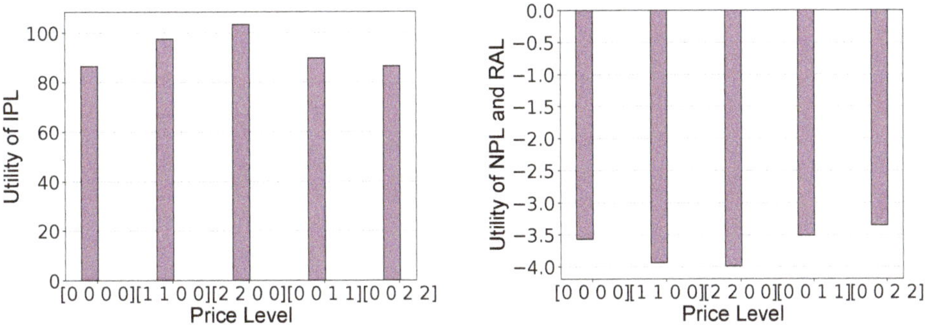

(c) (d)

Figure 13. The impact of price level on tenant behavior and system utility. (**a**) Numbers of deployed access functions and VNF chains with different price levels. (**b**) Bandwidth and computational resources applied by tenants with different price levels. (**c**) Utility of the IPL with different price levels. (**d**) Utility of the NPL and the RAL with different price levels.

7. Conclusions

In this paper, we design a pricing-driven joint MEC server orchestration and network slice deployment scheme. In the proposed system, the IPL handles pricing, the NPL handles MEC server orchestration as well as slice deployment, and the RAL handles allocation of radio, computational and storage resources. A three-stage Stackelberg game model is used to describe the relationships among these three layers. In order to efficiently achieve the Stackelberg equilibrium, we propose a three-layer DRL algorithm. D3QN is used to provide strategies for the IPL, while DMBDQ is used to make decisions for the NPL and the RAL to deal with large-scale action spaces. Simulations verify the convergence of the proposed D3QN-DMBDQ algorithm. It is also demonstrated that MBDQ with an illegal action modification capability is advantageous in large-scale action space problems. Moreover, numerical results show that our scheme outperforms other benchmarks in terms of the utilities of the InP and slices.

Author Contributions: Conceptualization, Y.H. and K.Z.; methodology, Y.H.; software, Y.H.; validation, Y.H. and K.Z.; formal analysis, Y.H. and K.Z.; investigation, X.C.; resources, G.C.; data curation, W.G.; writing—original draft preparation, Y.H.; writing—review and editing, S.L.; visualization, G.C.; supervision, W.G.; project administration, X.C.; funding acquisition, G.C. All authors have read and agreed to the published version of the manuscript.

Funding: This work was funded by the Beijing Natural Science Foundation under Grant L234025.

Data Availability Statement: The data presented in this study are available on request from the corresponding author.

Conflicts of Interest: The authors declare no conflicts of interest.

Abbreviations

$\mathcal{N}$	Set of slices
$\mathcal{M}$	Set of base stations
$\mathcal{V}$	Set of MEC servers
$\mathcal{Q}$	Set of subareas
$x_{m,n}$	Whether the access function of slice n is deployed on base station m
$k_{v,n}$	Whether the VNF chain of slice n is deployed on server v
p_v	Whether server v is activated

$a_{v,m}$	Whether base station m is associated with server v
$y_{n,q}^{m}$	Whether (n,q) is associated to base station m
$u_{n,q}$	Number of users of (n,q)
W_{m}^{max}	Bandwidth capacity of base station m
E_{m}^{max}	Computational capacity of server v
S_{m}^{max}	Storage capacity of server v
$w_{n,q}^{m}$	Radio resources allocated to (n,q) by base station m
$e_{n,q}^{v}$	Computational resources allocated to (n,q) by server v
$s_{n,q}^{v}$	Storage resources allocated to (n,q) by server v
$d_{n,q}^{tran}$	Transmission delay of (n,q)
$d_{n,q}^{prop}$	Propagation delay of (n,q)
$d_{n,q}^{comp}$	Computational delay of (n,q)
$d_{n,q}$	Total delay of (n,q)
L	Number of the levels of price
c_n	Cost of slice n
r^{InP}	Revenue of InP
p^{sum}	Number of activated servers
d_{n}^{aver}	Average delay proportion of slice n
c_{n}^{aver}	Average user cost of slice n
w_d/w_c	Weight of delay/cost

References

1. Poularakis, K.; Llorca, J.; Tulino, A.M.; Taylor, I.; Tassiulas, L. Joint Service Placement and Request Routing in Multi-cell Mobile Edge Computing Networks. In Proceedings of the IEEE International Conference on Computer Communications (INFOCOM), Paris, France, 29 April–2 May 2019; pp. 10–18.
2. Chen, S.; Wang, L.; Liu, F. Optimal Admission Control Mechanism Design for Time-Sensitive Services in Edge Computing. In Proceedings of the IEEE International Conference on Computer Communications (INFOCOM), London, UK, 2–5 May 2022; pp. 1169–1178.
3. Hou, Y.; Zhang, K.; Liu, X.; Chuai, G.; Gao, W.; Chen, X. An Inter-Slice RB Leasing and Association Adjustment Scheme in O-RAN. *IEEE Trans. Netw. Serv. Manag.* **2024**, *21*, 402–417. [CrossRef]
4. Khan, H.; Luoto, P.; Samarakoon, S.; Bennis, M.; Latva-aho, M. Network Slicing for Vehicular Communication. *IEEE Trans. Emerg. Telecommun. Technol.* **2021**, *32*, e3652. [CrossRef]
5. Spantideas, S.T.; Giannopoulos, A.E.; Trakadas, P. Smart Mission Critical Service Management: Architecture, Deployment Options, and Experimental Results. *IEEE Trans. Netw. Serv. Manag.* **2024**, 1. [CrossRef]
6. Filali, A.; Mlika, Z.; Cherkaoui, S.; Kobbane, A. Dynamic SDN-Based Radio Access Network Slicing with Deep Reinforcement Learning for URLLC and eMBB Services. *IEEE Trans. Netw. Sci. Eng.* **2022**, *9*, 2174–2187. [CrossRef]
7. Rost, P.; Breitbach, M.; Roreger, H.; Erman, B.; Mannweiler, C.; Miller, R.; Viering, I. Customized Industrial Networks: Network Slicing Trial at Hamburg Seaport. *IEEE Wirel. Commun.* **2018**, *25*, 48–55. [CrossRef]
8. Thiruvasagam, P.K.; Chakraborty, A.; Murthy, C.S.R. Resilient and Latency-Aware Orchestration of Network Slices Using Multi-Connectivity in MEC-Enabled 5G Networks. *IEEE Trans. Netw. Serv. Manag.* **2021**, *18*, 2502–2514. [CrossRef]
9. Mada, B.E.; Bagaa, M.; Tale, T.; Flinck, H. Latency-aware Service Placement and Live Migrations in 5G and Beyond Mobile Systems. In Proceedings of the ICC 2020—2020 IEEE International Conference on Communications (ICC), Dublin, Ireland, 7–11 June 2020; pp. 1–6.
10. Zhang, Y.; Wang, W.; Ren, J.; Huang, J.; He, S.; Zhang, Y. Efficient Revenue-Based MEC Server Deployment and Management in Mobile Edge-Cloud Computing. *IEEE/ACM Trans. Netw.* **2023**, *31*, 1449–1462. [CrossRef]
11. Zhang, X.; Li, Z.; Lai, C.; Zhang, J. Joint Edge Server Placement and Service Placement in Mobile-Edge Computing. *IEEE Internet Things J.* **2022**, *9*, 11261–11274. [CrossRef]
12. Ouyang, T.; Chen, X.; Zhou, Z.; Li, R.; Tang, X. Adaptive User-Managed Service Placement for Mobile Edge Computing via Contextual Multi-Armed Bandit Learning. *IEEE Trans. Mob. Comput.* **2023**, *22*, 1313–1326.
13. Mazloomi, A.; Sami, H.; Bentahar, J.; Otrok, H.; Mourad, A. Reinforcement Learning Framework for Server Placement and Workload Allocation in Multiaccess Edge Computing. *IEEE Internet Things J.* **2023**, *10*, 1376–1390. [CrossRef]
14. Chantre, H.D.; Saldanha da Fonseca, N.L. The Location Problem for the Provisioning of Protected Slices in NFV-Based MEC Infrastructure. *IEEE J. Sel. Areas Commun.* **2020**, *38*, 1505–1514. [CrossRef]

15. Li, M.; Zhang, Q.; Liu, F. Finedge: A Dynamic Cost-Efficient Edge Resource Management Platform for NFV Network. In Proceedings of the 2020 IEEE/ACM 28th International Symposium on Quality of Service (IWQoS), Hangzhou, China, 15–17 June 2020; pp. 1–10.
16. Gao, B.; Zhou, Z.; Liu, F.; Xu, F.; Li, B. An Online Framework for Joint Network Selection and Service Placement in Mobile Edge Computing. *IEEE Trans. Mob. Comput.* **2022**, *21*, 3836–3851. [CrossRef]
17. Luu, Q.T.; Kerboeuf, S.; Mouradian, A.; Kieffer, M. A Coverage-Aware Resource Provisioning Method for Network Slicing. *IEEE/ACM Trans. Netw.* **2020**, *28*, 2393–2406. [CrossRef]
18. Jin, P.; Fei, X.; Zhang, Q.; Liu, F.; Li, B. Latency-aware VNF Chain Deployment with Efficient Resource Reuse at Network Edge. In Proceedings of the IEEE Conference on Computer Communications (INFOCOM), Toronto, ON, Canada, 6–9 July 2020; pp. 267–276.
19. D'Oro, S.; Restuccia, F.; Melodia, T.; Palazzo, S. Low-Complexity Distributed Radio Access Network Slicing: Algorithms and Experimental Results. *IEEE/ACM Trans. Netw.* **2018**, *26*, 2815–2828. [CrossRef]
20. Hou, Y.; Zhang, K.; Chen, Z.; Liu, X.; Chuai, G.; Gao, W.; Chen, X. Joint Server Activation and Network Slice Deployment in Mobile Edge Computing Networks. In Proceedings of the 2024 IEEE 35th International Symposium on Personal, Indoor and Mobile Radio Communications (PIMRC), Valencia, Spain, 2–5 September 2024; pp. 1–7.
21. Cheng, C.; Zhu, Z.; Xin, B.; Chen, C. A multi-agent reinforcement learning algorithm based on Stackelberg game. In Proceedings of the 2017 6th Data Driven Control and Learning Systems (DDCLS), Chongqing, China, 26–27 May 2017; pp. 727–732.
22. Tran, T.D.; Le, L.B. Resource Allocation for Multi-Tenant Network Slicing: A Multi-Leader Multi-Follower Stackelberg Game Approach. *IEEE Trans. Veh. Technol.* **2020**, *69*, 8886–8899. [CrossRef]
23. Zhu, X.; Luo, Y.; Liu, A.; Xiong, N.N.; Dong, M.; Zhang, S. A Deep Reinforcement Learning-Based Resource Management Game in Vehicular Edge Computing. *IEEE Trans. Intell. Transp. Syst.* **2022**, *23*, 2422–2433. [CrossRef]
24. Wang, Z.; Schaul, T.; Hessel, M.; van Hasselt, H.; Lanctot, M.; de Freitas, N. Dueling network architectures for deep reinforcement learning. *arXiv* **2016**, arXiv:1511.06581.
25. Li, Y.; Aghvami, A.H.; Dong, D. Path Planning for Cellular-Connected UAV: A DRL Solution with Quantum-Inspired Experience Replay. *IEEE Trans. Wirel. Commun.* **2022**, *21*, 7897–7912. [CrossRef]
26. Tavakoli, A.; Pardo, F.; Kormushev, P. Action Branching Architectures for Deep Reinforcement Learning. In Proceedings of the AAAI Conference on Artificial Intelligence, New Orleans, LA, USA, 2–7 February 2018; pp. 4131–4138.
27. Abdel-Aziz, M.K.; Perfecto, C.; Samarakoon, S.; Bennis, M.; Saad, W. Vehicular Cooperative Perception Through Action Branching and Federated Reinforcement Learning. *IEEE Trans. Commun.* **2022**, *70*, 891–903. [CrossRef]
28. Sohaib, M.; Jeong, J.; Jeon, S.W. Dynamic Multichannel Access via Multi-Agent Reinforcement Learning: Throughput and Fairness Guarantees. *IEEE Trans. Wirel. Commun.* **2022**, *21*, 3994–4008. [CrossRef]
29. Shuai, H.; Li, F.; Pulgar-Painemal, H.; Xue, Y. Branching Dueling Q-Network-Based Online Scheduling of a Microgrid with Distributed Energy Storage Systems. *IEEE Trans. Smart Grid* **2021**, *12*, 5479–5482. [CrossRef]
30. Zhang, Q.; Liu, F.; Zeng, C. Online Adaptive Interference-Aware VNF Deployment and Migration for 5G Network Slice. *IEEE/ACM Trans. Netw.* **2021**, *29*, 2115–2128. [CrossRef]
31. Wu, S.; Liu, L.; Zhang, W.; Meng, W.; Ye, Q.; Ma, Y. Revenue-Maximizing Resource Allocation for Multitenant Cell-Free Massive MIMO Networks. *IEEE Syst. J.* **2022**, *16*, 3410–3421. [CrossRef]
32. Mitsis, G.; Tsiropoulou, E.E.; Papavassiliou, S. Price and Risk Awareness for Data Offloading Decision-Making in Edge Computing Systems. *IEEE Syst. J.* **2022**, *16*, 6546–6557. [CrossRef]
33. He, W.; Yao, H.; Mai, T.; Wang, F.; Guizani, M. Three-Stage Stackelberg Game Enabled Clustered Federated Learning in Heterogeneous UAV Swarms. *IEEE Trans. Veh. Technol.* **2023**, *72*, 9366–9380. [CrossRef]
34. Cao, Y.; Ren, X.; Qiu, C.; Wang, X. Hierarchical Reinforcement Learning for Blockchain-Assisted Software Defined Industrial Energy Market. *IEEE Trans. Ind. Inf.* **2022**, *18*, 6100–6108. [CrossRef]
35. Zarandi, S.; Tabassum, H. Delay Minimization in Sliced Multi-Cell Mobile Edge Computing (MEC) Systems. *IEEE Commun. Lett.* **2021**, *25*, 1964–1968. [CrossRef]
36. Bi, Y.; Meixner, C.C.; Bunyakitanon, M.; Vasilakos, X.; Nejabati, R.; Simeonidou, D. Multi-Objective Deep Reinforcement Learning Assisted Service Function Chains Placement. *IEEE Trans. Netw. Serv. Manag.* **2021**, *18*, 4134–4150. [CrossRef]
37. Sun, Y.; Peng, M.; Mao, S.; Yan, S. Hierarchical Radio Resource Allocation for Network Slicing in Fog Radio Access Networks. *IEEE Trans. Veh. Technol.* **2019**, *68*, 3866–3881. [CrossRef]
38. MOSEK Inc., Copenhagen, Denmark. Mosek Aps. [Online]. Available online: www.mosek.com (accessed on 8 January 2025).
39. Giannopoulos, A.; Spantideas, S.; Kapsalis, N.; Gkonis, P.; Sarakis, L.; Capsalis, C.; Vecchio, M.; Trakadas, P. Supporting Intelligence in Disaggregated Open Radio Access Networks: Architectural Principles, AI/ML Workflow, and Use Cases. *IEEE Access* **2022**, *10*, 39580–39595. [CrossRef]
40. Wei, F.; Feng, G.; Sun, Y.; Wang, Y.; Qin, S.; Liang, Y.C. Network Slice Reconfiguration by Exploiting Deep Reinforcement Learning with Large Action Space. *IEEE Trans. Netw. Serv. Manag.* **2020**, *17*, 2197–2211. [CrossRef]

41. Zhan, C.; Hu, H.; Mao, S.; Wang, J. Energy-Efficient Trajectory Optimization for Aerial Video Surveillance under QoS Constraints. In Proceedings of the IEEE Conference on Computer Communications (INFOCOM), London, UK, 2–5 May 2022; pp. 1559–1568.
42. Schaul, T.; Quan, J.; Antonoglou, I.; Silver, D. Prioritized experience replay. *arXiv* **2016**, arXiv:1511.05952.
43. Cui, Y.; Huang, X.; He, P.; Wu, D.; Wang, R. QoS Guaranteed Network Slicing Orchestration for Internet of Vehicles. *IEEE Internet Things J.* **2022**, *9*, 15215–15227. [CrossRef]
44. Ye, F.; Wang, J.; Li, J.; Zhu, P.; Wang, D.; You, X. Intelligent Hierarchical Network Slicing Based on Dynamic Multi-Connectivity in Cell-Free Distributed Massive MIMO Systems. *IEEE Trans. Veh. Technol.* **2023**, *72*, 11855–11870. [CrossRef]
45. Liu, Y.; Wang, H.; Peng, M.; Guan, J.; Wang, Y. An Incentive Mechanism for Privacy-Preserving Crowdsensing via Deep Reinforcement Learning. *IEEE Internet Things J.* **2021**, *8*, 8616–8631. [CrossRef]
46. Huang, S.; Ontañón, S. A closer look at invalid action masking in policy gradient algorithms. *arXiv* **2022**, arXiv:2006.14171. [CrossRef]

electronics

MDPI

Article

GLRM: Geometric Layout-Based Resource Management Method on Multiple Field Programmable Gate Array Systems

Hongxu Gao [1], Zeyu Li [1,2,*], Lirong Zhou [1,*], Xiang Li [3] and Quan Wang [1]

[1] School of Computer Science and Technology, Xidian University, Xi'an 710071, China; hx.gao@stu.xidian.edu.cn (H.G.); qwang@xidian.edu.cn (Q.W.)

[2] School of Computer Science and Technology, North University of China, Taiyaun 030051, China

[3] School of Decision Sciences, The Hang Seng University of Hong Kong, Hong Kong 999077, China; p233343@hsu.edu.hk

* Correspondence: 20230101@nuc.edu.cn (Z.L.); zlrong@stu.xidian.edu.cn (L.Z.); Tel.: +86-1500-343-9992 (Z.L.); +86-1882-955-0389 (L.Z.)

Abstract: Multiple field programmable gate array (Multi-FPGA) systems are capable of forming larger and more powerful computing units through high-speed interconnections between chips and are beginning to be widely used by various computing service providers. However, the new computing architecture brings new challenges to the system's task resource management. Existing resource management methods do not fully exploit resources in Multi-FPGA systems, and it is difficult to support fast resource request and release. In this regard, we propose a geometric layout-based resource management (GLRM) method for Multi-FPGA systems. First, a geometric layout-based task combination algorithm (TCA) was proposed to ensure that the final system can use the available FPGA resources more efficiently. Then, we optimised two resource management algorithms using TCA. Compared with state-of-the-art resource management methods, TCA increases resource flexibility by an average of 6% and resource utilisation by an average of 7%, and the two optimised resource management methods are effective in improving resource management performance.

Keywords: geometric layout; resource management; resource allocation; task combination; Multi-FPGA

1. Introduction

Field programmable gate arrays (FPGAs) are gradually replacing X86 or GPU in high performance computing platforms in resource-constrained environments due to their low power consumption, high parallelism, and fast computing speed [1,2]. As applications become larger and more complex, system-on-chip (SoC) architectures consisting of multiple FPGAs (Multi-FPGA) that combine faster inter-chip interconnections to form larger, more computationally intensive units have become popular [3,4]. In addition, the Dynamic Partial Reconfiguration (DPR) technology of FPGA allows the runtime to dynamically configure tasks to different reconfigurable partitions [5], further increasing the flexibility of Multi-FPGA systems and virtually increasing the availability of hardware resources [6,7].

Although the Multi-FPGA architecture and DPR technology provide great flexibility in system design, resource management and the overhead incurred during the reconfiguration process must be carefully considered, as they can easily compromise the performance gains achieved through hardware acceleration [8,9]. The multi-FPGA architecture is like a single FPGA chip, which is a "black box" and invisible to the user, but when implementing applications on it, some issues should be considered: task deployment location, resource constraints and resource reuse, etc. In addition to employing DPR technology, there is a need for further requirements regarding task segmentation and reorganization.

The original FPGA resource management algorithms utilize board-level granularity for management. A typical form of organisation is known as MPC-X [10], which has the advantage of the simplicity of operation and the disadvantage of very low resource flexibility. To improve the flexibility of resource usage, slot-based and BRAM-based resource management approaches have been proposed [11–13], which reduce the resource granularity compared to FPGA chip-based resource management, with the disadvantage of not being able to use the freed resources. With the development of dynamic partially reconfigurable technology, researchers have proposed centralised bus-based [14] and quadtree-based [15] resource management algorithms with a resource granularity of resource rectangles without fixed boundaries, which can effectively control resource fragmentation, but the flexibility and efficiency of resource utilisation are still low. In addition, with the emergence of Multi-FPGA systems as a new computing architecture, the existing single-chip resource management methods can no longer be adapted to multi-chip FPGA resource management [16–18].

Overall, existing resource management methods suffer from high resource wastage and are not applicable to Multi-FPGA systems. In response, we propose a geometric layout-based resource management method on Multi-FPGA systems, which includes a geometric layout-based task combination algorithm (TCA) and two resource management algorithms optimized by TCA. The proposed method is experimentally verified and demonstrates the effectiveness of resource management. In this context, the contributions can be summarised as follows:

1. A geometric layout-based task combination algorithm to make sure that the final system can make use of the available FPGA resources more efficiently. The available resources and tasks on the FPGA chip are abstracted into resource rectangle models and task rectangle models of specific length and width, and the optimal combination strategy of task rectangle models is generated with the aim of maximising the utilisation of the resource rectangle models.
2. Two resource management algorithms optimized by TCA to improve resource management performance. The improved quadtree resource management algorithm uses variables instead of resource layouts to simulate the allocation process to achieve fast resource request and recovery. The improved central bus resource management algorithm uses the resource fragments generated by task placement to place other tasks to improve resource utilisation.
3. The experimental results show that the task combination algorithm is able to effectively combine and place the tasks, with an average increase of 6% in resource flexibility and an average increase of 7% in resource utilisation; moreover, the two optimised resource management methods can effectively improve the resource management performance.

The paper is structured as follows. Section 2 discusses related work on FPGA resource management. In Section 3, we introduce the geometric layout-based task combination algorithm. In Section 4, we provide a detailed description of the two resource management algorithm optimized by TCA. In Section 5, we evaluate the performance of our method. Section 6 concludes the paper.

2. Related Work

The evolution of FPGA resource management can be abstracted as a process of changing resource granularity from large to small. In the early period, FPGA resource management was managed by using board-level granularity, where multiple FPGAs were grouped into a group and the minimum configuration unit (MCU) was a single-chip FPGA [19]. The advantage of the FPGA group is that it is easy to operate and meets the resilience requirements for high-performance computing platforms, but the flexibility of using the on-chip resource is very low [10,20].

With the huge resources of FPGAs and the maturity of DPR technology, the granularity of FPGA resource management gradually tends to parts of the on-chip resources. At this time, the MCU is called "slot", which is a fixed-boundary resource rectangle [11,12]. On this basis, ref. [13] proposed a resource management strategy, the MCU of which is a resource rectangle with no fixed boundary. Due to the lack of fixed shape constraint, the flexibility of resources is promoted, but the management of whole resources is lacking. In addition, the literature [15] proposed a quadtree algorithm (adaptive reconstruction region), the MCU of which is a resource rectangle with no fixed boundary, and the management mode is shown in Figure 1. This method can effectively control resource fragmentation and ensure connectivity between tasks, but the bus would consume some resources. Another resource management algorithm with no fixed boundary is based on a centralised bus (combined reconstruction region) [14], as shown in Figure 2. This method reduces the resource consumption of the bus, but the one-sided dimension is fixed.

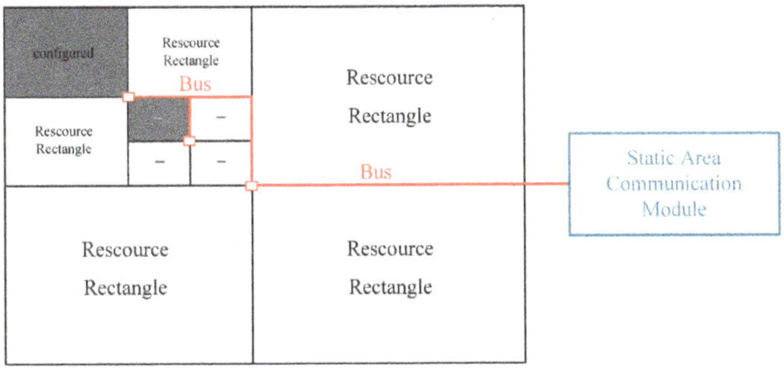

Figure 1. Quadtree algorithm.

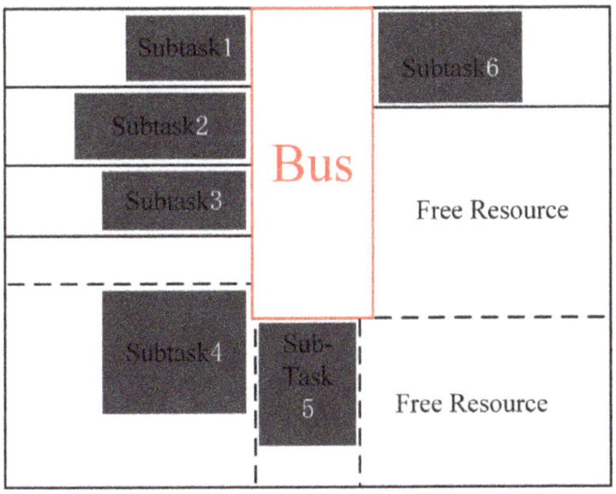

Figure 2. Centralized bus algorithm.

In [12], a task encapsulation strategy based on switch is proposed to place some subtasks of one large task on multiple FPGAs, thereby enabling one large task to be placed on multiple FPGAs. However, the configuration file and routing of the networked tasks are complicated, which makes resource management difficult. Ref. [21] proposed a novel area sharing method that leverages the exploratory capabilities of OpenCL, employing intelligent clustering and custom, task-specific partitioning and mapping to more effectively manage the resource requirements of tasks. By selecting the most appropriate distribution that best enhances the temporal computation density based on runtime workload demands, the system's throughput is improved. Mehrabi [22] highlighted the importance of considering spatio-temporal strategies in FPGA resource management to achieve long-term target allocations and optimize FPGA usage efficiency by tracking and correcting deviations.

In this work, we propose a task combination algorithm based on a geometric layout and combine it with two state-of-the-art resource management algorithms. By integrating applications for resources, the resource granularity is further reduced, the resource waste is reduced, and the resource utilization and resource flexibility are improved. In addition, the placement is accelerated by separating the allocation and relocation of resources.

3. Geometric Layout-Based Task Combination Algorithm

In this work, we propose a geometric layout-based task combination algorithm that reduces the number of resources occupied by the combination by allowing the tasks to use resource fragments from other tasks in the combination, thus improving the resource efficiency of the FPGA.

3.1. Task Combination Algorithm

FPGA resource management is constantly evolving towards more flexibility and less fragmentation. To simplify the resource management process, the task combination problem is abstracted as a rectangle combination problem by abstracting the tasks into a set of rectangles on the FPGA based on their resource requirements. The combined rectangle must contain all the tasks, as well as the buses needed to connect the tasks, to ensure that all the small rectangles can be connected to the system's buses. Suppose there are several small rectangles $S_{mission} = \{Rec_1, Rec_2, Rec_3, \ldots\}$; then, we need to find a set of layouts $S_{mission}\{C_1, C_2, C_3, \ldots\}$, each of which produces a large rectangle containing all the rectangles in which the layout is contained. If any two rectangles are combined, the length of the combining edges is not equal and there will be resource fragments. We set the rectangle set $S_{BIT} = \{Rec_1, Rec_2, \ldots\}$ and use (W_i, H_i) to represent the horizontal and vertical sides of the rectangle. Suppose $W_i > H_i$ and $Waste_{i,j}$ represents the size of the resource fragment generated when Rec_i and Rec_j are combined; then, $Waste_{i,j}$ can be calculated by Formula (1):

$$Waste_{i,j} = \begin{cases} max(H_i, H_j) * (W_i + W_j) - W_i * H_i - W_j * H_j, & HorizontalCombination \\ max(W_i, W_j) * (H_i + H_j) - W_i * H_i - W_j * H_j, & VerticalCombination \end{cases} \quad (1)$$

According to the existing resource management algorithm, if there are three subtasks a, b, and c, the amount of resources required for subtasks is R_a, R_b, and R_c, respectively. Then, the resources D_a, D_b, and D_c allocated for each task satisfy $D_a > R_a$, $D_b > R_b$, and $D_c > R_c$, and using the task combination algorithm proposed in this work, the system allocates the resource amount D_{a+b+c} to the combined three subtasks, which satisfies $D_{a+b+c} \geq R_a + R_b + R_c$. The parameter P is used to represent the product of the subtask and the product of the start–end time interval, that is, the weighted resource occupancy of the subtask. As shown in Figure 3a, the start and end times of each subtask in the system are (S_a, E_a), (S_b, E_b), and (S_c, E_c), respectively. The resources occupied in each task are P_a, P_b, and P_c , and the total resources occupied by the three subtasks is shown in Formula (2):

$$P_a + P_b + P_c = D_a * (E_a - S_a) + D_b * (E_b - S_b) + D_c * (E_c - S_c) \quad (2)$$

As shown in Figure 3b, after the combining tasks, the start and end times of the three tasks in the system are all (S_a, E_b), and the total weighted resource occupancy of the task is P_{a+b+c}. The calculation method is as follows:

$$P_{a+b+c} = D_{a+b+c} * (max(E_a, E_b, E_c) - min(S_a, S_b, S_c)) \quad (3)$$

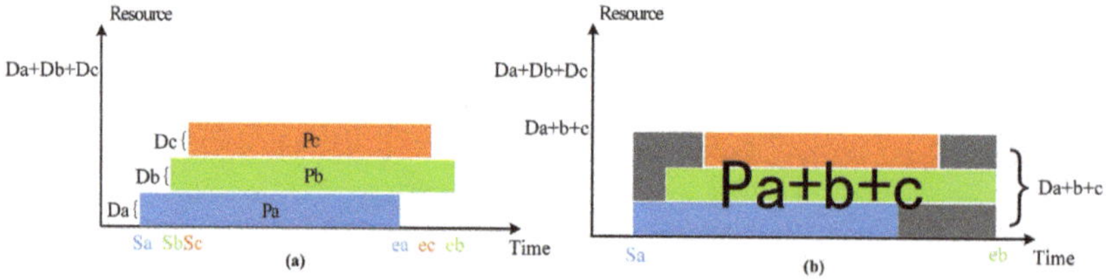

Figure 3. Optimization of resource management algorithm performance by task combination. (**a**) Resources occupied of each task before optimization, (**b**) Resource occupation time after task combination.

If the weighted resource occupancy of the resource allocation and the combined allocation meets $P_{a+b+c} < P_a + P_b + P_c$, the number of tasks accommodated by the system at the same time can be increased by the task combination, and the total resource cost of the task is reduced.

3.2. Implementation of Algorithm

3.2.1. Build the Sequence of Algorithm

The arrangement $Edge_{BIT} = \{E_1, E_2, E_3, \ldots\}$ of all sides is constructed when the combination of the adjacent sides is performed. If the adjacent edges correspond to different rectangles and are both horizontal or vertical, a new combined rectangle is generated. If the number of elements in S_{BIT} is n and the number of newly generated rectangles is N_{NEW}, then N_{NEW} satisfies $N_{NEW} \leq 2n - 1$. A combination of the two edges that satisfy $E_i < E_j$ produces a new rectangle whose side length can be expressed as Formulation (4).

$$Rec_{new} = \begin{cases} (W_i, H_i + H_j), & E_i = W_i \text{ and } E_j = W_j \\ (W_i + W_j, H_j), & E_i = H_i \text{ and } E_j = H_j \end{cases} \tag{4}$$

The maintenance of the edge sequence uses a greedy strategy, and under the premise of including all the rectangles in S_{BIT}, a new rectangle with the smallest $Waste_{i,j}$ can be generated.

3.2.2. Two-Dimensional Equilibrium Evaluation

After the rectangular combination operation, several new rectangles are generated, and it is necessary to select the acceptable combinations from these combinations and record the progress of the combination. The characteristics of the min heap satisfy the sorting method required for the rectangular combination selection. In order to compare the advantages and disadvantages of the rectangular combination, a min heap is established by sorting the unacceptable degrees.

We define the ratio of width to height (**RWH**) as the ratio of the lateral side length of the rectangle to the length of the longitudinal side. The formula is expressed as follows:

$$RWH_i = W_i / H_i \tag{5}$$

The standard ratio of width to height (**SRWH**) is the ratio of the horizontal and vertical edges of the resource layout generated by the resource management algorithm. Since the dynamic reconfigurable regions of different FPGA chips have different shapes, the **RWH** of the resource is used as the **SRWH**.

Moreover, combinations of smaller resource fragments and similar shapes and resource shapes should be accepted. We define the acceptance degree (**AD**) as a reasonable degree of the combination that can be expressed as Formulation (6):

$$AD_i = \alpha Waste_i + \beta |RWH_i - SRWH_i| \tag{6}$$

where α denotes the weight of the resource fragment when calculating the acceptability, β denotes the weight of the difference value between **RWH** and **SRWH**, and the range of α and β is all from 0 to 1.

3.2.3. Maintain the Rectangular Heap Sequence Completion Combination

The details of maintaining the heap structure include the maintenance of the overall progress of the layout, in-heap and out-heap strategies and end conditions, and the maintenance of the edge sequences. The interaction between the heap and the edge sequence, that is, the rectangular combination of the heap into the edge sequence and the new combination of rectangles into the rectangular min heap, covers the entire process of the rectangular combination.

(1) Heap-to-edge sequence operation: The roof element is the current optimal combination scheme and is recorded in the global combined process. The roof element is popped and the heap structure is reconstructed, the four sides of the two sub-rectangles are removed from the edge sequence, and the two sides of the new rectangle are added to the edge sequence.

(2) Edge sequence to heap operation: After the two new edges enter the sequence, respectively, based on the position, a new four-rectangular combination is generated by the new edges and the first edge can be combined, forwards and backwards. Then, the generated new rectangle enters the min heap in turn, and the min heap structure is reconstructed.

Since the rectangles to be combined are not added one by one to the final combination of rectangles, it is likely that the combination will be as shown in Figure 4. Rectangle A is first combined with rectangle B as rectangle E, and rectangle C is combined with rectangle D as rectangle F, and then rectangles E and F are combined. The final layout scheme is composed, so the current layout progress of the min heap record is a variable queue, and each element in the queue represents a segment of the combination process. In addition, once rectangle A has been combined with rectangle B as rectangle E, rectangle A is not accepted for other schemes to generate new rectangles. Only rectangle E and other rectangles are accepted to generate a new rectangle, because rectangle E is the current optimal solution. Furthermore, the combination of rectangle A and other rectangles belongs to the current sub-optimal solution. According to the greedy strategy, only the optimal solution is accepted. The complete procedure of the algorithm is described in Algorithm 1:

Algorithm 1 Combination process based on edge sequences and small top heaps

Input: Task Rectangle Collection *missions*
Output: Combined task shape

for *m* in *missions* **do**
    Add the edges of *m* to the collection of edges *edges*
end for
Ascending order edges
for *e* in *edges* **do**
    if *e* with a critical edge if it can be formed into a rectangle **then**
        Rectangle joins two-dimensional equilibrium small top heap *minHeap*
    end if
end for
while The top element of the heap does not contain all tasks **do**
    for s in *states* **do**
        while State of the top element of the heap and s != 0 and state of the top element of the heap and s != s **do**
            Element out of heap and rebuild heap structure
            break
        end while
    end for
    Accept the top element of the heap, exit the heap, and maintain the heap structure
    Update the side sequences
end while
Insertion of buses for task combinations

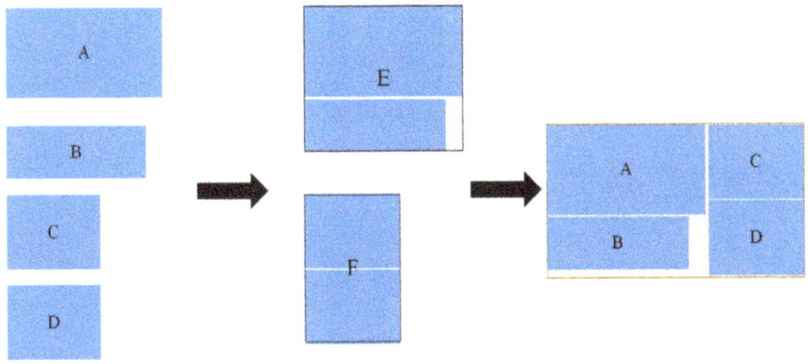

Figure 4. The process of rectangular combination.

3.2.4. Bus Insert

The insert bus operation is responsible for connecting each task to the global bus. When the rectangle combination is complete, the bus is inserted between the rectangles and all tasks are connected to the system bus.

Assume that no bus rectangle is located in the lower left corner of the blank resource rectangle in the reconfigurable area; then, the bus resource is added from the lower left corner to the upper right corner. As shown in the Figure 5, representing the two regions in coordinates, the space occupied by the busless rectangle is $(0,0) \rightarrow (W_i, H_i)$

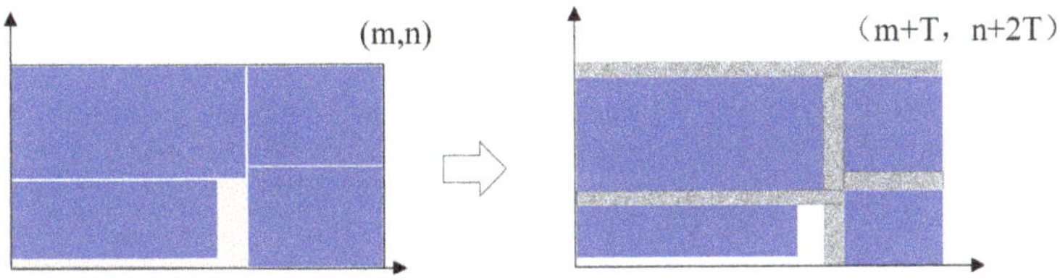

Figure 5. Schematic diagram of resource utilization by the bus.

For a rectangle R containing n sub-rectangles, the number of sub-rectangles in the column containing the largest number of sub-barrels in R is $Column_{max}$, and the maximum of the rows is Row_{max}. Then, the total height is increased by $Column_{max}$, and the width is increased by Row_{max}, so that the increased bus resources can be connected to all child rectangles with certainty. For a rectangle R containing n sub-rectangles, if the total height increase is less than $\lceil Column_{max}/2 \rceil$ or the total width increases by less than $\lceil Row_{max}/2 \rceil$, then it is not guaranteed that all rectangles are connected to the bus; meanwhile, when the total height is increased by $\lceil Column_{max}/2 \rceil$ and the total width is increased by Row_{max}, or when the total width is increased by $\lceil Row_{max}/2 \rceil$ and the total height is increased by $Column_{max}$, it can be ensured that the increased space can place a bus that can be connected to all rectangles.

As shown in Figure 6, we can choose to apply the bus resources along the positive direction of the x-axis or the positive direction of the y-axis. Select the corresponding resource application method according to the number of blank resources in both directions.

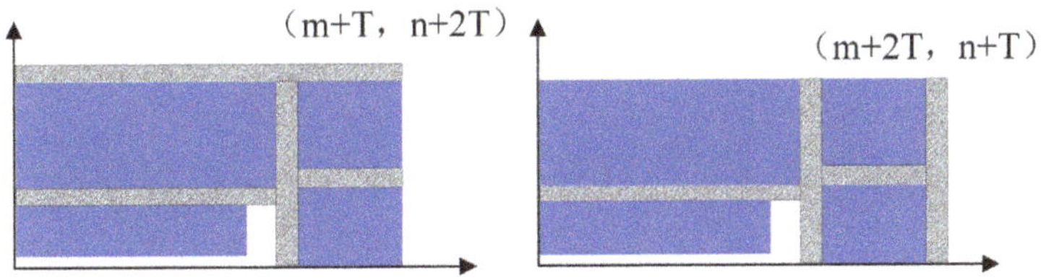

Figure 6. Horizontal application and vertical application.

The total amount of resources applied is expressed by the following Formula (7).

$$(W_{req}, H_{req}) = \begin{cases} (W + Row_{max}, H + \lceil Column_{max}/2 \rceil), & W/H < W_{req}/H_{req} \\ (W + \lceil Row_{max}/2 \rceil, H + Column_{max}), & else \end{cases} \tag{7}$$

As shown in Algorithm 2, the process of inserting the bus is described as follows:

Algorithm 2 The process of inserting the bus

Input: Collection of tasks, shape of resources
Output: Combination of tasks after insertion of bus

```
Combination according to uninserted and inserted buses
Calculate the shape difference between the two combinations to obtain the maximum
  number of row and column rectangles
if Follow the width and height of the no-bus to find the right resource then return false
end if
if More vertical white space in the selected resource area then
    Requests for resources under the vertical application modality
else
    Request for resources under the horizontal application modality
end if
if Failed application then return false
end if
```

3.3. *Complexity Analysis*

The algorithm strictly adheres to the optimal substructure and reduces the number of invalid combinations. Each combination will reduce the possible combination, with N indicating the number of tasks to be combined, the time complexity of the combined algorithm is $O(logN)$, the time complexity of maintaining the heap structure is $O(logN)$, and the final algorithm time complexity is $O(logN^2)$. The algorithm needs to create heap space for all possible combinations that occur during the combination process, with a space complexity of $O(N^2)$.

4. The Quadtree and Central Bus Resource Management Algorithm Optimized by TCA

4.1. *Improved Quadtree Resource Management Algorithm*

The traditional tree resource management structure has low efficiency due to the overhead of maintaining the tree structure and the resource waste caused by different aspect ratios of the task rectangle. To reduce the effect of rectangular aspect ratio, tasks are combined using task combination algorithms. This paper proposes an improved method of quadtree resource management that uses the count method instead of the tree structure to reduce the overhead of maintaining the tree structure. Using array-based containers instead of pointers can improve memory management efficiency and reduce program space and time complexity.

(1) CLB resource constraints: the CLB resources applied by different subtasks cannot overlap at the same time to prevent mutual interference. To satisfy the CLB resource constraint, the horizontal spacing of the starting coordinates of the two rectangles is greater than the width or longitudinal spacing of one of the rectangles, which is greater than the height of one of the rectangles. The formula is expressed as follows:

$$\begin{cases} |x_1 - x_2| < w_1 \,||\, |x_1 - x_2| < w_2 \\ |y_1 - y_2| < h_1 \,||\, |y_1 - y_2| < h_2 \end{cases} \tag{8}$$

where $|x_1 - x_2|$ represents the horizontal spacing between the starting coordinates of the two rectangles, w_i represents the width of rectangle i, and h_i represents the height of rectangle i.

(2) Bandwidth constraints: bandwidth constraints are divided into bus bandwidth constraints and on-chip resource bandwidth constraints. The division of the bus determines the communication time, further affecting the total length of execution time of the subtask. The formula is expressed as follows:

$$B_1 - B_2 > Trans_1 \tag{9}$$

(3) Storage constraints: the storage constraints need to consider the spacing of storage resources. For a subtask that requires on-chip storage resources, the spacing determines the minimum resource level that it can request, that is, the resource level contains at least one storage resource.

By taking the logarithm of the total resources with a base of 4, resource requests are graded, which is more in line with the quadtree resource management approach and also convenient for computation.The "level-resource amount" table is created with the level as the subscript, and the number of resources contained in the node of the current level is stored. As shown in Figure 7, the entire reconfigurable partition is treated as a level 0 resource, and the resource level is incremented by one each time. When the quadtree is in its initial state, the number of level 0 resources is 1, and the number of other equivalent resources is 0. Instead of maintaining the quadtree structure, use the resource node amount maintenance method. A container whose size is the total number of levels is a "level-node amount" table; the table entry stores the amount of resources corresponding to the current resource level and the number of remaining nodes. When a subtask requests a resource, it can obtain a level suitable for its own needs and request resources by checking the level-node amount table.

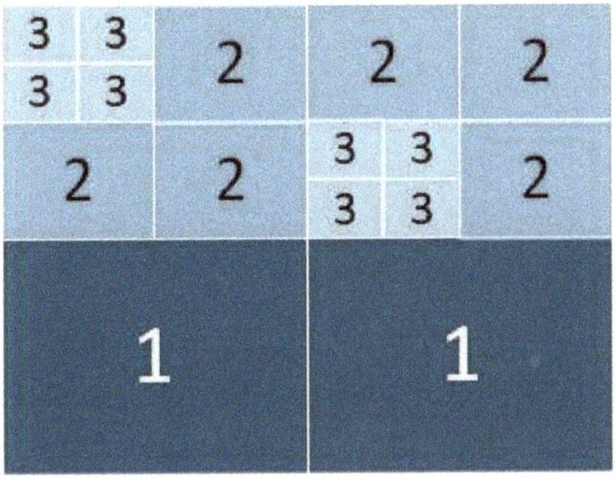

Figure 7. Resource level schematic.

The specific location of the resource is determined based on the task sequence. When the resource application process is saved by the vector, if there are four resource rectangles in a particular level, the resource rectangles are merged. When a quadtree is moved, a specific resource area must be allocated to the task in the order in which the resources are released.

A quadtree is generated according to the resource level and the occupied time period corresponding to the subtask rectangle. Sort each subtask rectangle by release time, which refers to the time when the task requests resources. For subtasks with the same release time, resources are allocated to subtasks with earlier application resources, and the quadtree is generated according to depth at first search. The complete procedure of the algorithm is described in Algorithm 3.

Algorithm 3 Delayed generation of quadtrees

Input: Interval during which the task is inside the device
Output: Generate a quadtree

```
Create a rectangular sequence of tasks for which resources are to be requested
Sort the task rectangles linearly in the order of when the tasks release their resources
Sorted in order of when resources were requested
Stable sorting by release time
Sort the task rectangle by the time heap of the task requesting resources
while All rectangles in the rectangle sequence are not all traversed do
    while Resource release time > time to request the top element of the heap do
        Release resources based on the level of resources requested by the mandate
        Remove nodes from the task heap for which resources have been requested
        Select subtrees in order of priority from smallest to largest numbering
        Add tasks to the heap of tasks for which resources have been requested, maintaining the heap structure
    end while
end while
```

4.2. Improved Centralized Bus Resource Management Algorithm

In this paper, we further propose an optimization method for the centralized bus resource management algorithm based on the task layout algorithm, which uses resource fragments generated by task placement to place other tasks to improve resource utilization. As shown in the Figure 8, the resources are shared after the tasks are combined.

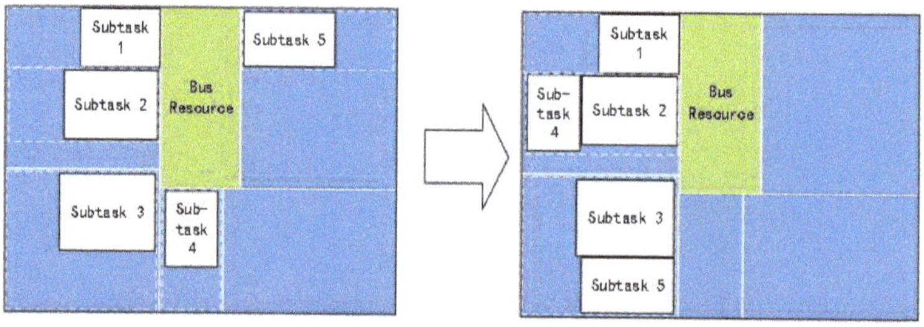

Figure 8. Task combination under centralized bus.

Unlike the improved quadtree algorithm, which uses the *RWH* of the reconfigurable area as the *SRWH*, the centralized bus resource management algorithm has no fixed *SRWH*, and the *SRWH* changes as the shape of the resource changes. Therefore, the improved algorithm accepts a combination of side lengths as close as possible to the resource to determine the side length, regardless of *SRWH*. The degree of non-acceptance can be expressed as follows:

$$AD_i = \alpha Waste_i + \frac{\beta}{RWH} \tag{10}$$

where AD_i is the unacceptance degree of rectangle i, α denotes the weight of the resource fragment when calculating the acceptability, and β denotes the weight of the difference value between RWH and SRWH.

There are different settings for the aspect ratio of the combination to adjust the tendency of the shape of the combined task to evolve. The limiting edge length makes the combined shape change towards the result of approaching a certain length as soon as possible to reduce the generation of resource fragments. If a combination makes the resource less efficient, the design is not accepted.

Since the resource size is not strictly granular, the resource management process cannot be simplified by simplifying the resource description. Therefore, the improved centralised bus resource management algorithm does not adopt the design of separating the allocated resources and determining the resource location. As a result, the time complexity of the centralised bus resource management algorithm for the resource application and release process is higher than that of the quadtree resource management algorithm.

5. Experimental Results and Analysis

In this section, we use the Task Graphs for Free (TGFF) to generate task DAG graphs. Then, based on the resource requirements of commonly used algorithms, the effectiveness of the improved resource management algorithm in improving performance was verified.

5.1. Testing Environment

We use C++ to build an experimental platform to provide the system framework and function preset interface for mentioned algorithms of task sorting, multiple sequence maintenance, resource management, task combination, and simulated annealing, based on which the algorithm proposed in this work and the comparison algorithm are implemented. The test task set and device network structure adopt three task topology diagrams and two physical FPGA chips to simulate the problem scenario of multi-task scheduling on Multi-FPGA, and the algorithm program is designed in C++ language.

We set the common algorithms for target recognition and image processing as task topology generated by TGFF [23]. The resource requirements of the tasks are shown in Table 1 [24]. In Table 1, common algorithms for target recognition include Debayer, Rectifier, Stereo match, Disparity, Flex-SURF, and Motor Control. Common algorithms for image processing include FPN correction, Dark field corr., FFT, Bad pixel/spike CCSDS 122, Binning, Hough Transform, and Median Filter. Slice represents the unit of measure for logic cells in FPGAs. The full name of BRAM is block RAM. BRAM is the predefined hardware resource in the FPGA that is dedicated to storage.

Table 1. List of common algorithm resource requirements.

	Algorithm	Slices	BRAM
Target Recognition	Debayer (2x)	200	2
	Rectifier (2x)	500	30
	Stereo match	2500	30
	Disparity	1000	15
	Flex-SURF	1000	0
	Motor Control (3x)	200	0
Image Processing	FPN correction	100	0
	Dark field corr.	200	1
	FFT	800	7
	Bad pixel/spike	100	2
	CCSDS 122	2500	12
	Binning	300	4
	Hough Transform	1800	14
	Median Filter	800	0

The width and height of the task are generated by random numbers based on the amount of logical resources in order to complete the simulation of the real shape of tasks. Considering that, the resource management algorithm studied in this work may be partially limited by the underlying layout and routing rules. Therefore, we validated the experiment in the reconfigurable virtual layer without considering the rule limitations of specific FPGA chips.

5.2. Evaluation Metrics

In order to evaluate the performance of resource management algorithms, three evaluation metrics are introduced below:

(1) Scheduling Flexibility (SF): Indicates the amount of tasks placed at the same time as a percentage of the total amount of tasks; the expression is as follows.

$$SF = \frac{1}{s}\sum_{i=1}^{s}\frac{M_i}{M} \tag{11}$$

where s represents the amount of sequences, N represents the maximum amount of tasks on the chip, and M represents the total amount of tasks.

(2) Resource Efficiency (RE): Indicates the rationality of the task M deployed in the resource area R. It is used to evaluate the resource utilization of different FPGA on-chip resource management algorithms. The expression is as follows.

$$RE = \sum_{i=1}^{p}\left(\frac{R_i}{\sum_{j=1}^{p} R_j} * \frac{M_i}{R_i}\right) = \frac{\sum_{i=1}^{p} M_i}{\sum_{j=1}^{p} R_j} \tag{12}$$

where p is the amount of tasks, M is the amount of resources requested by the task, and R is the amount of resources acquired by the task.

(3) Biggest Resource Area (BRA): It represents the largest available free resource rectangle on the FPGA chip, i.e., the maximum resource request that the FPGA chip can respond to. For quadtree resource management, the BRA is shown in area A in Figure 9a. For centralized bus resource management, the BRA is shown in area C in Figure 9b.

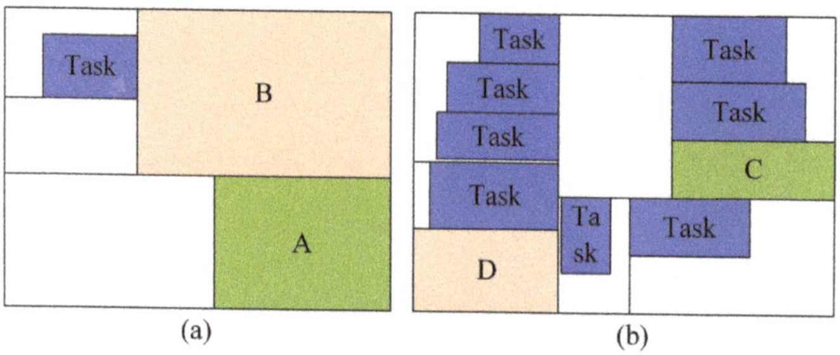

Figure 9. The BRA under the two resource management algorithms. (**a**) BRA for quadtree resource management, (**b**) BRA for centralized bus resource management.

5.3. Results and Discussion

We simulate the allocation of resources according to the task sequence, which is the sequence generated by the full alignment of the 11 tasks, and then generate resource layouts according to the resource management algorithms before and after improvement, respectively. Before simulating the allocation of resources, the device is considered empty, and while simulating the allocation of resources, it becomes non-empty. As mentioned above, the two improved algorithms have different advantages in managing resources in empty and non-empty devices. Therefore, in addition to comparing the performance indices of the two sets of original and improved algorithms, the design experiment also compares the performance of the four algorithms in the two resource scenarios. In the empty device, the comparison of the performance indices of the four resource management algorithms is shown in Table 2.

First, we compare the original algorithm with the improved algorithm. In response to the improvement of the quadtree resource management algorithm, the resource utilisation rate has increased by 3.6%, the resource utilisation rate of the centralised bus resource management algorithms has improved by 10.2%, and the performance improvement of the centralised bus algorithm is more obvious. The improved quadtree algorithm has a 6.2% increase in scheduling flexibility, and the improved centralised bus algorithm has an increase of 100%. Due to the increased resource utilisation, the improved algorithm can leave more space for more tasks. When resources are sufficient, the BRA is the largest task that the system can accommodate, and the data are the averages generated by different sequences. As can be seen from the table, the improved algorithm significantly increases the size of the free area.

Table 2. Experimental results of four resource management algorithms on a blank device.

Resource Management Algorithm	Resource Utilization Rate	Scheduling Flexibility	Largest Available Free Resource
Quadtree Resource Management algorithm [15]	26.8%	60.4%	1256
Improved Quadtree Resource Management Algorithm	30.4%	66.6%	3447
Centralized Bus Resource Management Algorithm [14]	46.4%	97.1%	5281
Improved Centralized Bus Resource Management Algorithm	56.6%	100%	5821

Second, we compare the two sets of algorithms. Although the improved quadtree algorithm has improved the indicator data, there is still a significant gap with the original centralised bus algorithm. According to the analysis, the centralised bus algorithm has obvious advantages in managing empty resources to complete the current space. However, if fragmentation occurs in the system, its performance will decrease.

For devices that have been working for some time, some discontinuous resources are already present in the device. In this case, the ability of the four algorithms to tolerate release is compared. The performance comparison of the four algorithms is shown in Table 3 and Figure 10.

Table 3. Experimental results of four resource management algorithms on non-blank devices.

Resource Management Algorithm	Average Resource Utilization Rate	Average Scheduling Flexibility
Quadtree Resource Management Algorithm [15]	26.9%	46.0%
Improved Quadtree Resource Management Algorithm	37.2%	75.6%
Centralized Bus Resource Management Algorithm [14]	45.3%	65.0%
Improved Centralized Bus Resource Management Algorithm	55.0%	96.3%

The changes in the scheduling flexibility of the application release sequence are shown in Figure 10. According to the results of the second set of experiments, it can be seen that the random application and release of resources changes the numerical relationship between the centralised bus algorithm and the quadtree algorithm. Figure 10 shows the reusability of the generation layout by the quadtree resource management algorithm. Since the task combination algorithm can change the rectangular shape of the application resource to adapt to the resource layout at different times, there is greater flexibility in managing non-empty devices than the original resource management algorithm, as the resource flexibility of the two improved algorithms is always higher than the two original algorithms. The quadtree algorithm is a resource management algorithm with fixed resource shape and size. Multiple tasks in the task sequence share the same task space, and the freed resources are more easily used by subsequent tasks, as shown in Figure 10 by the decreasing gap between the two quadtree algorithms and the original centralised bus algorithm.

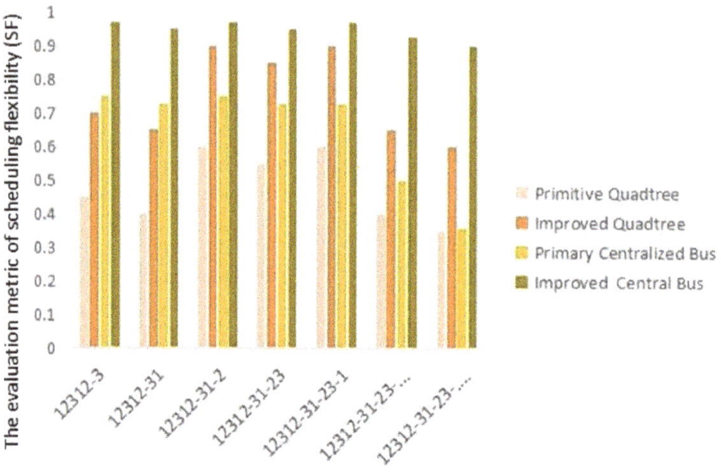

Figure 10. The change in scheduling flexibility for a set of release sequences.

6. Conclusions

In response to the issue of low resource utilization in multi-FPGA systems, we propose a geometric layout-based resource management method to improve the resource management efficiency of the system. By comparing the differences in performance indicators such as resource utilization, resource flexibility, and maximum available blank area among improved algorithms, quadtree-based resource management algorithms, and centralized bus-based resource management algorithms, the results showed that dynamic task combination can effectively combine and place tasks, with an average increase in resource flexibility of 6% and an average increase in resource utilization of 7%. In future work, we will focus on task placement methods under resource-constrained conditions to introduce appropriate constraints to ensure the effectiveness of resource management methods.

Author Contributions: Conceptualization, Q.W.; methodology, H.G. and Z.L.; software, H.G. and L.Z.; validation, Z.L. and X.L.; formal analysis, X.L.; investigation, H.G. and L.Z.; resources, Z.L. and H.G.; data curation, L.Z. and H.G.; writing—original draft preparation, H.G. and L.Z.; writing—review and editing, Z.L.; visualization, X.L.; supervision, Q.W.; project administration, Q.W.; funding acquisition, Q.W. All authors have read and agreed to the published version of the manuscript.

Funding: This work was supported in part by the National Natural Science Foundation of China under Grant 61972302, in part by the Guangzhou Municipal Science and Technology Project under Grant SL2022A04J00404, in part by the Fundamental Research Funds for the Central Universities under Grant XJS220306, in part by the Natural Science Basic Research Program of Shaanxi under Grant 2022JQ-680, and in part by the Key Laboratory of Smart Human Computer Interaction and Wearable Technology of Shaanxi Province.

Data Availability Statement: All data is contained within the article.

Conflicts of Interest: The authors declare no conflict of interest.

References

1. Saha, D.; Sur-Kolay, S. Minimization of WCRT with recovery assurance from hardware trojans for tasks on FPGA-based cloud. *ACM Trans. Embed. Comput. Syst. (TECS)* **2020**, *20*, 1. [CrossRef]
2. Wang, Y.; Liao, Y.; Yang, J.; Wang, H.; Zhao, Y.; Zhang, C.; Xiao, B.; Xu, F.; Gao, Y.; Xu, M.; et al. An FPGA-based online reconfigurable CNN edge computing device for object detection. *Microelectron. J.* **2023**, *137*, 105805. [CrossRef]
3. Bolchini, C.; Sandionigi, C. Design of hardened embedded systems on multi-FPGA platforms. *ACM Trans. Des. Autom. Electron. Syst. (TODAES)* **2014**, *20*, 16. [CrossRef]
4. Shan, J.; Lazarescu, M.T.; Cortadella, J.; Lavagno, L.; Casu, M.R. CNN-on-AWS: Efficient allocation of multikernel applications on multi-FPGA platforms. *IEEE Trans. Comput.-Aided Des. Integr. Circuits Syst.* **2020**, *40*, 301–314. [CrossRef]

5. Purgato, A.; Tantillo, D.; Rabozzi, M.; Sciuto, D.; Santambrogio, M.D. Resource-efficient scheduling for partially-reconfigurable FPGA-based systems. In Proceedings of the 2016 IEEE International Parallel and Distributed Processing Symposium Workshops (IPDPSW), Chicago, IL, USA, 23–27 May 2016; IEEE: Piscataway, NJ, USA, 2016; pp. 189–197.
6. Pui, C.W.; Young, E.F. Lagrangian relaxation-based time-division multiplexing optimization for multi-FPGA systems. *ACM Trans. Des. Autom. Electron. Syst. (TODAES)* **2020**, *25*, 21. [CrossRef]
7. Zheng, J.; Wu, N.; Yan, G.; Ge, F.; Zhou, L. Dynamically reconfigurable simulation platform for 3D NoC based on multi-FPGA. *IEICE Electron. Express* **2015**, *12*, 20150065. [CrossRef]
8. Najem, M.; Bollengier, T.; Le Lann, J.C.; Lagadec, L. A cost-effective approach for efficient time-sharing of reconfigurable architectures. In Proceedings of the 2017 International Conference on FPGA Reconfiguration for General-Purpose Computing (FPGA4GPC), Hamburg, Germany, 9–10 May 2017; IEEE: Piscataway, NJ, USA, 2017; pp. 7–12.
9. Irick, K.M.; DeBole, M.; Park, S.; Al Maashri, A.; Kestur, S.; Yu, C.L.; Vijaykrishnan, N. A scalable multi-FPGA framework for real-time digital signal processing. In Proceedings of the SPIE—The International Society for Optical Engineering, San Diego, CA, USA, 2–5 August 2009; pp. 28–31.
10. Iordache, A.; Pierre, G.; Sanders, P.; de F. Coutinho, J.G.; Stillwell, M. High performance in the cloud with FPGA groups. In Proceedings of the 9th International Conference on Utility and Cloud Computing, Shanghai, China, 6–9 December 2016; pp. 1–10.
11. Chen, F.; Shan, Y.; Zhang, Y.; Wang, Y.; Franke, H.; Chang, X.; Wang, K. Enabling FPGAs in the cloud. In Proceedings of the 11th ACM Conference on Computing Frontiers, Cagliari, Italy, 20–22 May 2014; pp. 1–10.
12. Caulfield, A.M.; Chung, E.S.; Putnam, A.; Angepat, H.; Fowers, J.; Haselman, M.; Heil, S.; Humphrey, M.; Kaur, P.; Kim, J.Y.; et al. A cloud-scale acceleration architecture. In Proceedings of the 2016 49th Annual IEEE/ACM International Symposium on Microarchitecture (MICRO), Taipei, Taiwan, 15–19 October 2016; IEEE: Piscataway, NJ, USA, 2016; pp. 1–13.
13. Khuat, Q.H.; Chillet, D.; Hübner, M. Considering reconfiguration overhead in scheduling of dependent tasks on 2D reconfigurable FPGA. In Proceedings of the 2014 NASA/ESA Conference on Adaptive Hardware and Systems (AHS), Leicester, UK, 14–17 July 2014; IEEE: Piscataway, NJ, USA, 2014; pp. 1–8.
14. Dörflinger, A.; Fiethe, B.; Michalik, H.; Fekete, S.P.; Keldenich, P.; Scheffer, C. Resource-efficient dynamic partial reconfiguration on FPGAs for space instruments. In Proceedings of the 2017 NASA/ESA Conference on Adaptive Hardware and Systems (AHS), Pasadena, CA, USA, 24–27 July 2017; IEEE: Piscataway, NJ, USA, 2017; pp. 24–31.
15. Fekete, S.P.; Reinhardt, J.M.; Scheffer, C. An efficient data structure for dynamic two-dimensional reconfiguration. In *Proceedings of the International Conference on Architecture of Computing Systems*; Springer: Berlin/Heidelberg, Germany, 2016; pp. 306–318.
16. Cui, J.; Deng, Q.; He, X.; Gu, Z. An efficient algorithm for online management of 2D area of partially reconfigurable FPGAs. In Proceedings of the 2007 Design, Automation & Test in Europe Conference & Exhibition, Nice, France, 16–20 April 2007; IEEE: Piscataway, NJ, USA, 2007; pp. 1–6.
17. Ammendola, R. A multi-FPGA high performance computing system for 3D FFT-based numerical simulations. *arXiv* **2022**, arXiv:2209.02314.
18. Kwon, Y.S.; Lee, J.G.; Kyung, C.M. Performance-driven event-based design mapping in multi-FPGA simulation accelerator. In Proceedings of the COEX Conference Center, Seoul, Republic of Korea, 1 October 2004 ; pp. 328–331.
19. Song, W.; Jiang, H.; Zhuang, W.; Shen, X. Resource management for QoS support in cellular/WLAN interworking. *IEEE Netw.* **2005**, *19*, 12–18. [CrossRef]
20. Yang, S.; Zhou, K.; Wang, J.; Liu, B.; Li, T. A partition method of SoC design serving the multi-FPGA verification platform. In Proceedings of the Advanced Computer Architecture: 10th Annual Conference, ACA 2014, Shenyang, China, 23–24 August 2014; Springer: Berlin/Heidelberg, Germany, 2014; pp. 43–57.
21. Minhas, U.I.; Woods, R.; Nikolopoulos, D.S.; Karakonstantis, G. Efficient, Dynamic Multi-Task Execution on FPGA-Based Computing Systems. *IEEE Trans. Parallel Distrib. Syst.* **2022**, *33*, 710–722. [CrossRef]
22. Mehrabi, A.; Sorin, D.J.; Lee, B.C. Spatiotemporal Strategies for Long-Term FPGA Resource Management. In Proceedings of the 2022 IEEE International Symposium on Performance Analysis of Systems and Software (ISPASS), Singapore, 22–24 May 2022; pp. 198–209. [CrossRef]
23. Dick, R.P.; Rhodes, D.L.; Wolf, W. TGFF: Task graphs for free. In Proceedings of the Sixth International Workshop on Hardware/Software Codesign. (CODES/CASHE'98), Seattle, WA, USA, 18 March 1998; IEEE: Piscataway, NJ, USA, 1998; pp. 97–101.
24. Zhang, H.; Bauer, L.; Kochte, M.A.; Schneider, E.; Wunderlich, H.J.; Henkel, J. Aging resilience and fault tolerance in runtime reconfigurable architectures. *IEEE Trans. Comput.* **2016**, *66*, 957–970. [CrossRef]

electronics

MDPI

Article

Towards Intelligent Edge Computing: A Resource- and Reliability-Aware Hybrid Scheduling Method on Multi-FPGA Systems

Zeyu Li [1,2,*], Yuchen Hao [1], Hongxu Gao [2] and Jia Zhou [3]

1 School of Computer Science and Technology, North University of China, Taiyaun 030051, China; s202307014@st.nuc.edu.cn
2 School of Computer Science and Technology, Xidian University, Xi'an 710071, China; hx_gao@stu.xidian.edu.cn
3 School of Microelectronics, Northwestern Polytechnical University, Xi'an 710071, China; zhoujia@eng-wx.com
* Correspondence: 20230101@nuc.edu.cn; Tel.: +86-1500-343-9992

Abstract: Multi-FPGA systems can form larger and more powerful computing units through high-speed interconnects between chips, and are beginning to be widely used by various computing service providers, especially in edge computing. However, the new computing architecture brings new challenges to efficient and reliable task scheduling. In this context, we propose a resource- and reliability-aware hybrid scheduling method on Multi-FPGA systems. First, a set of models is established based on the resource/time requirements, communication overhead, and state conversion process of tasks to further analyze the constraints of system scheduling. On this basis, the large task is divided into subtasks based on the data dependency matrix, and the Maintenance Multiple Sequence (MMS) algorithm is used to generate execution sequences for each subtask to the Multi-FPGA systems to fully exploit resources and ensure reliable operation. Compared with state-of-the-art scheduling methods, the proposed method can achieve an average increase in resource utilization of 7%; in terms of reliability, it achieves good execution gains, with an average task completion rate of 98.3% and a mean time to failure of 15.7 years.

Keywords: resource management; reliability; hybrid scheduling; Multi-FPGA

1. Introduction

The Commercial Off The Shelf (COTS) Field Programmable Gate Arrays (FPGAs) support partial run-time reconfigurability, which allows some FPGA resources to be configured without affecting the operation of other resources. This technology allows multiple tasks to be executed on the FPGA in a spatially and temporally multiplexed manner [1,2]. However, a single FPGA faces resource constraints. Therefore, the resource requirements of an application can often exceed the resources available on a single FPGA. Even if multiple run-time reconfigurations are allowed, this may not alleviate the resource constraints of end-side intelligent computing applications. Today, many edge computing applications require the simultaneous use of multiple FPGAs (also known as Multi-FPGA systems) to perform their operations [3,4], such as in urban smart transportation applications. There are multiple FPGAs required to perform tasks such as real-time traffic monitoring (camera image processing and traffic monitoring), traffic signal control optimization (signal control and dynamic switching), and abnormal event detection and response (traffic accidents and road construction). The system architecture is shown in Figure 1. A Multi-FPGA system is responsible for submitting and distributing tasks by a client controller, with multiple FPGAs serving as servers to execute tasks and return processing results to the client. Among them, multiple FPGAs are connected to the central client, and the link is built based on a dual backup method.

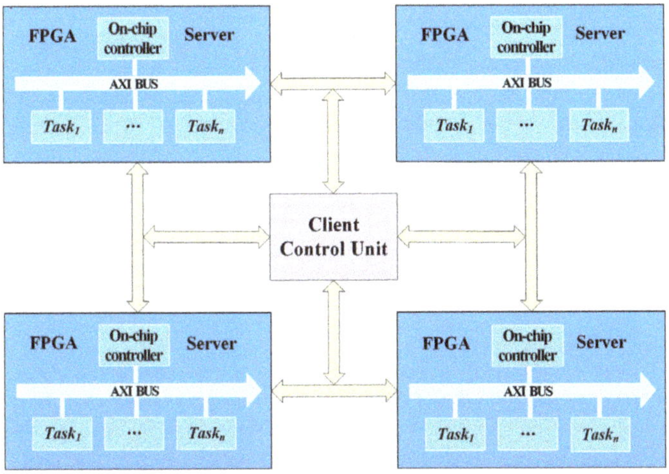

Figure 1. Multi-FPGA systems.

While Multi-FPGA system architectures and Dynamic Partial Reconfiguration (DPR) [5] techniques offer great flexibility, the overheads incurred during system scheduling management and reconfiguration must be carefully considered, as they can easily jeopardize the performance gains achieved through hardware acceleration [6,7]. The Multi-FPGA architecture is like a single FPGA chip, a 'black box' that is invisible to the user. Still, there are some issues that should be taken into account when implementing applications on it: scheduling order, deployment regions, resource constraints, and complex communication overheads between tasks. Combined with the application of DPR technology, further requirements for segmentation and reorganization of large tasks are presented.

Multi-FPGA systems have multiple FPGA resources, and each FPGA can be divided into different reconfigurable blocks for fine-grained resource control. Deploying tasks with different resource requirements and execution times to the corresponding blocks helps to efficiently utilize resources for further deployment of more hardware accelerators working simultaneously. Task scheduling implements resource resilience policies as well as management of task configuration and execution order [8–10]. The DPR technique can reuse the resources of each FPGA in a time-shared manner, providing more options and optimizations for resource management and task deployment. Therefore, it is a challenge to efficiently utilize multiple FPGAs and the resources on each FPGA for more efficient task execution.

Overall, the task scheduling problem is NP-hard because it is a more general optimization version of the Resource Constrained Scheduling Problem (RCSP), which is NP-complete. At the same time, existing research methods for resource scheduling suffer from problems such as low resource utilization, lack of reliable operation guarantees, and inapplicability to the Multi-FPGA system. In this work, we propose a resource- and reliability-aware hybrid scheduling method on a Multi-FPGA system. The proposed method is experimentally verified and the effectiveness of the management and scheduling is demonstrated. In this context, our contributions are summarized as follows.

(1) A resource-aware scheduler to make sure that the final system can make use of the available FPGA resources more efficiently. When scheduling tasks, it can provide the

minimum resources for each task as a service objective, i.e., to schedule as few on-chip resources as possible for all tasks received within a time unit to improve resource utilization.

(2) A reliability-aware scheduler to ensure the the successful execution of tasks and improve the expected lifetime in the Multi-FPGA system. The scheduler implements multi-task scheduling across multiple FPGAs, balancing makespan and reliability by placing tasks in a redundant and load-balanced manner while ensuring execution efficiency.

(3) The experimental results show that the resource management method is able to effectively combine and place the tasks, with an average increase in resource utilization of 7%; the reliability-aware scheduling method achieves good execution gains, with an average task completion rate of 98.3% and a system's lifetime of 15.7 years.

The paper is structured as follows. Section 2 discusses related work on FPGA task scheduling. In Section 3, we provide a detailed description of the resource- and reliability-aware task scheduler. In Section 4, we evaluate the performance of our method. Section 5 concludes the paper and proposes future work.

2. Related Work

Many previous studies have focused on task planning on a single FPGA. A few other studies in the literature specifically focused on task scheduling in Multi-FPGA systems. The research course of task scheduling on Multi-FPGA systems is mainly reflected in the task model, task sequence, and task state management. In application, the main difference between scheduling algorithms is whether the task execution mode is determined and whether the task has a deadline time. The scheduling goals of the algorithms are mostly to achieve shorter task execution time or less resource consumption.

Tang, Y. et al. proposed a method to build task queues based on task deadline and task slack time and to build a task model including required resources and task execution time [11]. Deiana, E. A. et al. proposed an improved method in which resources are requested as late as possible to reduce the amount of resources [12]. Sun, Z. et al. proposed a two-phase task scheduling approach to optimize task execution efficiency in a multi-FPGA system but did not consider load balancing of the system [4]. Unlike a software strategy, the simple hardware real-time scheduler can directly configure the tasks in the ready queue according to priority and achieve fast scheduling [13], which is simple and fast for scheduling, but cannot control global indicators such as load balancing.

Some scheduling algorithms are based on shape modeling, by modeling tasks/schedulable regions as rectangular blocks for task-resource mapping [14–16]. Task scheduling is modeled using Mixed-Integer Linear Programming (MILP) formulas based on an architecture with FPGA resources [17]. The grey correlation degree indicates the degree of correlation between two parameters in the system [18]. Using the grey relation theory, a task model including task size, task shape, execution time, and configuration time is established, which is a way to generate a scheduling sequence with the shortest execution time [19]. Considering the task shape and computation time in the task model [20], a task implementation that is slow to execute but suitable for the current resource is selected during scheduling. Therefore, the on-chip resources can satisfy the resource requirements of more tasks, improve resource utilization, and reduce the task waiting time.

In the above-mentioned studies on task scheduling for the Multi-FPGA system, most of them focus on improving the efficiency of task execution with little consideration of reliability assurance. In this work, we propose a reliability-aware, multi-task multi-device scheduling approach that aims to ensure fault tolerance during task execution and to balance the task load among multiple FPGAs to extend the system lifetime.

3. Resource- and Reliability-Aware Task Scheduler

In this section, we design a resource- and reliability-aware task scheduler that schedules multiple subtasks of a large task for execution in a load-balanced and fault-tolerant manner in a Multi-FPGA system. First, we build a task resource model and a timing model, and analyze the state changes during the task scheduling process. Second, we further analyze the impact of multiple FPGA systems on the communication process and establish a model for inter-FPGA task communication. On this basis, we propose the task hybrid algorithm for solving the multi-task scheduling problem on multiple FPGA chips.

3.1. Model

3.1.1. Resource Model of the Task

The task model includes the input and output of the algorithm and each task needs to be represented in the format of the model to generate a task vector. The task model is divided into a pre-scheduled model m_{pre} and a post-scheduled model m_{pos}, which are, respectively, used to describe the resource requirements of the task and the resource description obtained by the task. The m_{pre} includes width of the resources required by the task W_i and height of the resources required by the task H_i, processing time of the data in the current task $times_{exe}$, specified deadline $Deadline_i$, input data $Data_{in}$, output data $Data_{out}$, and task profile partial BIT bit_i. The m_{pre} is as follows: $m_{pre} = \{W_i, H_i, time_{exe}, Deadline_i, Data_{in}, Data_{out}, bit_i\}$. The m_{pos} includes the FPGA chip number at which the task is placed F_i, the coordinate range of the on-chip resources x_i, y_i the start time of the on-chip resources s_i and end time of the on-chip resources e_i, the required storage resources $Data_{max}$, and the time occupied by the bandwidth B_i. The m_{pos} is as follows: $m_{pos} = \{F_i, x_i, y_i, s_i, e_i, Data_{max}, B_i\}$.

3.1.2. Time Model of the Task

From a time perspective, the on-chip tasks go through four stages: task configuration time $time_{conf}$, data reception time $time_{train-in}$, execution data time $time_{exe}$, and data transmission time $time_{train-out}$, which constitute the shortest time $time_{min}$ for a single task to be on the FPGA chip. At different stages, there is an indefinite length of waiting time $time_{wait}$ due to data dependencies between tasks. So, the global time of the task $time_{total}$ is as follows: $time_{total} = time_{wait} + time_{min}$. When calculating the amount of resources occupied by a task, the amount of resources is multiplied by a $time_{total}$ way of reflecting the impact of resource occupation time on the total amount of system resources.

3.1.3. Overhead of Task Communication

The communication overhead of the tasks depends on the system architecture. This work is directed to a system using the AXI bus structure, where there is a continuously active master node that organizes all communication. The communication overhead can be divided into device internal communication overhead (Figure 2) and device-to-device communication overhead (Figure 1).

Communication between subtasks configured on the same FPGA is relatively simple. After the subtask in the pending receive data state receives the bus, the master node checks the task address of the data to be sent in the address mapping table and sends a read command to the task that is sending data. Then, the master node retrieves the data and sends it to the subtask that has pending received data. The communication overhead corresponding to the communication process is expressed as follows:

$$time_{train-i,j} = (Data_{out-i,j} / Rate_{AXI}) * 2 \quad (1)$$

Communication of subtasks configured on different FPGAs are more complicated. When the subtask in the state of pending receiving data obtains the bus, the master node checks the task location of the data to be sent in address mapping table and send a request of reading data to another device. It is needed to send a bus request to the CPU and the other device when sending data and keep the local bus occupied while waiting for the license. Finally, the communication overhead of local device $time_{tran-receive}$ and the communication overhead of the other device $time_{tran-send}$ are expressed as follows:

$$\begin{aligned}
&time_{cpu,j} = Data_{out-i,j}/Rate_{pcie} + Date_{out-i,j}/Rate_{AXI} \\
&time_{tran-wait} = max(Bus_{CPU}, Bus_{FPGA}) \\
&time_{tran-send} = time_{CPU,j} \\
&timetran - receive = \\
&max(Bus_{CPU}, Bus_{FPGA}) + time_{CPU,j}*2
\end{aligned} \tag{2}$$

By describing the two communication processes above, it can be seen that the communication overhead between devices is significantly higher than the communication overhead within the device. Therefore, by default, when the configuration sequence is generated, the subtasks belonging to a task are configured on the same device. Only if the current device does not have sufficient resources or the task cannot be completed before the deadline, is it necessary to try to configure the other devices. If all devices cannot meet the resource requirements of the subtasks, the subtasks must be reapplied the next time.

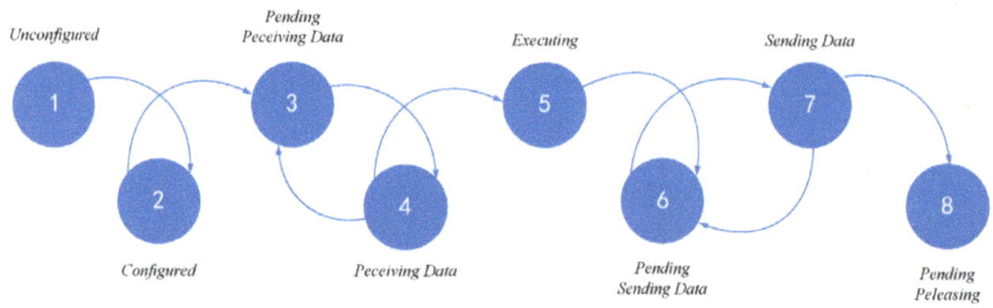

Figure 2. The state transition diagram of subtasks.

3.1.4. State Conversion Process of Task

Depending on the time structure of the subtask, the execution of the subtask can be represented by eight states: unconfigured, configured, pending receiving data, receiving data, executing, pending sending data, sending data, and pending releasing. The initialization state of each task is the unconfigured state, the end state is the releasable state, and the transition relationship between the start and end of the eight tasks is shown in Figure 3.

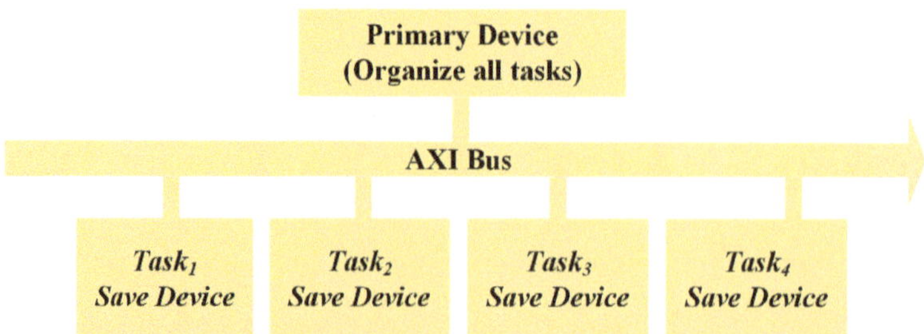

Figure 3. On-chip system structure diagram.

3.2. Subtask Sequence Division

Task scheduling requires time constraints on tasks. The main purpose of topological ordering is to generate a task order that transitions from an unconfigured state to a configured state, which is relied upon to carry the work forward. Because each branch in the DAG of a large task is of different lengths, the different topological ordering will affect the execution time of global tasks. In addition, topological ordering can also prevent resource deadlocks.

The generation of topological sorting is based on a data dependency matrix. According to the data dependency matrix, all feasible solutions for each large task are stored in a tree structure, and the tasks on which the pre-tasks depend are configured before configuration. Suppose there are five tasks A, B, C, D, and E, whose topology is generated by TGFF as shown in Figure 4.

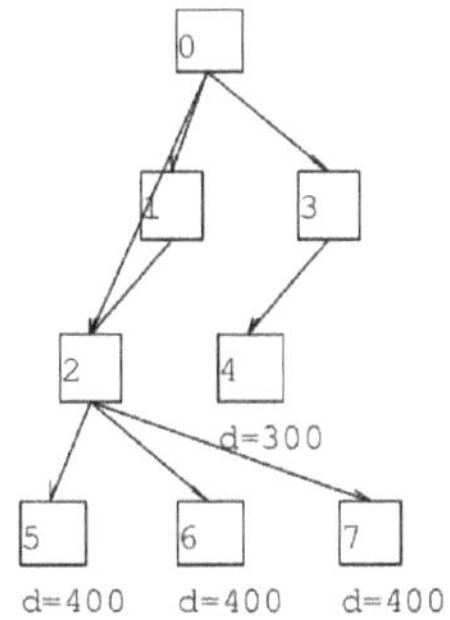

Figure 4. Task topology.

The data dependency matrix between tasks corresponding to the topology is as follows, assuming that the amount of data between tasks is 1:

$$\begin{bmatrix} 0 & 1 & 1 & 0 & 0 \\ 0 & 0 & 0 & 1 & 0 \\ 0 & 0 & 0 & 1 & 1 \\ 0 & 0 & 0 & 0 & 1 \\ 0 & 0 & 0 & 0 & 0 \end{bmatrix} \tag{3}$$

By analyzing the data dependency matrix and the task topology, it can be known that if the column vector corresponding to a subtask is a 0 vector, it indicates that there is no unconfigured predecessor task in the subtask, and the row vector of a particular task is a 0 vector, indicating that a subtask has no successor tasks, which signifies the end task of a large task. By decomposing the matrix, all possible task sequences can be obtained, and the decomposition process is as follows:

$$\begin{bmatrix} 0 & 1 & 1 & 0 & 0 \\ 0 & 0 & 0 & 1 & 0 \\ 0 & 0 & 0 & 1 & 1 \\ 0 & 0 & 0 & 0 & 1 \\ 0 & 0 & 0 & 0 & 0 \end{bmatrix} \rightarrow \begin{bmatrix} 0 \\ 0 \\ 0 \\ 0 \\ 0 \end{bmatrix} + \begin{bmatrix} 0 & 1 & 1 & 0 & 0 \end{bmatrix} + \begin{bmatrix} 0 & 0 & 1 & 0 \\ 0 & 0 & 1 & 1 \\ 0 & 0 & 0 & 1 \\ 0 & 0 & 0 & 0 \end{bmatrix} \tag{4}$$

There is no data dependency in the startup task that can be executed directly. First, the row and column vector corresponding to the start task is decomposed. From the decomposed row vector, it can be seen that the tasks of the subsequent positions of task A are B and C, and the column vectors corresponding to tasks B and C become the 0 vectors after decomposing the row and column vectors of task A. Priority to remove the first column:

$$\begin{bmatrix} 0 & 0 & 1 & 0 \\ 0 & 0 & 1 & 1 \\ 0 & 0 & 0 & 1 \\ 0 & 0 & 0 & 0 \end{bmatrix} \rightarrow \begin{bmatrix} 0 \\ 0 \\ 0 \\ 0 \end{bmatrix} + \begin{bmatrix} 1 & 1 & 0 & 0 \end{bmatrix} + \begin{bmatrix} 0 & 1 & 1 \\ 0 & 0 & 1 \\ 0 & 0 & 0 \end{bmatrix} \tag{5}$$

Priority to remove the second column:

$$\begin{bmatrix} 0 & 1 & 0 & 0 \\ 0 & 0 & 1 & 1 \\ 0 & 0 & 0 & 1 \\ 0 & 0 & 0 & 0 \end{bmatrix} \rightarrow \begin{bmatrix} 0 \\ 0 \\ 0 \\ 0 \end{bmatrix} + \begin{bmatrix} 0 & 1 & 0 & 0 \end{bmatrix} + \begin{bmatrix} 0 & 1 & 0 \\ 0 & 0 & 1 \\ 0 & 0 & 0 \end{bmatrix} \tag{6}$$

The above corresponds to two decomposition methods, i.e., decomposing tasks B or task C. Here, we select the first corresponding decomposition method since there is no new 0 vector after the decomposition, so the next one to enter the configuration queue can only be task C:

$$\begin{bmatrix} 0 & 1 & 1 \\ 0 & 0 & 1 \\ 0 & 0 & 0 \end{bmatrix} \rightarrow \begin{bmatrix} 0 \\ 0 \\ 0 \end{bmatrix} + \begin{bmatrix} 0 & 1 & 1 \end{bmatrix} + \begin{bmatrix} 0 & 1 \\ 0 & 0 \end{bmatrix} \tag{7}$$

After decomposing the row and column vector of task C, the column vector of task D becomes a 0 vector. Next, we decompose task D:

$$\begin{bmatrix} 0 & 1 \\ 0 & 0 \end{bmatrix} \rightarrow \begin{bmatrix} 0 \\ 0 \end{bmatrix} + \begin{bmatrix} 0 & 1 \end{bmatrix} + \begin{bmatrix} 0 \end{bmatrix} \tag{8}$$

At this point, there is only one task E left in the matrix. After E enters the configuration queue, all tasks enter the configuration state and an effective sequence is obtained through the decomposition of the matrix: $A \rightarrow B \rightarrow C \rightarrow D \rightarrow E$. It is a safe and effective configuration method to generate task sequences in strict accordance with matrix decomposition.

3.3. Deployment of Tasks on Multi-FPGA Systems

The implementation of dividing the subtask sequence corresponding to several large tasks into the configuration sequence corresponding to several FPGA chips is called maintaining multi-sequences. We propose a Maintain Multi-Sequence (MMS) algorithm as follows (Algorithm 1).

First, we set the default device number for each subtask sequence in a circular fashion. This reduces the overhead of inter-device communication. In a resource-rich environment, subtasks belonging to the same task should be configured in a default device to reduce the amount of data communication between devices. On the other hand, load balancing is beneficial. By distributing large tasks across individual FPGA chips, we prevent multiple large tasks from being concentrated on a single device, resulting in the under-utilization of the system's computing and interface resources. When selecting the default device, first sort the subtask sequence by Deadline, which prevents the larger Deadline task sequence from defaulting to the same device. Secondly, sort the devices in descending order of resources. By allocating resources to a device with more resources, the subtasks in the same large task will be more centralized on the same device, reducing the overhead of communication between devices.

In the next step, a deadline-based as-late-as-possible configuration strategy is used to generate configuration sequences, where each task is configured at the last moment in a timeframe that does not affect other tasks. Since the goal of the scheduling algorithm is to ensure that each task is completed before the deadline and that the same task is executed on different FPGAs in a dual-mode hot standby for fault tolerance, the time distance (DT) and resource usage between the current time and the deadline of each configuration sequence is first calculated. As shown in Figure 5, the process of requesting devices by subtasks uses back-to-front dynamic allocation. After comparing the deadlines, the largest deadline is used as the starting point for generating the configuration sequence.

Algorithm 1 Maintain Multi-sequences

Input: Task Collection, Device Collection

```
Sort the task sequence by Deadline and initialize the time
Sort devices by resource
for m in Task Collection do
   set the default number for every device
end for
while time- - do
   for tasks in Task Collection do
      if Separate successfully resources for tasks then
         Reduce the Deadline of tasks
      end if
   end for
   Reorder tasks
   if Allocation end then
      Break
   end if
end while{M}ove configuration sequence forward
if time < 0 then
   for mission in Device Collection do
      mission.time -= time;
   end for
end if
```

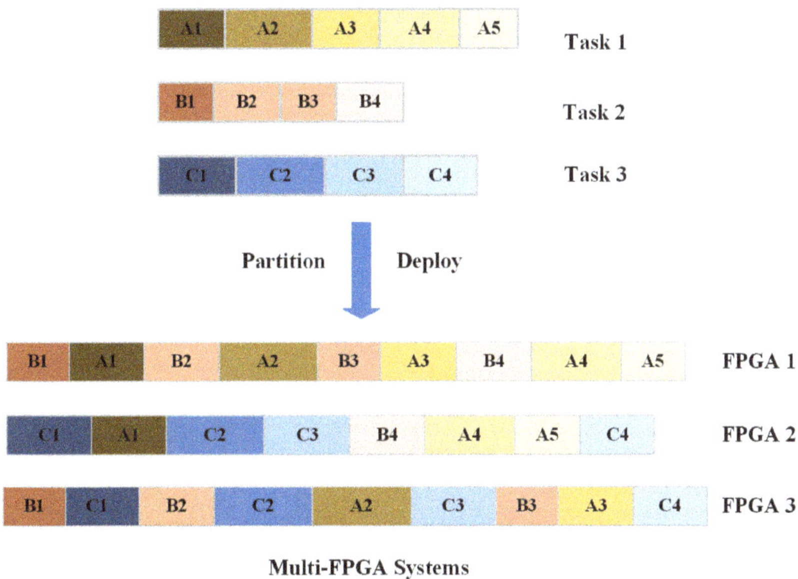

Figure 5. Task sequence partitioning and deployment on Multi-FPGA systems.

All subtasks form a Device Application Sequence and then enter the Device Configuration Sequence. The generation of the device application sequence starts with the last element of each task sequence, i.e., the end node in the task topology. The device application sequence is sorted in descending order of time distance. The task with the largest DT first selects the device and enters the device configuration sequence. After configuration, the next task in the same sequence is added to the Device Application Sequence and reordered. Iterating through the above rules dynamically generates the final configuration sequence. The last action before generating the final configuration sequence is to advance the configure sequence. Check that there is no downtime when all the tasks are scheduled; if there is, then the configuration time of all the tasks should be moved forward to eliminate the downtime.

4. Experimental Evaluation

In this section, we use the Task Graph for Free (TGFF) [21] to generate the Task DAG. The scheduler based on the Multi-FPGA system was tested to verify its performance and fault tolerance when scheduling multiple large tasks.

4.1. Testing Environment

We used C++ to build an experimental platform to provide the system framework and function preset interface for the proposed methods of task sorting, multiple sequence maintenance, resource management, and task combination, based on the algorithm proposed in this work and the comparison algorithm that is implemented. The test task set and device network structure adopt three task topology diagrams and two physical FPGA (XC7A200T-2FBG484I) to implement the scenario of multi-task scheduling on Multi-FPGA. The algorithm program is designed in C++ language and the FPGA project is designed in Verilog.

This work sets the common algorithms for target recognition and image processing as task topology generated by TGFF. The resource requirements of the tasks are shown in Table 1 [22]. The width and height of the task are generated by random numbers based on the amount of logical resources, in order to complete the simulation of the real shape of tasks.

Table 1. List of common algorithm resource requirements.

	Algorithm	Slices	BRAM
Target Recognition	Debayer (2×)	200	2
	Rectifier (2×)	500	30
	Stereo match	2500	30
	Disparity	1000	15
	Flex-SURF	1000	0
	Motor Control (3×)	200	0
Image Processing	FPN correction	100	0
	Dark field corr.	200	1
	FFT	800	7
	Bad pixel/spike	100	2
	CCSDS 122	2500	12
	Binning	300	4
	Hough Transform	1800	14
	Median Filter	800	0

4.2. Evaluation Metrics

In order to evaluate the performance of resource management algorithms, three evaluation metrics are introduced below.

Average Resource Vote (ARV): indicates the resource usage of the task and measures the effect of the scheduling algorithm to save resources. The expression is as follows:

$$ARV = \frac{1}{size_{total} * T_{total}} \sum_{i=0}^{N} (size_i * T_i) \tag{9}$$

Task Completion Rate (TCR): indicates the percentage of successfully executed tasks compared to all scheduled tasks.

Mean Time to Failure (MTTF): indicates the average time before failure. In systems where hard fault repair cannot be achieved, it is equivalent to the system lifetime.

4.3. Result and Analysis

We set up three sets of scheduling strategies for verification in three task DAGs. Regarding the first strategy, we do not use an additional task scheduling algorithm; we just let three large tasks enter the Single-FPGA one by one. In the second strategy, we use task hybrid scheduling to combine three large tasks into one large task set and apply for resources in the Single-FPGA. In the third experiment, we use a load balancing and fault tolerance strategy (resource- and reliability-aware scheduler) to schedule tasks and set default devices for large tasks, then mix subtasks scheduled in the same device and apply for resources in the Multi-FPGA. In the experiment, each device is set to have sufficient resources to respond to resource requests of subtasks.

Firstly, we evaluated the resource utilization and scheduling efficiency of the proposed method, and the experimental results are shown in Table 2 and Figure 6. In Table 2, the ARV, maximum resource utilization rate, and execution time of the three policies when scheduling three groups of tasks are shown. Among them, the Single-FPGA Task Continuous Placement strategy has no advantage in each of the metrics, while the Single-FPGA Task Mix Placement strategy has a higher ARV and maximum resource utilization rate than the Multi-FPGA Task Mix Placement strategy, but the execution time is much higher than the latter. Figure 6 shows the resource margin on each FPGA chip as the task group executes the three scheduling strategies. As a whole, it can be obtained that the task mix algorithm has a significant effect on improving the scheduling metrics.

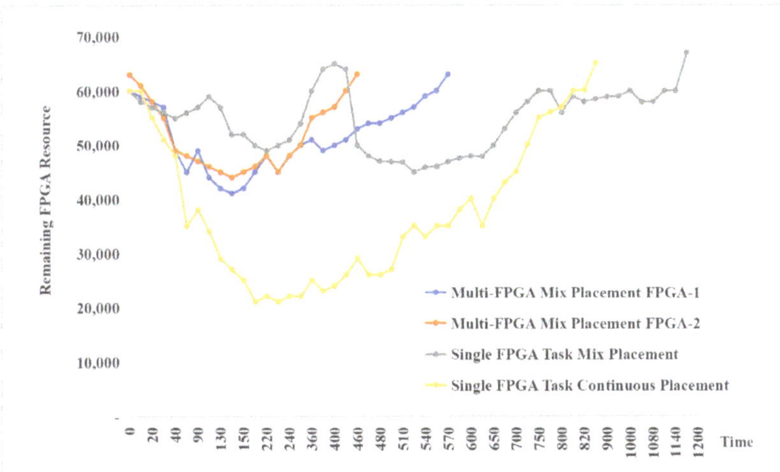

Figure 6. The resourcesurplus variation chart of the first group of experiments.

Table 2. The influence of the task hybrid algorithm and load balancing strategy on the scheduling effect.

Task Sequence Maintenance Approach	ARV			Maximum Resource Utilization Rate			Execution Time		
	1	2	3	1	2	3	1	2	3
Single-FPGA Task Continuous Placement	15.1%	16.2%	14.9%	34.4%	35.1%	31.1%	1141	1389	1312
Single-FPGA Task Mix Placement	42.6%	45.1%	43.0%	68.3%	74.9%	68.0%	858	1138	1140
Multi-FPGA Task Mix Placement	29.6%	30.4%	30.2%	34.3%	35.6%	34.9%	524	689	627

The above reasons are the task successive placement strategy causes the overall execution time of the tasks to become longer when dealing with the bursty task collection, and the much resources remaining indicates that FPGA's ability for parallel computing is not utilized to the extent that it is not possible to guarantee that the tasks that are leaning back will be executed before the deadline. When three tasks are mixed to apply for the resources of a single FPGA, the three tasks form a mixed task set, the overall execution time decreases, the resource utilization rises, and compared to sequential placement, the mixed placement configures more tasks in the FPGA, taking advantage of the FPGA's parallel nature. Three tasks are configured in two FPGAs through complex balancing and task mixing, which reduces the resource residual requirement for a single FPGA compared to mixing three tasks and reduces the total execution time by joint scheduling of the two FPGA devices, which can complete the task before the deadline.

Similarly, we use the above scenarios and three scheduling strategies to verify the reliability performance of the proposed method. The proposed method described in this paper also aims to extend the MTTF by load balancing to alleviate the stress accumulation on each FPGA device for a long time. Therefore, we used the method described in Section 3.3 of reference [23] to measure MTTF. The TCR and MTTF results are shown in Table 3. As shown in the table, the reliability-aware scheduling method proposed in this paper achieves an average of 98.3% on TCR and 15.7 years on MTTF, which is much higher than the other two scheduling methods.

The above reasons are due to: (1) simultaneous execution of redundant tasks through multiple FPGA placements ensures uninterrupted task execution after failures and (2) reduced spike stress on a single FPGA by a load-balanced mix of placement tasks on Multi-FPGA, resulting in extended system lifetime. The experimental results of the Single-FPGA task mix placement strategy are better than the Single-FPGA task continuous placement strategy due to the fact that the hybrid placement avoids fault accumulation and stress accumulation to some extent.

Table 3. The influence of the task hybrid algorithm and load balancing strategy on the scheduling effect.

Task Sequence Maintenance Approach	TCR			MTTF		
	1	2	3	1	2	3
Single-FPGA Task Continuous Placement	66.7%	62.5%	72.5%	5.2	6.0	5.8
Single-FPGA Task Mix Placement	85.0%	82.5%	90.0%	6.3	6.9	6.8
Multi-FPGA Task Mix Placement	100.0%	95.0%	100.0%	15.2	16.0	15.8

In addition, we further investigate the scalability of the scheduling strategy proposed in this paper on top of a multi-FPGA system and design the following experiments. By increasing the number of FPGAs to test the number of task groups that can be carried out by different scheduling strategies in a certain period of time, we have verified the scalability of the method. The scheduling strategies are Multi-FPGA Task Mix Placement, Single-FPGA

Task Continuous Placement, and Single-FPGA Task Mix Placement proposed in this paper. The task groups are then randomly combined from the tasks in Table 1.

From Table 4, it can be seen that as the number of FPGAs increases, the number of schedulable task groups increases for all scheduling policies, but the Multi-FPGA Task Mix Placement policy grows at a much higher rate than the other two policies. The reason is that the Single-FPGA Task Continuous Placement strategy can only schedule tasks sequentially and cannot execute tasks simultaneously on the chip. The Single-FPGA Task Mix Placement strategy can schedule different tasks to be executed on a single slice, so it can flexibly deploy tasks. The Multi-FPGA Task Mix Placement strategy cannot support more tasks when the number of FPGAs is small because it needs to deploy tasks redundantly, but with the increase of FPGAs, its scheduling strategy will be better able to support more tasks. Moreover, as the number of FPGAs increases, the scheduling strategy will make better use of the resources of each FPGA, and thus, the number of tasks completed can be significantly increased. The above experiments also demonstrate that the scheduling method described in this paper has good scalability on Multi-FPGA systems, which improves the adaptability of the system in large-scale edge computing scenarios.

Table 4. The number of task groups that can be scheduled with the increase of the amount of FPGAs under different scheduling strategies.

Task Sequence Maintenance Approach	The Amount of FPGAs				
	2	3	4	5	6
Single-FPGA Task Continuous Placement	4	6	9	13	16
Single-FPGA Task Mix Placement	10	14	19	27	38
Multi-FPGA Task Mix Placement	7	12	18	29	40

5. Conclusions and Future Work

In this paper, a set of task models is established based on the resource/time requirements, communication overhead, and state conversion process of the task; based on this, a resource- and reliability-aware hybrid scheduling method on the Multi-FPGA system has been proposed to fully utilize FPGA resources to cope with the deployment of bursty tasks. Experiments show that the method proposed in this paper significantly improves resource utilization by 7%, which achieves a task completion rate of 98.3% and extends system reliability with a mean time to failure of 15.7 years. In future work, we will design an exploration method to solve an appropriate proportion of FPGA usage in the system to balance reliability and makespan for different applications. In general, the more FPGAs are used as redundant resources to achieve fault tolerance, the longer the corresponding makespan. To ensure the main implementation goals of different applications, it is imperative to determine the right proportion of FPGA in the system for fault tolerance or operational tasks. In addition, we will further investigate the scalability and energy of scheduling strategies on Multi-FPGA architectures to more fully evaluate their applicability in large-scale edge computing environments.

Author Contributions: Conceptualization, Z.L. and Y.H.; methodology, Z.L. and H.G.; software, Y.H. and H.G.; validation, Z.L. and J.Z.; formal analysis, Y.H. and J.Z.; investigation, H.G. and J.Z.; resources, Z.L.; data curation, Y.H. and H.G.; writing—original draft preparation, Z.L. and Y.H.; writing—review and editing, Z.L. and J.Z.; funding acquisition, Z.L. All authors have read and agreed to the published version of the manuscript.

Funding: This work was supported in part by the Research Start-up Fund in Shanxi Province under Grant 980020066, in part by the Management Fund of North University of China: 2310700037HX, and in part by the Fundamental Research Program of Shanxi Province: 202403021212165.

Data Availability Statement: Data are unavailable due to privacy or ethical restrictions.

Acknowledgments: The authors would like to thank the editors and reviewers for their contributions to our manuscript.

Conflicts of Interest: The authors declare no conflicts of interest.

References

1. Bolchini, C.; Sandionigi, C. Design of hardened embedded systems on multi-FPGA platforms. *ACM Trans. Des. Autom. Electron. Syst. (TODAES)* **2014**, *20*, 1–26. [CrossRef]
2. Shan, J.; Lazarescu, M.T.; Cortadella, J.; Lavagno, L.; Casu, M.R. CNN-on-AWS: Efficient allocation of multikernel applications on multi-FPGA platforms. *IEEE Trans. Comput.-Aided Des. Integr. Circuits Syst.* **2020**, *40*, 301–314. [CrossRef]
3. Wang, Y.; Liao, Y.; Yang, J.; Wang, H.; Zhao, Y.; Zhang, C.; Xiao, B.; Xu, F.; Gao, Y.; Xu, M.; et al. An FPGA-based online reconfigurable CNN edge computing device for object detection. *Microelectron. J.* **2023**, *137*, 105805. [CrossRef]
4. Sun, Z.; Zhang, H.; Zhang, Z. Resource-Aware Task Scheduling and Placement in Multi-FPGA System. *IEEE Access* **2019**, *7*, 163851–163863. [CrossRef]
5. Wang, Z.; Tang, Q.; Guo, B.; Wei, J.B.; Wang, L. Resource Partitioning and Application Scheduling with Module Merging on Dynamically and Partially Reconfigurable FPGAs. *Electronics* **2020**, *9*, 1461. [CrossRef]
6. Najem, M.; Bollengier, T.; Le Lann, J.C.; Lagadec, L. A cost-effective approach for efficient time-sharing of reconfigurable architectures. In Proceedings of the IEEE 2017 International Conference on FPGA Reconfiguration for General-Purpose Computing (FPGA4GPC), Hamburg, Germany, 9–10 May 2017; pp. 7–12.
7. Iordache, A.; Pierre, G.; Sanders, P.; de F. Coutinho, J.G.; Stillwell, M. High performance in the cloud with FPGA groups. In Proceedings of the 9th International Conference on Utility and Cloud Computing, Shanghai, China, 6–9 December 2016; pp. 1–10.
8. Tianyang, L.; Fan, Z.; Wei, G.; Mingqian, S.; Li, C. A Survey: FPGA-Based Dynamic Scheduling of Hardware Tasks. *Chin. J. Electron.* **2021**, *30*, 991–1007. [CrossRef]
9. Ding, B.; Huang, J.; Xu, Q.; Wang, J.; Chen, S.; Kang, Y. Memory-aware Partitioning, Scheduling, and Floorplanning for Partially Dynamically Reconfigurable Systems. *ACM Trans. Des. Autom. Electron. Syst.* **2023**, *28*, 1–21. [CrossRef]
10. Ramezani, R. Dynamic Scheduling of Task Graphs in Multi-FPGA Systems Using Critical Path. *J. Supercomput.* **2021**, *77*, 597–618. [CrossRef]
11. Tang, Y.; Bergmann, N.W. A Hardware Scheduler Based on Task Queues for FPGA-based Embedded Real-time Systems. *IEEE Trans. Comput.* **2014**, *64*, 1254–1267. [CrossRef]
12. Deiana, E.A.; Rabozzi, M.; Cattaneo, R.; Santambrogio, M.D. A multiobjective reconfiguration-aware scheduler for FPGA-based heterogeneous architectures. In Proceedings of the IEEE 2015 International Conference on ReConFigurable Computing and FPGAs (ReConFig), Riviera Maya, Mexico, 7–9 December 2015; pp. 1–6.
13. Purgato, A.; Tantillo, D.; Rabozzi, M.; Sciuto, D.; Santambrogio, M.D. Resource-efficient scheduling for partially-reconfigurable FPGA-based systems. In Proceedings of the 2016 IEEE International Parallel and Distributed Processing Symposium Workshops (IPDPSW), Chicago, IL, USA, 23–27 May 2016; pp. 189–197.
14. Clemente, J.A.; Resano, J.; Mozos, D. An approach to manage reconfigurations and reduce area cost in hard real-time reconfigurable systems. *ACM Trans. Embed. Comput. Syst. (TECS)* **2014**, *13*, 90. [CrossRef]
15. Wang, G.; Liu, S.; Nie, J.; Wang, F.; Arslan, T. An online task placement algorithm based on maximum empty rectangles in dynamic partial reconfigurable systems. In Proceedings of the IEEE 2017 NASA/ESA Conference on Adaptive Hardware and Systems (AHS), Pasadena, CA, USA, 24–27 July 2017; pp. 180–185.
16. Kao, C.C. Performance-Oriented Partitioning for Task Scheduling of Parallel Reconfigurable Architectures. *IEEE Trans. Parallel Distrib. Syst.* **2015**, *26*, 858–867. [CrossRef]
17. Resano, J.; Mozos, D.; Catthoor, F. A Hybrid Prefetch Scheduling Heuristic to Minimize at Run-time the Reconfiguration Overhead of Dynamically Reconfigurable Hardware. In Proceedings of the IEEE Design, Automation and Test in Europe, Munich, Germany, 7–11 March 2005; pp. 106–111.
18. Liu, S.; Forrest, J.; Vallee, R. Emergence and development of grey systems theory. *Kybernetes* **2009**, *38*, 1246–1256. [CrossRef]
19. Wu, J.O.; Wang, S.F.; Fan, Y.H.; Chien, W. The scheduling and placement strategies for FPGA dynamic reconfigurable system. In Proceedings of the IEEE 2016 International Conference on Applied System Innovation (ICASI), Okinawa, Japan, 26–30 May 2016; pp. 1–2.
20. Wassi, G.; Benkhelifa, M.E.A.; Lawday, G.; Verdier, F.; Garcia, S. Multi-shape tasks scheduling for online multitasking on FPGAs. In Proceedings of the IEEE 2014 9th International Symposium on Reconfigurable and Communication-Centric Systems-on-Chip (ReCoSoC), Montpellier, France, 26–28 May 2014; pp. 1–7.
21. Dick, R.P.; Rhodes, D.L.; Wolf, W. TGFF: Task graphs for free. In Proceedings of the IEEE Sixth International Workshop on Hardware/Software Codesign (CODES/CASHE'98), Seattle, WA, USA, 15–18 March 1998; pp. 97–101.

22. Zhang, H.; Bauer, L.; Kochte, M.A.; Schneider, E.; Wunderlich, H.J.; Henkel, J. Aging resilience and fault tolerance in runtime reconfigurable architectures. *IEEE Trans. Comput.* **2016**, *66*, 957–970. [CrossRef]
23. Li, Z.; Huang, Z.; Wang, Q.; Wang, J. AMROFloor: An Efficient Aging Mitigation and Resource Optimization Floorplanner for Virtual Coarse-Grained Runtime Reconfigurable FPGAs. *Electronics* **2022**, *11*, 273. [CrossRef]

electronics

MDPI

Article

DGA-Based Fault Diagnosis Using Self-Organizing Neural Networks with Incremental Learning

Siqi Liu *, Zhiyuan Xie and Zhengwei Hu

School of Electrical and Electronic Engineering, North China Electric Power University, Baoding 071003, China; zhiyuanxie@ncepu.edu.cn (Z.X.); hzwwizard@ncepu.edu.cn (Z.H.)
* Correspondence: liusiqi@ncepu.edu.cn

Abstract: Power transformers are vital components of electrical power systems, ensuring reliable and efficient energy transfer between high-voltage transmission and low-voltage distribution networks. However, they are prone to various faults, such as insulation breakdowns, winding deformations, partial discharges, and short circuits, which can disrupt electrical service, incur significant economic losses, and pose safety risks. Traditional fault diagnosis methods, including visual inspection, dissolved gas analysis (DGA), and thermal imaging, face challenges such as subjectivity, intermittent data collection, and reliance on expert interpretation. To address these limitations, this paper proposes a novel distributed approach for multi-fault diagnosis of power transformers based on a self-organizing neural network combined with data augmentation and incremental learning techniques. The proposed framework addresses critical challenges, including data quality issues, computational complexity, and the need for real-time adaptability. Data cleaning and preprocessing techniques improve the reliability of input data, while data augmentation generates synthetic samples to mitigate data imbalance and enhance the recognition of rare fault patterns. A two-stage classification model integrates unsupervised and supervised learning, with k-means clustering applied in the first stage for initial fault categorization, followed by a self-organizing neural network in the second stage for refined fault diagnosis. The self-organizing neural network dynamically suppresses inactive nodes and optimizes its training parameter set, reducing computational complexity without sacrificing accuracy. Additionally, incremental learning enables the model to continuously adapt to new fault scenarios without modifying its architecture, ensuring real-time performance and adaptability across diverse operational conditions. Experimental validation demonstrates the effectiveness of the proposed method in achieving accurate, efficient, and adaptive fault diagnosis for power transformers, outperforming traditional and conventional machine learning approaches. This work provides a robust framework for integrating advanced machine learning techniques into power system monitoring, paving the way for automated, real-time, and reliable transformer fault diagnosis systems.

Keywords: multi-fault diagnosis; power transformers; artificial intelligence; dissolved gas analysis (DGA)

1. Introduction

Power transformers play a crucial role in electrical power systems, acting as the interface between high-voltage transmission and low-voltage distribution networks [1,2]. They are essential for the reliable and efficient transfer of electrical energy over long distances. As global energy demand continues to increase, ensuring the smooth operation of power transformers becomes even more critical. However, like all electrical machinery, power transformers are susceptible to faults, which can range from insulation breakdowns and winding deformations to more complex failures such as partial discharge (PD) and short circuits [3–5]. These faults can have serious consequences, including the disruption of electrical service, economic losses due to extended downtimes, and even safety hazards.

The failure of a power transformer can lead to significant financial losses. According to industry reports, transformer failures in electrical networks can cost utilities millions of dollars annually due to both the repair costs and the cascading impact on grid stability [6]. In addition, failure events often lead to power outages, which can disrupt industrial processes, commercial operations, and household services [7]. To prevent such catastrophic failures, early detection and diagnosis of faults in transformers are essential. A timely diagnosis can provide a window for preventive maintenance, reduce the need for costly repairs, and ultimately extend the transformer's service life.

Traditionally, fault diagnosis in transformers has been achieved through methods like visual inspection [8], oil sampling [9], dissolved gas analysis (DGA) [10], and thermal imaging [11]. However, these methods often have limitations. For example, visual inspection is subjective and may not detect latent faults, while oil sampling provides only intermittent information. Thermal imaging is also a non-invasive technique but does not provide in-depth analysis of fault mechanisms, particularly in complex electrical or mechanical failures [12]. These methods also tend to rely heavily on the expertise of operators, which may lead to human errors or oversights.

Given these limitations, there is a growing demand for automated, reliable, and real-time fault diagnosis systems. These systems are expected to detect incipient faults at an early stage, well before they escalate into major failures. With advancements in sensor technology and data analytics, there is now an opportunity to develop predictive fault diagnosis systems that can analyze a variety of operational parameters continuously. Over the years, several advanced methods have been proposed to detect transformer faults using data-driven approaches. These methods leverage a variety of data sources, including vibration [13], temperature [13], acoustic signals [14], and electrical measurements [15] such as current and voltage waveforms. Among these techniques, machine learning algorithms have gained popularity. They can analyze large volumes of data to detect patterns indicative of faults in a more automated, reliable, convenient, and accurate way. In recent years, deep learning has made significant progress in the field of visual inspection, especially in detecting insulation defects in transformers. For example, one study [16] designed a robotic inspection fish that uses deep learning networks to visually inspect the insulation paper inside transformers, identifying discharge carbon marks and cracks. Furthermore, the transformer architecture has demonstrated high fidelity in structural defect detection [17]. By incorporating learnable down-sampling and up-sampling modules, transformers achieve an excellent balance between global and local semantic information. These studies indicate that deep learning techniques, especially visual analysis methods, have been successfully applied to the automated health evaluation of transformers. Including these methods in the introduction aids in comprehensively showcasing the potential of deep learning in transformer condition monitoring.

However, several challenges remain:

- Data quality and imbalance issues: The quality of the data used in DGA can be compromised due to factors such as noise in gas concentration readings, instrument limitations, and sampling inconsistencies. These issues can negatively impact the performance of AI models in fault detection. Moreover, in many cases, fault data for specific failure modes are sparse, leading to a data imbalance that causes AI models to underperform, particularly in fault diagnosis for rare transformer issues.

- High computational complexity: Although using neural networks can improve diagnostic accuracy, the neural network models are complex and have high computational complexity.
- Real-time performance and adaptability: DGA data typically require significant time to be collected and processed, which can affect the real-time capabilities of fault diagnosis systems. Furthermore, transformer operating conditions can vary significantly across regions, affecting model performance and generalizability.

To address the above issues, this paper proposes a self-organizing neural network for multi-fault diagnosis of power transformers, combining data augmentation and incremental learning methods. The following key points characterize the originality of this contribution:

- A two-stage classification model that combines unsupervised and supervised methods is proposed. In the first stage, the k-means algorithm is used for unsupervised classification. Based on the classification results, a self-organizing neural network is trained in the second stage for fault diagnosis.
- A self-organizing neural network approach is proposed, which adaptively suppresses the activated nodes of the neural network based on the training process, dynamically constructing the neural network training parameter set, thereby significantly reducing the model's computational complexity while ensuring accuracy.
- The introduction of incremental learning allows the model to continuously learn new knowledge without altering the neural network architecture, improving the real-time performance and adaptability of the model.

The rest of this paper is organized as follows. Section 2 provides a review of related work in the field of transformer fault diagnosis, including traditional and machine learning-based methods. Section 3 describes the methodology for the proposed fault diagnosis system, detailing the data collection process, feature extraction techniques, and incremental learning. Section 4 presents the simulation results and outperforms the benefits of the proposed framework. Finally, we conclude the paper and discuss the future work in Section 5.

2. Related Work

The use of DGA for diagnosing faults in power transformers has been a standard practice for decades. By analyzing the concentrations of various gases dissolved in transformer oil, DGA provides insights into the internal health of transformers and can help in identifying fault types such as overheating, partial discharge, and short circuits. DGA is considered a reliable technique for early fault detection, but traditional methods of analysis often rely on heuristic rules and expert knowledge, making them subjective and limited in terms of scalability and automation. As such, there has been increasing interest in integrating artificial intelligence (AI) techniques with DGA to improve fault detection accuracy, automate the diagnostic process, and reduce the dependence on expert judgment.

In recent years, machine learning algorithms, such as support vector machines (SVM), decision trees (DT), and k-means, have been widely applied to DGA data for transformer fault diagnosis. These methods can classify fault types based on the concentration of dissolved gases, offering a significant advantage over traditional approaches by reducing human involvement in the analysis process. For example, Zhang et al. [18] applied an SVM-based model for classifying transformer faults using DGA data and achieved a high accuracy rate of over 90%. Their results demonstrated that machine learning models could effectively handle complex patterns in gas concentrations, which are often challenging for conventional methods. Similarly, in a study by Xiao et al. [19], a decision tree algorithm was used to classify fault conditions in transformers. The study showed that decision trees could accurately categorize faults such as arcing and overheating with high sensitivity.

Nanfak et al. [20] proposed a hybrid method that uses k-means clustering for data preprocessing and an SVM for fault classification, enhancing the accuracy and efficiency of transformer fault diagnosis.

Another important advancement in the field has been the use of artificial neural networks (ANNs), which are well-suited to handle nonlinear relationships between gas concentrations and fault conditions. Liu et al. [21] proposed an ANN model to diagnose transformer faults based on DGA data. The model was able to learn complex patterns in the data, outperforming traditional rule-based methods, and was particularly effective in detecting incipient faults before they manifested as major failures. Furthermore, Zhang et al. [22] demonstrated the use of a deep learning approach, leveraging a multi-layered neural network to process DGA data. Wang et al. [23] leveraged a brain-inspired neural-transformer architecture to achieve high-precision and robust fault diagnosis while maintaining low computational cost. The study incorporated a two-dimensional representation method, the frequency-slice wavelet transform (FSWT), to enhance the fault identifiability of vibration signals. Their results indicated that deep neural networks could significantly enhance fault detection accuracy compared to simpler machine learning models.

The integration of deep learning techniques such as convolutional neural networks (CNN) and recurrent neural networks (RNN) for transformer fault diagnosis has also gained traction. These advanced AI techniques offer the advantage of automatic feature extraction from raw data, which reduces the need for manual intervention and predefined features. For instance, Li et al. [24] proposed a hybrid model combining CNN and RNN to analyze time-series DGA data. Their model showed a remarkable ability to capture both temporal and spatial patterns in the gas concentrations, leading to improved diagnostic performance. The study found that deep learning-based models could provide higher diagnostic accuracy and robustness, but the neural network models are complex and have high computational complexity.

Despite the promising results of AI algorithms in DGA-based fault detection, some challenges remain. One key challenge is the need for large and high-quality datasets to train AI models effectively. In particular, the quality and consistency of DGA data can vary depending on operational conditions, making it difficult to develop generalized models. Several studies have explored methods to address this issue, such as using data augmentation techniques or transferring knowledge from other datasets [25]. Additionally, the operating conditions and fault types of transformers may vary in different regions and operating environments, leading to insufficient adaptability of existing models.

In conclusion, integrating AI with DGA for transformer fault diagnosis holds significant potential to improve fault detection accuracy, automate the diagnostic process, and reduce dependence on expert judgment. However, challenges related to data quality, imbalance issue, high computational complexity, and the need for real-time performance and adaptability remain important areas of current research.

3. Methodology

3.1. Problem Formulations

The data-driven transformer fault diagnosis can be described as a supervised classification problem based on labeled data. Let the input be an M-dimensional sample, where each sample contains M key performance indicators (KPIs) reflecting the transformer's performance, i.e., $X = [KPI_1, KPI_2, \ldots KPI_M] \in \mathbb{R}^M$. The output is a set of anomaly causes $Y = \{F_1, \ldots, F_i, \ldots F_N\}$, where F_i represents the i-th anomaly cause. The fault diagnosis process is to determine the correspondence between the input vector representing the transformer's performance state and the output set, i.e., $f(X) \rightarrow Y$. Let FX_i represent the distribution of the input vector $X = [KPI_1, KPI_2, \ldots KPI_M] \in \mathbb{R}^M$ when the i-th anomaly cause occurs, and let FC_i represent the distribution of the output F_i when the i-th anomaly cause occurs. Then, the anomaly diagnosis problem can be transformed into the expression $FX_i \rightarrow FC_i, \forall i \in N$, where N is the total number of anomaly causes.

3.2. Data Balancing

In fault diagnosis, there is often an imbalance in the data between samples from different fault causes. This class imbalance can significantly affect the classification performance of the model. Therefore, this section introduces several common data balancing methods and compares the impact of different data balancing techniques on the model's accuracy in the subsequent model training process.

(1) Random sampling

Random sampling methods are primarily divided into random over-sampling and random under-sampling. Random over-sampling balances the sample sizes of the minority and majority classes by duplicating data from the minority class and adding it to the original dataset. Since random over-sampling simply increases the number of minority class samples by copying, it can easily lead to overfitting, where the model learns overly specific information and performs poorly in terms of generalization. On the other hand, random under-sampling removes some data from the majority class to balance the number of samples in both classes. However, a drawback of this method is that it may result in the loss of important data.

(2) Synthetic Minority Over-sampling Technique (SMOTE)

SMOTE [26] is an improved version of the random over-sampling algorithm that selects neighboring samples using the k-nearest neighbor (KNN) algorithm and synthesizes new minority class samples based on these neighbors. A new minority class sample can be generated through the following process. First, for a minority class sample X_i in the sample set MMM, the k-nearest neighbors in the feature space are found. Then, a sample X_j is randomly selected from these neighbors, and the difference $diff = X_i - X_j$ is calculated. Finally, a new sample X_n is generated using the formula $X_n = X_i + \text{rand}(0,1) \cdot diff$, where rand(0,1) is a random number between 0 and 1.

(3) Adaptive Synthetic Sampling (ADASYN)

ADASYN [26] uses a systematic method to adaptively create different amounts of synthetic data according to their distributions. The main idea of the ADASYN algorithm is to use the density distribution as a criterion for automatically determining the number of synthesized samples that need to be generated for each minority example. The basic process of ADASYN is summarized as follows:

Firstly, calculate the total number of minority class samples that need to be synthesized:

$$G = (M_{\text{max}} - M_{\text{min}}) \times \alpha \tag{1}$$

where M_{min} is the set of minority class samples and M_{max} is the set of majority class samples. $\alpha \in [0,1]$ represents the expected balance level after the addition of the synthetic sample. When $\alpha = 1$, it means that the dataset is completely balanced after adding the synthetic samples.

Secondly, for each sample $X_i \in M_{\text{min}}$, find their k-nearest neighbors in the n-dimensional space and calculate the ratio:

$$r_i = \Delta_i / K, i = 1, 2, \cdots, m \tag{2}$$

where Δ_i is the number of examples in the k-nearest neighbors of X_i that belong to M_{max}.

Next, regulate r_i and express a

$$r'_i = r_i / \sum_{i=1}^{M_{\min}} r_i \tag{3}$$

Calculate the number of samples that need to be synthesized for each $X_i \in M_{\min}$:

$$g_i = r'_i \times G \tag{4}$$

Finally, for each $X_i \in M_{\min}$, generate g_i synthetic data samples according to

$$X_{new} = X_i + (X_j - X_i) \times \lambda \tag{5}$$

where X_j is one of the k-nearest neighbors for X_i and $\lambda \in [0,1]$ is a random number.

3.3. The Proposed Method

As shown in Figure 1, this paper proposes a two-stage classification model that combines unsupervised and supervised methods. In the first stage, the k-means algorithm is used for unsupervised classification; based on the classification results, a self-organizing neural network is trained in the second stage for fault diagnosis.

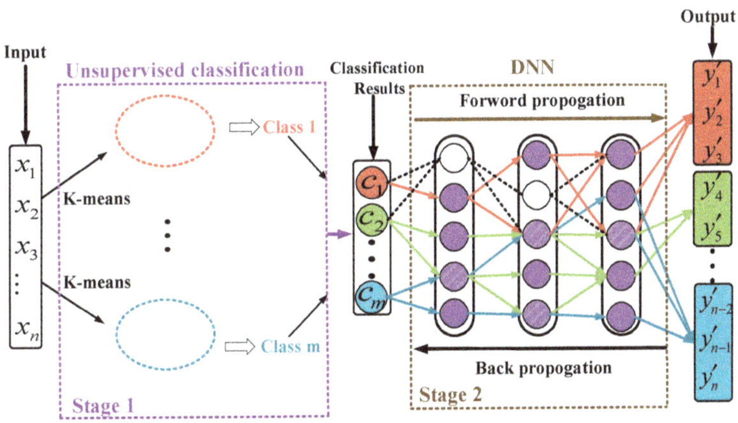

Figure 1. The framework of the proposed model.

(1) Stage 1

K-means is a popular unsupervised clustering algorithm that partitions a dataset into a predefined number of clusters *K*. The goal is to group similar data points together based on their features. In reference to [20], the study generates 120 clusters using the k-means algorithm. Since each cluster may contain one or more fault types, during the subset analysis phase, human experts employ a traditional sub-model based on gas ratios to distinguish between the different fault types within the same cluster. The various sub-models are then combined to form the final diagnostic model. In reference [20], R_1–R_{15} represent the ratios utilized by the human expert to differentiate between the fault types within the same subset.

(2) Stage 2

A fully connected neural network consists of an input layer, multiple hidden layers, and an output layer, with each layer containing multiple neurons. Let the input sample set be $\{x_i, y_i\}_{i=1}^{N}$, where N is the number of samples. The input vector X propagates forward through each hidden layer to the output layer. The output of each hidden layer is $h_i(\mathbf{x}) = g(w_i^T\mathbf{x} + b_i)$, where $w_i \in R^{d_i \times d_{i-1}}$, $b \in R^{d_i}$, d_i are the dimensions of the output vector, and g is the nonlinear activation function. The neural network output $f_W(\mathbf{x})$ can be expressed as

$$f_W(\mathbf{x}) = H_L(H_{L-1}(\cdots(H_1(\mathbf{x})))) \quad (6)$$

where L is the total number of hidden layers, and $W = (W_1, W_2, \ldots, W_l, \ldots, W_L)$ represents the total parameter vector of the neural network.

Fault diagnosis is essentially a multi-class classification problem. Let the total number of classification categories be C. The loss function is computed using cross-entropy, which can be expressed as

$$L_{CE}(W) = -\sum_{k=1,k\neq c}^{C} P(c_c/x) \cdot \log(P(c_k/x)) \quad (7)$$

where C is the total number of classes, $P(c_c/\mathbf{x})$ is the probability that the input x is predicted to y_c belongs to the true class c, and $f_W(x) = P(c_k/x)$ is the probability that the input is predicted to belong to any class k. If $k! = c$, it indicates the probability of misclassification.

To minimize the loss function $L_{CE}(W)$, the backpropagation algorithm is commonly used to reduce the error. The stochastic gradient descent (SGD) method trains the model by randomly sampling small batches of data, which is efficient and converges quickly. Therefore, it is often used to optimize the network parameters W. The parameter update can be expressed as

$$W^n = W^{n-1} - \alpha\nabla_W L_{CE}(W; \mathbf{x}_i^n, y_i^n) \quad (8)$$

where $\mathbf{x}_k^n, y_k^n \in \text{batch}_n = \{(\mathbf{x}_1^n, y_1^n), (\mathbf{x}_2^n, y_2^n), \ldots, (\mathbf{x}_k^n, y_k^n)\}$ represents the loss for the n-th batch $\text{batch}_{n(1 \leq n \leq N_{batches})}$ of training samples, x_i^n and y_i^n are the input vector and the sample class, respectively, $W^t = \{W_l^n\}_{l=1}^{L}$ is the network parameter vector after training on the n-th batch of samples, and α is the adaptive learning rate.

Reference [27] proposed two cascaded DNNs. The first-level DNN is used to partition the original dataset into multiple subsets, where each subset contains data with similar characteristics. In the second level, a DNN subnet is dynamically and adaptively created for each subset, with the selection of nodes and connections optimized to minimize training errors. Inspired by reference [27], in this paper, a self-organizing neural network method is introduced, which adaptively suppresses activated nodes during the training process. This approach dynamically builds the neural network's training parameter set, significantly lowering the model's computational complexity without compromising accuracy. Different appropriate partial networks are chosen for different categories to minimize the overall loss function $L_{CE}(W)$.

From Equation (2), it can be seen that the complexity of the backpropagation algorithm depends on the number of hidden layers and the number of nodes in each layer, i.e., it depends on the weight vector $W = (W_1, W_2, \ldots, W_l, \ldots W_L)$ of the network. Since there is currently no effective method to precisely estimate the required number of layers and neurons in a neural network in advance, the appropriate network configuration must be selected through multiple trial-and-error processes. To reduce the computational complexity of SGD, this paper proposes a novel self-organizing stochastic gradient algorithm. This algorithm can autonomously suppress the activation of inactive neurons as the training process evolves and automatically select the network parameters for backpropagation that need to be updated. This significantly reduces the parameter tuning required for the backpropagation network while ensuring training accuracy. Figure 2 illustrates the process of selecting activated neurons and autonomously constructing the neural network training parameter set in the self-organizing stochastic gradient descent method. The backpropagation network training parameter set is updated in epochs, with each epoch serving as the smallest update cycle. Figure 2a,b show the schematic diagrams of the selected backpropagation training parameter set and activated neurons at epochs $n-1$ and n, respectively. As training progresses, after each epoch, the neural network autonomously decides which inactive neurons to suppress at the beginning of the next epoch. Based on the current set of activated neurons, the backpropagation training parameter set is constructed. The suppressed inactive neurons, along with all the weight parameters connected to them, will not be updated in subsequent training processes. In this paper, whether a neuron is an inactive node is determined by checking if the change in its weights at $epoch_{n-1}$ and $epoch_n$ is smaller than a predefined threshold τ. Specifically, for the i-th hidden node in the l-th layer u_l^i, if the weight distance $d_{l_2} = \left\| w^n_{u_l^i} - w^{n-1}_{u_l^i} \right\|_2$ is smaller than the threshold, then the hidden node is considered inactive.

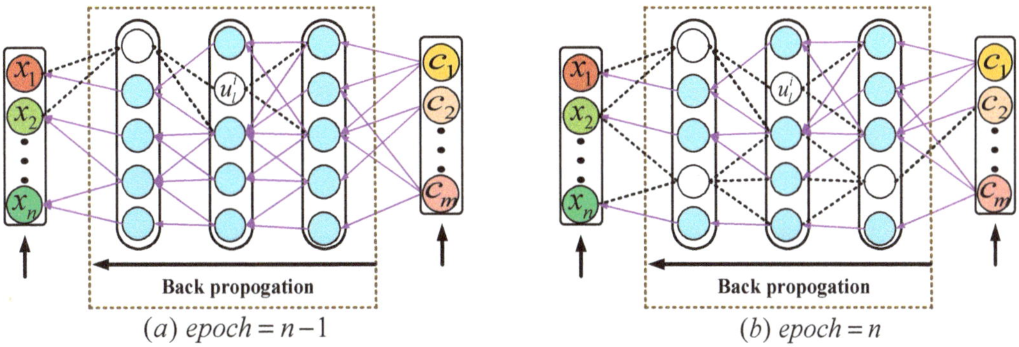

Figure 2. Illustration of autonomous node selection in backpropagation.

3.4. Incremental Learning

Incremental learning allows the model to continuously learn from new data while retaining its ability to generalize from previously seen examples. This is achieved by updating the model incrementally after each new batch of data is processed. Incremental learning with deep learning neural networks (DNNs) is a challenging task due to the complexity of neural networks and the problem of catastrophic forgetting (where the model forgets previously learned knowledge when new data is introduced). Fine-tuning is the most commonly used technique in incremental learning with deep neural networks. In this approach, a pre-trained model is used as a starting point, and the model is fine-tuned with new data. Fine-tuning allows the network to retain useful knowledge learned from previous tasks while adapting to new data. When new data arrive, some layers of the pre-trained model are frozen, and only the last few layers are updated to adapt to the new task or data distribution. However, if the new data differ greatly from the old data, fine-tuning may not be sufficient. To solve this problem, in this paper, we learn new knowledge by activating the previously frozen nodes from the previous step. Specially, for any active hidden units i at the l-th layer u_l^i, if the ℓ_2-distance ($d_{l_2} = \left\| w^t_{u_l^i} - w^{t-1}_{u_l^i} \right\|_2$) between the weight of u_l^i at time t and $t-1$ is larger than the threshold τ, we will randomly activate a frozen node at layer l. After all the actively hidden nodes have been checked, we need to retrain the weights of the new network. At the same time, due to the reasonable initial parameters from last training, the retraining convergence time will be greatly reduced. Unlike reference [27], which adds new neural nodes to the existing network to learn new knowledge, this paper adopts a method of activating existing frozen neural nodes for learning. In comparison, the proposed method features a simpler network structure and significantly lower computational complexity.

3.5. Training and Comparation

In order to highlight the performance of our proposed algorithm, several commonly used regression algorithms are used for performance comparison.

(1) Traditional DNN

To highlight the effect of a self-organizing neural network, we adopt the traditional DNN model to evaluate the performance of the dataset.

(2) Support Vector Regression (SVM)

SVM attempts to minimize the error bound and maximize the margin to get an optimal separating hyper-plane. For the decision function $f(x) = \langle \omega, \phi(x) \rangle + b$, we can get the SVM model by solving the following problem.

$$\begin{aligned} &\text{minimize} \frac{1}{2}\|\omega\|^2 + C\sum_{i=1}^{l}(\xi_i + \xi_i{}') \\ &\text{subject to} \begin{cases} y_i - \langle \omega, x_i \rangle - b \le \varepsilon + \xi_i \\ \langle \omega, x_i \rangle + b - y_i \le \varepsilon + \xi_i{}' \\ \xi_i, \xi_i{}' \ge 0 \end{cases} \end{aligned} \tag{9}$$

where C is the regularization parameter, $\phi(x)$ is the kernel function that maps the input date to a high-dimensional feature space, ε is the error tolerant threshold, ξ_i and $\xi_i{}'$ is the i-th slack variable.

(3) Decision Tree (DT)

DT observes input properties and learns the decision rules using a kind of tree structure to predict the continual output. Decision tree is constructed by recursive partitioning that starts from the root node (top node) and splits it into left and right child nodes. These child nodes will be further split themselves until the leaves are pure, i.e., leaf nodes. Each non-leaf node represents a test on a feature attribute. Each branch represents the output of this feature attribute in a certain value range, and each leaf node stores the output variable. The RMSE will be applied as a loss function to get the best division.

(4) Random Forest (RF)

RF is an ensemble learning algorithm that combines multiple decision trees for regression. Compared with DT, RF has better generalization performance and is less sensitive to outliers. The operation of RFR is to construct several decision trees during training and then output the average value as the prediction of all trees.

3.6. Computational Complexity Analysis

The computational complexity of a deep neural network (DNN) is generally represented by the number of floating-point operations (FLOPs) required for the forward propagation process. For each layer of a fully connected neural network, the FLOPs can be expressed as $F_i = (2I_i - 1) \cdot O_i$, where I_i and O_i represent the input and output dimensions of the i-th layer, respectively. For a fully connected neural network with L hidden layers, the forward propagation computational complexity is expressed as

$$FLOPs_{forward} = N_{epo}\sum_{i=1}^{L}(2I_i - 1) \cdot O_i \tag{10}$$

where N_{epo} is the number of epochs at convergence.

For a neural network with a symmetric structure in both forward and backward propagation, the computational complexity of backward propagation is the same as that of forward propagation. If some neurons are inactive during backward propagation (i.e., their gradients are set to 0), the computational complexity of backward propagation is directly proportional to the total number of active neurons.

4. Experiment

4.1. Dataset

The proposed model was evaluated on the dataset provided by reference [20], which contains 849 labeled DGA data. It utilized a dataset comprising gas concentration measurements from dissolved gases in transformer oil, which are key indicators of faults in power transformers. The dataset includes six main fault types, including low energy discharge (D_1), high energy discharge (D_2), low thermal fault (PD), partial discharge (T_3), medium thermal fault (T_2), and high thermal fault (T_1). The dataset specifically focuses on the gas ratios, including hydrogen (H_2), methane (CH_4), ethane (C_2H_6), ethylene (C_2H_4), and acetylene (C_2H_2), which are crucial for diagnosing transformer faults. In order to better capture the data features and improve diagnostic performance, like in reference [20], this paper has generated seven new features based on the original dataset. Table 1 presents the seven input feature vectors used in this paper. The importance and function of each vector are described below:

Table 1. Seven new features used in this paper.

New Features	Descriptions
$X = [X(i)]\ i \in [1,5]$	$X(i) = \frac{C_i}{\sum_{j=1}^{5} C_j}$ where C_i and C_j represent the concentrations of H_2, CH_4, C_2H_6, C_2H_4, and C_2H_2, respectively.
$X = [R_1, R_2, R_3]$	$R_1 = \frac{CH_4}{H_2}, R_2 = \frac{C_2H_2}{C_2H_4}, R_3 = \frac{C_2H_4}{C_2H_6}$
$X = [R_1, R_2, R_3]$	$R_1 = \frac{C_2H_2}{C_2H_4}, R_2 = \frac{C_2H_4+C_2H_6}{C_2H_2+H_2}, R_3 = \frac{C\ H_4+C_2H_2}{C_2H_4}$
$X = [R_1, R_2, R_3, R_4, R_5]$	$R_1 = \frac{H_2}{H_{2\ \mathrm{lim}}}, R_2 = \frac{C\ H_4}{C\ H_{4\ \mathrm{lim}}}, R_3 = \frac{C_2H_6}{C_2H_{6\ \mathrm{lim}}}, R_4 = \frac{C_2H_4}{C_2H_{4\ \mathrm{lim}}}, R_5 = \frac{C_2H_2}{C_2H_{2\ \mathrm{lim}}}$
$X = [R_1, R_2, R_3, R_4, R_5]$	$R_1 = \frac{H_2}{C_{MAX}}, R_2 = \frac{C\ H_4}{C_{MAX}}, R_3 = \frac{C_2H_6}{C_{MAX}}, R_4 = \frac{C_2H_4}{C_{MAX}}, R_5 = \frac{C_2H_2}{C_{MAX}}$
$X = [CH_4, C_2H_4, C_2H_2]$	$X(i) = \frac{C_i}{\sum_{j=1}^{3} C_j}$, where C_i and C_j represent the concentrations of CH_4, C_2H_4, and C_2H_2, respectively.
$X = [R_1, R_2, R_3]$	$R_1 = \frac{C_2H_2}{C_2H_4}, R_2 = \frac{C_2H_6+C_2H_4}{C_2H_2+H_2}, R_3 = \frac{C\ H_4+C_2H_2}{C_2H_4}$

Figure 3 shows the proportion of each fault type in the overall dataset. From the figure, it can be observed that there is a severe data imbalance between the PD (partial discharge) class and the other classes, which could significantly affect the training of the diagnostic model. As in [20], the data collected were randomly divided into two datasets: a test set and a training set with a 70:30 training-to-test ratio. Moreover, the IEC TC10 database containing 117 labeled DGA data [28] will be used for incremental learning.

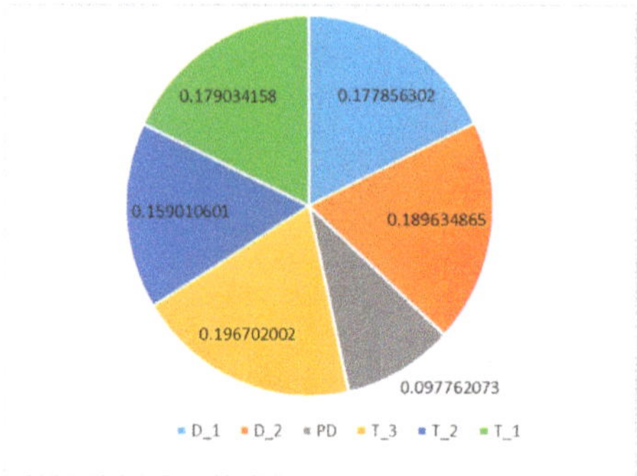

Figure 3. The proportion of each fault type in the overall dataset.

4.2. Evaluation Metrics

The diagnostic performance of the system is evaluated based on the accuracy of case diagnosis. In this paper, the diagnosis accuracy rate (DAR) is used to evaluate the performance of the diagnostic system. It is calculated by the ratio of correctly classified samples (N_{da}) to the total number of samples (N_{all}), i.e., $\frac{N_{da}}{N_{all}}$. A higher accuracy rate indicates better system performance. Additionally, considering only diagnostic accuracy is insufficient to assess the algorithm's performance on imbalanced data, so this paper introduces a confusion matrix to evaluate the algorithm's performance on imbalanced data by comparing the mapping probabilities between the predicted results and the true values. Each column of the confusion matrix represents the predicted class, while each row represents the true class, as shown in Figure 4. C_i, D_i, and $P(C_i/D_i)$ represent the true class label, the predicted class label, and the corresponding probability, respectively.

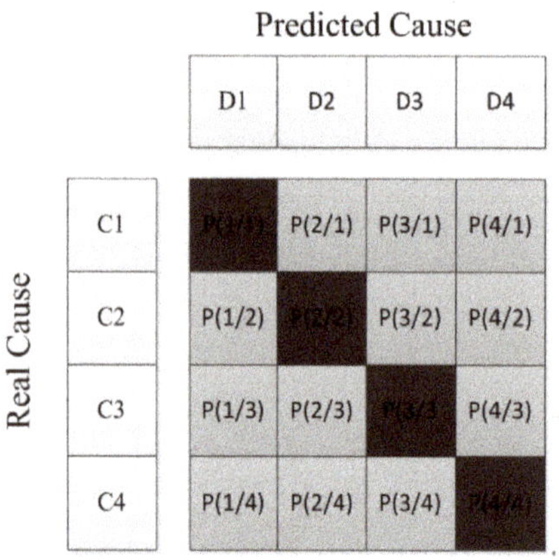

Figure 4. Confusion matrix.

4.3. Experiment Setting

To compare the performance of our proposed algorithm with traditional classification methods, several algorithms implemented by sklearn packet, traditional DNN, SVM, DT, and RF, are used. The output of the model is the RMSE estimated by the predicted value and actual output. The parameters of other commonly used classification algorithms were optimized with the grid search method. The optimal parameter settings of the models are shown in Tables 2 and 3.

Table 2. Parameter settings for DNN.

Parameters	Values
Number of nodes per layer	(100,100,6)
Activation function	ReLU
α	$0.01 * 0.5^{epoch/10}$
$epoch_{max}$	100
$N_{batches}$	100
τ	0.001
m	6

Table 3. The optimal parameter settings of other classification algorithms.

Model Type	Parameters	Iterations
SVM	C = 50, σ = 0.01	100
DT	max_depth = 8	100
RF	min_samples_split = 5, n_estimators = 100	100

4.4. Results and Comparation

(1) The results of data balancing

To further understand the differences between the ADASYN and SMOTE methods in terms of data balancing, Figure 5 presents 3D scatter plots of a portion of the dataset after processing with these two methods. The 3D scatter plot of the original training set is shown in Figure 5a, while the 3D scatter plots of the data after balancing with SMOTE and ADASYN are shown in Figure 5b,c, respectively. In Figure 5b, the SMOTE algorithm generates the same number of new samples for each minority class sample, but it does not consider the neighboring samples from other classes, which results in some overlapping of the generated new samples (highlighted in the black dashed box). In Figure 5c, the dataset generated by the ADASYN algorithm not only balances the data distribution but also pays more attention to the difficult-to-learn samples in the minority class. Compared to Figure 5b, ADASYN in Figure 5c reduces the amount of additional noise and overlapping samples, thus performing better than SMOTE.

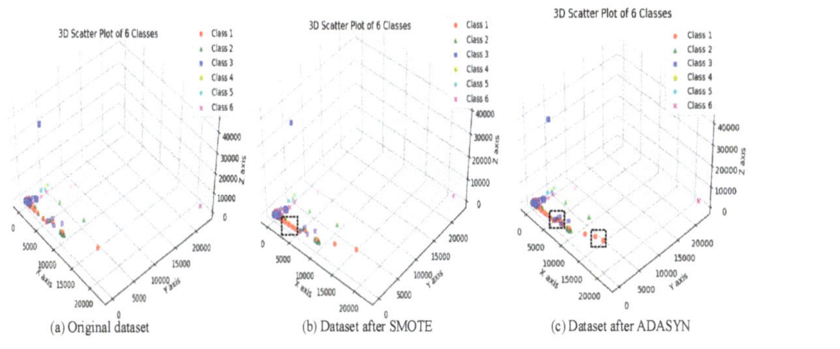

Figure 5. 3D scatter plots.

(2) The results of the proposed method

In stage 1, six clusters are generated using the k-means algorithm. The role of classification is to group samples with similar features together, so that in stage 2, different sub-networks can be selected and trained for different classes, thereby improving training accuracy and convergence speed. Based on the classification results, a self-organizing neural network is trained in the second stage for fault diagnosis. Traditional DNNs train samples with different features together, and the network structure and connections between hidden nodes are fixed. However, the significant differences between sample features can not only lead to large training errors but also make the training convergence process difficult due to the large number of neurons and network connections in DNNs. To address these issues, this paper adopts a differentiated dynamic sub-network selection training method to improve fitting accuracy and reduce the overall regression error of the model. This method primarily targets each classified sub-dataset, dynamically selects neurons, and constructs sub-DNN networks to minimize the overall loss function. Figure 6 shows the convergence process of the model on the training and testing sets. It can be seen that when the epoch is greater than 40, the curve changes smoothly and tends to converge, with an accuracy rate maintained at around 92%.

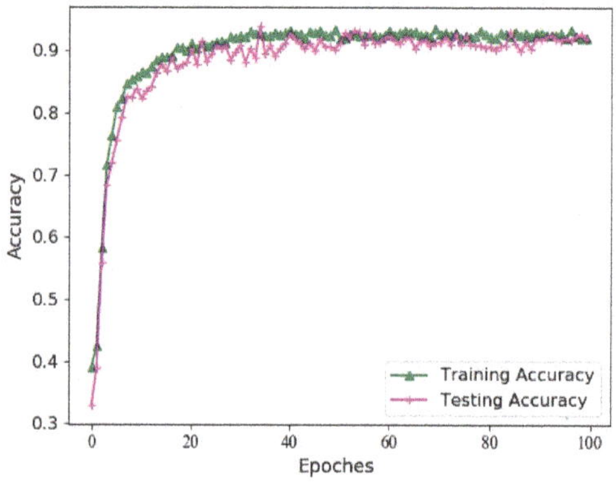

Figure 6. The convergence process of the model.

To visualize the suppression effect of the proposed algorithm on inactive nodes during training, Figure 7 shows the curve of the number of activated nodes in each layer of the neural network as the epoch increases. As can be seen in the figure, when epoch > 20, the number of activated neurons in each layer gradually decreases. When 20 < epoch < 30, nearly half of the neuron activations in layer 1 and layer 2 are suppressed, significantly reducing the number of network parameters that need to be updated. When epoch > 40, all neuron nodes are suppressed, resulting in no parameters needing to be updated, and the backpropagation complexity becomes zero, causing the training curve to converge.

Table 4 presents the confusion matrix of the proposed algorithm on the original dataset. The diagonal elements of the confusion matrix represent the number of correctly classified instances for each category, while the off-diagonal elements indicate the number of instances misclassified by the classifier. As shown in the table, the proposed algorithm achieves a high diagnostic accuracy of approximately 92.12%, which is close to the final convergence accuracy depicted in Figure 6. To verify that data augmentation techniques can improve model performance, Table 5 presents the confusion matrix of the proposed algorithm on the test set after augmenting the training data using the ADASYN algorithm. As shown in Table 5, after using the data augmentation technique, the number of misdiagnosed PD cases decreased from 6 to 2. Although the proportion of other categories misclassified as the PD category increased, the overall diagnostic accuracy improved. Specifically, the ADASYN data augmentation technique increased the accuracy from 92.12% to 93.7%. In addition, the test accuracies achieved using the SMOTE and random sampling data balancing methods are 92.91% and 84.25%, respectively.

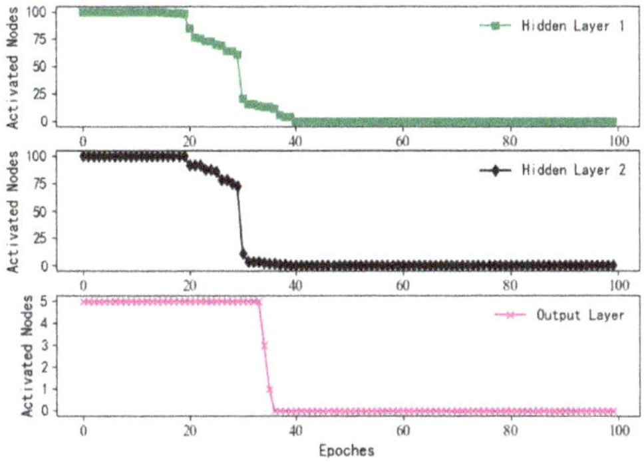

Figure 7. Activated nodes vs. epochs.

Table 4. The confusion matrix on original dataset.

True \ Predicted	D_1	D_2	PD	T_3	T_2	T_1
D_1	43	2				
D_2	2	45	1			
PD		2	19	4		
T_3			2	45		3
T_2		1		1	37	1
T_1					1	45

Table 5. The confusion matrix on dataset after ADASYN.

True \ Predicted	D_1	D_2	PD	T_3	T_2	T_1
D_1	42	1	2			
D_2	2	43	3			
PD		2	23			
T_3		1	3	45		1
T_2					40	
T_1					1	45

Incremental learning allows the model to continuously learn from new data while retaining its ability to generalize from previously seen examples. However, if the new data differs greatly from the old data, fine-tuning may not be sufficient. To solve this problem, in this paper, we learn new knowledge by activating the previously frozen nodes from the previous step. Specially, if the weight of u_l^i at time t and $t-1$ is larger than the threshold τ, the node i at layer l (u_l^i) will be activated. The IEC TC10 database containing 117 labeled DGA data [24] is used for incremental learning. Table 5 presents the sensitivity analysis of threshold τ to test accuracy. As shown in Table 6, as the threshold τ decreases, the number of activated nodes in each layer increases to facilitate learning new knowledge. When the threshold τ is reduced to 0.0001, the DAR reaches 100%, with all samples correctly diagnosed. However, when the threshold is further reduced to 0.00001, the DAR remains at 100%, but the number of activated nodes increases, leading to higher computational complexity. Therefore, the threshold is set to 0.0001 in this paper.

Table 6. The sensitivity analysis of threshold τ to test accuracy.

τ	0.01	0.001	0.0001	0.00001
DAR	94.01%	98.29%	100%	100%
Number of activated nodes in the k-th layer	layer 1: 42 layer 2: 37	layer 1: 65 layer 2: 52	layer 1: 82 layer 2: 69	layer 1: 94 layer 2: 82

(3) Performance comparations

To highlight the superiority of the proposed algorithm, we compared its performance with existing methods on the two datasets mentioned in the paper, as shown in Figure 8. The figure demonstrates that the proposed algorithm achieves the highest diagnostic accuracy, indicating its effectiveness and potential for further application and deployment in real-world scenarios. Although traditional DNNs can achieve relatively high diagnostic accuracy, the algorithm proposed in this paper features significantly lower computational complexity.

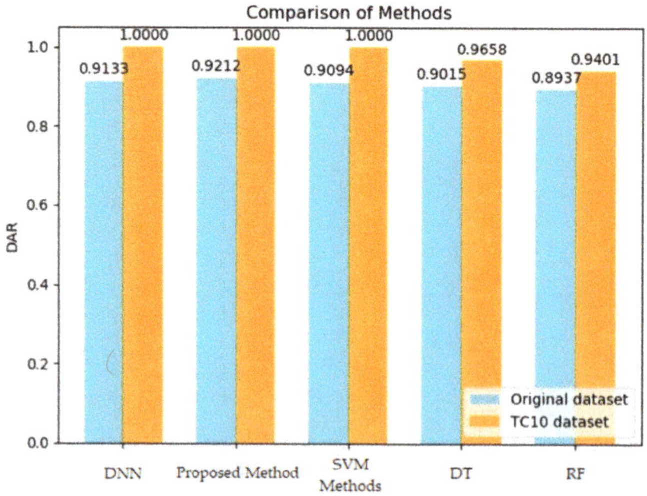

Figure 8. Performance comparation.

5. Conclusions

In conclusion, this paper proposes a novel fault diagnosis method for power transformers that combines data augmentation, clustering-based classification, and self-organizing neural networks with incremental learning. The ADASYN-based data augmentation effectively addresses data imbalance, improving diagnostic accuracy to 93.7%, while the two-stage classification framework enhances training precision and convergence speed. The dynamic optimization of the self-organizing neural network significantly reduces computational complexity, and the incremental learning mechanism ensures adaptability to new data while maintaining generalization. Comparative analysis demonstrates the superiority of the proposed method over traditional approaches, highlighting its potential for real-world deployment in power transformer fault diagnosis and grid reliability enhancement. The proposed method can be implemented as part of an online monitoring and diagnostic system, leveraging data collected from sensors installed on transformers, providing actionable insights for predictive maintenance and operational decision-making.

Author Contributions: Conceptualization, S.L. and Z.H.; methodology, S.L.; software, S.L.; validation, S.L.; formal analysis, S.L.; writing—original draft preparation, Z.X.; writing—review and editing, Z.X. and Z.H.; supervision, Z.H. All authors have read and agreed to the published version of the manuscript.

Funding: This work was funded by the General Program of National Natural Science Foundation of China (Grant No. 52177083 and 62001166) and by Major Science and Technology Projects in Hebei Province (Grant No. 23281701Z).

Data Availability Statement: The original contributions presented in this study are included in the article. Further inquiries can be directed to the corresponding author.

Conflicts of Interest: The authors declare no conflicts of interest.

References

1. Hossain, M.S.A.; Das, S.K.; Ghosh, A. Transformer fault diagnosis using vibration analysis and machine learning. *IEEE Trans. Power Deliv.* **2020**, *35*, 681–688.
2. Lee, J.M.; Choi, Y.H.; Lee, H.S. Application of machine learning algorithms for transformer fault diagnosis: A review. *IEEE Access* **2020**, *8*, 90873–90887.
3. Rahman, R.S.H.I.A.; Khaleed, H.M.G.D.A.; Krishnan, M.N.S.R.K. A study of transformer fault diagnosis using online monitoring and diagnostic systems. *IEEE Trans. Ind. Electron.* **2014**, *61*, 2617–2625.
4. Kumar, F.C.S.R.N.; Saravanan, P.M.G.R.; Sharma, P.B.S.R.H.K. Partial discharge detection and fault diagnosis in power transformers using wavelet transform. *IEEE Trans. Dielectr. Electr. Insul.* **2012**, *19*, 212–218.
5. Goh, R.S.; Tan, R.K.A.; Khilnani, A.G. Fault diagnosis of power transformers using advanced signal processing techniques. *J. Electr. Eng. Technol.* **2017**, *12*, 465–474.
6. Williams, B.J.; El-Sayed, R.A. Impact of transformer failures on utility performance and economy. *IEEE Trans. Power Deliv.* **2008**, *23*, 1283–1289.
7. Mark, P.B.G.; Patel, R.K.; Agarwal, P.B.S. Unsupervised learning for transformer fault detection: K-means clustering-based approach. *IEEE Trans. Power Syst.* **2018**, *33*, 2310–2321.
8. Parsa, S.M.; Kazemi, A.M.S.H.; Zadeh, H.B. A comprehensive review on the diagnostic techniques for fault detection and condition monitoring of transformers. *Int. J. Electr. Power Energy Syst.* **2012**, *43*, 1–10.
9. McDonnell, M.J.S.; Goulbourne, M.P.E. Evaluation of insulating oil and gas samples for transformer fault diagnosis. *IEEE Trans. Power Deliv.* **1998**, *13*, 1155–1161.
10. Hechifa, A.; Labiod, C.; Lakehal, A.; Nanfak, A.; Mansour, D.-E.A. A Novel Graphical Method for Interpretating Dissolved Gases and Fault Diagnosis in Power Transformer Based on Dynamique Axes in Circular Form. *IEEE Trans. Power Deliv.* **2024**, *39*, 3186–3198. [CrossRef]
11. Xie, S.J.; Zhao, Y.H.; Jin, Q.X. Application of infrared thermography for transformer fault diagnosis. *IEEE Trans. Power Deliv.* **2007**, *22*, 450–457.
12. Lee, C.M.; Lee, J.H.; Kim, J.G. Transformer fault detection and diagnosis using online monitoring. *IEEE Trans. Ind. Electron.* **2011**, *58*, 1214–1221.
13. Al-Dulaimi, S.A.; Raza, S.R.J.; Khokhar, A.Z. Condition monitoring and fault diagnosis of power transformers using vibration and temperature data. *J. Electr. Eng. Technol.* **2020**, *15*, 1703–1712.
14. Ezzat, H.M.; El-Gohary, H.M.; Hamed, A.R. Fault detection in power transformers using acoustic and vibration signal analysis. *IEEE Trans. Power Deliv.* **2020**, *35*, 584–591.
15. Zhang, Z.; Liu, H.; Li, Y. Transformer fault diagnosis using electrical data and machine learning techniques. *IEEE Trans. Smart Grid* **2020**, *11*, 2048–2057.
16. Qiao, L.; Zhang, X.; He, S. Visual Defect Detection and Analysis of Digital Robot Based on Virtual Artificial Intelligence Algorithm. *Procedia Comput. Sci.* **2024**, *243*, 601–609.
17. Wang, J.; Xu, G.; Yan, F.; Wang, J.; Wang, Z. Defect transformer: An efficient hybrid transformer architecture for surface defect detection. *arXiv* **2022**, arXiv:2207.08319.
18. Zhang, J.; Liu, T.; Wang, X. A machine learning approach to fault diagnosis of power transformers using dissolved gas analysis. *IEEE Trans. Power Deliv.* **2019**, *35*, 1784–1792.
19. Xiao, L.; Yang, C.; Zhao, J. Fault diagnosis of power transformers based on decision tree algorithm using dissolved gas analysis data. *Electr. Eng. J.* **2020**, *51*, 2321–2330.
20. Nanfak, A.; Hechifa, A.; Eke, S.; Lakehal, A.; Kom, C.H.; Ghoneim, S.S. A combined technique for power transformer fault diagnosis based on k-means clustering and support vector machine. *IET Nanodielectr.* **2024**, *7*, 175–187. [CrossRef]

21. Liu, Z.; Wang, J.; Zhang, H. Artificial neural network-based transformer fault diagnosis using dissolved gas analysis. *Int. J. Electr. Power Energy Syst.* **2018**, *102*, 73–80.
22. Zhang, Y.; Li, X.; Cheng, X. Deep learning approaches for fault diagnosis of power transformers using dissolved gas analysis. *IEEE Access* **2020**, *8*, 12345–12356.
23. Wang, C.; Tian, B.; Yang, J.; Jie, H.; Chang, Y.; Zhao, Z. Neural-transformer: A brain-inspired lightweight mechanical fault diagnosis method under noise. *Reliab. Eng. Syst. Saf.* **2024**, *251*, 110409. [CrossRef]
24. Li, M.; Chen, X.; Yu, Y. Hybrid deep learning model for transformer fault diagnosis based on time-series dissolved gas analysis. *IEEE Trans. Ind. Inform.* **2021**, *17*, 3971–3980. [CrossRef]
25. Chen, L.; Zhang, Q.; Wu, S. Data augmentation techniques for improving machine learning performance in transformer fault diagnosis based on dissolved gas analysis. *IEEE Trans. Power Syst.* **2017**, *32*, 3072–3080.
26. He, H.; Garcia, E.A. Learning from imbalanced data. *IEEE Trans. Knowl. Data Eng.* **2009**, *21*, 1263–1284.
27. Liu, X.; Chuai, G.; Wang, X.; Xu, Z.; Gao, W. QoE Assessment Model Based on Continuous Deep Learning for Video in Wireless Networks. *IEEE Trans. Mob. Comput.* **2023**, *22*, 3619–3633. [CrossRef]
28. Duval, M.; de Pabla, A. Interpretation of gas-in-oil analysis using new IEC publication 60599 and IEC TC10 databases. *IEEE Electr. Insul. Mag.* **2001**, *17*, 31–41. [CrossRef]

electronics

Article

A Hardware Trojan Diagnosis Method for Gate-Level Netlists Based on Graph Theory

Hongxu Gao [1], Guangxi Zhai [1], Zeyu Li [1,2,*], Jia Zhou [3], Xiang Li [4] and Quan Wang [1]

1 School of Computer Science and Technology, Xidian University, Xi'an 710071, China; hx_gao@stu.xidian.edu.cn (H.G.); gxzhai@stu.xidian.edu.cn (G.Z.); qwang@xidian.edu.cn (Q.W.)
2 School of Computer Science and Technology, North University of China, Taiyuan 030051, China
3 School of Microelectronics, Northwestern Polytechnical University, Xi'an 710071, China; zhoujia1989@nwpu.edu.cn
4 School of Decision Sciences, The Hang Seng University of Hong Kong, Hong Kong 999077, China; p233343@hsu.edu.hk
* Correspondence: 20230101@nuc.edu.cn; Tel.: +86-1500-343-9992

Abstract: With the increasing complexity of integrated circuit design, the threat of a hardware Trojan (HT) is becoming more and more prominent. At present, the research mainly focuses on the detection of HTs, but the amount of research on the diagnosis of HTs is very small. The number of existing HT diagnosis methods is generally completed by detecting the HT nodes in the netlist. The main reason is the lack of consideration of the integrity of HTs, so the diagnosis accuracy is low. Based on the above reason, this paper proposes two implanted node search algorithms named layer-by-layer difference search (LDS) and layer-by-layer grouping difference search (LGDS). The LDS algorithm can greatly reduce the search time, and the LGDS algorithm can solve the problem of input node disorder. The two methods greatly reduce the number of nodes sorting and comparing, and therefore the time complexity is lower. Moreover, the relevance between implanted nodes is taken into account to improve the diagnosis rate. We completed experiments on an HT diagnosis; the HT implantation example is from Trust-Hub. The experimental results are shown as follows: (1) The average true positive rate (TPR) of the diagnosis using KNN, RF, or SVM with the LDS or LGDS algorithm is more than 93%, and the average true negative rate (TNR) is 100%. (2) The average proportion of implanted nodes obtained by the LDS or LGDS algorithm is more than 97%. The proposed method has a lower time complexity compared with other existing diagnosis methods, and the diagnosis time is shortened by nearly 75%.

Keywords: gate-level hardware Trojan; graph theory; diagnosis

1. Introduction

Integrated circuits play a vital role in modern technology and industry. They are the core component of electronic devices, covering applications in various fields from smartphones to computers, automobiles and industrial control systems, and more [1]. However, integrated circuits injected with a hardware Trojan (HT) may lead to the following hazards: information leakage, functional damage, remote control, and economic loss [2–4]. These problems seriously endanger the security of individuals, enterprises, and countries. Therefore, it is essential to ensure the security and reliability of integrated circuits.

Nowadays, there have been many different HT-detection methods. Formal verification [5,6] is a logic verification method based on an algorithm, but it needs a gold netlist for comparison and has poor scalability. Logic testing [7,8] activates the HT by adding test vectors. However, the attacker can escape the test by adding rare trigger conditions. Side-channel analysis [9–11] detects an HT with the help of electrical parameters such as delay, power consumption, and electromagnetics during circuit operation. Based on reverse engineering [12–16], it is a kind of method in destructive detection, mainly through a series of reverse engineering to restore the design and details of the circuit. There are also some methods that combine machine learning for an HT detection [1,17–19], and these methods tend to have high detection rates.

Most of the existing HT-detection methods only detect whether there is an HT in the circuit and do not diagnose where the HT is implanted in the circuit [20,21]. However, HT diagnosis is also very important in integrated circuits. When a circuit is very large, just detecting it without diagnosing it may cause relevant personnel to spend a lot of time on comprehensive inspection and modification. The benefits brought by HT diagnosis mainly include the following aspects: (1) HT diagnosis can help designers to accurately find the infected part of the circuit, avoiding the overall inspection and modification of the whole circuit, reducing the time-to-market and cost. (2) HT diagnosis can help to exclude false detection and avoid false suspicion and the processing of normal circuit parts. (3) HT diagnosis can help designers understand the related mechanisms of an HT and improve defense strategies [22]. The deficiency of current diagnosis methods is the lack of consideration of the integrity of HTs, so there is a problem of low diagnosis accuracy.

In order to further improve the accuracy of gate-level HT diagnosis, this paper proposes a layer-by-layer difference search (LDS) and layer-by-layer grouping difference search (LGDS) algorithm based on [17]. Different from [17], this paper proposes two implanted node search algorithms, which reduce the amount of node sorting and comparing to reduce the time complexity. The specific steps are shown in Figure 1.

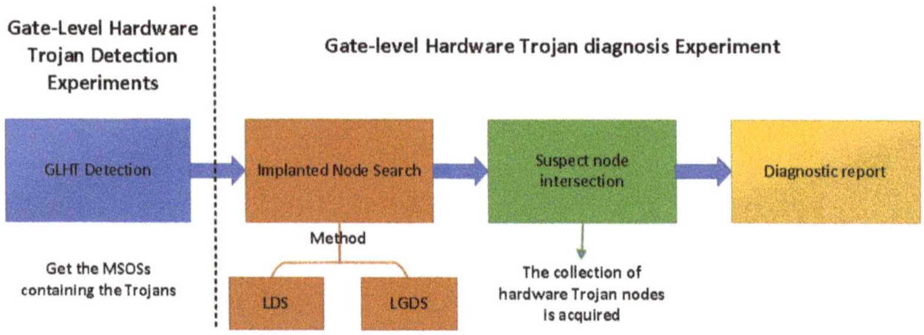

Figure 1. Gate-level HT diagnosis method based on graph theory.

The contributions of this paper are summarized as follows:

(1) In this paper, we propose a new method for an HT diagnosis based on graph theory.
(2) The LDS algorithm is proposed, which takes into account the hierarchical relationship of HT load nodes in the netlist; the LGDS algorithm is proposed to solve the problem of out-of-order input nodes.
(3) The proposed method reduces the number of non-implanted nodes and improves the diagnostic accuracy. Moreover, the amount of node sorting and comparing is reduced, which decreases the time complexity.
(4) Experimental results show that the proposed method has lower time complexity. The average true positive rate (TPR) for diagnosis is higher than 93% and the true negative rate (TNR) is 100%. Compared with other existing diagnostic methods, the proposed method has a higher diagnostic accuracy and lower time complexity.

The structure of this paper is divided as follows: Section 2 discusses the related work on HT detection and diagnosis. Section 3 shows the research on gate-level HT diagnosis. Section 4 presents the experimental process and analyzes the results. Section 5 concludes this paper.

2. Related Work

In the early stage, people focus on HT-detection technology, which is the most direct way to deal with the security threats caused by HTs. Ludwig et al. [13] designed a framework that introduces a data validation technique based on physical layout confirmation to evaluate the results of reverse engineering both qualitatively and quantitatively, taking into account all possible sources of error. The proposed framework can avoid the natural error of reverse engineering to adversely affect HT detection. Banga et al. [14] proposed an HT-detection method based on circuit region division and power consumption characteristic measurements. This method can be regarded as the first method based on electrical properties. Rajendran et al. [15] proposed a non-intrusive trusted design technique for detecting HTs by analyzing frequency variations of ring oscillators. The proposed technique is capable of detecting HTs implanted in the integrated circuit as a whole or locally in the presence of process variations and measurement errors. While proposing the concept of an HT for the first time, Agrawal et al. [23] also designed a method to construct side channel information such as the power, temperature, and electromagnetic profile as the circuit fingerprint through noise modeling by referring to the principle of side channel cryptanalysis for the first time. Wolff et al. [24] first proposed the method based on a logic test. They first analyzed and investigated the HT effect, then expounded the mechanism of HT detection based on the frequency analysis of rare signal values, and finally designed the generation program of the input trigger vector and HT test vector to detect the HT effect.

Recently, some researchers have begun to pay attention to HT diagnosis techniques that can locate the location of HT implantation or show the extent of HT implantation. Du et al. [18] divided the circuit into sectors and extracted HT-related features from each sector. The label of the sector is used to predict whether it contains an HT during diagnosis. This method can report which sector the HT is implanted in, but the size of the sector is uncertain and there may be overlapping areas between different sectors. Wang et al. [17] divided the circuit into multiple Maximum Single-Output Submodules (MSOSs). MSOSs refer to strongly connected components composed of nodes and their corresponding cells. This method can ensure the uniqueness of the partition and avoid the existence of common strongly connected components among any MSOS.

Although the diagnosis of [17] is simple and effective, the execution time complexity is high. In addition, it does not consider the relevance between implanted nodes, so there may be many non-implanted nodes in the execution result.

3. Gate-Level HT Diagnosis Based on Graph Theory

At present, most of the HT diagnosis methods lack the consideration of the integrity of an HT. On this basis, the gate-level HT diagnosis method based on graph theory is proposed in this paper. This section mainly describes the experimental process, graph theory analysis, and algorithm design.

3.1. Complete Experimental Process

Figure 1 represents the flowchart of the proposed gate-level HT diagnosis method, which is mainly as follows:

(1) The detection method of [17] was used to complete the detection of an HT and obtain the MSOSs containing an HT. If no HT is included, the diagnosis is terminated. The MSOS is obtained by the knowledge of graph theory. The MSOS is composed of a number of nodes and their corresponding units of strongly connected components. Then, the HT-related features in MSOSs are calculated and counted, and the hyperparameters in the machine learning algorithm are adjusted by the cross-validation method. We train a specific supervised learning model using the optimized hyperparameters. Finally, the MSOS containing HTs can be obtained through the trained model.

(2) Find the additional implanted nodes of the target netlist relative to the gold netlist using the LDS or LGDS algorithm. The additional implanted nodes are also called difference nodes. After removing these difference nodes and their corresponding cells, the target netlist should satisfy graph isomorphism with the gold netlist as much as possible.

(3) The MSOSs obtained in step (1) and the implanted nodes obtained in step (2) are intersected.
(4) The obtained node intersection is then the HT node set.

The difference between our method and [17] lies in the second step of the implanted node search. In [17], the implanted node search based on a breadth-first comparison is adopted, which has the characteristics of a simple principle and easy implementation. However, it does not take into account the relevance of implanted nodes, so there may be some non-implanted nodes or even some actual implanted nodes in the execution results. This paper adds two different algorithms based on it, as shown in Figure 2. Our method searches according to the concept of layers, taking into account the relevance between nodes, and the innovation is that the method design is different. The main steps are as follows:

(1) LDS or LGDS: by comparing the nodes in the target netlist and the gold netlist layer by layer, the difference nodes in each layer are found; that is, the load-tamper node pair.
(2) Input-side breadth-first comparison: for each load-tamper node pair, the breadth-first comparison technique of [17] is used with the load node and tamper node as the root, respectively.
(3) Implanted nodes search based on breadth-first comparison: taking the expansion set of payload nodes and the expansion set of tampered nodes as input, the implanted nodes search method based on a breadth-first comparison is executed to find the implanted nodes.

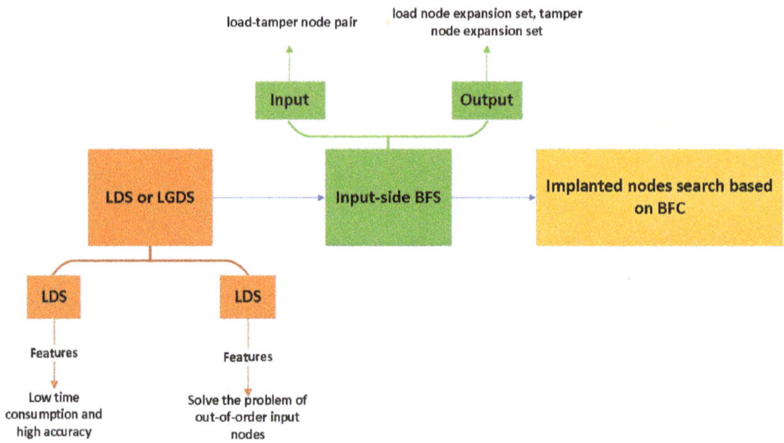

Figure 2. Implanted node search method based on LDS or LGDS.

3.2. Graph Theory Analysis

A netlist is a circuit graph composed of nodes and their corresponding units, which can be regarded as a weighted graph in graph theory to a certain extent. Figures 3 and 4 show the circuit diagram and its corresponding weighted graph. Nodes are vertices, cells are edges, and the type of the cell is the weight of the edge. The two nodes corresponding to cells T4 and G4 in Figure 3 are a load-tamper node pair. The node corresponding to unit T4 after the HT is implanted (i.e., the load node) and the node corresponding to unit G4 before the HT is implanted (i.e., the tamper node) are in the same layer, and they are the only pair of different nodes in their layer (i.e., difference nodes). Generally, HT features are not directly reflected in graph elements, but need to be mapped to specific vertex search conditions. Therefore, the key to study the graph theory of HTs is to determine the vertex search condition. The diagnosis method studied in this paper exploits a simple corollary: if the netlist does not contain HTs originally, but does after the addition of a specific module, then the added module must contain HTs. Therefore, the proposed method searches for additional implanted nodes of the target netlist with respect to the gold netlist. The corresponding vertex search criteria are present in the target netlist, but not in the gold netlist.

The method studied in this paper also addresses the problem of non-unique submodule partitioning schemes. We use the knowledge of graph theory: the MSOS partition is exactly unique. This shows that there exists only one scheme for partitioning MSOSs for any netlist. This is equivalent to no common strongly connected component existing between any two distinct MSOSs. The uniqueness of the partition can avoid the following situations: two submodules contain HT nodes, but the degree of influence of HT nodes on the characteristics of the two is too different, resulting in one submodule being judged as "with HT" and the other submodule being judged as "without HT".

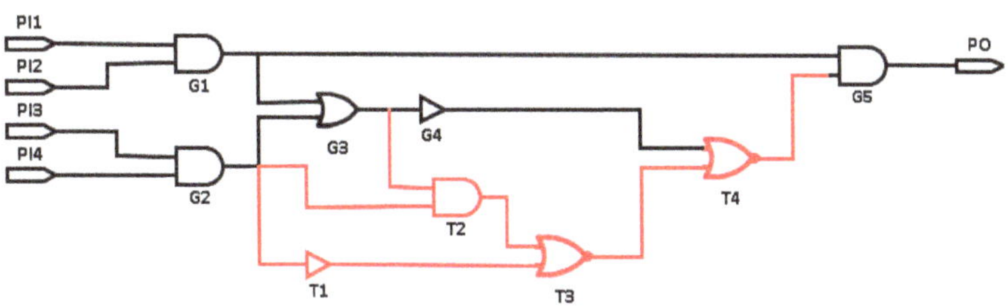

Figure 3. Example netlist circuit diagram.

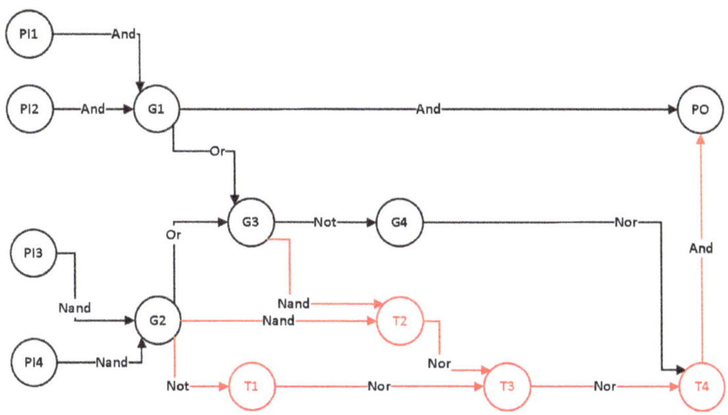

Figure 4. A weighted graph of a netlist circuit.

3.3. Gate-Level HT Implantation Methods

According to the circuit diagram structure, the nodes contained in gate-level HTs are divided into the following three categories in this paper:

(1) Load node: the main output node of the HT (such as the node corresponding to the T4 unit in Figure 3), masquerading as the input node of a specific node in the host netlist, so as to complete the HT function.

(2) Internal node: the internal node of the HT (such as the node corresponding to cell T3 in Figure 3) does not act as the input node or output node of any node in the host netlist.

(3) Trigger node: the secondary input node of the HT (such as the nodes corresponding to the T1, T2, and T4 cells in Figure 3) masquerades the output node of the host primary netlist-specific node (which can also be regarded as the primary input node of the HT) to activate the HT function.

Load node implantation mode: (a) A specific input node that replaces a specific node in the host netlist with a load node. (b) Replace a specific primary output node in the host netlist with a load node. (c) Add the load node as an additional input node for a specific node in the host netlist. (d) Add the load node as an additional primary output node for the host netlist. Among them, the two ways a and b essentially replace a specific node in the host netlist as a load node, and the replaced node can be used as the input node of the trigger node. In essence, in both ways, c and d add extra nodes to the host netlist, which have obvious influences on the function of the host netlist.

The implantation mode of the trigger node: (a) Add the trigger node as an additional output node for a specific node in the host netlist. (b) Add the trigger node as an additional output node for a specific primary output node in the host netlist. (c) A specific output node that replaces a specific node in the host netlist with a trigger node. (d) A specific output node that replaces a specific primary output node in the host netlist with a trigger node. (e) Add additional primary input nodes for the host netlist as input nodes for the trigger node. Among them, a and b only add an output branch for a specific node in the host netlist and basically do not affect the function of the host netlist. In essence, c and d replace a specific node in the host netlist as a trigger node, but it is usually necessary to use the replaced node as the output node of the load node to ensure that other functions of the host netlist are not affected. The effect of e on the function of the host netlist is too obvious.

The different implantation methods of load nodes and trigger nodes will affect the implantation node search, so the proposed method uses the corresponding difference analysis and non-implantation node filtering strategy. For example, if the designer implants the payload node with mode a or b when the gate-level HT is implanted, the replaced input node in the host (the host-tampered node) has an output branch without an end. In view of the HT designer's handling of this output branch, the analysis is as follows:

(1) This output branch is used as the input of a specific trigger node; that is, the trigger node is implanted in c way, as shown in Figure 3 by connecting the G4 unit with the T4 unit. When performing the implanted node search method of LDS, such host-tampered nodes are added as candidate implanted nodes because of the set of input-side breadth-first comparison nodes belonging to the load node.

(2) Connect this output branch to an additional input port for a specific cell in the host netlist: when the implanted node search method based on a breadth-first comparison is executed, the node corresponding to the cell with an added input port will be added as a candidate implanted node because of the change in the number of input nodes.

(3) Delete the output branch: Removing the line between G4 and T4 in Figure 3 and changing T4 to G4 or not is an example of this approach. This processing usually causes a big change to the function of the host netlist, but it is the simplest case for the implanted node search method of LGDS and does not need to be targeted.

3.4. Design of LDS and LGDS Algorithm

When a payload node of an HT is implanted, it replaces a specific node in a specific layer of the target netlist with itself. Therefore, if we compare this layer of the target netlist and the gold netlist, we can find a pair of difference nodes; that is, the load-tamper node pair. According to this principle, in this paper, the target netlist and the gold netlist are simultaneously traversed in layer order to find the difference nodes of the two in each layer, as shown in Algorithm 1. According to step 5, the LDS algorithm must be affected by the out-of-order problem of input nodes because it has to compare the nodes of each layer one by one in order. Figure 5 is an example of LDS. Observations show that the target netlist and the gold netlist are exactly the same in layers 1, 2, and 4, but there is a load-tampering node pair in layer 3, which is the two nodes corresponding to T4 and G3 cells.

The problem of out-of-order input nodes can cause two nodes that should be the same to have different results when performing a breadth-first comparison. Based on the LDS algorithm, in order to solve the problem of input node disorder, the nodes in each layer need to be divided into several groups according to the corresponding unit type and the number of input nodes, and then each node group is compared in turn to find out the difference nodes, as shown in Algorithm 2. Among them, step 9 is the key to finding the load-tamper node pair. It first compares two groups of nodes with the same number of corresponding cell types and input nodes, then finds one group of redundant nodes, and finally finds the tampered nodes or load nodes corresponding to the redundant nodes. This process is usually very difficult because the LGDS algorithm solves the problem of input nodes out of order, which leads to large time complexity and may introduce non-implanted nodes. It is difficult to guarantee absolute correctness while ensuring low time complexity. However, for an implanted example containing multiple HTs, step 9 must be performed correctly to further distinguish each implanted HT.

Algorithm 1: LDS Algorithm

```
Input: Target netlist T, Golden netlist G
Output: Set of load-tamper node pairs P
Initialize P as an empty set;
Initialize layers TL of T and GL of G as their respective primary output node sets;
while the number of compared layers has not reached a specific value do
    Initialize the next layer NTL of T and NGL of G as empty sets;
    foreach node t ∈ TL, g ∈ GL do
        if t and g correspond to the same type of cell and have the same number of input
          nodes then
            Add all input nodes of t and g to NTL and NGL respectively;
        end
        else
            Add the pair (t, g) as a load-tamper node pair to P;
        end
    end
    Update TL with NTL and GL with NGL;
end
```

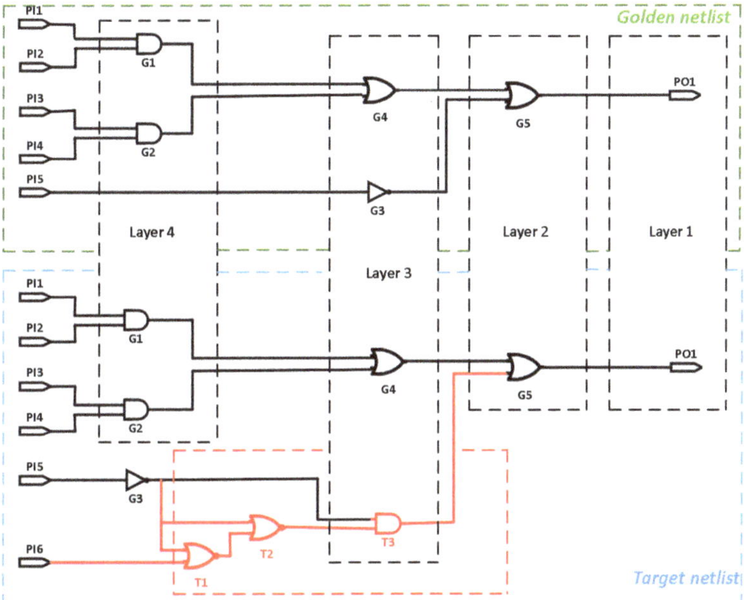

Figure 5. An example of LDS.

The time complexity of Algorithm 1 depends on the number of levels of alignment and the number of nodes and operations in each level. The number of layers is assumed to be L, and the number of nodes in the target netlist and gold netlist are T and G, respectively.

Then, the time complexity of Algorithm 1 is $O(L \times T \times G)$. The space complexity mainly depends on the size of the set P of load-tamper node pairs. Assuming that the number of load-tamper node pairs is P, the space complexity is $O(P)$. In Algorithm 2, the number of layers for alignment is assumed to be L, and the number of nodes for the target netlist and gold netlist are T and G, respectively. The time complexity of the algorithm is mainly composed of the grouping process and comparison process. The grouping process is $O((T \times G) \times \log(T \times G))$, and the comparison process is $O(N^2)$, so the time complexity is $O(L \times ((T \times G) \times \log(T \times G)) + N^2)$. The set size is P of load-tamper node pairs, an then the space complexity is $O(P)$.

Algorithm 2: LGDS Algorithm

```
Input: Target netlist T, Golden netlist G
Output: Set of load-tamper node pairs P
Initialize layers TL of T and GL of G as their respective primary output node sets;
while the number of compared layers has not reached a specific value do
    Initialize the next layer NTL of T and NGL of G as empty sets;
    The nodes in TL, GL are sorted and grouped according to the type of cell and
      the number of input nodes. Finally, the node grouping sets TGs, GGs are
      obtained;
    for node groups TG ∈ TGs, GG ∈ GGs do
        if the size of TG is equal to the size of GG then
            Add all input nodes of each node in TG and GG to NTL and NGL;
        end
        else
            Compare each node in TG and GG using Input-side breadth-first
              comparison;
            Add the input nodes of the same node respectively NTL, NGL;
            TG or GG redundant nodes as load or tamper with the nodes, build an
              incomplete load-tamper with the nodes to join P, or complete P
              existing in an incomplete load-tamper with nodes;
        end
    end
    Update TL with NTL and GL with NGL;
end
```

4. Experiments and Results

This section describes the experimental process, evaluation metrics, and results.

4.1. Evaluation Measures

Evaluation metrics for binary classification problems are used in this experiment, as shown in Table 1. A higher true positive (TP) indicates that more HTs have been correctly located, and a higher true negative (TN) indicates that it will not mislocate. A higher TPR indicates a better diagnosis, and a higher TNR indicates that it is less likely to cause misjudgment. The formulas for calculating the TPR and TNR are shown in Table 2.

Table 1. Binary classification evaluation.

	The Prediction Is Positive	The Prediction Is Negative
Positive Example	True positive (TP)	False Negative (FN)
Negative Example	False Positive (FP)	True negative (TN)

Table 2. TPR and TNR formulas.

Metric	Calculation Formula
TPR	$\frac{TP}{TP+FN}$
TNR	$\frac{TN}{TN+FP}$
Accuracy	$\frac{TN+TP}{TN+TP+FP+FN}$
Precision	$\frac{TP}{TP+FP}$
F1 Score	$\frac{2\times Precision\times TPR}{Precision+TPR}$
Balanced Accuracy	$\frac{TPR+TNR}{2}$

4.2. Experiment on Implanted Node Search

The CPU used in this experiment is AMD Ryzen 53600 with a main frequency of 3.6 GHZ. The memory is 16 G of DDR4 with a frequency of 3.2 GHZ. The HT example selected in this paper is from the combinational circuit designed in [17], and its naming rule is: "gold netlist name_T number". In this paper, MSOSs containing HTs were obtained after completing the HT-detection experiment in [17]. Subsequently, LDS and LGDS algorithms are used, respectively, to find the additional implanted nodes of the target netlist relative to the gold netlist. The HT benchmarks used in this paper include c2670 c3540, c5315, c6288, s1423, s13207, s15850, and s35932. That is about 900 different circuits. Table 3 presents the results obtained on netlist s35932_T607 using different algorithms. The proportion of implanted nodes represents the proportion of the number of implanted nodes in all the nodes obtained by the search. The netlist is implanted with 2 HTs, totaling 24 HT nodes. According to Table 3, LDS and LGDS obviously consume less time. Since LGDS needs to deal with the problem of out-of-order input nodes, it may introduce some non-implanted nodes, resulting in a reduction in the proportion of implanted nodes. Table 4 shows the implant node search results in netlist c6288_T209. The table is implanted with an HT with 15 nodes. From Table 4, we can see that the running time of the LDS and LGDS methods is lower than the remaining methods. The effect of LDS is superior, and the proportion of LGDS is lower due to the introduction of non-implanted nodes.

Table 3. Implanted node search results in s35932_T607.

Method	Method in [17]	Method in [18]	LDS	LGDS
Node cell name	trig23_0U1 trig23_0U2 . . . tri23_0U9 troj7_0state_reg_0_ troj7_0state_reg_1_ tro_0Trojan_out0_reg troj7_0U3 troj7_0U4 . . . troj7_0U9 trojan7_0 troj7_1U1 troj7_1U2 troj7_1U3 trojan7_1	trig23_0U1 trig23_0U2 . . . tri23_0U9 tro_0Trojan_out0_reg troj7_0U3 troj7_0U4 . . . troj7_0U9 trojan7_0 troj7_1U1 troj7_1U2 troj7_1U3 trojan7_1	trig23_0U1 trig23_0U2 . . . tri23_0U9 troj7_0state_reg_0_ troj7_0state_reg_1_ tro_0Trojan_out0_reg troj7_0U3 troj7_0U4 . . . troj7_0U9 trojan7_0 troj7_1U1 troj7_1U2 troj7_1U3 trojan7_1	trig23_0U1 trig23_0U2 . . . tri23_0U9 troj7_0state_reg_0_ troj7_0state_reg_1_ tro_0Trojan_out0_reg troj7_0U3 troj7_0U4 . . . troj7_0U9 trojan7_0 troj7_1U1 troj7_1U2 troj7_1U3 trojan7_1 U3783 U4537
Proportion	100%	91.7%	100%	92.3%
Time consuming (ms)	153	105	27	91

Table 4. Implanted node search results in c6288_T209.

Method	Method in [17]	Method in [18]	LDS	LGDS
Node cell name	troj9_0U1 troj9_0U2 . . . troj9_0U7 trojan9_0 troj9_1U1 . . . troj9_1U6 trojan9_1	troj9_0U1 troj9_0U2 . . . troj9_0U6 trojan9_0 troj9_1U1 . . . troj9_1U6 trojan9_1	troj9_0U1 troj9_0U2 . . . troj9_0U7 trojan9_0 troj9_1U1 . . . troj9_1U6 trojan9_1	troj9_0U1 troj9_0U2 . . . troj9_0U7 trojan9_0 troj9_1U1 . . . troj9_1U6 trojan9_1 U2415 U2416
Proportion	100%	93.3%	100%	88%
Time consuming (ms)	97	64	18	60

The results of the implanted node search for all netlists are shown in Table 5. The maximum proportion refers to the maximum proportion of implanted nodes searched in the netlist. If the ratio reaches 100%, it means that the proposed method can search all implanted nodes in a certain netlist. Similarly, the minimum proportion means that in a certain netlist, only a part of the implanted nodes are searched. The average ratio is the average of the percentage of implanted nodes in each netlist. According to the comparison of the time taken by method [17] and LDS method, it can be found that the time taken by the LDS method is reduced by nearly 75%. The circuit partitioning method is unified as MSOS partitioning. Nowadays, there are also methods to divide sectors [18], but there may be overlapping nodes in the sector. Although the method in [17] and the method proposed in this paper can complete the search of implanted nodes, it is obvious that the search method in this paper is more efficient. In [25], the authors directly detect whether each node in the netlist is an HT node, although they could complete the diagnosis. It is not accurate because normal nodes may be reported as HT nodes.

Table 5. Search results for all netlists.

	Method in [17]	Our Proposed LDS Method	Our Proposed LGDS Method	Method in [18]	Method in [25]
Minimum proportion	67.2%	84.6%	17.5%	-	-
Maximum proportion	100%	100%	100%	-	-
Average proportion	98.9%	99.9%	97.3%	-	-
Time consuming (ms)	45363	12145	34574	-	-
Circuit partitioning method	MSOS	MSOS	MSOS	Sector	Detecting nodes
Diagnosis or not	1	1	1	1	1

4.3. HT Diagnosis Experiment

The HT diagnosis experiment follows the implanted node search experiment. For each netlist, if there is no MSOS predicted as "HT", the diagnosis is terminated. Otherwise, the intersection between the nodes contained in the MSOS predicted as "HT" and the implanted nodes is obtained, so as to complete the diagnosis. The HT diagnosis results for all tested netlists are shown in Table 6. From this result analysis, it can be seen that the results of using KNN, RF, or SVM models with LGD or LGDS to diagnose achieve a sufficiently high level. The average TPR of both LDS and LGDS exceeds 93%, and the average TNR is 100%. It can be found that our method obtains the same experimental results because the essential difference between the LDS algorithm and the LGDS algorithm is not big. The most important difference is that the LGDS algorithm can solve the problem of input node disorder, but it will increase the time complexity. Therefore, the result is the same. The method in [17] can overcome the problem of out-of-order input nodes at the expense of some performance, and search to obtain enough complete and pure implanted nodes. However, since the average TPR is slightly lower than the method studied in this paper, some implanted nodes may be missing. Compared with [17], the proposed method takes into account the relevance between the implanted nodes and the concept of "layer" where the HT payload node is located in the whole netlist. Therefore, the average effect of the proposed method is better and the time consumption is shorter. Compared with [18], the detection effect of this paper is significantly better, which is because [18] does not search for implanted nodes. Compared with [25], the proposed method improves the average TPR and TNR of gate-level HT diagnosis by about 4% and 15%, respectively.

Table 6. HT diagnosis results

Principle of Search/ Machine Learning Mode	KNN		RF		SVM		DT		Bayes		Adversarial Training	
	TPR	TNR	TPR	TNR	TPR	TNR	TPR	TNR	TPR	TNR	TPR	TNR
Method in [17]	97.3%	100%	97.7%	100%	93.4%	100%	-	-	-	-	-	-
Method in [18]	90.91%	92.46%	-	-	-	-	86.36%	98.61%	100%	65.15%	-	-
Method in [25]	-	-	-	-	-	-	-	-	-	-	94.9%	85.3%
Our proposed LDS method	98.0%	100%	98.4%	100%	93.9%	100%	91.3%	100%	93.7%	100%	-	-
Our proposed LGDS method	98.0%	100%	98.4%	100%	93.9%	100%	95.6%	100%	96.0%	100%	-	-

5. Conclusions

This paper focuses on HT diagnosis and proposes a diagnosis scheme based on graph theory. LDS and LGDS algorithms are proposed to search the implanted nodes. It greatly reduces the number of nodes that need to be sorted for difference and reduces the diagnosis time. At the same time, considering the integrity of HTs, the non-implanted nodes are reduced and the diagnosis accuracy is improved. Tables 5 and 6 show that our proposed method has a good diagnostic performance. However, our method still has some shortcomings. For example, the LDS algorithm must be affected by the out-of-order problem of input nodes because it needs to compare nodes in each layer one by one in order. Secondly, the LGDS algorithm will miss the implanted nodes in some extreme cases. We will try to solve this problem in the future work.

Author Contributions: Conceptualization, H.G. and Z.L.; methodology, Z.L. and G.Z.; software, J.Z., X.L. and H.G.; writing—original draft preparation, H.G. and G.Z.; writing—review and editing, Z.L., J.Z. and Q.W.; funding acquisition, Z.L. All authors have read and agreed to the published version of the manuscript.

Funding: This work was supported in part by the National Natural Science Foundation of China under grant 61972302, in part by the Guangzhou Municipal Science and Technology Project under grant SL2022A04J00404, in part by the Fundamental Research Funds for the Central Universities under grant XJS220306, in part by the Natural Science Basic Research Program of Shaanxi under grant 2022JQ-680, and in part by the Key Laboratory of Smart Human Computer Interaction and Wearable Technology of Shaanxi Province.

Data Availability Statement: The data presented in this study are available on request from the corresponding author.

Acknowledgments: The authors would like to thank the editors and reviewers for their contributions to our manuscript.

Conflicts of Interest: The authors declare no conflicts of interest.

References

1. Huang, Z.; Wang, Q.; Chen, Y.; Jiang, X. A survey on machine learning against hardware trojan attacks: Recent advances and challenges. *IEEE Access* **2020**, *8*, 10796–10826. [CrossRef]
2. Li, H.; Liu, Q.; Zhang, J. A survey of hardware Trojan threat and defense. *Integration* **2016**, *55*, 426–437. [CrossRef]
3. Bhunia, S.; Hsiao, M.S.; Banga, M.; Narasimhan, S. Hardware Trojan attacks: Threat analysis and countermeasures. *Proc. IEEE.* **2014**, *102*, 1229–1247. [CrossRef]
4. Huang, Z.; Wang, Q.; Yang, P. Hardware trojan: Research progress and new trends on key problems. *J. Comput.* **2019**, *42*, 993–1017.
5. Qin, M.; Hu, W.; Mu, D.; Tai, Y. Property based formal security verification for hardware Trojan detection. In Proceedings of the 2018 IEEE 3rd International Verification and Security Workshop (IVSW), Costa Brava, Spain, 2–4 July 2018; pp. 62–67.
6. Ponugoti, K.K. *Formal Verification for Hardware Trojan Detection*; North Dakota State University: Fargo, ND, USA, 2023.
7. Mukherjee, R.; Rajendran, S.R.; Chakraborty, R.S. A comprehensive survey of physical and logic testing techniques for Hardware Trojan detection and prevention. *J. Cryptogr. Eng.* **2022**, 12, 495–522. [CrossRef]
8. Pan, Z.; Mishra, P. Automated test generation for hardware trojan detection using reinforcement learning. In Proceedings of the 26th Asia and South Pacific Design Automation Conference, Tokyo, Japan, 18–21 January 2021; pp. 408–413.
9. Farahmandi, F.; Huang, Y.; Mishra, P.; Farahmandi, F.; Huang, Y.; Mishra, P. Hardware trojan detection schemes using path delay and side-channel analysis. In *System-on-Chip Security: Validation and Verification*; Springer: Cham, Switzerland, 2020; pp. 221–271.
10. Amelian, A.; Borujeni, S.E. A side-channel analysis for hardware Trojan detection based on path delay measurement. *J. Circuits Syst. Comput.* **2018**, 27, 1850138. [CrossRef]
11. Yang, S.; Chakraborty, P.; Bhunia, S. Side-channel analysis for hardware Trojan detection using machine learning. In Proceedings of the 2021 IEEE International Test Conference India (ITC India), Bangalore, India, 18–20 July 2021; pp. 1–6.
12. Courbon, F.; Loubet-Moundi, P.; Fournier, J.J.; Tria, A. A high efficiency hardware trojan detection technique based on fast SEM imaging. In Proceedings of the 2015 Design, Automation & Test in Europe Conference & Exhibition (DATE), Grenoble, France, 9–13 March 2015; pp. 788–793.
13. Ludwig. M.; Bette, A.C.; Lippmann, B. Vital: Verifying trojan-free physical layouts through hardware reverse engineering. In Proceedings of the 2021 IEEE Physical Assurance and Inspection of Electronics (PAINE), Washington, DC, USA, 30 November–2 December 2021; pp. 1–8.
14. Banga, M.; Hsiao, M.S. A region based approach for the identification of hardware Trojans. In Proceedings of the 2008 IEEE International Workshop on Hardware-Oriented Security and Trust, Anaheim, CA, USA, 9 June 2008; pp. 40–47.
15. Rajendran, J.; Jyothi, V.; Sinanoglu, O.; Karri, R. Design and analysis of ring oscillator based design-for-trust technique. In Proceedings of the 29th VLSI Test Symposium, Dana Point, CA, USA, 1–5 May 2011; pp. 105–110.
16. Forte, D.; Bao, C.; Srivastava, A. Temperature tracking: An innovative run-time approach for hardware Trojan detection. In Proceedings of the 2013 IEEE/ACM International Conference on Computer-Aided Design (ICCAD), San Jose, CA, USA, 18–21 November 2013; pp. 532–539.
17. Wang, J.; Zhai, G.; Gao, H.; Xu, L.; Li, X.; Li, Z.; Huang, Z.; Xie, C. A Hardware Trojan Detection and Diagnosis Method for Gate-Level Netlists Based on Machine Learning and Graph Theory. *Electronics* **2023**, *13*, 59. [CrossRef]
18. Du, M.; Huang, Z.; Chen, Y.; Li, L.; Wang, Q.; Liu, J. A HT detection and diagnosis method for gate-level netlists based on machine learning. In Proceedings of the 2021 IEEE 6th International Conference on Signal and Image Processing (ICSIP), Nanjing, China, 22–24 October 2021; pp. 1070–1074.
19. Huang, Z.; Li, Z.; Xie, C.; Du, M.; Wang, Q. A hardware trojan detection and diagnosis method for gate-level netlists based on different machine learning algorithms. *J. Circuits Syst. Comput.* **2022**, *31*, 2250135. [CrossRef]
20. Zhang, Y.; Li, S.; Chen, X.; Yao, J.; Mao, Z.; Yang, J.; Hua, Y. Hybrid multi-level hardware Trojan detection platform for gate-level netlists based on XGBoost. *IET Comput. Digit. Tech.* **2022**, *16*, 54–70. [CrossRef]
21. He, J.; Zhao, Y.; Guo, X.; Jin, Y. Hardware trojan detection through chip-free electromagnetic side-channel statistical analysis. *IEEE Trans. Very Large Scale Integr. (VLSI) Syst.* **2017**, *25*, 2939–2948. [CrossRef]
22. Kampel, L.; Kitsos, P.; Simos, D.E. Locating hardware trojans using combinatorial testing for cryptographic circuits. *IEEE Access* **2022**, *10*, 18787–18806. [CrossRef]
23. Agrawal, D.; Baktir, S.; Karakoyunlu D.; Rohatgi, P.; Sunar, B. Trojan detection using IC fingerprinting. In Proceedings of the 2007 IEEE Symposium on Security and Privacy (SP'07), Berkeley, CA, USA, 20–23 May 2007; pp. 296–310.
24. Wolff, F.; Papachristou, C.; Bhunia, S.; Chakraborty, R.S. Towards Trojan-free trusted ICs: Problem analysis and detection scheme. In Proceedings of the Conference on Design, Automation and Test in Europe, Munich, Germany, 10–14 March 2008; pp. 1362–1365.
25. Hasegawa, K.; Hidano, S.; Nozawa, K.; Kiyomoto, S.; Togawa, N. R-htdetector: Robust hardware-trojan detection based on adversarial training. *IEEE Trans. Comput.* **2022**, *72*, 333–345. [CrossRef]

electronics

Article

A Blockchain and Zero Knowledge Proof Based Data Security Transaction Method in Distributed Computing

Bowei Zhang [1,*], Heng Pan [1,*], Kunyang Li [1], Ying Xing [1], Jiaxiang Wang [2], Dongdong Fan [1] and Wenjie Zhang [1]

1 Cyber Security Academy, Zhongyuan University of Technology, Zhengzhou 450007, China; likunyanggg@163.com (K.L.); xingying_vip@163.com (Y.X.); fanddong00@zut.edu.cn (D.F.); z972843100@gmail.com (W.Z.)
2 School of Advanced Technology, Xi'an Jiaotong-Liverpool University, Suzhou 215123, China; jiaxiang.wang21@student.xjtlu.edu.cn
* Correspondence: bll05444@163.com (B.Z.); panheng@zut.edu.cn (H.P.)

Abstract: In distributed computing, data trading mechanisms are essential for ensuring the sharing of data across multiple computing nodes. Nevertheless, they currently encounter considerable obstacles, including low accuracy in matching trading parties, ensuring fairness in transactions, and safeguarding data privacy throughout the trading process. In order to address these issues, we put forward a data trading security scheme based on zero-knowledge proofs and smart contracts. In the phase of preparing the security parameters, the objective is to reduce the complexity of generating non-interactive zero-knowledge proofs and to enhance the efficiency of data trading. In the pre-trading phase, we devise attribute atomic matching smart contracts based on precise data property alignment, with the objective of achieving fine-grained matching of data attributes between trading parties. In the trading execution phase, lightweight cryptographic algorithms based on elliptic curve cryptography (ECC) and non-interactive zero-knowledge proofs are employed for the dual encryption of trading data and the generation of attribute proof contracts, thus ensuring the security and privacy of the data. The results of experiments conducted on the Ethereum platform in an industrial IoT scenario demonstrate that our scheme maintains stable and low-cost consumption while ensuring accuracy in matching and privacy protection.

Keywords: blockchain; data trading; zero knowledge proof; privacy-preserving; smart contract

1. Introduction

With the rapid evolution of information technology, various connected devices are constantly generating massive amounts of data. For example, various distributed devices, social networks and other technologies have contributed enormously to increased data generation. According to media predictions, the number of IoT-related devices in everyday life is expected to increase to 41.6 billion within a year. This exponential growth makes it extremely challenging to perform complex retrieval and analysis from such vast and diverse data sources. However, with the rapid advancement of AI in recent years and the corresponding progress in related technologies, the potential of distributed computing has been unleashed. Distributed computing provides efficient computing power and resource management for handling large-scale data. Consequently, leveraging these cutting-edge technologies for model training on the vast amounts of data generated daily has become an inevitable trend [1–3].

Consequently, as data-driven approaches have become central to many distributed computing systems, data trading has emerged as a model for the circulation of data. By monetizing data resources, data trading facilitates the connection between data owners and data consumers, thereby enhancing the utilization of multi-source data and addressing the current issue of data silos. By leveraging large-scale AI models, the data demand side can analyze data acquired from various distributed scenarios through data transactions, thereby deriving greater benefits, enhancing efficiency, and reducing production costs. In this context, a typical distributed computing application, federated learning (FL) in edge computing, becomes a key technology for processing and exploiting massive data [4,5]. For instance, industrial sectors can subscribe to diverse types of industrial data (such as temperature and humidity data from assorted sensors) through data exchange platforms to train their models, resulting in enhanced efficiency and superior outcomes.

In traditional data trading systems, data owners and consumers are required to rely on trading service providers for the management of access control, authorization, and data retrieval. This centralized approach relies on third-party entities, lacks transparency, and increases the impact of issues arising from a single centralized node. This is inconsistent with the core concept of distributed systems. Blockchain is an emerging distributed technology that has been widely applied in data trading systems due to its decentralized, publicly verifiable, and tamper-resistant ledger characteristics [6]. Nevertheless, given the highly sensitive nature of the data being traded, relying on a single distributed technology alone does not fully address all issues. As an illustrative example, the low accuracy of trading group matching results leads to inefficient matching between data owners and consumers. Insufficient privacy protection for sellers may result in data breaches and misuse. A lack of security during data transmission renders the data vulnerable to tampering or theft. Furthermore, unfair data value exchange can harm the interests of both parties involved in the transaction.

In order to protect against potential privacy breaches that may occur during the course of a transaction, the prevailing approach to data protection in the context of data trading is to rely on cryptographic security mechanisms. A number of researchers have put forward a variety of cryptographic solutions with the aim of ensuring the security of data trading. For example, there are schemes based on digital signatures [7,8] and those based on zero-knowledge proofs [9,10]. Schemes based on digital signatures permit data providers and consumers to publish and purchase data without disclosing their true identities, and to authenticate data sharing under conditions of anonymity. Nevertheless, the act of signing a data entity primarily serves to confirm the ownership of the data, rather than to verify the accuracy of the data entity itself. Conversely, zero-knowledge proof technology can validate the integrity and legality of the transaction data while maintaining the confidentiality of the transactional details. The development of zero-knowledge proofs has seen them applied extensively in data trading scenarios, whether in the form of basic interactive zero-knowledge proofs or noninteractive zero-knowledge proofs [11]. This is due to the unique characteristics of the technology, which have yielded positive results.

Nevertheless, in the context of data trading, the application of zero-knowledge proofs still presents certain challenges, such as the construction of proofs for confidential data. Furthermore, two significant challenges must be addressed and resolved in the context of data trading. Firstly, there is a risk that the data seller may send the data without receiving payment, thereby enabling the data buyer to obtain the data without paying. Secondly, there is a possibility that the data buyer may be unable to access the data before payment, while the data seller, after receiving payment, may fail to deliver the data as per the contract.

To address the limitations of existing data trading systems in terms of privacy protection, transaction fairness, and storage scalability, we propose a blockchain-based data trading solution. This solution utilizes a systematic technology selection process to choose appropriate technologies for different requirements. In terms of privacy protection, we employ non-interactive zero-knowledge proofs (zk-SNARKs) to ensure that both parties can complete the verification process without exposing private data. For transaction fairness, we adopt elliptic curve cryptography (ECC) to provide higher computational efficiency and lower storage costs. To achieve precise matching of data attributes, we design an atomic matching-based smart contract mechanism to enhance transaction accuracy. Lastly, we utilize off-chain storage technologies (such as IPFS) to alleviate on-chain storage pressure and address user scalability issues. By storing encrypted data off-chain and using the blockchain for indexing, we enhance the system's scalability, making it suitable for large-scale and complex data trading scenarios.

The principal contributions of this paper are outlined as follows:

- This paper presents the design of a blockchain-based smart contract based on the concept of atomic matching, which enables the fine-grained matching of data sellers and buyers according to detailed data attributes. Furthermore, the model incorporates off-chain storage and the separation of parameter preparation phases, thereby enhancing the system's scalability in handling large volumes of data and increasing numbers of users.
- A fair end-to-end protection scheme is proposed, which employs lightweight cryptographic algorithms for dual encryption of transaction data prior to the completion of the transaction. Furthermore, zero-knowledge proofs are utilised to verify the nature of the transaction data, thereby safeguarding the privacy of sensitive information for transaction users.

Regarding the organization of this paper, Section 2 introduces the related work. Section 3 presents the overall model of the proposed system and the threat analysis. The Section 4 describes the system architecture. Section 5 conducts simulation experiments and experimental analysis of the system. Section 6 provides a summary and analysis of this work.

2. Related Work

The unique distributed nature of blockchain technology gives it great potential and application value in data transactions. At the present time, the applications of blockchain technology in conjunction with other scenarios can be broadly categorized into the following types.

The advent of blockchain technology has rendered the concept of peer-to-peer (P2P) energy trading a tangible reality. This has paved the way for consumers and small-scale energy producers, such as those utilizing home solar systems, to engage in direct trading, thereby reducing reliance on traditional intermediaries. This model serves to enhance the efficiency of energy trading and to reduce costs. In their paper, Shunrong Jiang et al. [12] put forth a proposal for a blockchain-based decentralized energy trading system. The system employs smart contracts and privacy-preserving technologies, including zero-knowledge proofs, to facilitate direct, secure, and private energy transactions between users and suppliers. Furthermore, it incorporates demand response capabilities, thereby enhancing the efficiency of energy management and system reliability. Aitzhan et al. [13] concentrated on the protection of decentralized energy trading in smart grid environments, seeking to eliminate the necessity for centralized third-party institutions. They employed distributed ledger technology and proof of concept, combining multi-signature and encrypted anonymous messaging methods to facilitate the anonymous negotiation of energy prices and the secure execution of transactions. In a further development of the concept, Ye-Byoul Son et al. [14] proposed a blockchain-based P2P energy trading system in which all bids are encrypted. The implementation of encrypted bidding and smart contracts based on functional encryption (FE) was also explored. In addition to cryptographic solutions, some energy trading scenarios employ non-cryptographic methods. To illustrate, Daghmehchi et al. [15] put forth a proposal for an IoT platform wherein the platform provider does not act as an intermediary. The platform allows users to securely and efficiently share credits with other users in need, thereby ensuring privacy protection through k-anonymity on network bridges.

Furthermore, the quantity of data in medical contexts is also expanding at a considerable rate, and the issues pertaining to the privacy and security of this data are becoming increasingly prominent. Blockchain technology provides a secure data-sharing platform for patients, hospitals, and research institutions, thereby ensuring data confidentiality and immutability while allowing authorized parties to access and utilize the data. Liang Xue et al. [10] put forth a solution tailored to the data generated in medical scenarios, which employs blockchain technology to facilitate fair and granular trading. This solution guarantees the secure transaction and protection of medical data through the use of verifiable attribute credentials and cryptographic techniques. Moreover, the utilization of Merkle hash trees and cryptographic knowledge safeguards the anonymity of data sellers, guaranteeing that the transaction process remains undetectable and providing a secure and efficient solution for medical data trading. Kumar et al. [16] devised a novel and secure data-sharing framework for industrial medical systems. This framework implements registration, verification (using zero-knowledge proofs), and consensus mechanisms based on smart contracts through a blockchain solution.

In the context of industrial Internet of Things (IIoT) data trading, Zhang [17] put forth a controlled IIoT data trading solution that employs automated smart contracts and hardware trusted execution environments. This approach enables data producers, or data owners, to retain complete control over their sovereignty throughout the trading process, while simultaneously reducing their own costs. In a further development of this concept, Akanksha Dixit et al. [18] introduced an innovative platform named FASTDATA, which utilizes blockchain technology to create a decentralized IIoT data trading marketplace. VerneMQ is employed as the data network layer to guarantee dependable hosting and fault-tolerant transmission of data flows. The integration of fully symmetric encryption schemes and digital signatures ensures the end-to-end encryption of data during transmission and storage, thereby safeguarding data privacy. Furthermore, a TrustScore mechanism was introduced to assess and enhance the credibility of network participants. Zhou et al. [19] devised the Federated Extreme Gradient Boosting (FedXGBoost) algorithm and a secure sharing mechanism for the aforementioned trading process. The STFS framework, which employs a range of technologies, including homomorphic encryption, secret sharing (SS), proxy re-encryption, and threshold aggregation signatures, effectively addresses issues of data privacy protection, model credibility and secure and controllable data sharing in the context of the Industrial Internet of Things (IIoT). Huang Cheng et al. [20] additionally proposed a traceable and efficient solution, employing an adaptive decentralised protocol for transmission and utilising relevant cryptographic technologies for other aspects.

The aforementioned scenarios represent some of the most prevalent avenues for the integration of blockchain technology with data trading. Of these, energy trading has been the subject of particularly extensive study, with research activity concentrated within the context of data trading within the Internet of Things (IoT). In general, regardless of the data trading scenario, the majority of solutions rely on cryptographic technologies, which are commonly referred to as soft environment solutions. These technologies include homomorphic encryption, asymmetric encryption, zero-knowledge proofs, and digital signatures.

Specifically, the integration of blockchain and zero-knowledge proof (ZKP) technologies has shown significant potential in privacy protection, security enhancement, and performance optimization. Refs. [21–23] delve into the combination of zk-SNARKs technology with blockchain, applied to account privacy protection and transaction verification for high privacy-demanding scenarios. These studies demonstrate how to achieve efficient and secure transaction verification mechanisms without disclosing transaction details, which is particularly applicable in finance and healthcare, where privacy requirements are extremely high. However, the performance overhead associated with the computation and verification processes of zk-SNARKs poses a significant challenge, especially in blockchain systems that need to handle a large volume of transactions. Refs. [24,25] further explore the integration of blockchain and ZKP in the Internet of Things (IoT) environment, proposing improvements to zk-SNARKs models to optimize performance, specifically by reducing proof sizes and shortening verification times to enhance the overall efficiency of blockchain systems. In addition, Ref. [26] introduces a method that utilizes ZKP to ensure privacy and fairness in a distributed IoT environment while maintaining system efficiency. Despite these studies revealing the considerable advantages of ZKP technology in protecting privacy within blockchain systems, it is evident that the limitations regarding performance overhead and trusted setup remain critical issues that require attention, and some work has already been completed in this regard. Furthermore, current research predominantly focuses on specific application scenarios, lacking in-depth exploration of the adaptability, flexibility, and scalability of the integration of blockchain and ZKP technologies in various complex scenarios.

Moreover, despite the plethora of proposed solutions, the majority of existing research primarily concentrates on the protection of bidding information or the pricing of data within the context of data trading. There is a paucity of research focusing on the specific content of the trading data itself. Furthermore, insufficient attention has been paid to the security of the data itself during the transaction process, as well as the growing issues related to device resource constraints and scalability.

The data transaction security scheme proposed in this paper builds upon existing research in the field, specifically the above research on data transaction work in different scenarios. The model proposed in this paper integrates data transaction privacy protection and ownership guarantee in these scenarios. Furthermore, this paper focuses on the proof of data protection in data transactions, differentiating itself from the various types of data transactions that are unique to specific scenarios. It aims to satisfy the majority of scenarios, including the use of this scheme for the transaction of medical electronic health records (EHRs), for the transaction of transactional data between financial institutions, and for the transaction of data among manufacturers, suppliers, and logistic companies in the manufacturing industry, promoting distributed computing for other applications.

The purpose of this paper is to address the most challenging problem in data transactions, i.e., how to ensure that the whole process of transactions is completed fairly and securely. We will solve this problem by combining advanced technologies used in existing working scenarios, such as elliptic curve cryptography (ECC), non-interactive zero-knowledge proofs, smart contracts, and IPFS, accompanied by a lightweight model design and combining technologies such as off-chain storage to keep the computational overhead and cost at a relatively low level in response to possible blockchain scalability and performance issues.

3. Scheme Analysis

3.1. System Model

In our system model, there are four types of entities: authority, IPFS, data seller, and data buyer. There also exists a class of execution tools smart contracts, as shown in Figure 1.

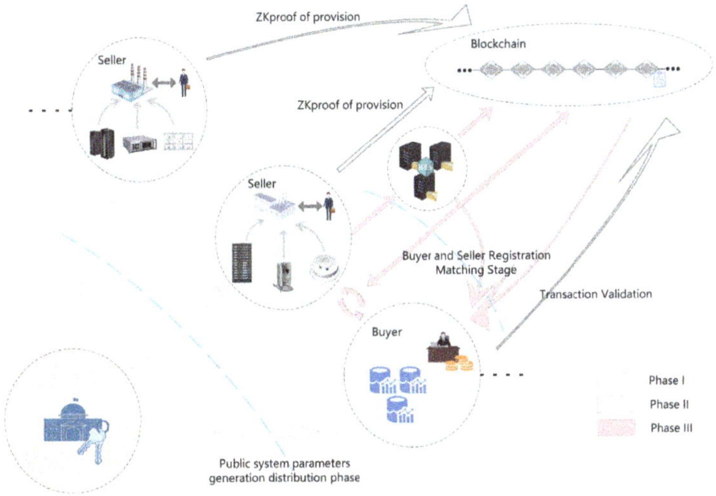

Figure 1. System model.

- Authority: The generation of zero-knowledge proof public parameters for data sellers, particularly those operating in resource-constrained environments such as the Internet of Things (IoT), can help to alleviate pressure on limited resources. Similarly, for data buyers, the generation of public system parameters and the publication of the buyer's public key can facilitate the transfer of data securely.
- IPFS: Relieves the storage pressure on the chain, saves the original data after double encryption of the seller, and provides a search function and encrypted data loading function for the buyer.
- Data Seller: The data seller is a user or agent who has data and wants to gain benefits from these data, but does not want to expose their original data information before the transaction is completed.
- Data buyer: A data buyer is a user or an agent who has a demand for these data; for example, a user under federated learning can obtain the demanded data through a data transaction to train his/her model.
- Smart contract: In the event that the pre-defined conditions are validated, the smart contract deployed on the blockchain will initiate its execution. Upon fulfilment of the stipulated conditions, the smart contract is capable of autonomously transferring funds, thereby ensuring the atomicity of the transaction.

The transaction is divided into three stages. In the initial stage, the authority generates two distinct types of public system parameters. Subsequently, the seller employs a zero-knowledge proof of these public parameters to generate their own proof, while the buyer returns their private key and publishes their public key. In the second stage, the data buyer and data seller invoke a matching smart contract on the blockchain. They input their attribute information such as data type, data size, and data price. The smart contract matches the best buyer and seller after receiving registration information. The third stage is the transaction phase. The data seller encrypts the original data twice: first with symmetric encryption, and then encrypting it with the buyer's publicly disclosed key, saving it on the IPFS, and returning the hash digest to the blockchain. The seller also uploads their zero-knowledge proof for verification. The buyer verifies the proof to ensure data integrity and correctness. Finally, the transaction is executed through the smart contract to ensure atomicity and fairness.

3.2. Threat Model

In the full-process fair data transaction scheme we designed, we assumed that the authority and the storage center IPFS are credible, and in addition, that the smart contracts in the blockchain are generally executed strictly according to the predetermined logic, so they can also be recognized as credible. However, data sellers and data buyers, who are the subjects in the model, are considered to be likely to act maliciously in order to gain more benefits because they are highly influenced by human factors, i.e., it is assumed that there is malicious behavior on the part of data sellers and data sellers.

This is modeled and analyzed to obtain a threat model as follows:

Sellers with data: There may be a situation where a seller does not have some actual characteristic data needed by the buyer, but in order to gain benefits, the seller will try to generate a zero-knowledge proof that can be verified by data characteristics by certain means, so as to deceive the data buyer to pay the cost, i.e., an act of misinformation and fraud. For example, a data seller does not have real industrial IoT data, but in order to obtain payment, he generates a zero-knowledge proof that seems to be valid to deceive the data buyer. The data buyer pays and then realizes that the data is invalid, resulting in wasted resources and financial losses.

The buyer of the demanded data: The buyer of the data may refuse to pay the corresponding monetary equivalent of the data after acquiring the data through certain means and may infer the real identity of the seller through some malicious means, thus compromising the the seller's privacy to gain more benefits, i.e., refusal to pay and fraud.

Blockchain network: Due to the distributed nature of blockchain networks, they consist of various types of nodes, where malicious users and legitimate users are mixed together. Malicious users may attempt to analyze the range of data transactions recorded on the blockchain ledger, such as the transaction information of buyers or sellers, and use this information to infer private details of the users.

Other potential attack vectors include smart contract vulnerabilities. While smart contracts are generally considered trustworthy, their code may still contain unknown vulnerabilities, allowing malicious users to exploit these weaknesses. For instance, logical errors or improper handling of boundary conditions within the contract can be exploited by attackers, leading to financial losses or inconsistencies in the contract's transaction state. Another type of potential attack vector comprises zero-knowledge proof vulnerabilities. Although zero-knowledge proofs (ZKP) are highly effective in protecting privacy during transactions, there may be potential vulnerabilities in the design and implementation of ZKP protocols. ZKP protocols rely on complex mathematical algorithms, and any small error in the proof generation, verification, or parameter setting processes could result in exploitable vulnerabilities. Furthermore, some ZKP protocols require a trusted setup, meaning that the system parameter generation process must be fully secure. If any part of this trusted setup phase is compromised, attackers could generate keys or parameters capable of forging proofs, thereby compromising the security of the entire system.

3.3. Security Objectives

Based on the traditional data transaction model, when designing a full-process fair data transaction model like the one in this paper, methods for how to prevent the above threats should be considered. The scheme should have these security attributes: fair exchange of data between the two parties participating in the data transaction, privacy protection for the data seller, and security of data transmission. Then, the security goals of the scheme design are as follows:

Fair exchange of data value: For both data buyers and sellers, in the case of malicious behavior, fair exchange needs to meet the requirement that the data seller can normally receive the equivalent value of the incentive on the basis of providing the correct data attributes requested by the other party. The data buyer needs to obtain correct and complete data that meets his/her demanded attributes while they pay the equivalent amount of the data value in monetary terms.

Data seller privacy protection: For data sellers, it is necessary that their private information will not be exposed, such as the real content of the original data, when the transaction has not been concluded or when proving the nature of the requested data. Steps must be taken to prevent other malicious nodes from obtaining the data seller's private information through various means across all aspects of the transaction.

Secure transmission of data: Ensuring the integrity, confidentiality, and reliability of data as it travels from seller to buyer is critical. Data is encrypted using symmetric encryption and/or asymmetric encryption to ensure that only authorized recipients can decrypt and access the data content.

Potential attack protection: To address vulnerabilities in smart contracts, code auditing and testing processes should be implemented to ensure that smart contracts are not affected by logical errors or unhandled boundary conditions during execution. For potential vulnerabilities in zero-knowledge proofs, we choose to use the widely validated zk-SNARKs protocol, which leverages its characteristics of uniqueness proof, integrity verification, and non-falsifiability to defend against potential attack vectors such as replay attacks, data tampering, and exploitation of protocol vulnerabilities .

4. Scheme Design

4.1. Overview

For the data security trading scheme described in this paper, the complete process is primarily divided into three stages: the public system parameter generation and distribution stage, the registration and matching stage, and the transaction execution stage. Throughout this process, ensuring data privacy and secure exchange is the core objective, guaranteeing that data remains uncompromised at every stage. The following provides a detailed description of each stage and the corresponding privacy protection measures, and the specific process can be seen in Figure 2. To more clearly distinguish the three phases, a green arrow is used in the first phase to represent the key generation and distribution phase for the data trading group. A yellow arrow is used to indicate the zero-knowledge proof parameter generation phase for the data sellers. The second and third phases are represented by blue and red arrows, respectively.

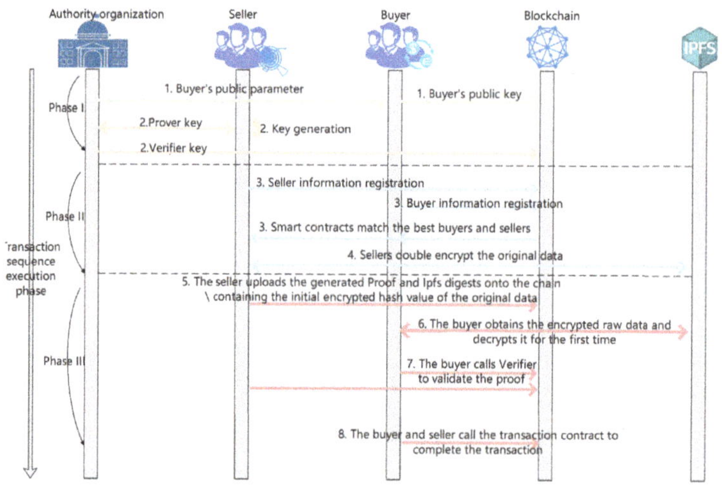

Figure 2. System flow chart.

a. In the public system parameter generation and distribution stage, an authority generates an asymmetric key pair for each buyer and returns the generated public and private keys to the buyer. The buyer will then upload their public key to the blockchain for the seller's use. Concurrently, the seller requests the system parameters necessary for zero-knowledge proofs from the authority based on their own parameters and receives a verification key. By ensuring that all key generation processes occur in a trusted environment and strictly controlling the distribution of keys, the buyer's privacy is effectively safeguarded, preventing potential key leaks.
b. In the registration and matching stage, both the seller group and the buyer group will register their information on the blockchain. This part involves the invocation of smart contracts, where both parties must fill in their data attribute information according to the provisions of the smart contract, without disclosing any raw data information. The smart contract will process the registration information and perform internal matching to identify suitable buyers and sellers. To further protect the seller's privacy, the seller uses their symmetric key to encrypt the raw data and generate a hash digest. Subsequently, the seller performs a secondary encryption using the publicly published buyer's public key and uploads the encrypted data to an off-chain storage IPFS center, returning a searchable hash digest for retrieval. This dual encryption mechanism and atomic attribute matching ensure that the seller's raw data remains undisclosed during the matching process.
c. In the transaction execution phase, the seller first generates the proof required for the buyer's verification using the zero-knowledge proof key generated in the first stage, and both the generated proof and the IPFS hash digest are recorded on-chain. The buyer retrieves the seller's uploaded data based on the on-chain IPFS index and uses their private key to perform the initial decryption of the data, obtaining the raw

data and generating a hash value for subsequent integrity verification. The execution rules of the transaction contract are pre-negotiated, and the buyer confirms the validity of the transaction contract based on the verification results of the zero-knowledge proof contract. This contract ensures the correctness and completeness of the data. Upon confirmation of the transaction, the buyer returns the agreed-upon currency to the seller, while the seller returns the key to the buyer. Through this series of processes, data privacy is effectively safeguarded at every stage of the transaction.

4.2. Detailed Programs

4.2.1. Phase I

In the data transaction scenario, in order to ensure that the key generation process is efficient and suitable for all kinds of resource-constrained devices under the premise of security, we choose an elliptic curve cryptography (ECC)-based encryption system to achieve higher security and smaller key sizes than traditional asymmetric encryption algorithms.

As shown in Figure 3, which illustrates the public system parameter generation and distribution phase, firstly, the authority selects a suitable elliptic curve E and a large prime number p, and the elliptic curve is defined over a finite domain $GF(p)$. A generating element G is chosen as the base point for generating the key pair, and the order of the generating element is n. $nG = O$ must be satisfied, where O is the infinity point of the elliptic curve. After that, a private key d_B (random large integer) is randomly generated for the buyer, making sure that it is complex enough to resist brute force decryption. We used a random number generator (CSPRNG) to create this and compute the public key $Q_B = d_BG$ for it in the set$(1, 2, \ldots, n-1)$. At the end of parameter generation, the public–private key pair is returned to the buyer.

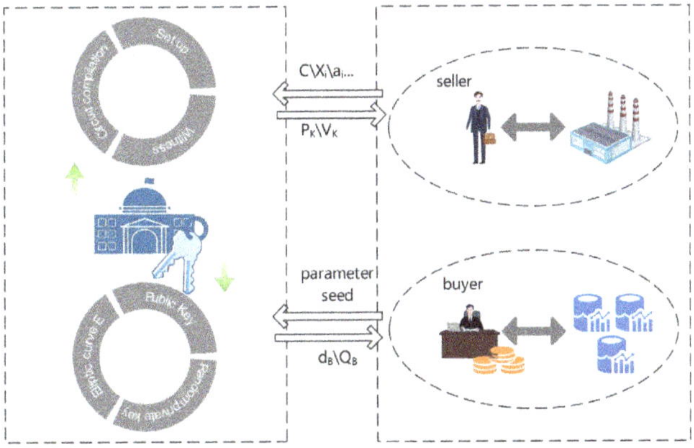

Figure 3. Security parameter distribution phase.

Secondly, based on the analysis of the zero-knowledge proof in the threat model, this paper selects zk-SNARKs (zero-knowledge succinct non-interactive argument of knowledge) as the zero-knowledge proof algorithm for implementation, primarily due to its significant advantages in terms of performance and security. Firstly, zk-SNARKs provide highly efficient verification times and compact proof sizes, making it well-suited for environments with stringent computational and bandwidth requirements. Additionally, zk-SNARKs offer strong security guarantees, including resistance to quantum attacks, which ensures a higher level of security for privacy-preserving systems. This algorithm has been widely adopted and extensively analyzed in cryptography, making it a reliable choice for securing transactions and ensuring privacy in the proposed design.

In the proposed scheme, the seller interacts with the authority, which uses its own deployed zk-SNARKs protocol to carry out the trusted setup phase, generating the public parameters of the system.

First, the system uses a random seed s and a selected elliptic curve parameter set to generate the system's public parameters $\{G, H\}$, among others. Here, $G \in$ the elliptic curve parameter set, and $H = s \cdot G$ is another point generated based on the random number s. This parameter will be used by all participants in the zero-knowledge proof system.

Secondly, the parameters that sellers need to upload to the authority include:

- Computational logic circuit definitions, C : For example, topological diagrams containing input wire definitions and logic operations.
- Input variables, $\mathbf{x} = \{x_1, x_2, \ldots, x_n\}$: These are the data attributes provided by the seller representing the values that need to be proven, such as data attributes collected by IoT sensor devices and case data from medical systems.
- Auxiliary information, $\mathbf{a} = \{a_1, a_2, \ldots, a_m\}$: These are the internal variables of the circuit, used to ensure the completeness of the computation.

Specifically, the circuit C represents the computational logic that the seller wants to prove, such as proving that certain data processing (e.g., hash computation) was performed correctly. The circuit C can be represented as a combination of gates through any Boolean or arithmetic circuit, and must satisfy the following condition: $C(x_1, x_2, \ldots, x_n) =$ true or false.

Finally, the authority generates the proving key <proving.key> based on the information uploaded by the data seller, which will be used by the seller to generate the subsequent proof. The formula is: <proving.key> $= H(C, x_i, a_i)$, where H is a hash function or a mapping on the elliptic curve, ensuring the immutability of the input circuit and data.

The authority simultaneously generates the verification key <verification.key>, which is used for the on-chain verification process. The formula is: <verification.key> $= H(s, C, x_i)$, where the verification key is related to the system's generated random seed s and ensures data integrity through hashing.

After the authority generates the keys and the zero-knowledge proof parameters, it returns the <proving.key> to the seller locally, which will be used later to generate the zero-knowledge proof. This proof will allow the data buyer to verify the claimed attributes through the blockchain platform. The <verification.key> is stored locally and will be used later for zero-knowledge proof contract generation when verification is required. At this point, the construction of the public parameters by the authority is complete.

4.2.2. Phase II

After the authority generates the public parameters for the buyers and sellers, the buyers and sellers need to invoke the on-chain smart contracts to establish the best buyer and seller matching in the second stage. In our design, the smart contract acts as a marketplace function. As shown in Figure 4, we designed a smart contract that can support fine-grained matching based on the linear search matching function, which defines the basic requirements of the transaction and the basic attribute set of the data. The registration information D_i can be as specific as the address of the buyer and seller, the amount of data, the type of data, the data threshold, and the price of the data, etc., and it can be changed according to actual buyer needs to achieve more specific and fine-grained matching.

After the buyer and seller groups have all registered their information, the smart contract will traverse all buyers, and for each buyer, traverse all sellers, looking for the seller that meets the data conditions preset by the buyer ahead of time. The seller's data thresholds should satisfy the buyer's threshold requirements, the seller's price requirements should meet the buyer's price thresholds, etc. If qualified sellers are found and the number of sellers is greater than or equal to two, the seller with the lowest price is selected as the best match. After successful matching, the MatchFound event is triggered and the matched buyer is removed from the buyer array to improve matching efficiency and avoid repeated matching, which satisfies the resource consumption problem in the vast majority of data transaction scenarios.

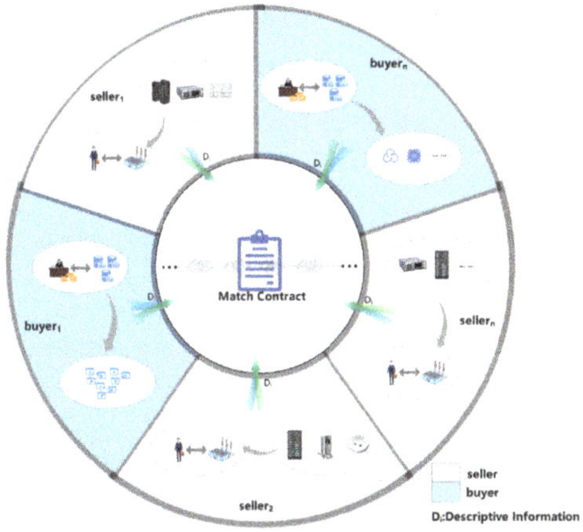

Figure 4. Matching of trading groups.

After the contract function successfully returns the best buyer and seller from the matching process, the seller first needs to encrypt the data for the first time. Here, the seller uses their own generated symmetric key to do so; the seller selects the key h and divides the plaintext into 128-bit data blocks and fills them. The plaintext data blocks are encrypted and the final output is the ciphertext M. Then, the seller will obtain the buyer's public key Q_B uploaded to the chain in the first stage, and assign it to the seller's initial encrypted data M for $0 \leq M \leq n-1$. Subsequently, the seller selects a random number k, and $k \in \{1, 2, \ldots, n-1\}$ calculates the point:

$$X_1(x_1, y_1) = kQ, \tag{1}$$

The seller re-selects $k$the random number if $x_1 = 0$ and calculates the point:

$$X_2(x_2, y_2) = kG, \tag{2}$$

and then calculates the ciphertext:

$$C \equiv Mx_1 modn, \tag{3}$$

(X_2, C) is to be used as the final ciphertext M.

After the seller performs double encryption, they will encapsulate the final ciphertext (X_2, C) into a file and upload it to the storage center IPFS to get its returned hash value summary CID, which can be used for subsequent data lookup and access. The storage center will divide the file into fixed-size data blocks, typically 256 KB, to ensure more efficient file distribution and storage. Each data block is assigned a unique content identifier (CID), generated by hashing the block using a cryptographic hash function (SHA-256). This guarantees that each block has a unique identifier and ensures the integrity of the data block. The storage center also creates a Merkle Directed Acyclic Graph (Merkle DAG) structure from these blocks, using hash values to represent the data dependencies. The hash value of each file block is used to generate higher-level hash values, eventually forming the root hash (Root CID) of the entire file, which serves as the unique identifier for the file. Any request for this file will be made through this root hash, which facilitates subsequent file lookup and retrieval.

Because the storage center can distribute each block of the file across different nodes rather than storing it centrally on a single server, this decentralized storage enhances the system's redundancy and fault tolerance. This process guarantees the confidentiality and integrity of the data during transmission and storage, and meets the strict requirements for data security and traceability in the data trading environment.

4.2.3. Phase III

This phase is the execution phase of the transaction between the buyer and the seller after the successful matching. As shown in Figure 5, Following the completion of the first two phases of preparation, the data trading scenario will enter the final execution phase of the transaction. The seller will use the zero-knowledge proof <proving.key> proof key generated in the first stage combined with their own proof parameters to generate verifiable proofs Π, including the specific nature of the data, the initial encryption of the data hash value, and other items. The construction of the proof is usually based on the definition of circuit C, along with the seller's private input x_i. It is a non-interactive proof Π that contains information about the correct execution of the circuit and does not reveal the specific value of x_i. The seller then uplinks both the generated proof file and the IPFS CID for the buyer to access. After the buyer obtains the CID, it will go to the IPFS to query, and after obtaining the correct return, it will capture the file locally, and then use its own key to decrypt it for the first time.

$$\Pi \leftarrow prove(< proving.key >, \{x_i\}, C, \{a_i\} \cdots >), \tag{4}$$

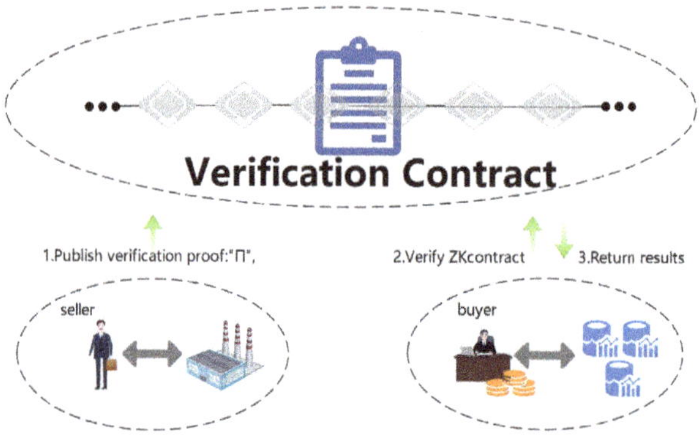

Figure 5. Transaction execution.

The buyer first calculates:

$$X_1(x_1, y_1) = dX_2 = d(kG) = k(dG) = kQ, \tag{5}$$

and subsequently can calculate to obtain, once encrypted, the ciphertext $M \equiv Cx_1^{-1} \bmod n$. Subsequently, the buyer calls the pre-prepared ZK verification smart contract for transaction verification, and they use the seller-uploaded Π as an input to the zero-knowledge proof contract to verify the nature of what the buyer wants to let the seller to prove. If the smart contract returns the correct response, it serves as proof that the seller's behavior is fair. In order to meet the relatively perfect requirements of full-process fairness and security, after the verification, the buyer can be assured based on the initial encrypted hash summary and the buyer's own, already obtained for comparison. If correct, this shows that the seller's behavior is safe and that the data transmission process is free of tampering.

$$true/false \leftarrow Verify(< verification.key >, \Pi), \tag{6}$$

After this, the buyer and seller jointly invoke the transaction contract, confirm the transaction according to the pre-determined rules, return the key that can unlock the data for the buyer, return the currency for the seller, and the transaction is successfully concluded. Through the above operations, the transaction is successfully completed, ensuring the security and integrity of the data as well as the fairness of the transaction. In the data trading environment, this solution not only guarantees the security of information transmission and storage, but also ensures the rights and interests of all parties involved in the transaction, and improves the overall trust and transaction efficiency of the system. Ultimately, efficient, secure, and trustworthy data exchange and value transfer is realized.

5. Experimentation and Evaluation

5.1. Experimental Environment

We implemented the proposed fair trade system and conducted a series of experiments to evaluate its performance. The system consists of two main components: a fine-grained matching module based on smart contracts, and a verification module based on zero-knowledge proofs and blockchain networks. For the verification module based on zero-knowledge proofs, the ZKP scheme is employed to perform several functions including witness generation, key generation, zero-knowledge proof generation, contract generation, and verification of contracts. These functions are programmed by using Zokrates 0.8.7, a toolkit for zero-knowledge proof implementations. The blockchain network is developed on the Ethernet public chain, using the Solidity language to implement smart contracts. We define multiple seller–buyers as participants in the blockchain network. The system has an Intel(R) Core(TM) i7-8700 CPU @ 3.20 GHz 3.19 GHz processor and 16.0 GB of RAM.

5.2. Experimental Results

To validate the feasibility of the proposed scheme, we simulated a real-world industrial IoT data trading scenario. The experiment was conducted on a small-scale blockchain network consisting of 10 participant nodes, including eight data buyers and two data sellers. Each data seller managed a set of 10 to 50 different types of industrial IoT devices, such as temperature and humidity sensors or pressure monitoring devices, which generated continuous data streams. In this simulation, each data seller held between 30 to 50 sets of data based on the actual data generated by their devices, with each set containing 100 sensor readings or other industrial equipment data. Specifically, Figure 6 illustrates the amount of data held by buyers and sellers and their respective data demands, while Figure 7 shows the price demands of buyers and sellers.

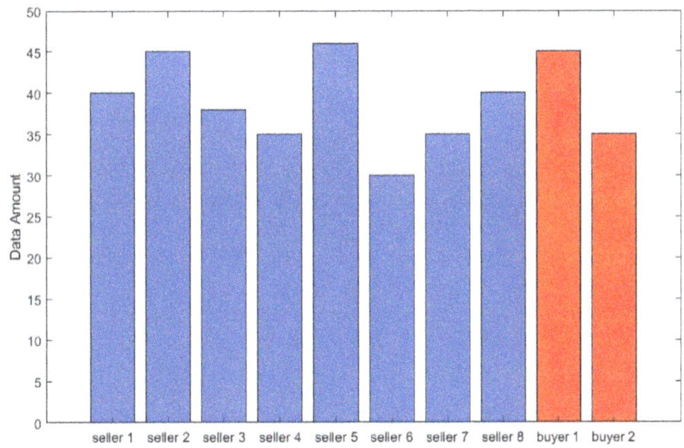

Figure 6. Data ownership requirements.

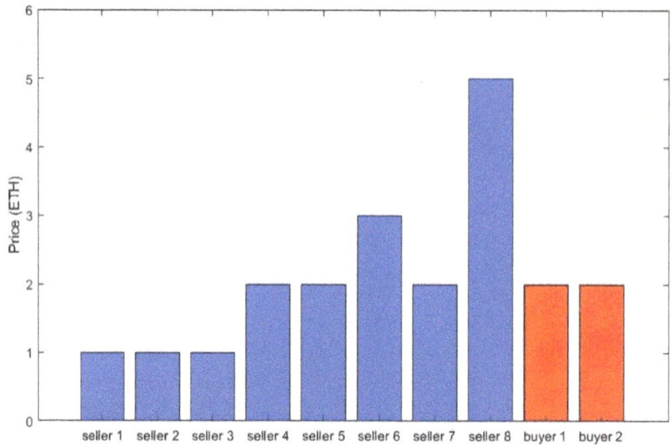

Figure 7. Data prices.

5.2.1. Matching Simulation

In our simulation, we assumed that all users had different data preferences or data type requests. By using the linear search matching mechanism, the smart contract firstly compared and excluded specific buyer and seller groups based on data preferences and types, and then selected the buyer and seller groups with matching preferences. Secondly, the time threshold requirements and price demands of buyers and sellers were matched to obtain the best buyer and seller pairs.

In the pre-transaction phase, that is, the matching phase, the seller and buyer groups simultaneously called the registration matching contract deployed on the blockchain to register the data information they had. We assumed that the eight sellers possessed types of data containing information about temperature, humidity, wind speed in different amounts, and that the price of the demand for each type of data was also high and low. The two buyers were defined as having different types of data requirements, namely, temperature and humidity. Figure 8 shows the gas fee required by a group of ten buyers and sellers when calling the registered matching contract. In order to facilitate the calculation, we uniformly set the Gas Price to 0.001 Gwei. From Figure 8, it can be seen that the gas required by our setup contract was maintained in a stable and low range, and the cost of the transaction members was also kept in a relatively low range. Figure 9 shows the execution cost of the matching function after the transaction group has registered its information, and the execution cost of the function in matching suitable sellers and buyers, which is the same as the cost of registering the information, and because we set the matching function to remove a buyer after it has been matched with a suitable seller, we avoided wasted resources due to repeated matching. Figure 9 shows that the execution cost of the matching contract in the first two phases of the linear search for suitable sellers was relatively high. Figure 9 shows that the execution cost incurred by the matching contract in the first two phases of the linear search of the transaction population for suitable sellers is relatively high, and after matching two buyers with suitable sellers, the transaction cost plummeted to a very low level due to the completion of successful matches for the subject buyers. This will be maintained until new buyers appear.

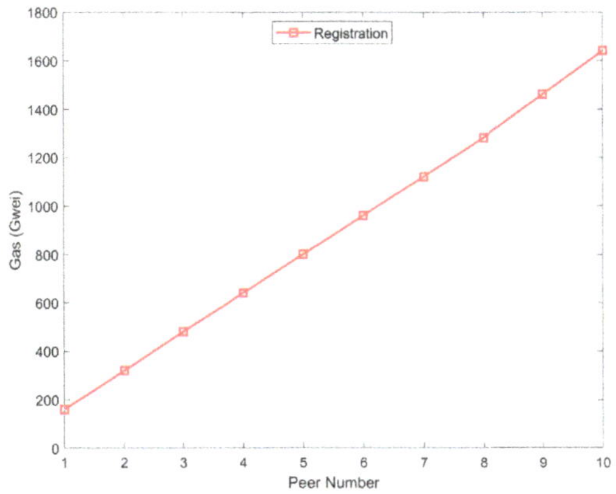

Figure 8. Registration cost.

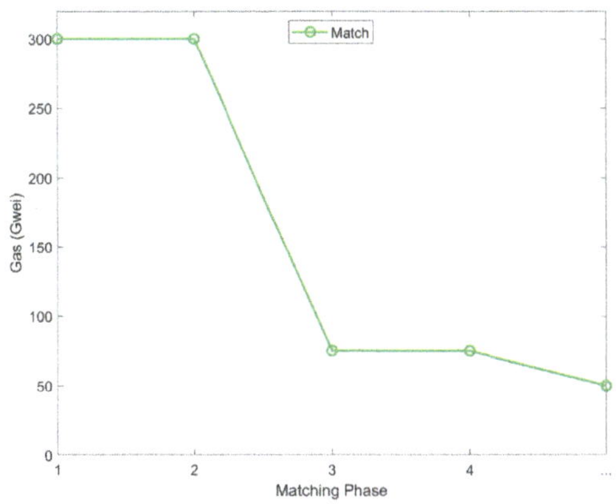

Figure 9. Matching phase costs.

5.2.2. Zero-Knowledge Proof Simulation

After going through the matching phase, the seller needs to verify the zero-knowledge proof of their data. We verify the assumptions about the nature of the data required by the buyer, such as the buyer needing the seller to prove that all the data in the dataset is contained in a specific threshold, the seller needing to prove that the amount of data in the dataset and the sum of the data satisfies a certain requirement, and the seller ensuring that the data, after initial encryption, satisfies the hash image matching requirement, etc.

For these hypothetical requirements, we carried out the actual simulation of matching buyers and sellers on the chain. First of all, in the previous simulation, we obtained the blockchain addresses of buyers and sellers, and then we used their addresses to generate high-level DSL code in accordance with the nature of the various hypothetical requirements.

As demonstrated in Algorithms 1–3, we present three logical verification methods that data buyers can utilize: verifying that the values within the dataset fall within a specified range, verifying that the dataset size meets the expected range, and verifying that the dataset's hash is correct. These three verification methods ensure that the data seller's requirements regarding the dataset's attributes are met.

Algorithm 1 Value Range Verification Process

Input: Array $a[N]$, $threshold\_min$, $threshold\_max$
Output: True or False

for each element $a[i]$ in array $a[N]$ **do**
  if $a[i] < threshold\_min$ **or** $a[i] > threshold\_max$ **then**
    return False
  end if
end for
return True

Algorithm 2 Dataset Size Verification Process

Input: Array $a[N]$, $expected\_size$
Output: True or False

if $N \neq expected\_size$ **then**
  return False
else
  return True
end if

Algorithm 3 Hash Verification Process

Input: Array $a[N]$, $hash$, $hash\_function$
Output: True or False

$computed\_hash \leftarrow hash\_function(a)$
if $computed\_hash \neq hash$ **then**
  return False
else
  return True
end if

This represents the process of constructing the validation properties of the premise assumptions, and in the process of constructing the DSL code for several properties, it can be found that the size of the DSL code is maintained at a very small level. The DSL code is compiled, witnessed, and proofed, resulting in a provable Proof.Json file that can be exported to the contract and then verified on the chain, as shown in Figure 10, where other participants can verify the smart contract's commitment to the industrial data in each match.

Figures 11 and 12 show the Solidity contract and verification result output corresponding to one of the verification logics. Upon input validation, the contract generates '0x0000. . . 00001', which signifies successful verification.

We have uplinked the validated contracts generated for several properties, and the Table 1 shows the size of the corresponding validation file and the corresponding DSL code generated for each property, which shows a trend in size that renders these more adaptable for the end-side nodes in industrial IoT scenarios. As shown in Figure 13, we have verified a total of four properties of contracts and divided the data into two parts: deployment cost and verification cost. Figure 13 demonstrates that the deployment cost increases with the number of contracts in a linear trend, and the execution cost required for the verification of each contract stabilizes at a smaller value.

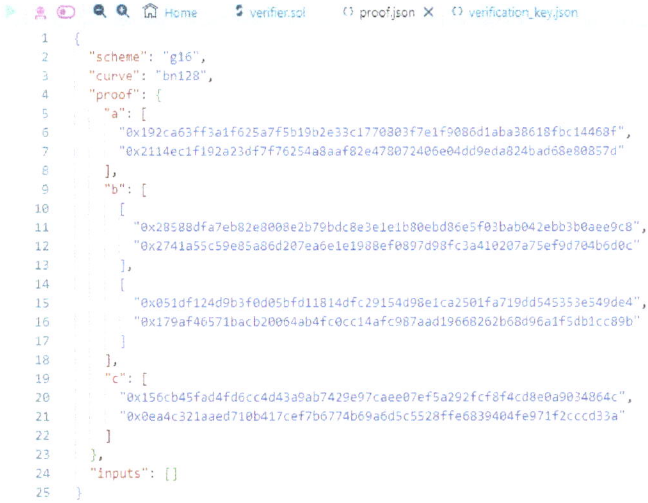

Figure 10. Proof file.

Figure 11. Verification of Contract Overview.

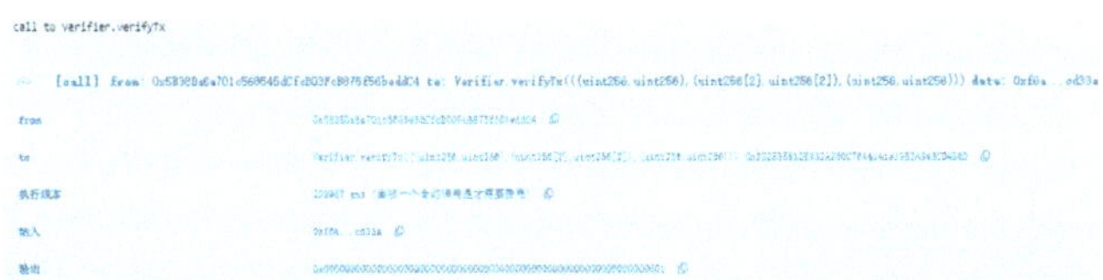

Figure 12. Verifier result.

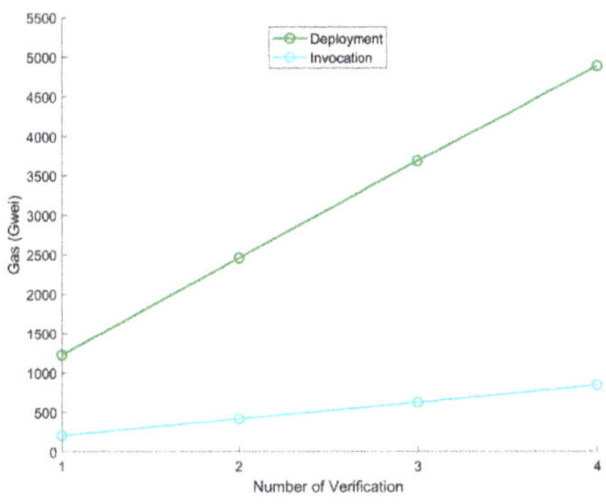

Figure 13. Verification cost.

Table 1. Verification sizes for different characteristics.

	Characteristic 1	Characteristic 2	Characteristic 3	Characteristic 4	...
DSL Code	330 bytes	324 bytes	274 bytes	285 bytes	...
Verification Size	10.3 kb	10 kb	9.63 kb	9.82 kb	...

Secondly, we compared the gas consumption required for different input data with the BZDIMS system [27], as shown in Table 2. BZDT represents the execution costs of our proposed scheme under three different input data sizes: 100 bytes, 200 bytes, and 300 bytes. The results indicate that the costs of the two schemes are roughly similar for different data inputs, demonstrating the strong stability of our approach.

Additionally, we conducted a comparative analysis of the gas used in our scheme with another relatively mature solution: the Aztec protocol, which is based on ZK Rollup technology. The fixed gas cost for a batch of ZK Rollup transactions is approximately 500,000 gas. In comparison, the execution cost of the verification contract for data sellers in our scheme is about 200,000 gas. However, due to the particular nature of the Aztec protocol, its cost applies to a batch of transactions, meaning the cost of ZK Rollup technology is significantly lower than that of our scheme. Nevertheless, in highly privacy-sensitive data trading scenarios, sellers may only need to prove the attributes of their data, and the trading groups often exhibit complex and dynamic changes. Our scheme, with its fixed cost structure, offers a more flexible proof generation method while ensuring both privacy and accuracy.

Table 2. Gas used Comparison for different data sizes.

Data (Bytes)	**Gas Used**	
	zk-SNARKs	
	BZDT	**BZDIMS**
100	149,675	153,859
200	187,924	195,061
300	208,967	215,663

We conducted a transaction simulation for industrial IoT data, and based on the simulation results of this experiment, it can be inferred that the scheme has high generality and can be applied to other scenarios. For example, in medical scenarios, the model can build a transaction bridge between hospitals and patients. First, both parties register their information through a common transaction platform and find the best buyer and seller through a fine-grained matching algorithm. Next, double encryption is utilized to protect the patient's private information, while the authenticity of patient-provided data, such as consultation information and results, is verified through non-interactive zero-knowledge proof. In the financial industry, the model enables credit data transactions between banks and credit bureaus, and the scheme's efficient matching and automated transaction mechanisms can significantly reduce transaction costs. In the manufacturing industry, the model can be used for transaction sharing of supply chain data. Manufacturers and suppliers register and match through the platform, and utilize encryption and zero-knowledge proof technology to protect trade secrets, making data transactions in each link of the supply chain safer and more efficient, while keeping transaction costs within a low range.

In conclusion, the scheme is highly versatile and practicable in different scenarios, which not only enhances the security and privacy protection of data transactions, but also reduces the transaction costs through efficient matching algorithms and automated transaction mechanisms, and provides a solution to the subsequent scalability problems that may exist in terms of the continuous growth of users through off-chain storage.

Of course, we have also noted that current blockchain systems often face limitations in transaction processing speed and throughput when handling large-scale data transactions. The computational complexity of zk-SNARKs is another challenge that needs to be addressed. While IPFS performs well in terms of data storage and access, it still encounters challenges such as network latency and node availability when dealing with large-scale data storage. These challenges require further optimization and improvement. In the future, we plan to introduce sharding technology, Layer 2 solutions, zk-SNARKs optimization models, and IPFS node expansion to further enhance the overall performance and scalability of the solution, ensuring its effectiveness in handling larger-scale data transactions.

6. Conclusions

In this paper, we propose a data transaction security mechanism that combines smart contracts and staged non-interactive zero-knowledge proof techniques to solve the fairness and security problems that exist in data transactions in distributed systems. We provide the amount of underlying data as well as the execution cost of the matching and proof phases in our proposed modeling scheme, demonstrating the low cost and feasibility of the model. Meanwhile, the scalability of the system in terms of handling large amount of data and a growing number of users is enhanced using an off-chain storage technique. The blockchain plays the role of a verifier in the authentication scheme, reducing unnecessary communication overhead. The participating nodes of the experimental setup are able to verify the correctness of the prover's statement through a contract in the blockchain. In our future research, we will focus on continuing to optimize the computational performance of zero-knowledge proofs by reducing their computational complexity to better accommodate resource-constrained devices. In addition, we will explore the applicability of the system in more application scenarios and further integrate advanced privacy protection techniques to enhance the level of privacy protection during data transactions.Concurrently, an investigation will be conducted into the potential for blockchain to be integrated with other distributed architectures, with the objective of enhancing the flexibility and compatibility of the system.

Author Contributions: Conceptualization, B.Z. and H.P.; methodology, B.Z.; formal analysis, B.Z., H.P. and K.L.; writing—original draft preparation, B.Z.; writing—review and editing, B.Z., H.P. and Y.X.; writing—review, J.W., D.F. and W.Z. All authors have read and agreed to the published version of the manuscript.

Funding: This research was funded in part by the National Key Research and Development Project of China under Grant 2023YFB2703603, Key Research Project for Higher Education of Henan Province 24A520059, Strength Enhancement Plan for Advantageous Disciplines of Zhongyuan University of Technology GG202425, and 2024 Scientific and Technological Research Project in Henan Province 242102210136.

Data Availability Statement: Data are contained within the article.

Conflicts of Interest: The authors declare no conflicts of interest.

References

1. Liu, J.; Zhang, J.; Song, S.H.; Letaief, K.B. Client-Edge-Cloud Hierarchical Federated Learning. In Proceedings of the ICC 2020—2020 IEEE International Conference on Communications (ICC), Dublin, Ireland, 7–11 June 2020; pp. 1–6.
2. Farahani, B.; Tabibian, S.; Ebrahimi, H. Toward a Personalized Clustered Federated Learning: A Speech Recognition Case Study. *IEEE Internet Things J.* **2023**, *10*, 18553–18562. [CrossRef]
3. Zhao, Y.; Zhao, J.; Jiang, L.; Tan, R.; Niyato, D.; Li, Z.; Lyu, L.; Liu, Y. Correction to "Privacy-Preserving Blockchain-Based Federated Learning for IoT Devices". *IEEE Internet Things J.* **2023**, *10*, 973. [CrossRef]
4. Fan, S.; Zhang, H.; Zeng, Y.; Cai, W. Hybrid Blockchain-Based Resource Trading System for Federated Learning in Edge Computing. *IEEE Internet Things J.* **2021**, *8*, 2252–2264. [CrossRef]

5. Wang, X.; Hu, J.; Lin, H.; Liu, W.; Moon, H.; Piran, J. Federated Learning-Empowered Disease Diagnosis Mechanism in the Internet of Medical Things: From the Privacy-Preservation Perspective. *IEEE Trans. Ind. Inform.* **2022**, *19*, 7905–7913. [CrossRef]
6. Chen, C.; Wu, J.; Lin, H.; Chen, W.; Zheng, Z. A Secure and Efficient Blockchain-Based Data Trading Approach for Internet of Vehicles. *IEEE Trans. Veh. Technol.* **2019**, *68*, 9110–9121. [CrossRef]
7. Li, T.; Wang, H.; He, D.; Yu, J. Blockchain-Based Privacy-Preserving and Rewarding Private Data Sharing for IoT. *IEEE Internet Things J.* **2022**, *9*, 15138–15149. [CrossRef]
8. Zhang, M.; Liu, J.; Feng, K.; Beltran, F.; Zhang, Z. SmartAuction: A blockchain-based secure implementation of private data queries. *Future Gener. Comput. Syst.* **2022**, *138*, 198–211. [CrossRef]
9. Pop, C.D.; Antal, M.; Cioara, T.; Anghel, I.; Salomie, I. Blockchain and Demand Response: Zero-Knowledge Proofs for Energy Transactions Privacy. *Sensors* **2020**, *20*, 5678. [CrossRef]
10. Xue, L.; Ni, J.; Liu, D.; Lin, X.; Shen, X. Blockchain-Based Fair and Fine-Grained Data Trading With Privacy Preservation. *IEEE Trans. Comput.* **2023**, *72*, 2440–2453. [CrossRef]
11. Hopwood, D.; Bowe, S.; Hornby, T.; Wilcox, N. *Zcash Protocol Specification*; GitHub: San Francisco, CA, USA, 2016.
12. Jiang, S.; Li, J.; Zhang, X.; Yue, H.; Wu, H.; Zhou, Y. Secure and Privacy-Preserving Energy Trading With Demand Response Assistance Based on Blockchain. *IEEE Trans. Netw. Sci. Eng.* **2023**, *11*, 1238–1250. [CrossRef]
13. Aitzhan, N.Z.; Svetinovic, D. Security and Privacy in Decentralized Energy Trading Through Multi-Signatures, Blockchain and Anonymous Messaging Streams. *IEEE Trans. Dependable Secur. Comput.* **2018**, *15*, 840–852. [CrossRef]
14. Son, Y.-B.; Im, J.-H.; Kwon, H.-Y.; Jeon, S.-Y.; Lee, M.-K. Privacy-Preserving Peer-to-Peer Energy Trading in Blockchain-Enabled Smart Grids Using Functional Encryption. *Energies* **2020**, *13*, 1321. [CrossRef]
15. Daghmehchi Firoozjaei, M.; Ghorbani, A.; Kim, H.; Song, J. Hy-Bridge: A Hybrid Blockchain for Privacy-Preserving and Trustful Energy Transactions in Internet-of-Things Platforms. *Sensors* **2020**, *20*, 928. [CrossRef]
16. Kumar, R.; Kumar, P.; Tripathi, R.; Gupta, G.P.; Islam, A.K.M.N.; Shorfuzzaman, M. Permissioned Blockchain and Deep Learning for Secure and Efficient Data Sharing in Industrial Healthcare Systems. *IEEE Trans. Ind. Inform.* **2022**, *18*, 8065–8073. [CrossRef]
17. Zhang, X.; Li, X.; Miao, Y.; Luo, X.; Wang, Y.; Ma, S.; Weng, J. A Data Trading Scheme With Efficient Data Usage Control for Industrial IoT. *IEEE Trans. Ind. Inform.* **2021**, *18*, 4456–4465. [CrossRef]
18. Dixit, A.; Singh, A.; Rahulamathavan, Y.; Rajarajan, M. FAST DATA: A Fair, Secure, and Trusted Decentralized IIoT Data Marketplace Enabled by Blockchain. *IEEE Internet Things J.* **2021**, *10*, 2934–2944. [CrossRef]
19. Zhou, Z.; Tian, Y.; Xiong, J.; Ma, J.; Peng, C. Blockchain-Enabled Secure and Trusted Federated Data Sharing in IIoT. *IEEE Trans. Ind. Inform.* **2022**, *19*, 6669–6681. [CrossRef]
20. Huang, C.; Liu, D.; Ni, J.; Lu, R.; Shen, X. Achieving Accountable and Efficient Data Sharing in Industrial Internet of Things. *IEEE Trans. Ind. Inform.* **2020**, *17*, 1416–1427. [CrossRef]
21. Guan, Z.; Wan, Z.; Yang, Y.; Zhou, Y.; Huang, B. BlockMaze: An Efficient Privacy-Preserving Account-Model Blockchain Based on zk-SNARKs. *IEEE Trans. Dependable Secur. Comput.* **2020**, *19*, 1446–1463. [CrossRef]
22. Singh, M.; Aujla, G.S.; Bali, R.S. A Deep Learning-Based Blockchain Mechanism for Secure Internet of Drones Environment. *IEEE Trans. Intell. Transp. Syst.* **2020**, *22*, 4404–4413. [CrossRef]
23. Huang, H.; Zhu, P.; Xiao, F.; Sun, X.; Huang, Q. A blockchain-based scheme for privacy-preserving and secure sharing of medical data. *Comput. Secur.* **2020**, *99*, 102010. [CrossRef]
24. Li, Y.; Tao, X.; Zhang, X.; Liu, J.; Xu, J. Privacy-Preserved Federated Learning for Autonomous Driving. *IEEE Trans. Intell. Transp. Syst.* **2021**, *23*, 8423–8434. [CrossRef]
25. Sun, X.; Yu, F.R.; Zhang, P.; Sun, Z.; Xie, W.; Peng, X. A Survey on Zero-Knowledge Proof in Blockchain. *IEEE Netw.* **2021**, *35*, 198–205. [CrossRef]
26. Li, Y.; Susilo, W.; Yang, G.; Yu, Y.; Liu, D.; Du, X.; Guizani, M. A Blockchain-Based Self-Tallying Voting Protocol in Decentralized IoT. *IEEE Trans. Dependable Secur. Comput.* **2020**, *19*, 119–130. [CrossRef]
27. Yang, X.; Li, W. A zero-knowledge-proof-based digital identity management scheme in blockchain. *Comput. Secur.* **2020**, *99*, 102050. [CrossRef]

electronics

MDPI

Article

Throughput Optimization for Blockchain System with Dynamic Sharding †

Chuyi Liu [1,2,3,‡], Jianxiong Wan [1,2,3,*,‡], Leixiao Li [1,2,3] and Bingbing Yao [1,2]

1 College of Data Science and Application, Inner Mongolia University of Technology, Hohhot 010080, China; lcy@imut.edu.cn (C.L.); lileixiao@imut.edu.cn (L.L.); 20201800637@imut.edu.cn (B.Y.)
2 Inner Mongolia Autonomous Region Engineering & Technology Research Center of Big Data Based Software Service, Hohhot 010080, China
3 Research Center of Large-Scale Energy Storage Technologies, Hohhot 010080, China
* Correspondence: jxwan@imut.edu.cn
† This paper is an extended version of our paper published in IEEE SMC 2023.
‡ These authors contributed equally to this work.

Abstract: Sharding technology, which divides a network into multiple disjoint groups so that transactions can be processed in parallel, is applied to blockchain systems as a promising solution to improve Transactions Per Second (TPS). This paper considers the Optimal Blockchain Sharding (OBCS) problem as a Markov Decision Process (MDP) where the decision variables are the number of shards, block size and block interval. Previous works solved the OBCS problem via Deep Reinforcement Learning (DRL)-based methods, where the action space must be discretized to increase processability. However, the discretization degrades the quality of the solution since the optimal solution usually lies between discrete values. In this paper, we treat the block size and block interval as continuous decision variables and provide dynamic sharding strategies based on them. The Branching Dueling Q-Network Blockchain Sharding (BDQBS) algorithm is designed for discrete action spaces. Compared with traditional DRL algorithms, the BDQBS overcomes the drawbacks of high action space dimensions and difficulty in training neural networks. And it improves the performance of the blockchain system by 1.25 times. We also propose a sharding control algorithm based on the Parameterized Deep Q-Networks (P-DQN) algorithm, i.e., the Parameterized Deep Q-Networks Blockchain Sharding (P-DQNBS) algorithm, to efficiently handle the discrete–continuous hybrid action space without the scalability issues. Also, the method can effectively improve the TPS by up to 28%.

Keywords: blockchain; sharding; deep reinforcement learning; hybrid action space

1. Introduction

In recent years, blockchain technology has emerged as a disruptive and transformational technology with high trust and security potential, and it has been widely used in various fields, such as identity management [1], supply chains [2], game systems [3], food tracing [4], value trading [5], etc. However, it is still challenging to apply blockchain systems in large-scale systems because of their slow data-processing speed. For example, Ethereum [6] can encompass thousands of blockchain nodes, but it can only process 14 Transactions Per Second (TPS); Hyperledger [7] achieves throughput of more than 3500 TPS. However, in some industries such as finance, the TPS of 3500 is still too low to process a large number of transactions.

At present, the most effective way to improve blockchain throughput is to apply sharding technology to a blockchain and redesign its architecture. Sharding splits the blockchain network into multiple disjointed networks called shards. In a so-called shard network, each node only communicates with a limited number of nodes within the same shard. This technique substantially reduces the storage, computation and communication cost [8]. At present, extensive research is being conducted, both in academia and the industry, to optimize sharding policies to improve blockchain TPS. Sharding policies fall under either of the following two categories: (i) static and (ii) dynamic. Static methods refer to unchanged sharding policies [9–12]. Dynamic sharding technology can provide dynamic sharding strategies for dynamic blockchain environments, improving blockchain throughput. Yun et al. [13] proposed a Deep Q-Networks enabled Shard-based Blockchain (DQNBS) scheme that dynamically selects the optimal configuration (i.e., the number of shards, block size and block intervals, etc.) to maximize TPS. Zhang et al. [14] proposed SkyChain, which consists of an adaptive ledger protocol to facilitate merging or spliting the block, and an optimization framework which can adjust the number of shards, the block size and block interval for a long-term balance between security and TPS. However, their works may yield sub-optimal solutions since the action space is discrete and the number of available actions is strictly limited for tractability. This is because the Deep Q-Network (DQN) algorithm did not solve the problem of action space explosion, resulting in difficulty in training neural networks.

In the blockchain computing process, tasks need to be sharded in real time according to the resources and system conditions, i.e., the state at that time, so as to improve the execution efficiency of the system. This is consistent with the logic of MDP in dealing with the dynamic planning problem. Therefore, we endeavor to find higher-quality sharding polices by reformulating the Optimal Blockchain Sharding (OBCS) problem into a Markov Decision Process (MDP) with discrete–continuous hybrid action space, where the number of shards is discrete-valued, while the block size and block interval are continuous. We use two different methods to solve this problem. In the first method, we discretize continuous variables and then process them according to the discretization method. The Branching Dueling Q-Network (BDQ) algorithm is used in the blockchain fragmentation problem, and we propose the Branching Dueling Q-Network Blockchain Sharding (BDQBS) algorithm. The BDQBS solves the problem of action space explosion and provides better action strategies for blockchain systems, thereby improving blockchain performance. However, the BDQBS discretizes continuous action to obtain discrete action space, which ignores precise action. So, we used another method, applying the Parameterized Deep Q-Networks (P-DQN) algorithm to solve the problem in the discrete–continuous hybrid action space and propose the Parameterized Deep Q-Networks Blockchain Sharding (P-DQNBS) algorithm. The P-DQNBS provides more precise action strategies for blockchain systems, further improving the performance of blockchain.

The main contributions of this project are summarized as follows:

1. Algorithm design: The BDQBS and P-DQNBS are proposed for blockchain sharding problems. Through the unique neural network structure of BDQ, BDQBS reduces the output dimension of the neural network, solving the problem of neural networks being difficult to train as a result of action space explosion. At the same time, it also shortens the time for parameter tuning and provides a fast sharding policy for blockchain. Compared to the BDQBS, the P-DQNBS provides a more accurate sharding policy for blockchain, which is more suitable for the real dynamic blockchain environment.
2. Extensive simulation-based evaluation: We use Python to build a blockchain sharding simulation environment based on existing blockchain sharding systems. We implemented BDQBS and P-DQNBS for different action spaces in the optimization of blockchain throughput based on sharding technology. By comparing throughput, average sub-action and security, the results show that the BDQBS and P-DQNBS are significantly superior to the baseline algorithm. P-DQN and BDQ have increased throughput by 1.28 and 1.25 times.

The rest of the paper is organized as follows. Section 2 reviews the related literature. In Section 3, the system model is presented. Our proposed sharding algorithm is presented in Section 4, followed by simulation results in Section 5. Finally, we conclude this paper in Section 6.

2. Related Work

This section reviews related studies on sharding technology, which are grouped into two categories: static sharding and dynamic sharding. Traditional blockchain networks usually use static sharding to process transactions, i.e., the entire network is divided into multiple fixed-size blocks, each of which processes a certain number of transactions. The static sharding process is relatively simple and easy to implement. However, static sharding is prone to network congestion and transaction latency problems. Dynamic sharding dynamically adjusts the size and number of shards based on the network load and the node availability, ensuring that the network is always able to handle highly concurrent transactions. Dynamic sharding is complicated to implement due to the complexity of parameter changes.

2.1. Static Sharding Technology

Typical static sharding techniques are Elastico [9] and OmniLedger [10]. Lu et al. [9] proposed Elastico, the first sharding technology for public chains, which combines the Proof of Work (PoW) [15] protocol with the Practical Byzantine Fault Toll (PBFT) [16,17] protocol. Nodes establish identification through PoW first, and then are randomly assigned to various committees. A committee can complete the PBFT protocol in each step as the number of nodes in each committee is small enough. Thus, the nodes in each committee can process transactions in parallel, which almost achieves linear scaling of throughput. However, Elastico cannot handle cross-sharding transactions.

The overall architecture of OmniLedger [10] is composed of one identity chain and multiple subchains. OmniLedger uses the RandHound [18] protocol to divide all nodes into different groups and randomly assign these groups to different sharding subchains. The consensus within each shard adopts the PBFT protocol. By removing the full sequence requirements of the blocks, OmniLedger organizes the blocks into a Directed Acyclic Graph structure, which increases the system throughput and reduces the transaction confirmation delay. In addition, OmniLedger uses atomic submission protocols to handle cross-sharding transactions. And by using ledger-editing technology, it sets checkpoints and prunes historical data before checkpoints to reduce the storage pressure on nodes. Using OminiLedger, the throughput of the blockchain increases linearly with the number of shards.

Based on Elastico and OmniLedger, researchers have made improvements to blockchain system architectures, such as Zilliqa [11] and Rapid Chain [12]. The Zilliqa team conducted architecture and performance optimization based on Elastico. In terms of architecture, they proposed a dual-chain architecture, with one transaction chain storing transaction data and one directory service chain storing miner metadata information. In terms of performance optimization, Zilliqa adopted CoSi multi-signature technology in the consensus phase. By using digital signatures instead of MAC in the PBFT protocl, the PBFT can be applied to hundreds of nodes, greatly improving its scalability. On the basis of OmniLedger, RapidChain [12] added information distribution technology based on erasure codes to accelerate the propagation speed of blocks, achieving full sharding technology covering communication computation and storage. In order to reduce the state cost, RapidChain adopts the Cuckoo protocol, which only needs to replace some nodes during each sharding switch. The RapidChain system mainly consists of three important phases, namely the bootstrapping phase, consensus phase and reconfiguration phase. The bootstrapping phase will only run once at the beginning of the RapidChain system, creating an initial random source and randomly selecting a special committee called the reference committee, whose members randomly allocate nodes to form a sharding committee.

2.2. Dynamic Sharding Technology

Although the static methods are easy to design and implement, they cannot adapt to the dynamic blockchain environment, such as a variation in the number nodes in the system and intermittent attacks from malicious nodes, etc. Dynamic sharding technology solves the problem that the sharding policy cannot be adjusted according to the situation. To address this issue, a popular approach is to formulate the OBCS problem as a Markov Decision Process (MDP) and integrate DRL into the sharding controller.

Yun et al. [13] proposed a scalable blockchain system based on fragmentation, which optimizes throughput while maintaining a high security level. They combined sharding technology with DRL, abstracted the blockchain sharding selection process into the MDP and proposed the DQNBS method. Sharding technology continuously delegates mining tasks to other nodes. By adjusting the number of shards, the security level can be changed proactively. It uses DRL to optimize the performance of the blockchain to meet large-scale and dynamic Internet of Things operations. In particular, based on the DRL framework, the concept of trust is integrated into the consensus phase. Thus, we can estimate the malicious probability of the network by monitoring the consensus result of each epoch. Based on network trust, the blockchain calculates the number of secure shards and adopts adaptive control to maintain optimal throughput conditions.

Zhang et al. [14] proposed a sky chain which combines blockchain with DRL. This is a new type of blockchain framework based on dynamic sharding, which achieves a balance between performance and security without affecting scalability in dynamic environments. Firstly, the sky chain adopts an adaptive ledger protocol to ensure that the ledger based on dynamic fragmentation policy can be effectively consolidated or split. Then, it proposes a fragmentation method based on DRL in order to optimize the fragmentation policy under the dynamic environment of a high-dimensional system state. The authors constructed a framework to evaluate blockchain sharding systems in terms of performance and security, achieving a long-term balance between the two by adjusting the sharding interval, number of shards and the block size. In addition, DRL can learn the characteristics of the system from previous experience and obtain long-term returns by adopting appropriate fragmentation strategies according to the current network state.

The above dynamic sharding technologies based on DRL generally adopts the basic DRL algorithm DQN, which solves the problem of state space explosion. However, when the action dimension increases and leads to an explosion in the action space, using DQN will result in the inability of neural network training.

3. System Overview

3.1. System Model

The blockchain sharding system containing N nodes is shown in Figure 1. The blockchain sharding system divides nodes into different shards, and nodes within the shards process transactions in parallel. Firstly, each node in the blockchain needs to solve a workload problem, PoW, to obtain its own identity (ID). The calculation process involves putting the "seed" of the PoW (i.e., EpochRand), the IP address, public key (PK) and the random number Nonce through the SHA-256 hash algorithm to obtain ID. The ID needs to be smaller than the target difficulty value d in the blockchain; i.e., the ID is a 256-bit value that starts with a certain number of 0 bits. Since the SHA-256 hash algorithm is irreversible, the only way to compute the hash value is that the node needs to keep trying to input different values of Nonce until it finds a hash value that meets the conditions. This process consumes a lot of computational resources and time in order to ensure the security of the algorithm. Then, a certain number of nodes are selected form the directory committee (DC) based on the speed of resolving the PoW. Once the nodes in the DC are identified, the blockchain is sharded and the nodes in the blockchain are divided into K shards based on the node's ID. The transactions are processed in parallel, and the nodes in the shards pack the transactions into blocks and execute the Practical Byzantine Fault Tolerance (PBFT) consensus algorithm. PBFT is used to solve the Byzantine Fault Tolerance problem in blockchain networks, i.e., how to guarantee the correctness of the consensus result in the presence of some malicious nodes in the network. The nodes in the shards verify the block and send it to the DC, which packages it into a final block, performs PBFT on it, uploads it to the blockchain after verification and returns the packaged information to all the nodes in the shards for updating.

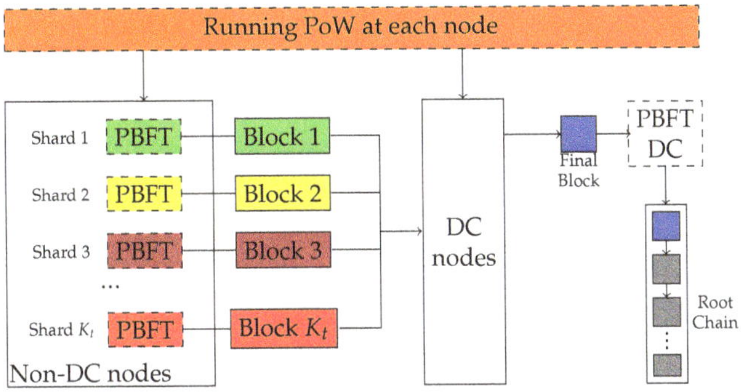

Figure 1. Blockchain sharding process in [19].

At epoch t, the computing capability of node i is denoted as $C_{i,t}$. Sharding begins from each node using its computing capability $C_{i,t}$ to run a computational-intensive task knows as PoW to obtain the identity in the blockchain. All nodes are then grouped as DC nodes and non-DC nodes:

- DC nodes. DC nodes are those who solve the PoW first. They receive local blocks from each shard, and a randomly chosen primary DC node generates the final block by merging all local blocks. The final block should be validated by all DC nodes via PBFT consensus protocol before being broadcast throughout the network and linked to the root chain.
- Non-DC nodes. Non-DC nodes in the blockchain are divided into K_t shards. Here we assume that a transaction can only be assigned to one shard, which is implemented in account-based sharding [20]. All shards process transactions in parallel and create local blocks of size B_t at interval T_t. Then, nodes in a shard broadcast messages through the communication channel with transmission rate $R_{i,j,t}$ to perform a local PBFT consensus protocol to validate that the information in the local block is correct.

3.2. Blockchain Sharding Mechanism

The blockchain sharding clustering mechanism is shown in Figure 2. Firstly, each node selects its own PK and IP address locally for future authentication. Nodes in blockchain networks can obtain their own IDs by solving a simple PoW. The identity ID of q node can be represented as

$$ID = H(EpochRand||IP||PK||Nonce) < d, \tag{1}$$

where EpochRand is the "seed" of the PoW, which needs to be generated at the end of the previous epoch to ensure that the PoW is not pre-caculated. d is the difficulty level of the PoW algorithm. It is a predefined parameter in the network which determines how much computing power is needed to solve the PoW. H is a hash operation.

A sharded blockchain consists of a DC and K shards. To share the sharding information, we need to select DC nodes first. The nodes in the DC are composed of the top C nodes that solve the PoW the fastest. To ensure that the number of nodes in the DC is similar to the other K shards, C=$\lfloor N/[K+1] \rfloor$. After the nodes in the DC are determined, the information is broadcast to other nodes. The non-DC nodes will check the information of the DC nodes. Then, the nodes are assigned into shards, according to the last L bit of the node ID. For example, if $L = 3$, the shard number is equal to the last three digits of ID, namely, $2^L = 2^3 = 8$. All nodes need to send their own information, namely PK, EpochRand, Nonce and ID, to the DC. The nodes in the DC collect all the information and broadcast it throughout the entire network, enabling the entire network to receive fragment information.

After each node knows its shard number, nodes within the same shard establish point-to-point connections.

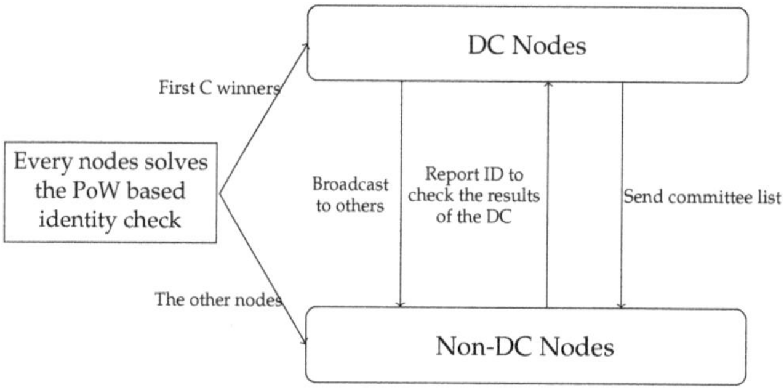

Figure 2. Sharding clustering mechanism in [13].

After the blockchain shard is complete, the division of transactions is determined based on the account UTXO, which means that the transaction is allocated to the shard that matches the last L-bit hash value of the sender's account. This is to prevent malicious users from generating transactions that exceed their balance and distributing them to different shards.

3.3. Markov Decision Process Formulation for Optimal Blockchain Sharding Problem

We model the blockchain sharding problem as an MDP. In our system, the state space, action space and reward function are defined as follows:

- State Space. The system state at epoch t can be expressed by

$$s_t = [\boldsymbol{R}_t, \boldsymbol{C}_t, \boldsymbol{H}_t, P_t], \tag{2}$$

  where $\boldsymbol{R}_t = \{R_{i,j,t}\}$ is the matrix of the data transmission rate, $i, j \in N$; $\boldsymbol{C}_t = \{C_{i,t}\}$ is the vector of the node computing capability; P_t is the probability of malicious nodes in the blockchain at time t, which is calculated based on consensus history [13]; and $\boldsymbol{H}_t = \{H_{i,t}\}$ is the vector of the consensus history of the previous epoch slot, which is a binary variable where $H_{i,t} = 0$ means that node i accepted the block to be linked to the blockchain at epoch $t-1$ and vice versa.
- Action Space. The throughput is closely related to the number of shards K_t, block size B_t (in bytes) and block interval T_t. Thus, we define the action at epoch t as

$$a_t = [K_t, B_t, T_t], \tag{3}$$

  where K_t is discrete and is selected from a finite enumerable set $\{1, 2, \ldots, k_{max}\}$; $T_t \in [T_{min}, T_{max}]$ is continuous. B_t is also discrete, but since the action space of B_t is quite large, e.g., several Megabytes, we assume that B_t is approximately continuous.
- Reward Function. We use the transaction throughput as our reward function. The reward r_t in epoch t can be defined as

$$r_t = \begin{cases} \dfrac{K_t \times \lfloor (B_t - B_H)/b \rfloor}{T_t} & \text{, constraints C1–C3 are satisfied,} \\ 0 & \text{, otherwise,} \end{cases} \tag{4}$$

$$\mathrm{C1}: k_{max} < (N[1 - 3P_t] - 1)/[3NP_t + 1] \tag{5}$$

$$\mathrm{C2}: k_{max} < (2N/[3P_t + 1]) - 1 \tag{6}$$

$$\mathrm{C3}: T_{latency} = T + T_c^k \leq uT, K = 1, 2, \ldots, k \tag{7}$$

where the numerator is the number of transactions processed by K_t shards in parallel and the denominator T_t represents the block interval. B_H is the size of the block head and b is the average size of transactions. In (4), constraints C1 and C2 are security constraints to ensure that after blockchain nodes are sharded, malicious nodes within the shard cannot threaten the security of the entire shard, and to prevent blocks generated by malicious nodes from being uploaded to the blockchain. Constraint C3 is a delay constraint. In order to meet the final attributes of the blockchain, the delay should be completed within several consecutive block intervals u. T_c is the time consumed for consensus.

3.4. The Optimal Blockchain Sharding Problem

The optimal blockchain sharding problem can now be written as the following optimization problem:

$$\max_{a_t=[K_t,B_t,T_t]} \mathbb{E}\sum_{t=0}^{T} \gamma^t r_t, \tag{8}$$

where $\gamma \in [0,1]$ is the discount rate.

Note that P_t can be determined based on $\boldsymbol{H}_t$, and T_c depends upon B_t and K_t. The details for calculating these variables can be found in [13], which we omit here due to space limitations. Problem (8) seeks to maximize the accumulated throughput. Given a policy π, which is a mapping between states and actions, the Q function is defined as the expectation of accumulated reward from state s_t after executing action a_t and following policy π, i.e.,

$$Q_\pi(s_t,a_t) = \mathbb{E}_\pi\left[\sum_{\tau=0}^{\infty} \gamma^\tau r_{t+\tau}|s_t,a_t\right]. \tag{9}$$

The optimal action can be selected once the optimal Q function is found. The optimal Q function satisfies the optimal Bellman equation defined as

$$Q^*_\pi(s_t,a_t) = \mathbb{E}_\pi[r_t + \gamma \max_{a_{t+1}} Q^*(s_{t+1},a_{t+1})]. \tag{10}$$

The traditional Q learning algorithm learns the optimal Q function by

$$\begin{aligned} Q_\pi(s_t,a_t) = {} & Q_\pi(s_t,a_t) + \\ & \alpha(r + \gamma \max_{a_{t+1}} Q_\pi(s_{t+1},a_{t+1}) - Q_\pi(s_t,a_t)), \end{aligned} \tag{11}$$

where $\alpha \geq 0$ is the learning rate, and the Q function is stored in a lookup table. An issue with Q learning is that it can only solve MDPs with discrete action space. However, our problem has a discrete–continuous hybrid action space. As such, it is impossible to directly apply the Q learning algorithm to estimate the optimal Q function. In the next section, we leverage the BDQ and P-DQN [21] to solve problem (8).

4. The Blockchain Sharding Algorithm

In order to improve the performance of the blockchain sharding system, we proposes two blockchain sharding control algorithms based on DRL for different action spaces, namely, blockchain sharding algorithms based on BDQ and P-DQN. The blockchain sharding algorithm based on BDQ not only solves the problem of discrete action space explosion, but also solves the problem of neural networks being difficult to train as a result of action space explosion. The BDQ proposes a new neural network structure with a shared decision module, which is connected to the network branches and state value branches of subactions in the action space. Moreover, it provides a certain degree of independence for each individual action dimension and has better scalability. The blockchain sharding algorithm based on P-DQN solves the problem of discrete–continuous hybrid action space in blockchain sharding decision making. P-DQN uses two different neural networks, namely the policy network and the value network, to predict action. The policy network outputs the continuous action parameters corresponding to a given discrete action, and obtains the continuous action value function from the continuous action parameters and state input value network. The optimal action is selected based on the value function.

4.1. The BDQBS Algorithm

When using DRL to deal with blockchain sharding problems, most studies use DQN to provide the blockchain sharding policy. DQN solves the problem of state space explosion, but when dealing with the problem of action space explosion caused by the combination of the number of actions and the number of action dimensions, DQN has the drawbacks of a complex neural network output and difficulty in training. BDQ is an extension of DQN that proposes a new neural network structure to approximate multidimensional action space functions, achieving a linear increase in network outputs with degrees of freedom. It enables the better training of neural networks, resulting in better action strategies. Therefore, we use BDQ to find the optimal solution to the blockchain sharding problem in the discrete action space.

The neural network structure of BDQ is shown in Figure 3. The state $s_t = (\boldsymbol{R}_t, \boldsymbol{C}_t, \boldsymbol{H}_t, P_t,)$ is input into the neural network. After the shared module, it outputs the dominant functions of $K, B, T, A(s_t, K_t), A(s_t, B_t), A(s_t, T_t)$ and the state value function $V(s_t)$. The dominant function is added to the state value function to obtain the Q value, which is used to select the optimal action.

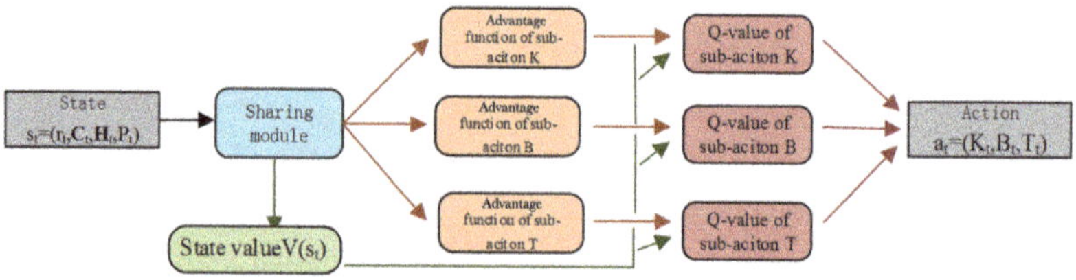

Figure 3. The neural network structure of BDQ.

4.1.1. Algorithm Design

Algorithm 1 shows the details of our BDQ algorithm. In each epoch t, the algorithm first initializes the experience replay pool $\boldsymbol{D}$ to store the experience samples generated by interactions between the agent and the blockchain environment. The experience samples are used to train the neural network. Two neural networks with the same structure, online network and target network, as well as weight θ and θ', are initialized. The status of the blockchain environment $s_t = (\boldsymbol{R}_t, C_t, \boldsymbol{H}_t, P_t)$ is obtained at the current time t (line 6). With the state s_t, the network outputs the advantage function (A_K, A_B, A_T) and state value function $V(s_t)$ of the subaction and adds them together to obtain the Q value of the action. Select $a_t = (K_t, B_t, T_t)$ of blockchain sharding based on the ϵ-greedy policy [22] (line 7). Input a_t into the blockchain (line 8). The blockchain nodes are divided into K shards based on K_t. According to B_t and T_t, the node processes transactions in parallel within time t and generates a block of size B. The DC collects the blocks generated by sharding, merges them into final blocks, and uploads them into the blockchain. The blockchain system proceeds to the next state $s_{t+1} = (\boldsymbol{R}_{t+1}, C_{t+1}, \boldsymbol{H}_{t+1}, P_{t+1})$ and obtains reward r_t, i.e., the throughput of processing transactions (line 9–10). The samples generated by the interaction between the agent and the blockchain system environment are stored in the experience pool to update the neural network (line 11). At last, the network is trained by the experience extracted from experience pool D and the parameters are updated (line 12).

Algorithm 1: The BDQBS Algorithm process

Input: the state of the blockchain system at time $t : s_t = (\boldsymbol{R}_t, \boldsymbol{C}_t, \boldsymbol{H}_t, P_t)$

Output: the action of blockchain system executed at time $t : a_t = (K_t, B_t, T_t)$

1 Initialize the experience playback pool D with size Z;
2 Initialize the online network and target network with the same structure;
3 Initialize the weights of both networks are θ and θ';
4 t=0;
5 **while** $t \leq N$ **do**
6 $\quad s_t \leftarrow$ current environmental status;
7 $\quad$ using the ϵ-greedy policy to select action

$$a_t = \begin{cases} argmaxQ(s_t, a_d), & 1-\epsilon; \\ \text{random generation action}, & \epsilon; \end{cases}$$

8 $\quad$ execute action a_t;
9 $\quad s_{t+1} \leftarrow$ the next state of the current environment;
10 $\quad r_t \leftarrow$ current reward;
11 $\quad$ store (s_t, a_t, s_{t+1}, r_t) in D to train the neural networks;
12 $\quad$ randomly extract the experience(s_t, a_t, s_{t+1}, r_t) of minibatch from D;
13 $\quad$ train the neural network;
14 $\quad$ update the parameters of the neural network by (12);
15 $\quad$ Waiting for t to move forward to $t+1$;
16 **end**

4.1.2. Approximation Architecture

According to Figure 3, the specific steps for updating the neural network parameters in line 8 of Algorithm 1 are as follows. The output of the BDQ neural network consists of the advantage function and state values of multiple action branches. The Q value of the action is obtained by adding the advantage function to the state value. According to (12), the loss values are calculated based on each Q value of multi-actions and the target function, respectively. They are added together to obtain the final loss value.The gradient descent method is used to update neural network parameters. The green arrows represent the flow of the state value, and the red arrows represent the function computation process for the sub-actions.

$$L = E_{s_t, a_t, R_{t+1}, s_{t+1}} D[\frac{1}{N} \sum_d (y_d - Q_d(s_t, a_d))^2] \tag{12}$$

where y_d is defined as

$$y_d = r + \gamma \frac{1}{N} \sum_d Q'_d(s_{t+1}, \underset{a'_d \in A_d}{argmax} Q_d(s_{t+1}, a_d)) \tag{13}$$

$Q'_d(s_{t+1}, \underset{a'_d \in A_d}{argmax} Q_d(s_{t+1}, a_d))$ obtains the Q value based on the state–action pair in the Q'_d network, and the sub-action a_d is determined by the maximum Q value based on the state s_{t+1} in the Q_d network. The Q function in (14) consists of the state value function $V(s_t)$ and the advantage function $A_d(s_t, a_d)$.

$$Q_d(s_t, a_d) = V(s_t) + A_d(s_t, a_d) \tag{14}$$

There are two neural networks with the same structure in the algorithm, where the online network updates in real-time and the target network is updated every C steps, using the parameters of online network.

4.2. The P-DQNBS Algorithm

In the real blockchain, the number of shards and the block size are discrete parameters. However, due to the large action space of the block size, such as $[0, 2^{23}]$, we approximately assume that the block size and block interval are continuous. Furthermore, the block size and block interval in the action space of the blockchain sharding problem can be regarded as continuous decision variables to construct a mixed-action-space MDP, further reducing the discrete action space. For the processing of mixed action spaces, previous work has approached the discrete action space by discretizing continuous action or relaxing discrete action into a continuous set to obtain a continuous action space. We used the P-DQN framework to solve the mixed action space problem and provide more accurate action for sharded blockchain networks. The P-DQN algorithm seamlessly integrates DQN for discrete action and Deep Deterministic Policy Gradient [23] for continuous action.

4.2.1. Algorithm Design

Algorithm 2 shows the details of our P-DQNBS algorithm. In each epoch t, it first computes the optimal continuous action $B^*_{K_t}$ and $T^*_{K_t}$ for each $K_t \in \{1, 2, ..., k_{max}\}$ based on the current state s_t (line 5), then selects the optimal K^*_t by

$$K^*_t = \arg \max_{K_t \in \{1,2,...,k_{max}\}} Q(s_t, K_t, B^*_{K_t}, T^*_{K_t}; \omega) \tag{15}$$

and obtains the optimal action $a^*_t = [K^*_t, B^*_{K^*_t}, T^*_{K^*_t}]$ (lines 6–7). Then, an action chosen from the ϵ-greedy policy

$$a_t = \begin{cases} \text{A random action, with probability } \epsilon, \\ [K^*_t, B^*_{K^*_t}, T^*_{K^*_t}], \text{ otherwise.} \end{cases} \tag{16}$$

is executed (line 8). The reward can be computed by (4) (line 9) since violation of constraint C1–C2 indicates that the ratio of malicious nodes is greater than the upper bound required by the PBFT consensus protocol, and consequently, no block is generated. Violation of constraint C3 means that the block cannot be verified within the threshold, which means the uploading of the block to the blockchain fails. Next, a system transition (s_t, a_t, r_t, s_{t+1}) is formed and stored in the replay buffer $\mathcal{D}$ (line 10), from which a minibatch $\mathcal{M}$ is sampled to train the policy network and value network, respectively (line 11). More specifically, the policy network is updated by maximizing the Q function; therefore, the loss function is set as

$$\mathcal{L}^{\Theta}_t(\theta) = \sum_{(s_\tau, a_\tau, r_\tau, s_{\tau+1}) \in \mathcal{M}} Q(s_\tau, K_\tau, B^*_{K_\tau}, T^*_{K_\tau}; \omega) \tag{17}$$

(line 9). The updating target for the value network is

$$y_\tau = r_\tau + \max_{K_{\tau+1} \in \{1,2,...,k_{max}\}} \gamma Q(s_\tau, K_\tau, B^*_{K_\tau}, T^*_{K_\tau}; \omega) \tag{18}$$

and is updated by minimizing the squared TD error, i.e.,

$$\mathcal{L}^{Q}_t(\omega) = \frac{1}{2} \sum_{(s_\tau, a_\tau, r_\tau, s_{\tau+1}) \in \mathcal{M}} [Q(s_\tau, K_\tau, B^*_{K_\tau}, T^*_{K_\tau}; \omega) - y_\tau]^2 \tag{19}$$

(lines 13–14).

In order to enhance the stability of P-DQNBS, we also use the target networks [24], which are periodically updated (line 15).

Algorithm 2: The P-DQNBS Algorithm process

Initialize the weights θ and ω for policy network $(B^*_{K_t}, T^*_{K_t})(s_t;\theta)$ and value network $Q(s_t, K_t, B^*_{K_t}, T^*_{K_t};\omega)$;
Initialize the weights θ' and ω' for target network $(B^*_{K_t}, T^*_{K_t})(s_t;\theta')$ and $Q(s_t, K_t, B^*_{K_t}, T^*_{K_t};\omega')$;
Initialize exploration parameter ϵ, minibatch size M, replay buffer $\mathcal{D}$, and stepsizes $\alpha_t, \beta_t \geq 0$;
for $t = 1, 2, ..., T$ **do**
  Observe the current state $s_t = [\boldsymbol{r}_t, \boldsymbol{C}_t, \boldsymbol{H}_t, P_t]$;
  $B^*_{K_t}$ and $T^*_{K_t} \leftarrow (B^*_{K_t}, T^*_{K_t})(s_t;\theta)$;`// Obtain the optimal continuous actions with respect to` K_t
  Select the optimal discrete action K^*_t by (15);
  Select action a_t according to the ϵ greedy policy by (16);
  Take action a_t, obtain the next state s_{t+1}, and calculate the reward by (4);
  Store the transition (s_t, a_t, r_t, s_{t+1}) into $\mathcal{D}$;
  Sample transitions $(s_\tau, a_\tau, r_\tau, s_{\tau+1})$ randomly from $\mathcal{D}$ to form a minibatch $\mathcal{M}$;
  Update the policy network by maximizing (17);
  Compute the updating target for value network by (18);
  Update the value network by minimizing (19);
  Update target networks by $\theta' \leftarrow \theta - \alpha_t \nabla_\theta \mathcal{L}^{\Theta}_t(\theta)$, $\omega' \leftarrow \omega - \beta_t \nabla_\omega \mathcal{L}^{Q}_t(\omega)$;
end

4.2.2. Approximation Architecture

To improve the algorithm's scalability, we use a neural network shown in Figure 4 to approximate the Q function. The neural network consists of two components, i.e., a policy network and a value network. The policy network parameterized by θ takes the system state s_t as input, and outputs $B^*_{K_t}$ and $T^*_{K_t}$, i.e., the optimal continuous actions with regard to a particular discrete action K_t; the value network parameterized by ω takes the system state s_t, $B^*_{K_t}$ and $T^*_{K_t}$ as input and outputs $Q(s_t, K_t, B^*_{K_t}, T^*_{K_t};\omega)$ of each discrete action $K_t \in \{1, 2, ..., k_{max}\}$.

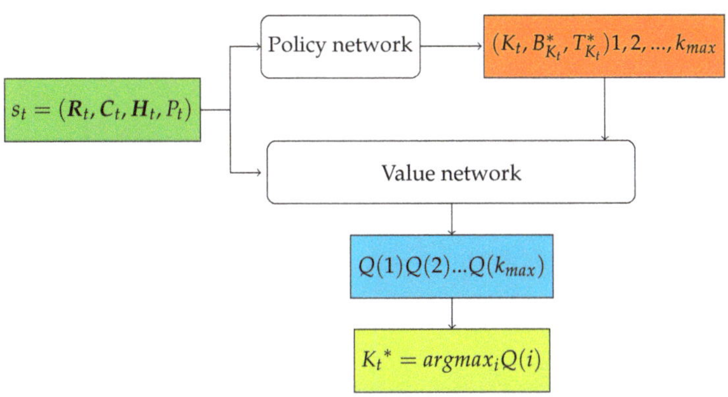

Figure 4. The neural network architecture of P-DQNBS.

The training of the policy network and value network by our Parameterized Deep Q-Networks Blockchain Sharding (P-DQNBS) algorithm is shown in detail as follows.

5. Simulations

In order to ensure the validity of the research findings, we used Python to build a blockchain simulation environment based on the fragmentation process of the blockchain system to simulate the actual sharding computation process. We used the Pytorch framework to implement the DRL. The proposed algorithms are implemented in the simulation environment to simulate the operation of algorithms under real conditions. Finally, we compared our algorithms with other algorithms under the same environmental parameters to obtain quantitative results. The interaction flowchart between the blockchain simulation environment and the algorithm is shown in Figure 5.

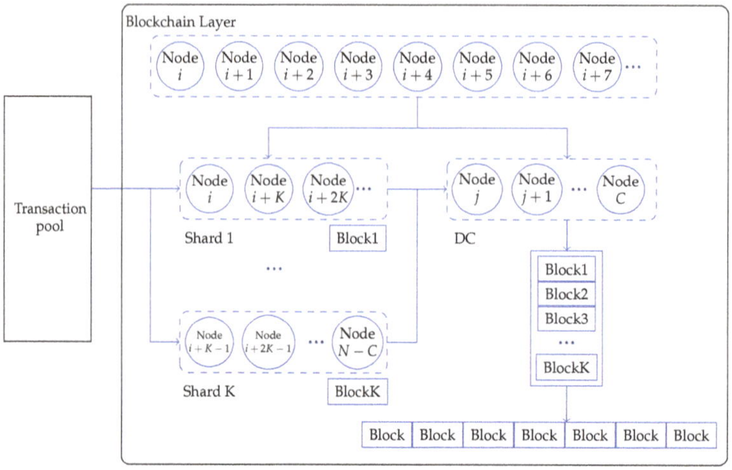

Figure 5. Simulation system structure of blockchain sharding.

After initialization, the transmission rate, computing power, consensus history and probability of malicious nodes between nodes in the blockchain at the current time are taken as the system state s_t. The state s_t is input into the neural network of the algorithm, and a random action or neural network action is selected through ϵ-greedy strategy is output as action a_t. Subsequently, the system enters the next moment s_{t+1} and calculates the immediate reward r_t. The experience (s_t, a_t, r_t, s_{t+1}) is stored in the experience pool. And the batch size of experience is selected to update the neural network parameters. All data are seaved and s_{t+1} is set as the current state s_t to start the next cycle.

5.1. *Parameter Settings*

This section mainly describes the setting of experimental environment parameters, as well as BDQBS and P-DQNBS parameters. Due to the different neural network structures of the two algorithms, the parameter settings are based on the experimental results of tuning the parameters of each algorithm.

5.1.1. Parameters for the Blockchain Environment

We use PyTorch [25] to build neural networks and implement our proposed algorithm with Python 3.6. The simulation environment is the same as [13], which includes 200 nodes. The maximum number of shards is 8. The maximum block interval and maximum block size are set to 16 s and 8 MB. The average transaction size and block header size are assumed to be 200 B and 80 B. The computing capability and data transmission rate follow uniform distributions. The policy network has three hidden layers, with the number of neurons being 256, 128 and 64, respectively; the value network has two hidden layers, with the number of neurons being 128 and 64, respectively. The policy network and value network use Adam optimization. Table 1 summarizes the parameter settings used in this paper.

Table 1. Parameters for the blockchain environment.

Symbol	Parameters	Value
N	Number of nodes	200
k_{max}	Maximum allowable shard number	8
T_{max}	Maximum block interval	16 s
B_{max}	Maximum block size of each shard	8 MB
b	Average transaction size	200 Bytes
B_H	Block header size	80 Bytes
$C_{i,t}$	Computing capability of node i at epoch t	10–30 GHz
$R_{ij,t}$	Data transmission rate between node i and j at epoch t	10–100 Mbps

5.1.2. Parameters for the Algorithms

As the Q-function is unknown, we incorporate neural networks in the reinforcement learning process, using the basic neural network Back Propagation for function approximation. For the BDQBS and P-DQNBS algorithm, we use the following settings. We set the number of neurons in the hidden layer to 256, 128 and 64, respectively. The discount factor γ is set to 0.9 to make the algorithms more inclined towards long-term optimization, which is beneficial for maximizing rewards. In order to explore better action in the early stage of the algorithms, the initial exploration probability of the algorithms is set to 0.9. After the algorithms explore 2000 steps, the exploration probability decreases by 0.01 per step until the exploration probability reaches 0.1. We set the experience pool size to 1000 and the update frequency of neural network parameters to update every 10 steps.

We set the number of hidden layers in the BDQBS algorithm neural network to 3, and set the learning rate r to 0.05. The number of experiences selected when updating the neural network is 32. In addition, dropout was introduced to prevent overfitting of the neural network, with a random inactivation ratio of 0.5.

The neural network of the P-DQNBS algorithm consists of a policy network and a value network. The number of hidden layers in both networks is set to 3. We set the learning rate r_p of the policy network to 0.001, and the learning rate r_v of the value network to 0.0001. We select 128 experiences when updating the neural network.

Table 2 shows the differences between the BDQBS and P-DQNBS settings.

Table 2. Parameters for BDQ and PDQ algorithm neural network.

Algorithm	Symbol	Parameters	Value
BDQBS	r	Neural network learning rate	0.05
	M	Number of experiences extracted	32
	δ	Random inactivation rate of neural networks	0.5
P-DQNBS	r_p	Policy network learning rate	0.05
	r_v	Value network learning rate	0.05
	M	Number of experiences extracted	32

5.2. Performance Comparison

We compared DQNBS as a baseline algorithm with our proposed P-DQNBS and BDQBS. The advantages and disadvantages of the three algorithms are shown in Table 3. They are compared from five aspects: TPS, sub-actions, TPS under different malicious node ratios, TPS under different transaction sizes and the average latency under different algorithms.

Table 3. Comparison of algorithm advantages and disadvantages.

Algorithm	Advantages	Disadvantages
DQNBS	It is capable of dynamically adapting sharding to meet large-scale and dynamic IoT operations based on the dynamically changing environment in the blockchain system.	Too many discrete actions may slow down the learning process and fail to handle continuous action spaces.
BDQBS	It can work with discrete action spaces and discretize continuous action spaces to indirectly process continuous action spaces.	The discretization of continuous space may lead to errors in results, as well as an explosion of the action space.
P-DQNBS	It is possible to handle the discrete–continuous hybrid action space directly in the sharding process, with a simpler processing and more accurate results.	It is complex and takes longer to process.

5.2.1. Throughput Analysis

Figure 6 plots the average TPS of three algorithms. All algorithms explore the action space for 2000 steps with $\epsilon = 0.9$ before ϵ decreases to 0.1 linearly in 100 steps.

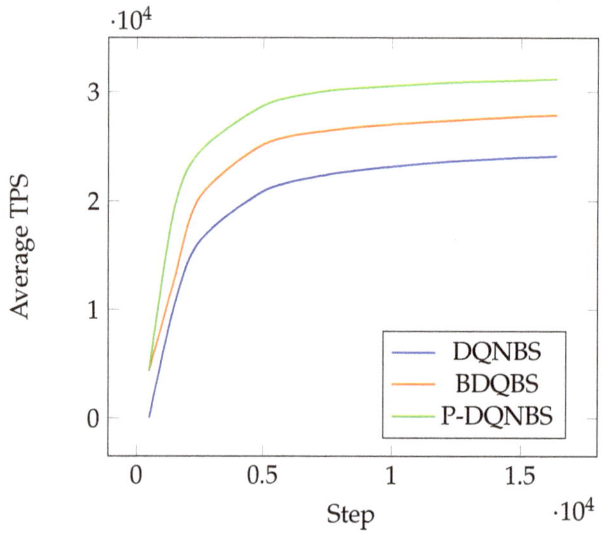

Figure 6. Average TPS under different algorithms.

The TPS of each algorithm first grows rapidly with the increase in the number of steps, then tends to stabilize, and approaches the limit value infinitely. P-DQNBS grows the fastest and has the highest limit value; in other words, P-DQNBS always has the largest TPS to a fixed number of steps. The TPS growth rate and instantaneous value of BDQNBS are inferior to P-DQNBS, which is better than DQNBS.

The average reward of the BDQBS algorithm is about 1.25 times greater than that of the DQNBS algorithm. When all algorithms converge, the average TPS of P-DQNBS is 28% and 11% higher than DQNBS and BDQ, respectively. Figures 7–9 show the average of the three sub-actions in different algorithms.

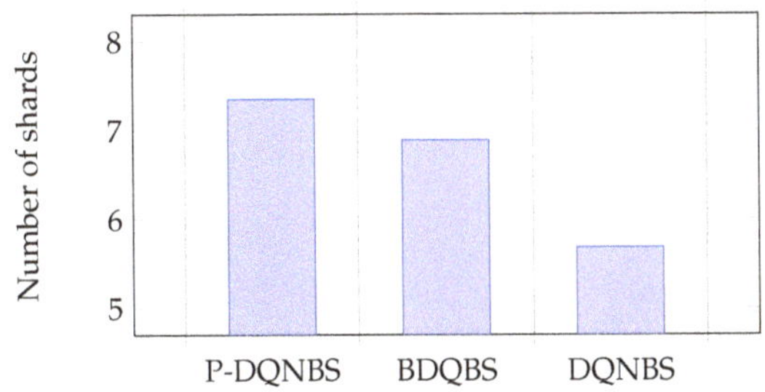

Figure 7. Average of sub-action K.

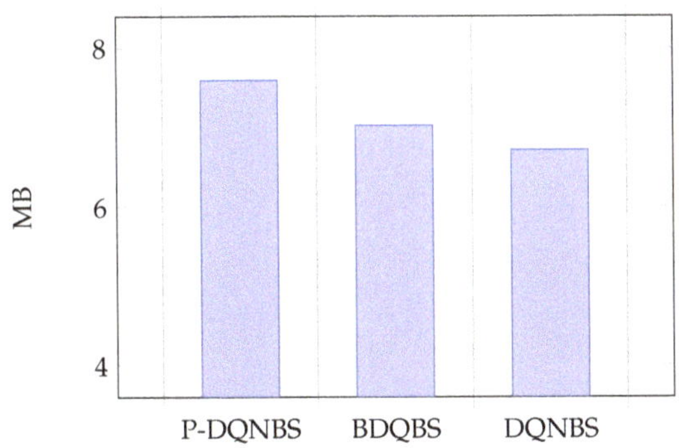

Figure 8. Average of sub-action B.

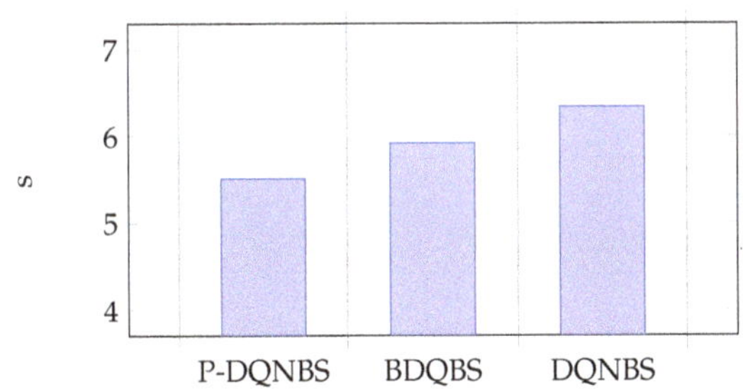

Figure 9. Average of sub-action T.

Sub-action K represents the number of shards. In Figure 7, the average value of sub-action K in the BDQBS is 21% higher than in the DQNBS, indicating that BDQBS can shard blockchain nodes into more shards and more transactions can be process in parallel within the shards. The average sub-actions K of the P-DQNBS are 29% and 7% higher than the DQNBS algorithm and BDQBS, respectively. Subaction B represents block size. In Figure 8, the average number of subactions B in the BDQBS is about 5% higher than in the DQNBS, which indicates that the BDQBS handles more transactions than the DQNBS. The average number of subactions B in P-DQNBS is approximately 8% higher than in BDQBS and 12% higher than in DQNBS, indicating that P-DQNBS can enable the blockchain to handle more transactions. The subaction T represent the block generation time. In Figure 9, the average number of subactions T of BDQBS is 7% smaller than that of DQNBS, indicating that using the BDQBS to process data is faster. The average number of subactions T in P-DQNBS is 7% and 13% less than in BDQBS and DQNBS, respectively, which indicates that P-DQNBS can process transactions in the shortest time and has the fastest processing speed. In summary, the BDQBS can improve the throughput of the blockchain compared to the DQNBS. The use of P-DQNBS can improve the performance of blockchain systems the best.

The average execution times per step of the DQNBS, BDQBS and P-DQNBS are 0.27 s, 0.31 s and 0.35 s, respectively. Since the execution times of the algorithms are very short, we output the execution times of twenty consecutive steps and calculate the average value to obtain the average execution time of each step of the algorithm.

5.2.2. Impact of Malicious Node Ratio

A malicious node rejects an honest block in the consensus process or creates a malicious block. Figure 10 shows the TPS under various malicious node ratios. When all nodes in the network are honest, the TPS of P-DQNBS is 1.12 and 1.17 times higher than BDQBS and DQNBS, respectively. As malicious nodes emerge, the performance of all algorithms drops, because K_t has to decrease to satisfy constraint C1 and C2 for increased P_t, and the number of transactions processed is concurrently reduced. We also observe that P-DQNBS is more robust to malicious nodes since it achieves higher TPS in all simulations.

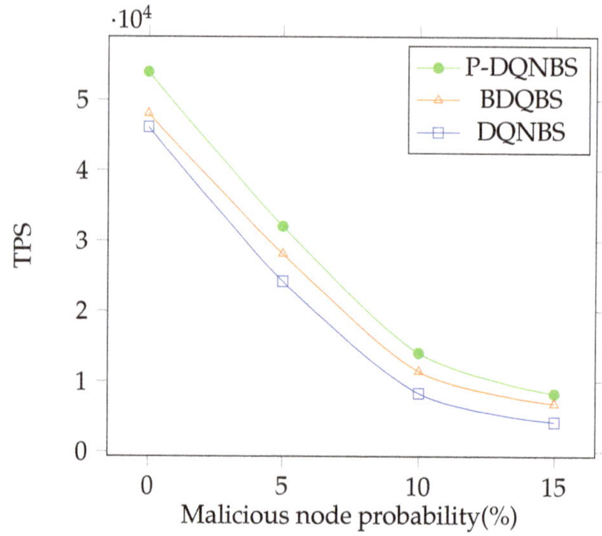

Figure 10. TPS vs. malicious node ratio.

5.2.3. Average Latency Comparison

To improve the throughput, an obvious approach is to increase the number of shards and the block size while maintaining a small block interval. However, arbitrarily large K_t and B_t values result in longer consensus time $T_{con}^{K_t}$, and together with a small T_t, will make constraint C1 and C2 easily violated. It can be shown in Figure 11 that all policies find feasible actions which keep the transaction latency under the threshold, but P-DQNBS learns the best policy with the highest throughput.

5.2.4. Throughput under Different Average Transaction Sizes

Figure 12 shows the throughput using different algorithms under different average transaction sizes. It can be seen that with the increase in transaction size, throughput significantly decreases because of the decreasing number of block packaged transactions. However, the P-DQNBS outperforms the BDQBS and DQNBS in any scale of transactions. When the average transaction size is 100MB, the throughput using the P-DQNBS algorithm is approximately 1.11 and 1.14 times that of the BDQBS and DQNBS. When the average transaction size reaches the maximum value of 500MB, the throughput using the P-DQNBS is approximately 60% and 89% higher than the BDQBS and DQNBS. This indicates that the P-DQNBS can provide better action for blockchains compared to BDQBS and DQNBS when processing transactions of any scale, resulting in an improvement in blockchain performance.

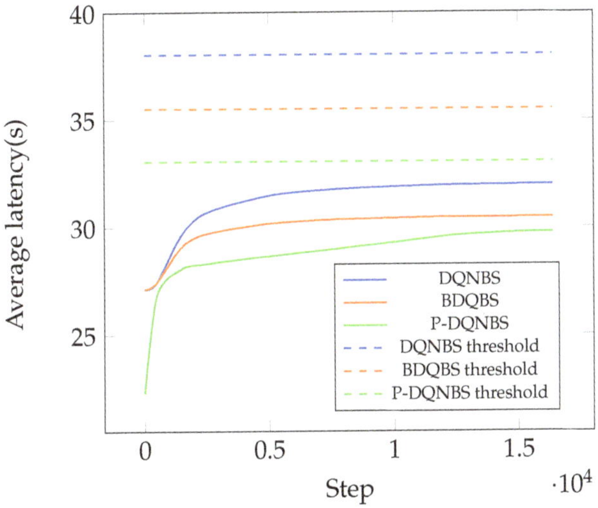

Figure 11. Average latency under different algorithms.

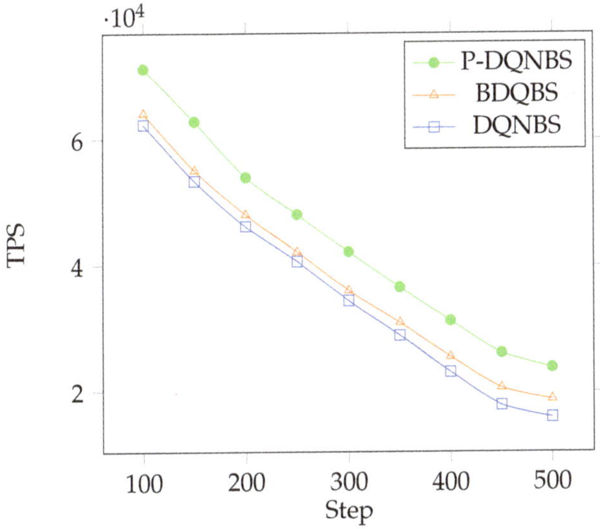

Figure 12. TPS vs. average transaction size

6. Conclusions and Future Work

According to the experimental analysis of P-DQNBS, BDQBS and DQNSB in Section 5.2, the throughput of the three algorithms is obtained in the blockchain simulation environment, and the average action of the three algorithms is compared and analyzed. The experimental comparison shows that the performance of the P-DQNBS is better than that of the BDQBS and the DQNSB. The average TPS of P-DQNBS is 28% and 11% higher than DQNBS and BDQ, respectively. When all nodes in the network are honest, the TPS of P-DQNBS is 1.12 and 1.17 times higher than BDQBS and DQNBS, respectively. When the average transaction size reaches the maximum value of 500 MB, the throughput using the P-DQNBS is approximately 60% and 89% higher than the BDQBS and DQNBS. Under a stochastic environment, the throughput of the three algorithms is compared, and the experimental results show that the P-DQNBS can provide the best strategy for the blockchain system and obtain the highest throughput under the condition of satisfying security. In addition, the average latency of the three algorithms is compared, and the experimental results show that the P-DQNBS algorithm has the smallest delay, indicating that the P-DQNBS algorithm can process transactions faster, so that the blockchain can achieve the highest throughput. Finally, the performance of the three algorithms is compared in terms of different average transactions, and the experimental results show that the P-DQNBS can provide the most accurate action strategies for the blockchain and make the blockchain's performance the best.

We proposed the BDQBS and the P-DQNBS as the optimal blockchain sharding policy. Compared with DQNBS and other algorithms, P-DQNBS does not need to discretize the continuous actions and thereby provides a higher-quality sharding policy for the OBCS problem. This topic mainly studies the research on blockchain performance optimization method based on sharding technology. Traditional blockchain sharding usually takes a static approach, which is not in line with a dynamic blockchain environment. Therefore, DRL is applied to the blockchain sharding problem to provide dynamic sharding decisions for the dynamic blockchain system, so as to improve the performance of the blockchain while establishing the blockchain sharding process as an MDP. The most common DRL algorithm used in the blockchain environment is the DQN, which solves the problem of state space explosion but does not solve the problem of action space explosion. This leads to difficulty in neural network training.

In view of the above problems, we used the BDQ and P-DQN in the blockchain sharding problem and proposed the BDQBS and P-DQNBS. The BDQBS algorithm solves the problem of action space explosion and provides a better action strategy for the blockchain system, thereby improving the blockchain's performance. The action space of the blockchain sharding problem is a discrete–continuous hybrid action space, and the BDQBS algorithm mainly solves the problem of discrete action space, so the continuous action is discretized to obtain the discrete action space. However, this approach ignores more precise action, so we applied the P-DQN to solve the problem, and proposed the P-DQNBS algorithm. The P-DQNBS algorithm provides a more accurate sharding strategy for the blockchain system, which further improves the performance of the blockchain.

This project takes optimizing the blockchain performance based on sharding technology as the main goal, and designs a blockchain sharding selection strategy based on DRL. Although certain results have been achieved, due to limitations on time and experimental conditions, there are still some shortcomings which need more in-depth research and improvement in the later stage. The experimental algorithm verifies the implementation based on the built blockchain shard simulation environment. However, the real blockchain system will inevitably have more dynamic changes. For example, the transmission rate between nodes and the computing power of nodes must be different. Due to the limited experimental conditions, it is necessary to perform algorithm verification in the real blockchain environment in the future. We use network sharding to partition blockchain nodes, and there is a problem of transaction cross-sharding when using network sharding, which leads to the problem of double spending. So, in the future, it will be necessary to supplement and improve the research on blockchain transaction sharding and state sharding. Blockchain transaction sharding and state sharding are research trends in improving blockchain throughput in the future.

Author Contributions: Conceptualization, L.L.; methodology, J.W.; software, C.L.; validation, B.Y.; formal analysis, B.Y.; writing—original draft preparation, C.L.; writing—review and editing, J.W.; supervision, L.L. All authors have read and agreed to the published version of the manuscript.

Funding: This research was funded in part by the scientific research project of the National Natural Science Foundation of China (62362055), the Inner Mongolia Autonomous Region Key R&D and Achievement Transformation Program Project (2022YFSJ0013, 2023YFHH0052, 2023KJHZ0001), the Research Program for Young Talents of Inner Mongolia Colleges (NJYT22084, NJYT23055), the Natural Science Foundation of Inner Mongolia (2023MS06008), the Key Research & Development Program of Erdos (YF20232328), the Scientific Research Program for Inner Mongolia Colleges (JY20220061, JY20230119, JY20230019), and the Basic Scientific Research Expenses Program of Universities directly under the Inner Mongolia Autonomous Region (JY20220078, 2022ZY0169).

Data Availability Statement: Due to the nature of this research, participants of this study did not agree for their data to be shared publicly, so supporting data are not available.

Conflicts of Interest: The authors declare no conflict of interest.

Abbreviations

The following abbreviations are used in this manuscript:

TPS	Transactions Per Second
OBCS	Optimal Blockchain Sharding
MDP	Markov Decision Process
DRL	Deep Reinforcement Learning
BDQBS	Branching 9 Dueling Q-Network Blockchain Sharding
P-DQN	Parameterized 13 Deep Q-Networks
P-DQNBS	Parameterized Deep Q-Networks Blockchain Sharding
DQNBS	Deep Q-Network enabled Shard-based Blockchain
DQN	Deep Q-Network
BDQ	Branching Dueling Q-Network
PoW	Proof of Work
PBFT	Practical Byzantine Fault Toll
DC	Directory Committee
PK	Public Key

References

1. Guo, S.; Hu, X.; Guo, S.; Qiu, X.; Qi, F. Blockchain meets edge computing: A distributed and trusted authentication system. *IEEE Trans. Ind. Inform.* **2019**, *16*, 1972–1983. [CrossRef]
2. Wan, J.; Li, J.; Imran, M.; Li, D.; Fazal-e-Amin. A blockchain-based solution for enhancing security and privacy in smart factory. *IEEE Trans. Ind. Inform.* **2019**, *15*, 3652–3660. [CrossRef]
3. Yun, J.; Goh, Y.; Chung, J.M.; Kim, O.; Shin, S.; Choi, J.; Kim, Y. MMOG user participation based decentralized consensus scheme and proof of participation analysis on the bryllite blockchain system. *KSII Trans. Internet Inf. Syst. (TIIS)* **2019**, *13*, 4093–4107.
4. Zheng, Z.; Xie, S.; Dai, H.; Chen, X.; Wang, H. An overview of blockchain technology: Architecture, consensus, and future trends. In Proceedings of the 2017 IEEE International Congress on Big Data (BigData Congress), Honolulu, HI, USA, 25–30 June 2017; pp. 557–564.
5. Yao, H.; Mai, T.; Wang, J.; Ji, Z.; Jiang, C.; Qian, Y. Resource trading in blockchain-based industrial Internet of Things. *IEEE Trans. Ind. Inform.* **2019**, *15*, 3602–3609. [CrossRef]
6. Wood, E. A secure decentralised generalised transaction ledger, Ethereum Proj. *Yellow Pap.* **2014**, *151*, 1–32.
7. Androulaki, E.; Barger, A.; Bortnikov, V.; Cachin, C.; Christidis, K.; De Caro, A.; Enyeart, D.; Ferris, C.; Laventman, G.; Manevich, Y.; et al. Hyperledger fabric: A distributed operating system for permissioned blockchains. In Proceedings of the Thirteenth EuroSys Conference, Porto, Portugal, 23–26 April 2018; pp. 1–15.
8. Nguyen, L.N.; Nguyen, T.D.; Dinh, T.N.; Thai, M.T. Optchain: Optimal transactions placement for scalable blockchain sharding. In Proceedings of the 2019 IEEE 39th International Conference on Distributed Computing Systems (ICDCS), Dallas, TX, USA, 7–10 July 2019; pp. 525–535.
9. Luu, L.; Narayanan, V.; Zheng, C.; Baweja, K.; Gilbert, S.; Saxena, P. A secure sharding protocol for open blockchains. In Proceedings of the 2016 ACM SIGSAC Conference on Computer and Communications Security, Vienna, Austria, 24–28 October 2016; pp. 17–30.
10. Kokoris-Kogias, E.; Jovanovic, P.; Gasser, L.; Gailly, N.; Syta, E.; Ford, B. OmniLedger: A Secure, Scale-Out, Decentralized Ledger via Sharding. In Proceedings of the IEEE Symposium on Security and Privacy, Francisco, CA, USA, 20–24 May 2018; pp. 583–598.
11. The Zilliqa Team. The Zilliqa Technical Whitepaper. 10 August 2017. pp. 1–14. Available online: https://docs.zilliqa.com/whitepaper.pdf (accessed on 4 December 2023).

12. Zamani, M.; Movahedi, M.; Raykova, M. RapidChain: Scaling Blockchain via Full Sharding. In Proceedings of the the 2018 ACM SIGSAC Conference, Toronto, ON, Canada, 15–19 October 2018.
13. Yun, J.; Goh, Y.; Chung, J.M. DQN-based optimization framework for secure sharded blockchain systems. *IEEE Internet Things J.* **2020**, *8*, 708–722. [CrossRef]
14. Zhang, J.; Hong, Z.; Qiu, X.; Zhan, Y.; Guo, S.; Chen, W. Skychain: A deep reinforcement learning-empowered dynamic blockchain sharding system. In Proceedings of the 49th International Conference on Parallel Processing-ICPP, Edmonton, AB, Canada, 17–20 August 2020; pp. 1–11.
15. Gervais, A.; Karame, G.O.; Wüst, K.; Glykantzis, V.; Ritzdorf, H.; Capkun, S. On the security and performance of proof of work blockchains. In Proceedings of the 2016 ACM SIGSAC Conference on Computer and Communications Security, Vienna, Austria, 24–28 October 2016; pp. 3–16.
16. Castro, M.; Liskov, B. Practical byzantine fault tolerance and proactive recovery. *ACM Trans. Comput. Syst.* **2002**, *20*, 398–461. [CrossRef]
17. Sukhwani, H.; Martínez, J.M.; Chang, X.; Trivedi, K.S.; Rindos, A. Performance modeling of PBFT consensus process for permissioned blockchain network (hyperledger fabric). In Proceedings of the 2017 IEEE 36th Symposium on Reliable Distributed Systems (SRDS), Hong Kong, China, 26–29 September 2017; pp. 253–255.
18. Syta, E.; Jovanovic, P.; Kogias, E.K.; Gailly, N.; Ford, B. Scalable Bias-Resistant Distributed Randomness. In Proceedings of the 2017 IEEE Symposium on Security and Privacy (SP), San Jose, CA, USA, 22–26 May 2017; pp. 444–460.
19. Yao, B.; Wan, J.; Shan, J.; Li, L.; Ma, Z.; Liu, C. Optimal Sharding for Dynamic Throughput Optimization in Blockchain Systems with Deep Reinforcement Learning. In Proceedings of the 2023 IEEE Conference on Systems, Man, and Cybernetics, Honolulu, HI, USA, 1–4 October 2023; pp. 1–5.
20. Król, M.; Ascigil, O.; Rene, S.; Sonnino, A.; Al-Bassam, M.; Rivière, E. Shard scheduler: Object placement and migration in sharded account-based blockchains. In Proceedings of the 3rd ACM Conference on Advances in Financial Technologies, Arlington, VA, USA, 26–28 September 2021; pp. 43–56.
21. Xiong, J.; Wang, Q.; Yang, Z.; Sun, P.; Han, L.; Zheng, Y.; Fu, H.; Zhang, T.; Liu, J.; Liu, H. Parametrized deep q-networks learning: Reinforcement learning with discrete-continuous hybrid action space. *arXiv* **2018**, arXiv:1810.06394.
22. Sutton, R.; Barto, A. *Reinforcement Learning: An Introduction*; The MIT Press: Cambridge, MA, USA, 1998.
23. Paul, L.T.; James, H.J.; David, S.; Tom, E.; Yuval, T.; Otto, H.N.M.; Pieter, W.D.; Alexander, P. Continuous control with deep reinforcement learning. *arXiv* **2018**, arXiv:1509.02971.
24. Mnih, V.; Kavukcuoglu, K.; Silver, D.; Rusu, A.A.; Veness, J.; Bellemare, M.G.; Graves, A.; Riedmiller, M.; Fidjeland, A.K.; Ostrovski, G.; et al. Human-level control through deep reinforcement learning. *Nature* **2015**, *518*, 529–533. [CrossRef] [PubMed]
25. Paszke, A.; Gross, S.; Massa, F.; Lerer, A.; Bradbury, J.; Chanan, G.; Killeen, T.; Lin, Z.; Gimelshein, N.; Antiga, L.; et al. Pytorch: An imperative style, high-performance deep learning library. *Adv. Neural Inf. Process. Syst.* **2019**, *32*, 8026–8037.

electronics

MDPI

Article

Access Control Strategy for the Internet of Vehicles Based on Blockchain and Edge Computing

Leixiao Li [1,2,3], Jianxiong Wan [1,2,3] and Chuyi Liu [1,2,3,*]

1 College of Data Science and Applicatioon, Inner Mongolia University of Technology, Hohhot 010062, China; lileixiao@imut.edu.cn (L.L.); jxwan@imut.edu.cn (J.W.)
2 Inner Mongolia Autonomous Region Engineering, Technology Research Center of Big Data Based Software Service, Hohhot 010062, China
3 Research Center of Large-Scale Energy Storage Technologies, Hohhot 010062, China
* Correspondence: lcy@imut.edu.cn

Abstract: Data stored in the Internet of Vehicles (IoV) face problems with ease of tampering, easy disclosure and single access control. Based on this problem, we propose an access control scheme for the IoV based on blockchain, trust values and weighted attribute-based encryption, called the Blockchain Trust and Weighted Attribute-Based Access Control Strategy (BTWACS). First, we utilize both local and global blockchains to jointly maintain the generation, verification and storage of blocks, achieving distributed data storage and ensuring that data cannot arbitrarily be tampered with. Local blockchain mainly uses Road Side Unit (RSU) technology to calculate trust values, while global blockchain is mainly responsible for data storage and access policy selection. Secondly, we design a blockchain-based trust evaluation scheme called Blockchain-Based Trust Evaluation (BBTE). In this evaluation scheme, the trust value of the vehicle node is based on four factors: initial trust, historical experience trust, recommendation trust and RSU observation trust. CRITIC is used to determine the optimal weights of four factors to obtain the trust value. Then, we use the Network Simulator version 3 (NS3) to verify the security and accuracy of BBTE, improving the recognition accuracy and detection rate of malicious vehicle nodes. Finally, by mining the association relationships between attribute permissions among various roles, we construct a hierarchical access control strategy based on weight and trust, and further optimize the access strategy through pruning techniques. The experiment results indicate that this scheme can effectively respond to gray hole attacks, defamation attacks and collusion attacks from other vehicle nodes. This method can effectively reduce the computing and transmission costs of vehicles and meet the access requirements of multiple entities and roles in the IoV.

Keywords: Internet of Vehicles; blockchain; edge computing; trust computing; access control; malicious attacks; attributes based on encryption

1. Introduction

The Internet of Vehicles (IoV) uses wireless communication technology to share information between vehicles, which helps to achieve automatic driving and maintain traffic safety [1,2]. IoV uses Vehicle to Vehicle (V2V) and Vehicle to Infrastructure (V2I) for communication [3]. The interactive information mainly includes road congestion, moving tracks, traffic accidents and entertainment consultation to create a safe and comfortable driving environment [4]. In order to prevent criminals from eavesdropping on and tampering with information, which may endanger the traffic system, information interaction must ensure the integrity and security of data, otherwise the system is vulnerable to malicious attacks, including replay, camouflage, message tampering attacks, etc. [5]. Therefore, the information resources in the IoV must be controlled to prevent unauthorized access and ensure the safe sharing of information resources. The goal of this paper is to build a more effective access control scheme to improve the security of IoV's information sharing.

Due to the widespread distribution and mobility of vehicles, it is difficult to expand the current centralized cloud model of the IoV system through a large number of weak devices, and it is difficult to meet the flexible access control requirements of multiple entities and roles in IoV [6]. In addition, the communication distance between IoV devices and the cloud is relatively long, which may consume a lot of bandwidth, time and energy. Cloud servers are the bottleneck of the current IoV network. A centralized server has a defect of single point failure, that is, a server failure will disrupt the entire network. On the other hand, blockchain is characterized by having distributed storage and being tamper proof, which can allow the realization of a trusted decentralized environment and provide a system with tamper resistance, traceability, fault tolerance and automatic execution strategies [7]. Thus, we utilize local blockchains (maintained by Road Side Units) [8] and global blockchains (maintained by trusted centers) to build an IoV network environment, with the goal of promoting secure access control for IoV and jointly addressing key challenges.

We proposed the Blockchain Trust and Weighted Attribute-Based Access Control Strategy (BTWACS) for controlling the access of IoV based on secure access. A trust evaluation mechanism, Blockchain-Based Trust Evaluation (BBTE), is introduced. BBTE takes into account four factors—initial trust, historical experience trust, recommendation trust and RSU observation trust—and is more comprehensive and efficient. It improves the accuracy and speed of identification of malicious nodes. A simulation environment is constructed to test the performance of the algorithm and compare it to other algorithms.

In sum, the main contributions of this paper are threefold:

- We propose BBTE, a trust evaluation mechanism that can identify malicious nodes faster and more accurately than other mechanisms.
- We propose the BTWACS, an IoV networking access control strategy that can make the communication process between nodes in the IoV safer, faster and more efficient.
- Extensive simulation studies are conducted to evaluate the effectiveness of the proposed strategy. Numerical results show that our strategy outperforms existing algorithms in terms of encryption and decryption efficiency and in the size of cipher-text.

The rest of the paper is organized as follows. Section 2 reviews the related literature. Section 3 describes the proposed trust evaluation method, BBTE. Section 4 presents the IoV access control strategy, the BTWACS. Section 5 details the experiment and the numerical studies. Section 6 concludes the paper.

2. Related Work

2.1. The Application of Blockchain in the Access Control of the IoV

The blockchain's own traceability, tamper-proof ability and anonymity, as well as other characteristics, can serve as a trusted third party in the access control of the IoV. Blockchain provides trusted computing and storage. It can not only store important data but can also use its computing power for access control decisions. The combination of blockchain technology and the IoV has become one of the current main research fields.

Since the 1970s, many access control methods have been implemented, such as Role-Based Access Control (RBAC) [9,10], Attributes-Based Access Control (ABAC) [11], Capability-Based Access Control (CapBAC) [12], etc. RBAC is a static model, which makes it difficult to adapt to frequent changes in IoV devices. For example, Cruz et al. [13] implemented role-based access control through smart contracts, but it required the maintenance of a large number of roles and authorization relationships, resulting in a heavy workload for administrators. Liu et al. [14] proposed ABAC for on-chain data, constructing a hierarchical access control strategy based on multiple attributes, implementing weighted attribute-based encryption and simplifying the complexity of access control strategies. However, without the trust evaluation of vehicle nodes, it is impossible to control the credibility of vehicles. Nakamura et al. [15] proposed CapBAC and used Ethereum smart contracts to store and manage capability tokens, which are special data structures for maintaining user-allowed actions for specific resources. But BAC focuses more on solving the dynamic network topology problem of IoV. These schemes lack evaluation abilities for malicious nodes and for the consideration of the reliability of on-chain data; attackers may send false or incorrect information. Thus, the reliability and security of data cannot be guaranteed.

2.2. Trust Computing

The IoV has high dynamism, and messages propagate between adjacent moving vehicles, making it susceptible to malicious attacks and security threats. Malicious vehicle nodes sending false or incorrect information in information exchange may lead to traffic congestion, even traffic accidents, and may threaten the safety of car owners' lives and property. To ensure the safe transmission of data between vehicle nodes and enable vehicle owners to make correct decisions based on reliable information, it is necessary to evaluate the trust of communication objects before exchanging messages between vehicles to ensure the reliability of information.

Existing trust management methods evaluate the trust value of vehicle nodes based on collecting and analyzing a large amount of the node's historical behavior and other data. Due to the high mobility of vehicles in the IoV, the interaction between vehicles is transient, and it is necessary to quickly and accurately identify malicious nodes to prevent malicious attacks and spread false information in the network to avoid traffic accidents. The trust management mechanism can effectively identify the level of trust of nodes. The higher the trust value, the more trustworthy the messages published by nodes. Chen et al. [16] constructed a data-sharing system consisting of a double-layer blockchain. In order to prevent malicious nodes from spreading false messages, a reasonable trust evaluation scheme was designed that evaluates the service quality of different providers by combining negative and positive shared records. Kang et al. [17] proposed an IoV data-sharing system based on federated blockchain, which utilizes a three weight subjective logic model to accurately manage the trust values of vehicles. Vehicles choose the best data provider based on trust values to choose more reliable data sources and improve data credibility. At present, many research works have discussed the problem of node safety improvement in the IoV. In reference [18], Zhang et al. used the blockchain to define the IoV framework. In a complex vehicle environment, considering the trust characteristics of blockchain nodes and the number of consensus nodes, the authors achieved node consensus based on the Practical Byzantine Fault Tolerance (PBFT) [19] to ensure node security. In reference [20], Yang et al. proposed a decentralized trust management system for a vehicle network based on blockchain technology, deployed smart contracts [21] on the vehicle blockchain, calculated the trust value of related vehicles on a Road Side Unit (RSU) based on the Proof of Work (PoW) [22] and cooperated in maintaining and updating the trust blockchain to achieve secure data sharing.

However, the above trust models cannot effectively resist various malicious attacks in all cases. Access control mechanisms based on trust management are still a hot topic in current research.

2.3. Cipher-Text Policy Attribute-Based Encryption

Cipher-Text Policy Attribute-Based Encryption (CP-ABE) is an encryption technology with fine-grained access control. It associates cipher-text with access control policies and can decrypt cipher-text only when the attributes of the data visitor meet the access control policies. This technology can flexibly control the attribute set of data visitors by changing the access control strategy structure, which is particularly suitable for a network environment where IoV nodes move at high speed and the topology changes rapidly. However, the more attributes in the access control policy, the higher its complexity. The encryption and decryption cost increases linearly with the increase in policy complexity, which has the drawback of a high computational cost.

CP-ABE can be used to formulate access control policies, which is convenient and flexible and is considered an effective access control method. The key is related to the attribute set, and the cipher-text is related to the access structure. Only when the attribute set matches the access structure can the cipher-text be successfully decrypted to plaintext, thereby achieving fine-grained access control for IoV data.

Porwal et al. adopted a combination of a CP-ABE scheme and a multi-chain platform to achieve easy and secure access control in an efficient, fine-grained, transparent and traceable manner [23]. However, the different types of entities in the IoV result in a large number of attributes involved in access policies, leading to a higher complexity of access control policies. Therefore, Liu et al. [14] proposed a weight-based access control strategy. It is different from that which Oham et al. [24] proposed, which divides regions based on the organization in advance, and is different from the density-based access strategy proposed by Kanumalli et al. [25]. The weight-based access control strategy does not require the identification of data visitors in advance and can flexibly formulate access control strategies. By mining the association of attribute permissions between different roles, it simplifies the complexity of access control policies and can access IoV data more efficiently.

3. Trust Evaluation Method

The purpose of trust assessment is to evaluate the trust value of vehicle nodes by collecting behavioral state information, and quickly and accurately identifying malicious vehicle nodes in the IoV. Using trust values as a basis for establishing communication, we can effectively respond to various attacks. BBTE comprehensively considers four core decision-making factors: initial trust, historical trust, recommendation trust and RSU observation trust. Next, we will introduce these four factors one by one.

3.1. Initial Trust

The vehicle stores some basic safety information in the Trusted Platform Module (TPM) [26], which includes the basic safety attributes of the vehicle, such as vehicle type, factory years, user information, digital certificates, etc. We can decompose the attribute information that affects vehicle safety performance into m indicators based on the system security strategy. The corresponding system security correlations are $S_i \in [0,1] (i = 1,2,\ldots)$. We can then assign weights to them. The initial trust of the vehicle is

$$IT = \sum_{i=1}^{m} \omega_i s_i \tag{1}$$

The basic safety attributes of vehicles may change with movement. Therefore, to ensure the authenticity of basic safety attributes, the vehicle will periodically calculate and update its basic safety attributes through RSU. After being verified by the RSU, it is stored in a distributed manner on the blockchain built by the RSU.

3.2. Historical Trust

Historical trust, also known as experiential trust, is established based on the historical interaction records of both parties. Due to the dynamic real-time nature of IoV, the time period of interaction needs to be taken as the calculation factor. The calculation formula for node historical trust is as follows:

$$HT(i,j) = \sum_{i=1}^{m} \frac{2e^{-\Delta t_i/r} SF_i}{e^{\Delta t_i/r} + e^{-\Delta t_i/r}} ES_{ij} \tag{2}$$

where SF_i is the weight of information resources, which is based on the correlation between information resources and security; m is the number of historical interactions of vehicles i and j; Δt_i is the difference between the current time and the access time; the larger the Δt_i, the smaller the weight; r is set according to the time unit; and ES_{ij} represents the trust evaluation of the message receiver j towards the sender i.

For the convenience of calculation, we set the total weight to 10. Because traffic safety is the most important attribute in the IoV, we classify and determine the weight according to the correlation between information and security. Therefore, the weight of strong safety information is the highest, accounting for half of the total, set to 5. The weight of non-safety-related information is the lowest, set to 2, and the weight of safety-related information is in the middle, set to 3. The classification of information resources in the IoV is shown in Table 1.

Table 1. The classification of trust value weight.

Information Classification	Example	Weight
Strongly safety-related	Collision warning, emergency braking, vehicle out of control, anchoring	5
Safety-related	Emergency vehicle yield, double flash, whistle	3
Non-safety-related	ETC, location services, information services	2

3.3. Recommendation Trust

When there is less or even no information interaction between vehicle nodes, the node needs to collect multiple recommendation nodes to calculate recommendation trust. The criteria for determining credibility vary depending on the type of recommendation node. Therefore, according to the degree of association between recommendation nodes k and evaluation nodes i, we divide them into three categories and calculate their respective recommendation trust. CRITIC [27] is used to determine the optimal weight of various types of recommendation trust. It multiplies different recommendation trust values with corresponding weights, incoming plus and, namely, for the final recommendation trust value, TR_{ij}.

3.3.1. Direct Recommendation Trust

We define recommendation nodes k that have had direct interaction with evaluation nodes i as direct recommendation nodes. The trust value of evaluation nodes towards such recommended nodes TD_{ik} can be directly used as their relationship credibility. The direct recommended trust is calculated as follows:

$$TR^d(i,j) = \sum_{i=1}^{m} \frac{C_{ik}M_{ik}}{\sum_{k=1}^{m} C_{ik}M_{ik}} TD_{ik} \tag{3}$$

where C_{ik} refers to the trust level of the recommendation trust given by the evaluation node i to the recommendation node k, $C_{ik} \in [0,1]$; m refers to the number of direct recommendation nodes; and M_{ik} refers to the number of interactions between the node i and the direct recommendation node k.

3.3.2. Indirect Recommendation Trust

We define recommendation nodes k that have had indirect interaction with evaluation nodes i as indirect recommendation nodes. The traditional recommended trust model takes the trust value of the node as the weight, as shown in Equation (4).

$$TR(i,j) = \sum_{k=1}^{m} TR(i,j)TR(k,j) \tag{4}$$

where $TR(i,j)$ indicates the trust value of node i towards node k. The higher the trust value, the more important its recommendations are. However, this mechanism ignores the possibility of collusive attacks and defamation attacks. If malicious nodes obtain high trust values through disguise, they will spread false information to normal nodes. TSMRP [28] uses the cosine similarity function to calculate the recommended trust value, but does not fully consider the difference between the information values. Based on this issue, we use the Pearson correlation coefficient to describe the difference between two views on the same question. The successful interaction score of vehicle node i on m nodes over a period of time t is $[r_{a1}, r_{a2}, \cdots, r_{am}]$, and the scores of vehicle node k on these m nodes is $[r_{o1}, r_{o2}, \cdots, r_{om}]$. The similarity scores equation for node i to node k is

$$P(i,k) = \frac{\left|\sum_{j-1}^{m} r_{aj} r_{oj} - \sum_{j-1}^{m} r_{aj} \sum_{j-1}^{m} r_{oj}\right|}{\sqrt{\sum_{j-1}^{m} (r_{aj})^2 - \left(\sqrt{\sum_{j-1}^{m} r_{aj}}\right)^2} \sqrt{\sum_{j-1}^{m} (r_{oj})^2 - \left(\sqrt{\sum_{j-1}^{m} r_{oj}}\right)^2}} \tag{5}$$

where the higher the value, the higher the score similarity between the two nodes, which means that when the score to other nodes in the network is more consistent, the calculation of indirect recommendation trust is as follows:

$$TR^{in}(i,j) = \sum_{k=1}^{m} p(i,k) TR(k,j) \tag{6}$$

3.3.3. Strange Recommendation Trust

We define recommendation nodes k that do not have interactions with evaluation nodes i as strange recommendation nodes. The evaluation trust level of the evaluation node towards this type of recommendation node is tru_i. We introduce feedback satisfaction FC_i to prevent defamation attacks, $FC_i \in [0,1]$. If $FC_i < 0.5$, the recommendation node is considered untrusted, and its recommendation trust will be discarded; otherwise, it is considered to be reliable. The filtered recommended trust set $B = [tru_1, tru_2, \cdots, tru_N]$. The strange recommendation trust is calculated as follows:

$$TR^{u}(i,j) = \frac{\sum_{i=1}^{N} tru_i}{N} \tag{7}$$

3.3.4. Final Recommendation Trust

TSMRP [28] used the fuzzy analytic hierarchy process based on the Entropy Method to determine the optimal weight of three types of recommendation trust but did not consider the correlations between data. We use CRITIC to determine the optimal weight. CRITIC is a better objective weighting method, which is calculated based on the volatility of data or the correlations between data [27]. n represents the number of vehicle node samples, and m represents the number of evaluation indicators of recommended trust. As above, the evaluation indicators of recommendation trust in this paper are direct, indirect and strange recommendation trust, that is, $m = 3$, forming the original indicator data matrix, as follows:

$$X = \begin{pmatrix} x_{11} & \cdots & x_{1n} \\ \vdots & \ddots & \vdots \\ x_{m1} & \cdots & x_{mn} \end{pmatrix} \tag{8}$$

where x_{ij} represents the numerical value of the ith sample for the jth evaluation indicator.

1. Dimensionless Processing

To eliminate the impact of different dimensions on the evaluation results, it is necessary to perform dimensionless processing on each indicator. The larger the value of the indicator used the better (using positive indicators).

$$\hat{X}_{ij} = \frac{x_j - x_{min}}{x_{max} - x_{min}} \tag{9}$$

2. Indicator Variability

The fluctuation of the internal values of each indicator is represented in the form of standard deviation. The larger the standard deviation, the stronger the evaluation strength of the indicator itself, and the indicator should be assigned more weights:

$$\begin{cases} \overline{x}_j = \frac{1}{n}\sum\limits_{i=1}^{n} x_{ij} \\ s_j = \sqrt{\frac{\sum\limits_{i=1}^{n}\left(x_{ij}-\overline{x}_j\right)^2}{n-1}} \end{cases} \quad (10)$$

where s_j is the standard deviation of jth evaluation indicator.

3. Indicator Conflict

The correlation coefficient is used to represent the correlation between indicators. The stronger the correlation with other indicators, the less conflicting it is with other indicators. The more information it reflects, the more repetitively the evaluation content can be reflected. Therefore, the weight assigned to this indicator should be reduced:

$$R_j = \sum_{i=1}^{m}(1 - r_{ij}) \quad (11)$$

where r_{ij} is the correlation coefficient between evaluation indicators i and j.

4. Amount of Information

$$C_j = S_j \times R_j = S_j \sum_{i=1}^{m}(1 - r_{ij}) \quad (12)$$

The larger the value of C_j, the greater the role of the jth evaluation indicator in the entire evaluation indicator system, and more weights should be assigned to it.

5. Weight

$$\omega_j = \frac{C_j}{\sum_{j=1}^{m} C_j} \quad (13)$$

We can calculate the weight assigned to each evaluation indicator through the method of weighted summation. From this, we can obtain the weights of direct, indirect and strange recommendation trust, ω_1, ω_2 *and* ω_3, respectively. The total recommendation trust is calculated as follows:

$$TR_{i,j} = \omega_1 TR_{i,j}^{d} + \omega_2 TR_{i,j}^{in} + \omega_3 TR_{i,j}^{u} \quad (14)$$

3.4. RSU Observation Trust

RSUs can act as observers to detect the behavior status of vehicles for trust evaluation and can transmit vehicle trust in real-time between RSUs. The relevant trust attributes of a vehicle are $\lambda_i = [\lambda_1, \lambda_2, \cdots, \lambda_k]$. Different trust attributes play different roles in credibility calculation, so it is necessary to assign different trust weights to each trust attribute, which can be expressed as $\varphi_i = [\varphi_1, \varphi_2, \cdots, \varphi_k]$, $\sum_{i=1}^{k} \varphi_i = 1$. The observation trust of a vehicle is

$$RT_i = \sum_{i=1}^{k} \varphi_i \lambda_i \quad (15)$$

RSUs are usually semi-trusted because they are distributed on the road without any strong security measures and are vulnerable to attacks from attackers. To ensure the authenticity and credibility of the RSUs, we conduct positive and negative evaluations on the RSUs to obtain a set of trusted RSUs, and then give a true and credible recommended trust value of the RSU according to the RSU stage trust and the latest trust value of the RSU. a^+ is a positive rating given by the vehicle to the RSU, and a^- is a negative rating. θ_n is the trust judgment for the nth RSU:

$$\theta_i = \frac{\theta_1 a^+ - \theta_2 a^-}{a^+ + a^-} \tag{16}$$

$\theta_n = [-1, 1]$, θ_1 and θ_2 are the weights of a^+ and a^-, respectively.

$$\theta_1 = \frac{F(a^+)}{F(a^+) + F(a^-)} \tag{17}$$

$$\theta_2 = \frac{F(a^1)}{F(a^+) + F(a^-)} \tag{18}$$

where $F(*)$ is the sensitivity to scoring. From Equation (16), it can be seen that the ratios of negative scores and different $F(*)$ will both affect the trend of θ_n changes. According to the consideration of time complexity and space complexity, within the range of error selection, $F(x) = x$, $F(x) = x^2$, $F(x) = x^3$, $F(x) = x^4$, $F(x) = e^x$ and $F(x) = e^{2x}$ are used to evaluate the impact of $F(*)$ on θ_n, as shown in Figure 1. When the negative score ratio is less than 50%, $F(x) = x^4$ is higher than other functions. This proves that a small proportion of the negative score has a small impact on the evaluation results, which is consistent with the evaluation results of most vehicles.

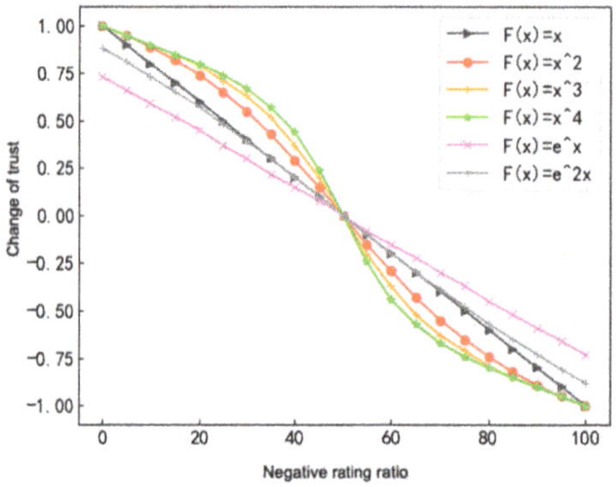

Figure 1. Changes in trust with the ratio of negative ratings under the $F(*)$.

Therefore, we choose $F(x) = x^4$ to control the change of trust θ_n in RSU. When the trust level of RSU is lower than the lower limit, it is considered untrustworthy. For the next moment, the RSU is removed from the trusted set and does not need to be recognized again, which improves the efficiency. From the vehicle entering the nearby RSU communication range until its exit, the RSU observes the behavior status of the vehicle and calculates the phase trust value of the vehicle and uploads it to the blockchain constructed by the RSU to update the trust value list, as shown in Table 2.

Table 2. RSU trust value update list.

RSU_{ID}	Stage Trust Value	Latest Trust Values	Time Period
RSU_1	RT_{D1}	RT_{R1}	$t_1 \sim t_2$
RSU_2	RT_{D2}	RT_{R2}	$t_2 \sim t_3$
...	...	...	...
RSU_n	RT_{Dn}	RT_{Rn}	$t_n \sim t_{n+1}$

The RSU observation trust value of the updated target node is calculated as follows:

$$RT_{Rn} = RT_{R(n-1)} + \frac{RT_{Dn} - RT_{D(n-1)}}{RT_{Dn} + RT_{D(n-1)}} \tag{19}$$

When the vehicle approaches the RSU, calculate the trust value for each behavior attribute of the vehicle using Equation (15), and then calculate the latest trust value RT_i according to Equation (19).

In summary, the initial trust value, historical trust value, recommended trust value and RSU observation trust value of the vehicle node are calculated. CRITIC is used again to determine the optimal weights of the four trust decision factors. At this point, the number of evaluation indicators $m = 4$, and the corresponding weight is obtained as $\varphi_i = \left[\varphi_i^{(1)}, \varphi_i^{(2)}, \varphi_i^{(3)}, \varphi_i^{(4)}\right]$. The overall trust value is calculated as follows:

$$Tr_i = \varphi_i^{(1)} IT_i + \varphi_i^{(2)} HT_i + \varphi_i^{(3)} TR_i + \varphi_i^{(4)} RT_i \tag{20}$$

4. BTWACS

Different types of entities in the IoV introduce more attributes involved in access policies, which leads to a higher complexity of access control strategy. The cost of encryption and decryption increases linearly with the complexity of the strategy, resulting in additional computational overhead for the vehicle. By mining the association of attribute permissions between different roles and simplifying the complexity of the access control strategy, the IoV system can achieve more efficient data access. Therefore, based on the advantages and disadvantages of current IoV access control models, we have designed a hierarchical access control strategy based on blockchain, trust and weighted attributes called the BTWACS.

The immutability of blockchain can provide more secure data protection for the system and increase its security. The evaluation mechanism based on trust values can achieve a reliable judgment of entities, improve the recognition rate of malicious nodes and thus improve the stability of the system. The hierarchical control of weighted attributes represents similar attributes through inclusion relationships through hierarchical division, simplifying the number of attributes and reducing computational and transmission costs, thereby improving system efficiency.

4.1. An IoV Network Model Based on Blockchain

The overall framework of the IoV network model based on blockchain is shown in Figure 2 and mainly includes five parts: (1) The Trusted Center (TC) is responsible for managing attributes and distributing keys. (2) The vehicle perceives data through the onboard unit and communicates with the RSU. (3) The RSU has storage space and good computing capabilities. Its main functions include communicating with vehicles, receiving uploaded data, calculating vehicle trust values, encrypting data and generating, verifying and storing blocks. (4) Global blockchain is built in the cloud, and its main functions include communication with RSUs and distributed storage of access policies and data uploaded. Decryption verification is required when accessing data. (5) Data visitors mainly refer to entities under IoV, such as insurance companies, traffic law enforcement agencies and car owners.

This model deploys smart contracts on the edge layer and network layer of the blockchain and achieves node consensus based on the Byzantine fault-tolerant algorithm to ensure the security of the blockchain nodes.

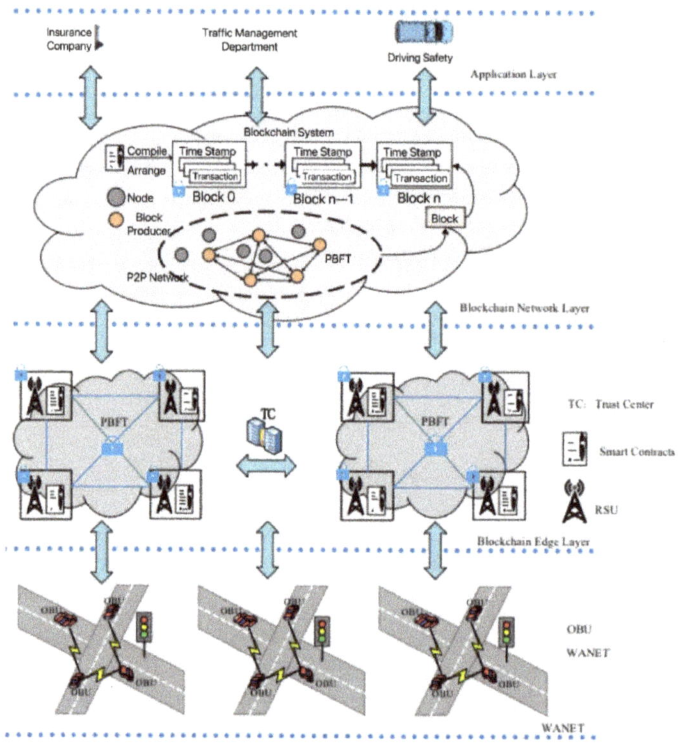

Figure 2. Overall framework of the IoV network model based on blockchain.

4.2. Access Control Policy

Trust assessments are mainly aimed at vehicles in the IoV, such as taxis, trucks, regular private cars and buses. Police vehicles, such as police cars and fire trucks, have higher-level user permissions and do not require trust assessment, and can access all shared data in the IoV. For example, when a vehicle encounters a traffic accident, it will upload the perceived data to the blockchain, which will be accessed by different entities. Traffic law enforcement departments use these data to investigate the cause of accidents and determine liability, while insurance companies use these data as the basis for claims and other car owners will use the data to replan their driving routes to avoid traffic congestion.

To avoid complex access control strategies that increase vehicle overhead, we design a weighted hierarchical access control strategy. The access permissions for data are not only divided by the attributes of vehicle type, the department to which the vehicle belongs and the position of the vehicle driver, but are also related to the trust attributes of the vehicle. Therefore, we also need to consider this attribute when dividing access permissions in order to achieve the trusted judgment of entities. Due to the numerous attributes contained by vehicle drivers, directly designing attribute-based access control strategies is highly complex. We intend to classify attributes into weighted hierarchies. For example, the relationship between job attributes in the truck transportation business department is truck driver$\subset$team leader$\subset$team leader$\subset$team manager. We assign weights to the attributes after hierarchical division and use the weighted attributes to represent similar attributes with continuous inclusion relationships in access permissions in the attribute set in order to simplify the number of attributes in access control policies and reduce the required computational and transmission costs, thereby improving encryption efficiency and ciphertext transmission rate.

Finally, we develop a hierarchical access control strategy through Algorithm 1.

Algorithm 1 BTWACS access control Strategy

Input: $AttrSet_i$, $Credit_i$

Output: Access Control Policy $\boldsymbol{T}$

1: Each entity is assigned different trust values: $Credit_i \in C$ (set trust threshold ***trust***). If entity is a vehicle, if $Credit_i >$ ***trust***, $AttrFlag_i = 1$, otherwise $AttrFlag_i = 0$. If the entity is the traffic management department, traffic law enforcement department or insurance company, $AttrFlag_i = 1$.

2: For each attribute$AttrSet_i \in U$, perform:

3: Classification attributes according to entity, vehicle type, department and position, and obtain $\boldsymbol{M}$ types of attributes $S = \{S_A, S_B, S_C, \cdots, S_M\}$;

4: $Classify(AttrSet_i) \rightarrow S_i$;

5: End.

6: Sort attributes based on access permissions. If there is an inclusion relationship between access permissions of similar attributes, that is, $S_{i,1} \subset S_{i,2} \subset S_{i,3} \subset \cdots \subset S_{i,N}$, weight them.

7: For $i = 1$ to M perform;

8: For $j = 1$ to N perform;

9: $S_{i,j}.\omega = j // \omega$ starting from 1;

10: End.

11: End.

12: For $i = 1$ to $AttrSet.length$ perform:

$//$Using weighted attributes to represent similar attributes with continuous inclusion relationships in access permissions in attribute sets.

13: if $S_{i,1} \subset S_{i,2} \subset S_{i,3} \subset \cdots \subset S_{i,M}$ in Staff, perform:

14: $S_{i,j}.\omega = m,\ S_{i,j} \rightarrow S_i : \omega_i,\ j \in [1, m]$;

15: End.

16: Use OR to connect different entities, and AND to connect different department and position attributes and trust values under the same entity.

17:$T = (Car_A\ AND\ (CarType_A \cdots OR \cdots)\ AND\ AttrFlag_A)\ OR$
$(Entity_B\ AND\ (Department_B \cdots OR \cdots)\ AND\ (S_B : \omega_1 \cdots OR \cdots)\ AND\ AttrFlag_B)\ OR$
$(Entity_C\ AND\ (Department_C \cdots OR \cdots)\ AND\ (S_C : \omega_2 \cdots OR \cdots)\ AND\ AttrFlag_C)\ OR \cdots$

The algorithm input is attribute sets and vehicle trust value sets defined by different entities, vehicle types, departments and positions, and output is the formulated hierarchical access control strategy T. According to entity, vehicle type, department and position, attributes are divided into different types of attribute: $S = \{S_A, S_B, S_C, \cdots, S_M\}$. If there is an inclusion relationship between access permissions for the same type of attribute, that is, $S_{i,1} \subset S_{i,2} \subset S_{i,3} \subset \cdots \subset S_{i,N}$, assign weight ω to them, increasing from 1, and then traverse. If there are continuous job attributes under the same physical department, replace these attributes with $S_i : \omega_i$. Use OR to connect different entities, and AND to connect different departments, job attributes and trust values under the same entity to generate hierarchical access control policies T. The structure of the access control policy is shown in Figure 3, where the attributes in the policy T are reduced to the $1/m$ of total attributes. However, the composition of data visitor attribute sets is complex, and there may be a risk of attribute redundancy. Therefore, we need to prune and optimize to obtain the final access control strategy T_a according to Algorithm 2.

Algorithm 2 BTWACS pruning

Input: Access Control Policy $\boldsymbol{T}$, *parameter* α

Output: Pruned Tree T_α

1: Calculate the empirical entropy of each node.

2: Recursively retract upwards from the leaf nodes of the tree.

3: The whole tree of a group of leaf nodes before and after retracting to its parent node is T_a and T_b, respectively. Calculate the loss function of T_a and T_b by (21) to obtain $Loss_\alpha$ (T_a) and $Loss_\alpha$ (T_b), respectively. If $Loss_\alpha$ $(T_a) \geq Loss_\alpha$ (T_b), then prune. Then, merge and reorganize the attribute sets in the leaf nodes, and retract them upwards to replace the parent node and become the new leaf node.

4: Return to 2 until it cannot continue, and obtain the subtree with the smallest loss function T_α.

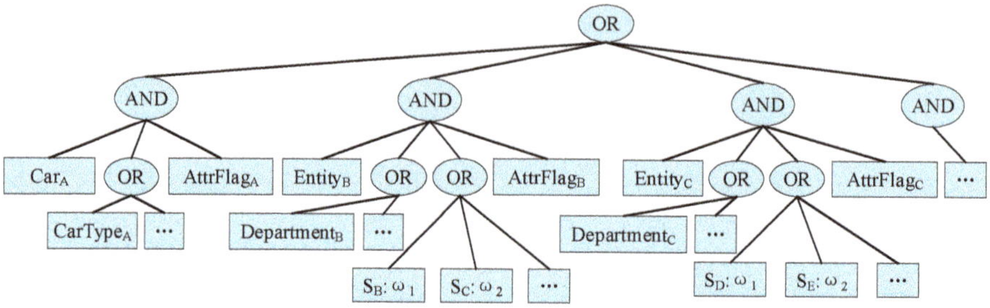

Figure 3. Access control policy.

Let the number of leaf nodes of the tree be $|T|$, with m as the leaf node of the tree T. The leaf node has N_m sample points, where the number of sample points of class k is N_{mk}, $E_m(T)$ is the empirical entropy on the leaf node m and $\alpha > 0$, and then the tree's loss function can be defined as:

$$Loss_\alpha(T) = \sum_{m=1}^{|T|} N_m E_m(T) + \alpha|T| \tag{21}$$

where the empirical entropy is

$$E_m(T) = -\sum_k \frac{N_{mk}}{N_m} log \frac{N_{mk}}{N_m} \tag{22}$$

4.3. Attribute-Based Encryption

The attribute-based encryption algorithm mainly consists of four parts: system initialization, generating user keys, generating encrypted files and decrypting.

4.3.1. System Initialization

The inputs of the system are the safety parameter γ and the attribute set U, and γ is publicly available. The output of the system is the public key PK and master key MSK. There is a bilinear group G_1 with prime P as the order, where g is the generator of G_1 and Z_p is the multiplication group of integer module P. This performs bilinear pairing operations $e : G_1 \times G_1 \rightarrow G_r$. We can generate the hash function $H : \{0,1\}^* \rightarrow G_1$ and attribute set $U = \{\alpha_1, \alpha_2, \alpha_3, \cdots, \alpha_n\}$, assign weighted attributes $\{s|s \in s_i\}$ to entities, select random number $\alpha, \beta \in Z_p$ and calculate $e(g,g)^\alpha$ and g^β.

The generated public key PK and master key MSK are as follows:

$$PK = \left\{G_1, g, g^\beta, e(g,g)^\alpha\right\} \tag{23}$$

$$MSK = g^\alpha \tag{24}$$

4.3.2. Generating User Keys

$Keygen(MSK, S, Tr)$ is a key SK that uses master key MSK, a group of weighted attributes S and trust value Tr as the input, and whose output is related to S and Tr. We can choose $t \in Z_p$ randomly, and every weighted attribute $i \in S$ has a weighted value ω_i. For each attribute i in the attribute set, calculate $D_i = H(i)^{\omega_i t}$ and generate the key for data visitors as SK:

$$SK = \left\{D = g^\alpha g^{\beta t}, g^t, \{D_i\}_{i \in S}, Tr\right\} \tag{25}$$

4.3.3. Encryption

In order to ensure the confidentiality and security of data and achieve effective access control effects, we adopt a hybrid encryption mechanism. Advanced Encryption Standard (AES) is used to encrypt data, and CP-ABE (See Section 2.3 for details) is used to encrypt symmetric keys and embed the encrypted data and symmetric keys into access control policies. The mechanism of mixing symmetric encryption AES and asymmetric encryption (CP-ABE) ensures the confidentiality of the data.

$Encrypt(PK, CK, M, T)$: Input the public key PK, plain text M, symmetric key CK and access control strategy T. Output the cipher-text CT. Choose the polynomial f_x for each node x in T. Choose a $d_x = k_x - 1$ degree polynomial for each node in T. From the root node R, $f_R(0) = s(s \in Z_p)$, s is random. For leaf node x, set $f_x(0) = f_{parent(x)}(index(x))$ and choose an f_x defined by d_x randomly. Every leaf node stands for a weighted attribute. ω_i is the smallest weight for each leaf node. Calculate $C = M \cdot e(g, g)^{\alpha s}$, $C_0 = g^s$. Make s a secret and split it along the tree. The corresponding secret sharding for the leaf node attribute i is $f_x(0)$. Calculate $C_i = H(i)^{-\omega_i s} \prod_{z \in S_i} g^{\gamma_z}$, $C_T = g^{f_x(0)}$.

$$CT = \{T, C, C_0, C_T, \{C_i\}_{i \in [1,n]}\} \tag{26}$$

4.3.4. Decryption

After the data requester obtains access permissions, AES is used to decrypt the data resources and CP-ABE is used to verify the legitimacy of the user. Only when the trust values and attribute sets match the access policy can the cipher-text be successfully decrypted to obtain plaintext, thus achieving fine-grained access control of the IoV data.

Only when the attribute set S and the trust value Tr of the key satisfies the T policy of the cipher-text access tree can the cipher-text be decrypted. Calculate $TP_x = MSK \cdot H \cdot \prod_{z \in S_x} g^{\gamma_z}$. Starting from the root node, perform recursive calculations. The partition of each sub node can be exponentially calculated based on the Lagrange difference factor, and then the multiplication operation can be performed. Construct decryption components as follows:

$$e(g, g)^{\alpha s} = \frac{e(P_x, C_0)}{e(C_T, C_i)} = \frac{e(P_x, C_0)}{e(g^{f_x(0)}, H \cdot \prod_{z \in S_x} g^{\gamma_z})} = \frac{e(g^{\alpha} \cdot H \cdot \prod_{z \in S_x} g^{\gamma_z}, g^s)}{e(g^{f_x(0)}, H \cdot \prod_{z \in S_x} g^{\gamma_z})} \tag{27}$$

We can then obtain plain text M through $M = \frac{C}{e(g,g)^{\alpha s}}$.

5. Experimental Results and Analysis

We use OpenStreetMap to construct a map of real traffic scenes and combine it with network simulators NS3 and Simulation of Urban MObility (SUMO) to simulate the motion trajectory of mobile vehicle nodes and the IoV environment of connected vehicles.

In the simulation environment, when vehicle A encounters an accident while driving, the program runs as follows: Firstly, the vehicle senses and generates access data M. Secondly, we can call Algorithm 1 to input the attribute set of the access object and the evaluated trust value, and then call Algorithm 2 to remove redundant attributes, and finally output access control policy T. Finally, the vehicle encrypts data using the access control strategy and uploads cipher-text to the blockchain network layer. After reaching node consensus based on the improved PBFT algorithm, the data are stored in the blockchain.

We validate the security and performance of the BTWACS and compare it to other access control methods. The simulation parameters are shown in Table 3.

Table 3. Parameter settings.

Parameter	Value
Scene	City street
Speed of vehicles	(5–50) m/s
Vehicle density within RSU	(10–70)
Communication range	0~300 m
OBU configuration	1.5 Ghz, 4 core CPU
RSU configuration	1.8 Ghz, 4 core CPU, 237 G hard disk

5.1. Safety Analysis

In order to ensure timely and reliable information exchange between vehicles, it is necessary to improve the recognition of malicious nodes, that is, to improve the recognition accuracy of untrusted nodes. We simulate and compare BBTE to TSMRP [28] and the scheme without trust evaluation, and the experimental results are shown in Figure 4. Figure 4a shows the accuracy of identifying malicious nodes with different node densities. Figure 4b shows the accuracy of identifying malicious nodes at different vehicle speeds.

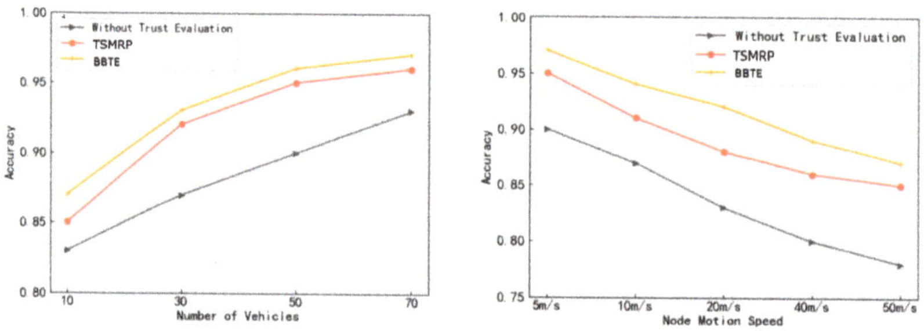

(**a**) (**b**)

Figure 4. Comparison of accuracy in identifying malicious nodes. (**a**) Identification accuracy of malicious nodes with different node densities; (**b**) identification accuracy of malicious nodes at different vehicle speeds.

As shown in Figure 4, a higher density of vehicle nodes, higher recognition accuracy and faster vehicle speed result in a decrease in the recognition accuracy of malicious nodes. TSMRP [28] combines direct trust and indirect trust to improve the accuracy of identifying malicious vehicle nodes but neglects the collection and calculation of vehicle experience trust and behavior observation information. BBTE combines direct trust, indirect trust, historical experience trust and behavioral observation trust, and the recognition accuracy of the BBTE is higher than the other two models.

This experiment simulates and implements a network using gray hole attack, on/off attack and defamation attack. BBTE is compared to trust models ART [29], CAT [30] and TSMRP [28] using the malicious node detection rate and malicious node recognition accuracy as two evaluation indicators. The accuracy of malicious nodes and the ratio of the real malicious nodes identify to the identified malicious nodes, as well as the detection rate of malicious nodes and the ratio of the identified real malicious nodes to the total number of malicious nodes are all used. We set the total number of nodes to 100, and the number of malicious nodes to 10, 20 and 30, respectively. The network attack scenario settings are shown in Table 4.

Table 4. Network attack scenario settings.

Attack Type	Description
Gray hole attack	50% probability of malicious packet loss.
On-off attack	Normal forwarding first, followed by mali-cious packet loss, alternating for a period of 30 seconds.
Defamation attack	In the process of trust recommendation, reduce the trust value of honest nodes and increased the trust value of untrusted nodes.

The comparison between the recognition accuracy and detection rate of malicious nodes under different attacks is shown in Figures 5 and 6.

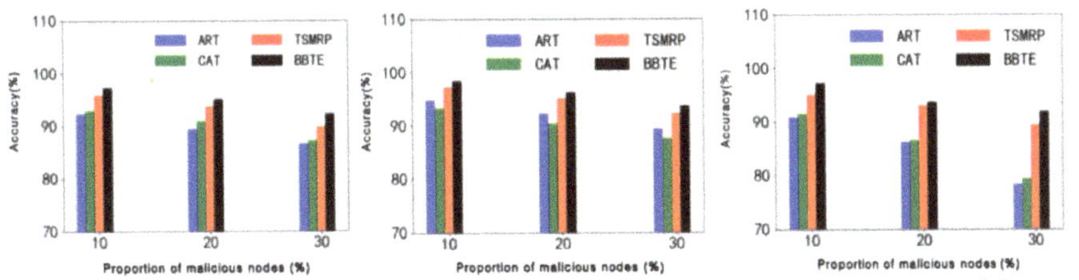

(a) Grey hole attack (b) On-off attack (c) Defamation attack

Figure 5. Comparison of malicious node identification accuracy under different attacks.

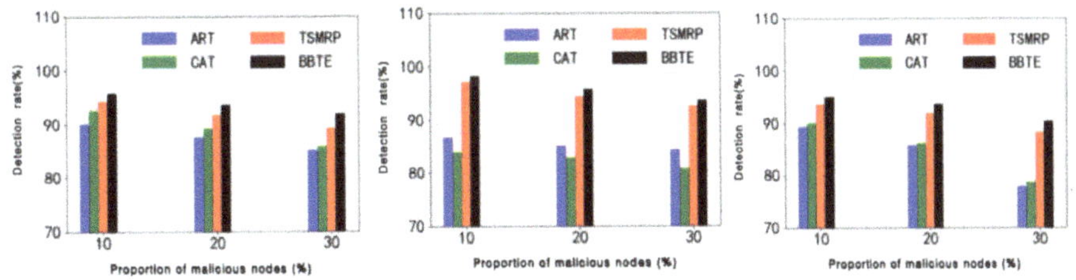

(a) Grey hole attack (b) On-off attack (c) Defamation attack

Figure 6. Comparison of malicious node identification detection rate under different attacks.

It can be seen from Figures 5 and 6 that CAT focuses on vehicle behavior detection and does not give enough consideration to historical experience trust and other vehicle recommendation trust information. ART relies on indirect trust and ignores the collection and calculation of direct trust. Neither ART nor CAT can effectively respond to temporal attacks. TSMRP combines direct trust and indirect trust and proposes a feedback mechanism to deal with temporal attacks but lacks consideration for the collection and calculation of vehicle experience trust and behavior observation information. BBTE combines direct trust, indirect trust, historical experience trust and behavioral observation trust, resulting in higher accuracy in trust calculation. Therefore, the recognition accuracy and the detection rate of BBTE are higher than the other three models.

5.2. Performance Analysis

The Trust Evaluation Method ensures the security and reliability of information transmission by judging the credibility of vehicle nodes and achieves the secure access control of data. We used the Java Pairing-Based Cryptography (JPBC) Library to perform comparative experiments on traditional CP-ABE [31], weighted CP-ABE [14] and BBTE. The number of attributes set in the experiment increases gradually from 1 to 100. In the access control strategy without pruning and restructuring, each attribute class contains an average of five attributes. After optimization, each attribute class contains an average of six attributes. The experimental results are shown in Figure 7. Figure 7a shows the change trend in encryption time with the number of attributes, and Figure 7b shows the change trend in cipher-text size with the number of attributes.

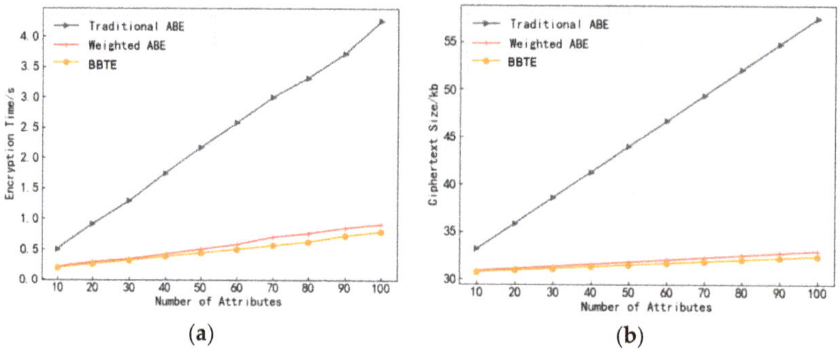

Figure 7. Comparison of encryption efficiency. (**a**) Encryption efficiency of vehicles; (**b**) cipher-text transmission size.

Calculation cost: As shown in Figure 7a, when the number of attributes is 100, the traditional CP-ABE encryption time takes about 4.26 s. Weighted CP-ABE constructs an access control policy by introducing weights, and the number of attributes can be reduced to 1/5, that is, the number of attributes in the policy is only 20, and the encryption time is reduced to about 0.91 s. In BBTE, not only are weights introduced to construct access control policies but trust value attributes are also introduced to improve the security of communication and interaction between vehicle nodes. After pruning optimization, redundant attributes are removed, resulting in an average of six attributes per attribute class. The encryption time is reduced to about 0.79 s, greatly reducing the complexity of the policy and significantly reducing computational overhead.

Transmission overhead: As shown in Figure 7b, when encrypting 100 attributes, the traditional CP-ABE cipher-text size is 57.5 kb. Weighted CP-ABE constructs an access control policy by introducing weights, and the number of attributes can be reduced to 1/5, which means that the policy only has 20 attributes and the cipher-text size is 33 kb. In BBTE, not only are weights introduced to construct access control policies but trust value attributes are also introduced to improve the security of communication and interaction between vehicle nodes. After pruning optimization, redundant attributes are removed, resulting in an average of six attributes per attribute class, reducing the cipher-text size to approximately 32.4 kb and reducing the transmission cost of vehicle data transmission to the blockchain network layer.

Weighted CP-ABE introduces weight to formulate hierarchical access strategies but does not consider factors such as entity trust values and attribute redundancy. BBTE adds trusted judgments to entities to further ensure secure access control effects and effectively reduces the complexity of access policies through pruning technology, saving computational costs.

6. Conclusions

In traditional IoV, data are easy to tamper with and leak. The BTWACS access control strategy achieves decentralized data security storage and access. This scheme evaluates the trustworthiness of accessing entities and introduces attribute-based encryption to achieve the flexible access control of on-chain data, ensuring the confidentiality and integrity of message transmission. It constructs a hierarchical access control strategy based on weight and trust by mining the association relationships between attribute permissions among various roles, and further optimizes the access strategy through pruning techniques. We evaluate the trust value to improve the security and efficiency of node interaction, and the results show that this scheme can effectively respond to gray hole attacks, defamation attacks and collusion attacks from other vehicle nodes. This method can effectively reduce the computing and transmission costs of vehicles and meet the access requirements of multiple entities and roles in the IoV.

It improves the communication performance of the IoV, enhances the security of the network and creates a safe and comfortable transportation environment. The algorithm improves the trust evaluation mechanism in blockchain technology, making it more efficient and accurate, and has a promoting effect on the development of blockchain technology. It is an application of blockchain technology in the actual IoT scenario IoV and is a good example of the practical application of blockchain. It is beneficial for the materialization and application of blockchain technology to play a role in real life.

We utilize the BTWACS to control the credibility of entities, ensuring the security of information transmission and avoiding security issues such as malicious attacks and data leakage. However, there is a lack of incentive mechanisms to promote the participation of selfish vehicle nodes. Moreover, although we preliminarily implement the attribute-based access control strategy, we still lack in-depth research on policy updates and the attribute revocation of on-chain data.

In future research, we will continue to conduct in-depth research on the policy update and attribute revocation of the data on the chain for the selfish vehicle node incentive problem, and further improve the access control effect of the IoV on the premise of ensuring data security and reliability.

Author Contributions: Conceptualization, L.L.; methodology, J.W.; formal analysis, L.L.; data curation, J.W.; writing—original draft preparation, C.L. All authors have read and agreed to the published version of the manuscript.

Funding: This research was funded in part by the scientific research project of the National Natural Science Foundation of China (62362055), the Inner Mongolia Autonomous Region Key R&D and Achievement Transformation Program Project (2022YFSJ0013, 2023YFHH0052), the Research Program for Young Talents of Inner Mongolia Colleges (NJYT22084, NJYT23055), the Natural Science Foundation of Inner Mongolia (2023MS06008), the Key Research & Development Program of Erdos (YF20232328), the Scientific Research Program for Inner Mongolia Colleges (JY20220061, JY20230119, JY20230019), and the Basic Scientific Research Expenses Program of Universities directly under Inner Mongolia Autonomous Region (JY20220078, 2022ZY0169).

Data Availability Statement: Due to the nature of this research, participants of this study did not agree for their data to be shared publicly, so supporting data is not available.

Conflicts of Interest: The authors declare that they have no conflict of interest to report regarding the present study.

References

1. Yu, B.; Bai, F. PYRAMID: Probabilistic Content Reconciliation and Prioritization for V2V Communications. *IEEE Trans. Veh. Technol.* **2018**, *67*, 6615–6626. [CrossRef]
2. Cheng, X.; Zhang, R.; Chen, S.; Li, J.; Yang, L.; Zhang, H. 5G enabled vehicular communications and networking. Wireless Communication over ZigBee for Automotive Inclination Measurement. *China Commun.* **2018**, *15*, 3–6. [CrossRef]
3. Lyamin, N.; Kleyko, D.; Delooz, Q.; Vinel, A. AI-Based Malicious Network Traffic Detection in VANETs. *IEEE Netw.* **2018**, *32*, 15–21. [CrossRef]
4. Khelifi, H.; Luo, S.; Nour, B.; Moungla, H.; Faheem, Y.; Hussain, R.; Ksentini, A. Named Data Networking in Vehicular Ad hoc Networks: State-of-the-Art and Challenges. *IEEE Commun. Surv. Tutor.* **2020**, *20*, 320–351. [CrossRef]
5. Zhao, L.; Li, X.; Gu, B.; Zhou, Z.; Mumtaz, S.; Frascolla, V.; Gacanin, H.; Ashraf, M.I.; Rodriguez, J.; Yang, M.; et al. Vehicular Communications: Standardization and Open Issues. *IEEE Commun. Stand. Mag.* **2019**, *2*, 74–80. [CrossRef]
6. Sharma, S.; Sharma, A.; Goel, T.; Deoli, R.; Mohan, S. Smart Home Gardening Management System: A Cloud-Based Internet-of-Things (IoT) Application in VANET. In Proceedings of the 2020 11th International Conference on Computing, Communication and Networking Technologies (ICCCNT), Kharagpur, India, 1–3 July 2020; pp. 1–5.
7. Liu, A.; Du, X.; Wang, N.; Li, S. Research progress of blockchain technology and its application in information security. *Ruan Jian Xue Bao/J. Softw.* **2018**, *29*, 2092–2115. (In Chinese)

8. Qazi, F.; Khan, F.H. Enhancing the security of vehicle to road side unit (RSU) communication with key generation and advanced encryption procedure in vehicular ad-hoc network (VANET). *Indian J. Sci. Technol.* **2017**, *10*, 36. [CrossRef]
9. Lee, T.; Moon, S.H.; Jang, J. Data encryption method using CP-ABE with symmetric key algorithm in blockchain network. In Proceedings of the 2021 International Conference on Information and Communication Technology Convergence (ICTC), Jeju Island, Republic of Korea, 20–22 October 2021; pp. 1371–1373.
10. Blundo, C.; Cimato, S.; Siniscalchi, L. Managing Constraints in Role Based Access Control. *IEEE Access* **2020**, *8*, 140497–140511. [CrossRef]
11. Xue, Y.; Xue, K.; Gai, N.; Hong, J.; Wei, D.S.; Hong, P. An Attribute-Based Controlled Collaborative Access Control Scheme for Public Cloud Storage. *IEEE Trans. Inf. Forensics Secur.* **2019**, *14*, 2927–2942. [CrossRef]
12. Ahamed, J.; Khan, F. An Enhanced Context-aware Capability-based Access Control Model for the Internet of Things in Healthcare. In Proceedings of the 2019 Sixth HCT Information Technology Trends (ITT), Ras Al Khaimah, United Arab Emirates, 20–21 November 2019; pp. 126–131.
13. Cruz, J.P.; Kaji, Y.; Yanai, N. RBAC-SC: Role-based access control using smart contract. *IEEE Access* **2018**, *6*, 12240–12251. [CrossRef]
14. Liu, X.; Yin, Y.; Chen, W.; Xia, Y.; Xu, J.; Han, L. Data security sharing scheme of Internet of vehicles based on blockchain. *J. Zhejiang Univ. (Eng. Ed.)* **2021**, *55*, 957–965. (In Chinese)
15. Nakamura, Y.; Zhang, Y.; Sasabe, M.; Kasahara, S. Capability-Based Access Control for the Internet of Things: An Ethereum Blockchain-Based Scheme. In Proceedings of the GLOBECOM 2019—2019 IEEE Global Communications Conference, Waikoloa, HI, USA, 9–13 December 2019; pp. 1–6.
16. Chen, C.; Wang, C.; Qiu, T.; Lv, N.; Pei, Q. A Secure Content Sharing Scheme based on Consortium Bolckchain in Vehicular Named Data Networks. *IEEE Trans. Ind. Inform.* **2019**, *16*, 3278–3289. [CrossRef]
17. Kang, J.; Yu, R.; Huang, X.; Wu, M.; Maharjan, S.; Xie, S.; Zhang, Y. Blockchain for secure and efficient data sharing in vehicular edge computing and networks. *IEEE Internet Things J.* **2018**, *6*, 4660–4670. [CrossRef]
18. Zhang, D.; Yu, F.R.; Yang, R. Blockchain-Based Distributed Software-defined Vehicular Networks: A Dueling Deep Q-Learning Approach. *IEEE Trans. Cogn. Commun. Netw.* **2019**, *5*, 1086–1100. [CrossRef]
19. Gu, W.; Li, J.; Tang, Z. A Survey on Consensus Mechanisms for Blockchain Technology. In Proceedings of the 2021 International Conference on Artificial Intelligence, Big Data and Algorithms (CAIBDA), Xi'an, China, 28–30 May 2021; pp. 46–49.
20. Yang, Z.; Yang, K.; Lei, L.; Zheng, K.; Leung, V.C.M. Blockchain-Based Decentralized Trust Management in Vehicular Networks. *IEEE Internet Things J.* **2019**, *6*, 1495–1505. [CrossRef]
21. Abuhashim, A.; Tan, C.C. Smart Contract Designs on Blockchain Applications. In Proceedings of the 2020 IEEE Symposium on Computers and Communications (ISCC), Rennes, France, 7–10 July 2020; pp. 15–26.
22. Wang, W.; Hoang, D.T.; Hu, P.; Xiong, Z.; Niyato, D.; Wang, P.; Wen, Y.; Kim, D.I. A Survey on Consensus Mechanisms and Mining Strategy Management in Blockchain Networks. *IEEE Access* **2019**, *7*, 22328–22370. [CrossRef]
23. Porwal, S.; Mittal, S. Design of Concurrent cipher-text Policy-Attribute Based Encryption Library for Multilevel Access of Encrypted Data. In Proceedings of the 2018 Fifth International Conference on Parallel, Distributed and Grid Computing (PDGC), Solan, India, 20–22 December 2018; pp. 42–47.
24. Oham, C.; Jurdak, R.; Kanhere, S.S.; Dorri, A.; Jha, S. B-FICA: BlockChain based Framework for Auto-Insurance Claim and Adjudication. In Proceedings of the 2018 IEEE International Conference on Internet of Things (iThings) and IEEE Green Computing and Communications (GreenCom) and IEEE Cyber, Physical and Social Computing (CPSCom) and IEEE Smart Data (SmartData), Halifax, NS, Canada, 30 July 2018–3 August 2018.
25. Kanumalli, S.S.; Ch, A.; Murty, P.S.R.C. Secure V2V communication in IoV using IBE and PKI based hybrid approach. *Int. J. Adv. Comput. Sci. Appl. (IJACSA)* **2020**, *11*, 466–472. [CrossRef]
26. Liu, Y.; Wang, Y.; Chang, G. Efficient Privacy-Preserving Dual Authentication and Key Agreement Scheme for Secure V2V Communications in an IoV Paradigm. *IEEE Trans. Intell. Transp. Syst.* **2017**, *18*, 2740–2749. [CrossRef]
27. Diakoulaki, D.; Mavrotas, G.; Papayannakis, L. Determining objective weights in multiple criteria problems: The CRITIC method. *Comput. Oper. Res.* **1995**, *22*, 763–770. [CrossRef]
28. Xia, H.; Zhang, S.; Sun, Y.; Xiao, F.; Li, Y.; Cheng, X. Design of Trust-Based Secure Multicast Routing Protocol in VANETs. *J. Comput. Sci.* **2019**, *42*, 961–979. (In Chinese)
29. Li, W.; Song, H. ART: An Attack-Resistant Trust Management Scheme for Securing Vehicular Ad Hoc Networks. *IEEE Trans. Intell. Transp. Syst.* **2016**, *17*, 960–969. [CrossRef]
30. Raghu, V.; Barnwal, R.P.; Ghosh, S.K. CAT: Consensus-assisted trust estimation of MDS-equipped collaborators in vehicular ad-hoc network. *Veh. Commun.* **2015**, *2*, 150–157.
31. Fan, K.; Pan, Q.; Zhang, K.; Bai, Y.; Sun, S.; Li, H.; Yang, Y. A Secure and Verifiable Data Sharing Scheme Based on Blockchain in Vehicular Social Networks. *IEEE Trans. Veh. Technol.* **2020**, *69*, 5826–5835. [CrossRef]

electronics

MDPI

Article

Analyzing Miners' Dynamic Equilibrium in Blockchain Networks under DDoS Attacks

Xiao Liu [1], Zhao Huang [1,*], Quan Wang [1], Xiaohong Jiang [2], Yin Chen [3] and Bo Wan [1]

[1] School of Computer Science and Technology, Xidian University, Xi'an 710071, China; cantona@stu.xidian.edu.cn (X.L.); qwang@xidian.edu.cn (Q.W.); wanbo@xidian.edu.cn (B.W.)
[2] School of Systems Information Science, Future University Hakodate, Hakodate 041-8655, Japan; jiang@fun.ac.jp
[3] Graduate School of Media and Governance, Reitaku University, Kashiwa 277-8686, Japan; ychen@reitaku-u.ac.jp
* Correspondence: z_huang@xidian.edu.cn; Tel.: +86-187-9261-0378

Abstract: Proof of work (PoW) is one of the most widely used consensus algorithms in blockchain networks. It mainly uses the competition between mining nodes to obtain block rewards. However, this competition for computational power will allow malicious nodes to obtain illegal profits, bringing potential security threats to blockchain systems. A distributed denial of service (DDoS) attack is a major threat to the PoW algorithm. It utilizes multiple nodes in the blockchain network to attack honest miners to obtain illegal rewards. To solve this problem, academia has proposed a DDoS attack detection mechanism based on reinforcement learning methods and static game modeling methods based on mining pools. However, these methods cannot effectively make miners choose the strategy with the best profit over time when facing DDoS attacks. Therefore, this paper proposes a dynamic evolutionary game model for miners facing DDoS attacks under blockchain networks to solve the above problems for the first time. We address the model by replicating the dynamic equation to obtain a stable solution. According to the theorem of the Lyapunov method, we also obtain the only stable strategy for miners facing DDoS attacks. The experimental results show that compared with the static method, the dynamic method can affect game playing and game evolution over time. Moreover, miners' strategy to face DDoS attacks gradually shifts from honest mining to launching DDoS attacks against each other as the blockchain network improves.

Keywords: blockchain; DDoS attacks; electronic transaction; network layer; PoW; security threat

1. Introduction

The PoW consensus algorithm is a widely used consensus algorithm for blockchain systems. PoW algorithm makes the blockchain nodes participating in the consensus through the network calculate a large number of unpredictable mathematical puzzles to prove the efforts of the nodes to obtain the right to get out of the block and the corresponding rewards. The process of competing with each other in terms of computing power to calculate the puzzle is called mining. The nodes in the blockchain network that participate in the mining process are called miners. The reward given to the miner that mines a new block is referred to as getting out of the block or mining reward [1]. Bitcoin is one of the most widely used blockchain systems that use PoW algorithms to maintain data consensus and ensure security [2]. The PoW algorithm can ensure the security of the Bitcoin system ledger and the impossibility of tampering with transactions [3]. However, many nodes (miners) must continuously compete to solve the puzzle to obtain the block reward. This competition, known as mining, consumes much computing power among miners and mining pools. Excessive competition and mining blocks can cause insecurity problems for miners. At the network layer, if malicious nodes forge IP addresses or send excessive numbers of network connection requests, the honest miners will lose their mining rewards. The malicious nodes will obtain an illegal block reward by launching several types of attacks, such as denial of service (DoS) attacks, blockchain DoS (BDoS) attacks, and distributed DoS (DDoS) attacks on blockchain networks [4]. The occurrence of such problems brings huge mining reward losses and security threats to blockchain networks [5]. Among them, DDoS attacks are the most important security threat [6].

A DDoS attack is when multiple attackers in different locations launch simultaneous attacks on one or more targets over a network [7]. In DDoS attacks, the attacker cuts off the connection between the target node and the network through the network, resulting in no external network requests and traffic access. This brings huge economic losses to the target node [8]. However, DDoS attacks also frequently occur on blockchain networks [9]. DDoS attacks on blockchain networks mainly refer to malicious mining nodes controlling multiple nodes through the network to attack other honest mining nodes to obtain illegal mining rewards [9]. In the PoW algorithm based on the mining process, malicious miners usually initiate excessive network requests to honest miners [7,10]. Therefore, it is necessary to implement effective models and algorithms in the blockchain network environment based on the PoW algorithm to resist or reduce the loss caused by malicious miners launching DDoS attacks. Academics have proposed many methods to solve the DDoS attack problem in the blockchain network layer. At present, these methods can be mainly divided into the following categories: DDoS defense methods combined with blockchain technology, DDoS combination attacks combined with other blockchain attacks, and static game strategies based on the blockchain mining pool [10–17]. Among these existing studies, the use of a static game approach to mitigate DDoS attacks is the most effective [18–21]. The Nash equilibrium solution is a static game strategy. It means that after the game, any player who unilaterally changes their strategy under this strategy combination (the other players' strategies remain unchanged) will not improve their own payoff. In other words, the Nash equilibrium state is an optimal state in which the static game method prevents all players from playing an additional game [22]. Therefore, the research of these static methods is mainly to obtain the Nash equilibrium state with the optimal profit of the mining pool. These static game modeling methods can utilize a finite number of games and implement the Nash equilibrium optimal profit strategy value of the mining pool when the mining pool faces different DDoS attacks under the blockchain network. Thus, they can alleviate the loss caused by DDoS attacks on the mining pools to a certain extent [23,24]. However, there are some drawbacks and problems with these static game approaches. First, the way of modeling and solving the stable strategy of these static methods cannot reflect the dynamic evolution of the strategies of both sides of the game over time. Second, these methods cannot effectively reflect the changing trend of miners' game strategy selection of mining strategy probability with time and parameter changes when miners respond to DDoS attacks under different network environment parameters. Third, there is a lack of effective game theory methods in the current research to model DDoS attacks miners face. Therefore, it is necessary to establish a dynamic game model to implement the dynamic selection of the miners and its optimal profit mining strategy when facing DDoS attacks in blockchain networks.

To solve the above problems, this paper proposes an evolutionary game approach to mitigate the DDoS attack for the miners. We use the evolutionary game method to build a model of two miners with the same computing power facing DDoS attacks. We then find the stable solution by replicating the dynamic equation. The Ode45 function is a function to solve differential equations in Matlab, which can be used to solve the equilibrium solution of dynamic differential equations in evolutionary game models [17]. In different network environments [25], we use the ode45 function of Matlab libraries to solve the stable strategy solution of the replicated dynamic equation. The experimental results show that the model designed by us can better reflect the evolution trend over time and the changing trend of game probabilities when miners face DDoS attacks in dynamic games than in static games. In particular, the main contributions of this paper are as follows.

- To the best of our knowledge, this paper is the first to use a dynamic method to study the selection of the profitable optimal strategy for miners under DDoS attacks.
- We construct the miners' profits tables and dynamic replication equation based on a DDoS attack.
- We obtain the optimal strategy in different cases by analyzing various attack situations on the dynamic replication equation.
- By comparing static and dynamic games, the experimental results show that dynamic games have the advantages of allowing multiple games and a better game evolution when miners face attacks. To be clear, the better the network environment is, the more the miners will choose to launch an attack to obtain the best profit when facing DDoS attacks.

The rest of the paper is organized as follows: Section 2 describes the related work. Section 3 presents our design of a DDoS attack game theory module and solutions for miners in blockchain systems. The analysis of the system performance is in Section 4. Conclusions and future work are provided in Section 5.

2. Related Work

2.1. DDoS Attacks in Blockchain Systems

In blockchain systems, many consensus algorithms use mining as an essential tool to generate blocks. The consensus layer of the blockchain system controls miners when they compete with each other to generate blocks based on mining [26]. PoW, proof of stake (DPoS), proof of activity (PoA), and other standard blockchain algorithms are the most common consensus algorithms in the consensus layer, ensuring the security and data consistency of the blockchain system. The PoW algorithm is the most widely used consensus algorithm for blockchain systems, which uses multiple nodes' arithmetic power to mine for block rewards in the blockchain systems. As the most basic mining unit, miners face many security threats when competing for mining. A malicious node obtains a miner's block reward by malicious means. Block withholding attacks, selfish mining attacks, and Sybil attacks are ways to withhold attacks by malicious nodes to use a higher mining computing power or forge IP addresses to attack honest miners to obtain illegal profits [27]. These attacks bring significant security threats and losses to the blockchain system. Therefore, we must protect miners in case of aggression.

A DDoS attack is one of the most common attacks encountered at the network layer of a blockchain system. A DDoS attack is usually caused by malicious nodes launching excessive network requests to disconnect the network of honest miners and obtain illegal block rewards. Honest miners suffer significant losses when attacked by malicious nodes. The occurrence of this DDoS attack scenario poses a security threat and financial loss to honest miners [28]. Therefore, the main target of DDoS attacks against blockchain systems is to illegally obtain mining income and block rewards from mining pools and miners. There are few kinds of research on miners against DDoS attacks. The current study is mainly embodied in DDoS defense methods and new DDoS attacks in two aspects.

2.2. The DDoS-Based Combination Attacks in Blockchain Systems

Combination attacks based on DDoS attacks mainly refer to malicious nodes launching DDoS attacks in combination with methods such as incentives, creating redundant blockchain forks (selfish mining), and other methods to obtain higher mining revenues than a single DDoS attack. Currently, academics have researched and made some progress on the aspects of new combinatorial attacks based on DDoS attacks. Hayat et al. [11] proposed a multilayer combination attack method (ML-DDoS) based on DDoS attacks and smart contracts, which was designed to obtain more rewards from attackers. Wang et al. [12] designed a new mining attack, a selfish mining-based denial-of-service (SDoS) attack, which targeted the blockchain system based on the PoW mechanism and analyzed the gains and strategies of the attacker and the honest miners through game theory. Mirkin et al. [13] implemented a novel DDoS attack based on blockchain incentives called blockchain denial of service

(BDoS). The attacks utilized the blockchain's reward mechanism to induce rational miners to stop mining, thus bringing the PoW-based cryptocurrency system to a standstill. The attack did not require control over a large portion of the mining capacity, nor did it require constant resource consumption, making it more effective and dangerous than traditional DDoS attacks. Yaish et al. [29] proposed a combination of DDoS attacks by combining the characteristics of blockchain and Ethereum. This combination attack consumed the victim's resources and reduced its benefits by executing context and verifying inconsistencies.

2.3. Defense and Mitigation Methods for DDoS Attacks

There are more current approaches to DDoS defense and mitigation strategies in blockchain systems. These methods are mainly categorized into two main categories: detection of DDoS attacks and mitigation of DDoS attacks. The first category mainly detects the presence of DDoS attacks by detecting the presence of excessive network requests or abnormal traffic in the blockchain system. The second type of research mainly uses static game theory methods to model and solve the Nash equilibrium's optimal profit strategy solution for the two mining pools facing DDoS attacks [30].

At present, the anti-DDoS attack methods in the blockchain system are mainly to detect and defend against DDoS attacks by detecting excessive network requests and abnormal traffic. Ilyas et al. [31] introduced an efficient technique using optimization-based deep learning by considering the blockchain network and a smart contract for the detection and prevention of DDoS attacks. The traffic was analyzed based on the user request, and a verification using a smart contract in the blockchain system was made to find the authenticated user. The network responses were provided for the authenticated user, and the suspicious traffic was utilized for the detection of DDoS attacks using the poaching raptor optimization-based deep neural network. Yakubu et al. [32] used blockchain-based smart contracts and single-server queuing systems to achieve secure authentication of communication between devices in smart homes and protocols to resist DDoS attacks. This method could detect whether blockchain devices launched DDoS attacks in IoT environments by verifying that abnormal traffic existed during authentication. Houda et al. [33] proposed a new framework based on blockchain technology. The framework protected the privacy of blockchain networks and mitigated the hazards of security threats such as DDoS attacks and DoS attacks. Jmal et al. [34] proposed an ANN DDoS attack detection model based on an artificial intelligence approach to identify malicious traffic and optimize the traffic load as a way to identify the presence of DDoS attacks on blockchain networks.

The research on DDoS game modeling in the academic community mainly focuses on the static modeling and solving of the mining pool revenue. These research studies use static modeling methods such as zero-determinant games or repeated games to study the benefits of mining pools facing DDoS attacks [35–37]. Wu et al. [18] expressed the interactive competition of mining revenue between mining pools under the blockchain network in the face of DDoS attacks as a general and random game model and proposed an efficient Nash learning algorithm to obtain a near-optimal DDoS attack strategy that maximized the expected long-term utility. Johnson et al. [19] first proposed a model and optimal strategy approach for static games when mining pools faced DDoS attacks in a blockchain system environment. This model effectively alleviated the mining losses caused by DDoS attacks on two mining pools with different computing power. Guo et al. [38] proposed a blockchain-based distributed collective entrance defense (DCED) framework in which network traffic characteristics could be recorded and aggregated at the entrances of the satellite Internet (SI). Their method used static game theory to model blockchain nodes and could effectively resist DDoS attacks. Wang et al. [39] proposed static game-based strategies for mining activity analysis to mitigate DDoS attacks in blockchain networks. By solving the Nash equilibrium point of the static game, the transaction fee dilemma of the mining pool and the transaction fee strategy of the end user was realized. Sood et al. [40] proposed a profit mitigation model for DDoS attacks in mining pools based on the stochastic game method. The model took the cost of launching DDoS attacks by mining pools into account in the modeling, which effectively mitigated the impact of changes in the network on the reduction in revenue that mining pools faced from DDoS attacks.

There has been some research on blockchain systems facing BWH attacks and selfish mining attacks in blockchain systems using dynamic games to solve the problem of decreasing their mining revenue. Huang et al. [5] proposed a dynamic evolutionary game model to mitigate the loss of revenue from BWH attacks faced by mining pools in blockchain systems. This dynamic game model was able to obtain the optimal solution for mining pools facing BWH attacks with different penalties and rewards. Kesavan et al. [41] presented a dynamic evolutionary game method of attacking the proof-of-work consensus based on selfish mining attacks. Their model used an evolutionary game for the first time to study the mining losses caused by selfish mining attacks to alleviate the reduction in mining pool revenue. Mighan et al. [42] used a dynamic evolutionary game model to model the probability of using the Ethernet data distribution network. The model allowed for the accurate modeling of data propagation and forks in blockchain systems. The authors also effectively addressed the issue of BWH attacks being able to degrade the performance of the Ethernet network using the dynamic game approach modeling.

2.4. Challenges in Current Research

The existing work on blockchain DDoS attacks can address the problems encountered to a certain extent. These types of approaches only boost the revenue of the mining pool that launched the attack. However, these efforts face more new issues and challenges. The DDoS-based combination attack methods can reduce attack costs while effectively enabling malicious mining pools to obtain higher mining revenues. However, these combination attack methods cannot alleviate, detect, and protect the losses of honest node mining benefits caused by combination attacks. These methods also cannot mitigate the revenue loss from DDoS attacks on mining pools that mine honestly and cannot effectively detect the presence of DDoS attacks in advance. To solve this problem, many research methods have been proposed to corrupt the DDoS attacks in blockchain networks. These methods can effectively use artificial intelligence to detect excessive network requests and abnormal traffic to prevent DDoS attacks. However, these methods only consider detecting the existence of DDoS attacks in advance and thus defending against them in advance. However, these methods do not consider the problem of revenue loss from honest mining when miners or mining pools face DDoS attacks during the mining process. In order to solve these problems, academics have gradually proposed static game models to mitigate the mining losses caused by DDoS attacks. The static game method is somewhat effective in mitigating the loss of mining revenue from mining pools. However, there are a number of problems and challenges associated with them. Static game modeling can only use a limited number of games. This approach is unable to perform multiple games dynamically and effectively reflect the convergence trend of parameter changes for different probabilities of honest mining pools or miners under different DDoS attack scenarios of game changes. Based on the research of BWH attack and selfish mining attack evolutionary game model, it can be proved that the dynamic evolutionary game method can effectively solve the problem of mitigating the reduction in revenue of mining pools or miners in the mining process when the blockchain system faces attacks. The success of the research work on these other attacks also suggests that dynamic games can similarly be used for the blockchain system's DDoS attack gain mitigation problem. However, current research work on DDoS attacks lacks effective dynamic modeling. This is the key issue that needs to be addressed in this paper.

Due to the above problems, we need to propose a new method to solve the problem that miners cannot effectively obtain the best benefits when facing DDoS attacks. In particular, we propose a dynamic evolutionary game model to establish the benefits of miners facing DDoS attacks under the blockchain network and find the optimal mining strategy according to different network environment conditions. The dynamic game model that we designed contains three main parts: model description, model building, and optimal strategy solving. In the following part of this paper, we specifically describe the design and solution process of the model.

3. The Proposed Evolutionary Game Theory Model and Solutions

3.1. Problem Description and Hypothesis

In this section, we assume a scenario where two miners with the same computational power face a decrease in revenue from DDoS attacks. We analyze the problems faced by this scenario and model the revenue problems faced by this scenario through parameters. In this paper, we consider the scenario where two miners with the same arithmetic power under the same mining pool face a DDoS attack. A typical scenario of a miner launching a DDoS attack in a blockchain network is shown in Figure 1. From Figure 1, we can see multiple mining pools competing for mining rewards through the network. Multiple mining pools perform honest mining to obtain the block rewards. However, they do not launch DDoS attacks to attack other mining pools over the network. Here, we assume pool 1 mines a block and receives a block reward from the pool manager, while the other pools do not receive the mining rewards. Mining pool 1 receives a mining reward value of R. Two miners of the same arithmetic power are mining under the same pool 1. When miner A and miner B both mine honestly in pool 1 at the same time, their share of the mining revenue is half of the revenue of pool 1, and the value is R. When miner A launches a DDoS attack on miner B, miner A cannot continue to mine honestly in the mining pool due to insufficient computing power. Mining pool 1 has only miner B mining honestly. At this time, the mining computing power of miners in mining pool 1 is half of the honest mining of miners, so the total mining revenue obtained by the miners is $\frac{R}{2}$. Therefore, miners A and B mine below pool 1 with an average return of $\frac{R}{4}$. However, the miner A does not want to spend arithmetic power to mine rewards honestly. Therefore, miner A consumes part of its arithmetic power to launch DDoS attacks on miner B through the network to gain illegal mining revenue. As shown in Figure 1, miner A launches DDoS attacks on miner B and receives a mining reward. Miner B loses wd's mining reward. w represents the network environment impact factor. d represents the illegal mining reward caused by miner A launching DDoS attacks when the network condition is very good (in the ideal network state, the value of w is 1). The pool manager penalizes the attacking pool and rewards the honest pool based on whether the miner attacks or not. The amount of reward and punishment is set to a. Finally, miner A launches an attack to gain mining revenue but is also punished by the pool manager for the attack. Miner B is rewarded for mining honestly but also suffers mining losses due to the attacks. The specific parameter description and four attack scenarios are elaborated and analyzed in the following contents.

We refer to this scenario and extend it to other DDoS attack scenarios for miners to make the following assumptions and analyze the whole problem. In this paper, Table 1 is established to explain the parameters and the corresponding description of the parameters. Through the relevant parameters in Table 1, we can conduct a rational analysis, and model, and find the solution to different situations facing DDoS attacks under the same mining pool. To simplify the establishment of the game model, this paper only considers the scenario of two miners with the same computing power in the same mining pool. The description of this problem and the assumptions are as follows.

(1) This paper assumes that all miners only mine in one mining pool and are not allowed to switch to other mining pools at will.

(2) We assume that the computing power of the entire mining pool is constant. The total block production reward obtained from the mining pool is assumed to be R. The mining pool only has two miners, A and B, with the same computing power. When miners A and B are both honest miners, the average payoff is $\frac{R}{2}$. When one of the miners launches a DDoS attack, the average honest mining gain for A and B is $\frac{R}{4}$. When A and B launch DDoS attacks on each other, miners A and B both earn 0 for honest mining.

(3) When a particular miner launches a DDoS attack, the loss of the honest miner is wd. The quality of the network environment is represented by the network coefficient w,

which is $0 \leq w \leq 1$. d is the damage caused by malicious miners to honest miners when the network is in an ideal state. Then, the network situation can cause malicious miners to launch DDoS attacks to incur damage. This paper assumes that the better the network condition, the higher the loss to honest miners. Thus, wd represents the illegal rewards obtained by the miner which launches a DDoS attack.

Figure 1. A scenario in which miners of a blockchain system face a DDoS attack.

Table 1. DDoS attack modeling parameters for miners.

Parameters	Description and Function of Parameters
R	The total profit allocated by the pool manager when a single mining pool mines in the blockchain system.
d	The illegal revenue gained by the attacker or the revenue lost by the attacked miner.
a	(1) When miners mine honestly with the same mining pool, the pool manager gives the reward to honest miners. (2) When a malicious miner launches a DDoS attack, the attacker is punished by the mining pool manager.
w	Network environment coefficient.
f_1	The miner returns from honest mining.
f_2	The miner returns when launching DDoS attacks.
$\overline{f}$	Average returns for miners facing DDoS attacks.
$F(x)$	The dynamic equation of replication for x and time t.
$F'(x)$	The first derivative of $F(x)$ with respect to the probability x of honest mining.
x	The probability that the miners mine honestly.
$x_i(i = 1,2,3\ldots)$	Solve the replicated dynamic equations to obtain the optimal policy values of multiple candidates that a miner may choose under the attack return model of this paper.
x^*	Deterministic mining strategies under different degrees of network environment.

(4) Because miners are mining in the same pool, the pool manager punishes miners with a penalty of a when they launch a DDoS attack. Similarly, when there is a DDoS attack in the same mining pool, the mining pool manager gives a reward of a to the honest miners.

(5) To simplify the establishment and solution of the model, this paper needs to meet the following restrictions. This paper does not consider the cost of DDoS attacks by miners. We also do not allow miners who mine in one pool to casually switch to mining in a different pool.

3.2. Design and Implementation of DDoS Attacks' Evolutionary Game Model for Miners

In this section, we need to build our evolutionary game model according to the above problem analysis. Our assumptions and analysis of DDoS attacks are similar to those in the literature [18,24,33]. We need to set up separate tables of block reward payoffs for miners A and B. Then, miners in the same mining pool will choose two strategies when facing attacks: launching a DDoS attack (D) and honest mining (H). According to whether miner A and miner B launch DDoS attacks or not, attacks can be divided into the following four scenarios: $(H, H), (H, D), (D, H)$, and (D, D).

(1) First, we consider the (H, H) case. This attack scenario is shown in Figure 2 below. The revenue that the entire pool receives from mining blocks is R. Miners A and B have the same computing power and mine under the mining pool. Therefore, the pool receives revenue R and splits it equally between miners A and B. Then, in this case, miners A and B both receive a block-producing reward of $\frac{R}{2}$.

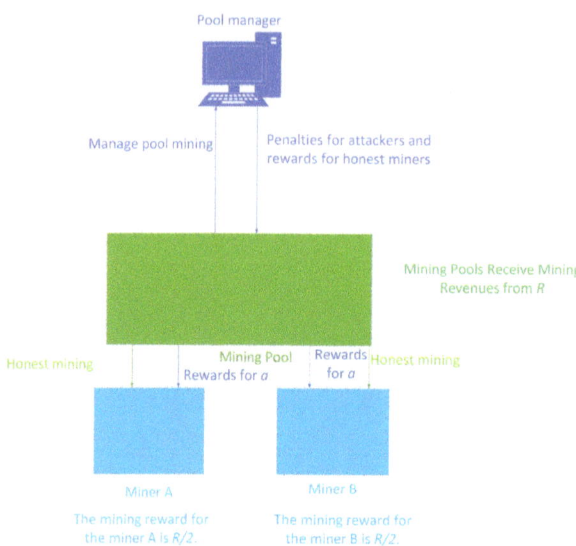

Figure 2. A scenario in which both miners mine honestly.

(2) Next, we consider the case of (H, D). This means that miner B launches a DDoS attack on miner A while miner A is mining honestly. In this case, only miner A mines honestly in the mining pool, and miner B can only sustain DDoS attacks on miner A due to insufficient computing power and cannot continue to mine honestly. At this point, there is only one miner A in the mining pool whose computing power is normal and honest. Therefore, the mining power of the miner, in this case, is half of the original mining power of both miner A and miner B. The total revenue from honest mining of the entire pool is R. Both miners earn an average payoff of $\frac{R}{2}$ by mining honestly. While the pool's honest mining power is cut in half in this case, the total mining profit to miners A and B is also cut in half by $\frac{R}{2}$. Therefore, each miner can only reap $\frac{R}{4}$ because the mining power is reduced

by half. Miner B launches a DDoS attack on miner A to obtain a mining reward of wd. Miner A suffers from a DDoS attack from B that loses wd's block reward. The pool manager rewards A with a for honest mining. Thus, miner A's payoff in this situation is $\frac{R}{4} + a - wd$. Miner B receives $\frac{R}{4}$ for honest mining. B launches a DDoS attack, and the mining pool manager penalizes it a. Miner B launches a DDoS attack and receives a block reward of wd from miner A. Thus, miner B's payoff in this situation is $\frac{R}{4} - a + wd$. The specific attack situation is shown in Figure 3 below.

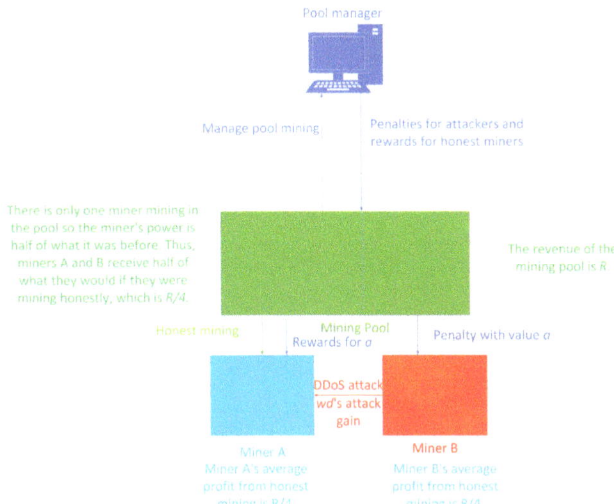

Figure 3. Miner B launches a DDoS attack on miner A, while A mines honestly.

(3) Then, we consider the case of (D, H). This means that miner A launches a DDoS attack on miner B while miner B is mining honestly. The miners in the pool currently have half the computational power of case 1. Miners A and B receive an average of R for honest mining. Similar to the case (H, D), except in this case, A is the attacker, and B is the victim. Similarly to case 2, A 's payoff in this case is $\frac{R}{4} - a + wd$. B 's payoff in this case is $\frac{R}{4} + a - wd$. The attack is shown in Figure 4 below.

(4) Finally, we consider the (D, D) case. In this case, miners A and B launch DDoS attacks and cannot mine honestly. Thus, the average return of A and B for honest mining in the pool is 0. Miner A suffers a DDoS attack from B and loses wd's block reward. However, A launches a DDoS attack and receives a block reward of wd from miner B. Since A launches a DDoS attack, the mining pool manager penalizes miner A with an amount equal to a. Thus, the reward of miner A in this case is $-a$. Since A and B both attack and A and B have the same amount of power, miner B and A have the same payoff in this situation. Thus, in this case, miner B 's payoff is also $-a$. This attack situation is shown in Figure 5 below.

After the above model is established, we can establish the profit and income tables of miner A and B, respectively, according to the profits under the four attack situations. In the game model of a DDoS attack, the income table of miner A is shown in Table 2 below.

Table 2. The revenue of miner A when attacked by DDoS attacks.

Pool A \ Pool B	Honest Mining (H)	DDoS Attacks (D)
Honest mining (H)	$\frac{R}{2}$	$\frac{R}{4} + a - wd$
DDoS attacks (D)	$\frac{R}{4} - a + wd$	$-a$

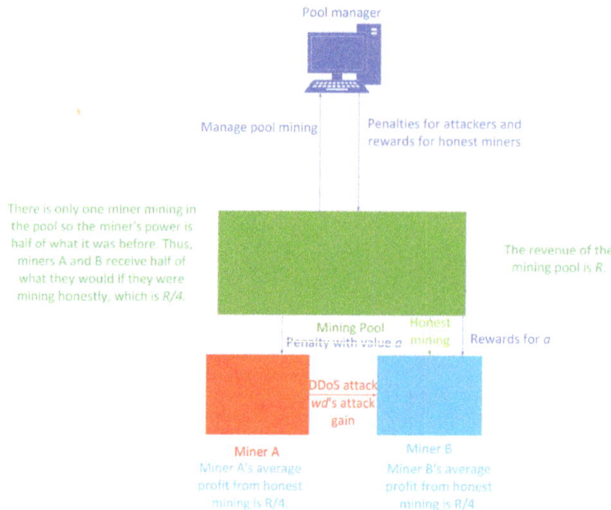

Figure 4. Miner *A* launches a DDoS attack on miner *B*, while *B* mines honestly.

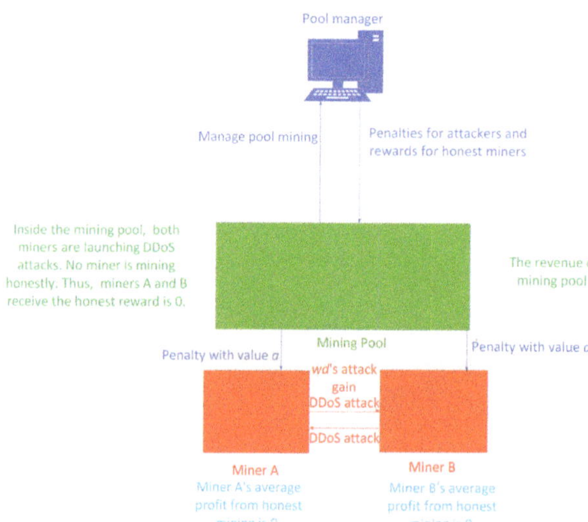

Figure 5. Miner *A* and miner *B* launch DDoS attacks on each other.

Each element in the table represents miner *A*'s payoff when miner *A* and miner *B* perform honest mining (H) or launch a DDoS attack (D). Similarly, the income table of miner *B* is described in Table 3 below.

Table 3. The revenue of miner *B* when attacked by DDoS attacks.

Pool A / Pool B	Honest Mining (H)	DDoS Attacks (D)
Honest mining (H)	$\frac{R}{2}$	$\frac{R}{4} - a + wd$
DDoS attacks (D)	$\frac{R}{4} + a - wd$	$-a$

After establishing the model and the income table of miners *A* and *B*, we need to develop a stable solution by setting the average income of miners to establish a dynamic replication equation [39]. We assume miners A and B mine honestly with probability x. The likelihood of an attack being selected is $1-x$. x is $0 \leqslant x \leqslant 1$. We use x^* as the stable solution to the dynamic equation. Then, this paper establishes the complementary strategies to obtain the optimal benefits through the values of each steady state. Through Tables 2 and 3, we can obtain the average earnings of honest mining by miners. We assume that a miner's average payoff of honest mining is f_1. The definition of f_1 is shown in Equation (1) below .

$$f_1 = x * \frac{R}{2} + (1-x) * (\frac{R}{4} + a - wd). \tag{1}$$

Similarly, we can use f_2 to represent the profit that a dishonest miner launches DDoS attacks, which is described in Equation (2).

$$f_2 = x * (\frac{R}{4} - a + wd) + (1-x) * (-a). \tag{2}$$

Therefore, from Equations (1) and (2), we can conclude that the average expected return of the miner is $\overline{f}$ in Equation (3).

$$\begin{aligned}
\overline{f} &= x * f_1 + (1-x) * f_2. \\
&= x * [x * \frac{R}{2} + (1-x) * (\frac{R}{4} + a - wd)] + (1-x) * [x * (\frac{R}{4} - a + wd) + (1-x) * (-a)] \\
&= x^2 * \frac{R}{2} + x(1-x) * \frac{R}{2} + (1-x)^2 * (-a)
\end{aligned} \tag{3}$$

From the above equation, we can conclude that the replication equation under this model is $F(x)$. $F(x)$ represents the steady state of honest mining probability x over time. Then, the dynamic replication equation $F(x)$ implemented in this paper is listed as follows in Equation (4).

$$\begin{aligned}
F(x) &= dx(t)/dt \\
&= x(f_1 - \overline{f}) \\
&= x[f_1 - x * f_1 - (1-x) * f_2] \\
&= x(1-x)(f_1 - f_2) \\
&= x(1-x)[x * \frac{R}{2} + (1-x) * (\frac{R}{4} + a - wd) - x * (\frac{R}{4} - a + wd) - (1-x) * (-a)] \\
&= x(1-x)(\frac{R}{4} - wd + 2a - ax)
\end{aligned} \tag{4}$$

We set the value of the dynamic replication equation $F(x)$ to 0, and we can obtain three steady-state deals of the evolutionary game, which is listed in the following Equation (5).

$$x_1 = 0, x_2 = 1, x_3 = \frac{R - 4wd + 8a}{4a} \tag{5}$$

We derive three possible stable states for this DDoS attack model by solving the dynamic replication equation. The three solutions of the dynamic replication equation, which are represented by $x_i (i = 1,2,3\ldots)$, are described in Equation (5). x_i denotes the multiple optimal policy values computed by the replication dynamic equation. When x_i is composed of uncertain values x_3, such as the network environment parameter w, the value range of $x_i = x_3$ is $x_3 \in R$. R is the whole set of real numbers. Next, we need to discuss the range of values of x_3 by comparing x_3 with the extreme values of probability 0 and 1. According to the method of solving the evolutionary game solution in reference [43], we divide it into three cases and discuss the stable state x^* in each case.

Through these three steady-state values, this paper can select the network coefficient w according to the situation of each steady-state solution. We also use the solution method of the evolutionary game to analyze which strategy benefits the miners best under each stable solution.

3.3. Steady-State Solutions

Through the three steady-state values, we can obtain the optimal mining strategy for different network environments w. By solving the problem of miners facing DDoS attacks and selecting the optimal mining strategy, we can also obtain the value range of the network environment coefficient w. Since the reward value a which is given by the pool manager must be positive, the case $a < 0$ is not considered in this paper. In the ideal state of the network case, the profit d of malicious miners launching DDoS attacks is also a fixed value. The range of d is $d \geq 0$. The first derivative of $F(x)$ with respect to x is $F'(x)$. We need to find out the unique mining strategy solution x^* under different network conditions through the change in network condition coefficient w. The value of x^* is chosen between the steady-state values x_1, x_2, and x_3. The $x_i(i = 1, 2, 3 \ldots)$ value satisfying $F'(x) < 0$ is the stable strategy solution x^* in each case of different network situations w when facing the DDoS attacks. However, among the three steady states obtained by the replication dynamic equation, $x_1 = 0, x_2 = 1$ are fixed values, and only the value of x_3 is uncertain. Therefore, we need to determine the value range of the network environment coefficient w by distinguishing the values of x_1, x_2, and x_3. At the same time, we also need to determine which steady-state solution makes $F'(x) < 0$ in x_1, x_2, and x_3 according to the range of values of x_3. This solution is the optimal mining strategy for miners with different x_3 values and the range of the network environment w. That is to say, we need to obtain the slope image of $F'(x)$ by discussing the value of x_3 in different cases to obtain the stable strategy [44].

Case A: $x_3 \leq 0$ means that $\frac{R-4wd+8a}{4a} \leq 0$, $d \geq 0$, and $a > 0$.

The reward and penalty a given to miners by the mining pool manager is a fixed value. The profit from successful pool mining is also a fixed value of R. DDoS attacks are launched at a fixed rate of d in the best network environments. The only parameter value that changes in steady state x_3 is the network environment coefficient w. The choice of miner strategy depends on the efficiency of network communication. The greater the value of w, the higher the damage inflicted by malicious miners on honest miners. In this case, simply setting $x_3 \leq 0$ takes the value range $\frac{R-4wd+8a}{4a} \leq 0$. The probability of honest mining can still be $x_1 = 0$ and $x_2 = 1$. From $\frac{R-4wd+8a}{4a} \leq 0$, we can conclude that the range of the network coefficient w is $\frac{R+8a}{4d} \leq w \leq 1$. The phase diagram of the replication dynamic is shown in Figure 6 below. We can analyze the optimal solution for DDoS attacks faced by miners in a relatively good network environment through Figure 6. The steady-state value is determined by replicating the dynamic equation with a negative slope at the intersection of the abscissa [44]. In this case, the equilibrium strategy solution satisfying $F'(x) < 0$ is $x^* = x_1 = 0$. Therefore, in case A, the best mining strategy for miners facing DDoS attacks is $x^* = x_1 = 0$. Therefore, in a good network environment, the optimal strategy for miners is to launch DDoS attacks against each other to obtain the optimal revenue.

$x^* = 0$ means that in a good network environment, miners choose to attack each other for the best profit over time. The main reason is that the network is excellent, malicious miners can launch DDoS attacks through the network and obtain more illegal block production rewards than when the network is in a harsh environment. The better the network environment, the more miners tend to choose to launch DDoS attacks to gain more revenue. Therefore, all miners will choose the best profit by launching DDoS attacks against each other.

Case B: $x_3 \geq 1$ means that $\frac{R-4wd+8a}{4a} \geq 1$, $d \geq 0$, and $a > 0$.

In this case, we can conclude by $\frac{R-4wd+8a}{4a} \geq 1$ that the value range of w is $0 \leq w \leq \frac{4a+R}{4d}$. This means that w is very small, and the network environment is poor. The phase diagram of the replication dynamic is shown in Figure 7 below. We can analyze it by replicating the phase diagram of the dynamic equation that the steady state, in this case, is $x^* = 1$. In case B, the equilibrium strategy solution satisfying $F'(x) < 0$ is $x^* = x_2 = 1$. Therefore, in a harsh network environment, miners will eventually choose the honest mining strategy to gain the best mining rewards.

The reason for the occurrence of case B is that miners receive fewer mining rewards by launching DDoS attacks when the network condition is harsh. If the miners profit less, they will choose the safe mining strategy with increasing games to gain the best profit. At the same time, when the network is not good, miners which do not know each other's mining status will not easily launch attacks. Therefore, all miners will eventually choose the honest mining strategy as the best way to profit over time.

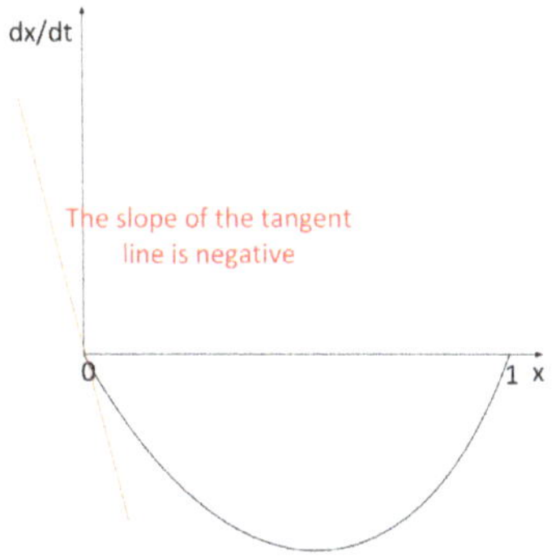

Figure 6. Replication dynamic phase diagram of attack case A.

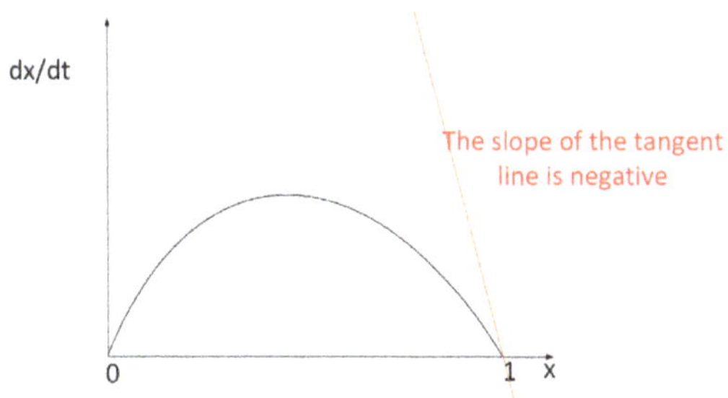

Figure 7. Replication dynamic phase diagram of attack case B.

Case C: $0 < x_3 < 1$ means that $0 < \frac{R-4wd+8a}{4a} < 1$, $d > 0$, and $a > 0$.

$0 < \frac{R-4wd+8a}{4a} < 1$ means that the network coefficient w ranges in $0 \leq \frac{4a+R}{4d} < w < \frac{8a+R}{4d} \leq 1$. This means the network is in a medium condition, The phase diagram of the replication dynamic is shown in Figure 8 below. From Figure 8, we can see that the optimal mining strategy, in this case, is $x_3 = \frac{R-4wd+8a}{4a}$. In case C, the equilibrium strategy solution satisfying $F'(x) < 0$ is $x^* = x_3 = \frac{R-4wd+8a}{4a}$. In a medium environment network, miners will choose the best profit from honest mining with a probability of x_3.

The reason for this is that because the network is under medium conditions, the miners will obtain almost the same payoff from launching a DDoS attack or from honest mining. All miners with different initial probabilities of honest mining will not choose the extreme option of honest mining or attack. Miners will eventually select the mixed strategy with the likelihood of honest mining with the best profit over time. Therefore, miners choose the mixed strategy in the medium network environment with an honest mining probability of x_3 to gain the best profit.

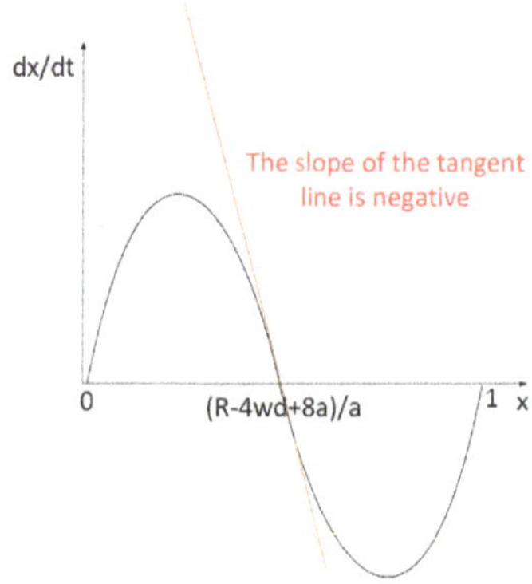

Figure 8. Replication dynamic phase diagram of attack case C.

Based on the above Section 3.3, we summarized the optimal strategy x^* for various network situations in Table 4. Table 4 describes the specific parameter ranges and optimal policy solutions in each network case. Table 4 lays a good foundation for the parameter setting and experimental analysis of dynamic and static game experiments in Section 4.

Table 4. Evolutionary stability strategy of miners facing DDoS attacks.

Network Environment Coefficient w	Evolutionary Steady-State Strategy x^*	Analysis
$\frac{R+8a}{4d} \leq w \leq 1$	$x^* = 0$	A good network environment corresponds to Case A
$0 \leq w \leq \frac{4a+R}{4d}$	$x^* = 1$	A harsh network environment corresponds to Case B
$0 \leq \frac{4a+R}{4d} < w < \frac{8a+R}{4d} \leq 1$	$x^* = \frac{R-4wd+8a}{4a}$	A medium network environment corresponds to Case C

4. Experiment and Results

The experimental simulation in this paper was divided into two main parts: a static game experiment and an evolutionary game experiment. In this section, our experiments' main goal was to validate the steady state of the evolutionary dynamic game model solution. We also implemented three static game experiments on the model to realize the Nash equilibrium point problem of miners facing DDoS attacks under static game conditions. The detailed description and performance analysis of the experiments is as follows. First, we selected the appropriate parameters and built the game experiment form according to the designed DDoS attack miner model. Second, we used the set model parameters to establish a static game model to solve the Nash equilibrium solution. Third, we conducted three static game experiments to achieve our designed model's optimal Nash equilibrium solution. We used Matlab R2022b to conduct evolutionary game modeling for miners in the same mining pool facing a DDoS attack in the blockchain system. Finally, we compared the design model in the static Nash equilibrium and the dynamic evolutionary game and analyzed the experimental results. The experimental results confirmed the correctness and effectiveness of the dynamic game model we designed.

We divided each part of the dynamic and static game experiment into three small experiments according to the strength coefficient w of the network. We also set the initial value parameters as $a = 6, d = 45, R = 60$. The actual game situations are shown in the following three experiments. We set the values of w to 0.1, 0.5, and 0.8, respectively, according to different network conditions. By comparing six experiments on static games and dynamic evolutionary games, this paper implemented the optimal selection strategy of miners under DDoS attacks in different network environments.

The settings of the six experimental parameter values and the solutions obtained are described in Table 5 below.

Our three settings of comparative static and dynamic evolutionary games experiments were assigned and solved according to Table 5. By changing the value of w to create separate network environments, we divided the whole experiment into three parts in both static game and dynamic evolutionary game. We set the corresponding parameters to observe the game state of miners facing DDoS attacks under different network environments. At the same time, we obtained the final miner's stable state x^* in each case under three other experimental conditions. Comparative experiments showed that the model designed by us had more game iterations in dynamic games than in static games and could show the trend of game evolution and convergence. The experimental results also showed that the experimental x^* was consistent with the theoretical value obtained by evolutionary game modeling and solving. The three experiments and analyses are described below.

Table 5. Comparison table of specific parameters and values corresponding to the static and dynamic game experiments.

One Miner Honest Mining Profit in One Same Mining Pool R	Illegal Profits of Miners Launching DDoS Attacks d	Degree of Punishment or Reward by the Pool Manager a	Network Environment Coefficient w	Evolutionary Steady-State Strategy x^*	Analysis
$R = 60$	$d = 45$	$a = 6$	$w = 0.1$	$x^* = x_2 = 1$	Nash equilibrium point for Experiment Section 4.1.1 of the static game and the solution obtained in experiment Section 4.2.1 correspond to case A in Section 3.3
$R = 60$	$d = 45$	$a = 6$	$w = 0.5$	$x^* = x_3 = \frac{R-4wd+8a}{4a} = \frac{60+0.5*45*4-8*6}{4*6} = 0.75$	Nash equilibrium point for Experiment Section 4.1.2 of the static game and the solution obtained in experiment Section 4.2.2 correspond to case C in Section 3.3
$R = 60$	$d = 45$	$a = 6$	$w = 0.8$	$x^* = x_1 = 0$	Nash equilibrium point for Experiment Section 4.1.3 of the static game and the solution obtained in experiment Section 4.2.3 correspond to case B in Section 3.3

4.1. Static Game Experiment

We mainly carried out three experiments in this section to realize the Nash equilibrium state of the static game of the designed model when miners face DDoS attacks according to references [45,46]. The purpose of the static game experiment was to serve as a contrast experiment for the following dynamic evolutionary game experiment. The main idea of the comparison experiment was to reflect the advantages of miners in realizing the dynamic evolutionary game when facing DDoS attacks by comparing our designed model in the case of static and dynamic games. As can be seen from Table 4 above, our static game experiment was divided into three subexperiments according to the different network environments w. The implementation and analysis of the three subexperiments are shown below.

4.1.1. Analysis of Game Strategy under the Bad Network Environment

After completing the experimental parameterization, we implemented the experiment on the optimal gain of miners facing DDoS attacks under the environment with bad network conditions in this section. The static optimal solution of DDoS attacks faced by miners in a bad network environment is realized by solving the Nash equilibrium. In the first subexperiment, we set the network environment coefficient to $w = 0.1$. According to Table 4 above, we set the global parameters as an honest miner mining gain to $R = 160$, the illegal gain for miners launching DDoS attacks to $d = 45$, and the penalty and reward for the mining pool manager to $a = 6$. The results of Experiment 1 are shown in Figures 9 and 10 below. We obtained the static Nash equilibrium solution of the designed model in the case of a bad network environment.

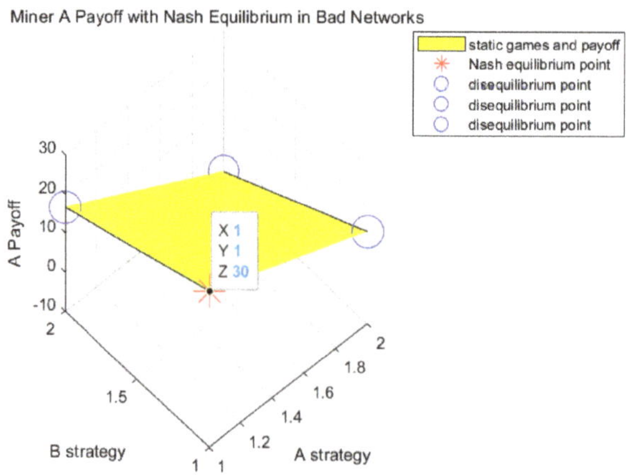

Figure 9. In a bad network environment, miner A faces the strategy of obtaining the best reward in a static game scenario by DDoS attacks.

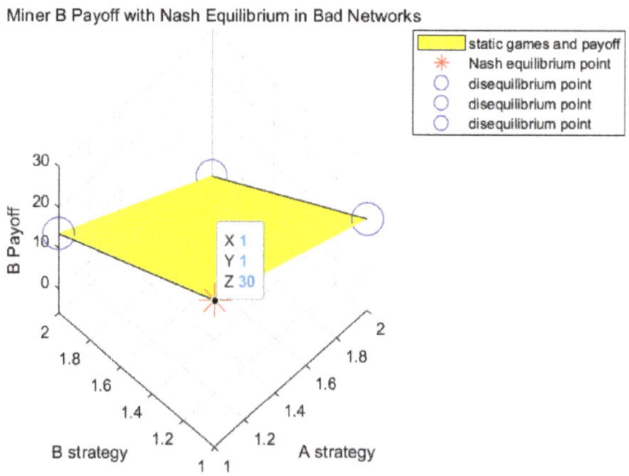

Figure 10. In a bad network environment, miner B faces the strategy of obtaining the best reward in a static game scenario by DDoS attacks.

In the following Figures 9 and 10, the red coordinates represent the Nash equilibrium optimal solution, and the blue coordinates represent the nonequilibrium points. A value equal to one on the X-axis in Figure 9 indicates that miner A chooses the honest mining strategy, and a value equal to zero indicates that mining pool A chooses to launch a DDoS attack. Similarly, a value of one on the Y-axis means that miner B chooses the honest mining strategy, and a value of zero on the Y-axis means that miner B chooses to launch a DDoS attack. The Z-axis represents the miner's optimal return when the Nash equilibrium is reached. As can be seen from Figure 9, the Nash equilibrium value of miners A and B is $(1, 1)$ when the network condition is not good. These results indicate that in the static game case, miners A and B choose honest mining for optimal profit when facing DDoS attacks. The optimal profit obtained by miner A is 30. Similarly, Figure 10 shows that miner B chooses honest mining for the best gain in the static game situation. Miner B's final optimal payoff is also 30.

4.1.2. Analysis of Game Strategy under the Medium Network Environment

When network conditions are harsh conditions, miners choose to mine honestly for optimal returns. As the network situation gradually improves, the changing scenarios occurring in the DDoS attack gains faced by miners will be reflected in the results of the medium static experiments. In this experiment, we set the value of the network environment parameter to $w = 0.5$. According to Table 4 above, we set the global parameters as an honest miner mining gain to $R = 160$, the illegal gain for miners launching DDoS attacks to $d = 45$, and the penalty and reward for the mining pool manager to $a = 6$. The static game experiment results of miner A and miner B are shown in Figures 11 and 12, respectively. In Figures 11 and 12, the coordinates marked in blue are nonequilibrium points, and the coordinates marked in red are Nash equilibrium points.

As can be seen from Figure 11, the Nash equilibrium points obtained by miner A in the static game when facing DDoS attacks in the revenue model designed in this paper are $(1, 2, -1.5)$ and $(2, 1, 31.5)$, respectively. This means that in the medium network environment, miner A faces DDoS attacks, and the optimal solution obtained using the static game approach to achieve the Nash equilibrium is a mixed strategy. The $(1, 2, -1.5)$ strategy means that miner A chooses to mine honestly, but miner B decides to launch a DDoS attack to achieve a static Nash equilibrium. Miner A's best payoff is -1.5. The $(2, 1, 31.5)$ strategy means that miner B chooses to mine honestly, but miner A chooses to launch a DDoS attack to achieve a static Nash equilibrium. Miner A's best payoff is 31.5.

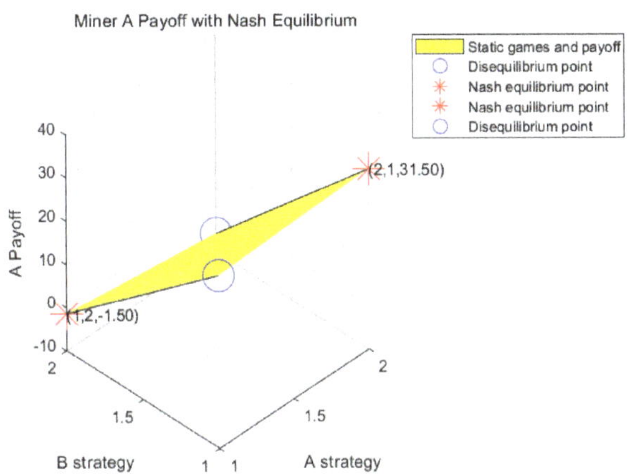

Figure 11. In a medium network environment, miner A faces the strategy of obtaining the best reward in a static game scenario by DDoS attacks.

As can be seen from Figure 12, the Nash equilibrium points obtained by miner B in the static game when facing DDoS attacks in the revenue model designed in this paper are $(1, 2, 31.5)$ and $(2, 1, -1.5)$, respectively. $(1, 2, 31.5)$ means that miner B chooses the optimal profit from launching DDoS attacks when reaching Nash equilibrium, and miner A chooses the optimal profit from honest mining. The optimal equilibrium return for both A and B is 31.5. $(2, 1, -1.5)$ means that miner B chooses to launch honest mining when the

Nash equilibrium is reached, and miner A chooses to launch DDoS attacks to make the best profit. The optimal equilibrium payoff for both A and B is -1.5.

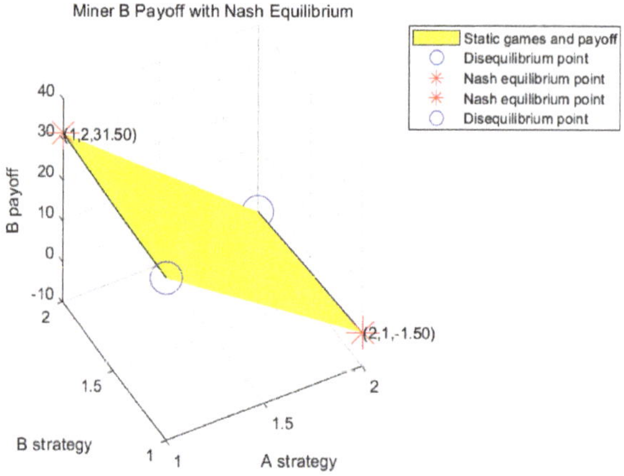

Figure 12. In a medium network environment, miner B faces the strategy of obtaining the best reward in a static game scenario by DDoS attacks.

4.1.3. Analysis of Game Strategy under the Good Network Environment

In medium network environments, miners facing DDoS attacks choose multiple mining strategies to coexist for optimal profits. How the network situation can be further improved in the medium case and how it can affect the miners' strategy changes is what needs to be achieved in this section of the static game experiments. The experimental results of the Nash equilibrium point performance of miners A and B facing DDoS attack to achieve a static game are shown in Figures 13 and 14 below. In this experiment, we set the value of the network environment parameter $w = 0.8$. According to Table 4 above, we set the global parameters as an honest miner's mining gain to $R = 160$, the illegal gain for miners launching DDoS attacks to $d = 45$, and the penalty and reward for the mining pool manager to $a = 6$. The specific experimental results are shown in Figures 13 and 14 below. We can see from Figures 13 and 14 that the coordinates marked in blue are nonequilibrium points, and the coordinates marked in red are Nash equilibrium points.

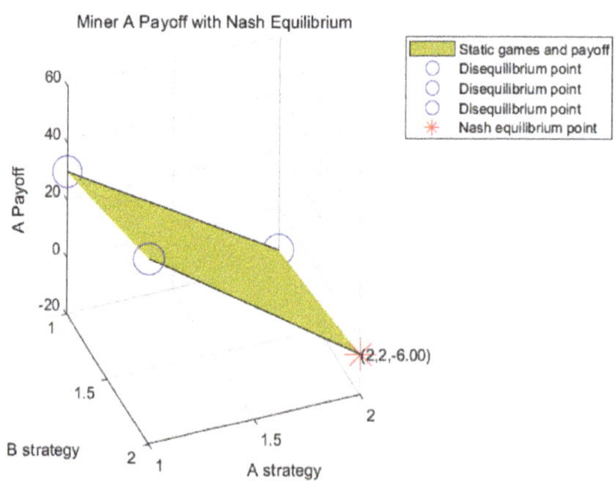

Figure 13. In a good network environment, miner A faces the strategy of obtaining the best reward in a static game scenario by DDoS attacks.

According to Figure 13 below, the Nash equilibrium point of miner A's static game when facing a DDoS attack is $(2, 2, -6)$. The strategy of $(2, 2, -6)$ means that in the case of good network conditions, miner A and miner B choose to launch DDoS attacks to obtain the best profit. Miner A's optimal payoff in the static Nash equilibrium is -6. Similarly, it can be seen from Figure 14 that the Nash equilibrium point of miner B is also $(2, 2, -6)$. Miner B also makes the best profit by launching DDoS attacks when the network is good. Miner B's best Nash equilibrium payoff is the same as miner A's, that is, -6.

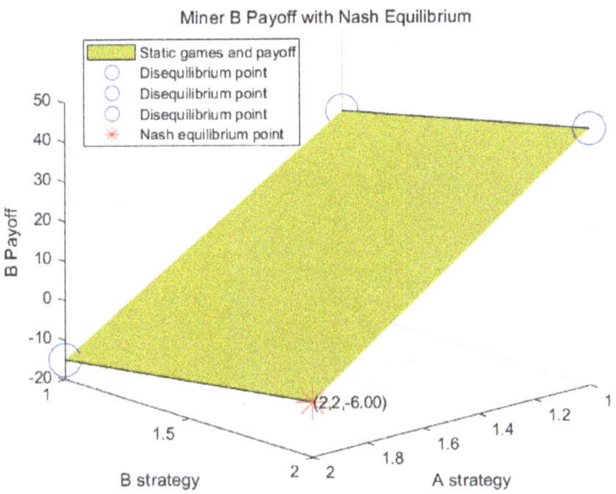

Figure 14. In a good network environment, miner B faces the strategy of obtaining the best reward in a static game scenario by DDoS attacks.

4.2. Evolutionary Game Experiment

4.2.1. Analysis of Game Strategy under a Harsh Network Environment

After completing the static game experiment, we needed to realize the advantages of the dynamic game by comparing the results of the dynamic game experiment with the static game experiment. We implement the analysis of the optimal strategy for the change in revenue of the dynamic game for miners facing DDoS attacks based on the harsh network environment in this section. We also compare the results with static game experiments in Section 4.1.1. In this case, we modeled the earnings of miners through Matlab. In the case of a bad network environment, we conducted an evolutionary game experiment for the miners facing a DDoS attack under the blockchain system. In that experiment, we set the network coefficient to $w = 0.1$. The experimental miner evolutionary game with a pool network environment is shown in Figure 15. From Figure 15 below, we can derive the strategy choice when the miners mining in the same pool face a DDoS attack under the condition of a poor network. We set the miners' initial honest mining probabilities from 0.1 to 0.9. Through the experiment, we observed and analyzed which strategies miners with different possibilities chose to make the best profit after being attacked.

Figure 15 presents the evolution trend of the miner strategy facing a DDoS attack in the same pool. From Figure 15, we can see that the horizontal coordinate represents the time t, and the vertical coordinate represents the initial probability x of honest mining in the mining pool. The curves of different colors in Figure 15 represent pools with different initial values for honest mining with different probabilities x. Initially, we set the miners to mine honestly with a probability from 0.1 to 0.9. The mining probability of honest miners with different probabilities changes over time, and after multiple game iterations, all probabilities eventually tend to one. Thus, the optimal strategy value of the iteration is one, and the convergence time of the game is about 0.35 s. This means that the final reward of the game is that all the miners will choose honest mining to gain the best profits. In the case of bad network conditions, the final strategy selected by the miners in the face of a DDoS attack has a probability of one to mine honestly in the last game time. The experiment corresponds to case B in Section 3.3 above, in which the result $x^* = x_2 = 1$ is consistent with the experiment.

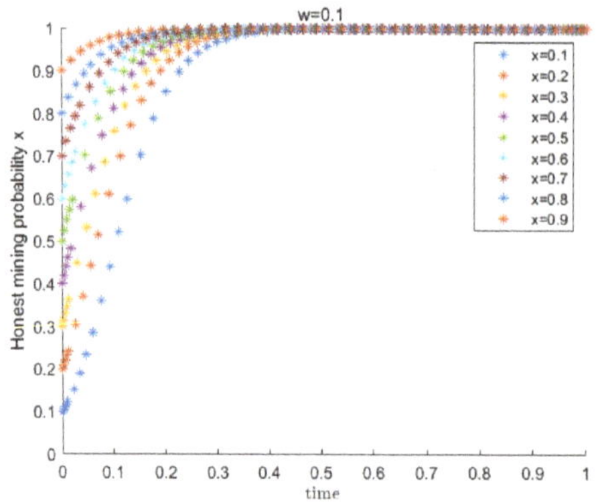

Figure 15. In a poor network environment, the miners face the strategy of obtaining the best reward with time t using DDoS attacks ($w = 0.1, x^* = 1$).

The reasons why miners face DDoS attacks in harsh network environments are as follows. First, due to the poor network environment, miners do not understand the network environment situation and dare not venture to launch DDoS attacks. Due to the unstable network environment, all miners choose honest mining strategies. Second, the illegal gains wd obtained by miners launching DDoS attacks in this experiment are proportional to the network environment coefficient w. The value of the network coefficient w becomes low if the network environment is bad. Miners which have to launch DDoS attacks in hostile network environments to gain illegal mining revenue wd will also have a smaller network coefficient value. This diminishing return on attacks can lead to miners launching attacks for far less illicit gain than they would bring in from their own peaceful and honest mining. In the end, all miners prefer the honest mining strategy that obtains more revenue rather than launching a DDoS attack.

Compared with the results of static game experiment Section 4.1.1 above, the results of our designed model in the dynamic evolutionary game experiment are the same as those of the static game. Both miner A and miner B choose the honest mining strategy to make the best profit under the harsh network conditions. However, the static game can only reflect that the honest mining strategy is the optimal strategy for miners in the harsh network environment through one game. There are some problems and defects in static game experiments under a bad network environment. First, the static game can only be played once in a bad network environment. The limit of the number of games can not effectively reflect the correctness of the optimal strategy when miners face DDoS attacks. Second, the static game can only obtain the optimal strategy by solving the Nash equilibrium solution. This method cannot reflect the game trend of the miner game with different probabilities of mining towards the optimal strategy over time through multiple game iterations. We realized the optimal strategy in multiple game environments by the method of game iteration in the harsh environment dynamic game experiments. At the same time, we set different initial mining probabilities by different colored curves. Through multiple game iterations in the dynamic experiments, we obtained the tendency of miners with different mining probabilities to converge to the optimal strategy over time.

4.2.2. Analysis of Game Strategy under a Medium Network Environment

When the network conditions are bad, miners change over time and choose honest mining strategies. Then, in this section, by increasing the value of the network environment coefficient w, we analyzed the trend of the change in the dynamic returns of miners. The purpose of this experiment was to verify whether the strategy selected by miners in the face of DDoS attacks in the medium network was consistent with the optimal strategy obtained in case C in Section 3.3 of the dynamic evolutionary game model analysis. In the case of the medium network environment, we conducted an evolutionary game experiment for the miners facing DDoS attacks under the blockchain system. In that case, we set the network coefficient to $w = 0.5$. The experimental miner evolutionary game with a medium network environment is shown in Figure 16. From Figure 16 below, we can derive the strategy choice when the miners mining in the same pool face a DDoS attack. We set the miners' initial honest mining probabilities from 0.1 to 0.9. Through this experiment, we observed and analyzed which strategies miners with different possibilities chose to make the best profit after being attacked.

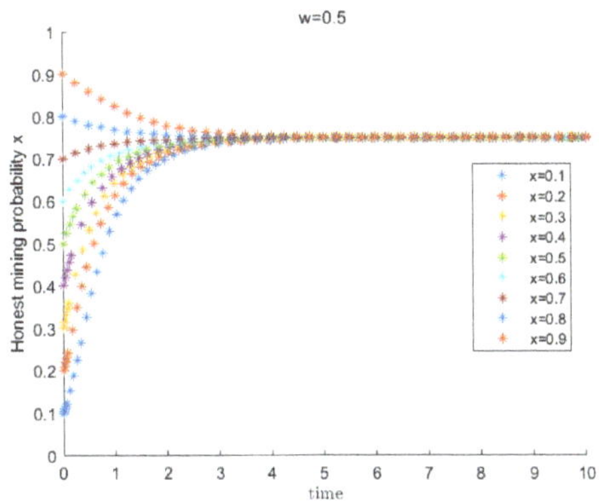

Figure 16. In a medium network environment, the miners face the strategy of obtaining the best reward with time t using DDoS attacks ($w = 0.5, x^* = 0.75$).

From Figure 16, we can see that in a medium network environment, all the miners with different probabilities will eventually choose to mine honestly with a certain probability and make the best profit. The probability of honest mining x^* depends on the values of a, d, R, w. We still set the initial miner's honest mining probability x from 0.1 to 0.9 on the Y-axis. The tendency of the initial values of these different probabilities to change over time in the game is represented by different colored curves on the Y-axis. We find that all miners finally approach honest mining with a probability of 0.75 in about 4 s. This means that the network miner chooses the mixed strategy of honest mining with a probability of 0.75 in the medium environment to gain the best profit. This means that the stable strategy chosen by the miner, in this case, is $x^* = x_3 = 0.75$. The experimental results are consistent with case C in Section 3.3 above, proving our experiment's correctness and validity.

The reasons why miners facing DDoS attacks choose a hybrid strategy of honesty and launching DDoS attacks in a medium network environment are as follows. First, some miners think that the network environment is good enough to launch attacks for better returns as the network situation improves. As a result, some of the miners decide to launch DDoS attack strategies. Other miners still believe that the current moderate network conditions are not enough to make them change their original honest mining strategy, so this group of miners does not easily change their strategy to stick to honest mining. Second, the value of the illegal revenue obtained by miners launching DDoS attacks increases as the network environment improves. This motivates some miners to abandon the strategy of mining honestly in the pool for revenue and willingly accept punishment from the pool manager for launching DDoS attacks for illegal revenue. This can lead to a situation where some miners decide to mine honestly while others decide to launch DDoS attacks.

Compared with the results of static game experiment Section 4.1.2 above, the results of our designed model in the dynamic evolutionary game are the same as those of the static game. In the medium network, miners A and B have two Nash equilibrium game points $(1,2)$ and $(2,1)$ in the static game experiment. This means that miners facing DDoS attacks in the static game scenario have a certain probability of making the best profit by launching a DDoS attack or a certain probability of making the best profit by honest mining. In the case of a medium network, the miners choose to use a mixed mining strategy. That means that the miners decide to mine honestly or launch DDoS attacks to obtain the best rewards. The Nash equilibrium solution of the static game strategy is consistent with the optimal strategy of the dynamic game in the medium network condition. However, the inability to effectively quantify the probability of a mixed strategy occurring is the most significant drawback of static games in medium network environments. In a medium-scale network environment, we cannot analyze through static game experiments the exact probability of the optimal miner strategy of honest mining and the probability of launching a DDoS attack. However, this problem was solved by a numerical simulation in our dynamic game experiments. We achieved this by setting the initial values to miners with different probabilities of honest mining. The probability values ranged from 0.1 to 0.9. We found that all miners mining with different probabilities eventually chose the strategy with honest probability $x = 0.75$ for optimal mining returns after many iterations of the game through a dynamic evolutionary game. This addresses the inability of static game experiments to quantify mixed-strategy probabilities in a moderate network environment. This solves the problem where static game experiments cannot effectively reflect the convergence trend and change in the game when miners face DDoS attacks.

4.2.3. Analysis of Game Strategy under a Good Network Environment

Mining pools in moderate network environments gradually shift towards launching DDoS attack strategies. Then, the dynamic trend of the optimal mining strategy for miners facing DDoS attacks under better network conditions than the medium environment is illustrated in the experiments in this section. In this case, we set $w = 0.8$ and the probability of miners to initially mine honestly x from 0.1 to 0.9. The experimental miner evolutionary game with a better network environment is shown in Figure 17. From Figure 17 below, we can see that the curves with different colors represent the game trend of honest miners with different probabilities over time. The game iteration changes over time with different colors for the initial probability of mining, but all the curves eventually tend to zero. Therefore, the value of x^*, in this case, is $x^* = x_1 = 0$. This means that in such a situation, miners would choose to launch DDoS attacks against each other to make the best profit.

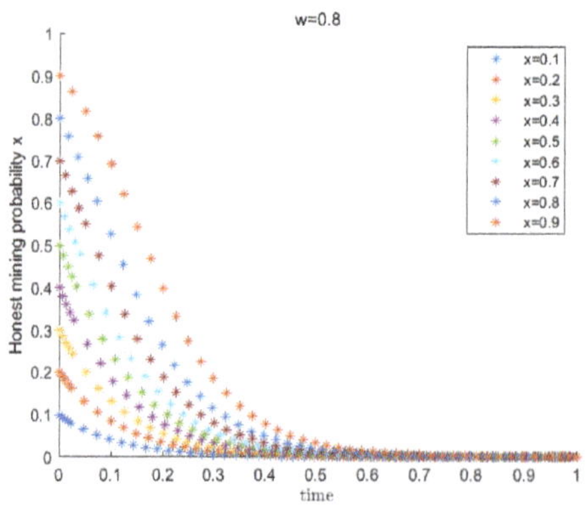

Figure 17. In a good network environment, the miners face the strategy of obtaining the best reward with time t using DDoS attacks ($w = 0.8, x^* = 0$).

From Figure 17, we can see that in the case of a good network environment, all the probabilities of miners mining with different honest mining probabilities eventually tend to $x = 0$ at about $t = 0.6$ s. The experimental results illustrate that miners facing DDoS attacks choose to launch DDoS attacks against each other to obtain optimal mining rewards when the network state w is relatively good. The experimental results are in agreement with the dynamic game stabilizing solution case B, which was obtained by the dynamic game analysis in Section 3.3 above. The optimal solution obtained from the experimental results and the optimal solution found in case B of Section 3.3 above are both $x^* = 0$, which shows the correctness of our experimental results and the validity of the model.

In a better network environment, miners choose to launch DDoS attacks against each other to gain optimal profits for the following reasons. First, the network environment becomes better than a medium network, and more miners abandon the strategy of spending arithmetic power to mine honestly in the pool for revenue. Miners assume that the network environment is better and that all other miners use the network to launch DDoS attacks themselves in order to maximize illegal profits. As time goes on and multiple iterations of the game are played, all of the miners choose to make the optimal profit by attacking each other's strategies. Second, the network conditions become better and the value of the gain wd for a miner launching a DDoS attack increases more than it does in the case of the medium network. Miners that initially followed an honest mining strategy in moderate network environments also gradually adopt the more profitable strategy of launching DDoS attacks through multiple iterations of the game. Eventually, miners in medium network environments choose a mixed strategy that gradually shifts to launching DDoS attacks to profit optimally due to changes in the network environment.

Compared with the results of static game experiment Section 4.1.3 above, the results of our designed model in the dynamic evolutionary game are the same as those of the static game. In a relatively good network environment, miners choose to profit optimally by launching DDoS attacks against each other. This result is consistent with the dynamic game experiment results under good network conditions. The inability to effectively characterize how miners with different probabilities of honest mining converge to an optimal strategy over multiple game iterations is the main drawback of static game experiments in a well-networked environment. In order to solve this problem, we also set up different colored curves to represent the miners with different initial values of the mining probability through the numerical simulation experiments within the dynamic game experiments. We obtained the evolution curves of the change in miners towards the steady state $x^* = 0$ with different probabilities of honest mining through multiple game iterations and a time-varying evolution in our dynamic game experiments.

4.3. Analysis of Experimental Results

Therefore, the condition of the blockchain network affects the choice of the optimal profit-making strategy for miners facing DDoS attacks. Meanwhile, the dynamic game can reflect the advantage of the convergence trend of the miner's game over the static game experiments in solving the problem of the miner's gain from facing DDoS attacks. Specific experimental phenomena and results are detailed in the following according to the three cases of network conditions, and the dynamic and static game comparison results are divided into four aspects of analysis and elaboration.

(1) When the network in the pool is good, miners know how each other is doing. Since the network coefficient w is directly proportional to the illegal blocking reward obtained by launching DDoS attacks, miners gain more profits by launching DDoS attacks. In this case, all miners with different honest probabilities eventually choose to launch DDoS attacks to earn higher returns as time goes by and the number of games increases. Therefore, in a good network environment, all miners attack each other within 0.6 s.

(2) When the network is in a moderate condition, all miners do not go to the extreme of simply honestly mining or launching DDoS attacks. This is because miners with a low initial value of honest mining profit even if they launch DDoS attacks. Since the illegal income from DDoS attacks is not as good as the network environment, miners with a high probability of honest mining also lower the value of x and gain higher rewards. Therefore,

miners of all possibilities choose the mixed game strategy to obtain the optimal block-out reward.

(3) When the network in the pool is bad, all the miners need to know each other's status. Since the network coefficient w is directly proportional to the illegal blocking reward obtained by launching DDoS attacks and the network condition is deplorable, miners receive little benefit from launching DDoS attacks, and attacking the mining pool manager also brings a certain degree of punishment to miners. As a result, miners at this point do not gain as much from launching DDoS attacks as they do from honest mining. Therefore, miners with different probabilities of initial mining value eventually choose the game strategy of honest mining to obtain the most block reward in the lousy network environment.

(4) The experimental results of static games are consistent with those of dynamic evolutionary games, proving our model's validity. Through comparative experiments in three different network environments, we can see that the dynamic game method used in this paper has more games than the static game method and can show the trend of multiple games over time by miners with different probabilities of honest mining.

5. Discussion

Discussion point 1: What is the practical impact of the DDoS gain mitigation model designed in this paper on the blockchain industry?

Answer:

The first discussion point is mainly to explain the practical significance of our model. Currently, there are security threats and hidden dangers in the blockchain system. Attacks such as selfish mining attacks, block interception attacks, and DDoS attacks exist in blockchain systems to illegally obtain mining rewards from honest-mining miners [5]. Selfish mining attacks are used to illegally gain access to the benefits of the public chain by creating a private chain outside of the public chain. Block retention attack is to attack miners to withhold the mining rewards of honest miners to achieve the purpose of their own illegal gain. DDoS attacks are the security threats present in blockchain networks that we focused on in this paper. Our model is effective in making blockchain systems using PoW consensus algorithms effectively mitigate mining losses from DDoS attacks without the need to detect the number of network requests and abnormal traffic in advance. This can increase the security of blockchain systems that use the PoW consensus algorithm, such as Bitcoin. At the same time, this paper analyzed different network situations through the game theory approach to make miners choose the optimal mining strategy through multiple game iterations. This is a useful reference for miners using the Bitcoin system to choose appropriate mining strategies under different networks when they face DDoS attacks.

Discussion point 2: What are the shortcomings of the model designed in this paper?

Answer:

The second issue is mentioned in our future work section. It is mainly about what are the shortcomings of our current work and what can be improved. Our model has not yet taken into account the cost of launching a DDoS attack, the distribution of proceeds from DDoS attacks faced by multiple miners, and the fact that miners do not have the same mining arithmetic power.

First, this paper only considered the problem of two miners with the same arithmetic power facing a DDoS attack. In a real situation, blockchain system cluster nodes' arithmetic power is different. At the same time, the number of mining cluster nodes is much more than two. In the next step, we will extend the model designed in this paper to the scenario of multiple miners with different arithmetic power for an in-depth study, in order to meet the demand for security in real blockchain systems.

Second, in order to simplify the modeling, we do not consider the cost of launching DDoS attacks in this paper. This modeling approach does not meet the complex security situaton of miners in an actual blockchain network. In following work, we will take the factors of attack cost and parameter representation of different values of punishment and reward into account to further improve the model designed in this paper.

6. Conclusions

In this paper, we proposed an evolutionary game model for miners facing DDoS attacks. The establishment and solution of this model can be effective enough to protect miners from DDoS attacks. We also obtained the optimal mining strategies of miners in different network environments by replicating the dynamic equation methods. We finally conducted comparative experiments between static and dynamic games for the designed model. The experimental results showed that miners facing DDoS attacks gradually shifted from an honest mining strategy to the profit optimization of launching DDoS attacks as the network conditions became better. The results of the dynamic and static comparison experiments showed that the dynamic game method had the advantage of being able to quantify the mixed strategies of miners facing DDoS attacks under medium network conditions and reflecting the trend of the change in the optimal strategy from multiple game iterations of mining pools with different probabilities. However, the static game approach could only represent the optimal strategies and returns of miners. The static game method could not realize the quantification of the probability of mixed strategies and the trend of game convergence dynamics. This suggests that the use of the dynamic game approach in this paper has advantages over the static game approach. The experimental results proved the effectiveness and correctness of the dynamic game model we designed.

7. Future Work

This paper effectively mitigates the revenue loss from DDoS attacks by modeling the dynamic game in the case of two mining pools with the same arithmetic power. However, there are many areas for improvement in the current work of this paper. First, the DDoS reward model's assumptions did not consider the cost of launching a DDoS attack by the miners. Second, the modeling assumed that the two pools had the same computational power. We did not consider the possibility of multiple mining pools with different computing power, which is not widely applicable. Therefore, we want to carry out the following in-depth research on this work in the future. Third, we modeled and solved the benefits of DDoS attacks faced by miners in a simulated environment. We did not conduct an actual experimental performance analysis of the model on a real blockchain system. In order to solve these problems, we need to carry out further in-depth research into the model of this paper to meet the requirements of real blockchain systems in future work. Future work will contain three main parts: research on asymmetric arithmetic miner game, research on the gain of multiminer game, and research on the security model of miner DDoS attacks under a real blockchain system. The specific work will be as follows:

(1) We will take the cost of launching DDoS attacks and the number of nodes launching attacks into consideration in a newly designed game model in the future so that the model establishment is more in line with the requirements of the existing blockchain system.

(2) We will add the case of multiple miners with different arithmetic power to the modeling and solving in this paper in future work. We will also provide an in-depth study of the problem of modeling multiple and solving the optimal gain of multiple miners and multiple mining pools facing DDoS attacks.

(3) In future work, we will improve the model designed in this paper so that it can be applied to real blockchain systems to meet the security requirements of real applications.

Author Contributions: Conceptualization, Q.W., X.J. and Z.H.; methodology, Z.H. and X.L.; software, Z.H. and X.L.; validation, Z.H., B.W., Y.C. and X.L.; writing—original draft preparation, X.L. and Z.H.; writing—review and editing, Z.H., Y.C., X.J. and Q.W.; supervision, X.J. and Q.W.; project administration, Z.H., Y.C., Q.W. and B.W.; funding acquisition, Q.W., B.W., X.J. and Z.H. All authors have read and agreed to the published version of the manuscript.

Funding: This work was supported in part by the National Natural Science Foundation of China under grant 61972302, in part by the Fundamental Research Funds for the Central Universities under grant XJS220306, in part by the Natural Science Basic Research Program of Shaanxi under grant 2022JQ-680, in part by the Science and Technology Program of Guangzhou under grant SL2022A04J00404, in part by the Foundation of National Key Laboratory of Human Factors Engineering under grant 6142222210101, in part by the key industry innovation chain projects of Shaanxi, China under grant 2021ZDLGY07-04, and in part by the Key Laboratory of Smart Human Computer Interaction and Wearable Technology of Shaanxi Province.

Data Availability Statement: No new data were created or analyzed in this study. Data sharing is not applicable to this article.

Acknowledgments: The authors would like to thank the Editors and Reviewers for their contributions to our manuscript.

Conflicts of Interest: The authors declare no conflict of interest.

References

1. Meneghetti, A.; Sala, M.; Taufer, D. A Survey on PoW-based Consensus. *AETiC* **2020**, *4*, 8–18. [CrossRef]
2. Lepore, C.; Ceria, M.; Visconti, A.; Rao, U.P.; Shah, K.A.; Zanolini, L. A Survey on Blockchain Consensus with a Performance Comparison of PoW, PoS and Pure PoS. *Mathematics* **2020**, *8*, 1782. [CrossRef]
3. Xu, J.; Wang, C.; Jia, X. A Survey of Blockchain Consensus Protocols. *ACM Comput. Surv.* **2023**, *55*, 278. [CrossRef]
4. Yadav, A.K.; Singh, K.; Amin, A.H.; Almutairi, L.; Alsenani, T.R.; Ahmadian, A. A Comparative Study on Consensus Mechanism with Security Threats and Future Scopes: Blockchain. *Comput. Commun.* **2023**, *12*, 102–115. [CrossRef]
5. Liu, X.; Huang, Z.; Wang, Q.; Wan, B. An Evolutionary Game Theory-Based Method to Mitigate Block Withholding Attack in Blockchain System. *Electronics* **2023**, *12*, 2808. [CrossRef]
6. Huang, Z.; Wang, Q. A PUF-based Unified Identity Verification Framework for Secure IoT Hardware via Device Authentication. *World Wide Web* **2020**, *2*, 1057–1088. [CrossRef]
7. Kumari, P.; Jain, A.K. A Comprehensive Study of DDoS Attacks over IoT Network and Their Countermeasures. *Comput. Secur.* **2023**, *127*, 103096. [CrossRef]
8. Mittal, M.; Kumar, K.; Behal, S. Deep learning approaches for detecting DDoS attacks: A systematic review. *Soft Comput.* **2023**, *27*, 13039–13075. [CrossRef]
9. Waseem, M.; Adnan Khan, M.; Goudarzi, A.; Fahad, S.; Sajjad, I.A.; Siano, P. Incorporation of Blockchain Technology for Different Smart Grid Applications: Architecture, Prospects, and Challenges. *Energies* **2023**, *16*, 820. [CrossRef]
10. Guru, A.; Mohanta, B.K.; Mohapatra, H.; Al-Turjman, F.; Altrjman, C.; Yadav, A. A Survey on Consensus Protocols and Attacks on Blockchain Technology. *Appl. Sci.* **2023**, *13*, 2604. [CrossRef]
11. Hayat, R.F.; Aurangzeb, S.; Aleem, M.; Srivastava, G.; Lin, J.C.-W. ML-DDoS: A Blockchain-Based Multilevel DDoS Mitigation Mechanism for IoT Environments. *IEEE Trans. Eng. Manag.* **2022**, *2022*, 1–14. [CrossRef]
12. Wang, Q.; Xia, T.; Wang, D.; Ren, Y.; Miao, G.; Choo, K.-K.R. SDoS: Selfish Mining-Based Denial-of-Service Attack. *IEEE Trans. Inform. Forensic Secur.* **2022**, *17*, 3335–3349. [CrossRef]
13. Mirkin, M.; Ji, Y.; Pang, J.; Klages-Mundt, A.; Eyal, I.; Juels, A. BDoS: Blockchain Denial-of-Service. In Proceedings of the 2020 ACM SIGSAC Conference on Computer and Communications Security, Virtual Event, 9–13 November 2020; pp. 601–619. [CrossRef]
14. Liu, J.; Wang, X.; Shen, S.; Yue, G.; Yu, S.; Li, M. A Bayesian Q -Learning Game for Dependable Task Offloading Against DDoS Attacks in Sensor Edge Cloud. *IEEE Internet Things J.* **2021**, *8*, 7546–7561. [CrossRef]
15. Baek, U.-J.; Ji, S.-H.; Park, J.T.; Lee, M.-S.; Park, J.-S.; Kim, M.-S. DDoS Attack Detection on Bitcoin Ecosystem Using Deep-Learning. In Proceedings of the 2019 20th Asia-Pacific Network Operations and Management Symposium (APNOMS), Matsue, Japan, 18–20 September 2019; pp. 1–4. [CrossRef]
16. Jiang, S.; Yang, L.; Gao, X.; Zhou, Y.; Feng, T.; Song, Y.; Liu, K.; Cheng, G. BSD-Guard: A Collaborative Blockchain-Based Approach for Detection and Mitigation of SDN-Targeted DDoS Attacks. *Secur. Commun. Netw.* **2022**, *2022*, 1608689. [CrossRef]
17. Zhang, Y.; Gai, K.; Zhu, L.; Qiu, M. An Auxiliary Classifier GAN-Based DDoS Defense Solution in Blockchain-Based Software Defined Industrial Network. In *Smart Computing and Communication*; Qiu, M., Lu, Z., Zhang, C., Eds.; Lecture Notes in Computer Science; Springer Nature: Cham, Switzerland, 2023; Volume 13828, pp. 319–328. [CrossRef]
18. Wu, S.; Chen, Y.; Li, M.; Luo, X.; Liu, Z.; Liu, L. Survive and Thrive: A Stochastic Game for DDoS Attacks in Bitcoin Mining Pools. *IEEE/ACM Trans. Netw.* **2020**, *28*, 874–887. [CrossRef]
19. Johnson, B.; Laszka, A.; Grossklags, J.; Vasek, M.; Moore, T. Game-Theoretic Analysis of DDoS Attacks Against Bitcoin Mining Pools. In *Financial Cryptography and Data Security*; Böhme, R., Brenner, M., Moore, T., Smith, M., Eds.; Lecture Notes in Computer Science; Springer: Berlin/Heidelberg, Germany, 2014; Volume 8438, pp. 72–86. [CrossRef]

20. Boreiri, Z.; Azad, A.N. A Novel Consensus Protocol in Blockchain Network Based on Proof of Activity Protocol and Game Theory. In Proceedings of the 2022 8th International Conference on Web Research (ICWR), Tehran, Iran, 24–25 April 2022; pp. 82–87. [CrossRef]
21. He, Q.; Wang, C.; Cui, G.; Li, B.; Zhou, R.; Zhou, Q.; Xiang, Y.; Jin, H.; Yang, Y. A Game-Theoretical Approach for Mitigating Edge DDoS Attack. *IEEE Trans. Depend. Secur. Comput.* **2022**, *19*, 2333–2348. [CrossRef]
22. Amini, H.; Bichuch, M.; Feinstein, Z. Decentralized payment clearing using blockchain and optimal bidding. *Eur. J. Oper. Res.* **2022**, *309*, 409–420. [CrossRef]
23. Khanum, S.; Mustafa, K. A Systematic Literature Review on Sensitive Data Protection in Blockchain Applications. *Concurr. Comput.* **2023**, *35*, e7422. [CrossRef]
24. Saad, M.; Njilla, L.; Kamhoua, C.; Kim, J.; Nyang, D.; Mohaisen, A. Mempool Optimization for Defending Against DDoS Attacks in PoW-Based Blockchain Systems. In Proceedings of the 2019 IEEE International Conference on Blockchain and Cryptocurrency (ICBC), Seoul, Republic of Korea, 14–17 May 2019; pp. 285–292. [CrossRef]
25. Tan, Y.; Huang, X.; Li, W. Does blockchain-based traceability system guarantee information authenticity? An evolutionary game approach. *Int. J. Prod. Econ.* **2023**, *264*, 108974. [CrossRef]
26. Bao, Q.; Li, B.; Hu, T.; Sun, X. A Survey of Blockchain Consensus Safety and Security: State-of-the-Art, Challenges, and Future Work. *J. Syst. Softw.* **2023**, *196*, 111555. [CrossRef]
27. Guo, H.; Yu, X. A Survey on Blockchain Technology and Its Security. *Blockchain Res. Appl.* **2022**, *3*, 100067. [CrossRef]
28. Shah, Z.; Ullah, I.; Li, H.; Levula, A.; Khurshid, K. Blockchain-Based Solutions to Mitigate Distributed Denial of Service (DDoS) Attacks in the Internet of Things (IoT): A Survey. *Sensors* **2022**, *22*, 1094. [CrossRef] [PubMed]
29. Yaish, A.; Qin, K.; Zhou, L.; Zohar, A.; Gervais, A. Speculative Denial-of-Service Attacks in Ethereum. *Cryptol. ePrint Arch.* **2023**, *2023*, 1–24.
30. Guo, T.; Han, Y.; Feng, C. A Survey on Attack and Defense of Block-chain System. *J. Softw.* **2021**, *32*, 1495–1525. [CrossRef]
31. Ilyas, B.; Kumar, A.; Setitra, M.A.; Bensalem, Z.A.; Lei, H. Prevention of DDoS Attacks Using an Optimized Deep Learning Approach in Blockchain Technology. *Trans. Emerg. Telecommun. Technol.* **2023**, *34*, e4729. [CrossRef]
32. Yakubu, B.M.; Khan, M.I.; Khan, A.; Jabeen, F.; Jeon, G. Blockchain-Based DDoS Attack Mitigation Protocol for Device-to-Device Interaction in Smart Home. *Digit. Commun. Netw.* **2023**, *9*, 383–392. [CrossRef]
33. Houda, Z.A.E.; Hafid, A.S.; Khoukhi, L. MiTFed: A Privacy-Preserving Collaborative Network Attack Mitigation Framework Based on Federated Learning Using SDN and Blockchain. *IEEE Trans. Netw. Sci. Eng.* **2023**, *2023*, 1985–2001. [CrossRef]
34. Jmal, R.; Ghabri, W.; Guesmi, R.; Alshammari, B.M.; Alshammari, A.S.; Alsaif, H. Distributed Blockchain-SDN Secure IoT System Based on ANN to Mitigate DDoS Attacks. *Appl. Sci.* **2023**, *13*, 4953. [CrossRef]
35. Li, Q.; Huang, H.; Li, R.; Lv, J.; Yuan, Z.; Ma, L.; Han, Y.; Jiang, Y. A comprehensive survey on DDoS defense systems: New trends and challenges. *Comput. Netw.* **2023**, *233*, 109895. [CrossRef]
36. Zheng, R.; Ying, C.; Shao, J.; Wei, G.; Yan, H.; Kong, J.; Ren, Y.; Zhang, H.; Hou, W. New Game-Theoretic Analysis of DDoS Attacks Against Bitcoin Mining Pools with Defence Cost. In *Network and System Security*; Liu, J.K., Huang, X., Eds.; Lecture Notes in Computer Science; Springer International Publishing: Cham, Switzerland, 2019; Volume 11928, pp. 567–580. [CrossRef]
37. Chaganti, R.; Boppana, R.V.; Ravi, V.; Munir, K.; Almutairi, M.; Rustam, F.; Lee, E.; Ashraf, I. A Comprehensive Review of Denial of Service Attacks in Blockchain Ecosystem and Open Challenges. *IEEE Access* **2023**, *10*, 96538–96555. [CrossRef]
38. Guo, W.; Xu, J.; Pei, Y.; Yin, L.; Jiang, C.; Ge, N. A Distributed Collaborative Entrance Defense Framework Against DDoS Attacks on Satellite Internet. *IEEE Internet Things J.***2022**, *9*, 15497–15510. [CrossRef]
39. Wang, C.; Chu, X.; Qin, Y. Dissecting Mining Pools of Bitcoin Network: Measurement, Analysis and Modeling. *IEEE Trans. Netw. Sci. Eng.* **2022**, *10*, 398–412. [CrossRef]
40. Sood, A. DDOS Attacks Against Bitcoin Mining Pools: A New Game-Theoretic Analysis With Defense Cost. In Proceedings of the 2023 3rd International Conference on Advance Computing and Innovative Technologies in Engineering (ICACITE), Greater Noida, India, 12–13 May 2023; pp. 2398–2402. [CrossRef]
41. Kesavan, R.; Pitchai, K.M. Modeling and Simulation of Selfish Mining Attacks in Blockchain Network using Evolutionary Game Theory. In Proceedings of the 2023 Third International Conference on Artificial Intelligence and Smart Energy (ICAIS), Coimbatore, India, 2–4 February 2023; pp. 1016–1021. [CrossRef]
42. Mighan, S.N.; Mišić, J.; Mišić, V.B.; Chang, X. An In-Depth Look at Forking-Based Attacks in Ethereum with PoW Consensus. *IEEE Trans. Netw. Serv. Manag.* **2023**, *2023*, 1–11. [CrossRef]
43. Sigmund, K.; Nowak, M.A. Evolutionary game theory. *Curr. Biol.* **1999**, *9*, 503–505. [CrossRef] [PubMed]
44. Hofbauer, J.; Sigmund, K. Evolutionary Game Dynamics. *Bull. Am. Math. Soc.* **2003**, *40*, 479–519. [CrossRef]
45. Ye, M.; Han, Q.-L.; Ding, L.; Xu, S. Distributed Nash Equilibrium Seeking in Games With Partial Decision Information: A Survey. *Proc. IEEE* **2023**, *111*, 140–157. [CrossRef]
46. Facchinei, F.; Kanzow, C. Generalized Nash equilibrium problems. *Ann. Oper. Res.* **2007**, *5*, 173–210. [CrossRef]

electronics

MDPI

Article

Lightweight Privacy Protection via Adversarial Sample

Guangxu Xie [1], Gaopan Hou [1,*], Qingqi Pei [1,*] and Haibo Huang [2]

1 The State Key Laboratory of Integrated Services Networks, Xidian University, Xi'an 710071, China; guangxxie@126.com
2 School of Electrical & Information Engineering, Hubei University of Automotive Technology, Shiyan 442002, China; huang7855@163.com
* Correspondence: gphou@stu.xidian.edu.cn (G.H.); qqpei@mail.xidian.edu.cn (Q.P.)

Abstract: Adversarial sample-based privacy protection has its own advantages compared to traditional privacy protections. Previous adversarial sample privacy protections have mostly been centralized or have not considered the issue of hardware device limitations when conducting privacy protection, especially on the user's local device. This work attempts to reduce the requirements of adversarial sample privacy protections on devices, making the privacy protection more locally friendly. Adversarial sample-based privacy protections rely on deep learning models, which generally have a large number of parameters, posing challenges for deployment. Fortunately, the model structural pruning technique has been proposed, which can be employed to reduce the parameter count of deep learning models. Based on the model pruning technique Depgraph and existing adversarial sample privacy protections AttriGuard and MemGuard, we design two structural pruning-based adversarial sample privacy protections, in which the user obtains the perturbed data through the pruned deep learning model. Extensive experiments are conducted on four datasets, and the results demonstrate the effectiveness of our adversarial sample privacy protection based on structural pruning.

Keywords: structural pruning; privacy protection; adversarial sample

1. Introduction

In recent years, deep learning models have received extensive research and application. Deep learning has effectively improved productivity and, to some extent, promoted societal development. However, science and technology are double-edged swords, and the automated inference of deep learning has posed unprecedented challenges to the personal privacy of Internet users.

Adversarial samples, as a weakness of deep learning, have been proposed [1]. By adding small perturbations to the input of a pre-trained deep learning model, it is easy to cause misclassification, and these inputs with added noise are referred to as adversarial samples. The existence of adversarial samples has had a significant impact on the practical application of deep learning and has become an important metric for evaluating the robustness of deep learning models.

However, in the field of data privacy protection, the emergence of adversarial samples could present a new opportunity for privacy protection techniques. Adversarial samples can cause misclassification in deep learning models, and if they can achieve misclassification specifically for sensitive attributes, they can protect the privacy of the underlying data. Now, there exist several approaches that utilize adversarial samples for privacy protection, including [2–4], and so on. In [2], inspired by [5], adversarial samples are generated by modifying the most influential elements of the input to achieve privacy attribute protection. Ref. [3] is a defense strategy against membership inference attacks [6], drawing inspiration from [7]. It employs multi-step gradients to generate adversarial samples and incorporates the magnitude of noise into the loss function, striking a balance between input utility and security.

Compared to traditional differential privacy [8], optimization-based approaches [9], and heuristic algorithms [10], it has been demonstrated that some adversarial sample-based privacy protections achieve better balance in terms of computational complexity, security, and data utility [2–4], making them more effective for privacy protection to some extent. Despite their own weaknesses, such as the attacks in [11], these approaches are still capable of altering the designs to enhance robustness. Privacy protections based on adversarial samples have their own advantages and can demonstrate their effectiveness in certain domains.

Inspired by the local differential privacy algorithm [12], we consider the question of whether privacy protection based on adversarial samples can be applied locally to better serve its privacy protection function. The greatest advantage of local differential privacy is that it does not require a trusted third party. We refer to the privacy protection based on adversarial samples deployed locally on the user's device as the local adversarial sample privacy protection (LASPP).

Although [2] mentions that the defender can be software or browser plug-ins deployed on the user side, which may suggest a local solution without the need for additional local solutions, a closer examination of the process reveals that the model has a large number of parameters, making it difficult for users with poor devices to deploy locally. This issue was not considered in [2]. Although the model can be placed on a cloud device and called by local users, the non-trusted third parties who fully understand the defense model may still be able to gain access to users' private information through backdoors. In addition, calling cloud devices locally will also bring about communication overhead and security issues. This paper prunes the deep learning model first and then distributes it to users locally, adding noise locally to reduce the threshold for users to use the model.

For [3], the defender itself is the model provider or the trusted third party. Hence, [3] is more likely to lean towards central deployment rather than on user devices. Deploying the defense locally on the user side can weaken the assumption that the defender is a trusted third party. However, user devices are limited, and deploying centralized models locally still faces challenges in making the models locally friendly. Therefore, this paper's solution has a certain promoting effect on deploying LASPP locally on users' devices. Furthermore, even in a centralized deployment of adversarial sample privacy protection solutions, the more lightweight ML model is more environmentally friendly.

Unlike the local differential privacy algorithm, the privacy protection based on adversarial samples requires a deep learning model, and generally, deep learning models have a large number of parameters, which poses a significant challenge for the LASPP. For example, in [2], the number of parameters in defending deep learning models exceeds 4×10^8, such a large parameter size will inevitably impose a significant burden on user devices. The limited computational capabilities of users' local devices may be the biggest challenge in applying adversarial sample privacy protections locally at present. Fortunately, model pruning techniques [13–24] may bring new possibilities for the LASPP. Model pruning is a technique used to reduce the size and complexity of deep learning models. Through model pruning, unnecessary parameters, connections, and layers can be removed from the model, reducing the storage requirements of the model, accelerating inference speed, and reducing the consumption of computing resources.

Mainstream model pruning techniques can be broadly categorized into structural pruning [13–21] and non-structural pruning [22–24]. Structural pruning is a pruning technique based on the model's structure. It reduces the size and complexity of the model by removing entire neurons, layers, or modules from the model. In non-structural pruning, thresholding is used to zero out or remove the parameters with smaller absolute values, resulting in a reduction in the number of parameters in the model. Non-structural pruning can significantly reduce the size and complexity of the model without altering its structure. Compared to non-structural pruning, structural pruning does not rely on specific AI accelerators or software to reduce memory overhead and computational costs, making it more widely applicable in practice [25,26].

The model pruning technique used in this article is structural pruning, mainly based on reference [15], which proposes using dependency graphs to enable structural pruning of any neural network. In this work, we apply the structural pruning technique to [2,3] to derive two privacy protections for adversarial samples based on the pruned model. We refer to these two privacy protections as structural pruning-based adversarial sample privacy protections (SP-ASPPs). Unlike [2,3], our scheme attempts to generate adversarial noise on the pruned model. As the pruned model has fewer parameters, it has the potential to be placed on the user side. To clearly illustrate our scheme, we illustrate our SP-ASPP in Figure 1. Through our attempt in this paper, we hope to provide some inspiration for future LASPPs.

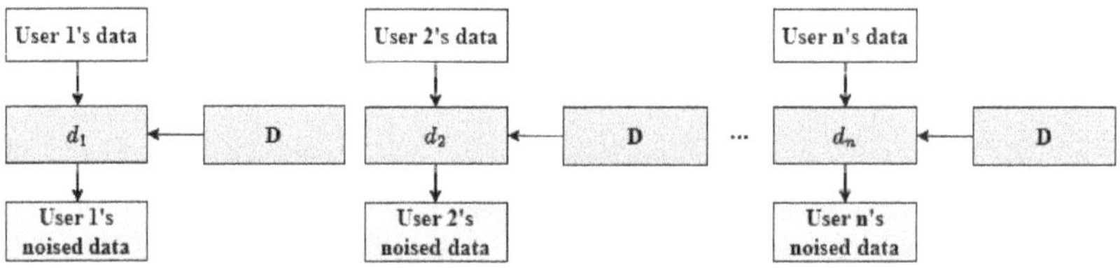

Figure 1. The privacy protection based on adversarial samples requires a deep learning model. In this paper, the model pruning technique is employed to prune the deep learning model D and obtain the pruned model d. The pruned model d is then used to generate adversarial noise. Through the pruning process, the threshold for using adversarial sample privacy protection is reduced, making it easier to deploy adversarial sample privacy protection locally and thus achieve better privacy protection.

We adopt four datasets to validate the SP-ASPPs. Building upon references [2,3], we have designed a lightweight adversarial sample-based privacy protection scheme for this paper. To demonstrate the effectiveness of our approach, we need to compare it with the original scheme. Therefore, the four datasets chosen in this paper are exactly the same as those used in [2,3]. The first dataset is used to validate the first SP-ASPP. The subsequent three datasets are used to validate the second SP-ASPP. The first dataset is derived from [2], while the subsequent three datasets are derived from [3].

We evaluate our SP-ASPP scheme by subjecting it to the attacks used in [2,3]. We compare our SP-ASPPs with [2,3] separately. For the same dataset, our first SP-ASPP uses the same attack model as [2], and our second SP-ASPP uses the same attack model as [3]. The inference accuracy of the attack model represents the effectiveness of the defense scheme, where a higher accuracy indicates a weaker defense effect, and vice versa. With the reduction in ML model parameters, if the decrease in defense model accuracy is minimal and the increase in attack model inference accuracy is also minimal, it demonstrates the effectiveness of the proposed SP-ASPPs in this paper.

The effectiveness of our approach is demonstrated by comparing the accuracy, size, and effectiveness of noising before and after pruning the defense model. The impact of noising is measured by the inference accuracy of the attack model. Thorough experiments demonstrate the effectiveness of our SP-ASPPs. The contributions of this article include the following.

- To our best knowledge, our research is one of the early considerations in weakening the contradiction between limited user device capabilities and a large number of parameters of deep learning models in privacy protection via adversarial samples.
- We use state-of-the-art model pruning techniques and combine them with advanced adversarial sample privacy protections to design two structural pruning-based adversarial sample privacy protections and verify their effectiveness.
- Thorough experiments on four real-world datasets demonstrate that the performance of the defense model after pruning is not significantly affected and prove the feasibility of the proposed locally-based privacy protection for adversarial samples.

The remaining parts of this paper are organized as follows. In Section 2, we discuss the related work. In Section 3, we introduce the participants and define the key issues of our work. In Section 4, we propose the pruning principle and our two structural pruning-based adversarial sample privacy protections. In Section 5, we describe our experimental setup, and provide the experimental results to validate the effectiveness of our work. Finally, in Section 6, we conclude our work.

2. Related Work

This section mainly introduces the related work of this paper, which mainly includes two aspects closely related to this paper. One is the privacy protection scheme based on adversarial samples, which forms the basis of this paper. The other is the related work on model structure pruning, which is the source of the pruning algorithm in this paper.

2.1. *Privacy Protection Based on Adversarial Samples*

Jia et al. [2] proposed a defense against attribute inference attack, which consists of two stages: noise generation and noise injection. In the noise generation stage, they draw inspiration from [5] and consider both the elements that have the most significant impact on the output and the degree to which these elements can be altered. They modify the elements that have a significant impact and can be changed substantially, iteratively altering one element at a time until the desired output is achieved and then stop the iteration and output the noised data that satisfies the requirements. In the second stage, random noise is added to make the inference of the attack model resemble random guessing.

Jia et al. [3] proposed a defense against membership inference attack, which consists of two stages: noise generation and noise injection. In the noise generation stage, they draw inspiration from multi-step adversarial sample generation methods [7]. However, their loss function takes into account three elements. The first element ensures that the attack model's binary classifier cannot obtain useful information. The second element ensures that the output label of the target model remains unchanged. The third element ensures that the magnitude of the noise is as small as possible. The noisy data are generated through multiple iterative steps. In the second step, random noise is added to prevent the attacker from inferring the added noise through the output.

Shao et al. [4] utilized adversarial samples to protect the text-based CAPTCHA. Their scheme consists of two stages: In the first stage, they construct foreground and background using randomly sampled fonts and background images and then combine them to create recognizable pseudo-adversarial CAPTCHA images. In the second stage, they design and apply a highly transferable text CAPTCHA adversarial attack method to better impede CAPTCHA solvers.

Li et al. [27] proposed a face image de-identification scheme, which includes four stages: face feature evaluation, privacy-oriented face obfuscation, targeted natural image synthesis, and adversarial perturbation. Their scheme demonstrates that adversarial samples can be used in the domain of face image de-identification.

Salman et al. [28] proposed PhotoGuard, which employs adversarial examples to protect users' private photos from malicious editing by large diffusion models. Two privacy protection mechanisms, Encoder attack and Diffusion attack, are developed for the encoder and the entire large diffusion model.

Shan et al. [29] proposed Glaze, a solution that adds imperceptible noise to images to prevent large models from learning their style, thus protecting the copyright of artists.

The above are all privacy protections based on adversarial samples. Although they have considered the security of the model and the availability of data, and have demonstrated that their solution achieves a good balance between security and usability, they have not taken into account the limitations of users' local devices and their knowledge. Knowledge limitations may arise because users may not be professional data security workers and may be unfamiliar with certain operations. In this paper, we have explored some issues that were not considered in previous research, with the expectation that our study can contribute to advancing the development of LASPP to a certain extent.

2.2. Model Pruning

Model pruning techniques can be divided into two categories: structural pruning and non-structural pruning. In this paper, we are solely concerned with structured pruning techniques.

Inspired by the linear properties of convolutions, Ding et al. [13] attempted to make filters gradually approach each other and eventually become identical to achieve network slimming. To this end, they proposed a new optimization method called centripetal SGD (C-SGD), which can train multiple filters to converge to a point in the parameter space. When training is complete, removing the identical filters can prune the network without causing performance loss, thus eliminating the need for fine-tuning.

You et al. [14] introduced a global filter pruning algorithm that transforms the output of a conventional CNN module by multiplying it with channel-wise scaling factors (i.e., gates). Setting the scaling factor to zero is equivalent to removing the corresponding filter. They utilized the Taylor expansion to estimate the change in the loss function when setting the scaling factor to zero and used the estimation to rank the global importance of filters. Subsequently, they pruned the network by removing unimportant filters. After pruning, all scaling factors were merged back into the original module, eliminating the need for introducing special operations or structures. Additionally, they introduced an iterative pruning framework called Tick-Tock to improve the accuracy of pruning. Extensive experiments demonstrated the effectiveness of their approach.

Shen et al. [16] combined the benefits of post-training pruning and pre-training pruning to propose a method that performs early pruning during training without compromising performance. Instead of pruning at initialization, this method quickly determines the model structure using a few rounds of training, evaluates the importance ranking of the main subnetworks, and then triggers pruning to ensure model stability and achieve early pruning during the training process.

Gao et al. [17] proposed a novel channel pruning method to reduce the computational and storage costs of convolutional neural networks. The target subnetwork is learned during model training and then used to guide the learning of model weights via partial regularization. The target subnetwork is learned and generated using an architecture generator, which can be effectively optimized. In addition, they also derived the proximal gradient for their proposed partial regularization to facilitate the structural alignment process. By these designs, the gap between the pruned model and the subnetwork is reduced, which improves pruning performance.

Shen et al. [18] proposed hardware-aware latency pruning, which formalizes structured pruning techniques as a resource allocation optimization problem aimed at maximizing accuracy while constraining latency within a budget on the target device. They ultimately solved the optimization problem using an enhanced knapsack problem solver, and this approach has been demonstrated to surpass previous work in achieving a balance between accuracy and efficiency.

Fang et al. [19] proposed a pruning scheme for large diffusion models, called Diff-Pruning, with the aim of learning lightweight diffusion models from existing models without extensive retraining. The essence of Diff-Pruning is encapsulated in a Taylor expansion over pruned timesteps, a process that disregards non-contributory diffusion steps and ensembles informative gradients to identify important weights.

Hou et al. [20] proposed a simple yet effective channel pruning technique, called pruning via resource reallocation (PEEL), to rapidly generate pruned models with negligible cost. Specifically, PEEL first constructs a predefined backbone and then conducts resource reallocation on it to shift parameters from less informative layers to more important layers in one round, thus amplifying the positive effect of these informative layers.

Ma et al. [21] addressed the compression problem of large language models (LLMs) within two constraints: task-agnosticism and minimizing reliance on the original training dataset. Their method, called LLM-Pruner, utilizes structured pruning techniques to selectively remove non-critical coupling structures based on gradient information while preserving a significant portion of the functionality of LLMs. To achieve this, with the help of the LoRA technique, the performance of the pruned model can be effectively restored in just 3 h with only 50 K data.

Fang et al. [15] investigated a highly challenging yet rarely explored task of general structure pruning for any architecture such as CNNs, RNNs, GNNs, and Transformers. The most prominent obstacle to achieving this goal is structural coupling, which not only forces different layers to be pruned simultaneously but also expects all deleted parameters to be always unimportant, avoiding structural issues and significant performance degradation after pruning. To address this issue, they proposed a generic fully automated method—DepGraph, which explicitly models the dependency relationships between layers and comprehensively groups coupled parameters for pruning. They extensively evaluated their method on several architectures and tasks, including ResNe(X)t, DenseNet, MobileNet, and Vision Transformer for images, GAT for graphs, DGCNN for 3D point clouds, and LSTM for language, and demonstrated that the proposed method consistently yields satisfactory performance even using simple norm-based criteria.

There exist many types of model pruning techniques, including those targeted at convolutional models and large diffusion models. In fact, these model pruning techniques can be applied to reduce the size of deep models. We ultimately chose [15] as our pruning scheme mainly because it demonstrated strong applicability and showed promising performance in their paper. However, other pruning schemes could also be explored, and this remains future work.

3. Model Preparation

This section mainly introduces the preparatory work for the lightweight adversarial sample privacy protection scheme, discussing the potential participants in the lightweight adversarial sample privacy protection scheme including three parties: defender, user, and attacker. In order to effectively propose a lightweight adversarial sample privacy protection scheme, three definitions are put forward to ensure the effectiveness of the model: the first one ensures that there is little change in the accuracy of the defense model before and after model pruning, the second guarantees a certain pruning ratio, and the third ensures the defensive effect of noise on the pruned model. Generally speaking, the first definition forms the basis for satisfying the second and third definitions.

3.1. Participating Parties

3.1.1. Defender

The defender designs and trains the defense model and distributes the obtained defense model to users assuming that the defender designs a larger model, denoted as D. To meet the diverse hardware requirements of users, assume that the defender can compress the model and control the pruning ratio, resulting in multiple pruned defense models $d^1, d^2, \ldots, d^M$. After obtaining the pruned models, the defender further trains each model and finally distributes them to the user. One key operation that the defender needs to perform during this process is:

$$D \longrightarrow d^j, j = 1, 2, 3, \ldots, M, \tag{1}$$

where the long arrow in Formula (1) represents the structural pruning operation. To facilitate the comparison of results, the defender also generated adversarial noise data using the unpruned defense model. We denote the data to which the noise is added as x. This process can be expressed as follows:

$$\{x, D\} \longrightarrow x', \tag{2}$$

where the long arrow in Formula (2) represents the defender's adversarial noise injection process.

3.1.2. User

For each user, distinguished by a subscript i, $i = 1,2,3,\ldots,N$. N represents the number of users. Firstly, user i has their own data x^i, which is a vector or matrix of a certain dimension that needs to be compatible with the defense models distributed by the defender. Based on the defense models, the user can generate adversarial samples and obtain a noisy vector $\hat{x}^i$. This process can be expressed as follows:

$$\{x^i, d^j\} \longrightarrow \hat{x}^i, i = 1,\ldots,N, j = 1,\ldots,M, \tag{3}$$

where the long arrow in Formula (3) represents the local perturbation process of user i.

3.1.3. Attacker

The attacker can train an attack model A to infer the noisy data. The information acquired by the attack model on $\hat{x}$ is defined as $A(\hat{x})$.

3.2. Problem Definition

We use $|\cdot|$ to represent the number of model parameters. In order to ensure that the pruned model maintains high accuracy, has a small parameter scale, and local noise addition is effective, we provide the following three definitions.

Definition 1. *Before and after model pruning, the models are represented as D and d, with their accuracy on the test set denoted as $Acc(D)$ and $Acc(d)$, respectively. If the model d has certain effects, there exists a small positive number $m > 0$ such that $|Acc(D) - Acc(d)| \leq m$.*

Definition 2. *Before and after model pruning, the models are represented as D and d, with their parameter sizes denoted as $|D|$ and $|d|$, respectively. If the model parameters of d are small enough to satisfy a certain condition, then there exists a positive number r such that $|d|/|D| \leq r$.*

Definition 3. *Before and after model pruning, the models are represented as D and d, with the obtained adversarial noisy data being x_D and x_d, respectively. For any attack model, its inference accuracy on x_D is represented as $Acc_A(x_D)$, and its inference accuracy on x_d is represented as $Acc_A(x_d)$. To ensure the effectiveness of the model pruning privacy protection, there exist two small positive numbers q and n such that $Acc_A(x_d) \leq q$ and $|Acc_A(x_d) - Acc_A(x_D)| < n$.*

4. The Proposed Scheme

This section mainly introduces the model pruning algorithm adopted in this paper, the first adversarial sample privacy protection scheme based on structural pruning, and the second adversarial sample privacy protection scheme based on structural pruning.

4.1. Model Pruning

The model pruning technique used in this study is referenced from [15], which involves dependency graph, grouping, and importance assessment. For ease of reference in the subsequent discussion, we denote this pruning process as $d = pruner(D)$, where D represents the defense model and d represents the pruned defense model.

4.1.1. Dependency Graph and Grouping

The neural network is represented as $\mathcal{F}(x; w)$, which is decomposed into finer and fundamental components, i.e., $\mathcal{F} = \{f_1, f_2, \ldots, f_L\}$. Here, each component f represents a parameterized layer such as convolution or a non-parameterized operation such as residual addition. The input and output of component f_i are denoted as f_i^- and f_i^+, respectively. Thus, for any network, the final decomposition becomes $\mathscr{F} = \{f_1^-, f_1^+, \ldots, f_L^-, f_L^+\}$. The network can be redefined as follows:

$$(f_1^-, f_1^+) \leftrightarrow (f_2^-, f_2^+) \cdots \leftrightarrow \cdots (f_L^-, f_L^+), \tag{4}$$

where the symbol $\leftrightarrow$ represents the connection between two adjacent layers, and L represents the total number of layers. This leads to the existence of inter-layer dependency and intra-layer dependency. Inter-layer dependency exists in the connected layers $f_i^- \leftrightarrow f_j^+$, denoted as $f_i^- \Leftrightarrow f_j^+$. Intra-layer dependency exists when f_i^- and f_i^+ have the same pruning scheme, represented as $sch(f_i^-) = sch(f_i^+)$, denoted as $f_i^- \Leftrightarrow f_i^+$. Based on the above symbols, the dependency model is constructed as follows:

$$D(f_i^-, f_j^+) = \mathbb{1}[f_i^- \leftrightarrow f_j^+] \vee \mathbb{1}[i = j \wedge sch(f_i^-) = sch(f_j^+)], \tag{5}$$

where the symbols $\vee$ and $\wedge$ represent logical *or* and logical *and*, respectively. The function $\mathbb{1}(\cdot)$ is an indicator function that returns *true* if the connection exists. Based on the above dependency graph, the components are divided into multiple groups, where there is no dependency relationship between each group, but there is a dependency relationship within each group.

4.1.2. Importance Evaluation

We assume there is a group $g = \{w_1, w_2, \ldots, w_{|g|}\}$ under L_1-norm, where the importance of each parameter is defined as $I(w) = |w|$ for each parameter w in group g. The importance of group g used in this article is defined as $I(g) = \Sigma_{w \in g} I(w)$. The survival of each group is determined according to their importance ranking.

4.2. *The First SP-ASPP*

We designed our privacy protection based on reference [2]. However, unlike [2], our scheme involves users performing the noise injection process themselves and uploading the perturbed data to the server, while attackers collect the user's perturbed data for final inference. Similar to [2], the first SP-ASPP consists of two phases: the noise generation phase and the random noise injection phase.

In the noise generation phase, the machine learning model is primarily pruned. The pruned model is then distributed to each user. Upon receiving the pruned and trained model, each user starts adding noise to their own data. For simplicity, this paper does not consider communication overhead and assumes that the defender performs model pruning and training tasks. Unlike [2], we assume that users have all the necessary permissions for modifying and adding privacy, which is reasonable locally since users have the most authority over their own data.

The algorithm is presented in Algorithm 1. The variable *maxiter* denotes the maximum number of iterations for generating adversarial noise, which is determined by user *i* and can be different for each user. The term *rand_mech* in the algorithm represents a random selection mechanism that chooses perturbed data with a probability of Ψ^i. The calculation of Ψ^i is obtained by solving the following optimization problem:

$$\begin{aligned} \hat{\Psi}^i &= \arg\min_{\Psi} KL(p^i \| \Psi^i) \\ s.t. \quad & \sum_{t=1}^{T} \|\hat{x}^{i,t} - x^i\| \le \beta^i \\ & \Psi_t^i > 0, \quad \forall t \in \{1, 2, ..., T\} \\ & \sum_{t=1}^{T} \Psi_t^i = 1, \end{aligned} \tag{6}$$

where p^i represents the probability distribution that user i wants the output to satisfy, Ψ^i is the optimal probability obtained by user i, and β^i is the noise amplitude set by user i with $\beta^i \geq \beta_{\min}$. The optimization problem above is solved by user i. "KL" refers to the Kullback–Leibler divergence [30]. The theoretical solution to the above optimization problem can be found in [2], and can be directly used to obtain Ψ^i.

Algorithm 1 The first SP-ASPP

Input: Number of users N, data of the ith user x^i, dimension of x^i K, defense model D, minimum perturbation magnitude $\beta_{\min}$.
Output: $\hat{x}^1, \hat{x}^2, ..., \hat{x}^N$.

DEFENDER:
  $d^j = pruner(D), j = 1, 2, 3, \ldots, M$
  send d^j to user i, $i = 1, 2, 3, \ldots, N$
USER i:
  for t in T **then**
    while $d^j(x^i) \neq t$ and $iter < maxiter^i$ **do**
      $e_{inc} = \arg\max_{k \in [1,K]} \{(1 - x^i_k) \frac{\partial(d^j_t(x^i))}{\partial x^i_k}\}$
      $e_{dec} = \arg\max_{k \in [1,K]} \{-x^i_k \frac{\partial(d^j_t(x^i))}{\partial x^i_k}\}$
      $v_{inc} = (1 - x^i_{e_{inc}}) \frac{\partial(d^j_t(x^i))}{\partial x^i_{e_{inc}}}$
      $v_{dec} = -x^i_{e_{dec}} \frac{\partial(d^j_t(x^i))}{\partial x^i_{e_{dec}}}$
      if $v_{inc} > v_{dec}$ **then**
        $x^i_{e_{inc}} = 1.0$
      else
        $x^i_{e_{dec}} = 0.0$
      end if
      $\hat{x}^{i,t} = x^i$
      $iter = iter + 1$
    end while
  end for
  $\hat{x}^i \leftarrow rand\_mech\{\hat{x}^{i,1}, \hat{x}^{i,2}, ..., \hat{x}^{i,T}; \hat{\Psi}^i\}$
  return $\hat{x}^i$
N users repeat the above operation.
return $\hat{x}^1, \hat{x}^2, ..., \hat{x}^N$

4.3. The Second SP-ASPP

We have designed a second structural pruning-based adversarial sample privacy protection based on [3]. The key difference is that users perform the noise generation process locally and then upload it to the server. This privacy protection also consists of two stages: noise generation stage and random noise addition stage. In the noise generation stage, the defender needs to train the defense model D and then perform pruning. The pruned model undergoes secondary training to obtain d. During this process, the defender needs to ensure that the model accuracy satisfies Definition 1. After receiving d, the user applies noise to the logits vector obtained from the target model, resulting in the noisy data.

We present the entire process in Algorithm 2. For the sake of uniformity, x is used to represent the data to be noised, and $\hat{x}$ is used to represent the noised data. The activation function of the output layer of the pruned defense model d is a sigmoid function, and the structure before the activation function is represented as h. Thus, the loss L can be expressed as:

$$L_1 = |h(softmax(x + e))| \tag{7}$$

$$L_2 = relu(-x_l - e_l + \max_{j|j\neq l}\{x_j + e_j\}) \tag{8}$$

$$L_3 = |softmax(\boldsymbol{x}) - softmax(\boldsymbol{x} + \boldsymbol{e})| \tag{9}$$

$$L = c_1 \cdot L_1 + c_2 \cdot L_2 + c_3 \cdot L_3, \tag{10}$$

where the values of $maxiter^i$ and β^i are chosen by the user i. c_1, c_2, and c_3 are constants that can be selected by the user. $rand\_mech$ refers to the one-time randomness mentioned in [3]. When sampling noise data, the user employs one-time randomness to ensure that they always return the same noised data for the same data sample.

Algorithm 2 The second SP-ASPP

Input: Number of users N, data of the ith user $\boldsymbol{x}^i$, defense model D.
Output: $\hat{\boldsymbol{x}}^1, \hat{\boldsymbol{x}}^2, ..., \hat{\boldsymbol{x}}^N$.

DEFENDER:
  $d^j = pruner(D)=\{h^j, sigmoid\}, j = 1, 2, \ldots, M$
  send $\{h^j, sigmoid\}$ to user i, $i = 1, 2, \ldots, N$
USER i:
  while True **do**
    $l = \arg\max\{\boldsymbol{x}^i\}$
    $\boldsymbol{e}^i = \boldsymbol{0}$
    $iter = 1$
    while $iter < maxiter^i$ and $\{\arg\max\{\boldsymbol{x}^i + \boldsymbol{e}^i\} \neq l$ or $h^i(softmax(\boldsymbol{x}^i)) \cdot h^i(softmax(\boldsymbol{x}^i + \boldsymbol{e}^i)) > 0\}$ **do**
      $\boldsymbol{u} = \frac{\partial L(h^i; \boldsymbol{x}^i)}{\partial \boldsymbol{e}}$
      $\boldsymbol{u} = \boldsymbol{u} / \|\boldsymbol{u}\|_2$
      $\boldsymbol{e}^i = \boldsymbol{e}^i - \gamma^i \cdot \boldsymbol{u}$
      $iter = iter + 1$
    end while
    $c_3 = 10 \cdot c_3$
    if $c_3 > 100000$ **then**
      break
    end if
  end while
  $\hat{\boldsymbol{x}}^i \leftarrow rand\_mech\{\boldsymbol{x}^i, \boldsymbol{x}^i + \boldsymbol{e}^i; \beta^i\}$
N users repeat the above operation.
return $\hat{\boldsymbol{x}}^1, \hat{\boldsymbol{x}}^2, ..., \hat{\boldsymbol{x}}^N$

5. Experiment

This section mainly introduces the experiments conducted in this paper, including the experimental setup and results. The setup section mainly covers the datasets used in the paper and the detailed configurations of the two SP-ASPPs. The results section presents the experimental results of the two SP-ASPPs.

5.1. Experimental Settings

5.1.1. Datasets

The used dataset consists of four parts, with the first dataset sourced from [2] and the following three datasets sourced from [3]. For distinction, the first dataset is referred to as "Att". Here, only a brief introduction to the datasets is provided, while specific usage instructions can be found in [2,3].

Att. This dataset can be obtained from GitHub (https://github.com/jinyuan-jia/~AttriGuard (accessed on 25 November 2023)). The dataset comprises 16,238 samples, with each sample consisting of 10,000 features. Each feature represents a user's rating for a specific app, and the rating values are normalized to 0, 0.2, 0.4, 0.6, 0.8, and 1.0. If a feature is missing, it is replaced with 0. The privacy attribute pertains to the user's city of residence or past residence, encompassing a total of 25 cities.

Location. This dataset can be obtained from GitHub (https://github.com/privacytrustlab/datasets/dataset_location.tgz (accessed on 25 November 2023)). This dataset contains 5010 samples, each with 446 binary features representing whether the user has visited a certain location or not. The samples are categorized into 30 classes.

Texas100. This dataset can be obtained from GitHub (https://github.com/privacytrustlab/datasets/dataset_texas.tgz (accessed on 25 November 2023)). This dataset comprises 67,330 samples, each with 6170 binary features representing external causes of injury, diagnosis, patient procedures, and general information. These samples are divided into 30 classes, with each class representing a common disease.

CH-MNIST. This dataset can be obtained from Kaggle (https://www.kaggle.com/kmader/colorectal-histologymnist (accessed on 25 November 2023)). This dataset contains tissue slice image data of colon cancer patients, with each image having dimensions of 64×64. There are a total of 5000 samples in this dataset, which are divided into eight classes.

5.1.2. The First SP-ASPP

The experimental settings include the defense model, the attack model, and the other settings.

The defense model. The defense model is trained by the defender. The structure of the defense model consists of a three-layer fully connected neural network with neuron counts of 10,000, 40,000, and 25, respectively. The activation function used in the middle layer is ReLU, while the output layer uses the softmax activation function. There is a dropout layer between the second and third layers, with a dropout rate of 0.7. The optimizer used is Adam, and the loss function is cross-entropy. The learning rate is set to 0.0005, and each training batch contains 200 samples. The training is performed for 100 epochs.

The pruned defense model is also trained by the defender. The only modification made is changing the neuron count in the middle layer while keeping the input and output layer neuron counts unchanged. A speed-up factor is introduced, defined as speed-up = (Base MACs)/(Pruned MACs), where MAC represents multiply–accumulate operations. In the experiments, the speed-up factor is set to 2, 4, 6, ..., 200 to observe the effect of different speed-up factors on the final noise addition. A speed-up factor of 1 corresponds to no pruning, and larger speed-up factors indicate higher pruning ratios. After pruning the defense model, it is further trained with parameters similar to those before pruning.

The attack model. To verify the defense effectiveness of the model, an attack model is also trained. The structure of the attack model consists of a three-layer fully connected neural network with neuron counts of 10,000, 30,000, and 25, respectively. The activation function used in the middle layer is ReLU, while the output layer uses the softmax activation function. There is a dropout layer between the second and third layers, with a dropout rate of 0.7. The optimizer used is SGD, and the loss function is cross-entropy. The learning rate is set to 0.05, and each training batch contains 100 samples. The training is performed for 50 epochs.

The purpose of training the attack model is to evaluate the defense effectiveness of the defense model by measuring its ability to resist attacks launched by the attack model.

The other setting. User i in the noise generation process has multiple options for the selection of p^i. In this paper, the selected p^i represents the proportion of users from the training set residing in the 25 cities. The value of $\beta_{\min}$ is set to 1.5. In Algorithm 1, $\beta_{min} = 1.5$, $N = 1631$, $M = 1$, $T = 25$, and $K = 10,000$.

5.1.3. The Second SP-ASPP

The experimental settings include the defense model, the attack model, and the other settings.

The defense model. The second local privacy protection is mainly validated using the last three datasets. The defense models are all fully connected neural networks, and for the three datasets, the intermediate and output layers are the same, consisting of $(256, 128, 64, 1)$. The input dimensions for Location, Texas100, and CH-MNIST are 30, 100, and 8, respectively. The activation function between layers is *relu*, and the activation function for the output layer is *sigmoid*. The defender compresses the defense model and then re-trains it. Throughout the process, the SGD optimizer is used, as well as binary cross-entropy loss, a learning rate of 0.01, and a batch size of 64. The number of training epochs for the defense model before and after compression is 400 and 100, respectively.

The attack model. The attack model is a fully connected neural network, and for the three datasets, the intermediate and output layers are the same, consisting of $(512, 256, 128, 1)$. The input dimensions for Location, Texas100, and CH-MNIST are 30, 100, and 8, respectively. The activation function between layers is *relu*, and the activation function for the output layer is *sigmoid*. The SGD optimizer is used, as well as binary cross-entropy loss, a learning rate of 0.01, and a batch size of 64. The number of training epochs for the attack model is 400.

The other setting. For Location, Texas100, and CH-MNIST, N is 2000, 20,000, and 2000, respectively. $M = 1$, $\gamma = 0.1$, $c_1 = 1.0$, $c_2 = 10.0$, and the initial value of c_3 is set to 0.1.

5.2. Experimental Results

5.2.1. The First SP-ASPP

We evaluate the first SP-ASPP from three aspects: defense model accuracy, model size, and attack inference accuracy, corresponding to Definitions 1–3 in the previous section, respectively.

The accuracy of the defense model. The accuracy of the defense model before pruning is 0.4549. After pruning, the speed-up ranges from 2 to 200, with the maximum defense model accuracy being 0.4697 and the minimum defense model accuracy being 0.4433. It can be observed that the accuracy of the defense model does not change significantly. The result is shown in Figure 2. In Definition 1, when $m = 0.0148$, the result satisfies the definition.

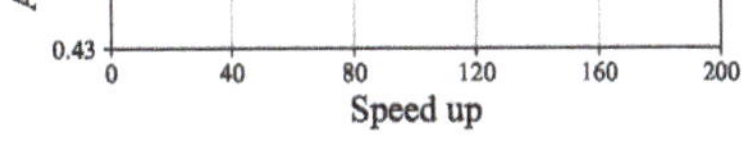

Figure 2. The accuracy of the defense model varies with speed-up. It can be roughly observed that the accuracy ranges from 0.44 to 0.47, with a variation range of [0, 0.03].

The number of parameters. The change in defense model parameter count with respect to speed-up is shown in Figure 3. The parameter count before model pruning is 401.04 Mb. After pruning, with speed-up ranging from 2 to 200, the minimum parameter count is 0.99 Mb, indicating a continuous decrease in parameter count. The minimum parameter count is achieved at a speed-up of 200. When $r = 0.002469$, the result satisfies Definition 2. In addition to defending model parameters, another metric is floating point operations (FLOPs). Since the defense model adopts a fully connected network, the amount of defense model parameters and FLOPs are equivalent, so we will not display it separately.

The inference accuracy of the attack model. The change in inference accuracy of the attack model with respect to speed-up under different noise budgets is shown in Figure 4.

Prior to defense model pruning, the attack model's inference accuracy at noise budgets of 1.5, 2.0, 3.0, 4.0, and 5.0 is 0.3721, 0.3603, 0.3492, 0.3439, and 0.3401, respectively.

- When the noise budget is set to 1.5, the maximum inference accuracy is 0.3771, and the minimum inference accuracy is 0.3283. When $n = 0.0437$, the results satisfy Definition 3.
- When the noise budget is set to 2.0, the maximum inference accuracy is 0.3666, and the minimum inference accuracy is 0.3020. When $n = 0.0583$, the results satisfy Definition 3.
- When the noise budget is set to 3.0, the maximum inference accuracy is 0.3569, and the minimum inference accuracy is 0.2707. When $n = 0.0785$, the results satisfy Definition 3.
- When the noise budget is set to 4.0, the maximum inference accuracy is 0.3518, and the minimum inference accuracy is 0.2548. When $n = 0.0890$, the results satisfy Definition 3.
- When the noise budget is set to 5.0, the maximum inference accuracy is 0.3480, and the minimum inference accuracy is 0.2459. When $n = 0.0942$, the results satisfy Definition 3.

At a speed-up of 80, the attack model's inference accuracy corresponding to noise budgets of 1.5, 2.0, 3.0, 4.0, and 5.0 are 0.3354, 0.3111, 0.2827, 0.2686, and 0.2607, respectively. All of these values are lower than the inference accuracy prior to defense model pruning, indicating that the defense performance is better than before pruning. It can be observed that the relationship between model pruning and defense performance is not strictly monotonic, and in some cases, model pruning may improve defense effectiveness. This also demonstrates the feasibility of adding noise to the pruned models locally. However, this study is only an attempt, and researchers can explore other related areas for further investigation.

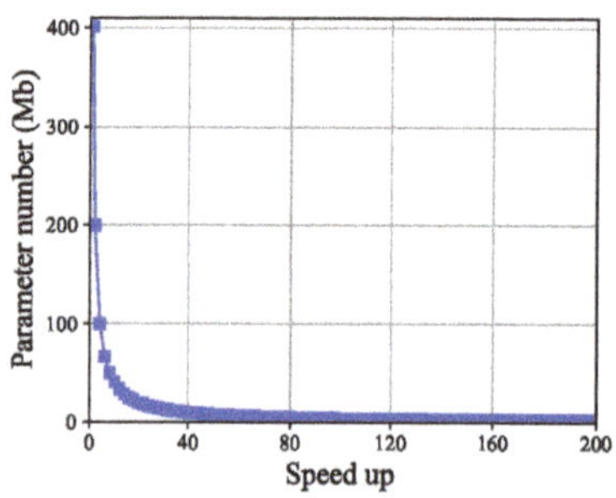

Figure 3. The change in the number of defense model parameters with respect to speed-up. The parameter count gradually decreases as the speed-up increases, approaching zero around a speed-up of 80.

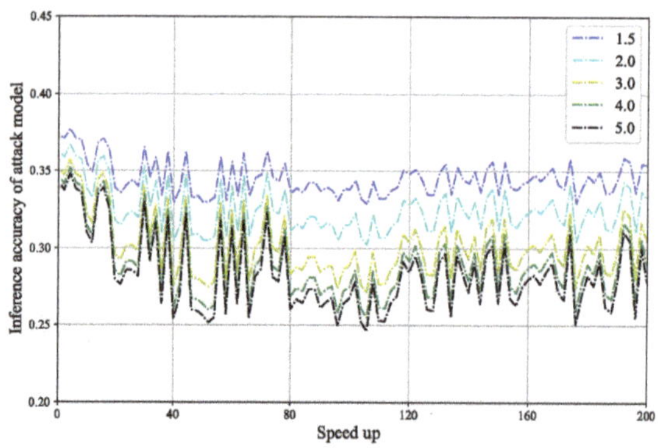

Figure 4. The change in inference accuracy of the attack model with respect to speed-up under different noise budgets is shown. As the noise budget increases, the defense performance improves. At the same noise budget, the inference accuracy of the attack model is not very stable, but some points can be found where the inference accuracy is lower than before pruning.

5.2.2. The Second SP-ASPP

We evaluate the second SP-ASPP from three aspects: defense model accuracy, model size, and attack inference accuracy, corresponding to Definitions 1–3 in the previous section, respectively.

The accuracy of the defense model. For Location, the accuracy of the defense model before pruning is 0.8575. When speed up is set to 20, 40, and 60, the maximum accuracy of the defense model is 0.8575, and the minimum accuracy is 0.8525. It can be observed that the accuracy of the defense model does not vary much. This result is shown in Figure 5a. In Definition 1, when $m = 0.005$, the result satisfies this definition. For Texas100, the accuracy of the defense model before pruning is 0.736. When speed up is set to 20, 40, and 60, the maximum accuracy of the defense model is 0.7355, and the minimum accuracy is 0.7353. It can be observed that the accuracy of the defense model does not vary much. This result is shown in Figure 5b. In Definition 1, when $m = 0.0007$, the result satisfies this definition. For CH-MNIST, the accuracy of the defense model before pruning is 0.7075. When speed up is set to 50, 100, 150, and 200, the maximum accuracy of the defense model is 0.7075, and the minimum accuracy is 0.7025. It can be observed that the accuracy of the defense model does not vary much. This result is shown in Figure 5c. In Definition 1, when $m = 0.005$, the result satisfies this definition.

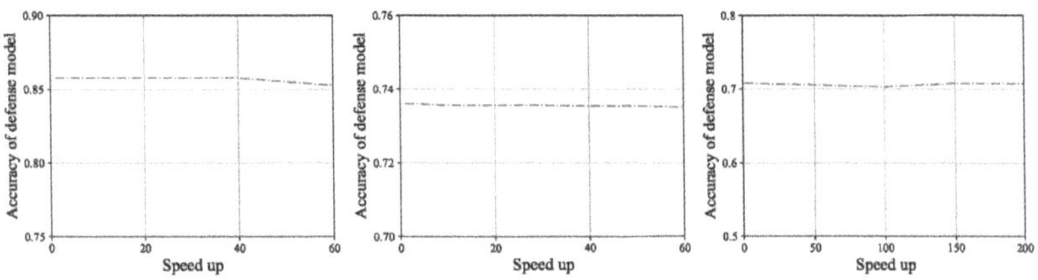

(**a**) Location (**b**) Texas100 (**c**) CH-MNIST

Figure 5. The variationof the defense model's accuracy with speed up for Location, Texas100, and CH-MNIST.

The number of parameters. The variation in the parameter size of the defense model with speed up is shown in Figure 6. For Location, the parameter size of the model before compression is 0.0492 Mb. When speed up is set to 20, 40, and 60, the minimum parameter size is 0.0008 Mb, which continuously decreases. The minimum parameter size is reached when the speed up is 60. When $r = 0.01626$ in Definition 2, the result satisfies this definition. For Texas100, before compression, the parameter size of the model is 0.0671 Mb. When speed up is set to 20, 40, and 60, the minimum parameter size is 0.0010 Mb, which continuously decreases. The minimum parameter size is reached when the speed up is 60. When $r = 0.01490$ in Definition 2, the result satisfies this definition. For CH-MNIST, before compression, the parameter size of the model is 0.0435 Mb. When speed up is set to 50, 100, 150, and 200, the minimum parameter size is 0.0002 Mb, which continuously decreases. The minimum parameter size is reached when the speed up is 200. When $r = 0.0046$ in Definition 2, the result satisfies this definition. It is expected that increasing the speed up will further reduce the model parameters. In addition to the parameter size of the defense model, another indicator is FLOPs. Since the defense model uses a fully connected network, the parameter size and FLOPs of the defense model are equal, so they are not shown separately.

The inference accuracy of the attack model. The inference accuracy results of the attack model are shown in Figure 7. For the three datasets, Location, Texas100, and CH-MNIST, the defense effect of the defense model has remained essentially unchanged before and after pruning. For Location, the defense effect of the defense model slightly deteriorates at speed-up = 20, and other values can be selected for speed up during pruning. For the CH-MNIST, the defense effect of the defense model deteriorates at speed up = 200, and other values can also be selected for speed up during pruning. Obviously, the inference accuracy of the attack model satisfies Definition 3. We found that the upper limit of compression by speed up is related to the model's own parameter size and the input and output dimensions of the model. The larger the model's parameter size and the smaller the input and output dimensions of the model, the greater the potential for model pruning. Therefore, in practical applications, it is necessary to develop an appropriate speed up based on the actual situation, which can satisfy local adversarial sample privacy protection while not reducing the defense effect. So far, we have also demonstrated the feasibility of the second structural pruning-based adversarial sample privacy protection.

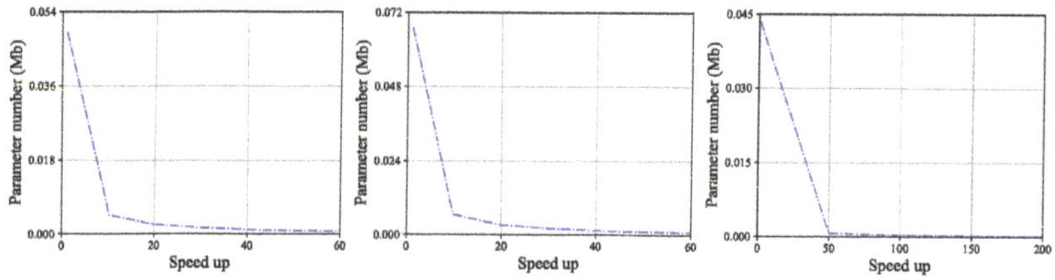

(a) Location (b) Texas100 (c) CH-MNIST

Figure 6. For Location, Texas100, and CH-MNIS, the parameter number of the defense model varies with the change in speed up.

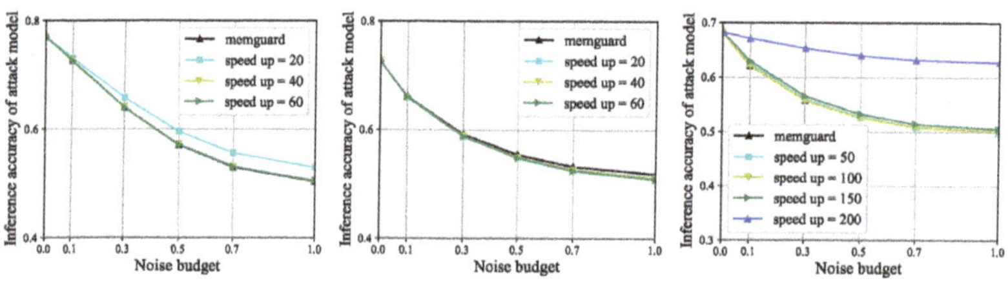

(a) Location (b) Texas100 (c) CH-MNIST

Figure 7. For Location, Texas100, and CH-MNIST, the inference accuracy of the attack model varies with the noise budget and speed up.

In order to present the effectiveness of our approach more clearly, we showcase the results in the table below. In Table 1, we compare our first SP-ASPP with [2] and our second SP-ASPP with [3]. We will conduct separate comparisons for the four datasets and different speed-up ratios. In the 'Methods' column of Table 1, the value in parentheses represents the magnitude of speed-up. The inference accuracy of the attack model varies under different noise budgets. Therefore, we take the average of the attack model's inference accuracy under different noise budgets to determine the final inference accuracy of the attack model. For Att, the considered noise magnitude budgets include 1.5, 2.0, 3.0, 4.0, and 5.0. For other datasets, the considered noise magnitude budgets are 0.1, 0.3, 0.5, 0.7, and 1.0.

It can be observed that as the model pruning parameter speed up increases, the accuracy of the defense model remains relatively stable, the model parameter size decreases significantly, and there is a slight increase in the inference accuracy of the attack model. The change in defense model accuracy and the change in attack model inference accuracy are both minimal, indicating that the defense model's effectiveness is relatively stable. This represents the SP-ASPPs proposed in this paper, which indeed significantly reduce model parameters while ensuring a certain level of defense effectiveness, demonstrating the effectiveness of the approach presented in this paper.

Table 1. The table displays the defense model accuracy, model parameter size, and inference accuracy of the attack models for different methods. In the 'Methods' column, the value in parentheses represents the magnitude of speed-up. The same attack model is applied to the same dataset. The inference accuracy of the attack model is the average value of inference accuracy under different noise magnitude budgets.

Datasets	Methods	Accuracy	Parameter Size (Mb)	Inference Accuracy
Att	AttriGuard [2]	0.4549	401.0400	0.3531
	1st-SP-ASPP (50)	0.4586	7.0100	0.2863
	1st-SP-ASPP (100)	0.4555	3.0000	0.2967
	1st-SP-ASPP (150)	0.4506	2.0100	0.2937
	1st-SP-ASPP (200)	0.4433	0.9900	0.3112
Location	MemGuard [3]	0.8575	0.0492	0.5946
	2nd-SP-ASPP (20)	0.8575	0.0024	0.6147
	2nd-SP-ASPP (40)	0.8575	0.0012	0.5951
	2nd-SP-ASPP (60)	0.8525	0.0008	0.5949
Texas100	MemGuard [3]	0.7360	0.0671	0.5715
	2nd-SP-ASPP (20)	0.7355	0.0033	0.5677
	2nd-SP-ASPP (40)	0.7353	0.0016	0.5673
	2nd-SP-ASPP (60)	0.7350	0.0010	0.5663
CH-MNIST	MemGuard [3]	0.7075	0.0435	0.5435
	2nd-SP-ASPP (50)	0.7050	0.0008	0.5442
	2nd-SP-ASPP (100)	0.7025	0.0004	0.5429
	2nd-SP-ASPP (150)	0.7075	0.0003	0.5495
	2nd-SP-ASPP (200)	0.7075	0.0002	0.6449

Through the above experiments, we found that using model pruning in adversarial sample privacy protections can significantly reduce the number of model parameters while ensuring a certain level of defense effectiveness. These findings indicate that structural pruning-based adversarial sample privacy protections have a certain degree of feasibility.

6. Conclusions

Previous adversarial sample privacy protections have mostly been centralized or have not considered the issue of hardware device limitations when conducting privacy protection, especially on the user's local device. This work attempts to reduce the requirements of adversarial sample privacy protections on devices, making the privacy protection more locally friendly. Advanced model structure pruning techniques are used to prune and train the defense model structure, which is then distributed to users. Users complete the privacy protection process on the pruned model to obtain the noisy data. Experiments on real datasets show that our SP-ASPPs are efficient. Through the solution of this article, the practical use of LASPP is promoted. In fact, the schemes in [2,3] are not secure because the defense schemes of adversarial samples [31–33] continue to be proposed, requiring more robust privacy protections. However, we are confident that robust models can still be pruned, and this is also a future direction for research.

Author Contributions: The model and methodology of this paper were proposed by G.X. and Q.P. The experiments were designed and conducted by G.X. and G.H.; H.H. was responsible for the graphical work of the paper. The writing of the paper was completed by G.X., G.H. and Q.P.; H.H. reviewed the paper. G.X. and G.H. made revisions to the paper. All authors have read and agreed to the published version of the manuscript.

Funding: This work is supported by the National Key Research and Development Program of China under Grant 2022YFB3-102700; the National Natural Science Foundation of China under Grants

62132013, 62102295, 62276198, and 61902292; and the Key Research and Development Programs of Shaanxi under Grant 2021ZDLGY06-03.

Data Availability Statement: Data are contained within the article.

Acknowledgments: Thanks to the development teams behind PyTorch and other toolkits for providing convenient experimental tools. Thanks to Featurize for offering a convenient and efficient cloud service, and thanks to the anonymous reviewers for their meticulous review.

Conflicts of Interest: The authors declare no conflicts of interest.

References

1. Szegedy, C.; Zaremba, W.; Sutskever, I.; Bruna, J.; Erhan, D.; Goodfellow, I.; Fergus, R. Intriguing properties of neural networks. *arXiv* **2013**, arXiv:1312.6199.
2. Jia, J.; Gong, N.Z. {AttriGuard}: A practical defense against attribute inference attacks via adversarial machine learning. In Proceedings of the 27th USENIX Security Symposium (USENIX Security 18), Baltimore, MD, USA, 15–17 August 2018; pp. 513–529.
3. Jia, J.; Salem, A.; Backes, M.; Zhang, Y.; Gong, N.Z. Memguard: Defending against black-box membership inference attacks via adversarial examples. In Proceedings of the 2019 ACM SIGSAC Conference on Computer and Communications Security, London, UK, 11–15 November 2019; pp. 259–274.
4. Shao, R.; Shi, Z.; Yi, J.; Chen, P.Y.; Hsieh, C.J. Robust text captchas using adversarial examples. In Proceedings of the 2022 IEEE International Conference on Big Data (Big Data), IEEE, Osaka, Japan, 17–20 December 2022; pp. 1495–1504.
5. Papernot, N.; McDaniel, P.; Jha, S.; Fredrikson, M.; Celik, Z.B.; Swami, A. The limitations of deep learning in adversarial settings. In Proceedings of the 2016 IEEE European Symposium on Security and Privacy (EuroS&P), IEEE, Saarbrücken, Germany, 21–24 March 2016; pp. 372–387.
6. Shokri, R.; Stronati, M.; Song, C.; Shmatikov, V. Membership inference attacks against machine learning models. In Proceedings of the 2017 IEEE Symposium on Security and Privacy (SP), IEEE, San Jose, CA, USA, 22–24 May 2017; pp. 3–18.
7. Madry, A.; Makelov, A.; Schmidt, L.; Tsipras, D.; Vladu, A. Towards deep learning models resistant to adversarial attacks. *arXiv* **2017**, arXiv:1706.06083.
8. Dwork, C. Differential privacy. In *Proceedings of the International Colloquium on Automata, Languages, and Programming*; Springer: Cham, Switzeland, 2006; pp. 1–12.
9. Shokri, R.; Theodorakopoulos, G.; Troncoso, C.; Hubaux, J.P.; Le Boudec, J.Y. Protecting location privacy: Optimal strategy against localization attacks. In Proceedings of the 2012 ACM Conference on Computer and Communications Security, Raleigh, NC, USA, 16–18 October 2012; pp. 617–627.
10. Salamatian, S.; Zhang, A.; du Pin Calmon, F.; Bhamidipati, S.; Fawaz, N.; Kveton, B.; Oliveira, P.; Taft, N. Managing your private and public data: Bringing down inference attacks against your privacy. *IEEE J. Sel. Top. Signal Process.* **2015**, *9*, 1240–1255. [CrossRef]
11. Xie, G.; Pei, Q. Towards Attack to MemGuard with Nonlocal-Means Method. *Secur. Commun. Netw.* **2022**, *2022*, 6272737[CrossRef]
12. Wang, T.; Blocki, J.; Li, N.; Jha, S. Locally differentially private protocols for frequency estimation. In Proceedings of the 26th USENIX Security Symposium (USENIX Security 17), Vancouver, BC, Canada, 16–18 August 2017; pp. 729–745.
13. Ding, X.; Ding, G.; Guo, Y.; Han, J. Centripetal sgd for pruning very deep convolutional networks with complicated structure. In Proceedings of the IEEE/CVF Conference on Computer Vision and Pattern Recognition, Long Beach, CA, USA, 15–20 June 2019; pp. 4943–4953.
14. You, Z.; Yan, K.; Ye, J.; Ma, M.; Wang, P. Gate decorator: Global filter pruning method for accelerating deep convolutional neural networks. *Adv. Neural Inf. Process. Syst.* **2019**, *32*. [CrossRef]
15. Fang, G.; Ma, X.; Song, M.; Mi, M.B.; Wang, X. Depgraph: Towards any structural pruning. In Proceedings of the IEEE/CVF Conference on Computer Vision and Pattern Recognition, Vancouver, BC, Canada, 17–24 June 2023; pp. 16091–16101.
16. Shen, M.; Molchanov, P.; Yin, H.; Alvarez, J.M. When to prune? a policy towards early structural pruning. In Proceedings of the IEEE/CVF Conference on Computer Vision and Pattern Recognition, New Orleans, LA, USA, 18–24 June 2022; pp. 12247–12256.
17. Gao, S.; Zhang, Z.; Zhang, Y.; Huang, F.; Huang, H. Structural Alignment for Network Pruning through Partial Regularization. In Proceedings of the IEEE/CVF International Conference on Computer Vision, Paris, France, 2–3 October 2023; pp. 17402–17412.
18. Shen, M.; Yin, H.; Molchanov, P.; Mao, L.; Liu, J.; Alvarez, J.M. Structural pruning via latency-saliency knapsack. *Adv. Neural Inf. Process. Syst.* **2022**, *35*, 12894–12908.
19. Fang, G.; Ma, X.; Wang, X. Structural Pruning for Diffusion Models. *arXiv* **2023**, arXiv:2305.10924.
20. Hou, Y.; Ma, Z.; Liu, C.; Wang, Z.; Loy, C.C. Network pruning via resource reallocation. *Pattern Recognit.* **2024**, *145*, 109886. [CrossRef]
21. Ma, X.; Fang, G.; Wang, X. LLM-Pruner: On the Structural Pruning of Large Language Models. *arXiv* **2023**, arXiv:2305.11627.
22. Dong, X.; Chen, S.; Pan, S. Learning to prune deep neural networks via layer-wise optimal brain surgeon. *Adv. Neural Inf. Process. Syst.* **2017**, *30*. [CrossRef]
23. Guo, Y.; Yao, A.; Chen, Y. Dynamic network surgery for efficient dnns. *Adv. Neural Inf. Process. Syst.* **2016**, *29*. [CrossRef]

24. Park, S.; Lee, J.; Mo, S.; Shin, J. Lookahead: A far-sighted alternative of magnitude-based pruning. *arXiv* **2020**, arXiv:2002.04809.
25. Luo, J.H.; Wu, J. Neural network pruning with residual-connections and limited-data. In Proceedings of the IEEE/CVF Conference on Computer Vision and Pattern Recognition, Seattle, WA, USA, 13–19 June 2020; pp. 1458–1467.
26. Yao, L.; Pi, R.; Xu, H.; Zhang, W.; Li, Z.; Zhang, T. Joint-detnas: Upgrade your detector with nas, pruning and dynamic distillation. In Proceedings of the IEEE/CVF Conference on Computer Vision and Pattern Recognition, Nashville, TN, USA, 20–25 June 2021; pp. 10175–10184.
27. Li, T.; Lin, L. Anonymousnet: Natural face de-identification with measurable privacy. In Proceedings of the IEEE/CVF Conference on Computer Vision and Pattern Recognition Workshops, Long Beach, CA, USA, 16–17 June 2019.
28. Salman, H.; Khaddaj, A.; Leclerc, G.; Ilyas, A.; Madry, A. Raising the cost of malicious ai-powered image editing. *arXiv* **2023**, arXiv:2302.06588.
29. Shan, S.; Cryan, J.; Wenger, E.; Zheng, H.; Hanocka, R.; Zhao, B.Y. Glaze: Protecting artists from style mimicry by text-to-image models. *arXiv* **2023**, arXiv:2302.04222.
30. Kullback, S.; Leibler, R.A. On information and sufficiency. *Ann. Math. Stat.* **1951**, *22*, 79–86. [CrossRef]
31. Ma, X.; Li, B.; Wang, Y.; Erfani, S.M.; Wijewickrema, S.; Schoenebeck, G.; Song, D.; Houle, M.E.; Bailey, J. Characterizing adversarial subspaces using local intrinsic dimensionality. *arXiv* **2018**, arXiv:1801.02613.
32. Liu, Y.; Qin, Z.; Anwar, S.; Ji, P.; Kim, D.; Caldwell, S.; Gedeon, T. Invertible denoising network: A light solution for real noise removal. In Proceedings of the IEEE/CVF Conference on Computer Vision and Pattern Recognition, Nashville, TN, USA, 20–25 June 2021; pp. 13365–13374.
33. Meng, D.; Chen, H. Magnet: A two-pronged defense against adversarial examples. In Proceedings of the 2017 ACM SIGSAC Conference on Computer and Communications Security, Dallas, TX, USA, 30 October–3 November 2017; pp. 135–147.

MDPI AG
Grosspeteranlage 5
4052 Basel
Switzerland
Tel.: +41 61 683 77 34

Electronics Editorial Office
E-mail: electronics@mdpi.com
www.mdpi.com/journal/electronics

www.ingramcontent.com/pod-product-compliance
Lightning Source LLC
Chambersburg PA
CBHW041939260926
51850CB00018B/301
* 9 7 8 3 7 2 5 8 4 5 8 2 8 *